The Asian Pacific

Political and Economic Development in a Global Context

SECOND EDITION

Vera Simone
California State University, Fullerton

Longman

New York   San Francisco   Boston
London   Toronto   Sydney   Tokyo   Singapore   Madrid
Mexico City   Munich   Paris   Cape Town   Hong Kong   Montreal

To Jameen and Lisa

Publisher: Priscilla McGeehon
Senior Acquisitions Editor: Eric Stano
Associate Editor: Anita Castro
Marketing Manager: Megan Galvin-Fak
Supplements Editor: Kristinn Muller
Production Manager: Mark Naccarelli
Project Coordination, Text Design, and Electronic Page Makeup: Pre-Press Company, Inc.
Cover Design Manager: Nancy Danahy
Cover Designer: Wendy Stolberg
Cover Photo: © PhotoDisc, Inc.
Photo Researcher: PhotoSearch, Inc.
Manufacturing Buyer: Al Dorsey
Printer and Binder: The Maple-Vail Book Manufacturing Group
Cover Printer: Coral Graphic Services, Inc.

Library of Congress Cataloging-in-Publication Data

Simone, Vera.
    The Asian Pacific : political and economic development in a
global context / Vera Simone.—2nd ed.
        p. cm.
    ISBN 0-8013-3021-1
    1. Asia—Economic conditions—1945– 2. Economic forecasting—
Asia. 3. Pacific Area—Economic conditions. 4. Economic
forecasting—Pacific Area. I. Title.
HC412 .S583 2000
330.95—dc21
                                                00-046138

Please visit our website at http://www.ablongman.com

ISBN 0-8013-3021-1

2 3 4 5 6 7 8 9 10—MA—03 02 01 00

Contents

Illustrations and Tables

MAPS AND BAR GRAPHS

TABLES

Preface

Preparation of this edition began during the most severe economic recession experienced by Asian Pacific nations since their remarkable ascent to high-growth, "miracle" economies. Contrary to the generally grim expectations of many observers, the recession was relatively short-lived. As this second edition goes to press, even the hardest hit countries, with the exception of Indonesia, have recovered. Much of the new material in this edition, therefore, addresses two questions: what impact has the economic crisis had on political and economic development in the region? and have there been fundamental changes in institutions as a result of the economic crisis?

Some of the changes in this second edition warrant mention at the outset.

- The developmental state (or statist) theory previously explained in Chapter Five has been incorporated into Chapter One. The inclusion in the first chapter of all three theoretical approaches—modernization, dependency-world systems and the developmental (or statist) approach—has produced a more comprehensive theoretical framework. The speculative section on the possibility of convergence between modernization and world system theories in the first edition has been dropped from this edition, sharpening the contrasts among the three theoretical alternatives.

- The cross-national comparisons of Asian Pacific countries in Chapter One have been expanded to include comparative PPP (Purchasing Power Parity) which provides a more meaningful comparison of standard of living in different countries than do per capita income figures.

- A description of Japanese colonial rule in Taiwan has been added to the (renamed) section "The Diversity of Colonial Rule" in Chapter Two and an extended consideration of the Taiwanese movement for independence has been added to Chapter Seven.

- The terms "authoritarian" and "democratic"—conventionally used to denote mutually exclusive "types of state"—have been reconceptualized as opposing but complementary attributes of all nation states in differing proportions at different stages of their development.

- A new term—authoritarian pluralism—has been introduced to characterize the process of political reform (democratization) in Japan and South Korea.

- The sections on North Korean economic reform in Chapter Five and North Korea's nuclear and security issues in Chapter Seven have been expanded to elucidate that country's "coming out from under" to join the world community of nations.

- The Asian financial crisis in all its ramifications receives coverage throughout this revision with a special section specifically devoted to a description of what transpired in Chapter Five and an extensive assessment of its impact on the prospects for change in Chapter Nine.

These changes, if anything, reinforce the tenor of a book that necessarily reflects the uncertainties of the times we live in. Its purpose, however, remains the same: to serve as a springboard for readers to pursue their own varied interests in the Asian Pacific region. By promoting an empathetic and thoughtful understanding of the diverse peoples of the Asian Pacific and their historically distinctive trajectories, it is hoped, this book will contribute to furthering the capabilities of the human race to forge a common identity for itself.

This revision has benefited from the support and assistance provided by members of the Economics and Business Department of Wuxi University of Light Industry who generously gave of their time and expertise to enhance my research into township-village enterprises (TVEs) as part of the economic reform process in the Wuxi area of China. I am also grateful to the Waiban (Foreign Affairs Office), the English Department and the staff of the Foreign Expert Building of Wuxi University for making my year's residence in China absorbing and enlightening. To all the reviewers of the first edition I am indebted for their careful reading and helpful comments on how to improve that edition. The staff at Longman have persevered in their dedication to the book throughout the long process of working on the second edition. I am also grateful to the Political Science Department of California State University, Fullerton for enabling me to spend the year 1997–98 in China and to the CSUF Foundation for assisting my research with a timely summer grant. The encouragement of family, friends and colleagues has contributed incalculably to my completing this revision and my friend and co-author of the first edition, Anne Feraru, continues to inspire me. Without her wise counsel I would undoubtedly still be revising the manuscript.

Preface to the First Edition

The Asian Pacific has entered world history as a new frontier. The dynamic center of this new frontier is Japan, a small resource-poor island nation culturally indebted in earlier times to China, for centuries the dominant power in the region. Following its defeat in World War II Japan emerged in the technological forefront of modern knowhow and has replaced the United States as the world's leading creditor nation. Not far behind are the newly industrializing countries, or NICs, as they are known. These four "littler tigers"—South Korea, Taiwan, Singapore, and Hong Kong—together with Japan have been responsible for much of the current U.S. trade deficit. Equally dramatic is the new wave of Japanese protégés in Southeast Asia—Indonesia, Mayalsia, and Thailand. These countries are on the verge of parlaying international capital into world-wide exports on an unprecendented scale. In China, the ancient ideas of the world's oldest continuous civilization are being recast into modern form. Even in China's present transitional state, the sheer size of its material and human resources guarantees it a place among the great powers of the world. And just over its border awaits the Siberian and Far Eastern hinterland of Russia, whose development remains an untapped extension of this new frontier.

The region has become the fastest growing economic area in the world, turning the skyways of the Pacific Ocean into one of the most traveled paths of modern moguls. After being overshadowed in the last few centuries by the dominance of Europe and North America, the countries of the Asian Pacific have come into their own as important members of the global network of economic and political relationships.

This book is designed to respond to, and to stimulate further, the growing interest in this area of the world among students, business people, media practioners, and the general public. It assumes little prior knowledge of the history, geography, politics, or foreign relations of the region. The geographic area chosen for study here, the "Asian Pacific," is more limited in scope than either the "Pacific Rim" or the "Pacific Basin." The "Rim" in its broadest definition includes all countries along both western and eastern shores of the Pacific, and the "Basin" adds to these the island countries in mid-ocean. Our choice is to focus on the countries of East and Southeast Asia—China, North and South Korea, Japan, Taiwan, Vietnam, Laos, Cambodia, Thailand, Malaysia, Singapore, Myanmar (formerly Burma), Indonesia, the Philippines, and to a lesser degree Brunei and the colony of Hong Kong. Other countries in the region are brought into the discussion where their actions significantly affect these countries. And of course the impact of American and Russian foreign policy interests and actions is inescapably part of the story.

Justification for adding this book to the already crowded shelves in bookstores and libraries is that it meets the need of nonspecialists for an up-to-date introduction to the politics of the whole region, that it incorporates economics, history, and cultural elements, and that it includes both national and international politics.

Our approach is analytic rather than simply descriptive. Instead of proceeding country by country, we identify and analyze patterns of similarities and differences among them, using descriptive material about particular countries to illustrate the patterns. Our hope is that this strategy will give the reader a grasp of the whole region and sufficient knowledge about each country to serve as the foundation for more intensive study.

The perspective of the book is interdisciplinary, because we are convinced that to understand contemporary politics in Asian countries one needs to know something about their history, especially their experiences with Western colonialism, and about the cultural traditions and modern beliefs that underlie their political institutions. A grasp of the close connection between economics and politics in the socialist countries as well as those with predominantly market economies is also essential.

Finally, politics as analyzed here crosses over the conventional separation in political science between comparative (that is, internal) politics and international relations. We show how a country's domestic political and economic policies influence its foreign relations and how both are influenced by the actions of other states, all operating within the context of a changing international environment in which they act and are acted upon.

The book is organized into nine chapters. Chapter 1 sketches the demographic and economic features of countries in the region and introduces the major theories of development that are applied and evaluated in subsequent chapters. Chapters 2 and 3 are historical, analyzing the effects of colonialism and the transition from colonial rule to independence. The next three chapters focus on politics, economics, and culture in these countries since independence. Contemporary political institutions and processes are compared in Chapter 4, with discussion of why authoritarianism in various forms characterizes them. Chapter 5 looks at their political economies, considering the reasons for their differing degrees of economic success and whether the Japanese pattern of development is transferable. Chapter 6 concludes the analysis of the process of modernization by showing how traditional Eastern cultures have interacted with Western-derived ideologies to affect political and economic change. The last three chapters shift to foreign policies and international relations. Chapter 7 focuses on the impact of the cold war and the effects of its end on political and military relations among Asian Pacific states and between them and the superpowers. Chapter 8 deals with the international political economy of the region, analyzing patterns of trade, aid, and investment and regional economic integration. In the concluding chapter, after reviewing the progress Asian Pacific countries have made thus far in political and economic development, we look to the future, at problems of succession in leadership, at prospects for human rights, and finally at the changing relationship between the region and the global system.

The Asian Pacific

Source: Adapted from John Andrews. *The Asian Challenge.* Hong Kong: Longman Group (Far East) Ltd., 1991.

1

Comparing Asian Pacific Countries
Some Facts and Some Theories

One way of learning new things is to make comparisons between what we are familiar with and what we are trying to get to know. Making comparisons involves identifying differences and recognizing similarities between the familiar and the unfamiliar, whether they are kinds of food or colleges or works of art or people or—in this book—groups of people organized into countries. Each country has its own history, worldview, social customs and relationships, ways of producing to meet material needs, ways of distributing and exercising political power, ways of managing relations with other countries. Yet every country is unique, both similar to and different from other countries. That is what comparative political analysis is about: comparing political processes, structures, policies, and other features of nation-states. In what ways are they similar? In what ways different? What theories can be used to explain those similarities and differences? We shall try here to make our comparisons systematically, not haphazardly, in order to detect patterns, to make generalizations, to see possible connections between politics and the economic, cultural, historical, and other characteristics of the countries under study.

For Americans and Canadians, studying the politics of the Asian Pacific region is probably more difficult than studying the politics of Europe. There are at least two reasons for this. One is that Europe is more familiar to most North Americans than Asia; the ancestors of most people in the United States and Canada, their dominant languages, and their political heritage have been from Western Europe; and their educational systems are still decidedly "Eurocentric." Asia, in contrast, is based on a different set of roots. Influenced by Confucianism, Hinduism, Buddhism, Islam, and the tradition of ancestor worship and ritualized reverence for symbols of authority, it is much less familiar to North Americans and more likely to be stereotyped by them as "backward," "inscrutable," "not like us"—hence more difficult to understand.

In addition to being culturally different from either Europe or North America, Asian countries are quite a bit more different from each other than are the countries of Europe, especially Western Europe. While Europe has a common religious tradition, Judeo-Christianity, the Asian Pacific has three major religions and one very powerful secular ethical tradition, Confucianism. European countries also have the shared experience of "modernization" and (especially in Western Europe) of "democratization," whether of the liberal or socialist variety; but Asian countries cover a vast range—from "modernized" Japan and Singapore at one end of the continuum to the traditionalism of Burma (renamed Myanmar in 1989) on the other, from the absolute monarchy of Brunei to the elective politics of the Philippines and Japan.

To help you overcome those initial obstacles to learning about the Asian Pacific and to introduce you to the adventure of comparative political analysis, we shall do two things in this chapter. The first is to quickly introduce the region with a preliminary sketch in broad brush strokes showing the variety (and occasional similarities) that characterizes these countries. That preliminary sketch will be filled out in more detail in the chapters that follow, but in this chapter you will be given enough information to begin comparing Asian countries with your own country, and with each other. The second thing we do in this chapter is to introduce three distinct theories that have been devised by social scientists to explain the process of "modernization": (1) modernization theory, (2) world system theory, and (3) developmental state or statist theory.

This process by which "traditional" societies (such as 14th century England and France) became "modern" economically and "developed" politically and socially (as Europe, the United States, Canada and Japan are today) is explained differently by each of these theories. When applied to our study of Asian countries, therefore, the distinctive focus each theory brings to the canvas, separately or in some combination, should illuminate for us how and why some countries have succeeded in modernizing and developing, while others have not. These theories are supplemented in Chapter 6 with a cultural perspective on development in the Asian Pacific.

THE ASIAN PACIFIC REGION: DIVERSITY AND COMMONALITIES

Cultural Heritage

Unlike Europe, the Asian Pacific countries do not share a single common cultural heritage. Several different civilizations have shaped the cultural mosaic that gives Asia its exotic allure for Westerners. East Asia is comprised of countries with a predominantly Confucian culture; Confucianism originated in China and spread to Korea and Japan and into the part of the Indochinese peninsula that today is Vietnam. Hinduism and Buddhism moved eastward from India before the ninth century, shaping the dominant belief systems of Burma, Siam (renamed Thailand in 1939), Cambodia, and the island of Bali in Indonesia, and also gathered adherents to various sects of Buddhism in China, Japan, and Korea. In a subsequent wave of traders from the Middle East and India, Islam found its way into the Asian Pacific, becoming the prevailing religion in Malaysia, Indonesia, Brunei, and the southern part of the Philippines. Christianity followed later, brought in by European and American traders, missionaries, and colonial officials, although it did not supplant the earlier traditions and, except in the Philippines and South Korea, now has only a small number of adherents. Thus the underlying belief systems of the Asian Pacific countries come from more varied traditions than do the belief systems of Europe.

If there is a common cultural characteristic stemming from that richly diverse past, it is the high value placed on consensus in social relations that distinguishes Asian Pacific peoples from Europeans, Americans, and Canadians. Unlike Westerners, who are accustomed to the rule of the majority in group decision making, in Asian Pacific cultures people prefer to deliberate until decisions acceptable to all can be reached. Consensus serves to maintain harmony among members of the group, who are expected to put the community's welfare above their individual interests. This emphasis on community is reinforced by the ethical beliefs of Confucianism, Buddhism, and Islam, and by the agricultural imperatives of wet rice cultivation practiced in much of the region, which requires community cooperation in maintaining the dikes and controlling the flow of water.

Colonial Experience

Different parts of the region were colonized in modern times by Europeans and Americans and later by the Japanese. The Dutch colonized the East Indies (now Indonesia); the Portuguese took modest holdings on the island of Timor, the port of Macao in south China, and Malacca, which later passed to the Dutch and then to the British; the Spanish and later the United States took the Philippines; Britain acquired Hong Kong, Burma, peninsular Malaya including Singapore, Brunei, Sarawak, and North Borneo (now Sabah); France conquered Indochina (now Vietnam, Laos, and Cambodia). Britain, France, tsarist Russia, Germany, and later Japan carved out semicolonial "spheres of influence" in China, and the United States through the Open Door policy exacted access to the spheres held by the other powers.

Thailand and Japan escaped Western colonization. Thailand accomplished this through the wily diplomacy of King Rama IV and the willingness of France and England to have his country serve as a buffer between their holdings in Southeast Asia. Japan, deducing that successful resistance to the West's superior military and economic power required it to emulate the West and become "modern" as rapidly as possible, undertook a crash program that by the early twentieth century had made it powerful enough not only to have escaped colonial rule but also to have acquired Taiwan and Korea as colonies of its own. Further conquests by Japan in the 1930s and 1940s gave large areas of China and Southeast Asia the experience of Japanese occupation.

Although the imperial powers' colonial policies varied in the impact they had on the traditional societies over which they ruled, the Asian colonies shared the common experience of alien domination and contact with modern institutions and Western ideas, especially the institutions of capitalism and the concept of nationalism. That experience stimulated the desire to become technologically advanced and to exercise the right of national self-determination. Nationalist independence movements challenged the legitimacy of colonialism and, after independence was achieved by most of the colonies in the two decades following World War II, those movements provided the first generation of postcolonial political leaders.

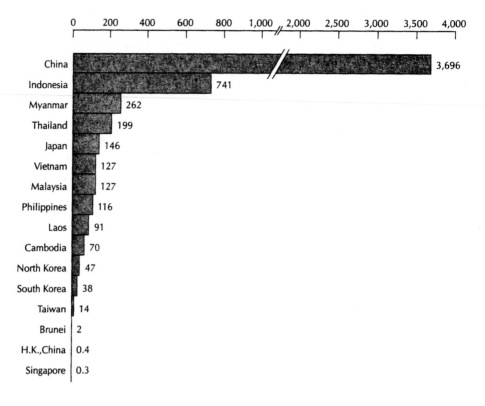

FIGURE 1.1 Land Area (1,000 sq. miles)

Source: The World Almanac and Book of Facts 1999

Geographic and Demographic Features

The countries of the Asian Pacific vary greatly in land area, population, and natural resources. As shown in Figures 1.1 and 1.2, China, with a land area similar to that of the United States and with over 1.2 billion people, is five times larger than the next largest Asian Pacific country, Indonesia, with 735,000 square miles and 200 million people. Other countries with land area over 100,000 square miles are (in descending order) Myanmar, Thailand, Japan, Vietnam, Malaysia, and the Philippines. Between 100,000 and 70,000 square miles in area are Laos and Cambodia, and under 50,000 square miles are North and South Korea, Taiwan, Brunei, and the city-state of Singapore. In addition to being a city-state, Singapore is an island, separated from the mainland of Malaysia by the Johore Strait. There are two other island-states in the Asian Pacific: Indonesia, which consists of over 13,500 islands, only 6,000 of which are inhabited, and the Philippines, which consists of 71,000 islands, with 95 percent of the population living on the 11 largest islands.

Population size roughly parallels land area, with some exceptions. The smallest in population is Brunei, with just under 300,000; countries with 12 million or less are

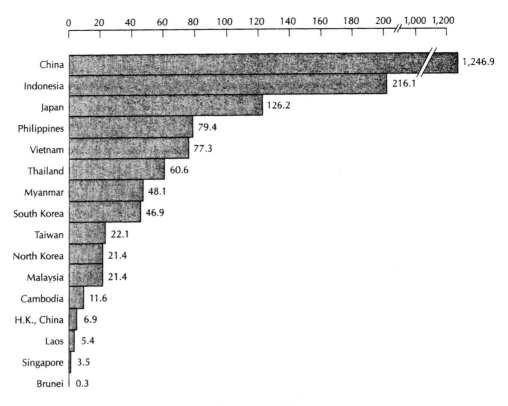

FIGURE 1.2   Population,1999 (July, est.) (in millions)

Source: The World Factbook 1999 (CIA) (from Internet)

Singapore, Laos, and Cambodia. Next are those with 20 to 50 million (Malaysia, Taiwan, North Korea, South Korea and Myanmar), from 60 to 80 million (Thailand, Vietnam, and the Philippines), and over 100 million (Japan and Indonesia). The single "giant" is China with over 1.2 billion people, of whom 7 million live in the former British colony of Hong Kong.

The countries also vary in natural resource endowment, another indicator—like land area and population size—of potential for economic development. Rich mineral resources are found in China, Malaysia, Indonesia, and Brunei, for example; natural resources such as good harbors, navigable rivers, and hydroelectric power capability are other potentially significant assets. However, the examples of economic success achieved by relatively resource-poor countries such as Japan, Singapore, and South Korea suggest that having resources in one's own country may be less crucial than having the means to buy them from others.

Apart from sheer numbers, another difference among the populations of Asian countries is in the variety and size of ethnic and religious groups, shown in Table 1.1. In countries like China, Korea, Japan, and Vietnam, which had long precolonial histories as distinct (though not always unified) states, the great majority belongs to a

TABLE 1.1   Populations, Ethnic and Religious Groups in Asian Pacific Countries

Country	Ethnic Groups	Percent	Religions	Percent
Brunei	Malay	64	Muslim (Official)	63
	Chinese	20	Buddhism	14
	Other	16	Christianity	8
			indigenous beliefs	
Population: 322,982 (July 1999 est.)			and other	15 (1981)
Cambodia	Khmer	90	Theravada Buddhism	95
	Vietnamese	5	other	5
	Chinese	1		
	Other	4		
Population: 11,626,520 (July 1999 est.)				
China	Han Chinese	91.9	Daoism (Taoism),	
	Zhuang, Uygur, Hui, Yi,		Buddhism, Muslim	2–3
	Tibetan, Miao, Manchu,		Christianity	1 (est.)*
	Mongol, Buyi, Korean,			
	and other nationalities	8.1		
Population: 1,246,871,951 (July 1999 est.)				
Hong Kong,	Chinese	95	eclectic mixture of	
China	Other	5	local religions	90
			Christianity	10
Population: 6,847,125 (July 1999 est.)				
Indonesia	Javanese	45	Muslim	88
	Sundanese	14	Protestant	5
	Madurese	7.5	Roman Catholic	3
	coastal Malays	7.5	Hindu	2
	other	26	Buddhism	1
			other	1 (1998)
Population: 216,108,345 (July 1999 est.)				
Japan	Japanese	99.4	observe both Shinto	
	other (mostly Korean)	0.6	and Buddhism	84
			other	16
			(including Christianity 0.7)	
Population: 126,182,077 (July 1999 est.)				
Korea, N.	racially homogeneous; there is		Buddhism and Confucianism, some	
	a small Chinese community		Christianity and syncretic Chondogyo	
	and a few ethnic Japanese			
Population: 21,386,109 (July 1999 est.)				
Korea, S.	homogeneous (except for about		Christianity	49
	20,000 Chinese)		Buddhism	47
			Confucianism	3
			pervasive folk religion (Shamanism),	
			Chondogyo (Religion of the Heavenly	
			Way), and other	1
Population: 46,884,800 (July 1999 est.)				
Laos	Lao Loum (lowland)	68	Buddhism	60
	Lao Theung (upland)	22	animist and other	40
	Lao Soung (highland) including			
	the Hmong ("Meo")			
	and the Yao (Mien)	9		
	ethnic Vietnamese/Chinese	1		
Population: 5,407,453 (July 1999 est.)				

TABLE 1.1   *(Continued)*

Country	Ethnic Groups	Percent	Religions	Percent
Malaysia	Malay and other indigenous	58	Islam, Buddhism, Daoism, Hinduism,	
	Chinese	26	Christianity, Sikhism**	
	Indian	7		
	others	9		
Population: 21,376,066 (July 1999 est.)				
Myanmar	Burman	68	Buddhism	89
	Shan	9	Christianity (Baptist 3,	4
	Karen	7	Roman Catholic 1)	
	Rakhine	4	Muslim	4
	Chinese	3	animist beliefs	1
	Mon	2	other	2
	Indian	2		
	other	5		
Population: 48,081,302 (July 1999 est.)				
Philippines	Christian Malay	91.5	Roman Catholic	83
	Muslim Malay	4	Protestant	9
	Chinese	1.5	Muslim	5
	other	3	Buddhist and other	3
Population: 79,345,812 (July 1999 est.)				
Singapore	Chinese	76.4	Buddhism (Chinese), Muslim (Malays),	
	Malay	14.9	Christianity, Hinduism, Sikh, Taoism,	
	Indian	6.4	Confucianism	
	other	2.3		
Population: 3,531,600 (July 1999 est.)				
Taiwan	Taiwanese (including		mixture of Buddhism, Confucianism,	
	Hakka)	84	and Taoist	93
	mainland Chinese	14	Christianity	4.5
	aborigine	2	other	2.5
Population: 22,113,250 (July 1999 est.)				
Thailand	Thai	75	Buddhism	95
	Chinese	14	Muslim	3.8
	other	11	Christianity	0.5
			Hinduism	0.1
			other	0.6
Population: 60,609,046 (July 1999 est.)				
Vietnam	Vietnamese	85–90	Buddhism, Taoism, Roman Catholic,	
	Chinese	3	indigenous beliefs, Islam, Protestant,	
	Muong Tai, Meo, Khmer,		Cao Dai, Hoa Hao	
	Man, Cham			
Population: 77,311,210 (July 1999 est.)				

*Note: officially atheist, but traditionally pragmatic and eclectic
**Note: in addition, Shamanism is practiced on East Malaysia

Source: The World Factbook 1999 (CIA) (from Internet)

single ethnic group. In contrast, Indonesia and Malaysia, which did not exist as political entities before colonial times, have greater diversity among their people. Divisions along ethnic, religious, and linguistic lines are thought to pose problems in creating national unity and loyalty to the central government and in developing a nationally oriented bureaucracy and nationally based political parties and interest groups. Ethnic differences often accompany religious differences within countries, and in a number of cases the religion of the ex-imperial power continues to have practitioners.

Political and Economic Systems

Postcolonial political and economic systems combine, in varying mixes, elements of precolonial traditional institutions with "modern" elements adopted—and adapted—from Western models. China, North Korea, Vietnam, and Laos have political institutions of Soviet origin, under the leadership of one ideologically based Communist party (though minor "parties" may be allowed to exist, they do not constitute a challenge to the Communist parties); their economies began as centrally planned and publicly owned systems, but they are all in different stages of market reform, which in the West is known as *liberalization*.

Japan and the Philippines have more recognizably Western democratic features with several major parties, though until 1993 the Liberal Democratic Party held power in Japan for all but a few months in the postwar period, and in the Philippines electoral competition was suspended during the period of martial law by former President Ferdinand Marcos. Both countries have economies based on private ownership of productive property, though in Japan the government has a major role in guiding the economy, which makes it arguably different from the Philippines whose capitalist ownership system is cast more unambiguously in the U.S. mold.

South Korea and Taiwan—whose governments began as bureaucratic, authoritarian regimes in which the military had important influence—have democratized political rule. South Korea in 1992 brought in the first civilian president in 30 years, and in 1998 elected its first opposition leader, a former political prisoner, to the office of president. Taiwan held its first direct presidential election in March 1996, completing its formal adoption of a democratic process. The military also has been politically involved in Indonesia, Thailand, Myanmar, and the Philippines. Private enterprise characterizes their economies, although in Indonesia the government controls oil and other extractive industries.

Singapore has a one-party-dominant civilian government, actively pursuing policies to promote economic expansion. Thailand and Cambodia are constitutional monarchies; Malaysia has a ceremonial sultan elected by the rulers of the former Malay states now incorporated into the Federation of Malaysia; and Brunei's sultan exercises supreme executive authority. Malaysia's multiethnic society is reflected in a ruling coalition of Malay, Chinese, and Indian parties in which the Malay Party is dominant. Hong Kong returned to Chinese sovereignty on July 1, 1997, to be governed for 50 years as a Special Administrative Region by its own inhabitants and in accordance with its own legal code, except in matters of foreign policy and defense. Under China's "one country, two systems" policy, Hong Kong retains its status as a free port and separate customs territory, with the Hong Kong dollar remaining a

Source: Clockwise form top right: United Nations photo 149070/Andrea Brizzi; United Nations photo; United Nations photo by J. Corash; United Nations photo 159497/J. Bleibtreu; photo by Vera Simone. Center: United Nations photo by G. Cohen.

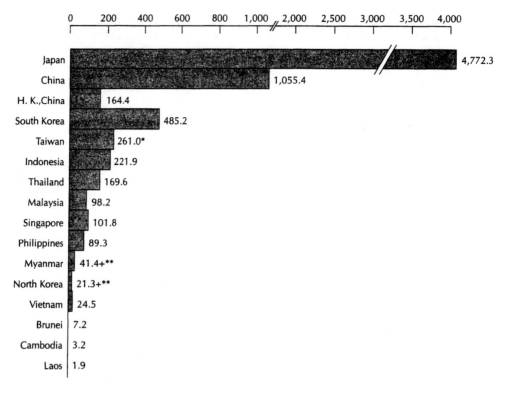

FIGURE 1.3   Gross National Product, 1997 (billions of dollars)

Sources: Asia 2000 Yearbook, for Taiwan; Handbook of the Nations, 15th ed. for Brunei, Myanmar, and North Korea; World Development Report 1998/1999, Tables 1 and 1a, for other countries.
+estimate
*1998 figure
**1994 figures are the last figures available

freely convertible currency. Its economy is capitalist though it has inherited a colonial government that was heavily involved in providing social services such as public housing.

This quick overview of the variety of political institutions in the Asian Pacific is followed up with a more thorough discussion in Chapter 4.

Economic Indicators

As shown in Figures 1.3 and 1.4, Asian Pacific countries range from wealthy Japan and China to poor Cambodia, Vietnam, and Laos. Japan, with a GNP of $4.8 trillion, ranks at the top of the Asian Pacific, second in the world behind the United States. With Hong Kong's GNP added to that of the mainland, China's GNP of $1.2 trillion, ranks it second largest in the Asian Pacific. South Korea's GNP of $485.2 billion ranks it third largest. Taiwan, Indonesia, and Thailand are all above $150 billion while Malaysia, Singapore, and the Philippines have GNPs between $50 billion and

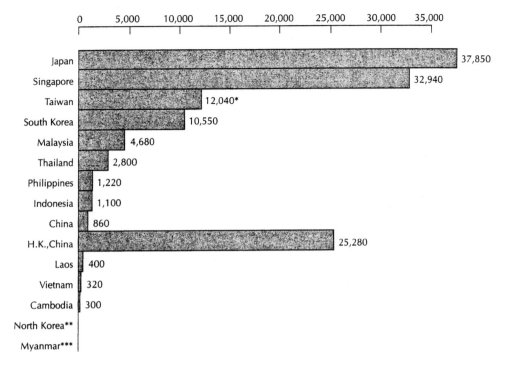

FIGURE 1.4 Gross National Product per capita, 1997 (in $US)

Sources: World Development Report 1998/1999 (New York: Oxford University Press, 1999) Table 1,
pp. 190–191; Table 1a, p. 232; *Far Eastern Economic Review: Asia Yearbook 2000,* p. 12 for Taiwan.
*Taiwan's per capita GNP or PCI is for 1998.
**Estimated to be lower middle income ($786 to $3,125)
***Estimated to be low income ($786 or less)

$100 billion. Myanmar, Vietnam, and North Korea are between $20 billion and
$50 billion. Below $10 billion are Brunei, Cambodia, and Laos.

As with GNP, GNP per capita—more simply, per capita income (PCI), which
is a country's income in U.S. dollars divided by the country's population—shows a
wide range, from the lowest average annual individual income of $320 in Vietnam
to Japan's $37,850. A country's rankings on GNP and PCI tend to be similar, ex-
cept for a few countries with the smallest and largest populations. Singapore, with
a population of only 3 million, has a rank of 8 in GNP but 3 in PCI and Brunei with
fewer than 300,000 people has a rank of 13 in GNP but 2 in PCI. Three of the most
populous countries—China, Indonesia, and Vietnam—rank 2, 5, and 12 in GNP but
8, 7, and 9 in PCI.

Another measure of income that gives a better comparison of standards of living than PCI is purchasing power parity (PPP), which calculates PCI in terms of
price comparisons of comparable goods and services in various countries. PPP is expressed in *international* dollars, a unit with purchasing power equal to the U.S. dollar, while PCI is expressed in U.S. dollars using the official exchange rate for the

country's currency. The differences between PCI and per capita PPP are striking, as shown in Figure 1.5. Of the ten countries plus Hong Kong, China, for which the World Bank provides PPP estimates, PCI understates the purchasing power of six countries and overstates it for two of them.

So while Japan's per capita income of nearly $38,000 appears enviably high (compared to the U.S. PCI/PPP of $28,740), it actually buys only $23,400 worth of goods and services. China's $860 PCI seems dismally low, but its PPP of $3,570 gives a more encouraging picture. The largest discrepancy between PCI and PPP values occurs in Malaysia, where the PCI understates purchasing power by over $6,000.

It should be noted that both PCI and per capita PPP are averages and that neither tells us how equally or unequally income is distributed among individuals in a country. In Malaysia and Thailand, for example, the wealthiest 20 percent of the population receives more than half (53.7 percent and 52.7 percent, respectively) of the total national income, while in Indonesia and Laos about 40 percent goes to the top 20 percent.[1] The existence of income differences between regions *within* a country is indicated by looking at the PPP of $24,540 in Hong Kong, which is eight times that of the rest of China.

Labels are often given to distinguish the levels of economic development reached by countries. The World Bank classifies Cambodia, Laos, Vietnam, and Myanmar as "low-income" economies. China, Indonesia, the Philippines, North Korea, and Thailand are "lower-middle income" and Malaysia is "upper-middle income." Brunei, Japan, South Korea, and Singapore are "high-income" economies (although Brunei's oil wealth and small land area and population put it in a separate category of "rich but underdeveloped," very similar to Middle East oil sheikdoms). Taiwan, which is omitted from World Bank reports, is also a high-income economy.

	Per Capita Income (PCI) 1997	Purchasing Power Parity (PPP) 1997	Difference
Japan	$37,850	$23,400	–$14,450
Singapore	32,940	29,000	–3,940
South Korea	10,550	13,500	+2,950
Malaysia	4,680	10,920	+6,240
Thailand	2,800	6,590	+3,790
Philippines	1,220	3,670	+2,450
Indonesia	1,100	3,450	+2,350
China	860	3,570	+2,710
Hong Kong, China	25,280	24,540	–740
Laos	400	1,290	+890
Vietnam	320	1,670	+1,350

FIGURE 1.5   Comparison of GNP per capita (PCI) and PPP, 1997 (in $US)

Sources: World Development Report 1998/1999 (New York: Oxford University Press, 1999), Table 1, pp. 190–191; Table 1a, p. 232.

Summing Up Similarities and Differences

To sum up this brief survey of the characteristics of Asian Pacific countries, we have found that all of them reached the modern era as traditional, agricultural societies. Although shaped by different belief systems, their cultures shared the social value of consensus. Some of them had had long histories as organized and distinct political entities, while others had not established a separate unified identity.

All Asian Pacific countries have felt the impact of colonialism to some degree. Although a few managed to escape colonial rule, the others did not, and all experienced the traumatic encounter between the indigenous traditional order and the new "modern" ways brought in by the Westerners and later by the Japanese. While the colonies each had different imperial masters pursuing somewhat different policies toward their "wards" with varying impact on the traditional political, economic, and social systems in the colonies, the common outcome in all was the awakening, or revival, of a sense of national identity and the demand for independence from alien rule.

When we look at the Asian Pacific countries now, four or more decades after independence was achieved, we are struck by the great differences among them, and generalizing about them is difficult. The region consists of very large countries and tiny ones, some resource-rich and others resource-poor, one with a billion people and one with fewer than a third of a million, some with relatively homogeneous populations and others a veritable patchwork of ethnically diverse people. The political and economic systems, though also quite varied, are typified by some form of authoritarianism and by a substantial degree of government direction of the economy in both the socialist and capitalist systems. Economic development in these countries is far from uniform: a cluster of affluent countries has reached a level rivaling the older developed states in Europe, a larger group of countries is moving up the economic ladder, and another smaller group is still struggling to raise its standard of living.

Having looked briefly at the variety of characteristics found among countries in the Asian Pacific region, we now move to the second part of this chapter: an explanation of the three different theories or frameworks to apply in comparing these countries with each other and with your own, the objective being to see which theory better explains why and how some countries have made progress in modernization and development and others have lagged behind.

THEORIES OF DEVELOPMENT

Development is the central organizing principle of this book, and it is also at the center of theories that have dominated the study of comparative politics in the last five decades. Let's begin by looking at an explanation of how development is defined and why it is the organizing principle of our comparison of Asian Pacific countries.

What Is Development and Why Is It Important?

Development, like *modernization*, is a term that describes the structural and behavioral changes that a society undergoes in the process of acquiring an industrial system of production and distribution. Technologically, development requires the knowledge and use of increasingly complex and sophisticated machinery and techniques with which to control the environment and produce a variety of goods and services. Organizationally, development results in the increasingly specialized nature of political, social, and economic institutions and the multiple roles they impose on human beings in the course of carrying out diverse responsibilities as workers, parents, and citizens. Behaviorally, development involves a broad range of new beliefs and attitudes that individuals must acquire to adjust to the demands placed on them by social and geographic mobility, broader political allegiances, economic growth, and a technology that requires literacy, openness to new experiences, punctuality, and working with people in close proximity and under conditions fixed by large organizations rather than landlords and the dictates of nature.

What makes newly independent nation-states like those that are the subject of this book pursue development? Part of the answer is that modern knowledge and technology were almost invariably seen by the conquered as the source of the Westerners' power to subjugate them. This dictated their mastery as a means of sheer survival, their development as a means of self-defense. A second reason that non-Western people aspire to the "modernity" of the Western way of life is the affluence and comfort afforded by modern know-how and organization. The conveniences that those of us who have them consider necessities—plumbing, electricity, refrigerators, telephones, and so on—are compelling wants in and of themselves for most human beings who carry their water from wells, live and work by the light of day, and otherwise labor with primitive tools. It was enough, even without the aid of mass media, to have heard about the exceptional exploits of white men and women. And though not all or even a majority of traditional people living throughout Asia (or Africa or Latin America) necessarily admired or coveted a modern way of life when introduced to it, they were inescapably propelled toward it by the glitter of its promise and its subversion of their traditional way of life.

But if development is irresistible it is also more complicated and problematical than it appears, both to those who consider themselves modern and those who aspire to join them. For one thing, "development" is a moving target. The rapidity with which not only technology but also organization and behavior change in the modern age makes it difficult to know which elements of modernity are enduring and which are ephemeral. What are the essential as distinct from the merely cosmetic components of modernization? Are some aspects of modern life as practiced by westerners culturally specific and therefore dispensable? A second dilemma is determining the question of who or what agent can bring about effective and desirable development. For those of us besieged by the relentless pressures of surviving in a modern environment, the question of how *to promote* development may already have given way to the question of how *to curtail* it; to us development seems preordained if not necessarily desirable, an inevitable outgrowth of human ingenuity and restlessness. But for most of the world's population, who or what can bring about a better life *for them* makes "development" not only theoretically pertinent but practically imperative.

When colonialism came to an end after World War II, Asian Pacific countries, like other countries of the Third World, began their excursion as newly independent nation-states with "development" as the central item on their agenda. But there were no blueprints for erecting a modern edifice or even much advice on what materials were necessary or where to begin the process of construction. The apparently simple question of "How to modernize?" masked a number of complex theoretical as well as practical issues. How feasible is it to modernize by borrowing the institutions and procedures of highly industrialized countries? What kind of political order most effectively promotes economic growth and social cohesion? Is a market-oriented economic strategy or a state-driven political economy more promising? To what extent does a development strategy closely aligned with international capital inhibit a young state from following independent domestic and foreign policies? How does a state's national security policy affect its developmental strategy? How is a state's need for political order balanced with its need for democratic expression and input?

While policymakers in the new states faced the task of finding practical answers on how best to proceed toward modernization, scholars faced the thorny theoretical problem of how to analyze the politics of "developing" countries with the analytic tools used for comparing modern Western countries. In a world sharply split between rich modernized nations and poor backward nations struggling to develop with either hand-me-down colonial institutions or experimental revolutionary ones, the question of how best to vanquish poverty and backwardness to become modern and rich had to be redefined. This redefinition led to three major questions: (1) What was the process by which capitalist modernization in the West had originally taken place? (2) Was that process similar or different for latecomers? (3) Why did development occur more readily in some countries than others?

The effort to answer these questions has produced three quite distinctive theoretical approaches. One has its roots in Western historical experience and will be referred to as *modernization theory,* even though it exhibits a number of different versions. The second is *world system theory,* which emerged in opposition to Western-centric assumptions and in its first incarnation was known as *dependency theory.* The third theoretical approach reflects more recent experiences in the Asian Pacific and is referred to as *developmental state or statist theory.* At the core of all three theories are ideas about the function of the state and of the marketplace. Basic to understanding these contemporary theoretical approaches, therefore, is a grasp of the European intellectual tradition on which they draw—that is, the theoretical principles, premises, and concepts that laid the groundwork for understanding development in modernizing Europe. The three leading contributors to that tradition are Thomas Hobbes, Adam Smith, and Karl Marx, and it is to their ideas on the modern state and the modern marketplace that we now turn.

Thomas Hobbes's Theory of the State

The concerns that prompted Thomas Hobbes (1588–1679) to construct his theory of the state in the seventeenth century are the same ones that faced the newly independent countries of the Asian Pacific at the end of World War II: civil war, ensuring the stability of a unified state, and securing the legitimacy of a regime. Dismayed at the horror of civil war in England, Hobbes undertook a scientific analysis of the causes of political disorder. Applying logic to the hypothetical situation of a "state of nature," Hobbes described human life without a government to maintain order as "solitary, poore, nasty, brutish, and short."[2] To avoid this perpetual state of civil strife, Hobbes argued, rational individuals agree to relinquish their natural rights to decide for themselves what is in their best interests to a state strong enough to secure political order. Thus Hobbes explained and justified citizens' obedience to a strong, authoritarian, and stable state as a rational alternative to the chaos of all individuals seeking their rights on the basis of might. Each individual with his or her own natural, self-interested agenda of desires and fears enters a social contract with all the others to obey the rules of the state.

Hobbes's objective—to prevent disorder—remains ours, and his solution—a national state strong enough to command political order and stability—has been extraordinarily enduring. Three centuries later Westerners still believe the state gets its legitimate mandate to decide right and wrong for everyone under its jurisdiction from the consent of the individuals over whom it rules. This seventeenth-century social contract conception of the authority of the state based on the self-interest of individuals is one of the two pillars of modern (Western) development theory. With its emphasis on the human (rational) need for a strong centralized authority, the Hobbesian idea of the state has considerable resonance for the Asian political world.

Adam Smith's Theory of the Market

The second pillar of modern development theory is the *free market*. If the state provides political order on the basis of individuals' consent, the market provides economic growth on the basis of individuals' choices to produce, sell, and buy. Living more than a century after Hobbes, Adam Smith (1723–1790) laid the groundwork for today's popular version of modernization theory: neoliberalism. He argued that the "natural" development of the market unencumbered by undue restrictions of the state best provides for economic growth and human welfare; what is in the economic self-interest of each individual operating in the marketplace coincides with the welfare of society as a whole. In other words, by producing a better mousetrap or a better automobile to outsell your competitor you not only enrich yourself but contribute to the economic growth and prosperity of the entire society. This is referred to as "the invisible hand."

Adam Smith's free market theory of development has been a favorite both among Asians eager to hasten their countries' modernization and among scholars keen on claiming universal validity for Smith's free market principles. International financial organizations like the IMF and World Bank have long prescribed neoliberalism as necessary for economic growth. When countries like South Korea, Thailand, and Indonesia exhibited phenomenal growth rates, they were hailed as examples of market-inspired economic success. When these very same economies were plunged into recession in 1997, the diagnosis was insufficient reliance on market requirements like transparency. Scholars using the developmental state or statist theory disputed the entire claim that astounding economic growth in the Asian Pacific stemmed from reliance on the unfettered market. According to this statist perspective, it was in fact precisely *because* East Asian *governments actively intervened in the market*, contrary to Adam Smith's advice, that they displayed such astonishing economic growth.

The experience of Asian Pacific nations has thus assumed theoretical significance as a test of the validity of Smith's theory, and debate continues on the question of how applicable neoliberalism is as a mechanism for latecomers to modernization. If anything, the debate has been intensified by the post–cold war conversions to market reforms on the part of the communist nations in the Asian Pacific—China, Vietnam, Laos, and even North Korea. The exact role of Adam Smith's free market in promoting economic prosperity in newly industrializing countries is a major bone of contention among the three modern development theories to be discussed in the next section. The reader will have the remainder of the book to consider which of the three contemporary development theories provides the most compelling explanation for how the market functioned in the national development of Asian Pacific states.

But first, one last piece of the Western European Enlightenment tradition must be put into place as the foundation of our ensuing discussion of the three contemporary theoretical approaches to development: the Marxian frame of analysis. World system theory is a direct descendant of Marx's theory of historical evolution. Without understanding Marx, therefore, the issues separating modernization theories from both the world system and developmental state approaches are difficult to comprehend.

Marx's Theory of Historical Evolution

Karl Marx (1818–1883) was almost as avid an admirer of the market as was Adam Smith. He was certainly as devout a believer in progress. But in two important ways his vision of the marketplace was markedly different from Smith's. First, he took a historical view of the market as a relative newcomer itself and therefore as vulnerable to decrepitude as earlier social systems that had disappeared from European history. Just as the bourgeoisie had ushered in the marketplace, according to Marx, the working class would usher in its nemesis: a humanitarian communism. The second characteristic of Marx's vision of the marketplace distinguishing it from Smith's was its ceaselessly dynamic motion. In an endless search for profits, the market was an irrepressible, globally expansive phenomenon that would spread into every nook and cranny of the earth's surface, breaking down national barriers indiscriminately and replacing them with an international class struggle of capitalists against the working class.

In his view of the state, Marx differed not only from Smith but also from the classic contract theory of Hobbes. In contrast to Smith's minimalist notion of the state's role in satisfying the needs of an expansive marketplace, Marx saw the state as a powerful agent of the capitalist class. If the bourgeois class was the engine of economic progress, of necessity it had to have the cooperation of the state in its activities, especially when it struck out for new lands to conquer and new shores from which to embark on its journeys throughout the world. In contrast to Hobbes's notion of the state as an autonomous neutral force subjecting all individuals equally to its authority, freeing them to participate in the economic activities of the marketplace under secure rules of political order, the state for Marx was an instrument of the business class for whom the market was a private benefit as well as a public arena of economic growth.

Their view of the state—in particular, its relationship to the market—distinguishes the three theoretical approaches we will be using in this book. It is the basis of the opposition between *modernization theory* and *world system theory*: In the former, when the state functions properly, it represents and serves the interests of all people equally; in the latter, when the state operates to support the marketplace, it becomes an ally of the capitalist class, which is its major beneficiary. Even when access to the state is never formally denied to anybody, the state's interests naturally coincide with the class that makes (and keeps) the state healthy, wealthy, and wise. Proponents of *developmental state theory* share this view of the state as serving the interests of its capitalist class but in their perspective, the state in *late industrializing* countries must first stimulate and nurture a capitalist class. To carry out this creative function, the state must be independently strong and decisively interventionist in the market so as to stake out a profitable position in the international division of labor among the world's nation-states.

Modern Theories of Development

Theories of development are, in the final analysis, contingent on how useful they are in explaining real events. Although the three theories we are about to discuss are not necessarily mutually exclusive on every issue, they do provide three distinct lenses through which to understand development in the Asian Pacific. The central focus of *modernization theory* is on the *internal* changes of singular nations as they centralize political rule, adopt market economies, and foster the values that propel individuals to rational market behavior. While the external or international context plays a part in providing opportunities for trade, investment, and expansion, national development as a whole is understood as internally generated by enterprising individuals and a neutral state apparatus capable of protecting property and securing domestic tranquillity.

On the other hand, *world system theory* views development as an outcome of the international process. As the world system expands—incorporating new territories and peoples—it leaves in its wake powerful *core* countries that dominate and exploit the weakest, most *peripheral* countries whose access to development is severely constrained by the more powerful actors in the international market. From this theoretical perspective, national development occurs only when the state structures of peripheral countries are strong enough to resist the self-serving interests of the more powerful players in the international market. Enter the statist approach, which focuses on the nation-state as an independent political entity at the intersection of a global market and a developing national economy. The developmental state insulates itself from both external and internal deterrents to national economic growth, exercising the kind of authority over the economy and society that propels it toward industrial production for an international market.

These three theoretical perspectives to be explored in greater detail in the following section may not all embrace progress with the same unalloyed optimism, but they do begin with the same two human constructions—the state and the marketplace—as their Enlightenment heritage. All three understand development as the outcome of the capitalist marketplace's transformation of small-scale subsistence agricultural societies under traditional local forms of rule—kingship, aristocracy, or chiefdoms—into ever-expanding, large-scale industrial societies with nation-states governed by competitive elections. But two characteristics stand out as sharply dividing these contending theories of development: their understanding of "time" and their outlook toward national versus global "space." Dependency theory, often considered a separate approach, is here treated as an antecedent of *world system theory*.

Modernization Theory.   Like Newtonian physics, *modernization theory* does not see the passage of time as changing the fundamental equation of how the capitalist marketplace works. Nor does it entertain the idea that beyond the individual there is an additional motor of change like social class or political party. From this perspective of modernization, therefore, it matters little when nations embark on the process of development; the rules, the relationships, and the consequences must of necessity remain pretty much the same. Countries like Indonesia or Malaysia that have pursued modernization in the latter half of the twentieth century confront an agenda similar to that of England, France, or Japan in the eighteenth and nineteenth centuries: capital accumulation, investment, and externally open trade relations relying on unfettered market mechanisms for exchange.

There has been a variety of modernization theories, some deriving from economics, some from sociology and anthropology. All of them divide social organizations into two ideal types: traditional and modern or agricultural and industrial. It is assumed that societies move from traditional to modern forms of organization and behavior in an incremental, unilinear "development" as peoples' inherited attachments to land, family, and tradition are replaced by industrial occupation, individual achievement, and human liberty. The central focus of modernization theories is on the *internal* changes of particular nations as they centralize political rule, adopt market economies, and reward individual efforts. The external or international context of course plays a role in providing opportunities for trade, investment, and expansion. But in the final analysis, according to this theoretical approach, national development is internally generated by enterprising individuals and a neutral state apparatus capable of protecting property and securing domestic tranquillity. In today's world, the version of this theory with the widest popularity is known as *neoliberalism*.

The state in general does not play a significant role in modernization theory because the market is assumed to be most vibrant when left unencumbered. But it is considered necessary as a neutral guardian of the institutions and values essential for the free market to function. Modernization in this theoretical conception is a *national* responsibility, requiring a state strong enough to protect and promote national interests but aloof enough to remain outside the arena of economic policymaking. Its sole function is to represent the interests of its citizens and maintain public order. Although in the early stage of the modernization process, the state may be called upon to support "infant" industries against external competitive pressures, it is expected to retreat to an impartial position above all classes.

A note of caution regarding the use of the "state" is in order. In these theoretical discussions of the state's role in the development process, the state seems to take on a life of its own, as if it were a single actor. We talk about it as being strong or weak, intervening to a greater or lesser extent in the economy, and so on. For a number of reasons, including the fact that the state plays such an important role in our lives as modern citizens, like a parent writ large who authors the rules that govern us, it is important to remember that the state is an abstraction; it does not actually exist as a substantial "thing." Rather, it refers to an extraordinarily complex organization made up of many people, often appointed, sometimes elected, usually representing others and functioning in diverse institutional settings that frequently pull in different directions. As an expression of authority, therefore, it neither speaks in a single voice nor does it actually represent the nation as a whole, except in the metaphorical or symbolic sense.

World System Theory.   Within the framework of *world system theory*, "late developers" face an entirely different dilemma from "early developers" when they confront the task of modernizing. Their lack of an internal bourgeois-driven developmental dynamic in the first place makes these nations subservient and vulnerable to the depredations of the advanced nations. This results in unequal relationships between strong states protecting the interests of their international investors and weak states unable to protect either their human or material resources from the ravages of an exchange system that favors the strong and the wealthy. Because this new dilemma is an internationally determined one in which starkly unequal players compete freely in an open match without handicaps, the weak players never get a chance to strengthen their game, while the already skillful players win not only all the games but eventually also the other players and the ballpark.

According to the early dependency version of this theoretical approach, expressed in the 1960s by scholars specializing in Latin America, exporting capitalism becomes part of the problem rather than being part of the solution to poverty and backwardness. Unlike Lenin's more optimistic scenario of imperialism as a process in which capitalists turn backward countries into the international equivalents of revolutionary workers who eventually break the chain of exploitation, dependency theorists held a pessimistic outlook for the Third World. Western investors in developing countries may see their activities as modernizing backward peoples—bringing them new ideas, superior sources of wealth, and the skills and attitudes required to produce them. But dependency theorists look not at the activities themselves but their consequences and see a bleak picture of unremitting impoverishment for third world peoples with the profits they produce returning to the already prosperous developed nations. The dependency perspective thus dramatically countered the optimistic liberal prospects of effective charitable assistance to help the weak become stronger. In its place was a grim depiction of a perverse umbilical cord by which the strong advanced country saps the nutrients of the underdeveloped dependent nation, permanently impairing its ability to develop at all.

In Immanuel Wallerstein's more fully elaborated theory of the *modern world system*, the same idea is the central premise: that there is a world capitalist system much larger than any single nation-state whose expansion drives and shapes development in the still underdeveloped parts of the world.[3] This world market system has been steadily incorporating more and more areas of the globe since its inception in the sixteenth century, giving rise to a three-tiered global "class system" among nation-states. The interrelationships among these three spatially distributed "classes" of nations provide the focus of analysis. At the *core* of this international political economy are the highly developed nations, which act as an external constraint on the internal economic and political structures of weak, *peripheral* nation-states in the international system. But if this postulate is similar to that of its earlier dependency version, the outlook for underdeveloped nations is not equally grim from the world system perspective.

Wallerstein's three-tiered system of nation-states leaves the theoretical door open to both upward and downward mobility of individual states from the lowest and highest tiers to the middle tier, the *semiperipheral* or "middle-class" level of nations. Over time with strong enough internal state structures and optimal international conditions, *some* states in the periphery can be observed to move upward into semiperipheral status. Core countries, of course, may also drop down into the semi-periphery. From the world system perspective, therefore, even relatively weaker states may be able to increase their bargaining chips in the international marketplace by generating policies in support of local initiatives that counteract the pressures from externally powerful players to their own advantage. Such a modified model of "dependent development" suggests that peripheral states can assist development by forging effective alliances between local bourgeoisie in dependent countries and the powerful multinational bourgeoisie combing the world for new investment opportunities.

World system theory thus provides conceptual space for *some* states to avoid being stifled by the profiteering of core countries, principally because the world capitalist system is seen historically as a continually expanding pie or non–zero-sum game. A key question is, however, left unexplored by world system theory: What exactly enables some states to exploit world system opportunities to propel themselves toward successful development? This question is addressed by the third theoretical framework of analysis: developmental state theory.

Developmental State Theory.   Also referred to as the *statist approach, developmental state theory* differs from both modernization theory and world system theory because it considers the state rather than the market the essential institution that enables late industrializing nation-states to achieve successful economic development.[4] Because of the competitive weakness of late developers in an already crowded international market, a capable and authoritative state is required to steer a course of economic growth that reconciles national capabilities with international opportunities. Such a developmental state exercises considerable authority over the market by shaping the business decisions made by private owners of productive property. In this theoretical scenario, while economic growth is propelled by a market economy, the driver of the (market) engine is a state bureaucracy which has a high degree of autonomy from the political demands and pressures of both elected officials with their divergent constituencies and powerful vested interests.

But the "autonomy" envisioned by the developmental state or statist approach does not refer to a state that is isolated from all social forces of civil society. On the contrary, the developmental state achieves its autonomy by being closely embedded in civil society. The state relies on its moral and material support from the population to maintain legitimate informal linkages between specialized governmental agencies and privately owned industrial enterprises. These informal linkages enable the government to rely on the price mechanisms of the market rather than administratively assigned prices to carry out its will. Through the close collaboration of public and private sectors, therefore, the sum of market decisions is not left to the vagaries of an "invisible hand," reflecting instead the agenda of powerful planning agencies. Peter Evans refers to the capability of this kind of developmental state as "embedded autonomy."[5]

The developmental state is defined by the scope and direction of its intervention in the market. Rather than limiting its exercise of power over the economy to regulatory oversight, the developmental state pursues what has come to be known as "an industrial policy."[6] It intervenes not only to remove serious obstacles to the operation of market mechanisms but also to orchestrate market forces in the direction of achieving national economic goals and ensuring international economic competitiveness. For example, the state can assume the role of surrogate for a missing capital market by raising and providing capital for private economic actors. In this way, it can induce transformative investment decisions that are in the best interests of the emergent private sector. It also assumes responsibility for sustained investments in education and policies to ensure equitable distribution of the wealth gained through high-speed growth.

As a broker of rapid national economic growth, the developmental state must have a highly organized and effective bureaucracy. This includes a number of key elements. First, the state must have a highly selective system for recruiting "the best and the brightest" into government bureaucratic service. Recruitment must be on the basis of merit requiring not only the highest level of education from the most prestigious universities but scoring high on national examinations. Second, government bureaucracy must provide long-term career rewards associated with the high prestige, honor, or respect afforded such public service. Third, there must be a "corporate coherence" for bureaucrats in high government service, an esprit de corps that endows incumbent bureaucrats with a defensive shield against pressures from individual constituents with personal agendas. This ensures the "autonomy" that enables developmental states to generate industrial policy decisions insulated from the clientelist pressures of particular vested interests. On the other hand, this autonomy of government bureaucracy needs to be "embedded" in the business community so that its "recommendations" will be compatible with the objectives of market players. This "embeddedness" naturally carries its own burden or costs for the developmental state. A fuller discussion of this aspect is covered in Chapter 5 as part of the analysis of Japan's extended economic downturn and the "Asian" financial crisis.

Throughout the remainder of this book, you will find evidence that favors one or another of these three theoretical contentions. Likewise the circumstances and experiences of development in the Asian Pacific raise significant questions for each of the theoretical approaches. In the case of modernization theory, its neoliberal version in particular, there is the question of whether and to what extent "free market" mechanisms are sustainable as the cornerstone of development anywhere in the world in the twenty-first century. For world system theory, the question is what effects the capacity of peripheral countries' development have on the limits of expansion of the world capitalist system. And the question for developmental state or statist theory is whether developmental states are enduring solutions for national political entities or merely transitional states that usher in the same problems that all so-called developed states face in adjusting to the new global order.

SUMMARY

The preliminary sketch of the countries in the Asian Pacific covered in the first half of this chapter demonstrates how richly varied the region is in almost all dimensions—area, population, geography, natural resources, cultural legacy, colonial experience, and system of government since independence.

   This diversity is in marked contrast to the aspiration all these countries share, that of development into prosperous, modern nation-states. With a resource base ranging from rich (Brunei with its oil) to poor (Japan), with belief systems including among others animism, Confucianism, Buddhism, Islam, and Catholicism, and with colonial structures inherited from Western European countries stretching from Portugal to Britain and the United States, it is difficult to imagine a single path of development for them all. And indeed the disparities among them with respect to how prosperous and modern they have become are enormous. If the astounding economic growth of the "four tigers" has made the Pacific Rim a household term in the West, the stagnation of a country like Myanmar or the slow pace of change in a country like Laos raise a key question: What factors explain why some countries develop rapidly and others seem to resist the process?

   A number of possible answers to this question can be derived from the theoretical frameworks discussed in the second half of this chapter. *Modernization theory* bases its analysis on the original Western experience with capitalist development, while the other two begin with the difficulties developing countries have had in adopting this model. Like modernization theory, *world system theory* is deductive in nature reasoning from the general to the specific though it is time-specific and historical. *Developmental state* or *statist theory*, which is also historical, is different from the other two because it is inductive and attempts to generalize from the particular experiences of Asian Pacific countries that have developed more rapidly than others by virtue of a strong, autonomous, and activist state. In the next chapter the diverse colonial legacy of Asian Pacific countries will be explored as a possible factor that influences how strong or weak modern states in the region are today.

QUESTIONS FOR DISCUSSION

1. In what ways are Asian Pacific countries different from each other? Similar to each other? Different from your own country? Similar to it?
2. What are the differences between living in a "developed" and an "underdeveloped" society? Why is development so appealing to people everywhere?
3. During the rise of modern capitalism in Europe, what contribution did government make? The market?
4. Can developing countries follow that same formula for success?

NOTES

1. *World Development Report 1998/1999* (New York: Oxford University Press, 1999) table 5, pp. 198–199.
2. *Hobbes's Leviathan* (Oxford: Clarendon Press, 1909), p. 97.
3. Immanuel Wallerstein, *The Modern World-System: Capitalist Agriculture and the Origins of the European World-Economy in the Sixteenth Century* (New York: Academic Press, text ed., 1976).
4. Two outstanding examples of the developmental state approach are Alice Amsden, *Asia's Next Giant: South Korea and Late Industrialization* (New York: Oxford University Press, 1989).
5. Peter Evans, *Embedded Autonomy: States and Industrial Transformation* (Princeton, NJ: Princeton University Press, 1995).
6. Chalmers Johnson, *MITI and the Japanese Miracle: The Growth of Industrial Policy, 1925–1975* (Stanford, CA: Stanford University Press, 1982.)

FOR FURTHER READING

Randall, Vicky, and Robin Theobald. *Political Change and Underdevelopment: A Critical Introduction to Third World Politics,* 2nd ed. Durham, NC: Duke University Press, 1998.

Seligson, Mitchell A., and John T. Passe-Smith, eds. *Development and Underdevelopment: The Political Economy of Inequality.* Boulder, CO: Lynne Rienner, 1993.

Evans, Peter. *Embedded Autonomy: States and Industrial Transformation.* Princeton, NJ: Princeton University Press, 1995.

Schuurman, Frans J., ed. *Beyond the Impasse: New Directions in Development Theory.* London: Zed Books, 1993.

2

The Imposition
of Colonialism

Modernization in the Asian Pacific began with colonialism. Although foreign ideas had contributed layers of cultural influence throughout East and Southeast Asia for thousands of years, Western colonialism was unlike anything that had preceded it. The Arabs, Indians, Malays, and Chinese who had set themselves up as rulers and had conducted trade and settled throughout the Asian region had never been accountable to monarchs elsewhere; the Europeans who arrived after the sixteenth century came to build empires for their monarchs in Portugal, Spain, England, and France, creating colonies out of other people's territory and incorporating them into the world market system.

The story of how the modern world insinuated itself into Asia, transforming the lives of those it subjugated, is complex. It has been told by different people in different ways and continues to be the subject of intense controversy, although for the most part the outward forms of colonialism have disappeared. The nations that exist in Pacific Asia today are in one way or another products of the intercourse between East and West over the past four centuries. During this time, the system we call *colonialism* swept through the world, altering everything in its course. But in the process of incorporating the world's people into a global economy, the originators of capitalism—Britain, France, the United States—were themselves undergoing continual changes that turned modernization at the center into a moving target and resulted in variations of the colonial enterprise on the periphery. Under Portuguese and Spanish rule, colonies fared quite differently than they did under Britain and France in the nineteenth century and under Japanese and American colonial administration in the twentieth century. Not surprisingly, responses to the challenge of modernization have varied with both time and circumstance.

But for Asians, as for all non-Western people, modernization was brought by outsiders who considered themselves superior both materially and spiritually. The merchant-adventurers from Portugal, Spain, Holland, England, and France were accompanied by Christian missionaries armed with the faith that conversion to belief in their God would rescue the heathen Asians from the errors of Hinduism, Buddhism, Confucianism, Islam, or the nature-worship, magical beliefs of animism. By its very nature, the Christian religious enterprise was an economic, political, and social form of Western intrusion quite distinct from the Indianizing influences that had followed in the wake of Arab and Indian trade throughout the region.

Trade and religion brought Western values, ideas, technology, and goods, the instruments for breaking down the natural contours of the old Asian world to prepare the way for a revolutionary process of change that continues to this very day. From the Asian perspective this Western intrusion was at once appealing and threatening to their established way of life. To Westerners, prying open Asian societies was somewhere between a duty and a blessing, bound to yield economic enrichment and spiritual salvation.

Merchants and missionaries were followed, especially in the nineteenth century, by administrators, governors, and resident advisers as well as the armed forces of the Western powers. The idea that political and socioeconomic development would also flow from the contact between Western imperialism and the "backward" peoples of Asia justified taking control of Asia as colonies. Colonialism in this phase entailed the remaking of Asia in the image of the West. By establishing political and administrative rule, Englishmen and Frenchmen would be modeling the benefits of modern society to stir in primitive peoples the desire to become modern. The result would be a world enriched by representative institutions and individual freedoms. We will not elaborate here on the destructive and rapacious aspects of Western colonial rule. The underlying problem for Asians with this benign view of colonialism's purpose was the assumption that modernization meant Westernization. How were Japanese, Chinese, Koreans, Thai, Vietnamese, or Javanese to become modern without also becoming Western? Was it possible for a nation to become Western without losing its own identity? What exactly was the Western experience of modernization that formed the basis of expectations for Asians?

The story of colonialism as the stimulus to modernization in Asia really begins in Europe, where great economic and political changes from the fifteenth century on impelled the people of that continent outward to assert control over the rest of the world. So in the first sections of this chapter, we uncover and examine the European roots of colonialism in the light of the three theories of development that were introduced in Chapter 1. We then describe the traditional societies of Asia as they were, before recounting the history of how the Europeans came and carved out their empires in Southeast Asia and exerted their influence in East Asia. The rest of the chapter looks first at the puzzling issue of why China and Japan responded so differently to the challenges of colonialism's demands for modernization and finally at the character of colonial rule in Southeast Asia as experienced by five of the colonies in that region.

THE EUROPEAN ROOTS OF COLONIALISM

Five hundred years ago living conditions worldwide were very similar; most people did hard physical labor, relying on their own power and that of animals to raise food and produce necessities for themselves. A few people, the elites of society, did brain work: making political decisions, directing wars, collecting taxes, supervising religious and educational institutions. But the gap between the haves and the have-nots was not as great as it is today. According to one estimate,[1] differences in income levels between the poorest and the richest countries were in the range of 1.0 to 1.6 before the industrial revolution, and the standard of living in Europe as a whole was lower than in China and about the same as in the rest of the world. Capitalism changed all that.

Colonialism grew out of the extraordinary changes that ushered in capitalism in Western Europe in the fifteenth century: the scientific, Protestant, and commercial revolutions. The Renaissance had released human energies for improving life on earth rather than preparing for life in heaven. The scientific revolution made the physical world more comprehensible to and controllable by human intelligence. And the Protestant revolution shattered the secular power of the Catholic Church, strengthening the individual nation-states of Europe. When the Portuguese and Spaniards started crisscrossing the seas in search of precious metals, valuable spices, and quality fabrics, they reduced the globe to a single market, centered in Europe. By the middle of the seventeenth century, the king of England had chartered companies to establish colonies in North America and India. Colonialism—the process of incorporating peoples in Asia, Africa, and the New World into the commercialized web of political life in Europe—had begun.

The transformation of Europe from feudalism to capitalism occurred in stages. In the mercantilist stage, the precious metals brought to Portugal and Spain from their colonies in the Western Hemisphere went to buy commodities from England and the Netherlands, becoming available as productive capital in those more advanced economies. There feudal manors were giving way to commercialized agriculture, mills, and mines. Merchants and lords were becoming capitalists who no longer saw land as an inheritance to support a way of life but as a means to make a profit. As land was enclosed, peasants were forced into cities where they became wageworkers. Artisans and craftsmen were also driven into the working class when the commodities they produced could not compete with goods produced more cheaply in greater volume in the new factories built by the capitalists.

With the industrial revolution in the late eighteenth century, capitalism moved into higher gear. In this second stage, manufacturing greatly increased productive capacity, and the voracious appetites of machinery for raw materials to continually expand production changed the nature of colonial undertakings. Under mercantilist colonialism, exotic luxury items like tea, porcelain, spices, and silks had been imported from the colonies into Europe. Now with the industrial stage of capitalism, there was a two-way trade. Minerals, fibers for manufacturing, oil, rubber, and tin as well as increased quantities of tea, coffee, and tobacco flowed into Europe and the United States to satisfy the vastly expanded population of consumers and producers,

In the other direction cotton goods, iron and steel products, alcoholic beverages, and cigarettes were exported to the colonies. In addition to this European commodity trade, the colonies provided opportunities for lucrative capital investments. Between 1880 and World War I, there was a virtual frenzy of competition among imperialist nations to acquire exclusive control of territory in Asia and Africa.

The colonial knots tied in the late nineteenth and early twentieth centuries are central to the discussion of modernization in non-Western areas. The question of what impact colonial status had on the traditional economies of non-Western peoples is bound to elicit a variety of answers. Did colonialism impair or enhance the chances for subsequent modernization after colonies achieved their independence? Some scholars deflate the significance of economic exploitation in the colonies, noting that European countries needed neither raw materials nor market outlets for their manufactured goods to any substantial degree.[2] Others argue that mere size (in absolute terms) of foreign trade or investment is not as critical in assessing their importance as their interrelatedness—that is, the degree to which a country has been incorporated as a dependent satellite into the world economic market. Differences such as these are at the core of the three alternative theoretical perspectives introduced in Chapter 1. Each perspective approaches the question of colonialism from a distinctive angle and interprets the facts of the colonial period of Asian history differently, as will be seen in the next section.

THREE THEORETICAL VIEWS OF COLONIALISM

Modernization Theory

Modernization theory approaches colonialism as an export commodity of the Western industrializing nations. Through colonial rule, advanced industrial nations export the productive, scientific, and social potential of modern liberal society to "backward," outlying areas. In their colonial outreach, capitalist nations extend their accomplishments beyond their national boundaries, thus opening up "backward" or traditional societies to the progressive potential of modern development. The initial motivation for foreign capitalist ventures may have been to expand markets and profits for their own domestic benefit, but the long-range consequences were to sow the seeds of modernization among insular and custom-bound peoples in backward parts of the world. The very term "opening up" to refer to Western encroachments suggests a liberating force, a loosening of the restrictions of tradition-bound peoples from their ancient moorings.

This does not necessarily mean excusing the more unsavory aspects of colonial exploitation or political subjugation; what it does mean is that colonialism is envisioned as an extension of modern civilization, which confronts traditional societies with the challenge of fundamental changes to their ancient way of life. These fundamental changes are identified as national—not regional or global—developments. As each colony obtains its independence, having spent a tutelary period under the wings of a more advanced industrial nation, it is expected to replicate, albeit in modified form, the original European pattern of national development, following a sequence of steps considered necessary to transform a traditional way of life into a modern one.

According to this theory, colonization is a process of cultural diffusion. Under the aegis of colonial rule, modern know-how and techniques are dispersed across an ever-widening geographical area. It is through colonization, therefore, that modernization as a potentiality is made available to people in "backward" areas of the globe. If "backward" societies are unable to benefit from the opportunity, an explanation must be sought in the internal factors that impede progress—the resistance to change of enduring traditions, for example. By focusing almost exclusively on the domestic socioeconomic and political aspects of change, the approach ignores the constraints on developmental resourcefulness that derive from the complex international web of dependency relations.

World System Theory

From the world system perspective, colonialism is the incorporation of new territories and people into the global network of market relationships. When precapitalist societies are brought into the existing order of the world market, they come in at the "periphery." In their relationship with the powerful "core" of advanced capitalist nations, these colonies, even when they gain their political independence, remain economically and politically weak. In between core and peripheral nations lies an intermediate or "semiperiperhal" zone of nations either moving up from their backward status as low-production, low-paid economic areas to high-production, well-paid economic areas or moving down from more advanced to less advanced economies.

At its inception in the sixteenth century, the world system was coterminous with Europe. Since then, core nations (or those attempting to move into that position) have used a combination of force and guile to continually enlarge the global market. Core nations are compelled to expand in order to remain competitive in a dynamically charged international market. This competition among core nations to supersede one another drives the expansion of the capitalist world system. But for newly incorporated or peripheral countries (whether they are formal colonies or not), however, it means dependence on the core and exploitation as the price of admission. As in the case with lower-class people within capitalist society, this theory suggests that peripheral nations face overwhelming odds against becoming truly independent and prosperous members of the world community. From their perspective, development or improvement is not merely a question of becoming politically independent or economically and culturally modernized; it is a question of how many cards one has to play in the mobility game within a worldwide system, which for the most part is stacked in favor of those who are already on top.

Developmental State (or Statist) Theory

Colonialism, from the statist perspective, is not viewed as the beneficent dissemination of modern ideas and practices by more advanced countries to backward areas, as modernization theory implies. Nor, from this perspective, can colonizing powers be held responsible for impeding the industrial development of "backward" countries, as world system theory suggests. Colonialism is merely part of a historical process of evolution. What needs to be explained are not the origins or purpose of the new industrial "species" of human society that was first discovered in sixteeth-century Europe, but the pattern of adaptations required by subsequent countries faced with the challenge of surviving in an already industrialized world order. Countries like Japan, Korea, and Taiwan are examples of successful adaptation by "late industrializers" and therefore offer instructive insights into the new institutional arrangements that have enabled them to survive.

From the statist perspective, as its name indicates, the central institution for understanding why and how these "late industrializers" have succeeded in adapting to modernization is the state. Colonialism posed the initial challenge or test of survival for most countries in the world. For countries such as the United States and Japan, which fashioned a strong enough state to either avoid or extricate themselves from subjugation to colonial status early in the game, industrial modernization proceeded both smoothly and relatively easily. For those less developed societies that were precluded by internal cultural, economic, or political conflicts from forming a strong centralized state, colonial rule exacted a higher cost: oppression, exploitation, and the complications of being subjected to the full brunt of market forces controlled by the industrial development of other countries. From this perspective, colonialism was the conquest of backward countries too weak internally to defend themselves against external aggression.

By delivering agrarian societies into the vortex of the international market, colonial rulers indefinitely postponed the capacity of their colonies to initiate and control their own internal industrial development. As colonies, these agrarian societies were "developed" by colonial interests on the basis of whatever comparative advantage they happened to possess that supplied the demands of the international market. The colonized people, however, could benefit only from the promise but not from the fulfillment of the fruits of their industry. So long as they were bereft of a strong developmental state of their own, colonies such as Korea and Taiwan were unable to encourage *local* industry and remained backward, agricultural producers. Furthermore, the end of colonial status did not automatically bring "backward" countries any closer to fulfilling the promise of development. For it was not primarily political independence from outside forces that mattered but erecting a state "strong" enough to direct, assist, and protect an internal industrial development geared to competing in the international market.

If the key factor in avoiding colonial ("backward") dependence on a world industrial market system is securing the institution of a strong developmental state, then the significant question is What characteristics does a state need to be "strong and developmental"? Clearly, the strength of a developmental state is not in the military might it can muster to enforce its will, though doubtless that is a necessary requisite. A "strong" state must have centralized authority to orchestrate and conduct a large, complex political economy. This means not only providing investment funds when necessary but also exacting a high level of industrial performance on the part of the privately owned sector in return.

And to effectively intervene in developing a strong, privately owned, internal industrial sector operating in conjunction with international market forces, the developmental state must also have the support of a merit-based bureaucracy, a literate workforce and a pool of managers equipped to work with borrowed technology.

By emphasizing the centrality of a developmental state strong enough to stand up to both internal and external impediments to national economic development—prompting some to call this system "command capitalism"—the statist perspective while displaying some affinities to both modernization and world system theories provides an understanding of colonialism that is distinctively its own. Which of these three theories—or what combination of them—are most persuasive as explanations for understanding colonialism? It will be left up to the reader to determine this in the remainder of the chapter.

TRADITIONAL SOCIETIES ON THE EVE OF COLONIALISM

What were societies like in East and Southeast Asia before Western colonialism hit them? Why did some traditional societies succumb more easily to colonial rule than others? To understand the impact of Western colonialism, it helps to have an understanding of the sum of earlier influences, sometimes referred to as traditional society, that the Europeans discovered when they arrived.

Economically and socially, societies throughout the Asian Pacific were quite similar prior to the seventeenth century. They were agrarian societies, many of them dependent on rice cultivation with its requirements for substantial irrigation, intensive labor, and community cooperation. The family was the basic unit of production; land was divided equally among sons in China but inherited by the eldest son in Japan. Within the family, as in the larger society, rigid social hierarchies favored male over female, old over young.

Belief Systems

The oldest and most enduring beliefs were in spirits attached to the variety of elements upon which people depended but over which they had no control; especially in rural areas these "superstitions" continued to coexist with the more organized and sophisticated religious doctrines that fanned out from the great civilizations in China and India.

Three great religious traditions—Hinduism, Buddhism, and Islam—had spread eastward from India and Arabia throughout Southeast and East Asia, while Confucianism had made its way from China to Korea, Japan, and Vietnam, where its principles were adapted to the distinctive conditions in each society. By the time Europeans began arriving in the sixteenth century, Hindu influence—once pervasive in most of Southeast Asia—was still visible only in Bali. Buddhism, which had followed Hinduism from India, was still dominant in Burma, Thailand, Laos, and Cambodia, and it had left traces of its presence in parts of Indonesia. Islam, having arrived in the fourteenth century, was established in Malaya, Indonesia, and the

Rice farming requires cooperation to build and maintain the paddies, as in the terraced fields in Indonesia.

Source: United Nations photo 154948/Ray Witlin.

southern Philippines. The only place where animism prevailed untouched by any of the major belief systems from either India or China was the Philippines; when Christianity was brought there by the Spaniards, it swept through the society like a brushfire.

An ethical system emphasizing propriety in earthly affairs, Confucianism was able to coexist with religious belief systems: in China with Taoism and Buddhism, and in Korea, Vietnam, and Japan with Buddhism. Chinese Confucianism was reshaped into a distinctively Japanese form by the additional influence of Shinto, the belief in the divinity of the emperor, and Bushido, a strong warrior code of honor. Although Confucianism and the religious beliefs of Hinduism, Buddhism, and Islam differ substantially from each other, they share a powerful common denominator: a fatalistic acceptance of the human condition.

Political Organization

In politics, authoritarian rule was the norm among traditional peoples in the Asian Pacific. There were enormous differences in the scale of political organization from the atomistic village communities of the Philippines to the highly centralized state bureaucracy of the Chinese empire. But even in China, where the central government ruled over a large land area, it did not penetrate down into the villages where most of the people lived. And the actual power wielded by the central government waxed and waned over the centuries; when the emperor's power waned, regional leadership exercised by a middle tier of provincial administrators filled the vacuum. In the nineteenth century, the Qing or Manchu dynasty's power was on the decline, increasing China's susceptibility to penetration from outside as well as to challenges from within.

Kingdoms similar to the Chinese existed, though on a smaller scale, in the other Confucian states and in Buddhist Burma, Thailand, Cambodia, and Laos, and they had existed earlier in Sumatra. The political institutions of Hindu and Islamic societies were typically small in scale as, for example, the Malay sultanates. In all these societies, the village was the lowest level of social organization. In the north and central Philippines, atomistic village communities were the only political structures, and this lack of cohesiveness may have made the Philippines more susceptible to foreign cultural penetration than other more cohesive societies.

The basis of the rulers' legitimacy and the ranking of different classes in the social hierarchy were also influenced by the dominant belief systems. In Hindu, Buddhist, and Islamic politics, divine will legitimized unlimited personalist monarchs, but detachment from worldly affairs kept the Hindu and Buddhist priesthood largely out of the political realm, and they did not challenge kingly authority. Islam, on the other hand, views this world as important and religion as governing all aspects of life, so the notion of separation of church and state is quite alien to the Moslem worldview. Although Confucianism, like Islam, is "this-worldly," it is decidedly secular in its teachings. Its rules and rituals outlined the moral order that guided everything in the universe. When there was widespread hunger and disorder in the realm, the emperor was said to have lost "the mandate of Heaven," which served notice that a new political leadership was required to restore the moral order.

Social Hierarchy

The ranking of classes below the emperor, king, or sultan put the military and merchants higher in the Hindu and Islamic social hierarchies than in the Buddhist; in the simple village structures of the Philippines, the village leader, the *datu,* occupied the top of the pyramid. Peasants in all societies were low in rank, the very bottom being occupied by slaves, outcasts, untouchables, and in Islamic societies the non-Moslems, the "infidels." In Confucian China, the emperor's legitimacy rested in practice on performance; if the emperor and his civil service of scholar-bureaucrats met their moral obligations to the classes beneath them, the inferiors owed their superiors obedience and respect. If there was disorder in social relationships, a new moral order was required to restore people's loyalty. Below scholar-officials in the Chinese social hierarchy, land-owning peasants ranked higher than artisans and merchants, the latter not at all well regarded. Landless workers and servants occupied the bottom position.

In Japan, the Confucian social hierarchy was modified to incorporate the pre-Confucian Shinto belief in the divine descent of the emperor from a sun goddess. Also unlike China, the Japanese emperor had for centuries symbolized the unique identity of Japan, though until 1868 actual power was exercised by the *shogun,* a military leader who reached his preeminent position in wars with several hundred other feudal clan leaders, the *daimyo.* The emperor was the ceremonial head of the social order and the *shogun* the head of the political order. Next came the *daimyo* and their armed supporters, the *samurai,* followed by the peasants. Below them—as in China—came artisans and merchants, and at the bottom the *eta* or outcasts, whose low status as the handlers of animal carcasses and leather remains in effect still. In Japan, the military tradition carried on by the shogun, daimyo, and samurai was much more powerful and respected than in China where military force played a major role in settling the issue of dynastic succession, but the military profession as such was not highly valued.

These characteristics, it is speculated, made traditional societies more or less resistant to Western influence and the conditions imposed by colonialism. Darling ranks China as the most resistant to foreign influence;[3] the Chinese-penetrated states of Korea, Vietnam, and Japan are somewhat less so and the least resistant are the Southeast Asian countries that had experienced the cultural impact of Hinduism, Buddhism, and, in the cases of Malaya and Indonesia, Islam as well. Cohesiveness of societal structures was highest in Korea, Vietnam, and China, and it was least in the pre-Spanish Philippines and in Japan.[4] Resistance to change may also have been greater in those societies in which people had the collective memory of a long, shared history than in societies of shorter duration. Countries that had existed for a thousand or more years prior to the arrival of Western colonialism include China, Vietnam, Korea, Cambodia, and Japan,[5] although their boundaries were much more fluid and permeable than those of modern European states.

Geography also impeded or enhanced the Western impact. Size may account in part for China's escaping colonization by a single foreign power, and the 3,000-mile extent of the Indonesian archipelago meant that Dutch rule spread only gradually from Sumatra and Java to the other islands. Topography also plays a role: For example, landlocked Laos was relatively inaccessible to the seagoing imperial powers as compared to countries with coasts. The presence of natural resources, such as tin and rubber in Malaya, and soil suited for crops in southern Burma, Java, and Sumatra added to their appeal.

THE CONQUEST OF SOUTHEAST AND EAST ASIA

In colonizing Southeast Asia, Europeans brought people together under one foreign government without regard for either natural boundaries or ethnic affinities. Indeed ethnic, linguistic, and religious divisions among colonized peoples facilitated their subjugation and were reinforced by divide-and-rule colonial policies and the importation of Chinese and Indians to work on the coffee and rubber plantations and in the mines. When these artificially created colonial states later became independent, their governments and leaders inherited all the attendant problems of trying to forge nations out of states arbitrarily imposed to serve European interests.

In China, Korea, and Japan, on the other hand, strong sovereign states with enduring boundaries predated European domination. Each had a long history of unified rule, a homogeneous population, and a highly developed and sophisticated civilization rivaling that of Europe. They were capable of effectively resisting the encroachments of Western colonizers, forcing them to pay higher costs for economic and political control. Unlike Southeast Asia, none of the East Asian countries became outright European colonies. Japan escaped colonization altogether and joined the Europeans in their own game, making Taiwan and Korea its imperial possessions. China came close to being colonized; the term semicolony seems a fitting description of its status in the nineteenth century, when the European countries (later joined by Japan) carved out for themselves special "spheres of influence" in parts of that vast country.

Western colonialism occurred in two phases, the mercantilist and the capitalist, as different motives reflective of economic changes in Europe impelled Western countries to conquests in Asia. Major events in the history of colonialism in the Asian Pacific are identified in Table 2.1.

The Mercantilist Phase

The Portuguese and Spanish arriving in the sixteenth century plied their trade quite differently from earlier Westerners who, since Marco Polo's time, had traveled overland between the Mediterranean and Asia in pursuit of silks and spices. In this early mercantilist phase of capitalism, the Dutch and the British, following closely on the heels of the Portuguese, vied with one another for control of key ports and sea lanes. Merchants typically negotiated or coerced local rulers into granting them an array of trading rights: the freedom to move in and out of Asian ports, favorable tariff treatment, a small foothold on shore for residence, storage, and ship provisioning. With their modest goal of acquiring desired Asian products, the European traders in this period did not need to penetrate extensively into the hinterland, nor did they usually assume responsibility for carrying on governmental functions. Exceptions were the Spanish in the Philippines and the Dutch East India Company in some of the islands now making up Indonesia, where control was extended in varying degrees.

The Portuguese and the Spanish.   The Portuguese captured Malacca (in what is now Malaysia) from the Malays of neighboring islands (now Indonesia) in 1511. Control over this important collection point for spices enabled them to increase their earnings by making the ships of other countries pay for protection as they passed through the narrow straits into the South China Sea and beyond. The Portuguese extended their interests into the Indonesian archipelago eastward to Timor and north to China, in 1557 acquiring Macao (which they still hold). The Spanish, moving westward from Mexico across the Pacific, took over the Philippines in 1564, holding them until 1898.

The Dutch and the British.   European nations fell over one another in the colonial hunt. The Dutch replaced the Portuguese in the Malay-Indonesian area, taking Jakarta on Java, the port of Malacca, and the Moluccas in 1641. The British successfully challenged the Dutch in the eighteenth century, moving from India on

TABLE 2.1 Important Dates in the Era of Colonialism

1511	Portuguese capture Malacca
1557	Portuguese take Macau
1564	Spanish take the Philippines
1637	Shimabara Rebellion by Japanese Christians against Tokugawa shogunate
1640	Japan bans contact with foreigners
1641	Dutch East India Company takes Jakarta, Malacca, Moluccas
1682	Dutch government takes over from Company
1786	British take Penang
1819	British take Singapore
1824	Dutch and British settle conflict over colonies by agreeing to Dutch control of the East Indies and British control of Malay peninsula
1842	First Anglo-Chinese ("Opium") War; Treaty of Nanjing: Hong Kong ceded to Britain
1850–1864	Taiping Rebellion against Qing Dynasty
1853	Admiral Perry's fleet arrives in Japan
1857	Second Anglo-Chinese War; Yangtze Valley opened, China cedes territory to Russia
1862	French take Cochin China
1863	French protectorate over Cambodia
1867	British protectorate over Kingdom of Burma
1868	Tokugawa shogunate overthrown; Meiji Restoration
1874	French protectorate over Kingdom of Annam-Tonkin
1885	British abolish Kingdom of Burma and administer as part of India
1887	French consolidate rule over Vietnam
1888	British protectorates over Brunei, North Borneo, Sarawak
1893	French protectorate over Laos
1894–1895	Sino-Japanese War; China cedes Taiwan to Japan; Japan gets rights in Korea, France gets sphere of influence in south, Russians in Manchuria
1896	British establish Federation of Malay States
1898	Spanish-American War, United States takes the Philippines; in China, Germany gets sphere of influence in Shandong Peninsula, Russia in Liaodong Peninsula, French in Guangzhou
1900	Boxer Rebellion (China)
1904–1905	Russo-Japanese War; Japan gets southern Sakhalin, sphere of influence in Manchuria, and more rights in Korea
1910	Japan annexes Korea
1911	Qing Dynasty ends; Republic of China proclaimed
1913	Russia establishes protectorate over Mongolia
1914–1918	World War I; Japan gets German interests in Shandong and influence in eastern Inner Mongolia and in Fujian Province

TABLE 2.1 *(Continued)*

1917	Russian Revolution; Japan expands influence in Manchuria
1931	Japanese begin military conquest of China
1934	Japanese create puppet state, Manchukuo
1941–1942	Japanese occupy the Philippines, Malaya, Singapore, Indonesia, Burma, French Indochina; by agreement with government, Japanese forces enter Thailand

to Burma and down the Malay Peninsula, where local sultans granted them the islands of Penang and Singapore. Competition between England and Holland heightened when they took opposing sides in the Napoleonic Wars and the British occupied Malacca, Java, and Sumatra. The rivals finally settled their differences through an 1824 treaty acknowledging Dutch possession of the East Indies and British dominance in the Malay Peninsula. As the result of wars in 1824 and 1852, the British obtained control of parts of Burma. Meanwhile, beginning in the eighteenth century, French missionaries and traders were displaying interest in the eastern part of Southeast Asia.

China. China responded with disdain to European traders' demands for entry, granting limited rights first to the Portuguese at Macao and later to the Dutch and British at Canton (now Guangzhou). By the early 1800s, however, the British urgently needed to expand their access to the China market. In an effort to correct a trade deficit caused by their purchases of Chinese tea, for which Britons had acquired an ever-growing thirst, the British East India Company brought opium from India to China. When the Chinese, alarmed by the growing addiction of their people, decided to curb that trade, Britain launched the first Opium War and defeated the Chinese handily. By the Treaty of Nanjing of 1842 China agreed to open five "treaty ports" to trade and ceded the island of Hong Kong to Britain outright.

The "Opening" of Japan. Initially receptive to both trade and Christian missionaries, the Japanese decided on a policy of isolation and by 1640 banished all foreigners except for a small number of Dutch who were allowed to reside on an island in Nagasaki Bay. Japan remained "closed" until 1853, when the American navy came to "open" it. "Manifest destiny" had propelled the United States westward across the continent and around Cape Horn to California and out into the Pacific. With an eye on Japan as a fueling station for ships on their way to Shanghai from San Francisco, the United States sent Admiral Matthew Perry with four warships to ask for better treatment of shipwrecked sailors, for permission for vessels to take on coal and provisions at Japanese ports, and for trade between the two countries. Perry gave the Japanese authorities a year to consider the requests, all of which, except the trade, were accepted upon his return in 1854. A few years later, however, commercial treaties were signed with the United States, Great Britain, France, Russia, and the Netherlands, opening up certain ports to trade and foreign residents.

Commodore Perry as portrayed by a Japanese artist.

Source: Detail from the Black Ship Scroll, 1853, with permission from the Honolulu Academy of Arts.

But Japan managed to avoid the indignity of becoming either a colony or a quasi colony by purposefully undertaking its own modernization (discussed later in this chapter).

The concessions won by the Europeans in East and Southeast Asia were sufficient to satisfy them until the industrial revolution enlarged their appetite for trade and led to the demand for expanded control over territory. In the latter part of the nineteenth century, colonialism turned into a virtual frenzy of competition for the remaining chunks of Asian real estate.

The Capitalist Phase

Appetites in this phase of colonial expansion were for grain to feed Europe's growing population, raw materials and minerals to feed Europe's mills and factories, markets for their manufactured goods, and places to invest their capital. Simply trading in available goods to satisfy existing needs was no longer sufficient. Supply had to be increased, demand created, and investments secured against civil disorder, war, and default on debt. This required control of areas where rice, tea, coffee, sugar, fibers, and rubber could be intensively cultivated by Asian laborers under

European direction; where tin and other mineral resources could be discovered and extracted; where investments could be made in plantations, mines, and the infrastructure of roads, railways, and harbor facilities to bring the local products out and European goods in; and where these varied economic activities could be pursued with a minimum of competition from other foreigners and interference from the Asian authorities. The answer was to make colonies of these areas, either outright or under the fig-leaf guise of "protectorates," drawing borders around them to mark the exclusive jurisdiction of each imperial power, or in the case of China, carving out quasi-colonial spheres of influence for the predator states.

Southeast Asia.   The Dutch, having concentrated their interests on the Indonesian archipelago, extended their effective control from Java and Sumatra to the outer islands, except for parts of Borneo, where between 1846 and 1888 the British established protectorates over North Borneo, Sarawak, and Brunei. They followed up on their earlier acquisitions in Burma by pressuring the king to make his country a British protectorate in 1867. When his successor tried to counter British influence by encouraging French trade and investment, the British invaded and in 1886 annexed Burma to India. Further down the Malay Peninsula, the British meddled in local conflicts among the sultans, giving advice, deposing and replacing rulers, until four of the sultanates came together as the Federated Malay States under a British resident-general. Five remaining Malay states, which had been under loose Thai suzerainty, accepted the status of protectorates. Added to the three Straits Settlements (Singapore, Penang, and Malacca) already under British rule, this completed England's domination of the Malay Peninsula.

France, having lost out to Britain in the competition for India at the end of the eighteenth century, was busy in Indochina, starting with Vietnam, which it saw as a potential route to trade with interior southwestern China. French advisers and mercenaries aided the emperor of Annam, the central segment of Vietnam, in uniting Cochin China and Tonkin, the southern and northern parts of the country, under his rule. During his reign, French traders and missionaries were allowed to enter, but successor Vietnamese emperors imposed restrictions on them and persecuted their subjects who had converted to Christianity. The murder of Christian missionaries provided the French with justification for military intervention, leading to the acquisition of part of Cochin China by cession in 1862 and the rest by conquest later. In 1874 a protectorate was established over the Kingdom of Annam including Tonkin, with French advisers to assist in reorganizing its armed forces, maintain order, and help with government finances. Antagonized by French influence in states it regarded as vassals, China was drawn into a losing war with France in 1883. In Cambodia King Norodom was induced to put his realm under French "protection," permitting the usual rights to residence, missionary activity, and the importation of goods duty free. Conquest of the kingdom of Laos completed France's colonial acquisitions, known collectively as French Indochina.

Thailand, alone in Southeast Asia, managed to escape formal colonization by taking advantage of the rivalry of France and England. Through skillful diplomacy, Siam, as it was then known, remained as an independent buffer between British and French colonies. It was, however, pressured to relinquish territory to British

Burma and Malaya and to French Laos and to grant extraterritoriality to foreign residents.

To complete the story of colonial acquisitions in Southeast Asia during the capitalist phase, sovereignty over the Philippines passed from Spain to the United States at the end of the Spanish-American War in 1898. Filipino revolutionaries who had fought along with American forces to liberate their country from Spain resisted the imposition of American rule until the armed struggle for Philippine independence was finally suppressed in 1902.

By drawing the strings tightly around Southeast Asia, Western nations were closing in on China. As Burma, Annam, Tonkin, and Laos were incorporated into the colonial empires of England and France, China's influence was further enfeebled. In the last half of the nineteenth century and the first four decades of the twentieth, China's territory and sovereignty were encroached on by competing Western powers, joined at the turn of the century by a newcomer to the imperialist game, Japan. Table 2.2 lists the colonies held by the Western powers and Japan around 1910.

Spheres of Influence in China.   The Anglo-Chinese War of 1857, often referred to as the Second Opium War, illuminated the pattern of collaboration by which Western powers extorted additional territorial rights in China. Initiated by Britain and joined by France, the war ended with China's agreeing to pay a huge indemnity, to open more treaty ports, and to grant rights to trade and travel the length of the Yangtze River deep into the interior of China. For her efforts in mediating the conclusion of the war, Russia received an additional large piece of Chinese territory in the northeast, which became the Maritime Province and included the valuable port of Vladivostok.

The next military encounter, in 1894, pitted China against Japan, challenger to Chinese influence over the Korean Peninsula. Again the Chinese lost to superior firepower, the Japanese getting control not only of Korea, which it annexed in 1910, but the Chinese island of Taiwan and the Liaodong Peninsula at the tip of

TABLE 2.2   Colonial Possessions Around 1910

Colonial Power	Colonial Possession
France	Cambodia, Laos, Vietnam (Cochin China, Annam, Tonkin)
Japan	Korea, Taiwan
Netherlands	Dutch East Indies (Sumatra, Java, Bali, most of Borneo, Moluccas, western Timor, Celebes, western New Guinea)
Portugal	Macau, East Timor
United Kingdom	Burma, Malay states, North Borneo, Brunei, Sarawak, Malacca, Penang, Singapore, Hong Kong
United States	Philippines (Spanish colony from 1564–1898)

Manchuria. This dramatic entry of Japan into the imperialist camp was too much for France, Russia, and another newcomer on the scene, Germany, and they used diplomatic pressure on Japan to return Liaodong to China. As a reward the French received various railroad, mining, and tariff concessions in South China adjacent to French Indochina, and the Russians got similar railroad and mining rights to Manchuria. The Germans, after applying additional military pressure in 1898, got exclusive leases on territory in Shandong along with railroad and mining rights, setting off another round in which similar privileges were granted to the Russians in the Liaodong Peninsula and the French on Guangzhou (Canton) Bay in the south. The British were given mainland territory adjacent to Hong Kong Island as well as the port of Weihaiwei in Shandong, from which to keep an eye on the Russians in Liaodong.

Acquisition of exclusive leases in ports and coastal areas signaled the beginning of the struggle for such rights in the interior, which reached a peak between 1895 and 1900. At stake were investment opportunities in the lucrative enterprises of building and operating railroads, which also opened up the hinterland to trade, missionary activity, and the exploitation of mining rights granted along with the railroad concessions. Protection for these substantial interests and the foreigners who came to work in China was provided for by European naval, land, and police forces in China.

Seeing the encroachment of other governments in China, the United States, which had not staked out a claim for itself to a sphere of influence at this point, asked the other powers to pledge themselves to an Open Door policy—that is, not to discriminate against other countries' products in tariffs, harbor duties, and railroad rates in their respective spheres. Competition among the foreign powers was thus moderated by acceptance of each other's concessions and by collaboration in multinational joint financing as well. Their common interest in protecting their positions in China found visible expression during the Boxer Rebellion in 1900, when antiforeign elements attacked the foreign settlement area of the capital, Beijing, and sacked the embassies. With the Chinese authorities either unable or unwilling to stop the rebels, five powers whose diplomats and citizens were under attack— England, Russia, Germany, the United States, and Japan—formed a military force to suppress the Boxers. They then extracted from the Manchu government sizable indemnities for damages, putting China further into debt. Within a few years Japan, with British approval, took on Russia between 1904 and 1905 and won the war in a costly but spectacular display of naval power. Though drained by the effort, Japan gained control over the southern part of Sakhalin Island and a commanding position in Manchuria.

China continued to suffer losses even after the abdication of the emperor in 1911 and the formation of the Republic of China government. Russia took Mongolia as a protectorate in 1913, and Britain drew Tibet into its sphere. In the aftermath of the 1917 Russian Revolution, Japan expanded its holdings in northern Manchuria and took part in the Allied intervention in Siberia against the Bolsheviks. And, having joined the winning side in World War I, Japan was rewarded (in secret treaties) with Germany's former rights in Shandong and the Pacific Islands, as well as gaining recognition of her expanded railway and mining interests in

Manchuria. All these acquisitions were a prelude to the military conquest of China by Japan, which began in Manchuria in 1931. The invading forces defeated the Chinese defenders and set up a puppet state, Manchukuo, in 1934. During the rest of the decade the Japanese conquered much of eastern China, evicting the Westerners from their privileged positions and forcing the republican government to move its capital from Nanjing far inland to Qongqing. The widest extent of Japanese imperialism came between 1940 and 1942, when its armed forces moved into Southeast Asia and many of the western and central Pacific islands. The effects on Southeast Asia of this relatively brief but significant experience of Japanese occupation will be discussed in Chapter 3.

MANCHU AND MEIJI: ALTERNATIVE RESPONSES TO COLONIALISM

The dramatically different outcome of the confrontation between East and West in China and Japan has intrigued and puzzled scholars for half a century. Why did China, a large and rich country with a more advanced civilization, disintegrate under the weight of Western imperialism, while Japan, a small, resource-poor island nation, consolidated its disparate feudal principalities to emerge in the space of 40 years as a modern, imperialist aggressor on the doorsteps of Asia? What accounts for Japan's rapid industrialization after the arrival of Admiral Perry while China, like Humpty Dumpty, had a great fall from which it is still recovering? These questions continue to be relevant to understanding the differences and complex interrelationship between Japan and China today. The two countries have followed very different paths to modernization despite remarkable similarities in historical and cultural experiences.

Early Responses of China and Japan to Western Demands

When the first wave of European merchants and missionaries appeared on the shores of Japan and China, the idea of trade had some appeal, more to the Japanese than to the Chinese, and Catholic missionaries of the Jesuit, Dominican, and Franciscan orders were allowed entry.

Reception of Christian Missionaries.   Among the missionaries, the Jesuits acted as "goodwill ambassadors" for Western learning in both Japan and China, where they were admired for their self-discipline as well as their education. Their rigorous training suited them for their top-down task of converting the Chinese and Japanese populations. Mastery of the language and customs of their hosts gained the Jesuits entry into elite circles as social equals. Father Francis Xavier, founder of the Jesuit order, won the confidence of Hideyoshi, a powerful Japanese general and contender for the position of shogun, who was known for sporting Portuguese clothes and a rosary. In China, another cleric, Matteo Ricci, was honored with a position in the imperial palace on account of his familiarity with both Chinese classics and Western science. Although the Jesuits never made the number of converts they had envisioned, they brought credit to Western civilization among Chinese and Japanese elites in this early period of contact with Westerners.

Japan and the Traders.   To the Japanese, Western trade at first appeared profitable and compelling. The introduction of novelties like tobacco and eyeglasses caught their fancy, setting off a "veritable craze for European things," including Western dress and Portuguese phrases.[6] European weaponry found buyers among feudal clan leaders who put them to use in their conflicts with one another. But the size of the trade with the West remained relatively small, as did the number of resident foreign traders. But foreign missionaries and merchants soon wore out their welcome in Japan. Conflicts among Europeans of different nationalities and a variety of Christian sects became disruptive, and the tendency of poor Japanese converts to translate the gospel into campaigns against their rich overlords led the daimyo to a change of heart toward Christianity. And when Spanish missionaries from the Philippines arrived, the Japanese began to suspect territorial designs. The shogunate (controlled by the Tokugawa clan after 1603) moved systematically and forcefully to isolate Japan totally from the outside world. European ships were restricted to only two ports, all Japanese were prohibited from going abroad or returning home, and a ban was placed on building ships any larger than the small vessels suitable for coastal transport. When 20,000 Christianized peasants led by unemployed samurai rose in revolt in 1637 against oppressive taxes, the Tokugawa government's worst fears about the subversive effects of Christianity were confirmed. The Shimabara Rebellion, which in its blend of Christianity and demands for economic justice foreshadowed the Taiping Rebellion in mid-nineteenth-century China, led to the expulsion of all foreigners in 1639. For the next 200 years, the only contact Japanese had with the outside world was with the handful of Dutch allowed to remain, confined to an island in Nagasaki Bay. Through this window, the Japanese kept up with news from the West.

China and the Traders.   China's reception of European traders up to the nineteenth century swung from first allowing the Portuguese in and then expelling them, to opening Chinese ports to all Western traders and missionaries and, in the eighteenth century, to forbidding Catholicism and confining the merchants to operating under severe restrictions from warehouses (called "factories") outside the port city of Canton.

By the end of the eighteenth century, the British found Chinese restrictions on their trade intolerable. Canton, the exclusive port for international trade conducted on the Chinese side by a number of chartered firms known as *cohongs*, no longer offered Great Britain sufficient trade opportunities. Three government missions in 1787, 1793, and 1816 were sent to persuade the Chinese government to change this policy. The emperor, with characteristic nonchalance, saw no need for either British representation in Peking or increased trade since "we possess all things . . . set no value on objects strange or ingenious, and have no use for your country's manufactures."[7]

Beneath the polite diplomatic impasse was a profound conflict of cultures. For their part, the British had neither admiration for nor patience with the Chinese, insisting upon their inalienable right to trade. Like other Europeans, they made no attempt to learn much about Chinese culture and derided the Asian customs as barbaric. For their part, the Chinese had for so long been governed by the assumption that foreigners were inevitably inferior, to be treated kindly but firmly. They saw all foreigners as "devils"; the English were "red-headed devils," the Americans "flowery-flag devils." Western dress and manners were a source of amusement to the Chinese, and even Westerners' physical features evoked laughter. The following reaction of a Chinese scholar to Western dress is not without wit:

> Their thick coats fit tightly around their arms and body, narrow trousers restrict the movements of their knees, tough leather pinches their feet, and hats unyielding in shape grip their heads. Their movements, nevertheless, are quick and abrupt; what they would do without the restraint of their garments, I do not fancy; perhaps, these cramping clothes are a necessary check to their fury, instituted by their sages.[8]

The clash between Chinese resistance to the blunt uncultured barbarians and European determination to do business moved from diplomacy to war in 1839.

Tea and Opium: The Foreigners Come to Stay

However comical their appearance was to the Chinese, the British merchants had a serious reason for wanting to broaden the terms of trade: tea. Not long after tea was first introduced into Europe by the Dutch in 1644, it became the Britons' national drink, and imports of tea from China created an unfavorable balance of trade for London. The Chinese felt no need for British woolens, and the market in China for ornamental clocks and curios from England was limited, so there was a huge outflow of silver to pay for the increasing imports of tea. The solution to Britain's problem was opium, grown in India under British East India Company monopoly, shipped to Canton by private firms under contract to the company, and imported illegally into China. The profit from the opium trade more than paid for the purchase of tea, saddling China with both a balance of payments deficit and a debilitating drug problem. The outflow of silver from China reached giant proportions when the British East India Company lost its monopoly in 1834, and the triumph of free traders opened the floodgates to opium trade.

Chinese efforts to eradicate the opium-smuggling traffic that was undermining both the economy and the morality of China provoked open conflict with the British, at heart a struggle over who would decide important issues of China's domestic affairs. China's defeat in the first of the Opium Wars, between 1839 and 1842, forced the opening of China and signaled the total convergence of external colonial interests and the internal sources of decay that led to the final collapse of the dynastic system in 1911. The intervening period is punctuated by "unequal treaties," each prompted by the recalcitrance of the imperial Manchu government and the retribution of frustrated Westerners.

Politically, these treaties gave free rein to foreign residents in China who were protected by "extraterritoriality," which meant they lived under the laws of their own country, not China's. Entire areas of the treaty ports (Figure 2.1) were outside the jurisdiction of Chinese courts, which made them a haven for Chinese criminals

FIGURE 2.1 Treaty Ports and Other Chinese Cities Opened to Foreigners in the Nineteenth Century

as well as for Westerners. To the Chinese, the very existence of these islands of foreign nationals without any allegiance to or respect for their civilization was an offense as well as a source of humiliation. The economic advantages these treaties afforded foreign manufacturers and merchants were considerable. Foreigners had control over the tariffs set on goods imported from European factories. This allowed cotton textiles manufactured in England to be sold cheaply enough to compete with homespun materials, undermining the Chinese handicrafts industry, a major supplement to peasants' income. By the end of the nineteenth century, foreign competition from India and Japan resulted in wiping out two of China's traditional exports, tea and silk, worsening China's unfavorable balance of trade. Indemnities attached to each treaty, punishing the Chinese regime for failure to live up to the previous one, further added to China's balance of payments problem.

Not speaking the Chinese language, resident foreign merchants and business-men depended on Chinese to negotiate both their businesses and their comforts in China. This gave rise to a class of Chinese whose livelihood was providing a wide range of services to Europeans; they were maids, cooks, nannies, and streetsweepers as well as subcontractors, translators, and Chinese who had connections and under-stood how to do business in China. This latter group who profited from playing by the foreigners' rules became known as *compradors* (or *comprador bourgeoisie*); as agents of foreign capital, these Chinese constituted a class whose well-being was in-tricately linked to and dependent on the foreigners.

Along with settlements of foreign merchants came a new breed of missionar-ies, their right to wage war against the cultural fabric of Confucianism protected by treaty. Protestant and Catholic missionaries ran schools, hospitals, and orphanages, making converts by attacking Confucianism as the source of superstition and cru-elty. Although they were only somewhat more successful than the Jesuits had been in winning converts, they were far more visible in the society, proselytizing mostly among the common people. On the one hand, their activities provided opportuni-ties for ordinary Chinese to obtain an education and health care otherwise unavail-able. On the other hand, they planted doubts among some Chinese about their own cultural heritage and evoked resentment among others who were quick to suspect the Christians of kidnapping their children or poisoning their relatives.

Rebellion Within: Taiping and Boxers

By the middle of the nineteenth century, the disruptive effects of Christianity and other Western activities along with the Manchu regime's inability to maintain the territorial integrity of the country and growing dissatisfaction with corruption in the bureaucracy conspired to bring the dynasty to the brink of being overthrown by the Taipings in a rebellion that lasted from 1850 to 1864. Founded by a young scholar whose repeated lack of success in passing the arduous civil service examina-tion had led him to convert to Christianity, the Taiping movement combined ele-ments of Christian ideology with an agenda for modernizing China, a traditional scheme of redistributing the wealth, and some Western ideas about manufactures and weapons. The Taipings came close to toppling the Manchu dynasty and perhaps replacing it with a regime capable of reforming and modernizing China's govern-ment. Western powers, at first favorably impressed by the Taipings' Christianity, soon became suspicious of their radical designs and mistaken religious notions, prompting the foreigners to support the Manchus' suppression of the rebellion.

The dynasty continued to decline in the face of military defeat by the British and French in 1857 and by the Japanese, whose victory over the Chinese between 1894 and 1895 underscored the failure of the government to undertake effective re-forms toward modernization. Manchu rulers obstructed and subverted the changes of progressive Chinese officials with the same determination they deflected Western demands. For example, funds appropriated to build a modern Chinese navy were used instead by the empress dowager to restore the marble boat and the Summer

With funds intended to build up the Chinese navy, the empress dowager had this marble boat reconstructed at the Summer Palace.

Source: Photo by Vera Simone.

Palace that had been destroyed by Western forces. The final blow to the imperial dynasty came when the empress dowager, against the advice of her officials, gave succor to the Boxer Rebellion, a popular antiforeign and virulently anti-Christian uprising in the northern provinces, and declared war on the foreign powers in June 1900. When the Boxers (the name of their secret society) besieged the foreign legations in Beijing, the Western powers sent an international expedition to rescue their diplomatic personnel. The dynasty once again put its seal on a peace treaty that included a large indemnity.

When the regime was finally left with no alternative but to implement a reform program similar to those attempted prior to the Boxer Rebellion, it was too late. China had already been partitioned into spheres of influence: The French were in Southwest China, the Japanese in Fujian, the British in the Yangtze River Valley, the Germans in Shandong, the Russians in Manchuria. The United States, arriving too late to claim a particular sphere and eschewing the violation of China's territorial integrity, treated all of China as open to American trade and economic activity.

Tokugawa Japan and the Outcome of Seclusion

While China was on the verge of dismemberment, Japan was emerging from 200 years of self-imposed isolation. During that time, internal peace and the far-reaching changes brought about by the Tokugawa regime prepared the way for its successors, the Meiji reformers, to carry out "a revolution from above." To centralize the military and political power of the shogunate, the Tokugawa rulers implemented economic and social policies restricting the autonomy of the daimyo, the feudal lords. A substantial amount of their land was transferred or confiscated, more than tripling the size of Tokugawa holdings. The daimyo were permitted only one castle each and only a fixed number of armed men, the samurai. To prevent the formation of political coalitions against him, the shogun insisted on prior approval of daimyo marriage plans, and daimyo were required to spend alternate years in residence at the shogun's capital, Edo (now Tokyo), where they were under surveillance, their wives and children remaining as hostages when they left. By the end of the Tokugawa period, the expenses of maintaining dual residences and traveling back and forth with their retinues had drained daimyo finances.

Economic and Social Changes.   The long period of internal peace resulting from centralization of power by the shogun transformed the samurai from warriors into paid government administrators residing in the capital of their lord's domain. By freezing class lines and eliminating social mobility while reducing the number of samurai on the land, Tokugawa policies were simultaneously enhancing samurai status and changing their function. With the samurai removed from the land, villages became autonomous units in which wealthy peasants prospered and became rural entrepreneurs engaged in vegetable oil processing, soya sauce production, and other household industries, as well as moneylending. Poorer peasants, on the other hand, left the land and moved into the cities to provide labor for the commerce and industry that developed there. A market network based on money, contractual relationships, and commercialized agriculture made the merchant class wealthier and more powerful, although it remained low in status and under the political control of the daimyo and samurai.

The changes brought about by Tokugawa rule, similar to changes that had occurred in China earlier but over a much longer time, generated serious problems. Samurai found themselves increasingly impoverished on stipends that were frequently cut by their financially pressed daimyo. Both were at the mercy of a fluctuating market, which further oppressed a growing number of poorer peasants while encouraging an increasingly prosperous class of rural entrepreneurs and city merchants. Watching merchants—whose activity they viewed with disdain—prosper, while they—warriors whose life was dedicated to service—became indigent, kindled the discontent of the samurai, who blamed their misfortunes on the corruption and incompetence of Tokugawa officials.

Attempts by the Tokugawa and the daimyo to address the problems of mounting deficits, inflation, and economic chaos failed, except those of the lords of Satsuma and Choshu. Their domains were in Kyushu and the western end of Honshu, which, as the map of Japan on page 104 shows, were most remote from the shogun's headquarters in Edo (Tokyo). The two clans adopted innovative programs to cut costs, put finances on a solid footing, and ensure profits. Though different strategies were used to achieve these results, both Satsuma and Choshu exhibited two characteristics that played an important role in shaping the conservative nature of Japan's modernization. One was the dynamic leadership of independent, progressive daimyo who promoted young low- and middle-ranking samurai of talent and ability to positions of responsibility. The second was a strong feudal tradition that had set these two domains in opposition to Tokugawa rule from its inception, placing them on an "outside" list of mistrusted daimyo. The enduring effect of this estrangement from the central government was to perpetuate an adherence to orthodox samurai traditions that, together with the special family ties Satsuma and Choshu enjoyed with the emperor's court in Kyoto, gave a distinctively conservative stamp to the overthrow of the Tokugawa and to the Meiji Restoration, which they later led.

Challenges to Tokugawa Rule.   The impetus for criticism of Tokugawa rule in early nineteenth-century Japan came from two directions: Western influences and Shinto revivalism, a school of thought that glorified the emperor. Foreign books on all subjects except Christianity could be legally imported after 1720, and scholars of "Dutch learning" translated Western works on science, astronomy, and geography into Japanese. They began to write treatises of their own, even turning (at some risk to themselves) to political, military, and economic subjects by the end of the eighteenth century. Some scholars suggested a formula similar to one the Chinese adopted in the 1860s: "Eastern ethics and Western science." Others argued for a synthesis of Confucianism, Bushido ethics, and Shinto beliefs, emphasizing the emperor's unique right to rule by divine descent, as grounds for ousting the shogun. Many of these ideas found acceptance among a wider audience in the aftermath of Admiral Perry's expedition to open Japan in 1853.

Occurring only eleven years after China's humiliating defeat in the Opium War, the armed U.S. expedition left no doubt in the minds of the Tokugawa that they had no choice but to accede to U.S. demands. Yet the popular outcry for expelling the foreigners made the obvious impossible. For the first time in 600 years the shogun's government consulted with the emperor and the daimyo, only to hear the same futile advice: Reject Perry's demands, but avoid war with the United States. The intrigue and internecine conflicts that followed the signing of the treaties with the United States and other Western countries created an irreparable crack in the Tokugawa armor. As the movement to "Revere the Emperor and Expel the Barbarian" accelerated, the leadership in Satsuma and Choshu, whose slogan was "Enrich the country and strengthen the army," moved closer to ending the Tokugawa regime.

Self-Modernization in Meiji Japan

In 1868, with minimal bloodshed, the Tokugawa were ousted by a coalition led by the Satsuma and Choshu clans. Having learned to appreciate the superior weaponry of the Westerners, the new elite, numbering fewer than a hundred people, most of samurai origin, veered away from any attempt to oust the foreigners. Instead, they set Japan on a revolutionary course of self-strengthening by learning from the West. Following the official installation of the Emperor Meiji as direct ruler of Japan and moving the capital to Tokyo, the samurai oligarchy proceeded to dismantle the feudal system and embark on a crash program of modernization.

Wielding power in the name of the emperor, using a combination of the carrot and the stick, the oligarchs abolished the feudal principalities and divided the

A few years after Perry's arrival, Japan signed treaties with foreign governments. This is the first Japanese Treaty Commission sent to the United States in 1860, pictured at the Washington Navy Yard.

Source: National Archives photo.

country into prefectures controlled by the central government. The daimyo were rewarded with "severance" money and newly created titles of nobility. A system of universal military service was adopted to create a powerful new national army and navy modeled on the Prussian military and the British navy. The samurai, already stripped of their warrior function, were now systematically abolished as a class. Their hereditary stipends were first converted into pensions and reduced, then commuted into small lump payments or government bonds. The final symbolic blow to both samurai and the feudal system was the prohibition against wearing their traditional swords. Reduced to ordinary subjects of the emperor, samurai now had to fend for themselves. Many rose in government offices, others used their lump-sum payments to start businesses; some entered the professions, joined the new military, or became policemen, which entitled them to wear swords. Those unable to adjust engaged in revolts, the most serious of which occurred in Satsuma in 1877 and was defeated at considerable cost by the new peasant soldiers of the Meiji army.

Modern Political Institutions.   The Meiji years were spent studying, borrowing, and assimilating those elements of the West that fit the leaders' vision of a militarily strong, politically centralized, and economically powerful Japan. They grafted

Western institutions of parliamentary government onto the authoritarian imperial system to which Japan was accustomed and in whose name they ruled. A constitution bestowed on the Japanese people by the emperor established a legislature, the Diet, composed of the House of Peers, appointed by the emperor, and the House of Representatives, elected by the highest taxpaying bracket of male citizens, estimated to have been slightly over 1 percent of the population. The cabinet system as well as commercial and civil laws were copied from Germany, criminal law from France, municipal government from Prussia. Political parties formed and elections were held, but the personalities and views of the oligarchs prevailed. Although "a group larger than the original oligarchy now participated in the work of government, . . . the young founders of the new government, now grown to solid middle age, still controlled Japan."[9]

Government and Business.   Government played a prominent and pragmatic role in Japanese economic development by creating a new institutional framework and a technologically advanced physical infrastructure. The police, the currency, and the postal system were modernized. A system of universal education was adopted, which made Japan the first country in Asia to have a literate people. A national banking system was adopted along American lines, and the tax system was standardized. To promote investments, the government took the lead in establishing and operating shipyards, mines, munitions works, textile mills, and other enterprises it considered essential to strengthen Japan for which sufficient private capital was not forthcoming. Foreign loans and government subsidies were used to build railways, roads, and telegraphic communications. Advisers, technicians, and other foreign personnel were imported to help with development but were dispensed with as soon as Japanese could be trained to replace them.

By the 1870s and 1880s, when the government found itself in financial difficulties with an adverse balance of trade, serious inflation, and overextended capital expenditures, it auctioned off most of its enterprises (except for munitions) to private businessmen, friends of government leaders, at bargain prices. Mitsubishi, for example, "acquired the Nagasaki [ship]yard for less than half of what the government had invested in it."[10] Through a combination of buying out businesses that were not immediately profitable but had the potential to be and doing business with the government, huge industrial and financial combines, the *zaibatsu,* emerged. Thus it was during the Meiji period in the late nineteenth century that the association of business with government—business in the service of the state—became the dominant ethos of Japan's economy.

China's Fate and Japan's Fortune: Some Different Explanations

The contrast between Japan's rapid and peaceful transformation into a modern society and China's painful and protracted collapse under the combined weight of Western pressure and domestic decay is overwhelming. How can this contrast be explained? The Japanese and the Chinese demonstrated the same antagonism toward the Western threat; each expressed profound satisfaction in the superiority of its own way of life in countering the Western challenge. Yet within twenty years of Admiral Perry's visit, the Japanese had done an about-face of unbelievable proportions. How it was accomplished has been described; what remains difficult to explain is what made it possible in Japan and impossible in China.

Different Historical Experiences?   The most obvious answers are also the most alluring. An example is the argument that draws on a difference between Japan's and China's historical experiences. China evolved independently of any external influences, in splendid isolation. Japan, on the other hand, borrowing heavily from China in the development of its civilization, was able to acknowledge the strength of the West, rendering resistance on its part futile and promoting imitation of the West in its stead. The Chinese remained historically so blinded by their own sense of hubris and complacency that neither the appreciation nor the adoption of Western techniques was possible.

The grounds for rejecting the historical argument are numerous, among the most important being that it is a single-factor explanation of an extraordinarily complex issue. But the appeal of such an argument is powerful enough to warrant illustrating the difficulties with it. While it is true that Chinese civilization developed without benefit of self-consciously borrowing from other civilizations, it was nonetheless capable of absorbing outside influences, even those that might be imposed by force. Wave after wave of foreign influences have not only passed through China but been peacefully absorbed by the Chinese into their civilization. Buddhism and Islam were mentioned earlier; there was even a community of Jews who flourished in the city of Kaifeng in the eleventh century whose only misfortune was to become so accepted that they totally assimilated, losing what had made them different from their Chinese brethren. Twice in Chinese history outsiders, the Mongols and the Manchus, conquered and ruled the Chinese long enough for them to become assimilated and indistinguishable from their subjects. The precedent the Japanese had for so readily adopting the West as a model for change may well be one among many influential factors, but it is not by itself sufficient explanation for the different impacts the West had on China and Japan.

Different Indigenous Institutions?   In assessing the different impact Western colonialism had on Japan and China, the internal conditions as well as the external pressures are essential components in the interaction. Both modernization theory and statist theory emphasize the internal institutional differences between Japan and China to explain their dissimilar responses to the confrontation with modernity, though for somewhat different reasons. Both modernization theories and statist theory assume that, because the singular pattern of modern ideas and practices brought by particular Western nations to Japan and China were similar, their dissimilar responses must be attributable to the differences in their indigenous institutions prior to the arrival of westerners. For modernization theory, it is the institution of feudalism that differs markedly in Japan and China; for statist theory it is the presence or absence of a developmental state that differentiates the preexisting situation in Japan and China.

Adherents of modernization theory point to the structural differences between feudal society in Japan and its counterpart in China as decisive for understanding Japan's successful early adaptation to modernity.[11] Feudalism in Japan was closer to its European form in the fourteenth or fifteenth centuries than to its Chinese counterpart in the sixteenth century. Unlike China, where intellectuals constituted a nonhereditary scholar-official elite, the feudal elite in Japan was a hereditary class of warriors, the samurai. Similarly in the inheritance of land, primogeniture was characteristic of both Japan and Western Europe, where the eldest son inherited the total family holding, while in China, land was equally divided among all the sons.

For statist theorists, it was not Tokugawa feudalism in Japan that was the significant institution responsible for Japan's modernizing feat but rather the creation of a strong, centralized political authority, a developmental state, by the Meiji "reformers" who overthrew the Tokugawa feudal state. Though clearly the two are closely interrelated, since the feudal social structure in Japan provided the historical backdrop that enabled the Meiji reformers to carry out their revolutionary creation of a developmental state, for our purposes, the point to be made is that both theories set their sights on the internal rather than external differences to account for Japan's success and China's failure to respond effectively to the Western challenge.

Different External Pressures?   From the world system perspective, on the other hand, external factors weigh more heavily in explaining the difference between Japan's and China's reactions to Western provocation. Colonialism, viewed through this theoretical prism, is not merely each Western country imposing its particular pattern of modern life on its acquired territories, but an overall process by which the international capitalist market as a whole expands. Laying claim to and reordering economic life in distant parts of the world, whether it is done by Portugal, the Netherlands, Great Britain, France, or the United States, is all part of the evolution of a single world-capitalist market system of exchange. Passing through a variety of stages, this world system incorporates more and more of the earth's surface, reorienting the production activities of people toward the international market. At each successive point in time, the demands that steer principal actors in the international market toward one location or another change in accordance with what has already transpired as well as the appearance of new opportunities. Thus it is not only the spatial imagery of a single world economy expanding amoeba-like around the globe by bringing more and more actors into its sphere of economic activity that makes world system explanations different from those proffered by modernization and statist theorists. It is also the notion of time, the passage of time, as a causal factor in explaining both the transformations in the world economy and how demands of the world economy interact with the experiences and resources of people at the periphery.

To explain why China resisted and Japan accepted the challenge of incorporation into the world economic system, therefore, hinges on a chronological or historical analysis not only of the conditions existing in peripheral countries like China and Japan, but the exigencies of the international market at different points in time. China was initially a far more compelling market for conquest by core interests than Japan. Because China with its vast market potentiality was a far more powerful magnet for European traders at least a half-century before Japan was of much interest, the high cost China had to pay for resisting Western intrusion acted as a cautionary lesson for the Japanese when their island nation became valuable to the United States as a way station for trade with China. Historically, then, because China was first to feel the full brunt of the capitalist world system, external pressure on China was greater than elsewhere at a time when there was no way of knowing the disastrous consequences of resisting Western demands.

The argument from a world system perspective is that variations in its impact on individual countries like China and Japan result from different pressures exerted by external forces at different times in the evolution of the international political economy. From this perspective, the internal differences between feudalism in Japan and China are negligible compared to the different pressures exerted on them at different times by the international network of colonial powers. This sheds a different light on a paradoxical observation about Japan's response made by adherents of modernization theory, that "a milder foreign challenge provoked a stronger domestic response."[12] For adherents of world system theory this observation, far from being incongruous, is literally accurate: It describes the disparity between the degree of external pressure that enabled Japan to respond more effectively than China to a different vector of global pressures.

DIVERSITY OF COLONIAL RULE: SOUTHEAST ASIA AND TAIWAN

Colonial institutions and policies were designed to serve the economic and political interests of the home country, or at least of vocal and influential elements in it. The primary concern, therefore, was to find the most "efficient" administrative means for securing the political stability necessary to exploit the economic resources and to secure the maximum cooperation of the indigenous peoples. Although considerable variations among colonies existed, depending on such circumstances as the stage of capitalist development of the colonizer and conditions in the Asian societies when they were colonized, the process of colonial state formation exhibited certain common features that will be identified and then illustrated in case studies of five colonies, each under the rule of a different imperial power.

Features of Colonial Rule

Several features typified the establishment of colonial rule in Southeast Asia. First, having been created by the use or threat of force, colonial states were maintained by the exercise of coercive power, including military power, over the subject people. Units of the armed forces of the imperial country, sometimes augmented with colonials at lower ranks, as well as police, were typical features of colonial administration through which internal order was maintained.

Second, administrative structures were created to raise the revenues necessary for colonies to be self-supporting. Policies were pursued to further the availability of commodities, access to markets, and opportunities for investments. These institutions and policies, designed primarily for the benefit of the imperial center, had unintended and often detrimental effects on the colonized population.

Third, methods of legitimizing colonial rule and winning over the support of indigenous people were adopted in order to reduce the cost of ruling over populations actively or potentially resistant to alien domination. Techniques of co-optation included jobs in the colonial civil service, grants of land, and other material advantages, as well as through the psychological bonds of Western education, fluency in a Western language, and conversion to Christianity. In some cases native rulers could be persuaded to accept incorporation into the colonial structure in return for the benefit of retaining, if not the substance of authority, at least some of the perquisites of their traditional position. For the imperial powers, the hope was that "indirect rule," working through precolonial authority structures, would lend legitimacy to the colonial state they had created, thereby reducing the need for and the costs of using coercive means to maintain order.

A final feature common to colonial rule was the effort by the colonizers to introduce political, economic, and cultural changes intended to serve their goals while at the same time keeping the colonized societies stable and thus easier and less expensive to control. The difficulty was that seemingly modest and even beneficial changes, such as education, simple public health measures, and road building, could have large unintended effects, disruptive to the social fabric of the colonized societies. Even where explicit colonial policy was to leave the traditional order as untouched as possible, the mere presence of outsiders served as a change maker, leading finally—as hindsight reveals—to organized anticolonial resistance under the banner of nationalism. But that outcome is the subject of Chapter 3. Here we will try to bring to life these generalizations about colonial rule by illustrating them with some specific examples of colonial policies and their effects.

The Philippines Under Spanish and American Rule

Of the Asian Pacific countries, Philippine society was perhaps the most transformed by colonialism. Living in separate villages, *barangays,* ruled by headmen, *datu,* Filipinos lacked the political and cultural cohesiveness of other Asian societies that had experienced Hindu, Buddhist, or Confucian influences and some degree of unification into small states or larger kingdoms. These factors made the Philippines more vulnerable to Spanish zeal for converting the "heathen" nature worshipers to Catholicism (thus resisting the spread of Islam and carrying on the battle waged successfully in Spain itself to end centuries of Moorish occupation). For similar reasons, the Spanish were able to harness Filipino agricultural labor by putting an end to traditional slash-and-burn subsistence farming on communal lands and turning peasants into serfs on large estates, the *encomiendas,* to produce commodities for the benefit of landowners (the religious orders were among the largest) and traders.[13]

The Spanish ruled through a mixture of civil, military, and ecclesiastical institutions. A governor-general with a civil bureaucracy assisted by provincial officials was superimposed over the grassroots village-level datu, thus incorporating the traditional headman into the Spanish civil structure. The mission of the military was to carry on operations against the Filipino Moslems of Mindanao and Sulu and to suppress nationalist unrest when it began to emerge toward the end of the nineteenth century. Catholic religious orders, in addition to being major landowners, spread not only Christianity but also Spanish culture through the educational institutions they created. Over the four centuries of Spanish colonialism the indigenous elites, who became officials and landowners during the expansion of sugar and rice plantations in the nineteenth century, had totally assimilated, wiping out consciousness of much of the precolonial Malay culture. Their assimilation, paradoxically, also had the effect of awakening in them a sense of Filipino identity, which led in the last quarter of the nineteenth century to a revolutionary movement for independence.

When the United States entered the picture in the war with Spain in 1898, it accepted the help of the revolutionaries in defeating the Spanish forces, but President McKinley rejected the Filipino declaration of independence as a republic and decided instead to make the islands an American colony. The consolidation of U.S. rule was accomplished after several years of warfare against the independence forces of Emilio Aguinaldo at the cost of more than 4,000 American lives and the lives of almost 200,000 Filipino guerrillas and civilians.[14] Within a short time the United States inaugurated steps leading to a large measure of self-government through institutions modeled on the American pattern; an elected legislature, political parties, recruitment of Filipinos into the civil service, an expansive school system using English as the language of instruction, and Philippine control over domestic policymaking all came into operation during the first decades of American rule.

U.S. involvement in the economy was less activist. Large church-owned estates were bought up and sold to Filipinos, but no steps were taken to prevent concentration of the property in the hands of big landlords who became part of the politico-economic elite. U.S. tariffs allowed free trade between the United States and the islands, with the double effect on the colonial economy of encouraging agricultural production for export and retarding the development of manufacturing enterprises unable to compete with imports from the United States. It was not until the depression of the 1930s that domestic economic interests in the United States—the sugar beet industry affected by cheap Philippine sugar cane, dairy farmers unhappy over importation of coconut oil for margarine, trade unions opposed to cheap Filipino labor—pressured the U.S. government to prepare the colony for independence. As a result, a ten-year transitional period of commonwealth status leading to independence began in 1935. A constitution was drawn up by an elected Filipino convention and a president and vice president elected, the constitution and presidential powers modeled on the American pattern. Despite the interruption of Japanese occupation from 1942 to 1945, the process leading to independence was completed in 1946.

Americans often congratulate themselves on having pursued enlightened colonial policies and prepared their wards for self-government and independence. It is true that the legalization of political parties, the establishment of an elected legislature, the opening of public educational opportunities to a wide segment of the people, the indigenization of the civil service, and the rise of a middle class all were positive innovations not often promoted (or as early) in other Asian colonies. One scholar explains the underlying political reality as follows:

> The party system had merely strengthened the political hold of dominant, landed families, which had used quasi-feudal techniques to gain an electoral following and could hold national power through a system of one-

party dominance ... [and that] the primary beneficiaries of American educational, commercial, and agrarian policies were those who already had superior wealth and education, men whose political power grew rapidly under American tutelage.[15]

So during both the Spanish and American colonial periods, but especially during the latter, the Philippine islands were unified for the first time and incorporated into the world capitalist system. The terms of that incorporation advanced the interests of both the colonial power and the elites of the colony at the expense of the peasants, who expressed their discontent violently in the 1930s and continued to do so after independence.

Laos Under French Rule

If the Philippines is the Asian Pacific country that experienced the maximum impact of Westernization under colonialism, the other extreme is Laos where, thanks to topography and the limited nature of French objectives, the impact of Western capitalist colonialism was modest. Landlocked and with a small multiethnic population of Lao, Tai, Khmer, and Meo people living in scattered settlements in the narrow valleys, uplands, and forested mountain areas, the country in precolonial times had been the site of a series of kingdoms in the valleys centered around Luang Prabang, Vientiane, and Champassak. These kingdoms survived and fell through a complicated and shifting network of vassal relationships with neighboring Thailand, Burma, and Vietnam.

French interest in Laos stemmed from their colonial control of the regions of Vietnam and Cambodia. Starting with the negotiation of a protectorate over the Laotian kingdom of Luang Prabang, French ambitions were challenged by Thailand and aroused the attention of the British as heirs to Burma's interests in Laos. After several years of demonstrations of force and ultimatums from France, three-cornered diplomacy among France, England, and Thailand decided Laos's fate, fixing its boundaries "in accordance with the desires and accommodations of the European colonialists"[16] and leaving in Thai territory a Lao population larger than that remaining in French Laos.

Selecting Vientiane as the colonial capital, the French divided the country into provinces administered by French *résidents* directed by a *résident supérieur,* who in turn was under the French governor-general for all of French Indochina. By using existing local government structures and by staffing the colonial civil service with Lao people and with imported Vietnamese who also staffed the police force and militia, France was able to run the colony with only a small cadre of French personnel.

Colonial policy was to develop Laos as a hinterland serving the needs of coastal Vietnam. Some roads linking Laos with Vietnamese cities were built using forced labor, but plans to put in a railroad from the coast inland to the Mekong River and to resettle in Laos large numbers of farmers from crowded Vietnam failed to materialize. Development lagged, and income from a head tax, forced labor, and the state monopoly on sales of opium were insufficient to meet the costs of administration and public works. An additional expense was incurred for military expeditions to suppress periodic rebellions by mountain tribes resentful of the taxes, French interference with their opium trade, and the subordination of their interests to those of the Lao and Vietnamese in the colonial government.

The impact of French colonial rule in Laos up to World War II was minor; most of the population continued to engage in subsistence farming in scattered settlements. Little was done to develop the economy, to encourage industry, to improve agriculture, to provide schools and health care, or to bridge the long-standing chasms dividing the various ethnic and linguistic segments of the population collected haphazardly as the result of past migrations within boundaries set by the colonial powers. Depending on one's perspective, French treatment of their colony could be condemned as neglectfully retarding Laos's development or applauded as benignly, if unintentionally, sparing the country from forced incorporation on unfavorable terms into the world capitalist system.

In Laos, and Cambodia too, French rule did little to promote economic, political, or social change, but in the Vietnamese segments of Indochina, French colonial policies had much greater impact. Railroads were built, mining companies formed, mills and factories established to supply local markets, and sugar, tea, coffee, rice, and rubber plantations were developed by European landowners. Through private commercial and capital investment and public financing of infrastructure, the colonial economy was integrated into the world economy. Those sections of the economy that produced primary commodities for export expanded, while others, like small-scale farming and traditional industries and crafts that competed with French manufactures, lost ground.

French cultural impact was felt strongly in Cochin China and in the urban centers of Tonkin, imparted by civilian and military officials, clerics, French schools, and the University of Hanoi. Some of the Westernized Vietnamese came to resent their colonial status and eventually joined forces with the traditionalists to oppose its continuation.

Malaya Under British Rule

In Malaya—the colonial possession that became Malaysia and Singapore after independence—British rule gave the Malays their first experience of political unity, but it also made Malaya a multinational society. Traditional Malay political organization had consisted of many small Islamic kingdoms on the mainland and also on the islands of the East Indies from Sumatra to Mindanao. Despite sharing cultural affinities of religion, language, race, and political organization, the Malay states had not been united in a pan-Malay empire. One result of Western colonialism was to divide the Malay states among the British on the mainland and in north Borneo, the Spanish in Mindanao, and the Dutch in the other islands.

British colonial structures were a complex patchwork combining direct rule over Penang, Malacca, and Singapore, indirect rule over the Federated Malay States, and looser supervision of the four other Malay states in the north. However different these arrangements were in each of the components of British Malaya, they did for the first time link them through the superstructure of colonial rule into a single political entity.

This unity was at the same time challenged by the introduction into Malaya of Chinese and Indians, who played vital roles in the colony's economic development but who were not, both by choice and especially by the British policy of preferential treatment for Malays over non-Malays, assimilated into Malay society. Migration of Chinese into the area began even before Malaya became a British colony, drawn by opportunities to do work shunned by the Malays, who engaged in fishing and subsistence agriculture. The Chinese became traders, construction workers, tin miners, and farmers, and by 1858 they constituted four-fifths of the population of Singapore, a major entrepôt for trade among India, Southeast Asia, and China. Expansion of tin mining under the British in the second half of the nineteenth century brought even more Chinese as indentured workers recruited mainly by earlier Chinese arrivals who had become well-to-do. The economic effects of the influx of Chinese were quite important but, in the words of one historian, "The political impact of Chinese immigration in the Malay Peninsula was almost as important as the economic. . . . Chinese entry in large numbers generated an increasing amount of friction between sultan and sultan, Malay and Chinese, and, even more seriously, Chinese and Chinese."[17]

The demographic shift caused by the arrival of large numbers of Chinese who outnumbered the indigenous Malays in certain areas aroused British concern about maintaining the social tranquillity needed for profitable economic exploitation of the colony. To counterbalance the Chinese and also to recruit tractable workers for the expansion of coffee and rubber plantations, importation of Tamil laborers from India was officially encouraged under a government-regulated contract system that in principle provided better terms for the Indian "coolies" than the unregulated indenture system the Chinese had known.

The result of the migration of Indians and Chinese was that at the time of independence the Malays constituted slightly under 50 percent of the population. The three major groups lived in separate communities, engaging in different occupations, speaking different languages, practicing different religions, attending different schools, and forming different social organizations. British policy favored high-ranking Malays with Western education and preference in government jobs while encouraging ordinary Malays to be content with schooling in agriculture and the manual arts. Business was the Chinese sphere and the Indians worked as laborers on large estates owned by Europeans and some Chinese. Tensions among these groups retarded the development of the movement for political independence that swept other colonial possessions in Southeast Asia after World War I. Those tensions eventually led to the split of Malaya into two states, Malaysia and Singapore.

The East Indies Under Dutch Rule

Across the Malacca Straits from Malaya lies Sumatra, the westernmost of the island chain that became the Dutch East Indies. As with Malaya, the islands lacked the experience of political unification in the precolonial period, although two sizable states, Sri Vijaya and Majapahit, had existed. The former, a maritime trade-based kingdom centered on Sumatra, was at its zenith in the eleventh century, while the latter was a land-based agrarian kingdom originating on Java and reaching its peak somewhat later. Its successor, the Mataram empire, ruled part of Java when the Europeans came, but none of the three kingdoms encompassed all the islands, which were eventually united as the Netherlands East Indies, defining the boundaries of the independent state of Indonesia.

Political unification under Dutch rule came in stages, moving slowly from Javanese coastal footholds acquired to serve as collecting points for spices from parts of the eastern islands to the inland areas of Java and to other islands as Dutch economic interest shifted in the capitalist phase to plantation farming and mineral extraction. The gradual extension, by conquest and by political manipulation, of effective Dutch control over various parts of the island chain was not completed until the twentieth century. This meant that some areas were subject to more than three centuries of colonial rule and others only decades by the time independence came in 1949.

As a result, although under colonial rule the people of the islands experienced unification for the first time, the traditional differences among them continued and were sharpened by differing lengths of subjection to the Dutch, by differing degrees of intrusion into traditional life to serve the colonizers' economic objectives, and by the Dutch policy of differential treatment for various Indonesian ethnic groups and the resident Chinese community. Java was most impacted by colonial policies, and the contrast between it and the other parts of Indonesia became more marked. It was the site of Jakarta, renamed Batavia when the Dutch East India Company chose it for its headquarters; the city later became the capital of the Netherlands East Indies and, as Jakarta again, the capital of independent Indonesia.

The pattern of expansion of Dutch control, the institutions created, the policies pursued, and the effects of colonialism on the islands all were important manifestations of the Dutch reason for being there, which was profit. Unlike other colonial powers, they had no ambition to make the natives into "proper brown Dutchmen" nor, for the most part, to convert them to Christianity nor to transfer the Dutch form of representative government to the colony nor to replace the customary law of the islands with the Dutch legal system. Their goal was to enrich the motherland by making money, first for the company while it ran the show during the seventeenth and eighteenth centuries and then for the Dutch government, which took over when the company was dissolved in 1798. In relentless pursuit of the goal of making money, the Dutch radically transformed the islands' economy, especially in Java.

With economic gain as the prime objective, the company was not really interested in governing for its own sake, but rather in controlling the supply of spices and later in introducing the cultivation of sugar and coffee for the global trading network of company ships carrying goods between Europe and Asia and within Asia as well. To keep this trading empire afloat, the Dutch worked at first through local chiefs to whom villagers customarily paid tribute in the form of labor and shares of their crops; the chiefs collected spices produced by their subjects and passed them on to the company. But when the market developed for items not traditionally cultivated, such as sugar and coffee, the company took a more active role, distributing seedling coffee bushes and using village labor supplied by the chiefs under company compulsion to clear land for plantations and build roads. Cultivation of coffee required a heavy investment of capital by the company and by resident Chinese, and thus the fastest-growing segment of the economy came under alien control.

The tribute system worked well enough from the company's point of view, but when its trade hegemony in Asia was successfully challenged by other Europeans, the company dissolved and the Netherlands government took over control of the colony. On the verge of bankruptcy because of debts from the Napoleonic Wars, the government in 1830 instituted the Cultivation System, a new variant of the tribute system for extracting income from Java with the collaboration of the indigenous elite. One-fifth of village lands were set aside for the production of export crops selected by the government; as part of their duty to their chiefs, the villagers cultivated the crops and worked on other projects such as road building, all without compensation. The arrangement was very profitable for the Dutch and benefited the local elites by maintaining their positions of authority and increasing their wealth. For the Javanese peasant, the blessings were mixed: More and more of them, while continuing to live "inside the shell of a familiar cultural and psychological universe," became participants in "one of the world's largest and most modern agricultural industries."[18] The population on Java increased rapidly, but among the costs to the peasants were episodes of famine, as their labor was diverted from rice production for their own consumption, and economic and political subservience bordering on slavery.

A change in government in the Netherlands led to changes in colonial policy and the Cultivation System was gradually dismantled. Payment of taxes in cash replaced payments in commodities; large private estates increased production of export commodities, and the workers on them were paid wages for their labor. This trend away from government monopoly and essentially feudal production toward a freer market and modern agricultural practice spread to Sumatra and other islands. Its success led paradoxically in the early twentieth century to another change in colonial policy, known as the Ethical policy.

Initiated by Dutch civil servants, the Ethical policy aimed at returning some of the benefits of increased productivity to the people of the islands in the form of education and other measures to improve their lot. The results were modest, however, limited by the resistance to change of traditional elites, the reluctance of the European business community, and inadequate funding for schools, a public credit program, and other reforms. In the realm of political institutions, this period saw the establishment of local councils elected by taxpaying, Dutch-speaking voters; the councils selected half of the members of a colonywide Assembly to advise the Dutch governor-general, who appointed the other members. A limited number of Indonesians gained experience as civil servants and council members, but most of the opportunities went to the sons of the aristocracy.

The effects of World War I, another change of government in the Netherlands, and the appearance of nationalist organizations demanding further reforms (their rise is described in Chapter 3) all contributed to the demise of the Ethical programs. One scholar offers this assessment of Dutch stewardship in the East Indies:

> In the crucial test of the beneficence of their rule, the Dutch failed, not apparently from any malicious design or from hypocrisy, but rather because the system which they developed was so completely alien to Indonesian experience and desires. . . . The tragedy of Dutch colonial rule was that it

afforded little indigenous experience in handling such a system and also it tended to exploit and perpetuate the problems of Indonesian cultural and regional disunity. These problems survived to embarrass the efforts of Indonesia to function as an independent economic and political entity after World War II.[19]

Taiwan Under Japanese Rule

The last example of colonial rule in this chapter is the island of Taiwan (named Formosa by Portuguese explorers). Taiwan was Japan's first colony and the first Asian territory to experience modern colonialism under an *Asian* power. Prior to 1624 when the Dutch East India Company took control, the island was inhabited by aborigines and visited sporadically by Chinese and Japanese pirates and fishermen, but it was unclaimed by any country. The Dutch encouraged the migration of farmers from China to grow sugar for export, offering them protection from the aborigines into whose lands the settlers moved.

The brief period of Dutch rule ended in 1662 when the island was occupied by military forces fleeing from China after the overthrow of the Ming dynasty by the Manchus, who founded the Qing dynasty. When the Ming loyalists finally surrendered in 1683, the island came under Chinese government jurisdiction for the first time. Qing authority over Taiwan lasted for two centuries but was tenuous, challenged by frequent rebellions against mainland rule, fighting between communities of Chinese settlers from different areas of China, and attacks by the aborigines resisting settler encroachment into their traditional lands. When the island was ceded to Japan after China's defeat in the Sino-Japanese War of 1894–1895, Chinese officials in Taiwan opposed the transfer and declared an independent "Republic of Formosa," but the Republic soon collapsed and its leaders fled to the mainland.

Japan's principal objective with respect to its first and longest-held colony was that it should serve the homeland's need for agricultural products, at first mainly sugar, and that it be financially self-sufficient. After a pacification campaign against Chinese and aboriginal resistance brought a degree of internal order, the military governor-general undertook measures to modernize Taiwan's subsistence agriculture: small farmers were encouraged to produce for sale rather than consumption, a comprehensive land survey was conducted to clarify boundaries and ownership, absentee landlords were bought out with government bonds and title given to the long-term tenants who had been tilling the land. Improved farming methods—fertilizers and higher-yielding varieties of sugarcane and rice—were introduced through demonstration farms; irrigation and flood control projects were undertaken, at first with government funding, later becoming the responsibility of farmers' associations. Railroads and roads were built and harbor facilities developed.

Simple and inexpensive health measures, by curbing epidemic diseases that before 1895 had contributed to a high death rate, resulted in a doubling of Taiwan's population during the colonial period. The Japanese incorporated into their colonial government the existing self-policing village system, known as *bao-jia*. Ten households made up a *jia* and ten *jia* made up a *bao*; their leaders were elected by the heads of households. Each *jia* and *bao* were responsible collectively for the behavior of the individuals in them. They worked closely with the local colonial police authorities in law enforcement and also in carrying out public health projects and in organizing labor for large-scale public works, such as roads and bridges. Through the *bao-jia* system, the colonial government was able to reach down to the lowest levels of Chinese Taiwanese society.

Although the initial costs of administering the colony were high, it became self-supporting by 1904, financed by the earnings of government monopolies of salt, alcoholic beverages, tobacco and camphor, and from land and income taxes. Private investment, which accounted for about half of the total investment in development, came from Japan and, as the island prospered, from local sources. Japan displaced China as the colony's principal trading partner and exports of agricultural products contributed to its favorable trade balance.

Japan's initial interest was in getting low-cost sugar for home consumption. The cane was produced by the island's small-scale farmers while Japanese capital concentrated on the milling phase of sugar production. Government subsidies helped Japanese companies to build large, modern sugar mills, driving the smaller Taiwanese-owned mills out of business, and the Japanese sugar millers were given monopoly rights to contract with Taiwanese farmers for the purchase of their cane. The price paid for sugar cane was kept low by the stagnant market and consequently the price for Taiwanese rice was also low. With favorable growing conditions, farmers had the option of raising either sugarcane or rice but they had no incentive to switch to growing rice instead. So the wealth derived from sugar went to Japanese investors, while the living standards of Taiwanese producers both of cane and rice remained low. These circumstances support the following argument about Taiwan under Japanese rule:

> Colonial Taiwan's economic development was consistent with the structural features of "peripheral capitalism": a hierarchical international division of labor between industrial Japan and agricultural Taiwan and a disarticulated colonial economy in which the development of the capitalist export (sugar) sector brought no spread effect to the subsistence (rice) sector. The result was the uneven development of productivity between these sectors, while low incomes for farmers prevailed in both.[20]

This situation lasted until the mid-1920s when Japan's growing industrialization led to a rising demand for rice imports to feed its expanding urban industrial workforce. The introduction of better quality strains of rice more palatable to Japanese tastes and of modern farming techniques that increased productivity meant that Taiwanese rice farmers could now command a higher price for rice, pushing up the price of sugar as well. After 1925, therefore, farmers in Taiwan enjoyed a rising standard of living that ameliorated the very uneven development of the earlier decades. But industrial development was limited mainly to food processing, and preferential treatment for Japanese-owned industries discouraged local industries. Opportunities for islanders to acquire entrepreneurial and managerial skills were limited by the fact that Japanese held those positions, as well as administrative positions in the colonial government. The war effort gave some impetus to industrial development but Taiwan remained largely an agricultural-based economy.

SUMMARY

In this chapter, colonialism as the source of modernization in the Asian Pacific region was traced back to its Western European origins. The differences in the impact of colonialism on Southeast Asia and on East Asia were contrasted. In Southeast Asia the imperial powers had the opportunity to determine the size and ethnic composition of future states by defining the boundaries of their colonial territories. In East Asia, in contrast, preexisting states of long standing resisted colonization, forcing the colonial powers to use different means to gain entry and achieve the purposes that had brought them to the region. A comparison between Japan's and China's confrontations with the West showed the complex interaction between external pressures and internal dynamics in the meeting between ancient and modern civilizations. The contending perspectives on the effects of colonialism provided by modernization, statist, and world system theories remind us of the difference that the angle of vision makes in the way we see the world, past and present. This difference becomes even more pronounced in the period of nationalist independence movements, which is the subject of the next chapter.

QUESTIONS FOR DISCUSSION

1. What were the Westerners' reasons for acquiring colonies and spheres of influence in Asia?
2. How did Japan and China respond to the threat of colonialism in the nineteenth century? Why did Japan avoid China's fate?
3. What different effects did colonial rule have on the Philippines, Laos, Malaya, and the Dutch East Indies? Why did such differences exist?

NOTES

1. Paul Bairoch, "Historical Roots of Underdevelopment: Myths and Realities," in *Imperialism and After: Continuities and Discontinuity,* ed. Wolfgang J. Mommsen and Jurgen Osterhammel (London: Allen and Unwin, 1986), pp. 192–194.
2. Ibid., pp. 209–10.
3. Frank C. Darling, *The Westernization of Asia* (Boston: G. K. Hall, 1979), p. 75.
4. Ibid., p. 78.
5. Ibid., p. 83.
6. John Fairbank et al., *East Asia: Tradition and Transformation* (Boston: Houghton Mifflin, 1989), p. 394.
7. The Emperor Ch'ien Lung's "Mandates," quoted in Vera Simone, *China in Revolution* (Greenwich, CT: Fawcett Publications, 1968), p. 72.
8. A Chinese scholar's letter, quoted in Roger Pelissier, *The Awakening of China 1793–1949,* ed. and trans. Martin Kieffer (New York: G. P. Putnam, 1967), p. 45.
9. Edwin O. Reischauer, *Japan: Past and Present* (New York: Knopf, 1947), p. 126.
10. W. J. MacPherson, *The Economic Development of Japan c. 1868–1941* (London: Macmillan Education, 1987), p. 38.

11. There is some controversy over whether China's "feudal period," so called by the communist modernizers, is actually feudal in character or requires an alternate label.

12. Conrad Schirokauer, *Modern China and Japan: A Brief History* (New York: Harcourt Brace Jovanovich, 1982), p. 106.

13. David Wurfel, *Filipino Politics* (Ithaca, NY: Cornell University Press, 1988), p. 5.

14. Ibid., p. 7.

15. Ibid., pp. 11–12.

16. MacAlister Brown and Joseph Zasloff, *Apprentice Revolutionaries: The Communist Movement in Laos, 1930–1985* (Stanford, CA: Hoover Institution Press, 1986), p. 9.

17. John F. Cady, *Southeast Asia: Its Historical Development* (New York: McGraw-Hill, 1964), p. 443.

18. David Joel Steinberg, ed., *In Search of Southeast Asia: A Modern History,* rev. ed. (Honolulu: University of Hawaii Press, 1987), p. 158.

19. Cady, *Southeast Asia,* pp. 378–79.

20. Chih-ming Ka, *Japanese Colonialism in Taiwan–Land Tenure Development, and Dependency, 1895–1945* (Boulder: Westview Press, 1995) p. 183.

FOR FURTHER READING

Bellah, Robert N. *Tokugawa Religion: The Cultural Roots of Modern Japan.* London: Collier Macmillan, 1985.

Chandler, David, *A History of Cambodia,* 3rd ed. Boulder: Westview, 2000.

Fairbank, John K., et al. *East Asia: Tradition and Transformation,* rev. ed. Boston: Houghton Mifflin, 1989, pp. 435–596.

Steinberg, David Joel, ed. *In Search of Southeast Asia: A Modern History,* rev. ed. Honolulu: University of Hawaii Press, 1987, parts 1–3.

Wolf, Eric R. *Europe and the People Without History.* Berkeley: University of California Press, 1982.

3

Nationalism and the Movement for Independence

Nationalism is a powerful and elusive force with roots in the human heart. The emotional attachment individuals can and do feel to their nation and to one another as members of that exclusive association can defy rational explanation. But nationalism as we use the term is more than a sentiment; it is the impetus to a potent form of mass politics inspired by an intense personal identification between "a people" and the modern, abstract idea of "their state." In this sense of the term, nationalism first appeared in Europe as a *consequence* of the creation of the modern state. By the time Europeans colonized the Asian Pacific, they brought this modern European conception of nationalism with them. So it was only a matter of time before Western-educated colonial subjects applied Western nationalist logic to their own situation to oppose the rule of Westerners.

But just as colonial rule in the Asian Pacific differed markedly from one place to another, nationalist reaction against colonialism also varied widely, depending both on the colonizing power and the culture and history of the people being overpowered. Nationalism in the Asian Pacific, therefore, is as diverse as the region itself. In Japan and Thailand, traditional elites transformed the indigenous state and used it to promote nationalism, thereby avoiding colonial rule in their countries. For the colonies in Southeast Asia the outcome of the nationalist struggle was political independence and statehood. In China the nationalist movement split into traditionalist and radical alternatives, impeding the processes of both nation- and state-building.

In this chapter nationalism will be portrayed as an element in the struggle of Asian Pacific peoples to transform themselves into modern nation-states. In the first section nationalism will be defined and its European origins explained. Next, the transmission to Asia of the Western concept of nationalism and the rise of nationalist movements in reaction to colonialism will be discussed in general terms.

Then the specific experiences of four pairs of countries will be compared. The concluding section describes the termination of colonial rule after World War II.

NATIONALISM AND THE MODERN NATION-STATE

Two elements converge to form the modern state: the nation and the state. The modern state is characterized by its "sovereignty," meaning that it is the supreme power. Its government is (or is supposed to be) capable of enforcing the state's authority down to the lowest level, the individual, and its rules are binding on all individuals within its borders. While *state* refers to the supreme power exercised by government within a given territory, *nation* refers to a group of individuals who feel they are "a people," a singular community, membership in which transcends in importance all local, more parochial attachments such as those of family, clan, village, tribe, or city. *Nationalism* is the emotional attachment an individual feels toward his or her nation; it is expressed in the belief that members of a nation ought to have the right to national self-determination and to a state of their own.

But nation and nationalism are indeterminate concepts, subject to widely varying interpretations. The affection for one's group, or one's "country" and the loyalty one feels to its institutions probably have characterized human beings for as long as they have inhabited the earth. *Patriotism* is a term generally used to describe it. *Nationalism* as it is used here, however, is distinct from *patriotism*. It refers to a doctrine as well as a form of politics that is promoted to explain, justify, and mobilize political action in support of the modern nation-state. What makes nationalism distinguishable from patriotism is its specific historical referent to the kind of relationship between citizens and the modern nation-state that crystallized in nineteenth-century Europe.

Three characteristics set the modern nation-state apart from earlier political communities—city-states, tribes, empires, and feudal principalities—with which people felt emotionally bonded. The first is the concept of uniform citizenship. In modern nation-states, individuals are citizens rather than subjects or appendages of a particular family, social class, status rank, or regional affiliation. As citizens, no individuals are superior to any others; all occupy the same position in relationship to the state. Each owes an oath of allegiance in return for citizenship, which either by birth or by naturalization entitles every individual uniform civil rights. The second characteristic is the principle of equality. All citizens are by definition equal members of the modern state and fully expect equality of treatment in the eyes of the law. The third characteristic is a presupposition implicit in the conception of the modern nation-state: that it is only one among many. This premise arises from the historical context in which such states emerged. Unlike empires, nation-states in the modern world are bred in the awareness that they coexist with and are also in opposition to other nation-states in an international state-system.

In actuality, of course, modern nation-states come in all sizes, shapes, and constitutions. The oldest examples among them are the result of centuries of experimentation. Collectively, however, they have given rise to an "ideal type" of nation-state, which is a purely abstract form or normative standard to which peoples in the

Asian Pacific, as elsewhere, have aspired in the twentieth century. But between the ideal and the real falls the shadow. In the ideal to which nationalists in the twentieth century have aspired, it is often taken for granted that nationalism as an ideology *precedes* and *inspires* the mass political action required to bring about the creation of the nation-state. In reality, however, it may more often be the case that nation-states are created *before* there is a common national identity among its people. With the exception of England, this was true in Western Europe where nationalism made its appearance long *after* the consolidation of the first dynastic states.

In a comparison of the new nation-states that in the second half of the twentieth century have replaced western colonial regimes with the earliest nation-states in Europe, the significant difference between them is not the timing but the self-consciousness of "fit" between state and nation(s). In other words, when western Europeans experienced the consolidated power of a centralized state in the sixteenth century, they were unaware that they had yet to encounter the nationalism that would transform them all into emotional participants in the exercise of that power. By contrast, the new nation-states that emerged in the late twentieth century and have continued to proliferate at the start of the twenty-first century are extremely self-conscious of the presence or absence of nationalism among their citizens. Nationalism, in this sense, is both an enduring and changing modern phenomenon. It is not merely a feeling of solidarity that people share on the basis of particular cultural or institutional traits and a common historical mythology, but a consciousness of themselves as "a unique people" who demand recognition from the state as such.

The *politics of nationalism* consists of the totality of ways in which nationalist sentiments arouse political action and mobilize popular support to acquire and use state power for national objectives. The successful outcome of nationalism is a modern nation-state where government represents "a sovereign people" identified as a "nation." When *state* and *nation* perfectly coincide—that is, when all (or a large majority) of the citizens of a state consider themselves members of *one* nation (as in the case of Japan)—the resulting nation-state is often seen as reaping benefits from this cultural homogeneity; it may also run exceptional risks. But not all states are so fortunate. In the Asian Pacific, there are several racial or ethnic groups that do not share the sense of belonging to one nation (in Malaysia and Indonesia, for example). Under some circumstances, they nonetheless coexist closely in one state, as is still the case in Malaysia. Under less (favorable) circumstances, as in Indonesia since Suharto was overthrown, different ethnic, racial, and religious groups have intensified their mutual hostilities. Singapore, another example of a multinational state, has been unusually successful in forging a national identity of its multinational character. And two national communities, the Chinese and the Koreans, suffer the unmerited burden of being divided into two states.

The European Origins of Nationalism

The singular origins of nationalism, as already mentioned, are found in sixteenth-century Europe. Although people have undoubtedly long owed loyalty to a "homeland," in Europe the nation-state evolved into a special kind of homeland. Initially the state belonged to the king in the way manors in the Middle Ages belonged to feudal lords. The state was identified with the person of the king, who set himself above his fellow feudal lords by enlarging his domain, increasing its wealth, and centralizing its administration. In reducing the power of the nobility, the absolute or "divine right" monarchs of Europe allied themselves with the ascendant power of the bourgeois or "middle" (between the nobility and the serfs) classes, for whom a centralized state was a necessary condition for economic development.

In this early stage of state building undertaken by royalty, people of all classes were subjected to the power of the monarch, and in this way parochial loyalties to lesser lords were transferred to the king. Nationalism as a popular force followed, culturally transforming serfs, noblemen, artisans, and merchants into citizens with a national identity. In the early nation-states—England, France, Sweden, and the Netherlands—a substantial core of the population already shared the elements of a single culture, which the state then reinforced and expanded. Although these states represented as yet only the propertied elite among their citizenry, they were able to arouse the masses' national sentiments and loyalties.

Political nationalism followed cultural nationalism as the bourgeois class became economically powerful enough to demand political control of the national assemblies, doing so in the name of all the people. Modern mass nationalism was born in the conflict between the sovereign power of absolute monarchs and the middle-class champions of representative assemblies, in the course of which two kings, Charles I of England and Louis XVI of France, literally lost their heads. To promote their cause, revolutionary leaders ignited ordinary citizens' enthusiasm for a state that would represent the aspirations of all its citizens, not merely the privileged. Thus seized on by revolutionary movements to legitimize their claims against unjust governments, as in the Declaration of Independence by the American states in 1776 and the Declaration of the Rights of Man in France in 1789, modern mass nationalism penetrated the lower classes to become the basis for political revolutions ushering in republicanism and democracy.

Modern Nationalism's Characteristics

As the ideology of cultural and political nationalism spread throughout Europe and to the rest of the world in the nineteenth and twentieth centuries, it exhibited two characteristics that are important to an understanding of its impact on the Asian Pacific. First, nationalism has adapted successfully to the appeal of other modern ideologies such as fascism, conservatism, liberalism, socialism, and communism by allying itself with each of them in various times and places. Nationalism inspired both Hitler's Fascist supporters and his Social Democrat opponents, for example, and in China, nationalism inspired both the National People's (Nationalist) Party and the Chinese Communists in their conflicting programs to rid their country of foreign domination.

The other characteristic of nationalism with significance for the Asian Pacific is its contradictory effects on political life. It is both a unifying and a fragmenting force. Within a country, nationalist sentiment can be the cement that binds people of diverse economic and political interests together, as occurs when a divided population goes to war against a common external enemy. More often in today's world, nationalism splits states apart as national groups pit themselves against one another for control of territory, as in the former Yugoslavia, Soviet Union, and Czechoslovakia. Nationalism can be a disruptive force on a vast scale internationally, setting country against country in competition for resources, markets, and international status, perhaps even threatening the entire international system based on nation-states.

THE ROOTS, TRUNK, AND BRANCHES OF ASIAN NATIONALISM

Western colonialism had the unintended effect of planting the seeds of nationalism in the minds of its subjects. While in some colonies there had been armed resistance to the imposition of colonial control and sporadic outbursts of rebellion afterward, that resistance was typically localized and spontaneous, in response to specific grievances, and ultimately ineffective in the face of colonial military repression. As colonial administrators, the British, Dutch, and French "saw no contradiction between their powers to rule an alien land and their preachments about creating self-government in that country."[1] But if this duplicity was opaque to Western colonial administrators, it became crystal clear to the native denizens over whom they ruled. It was not long before people in the colonies began to use ideas of nationalism and of the right to national self-determination to challenge the legitimacy of colonial rule.

Once taking root, the concept of nationalism opened the way to more systematic, sustained, and finally successful action, not just to resist but to offer an alternative to foreign rule. The contradiction between the Western principle of self-government and the practice of imperialism was obvious. If the English and the French as well as the Dutch, the Spanish, and the Americans had the right as members of nations to be governed by their own people and to have their own sovereign nation-states, why were those rights denied to the people in the colonies? Once the colonials became aware of themselves as members of a nation, they could be mobilized more effectively to throw off the yoke of imperialism and exercise their right to self-determination.

Thus the European idea of nationalism served the leaders of anticolonialist nationalist movements in several ways. It could be used to expand the parochial loyalties of their compatriots to embrace an identification with the whole country, creating a nation where none had existed before. The establishment of such an identity would increase the unity and the strength of the resistance to colonialism; and it could be used to demonstrate to the colonial overlords that their rule was both illegitimate and untenable.

Nationalism and Development: Three Lenses

Nationalism can be both a constructive and destructive force for new nation-states as well as older ones. And its relationship to development remains as puzzling and salient for nation-states in the twenty-first century as it has been in previous centuries. It may be useful, therefore, to view the significance of nationalism through the interpretive lens of each of the three theoretical perspectives that have framed our comparative analysis of development.

Modernization Theory.   From the perspective of modernization theory, nationalism is an essential ingredient for the successful transition of all traditional societies into modern nation-states. The forms it takes and the outcome it produces depend on the internal conditions of each political entity. As they are introduced to new ideas and practices, people in traditional societies gradually transform their lives, adapting to new beliefs and behaviors. As part of that process people learn to think and feel differently about themselves and those around them. In particular, they begin to think politically in broader terms than their own families or villages. As they develop more extensive relationships of trust based on wider common experiences and shared interests, they form new (modern) identities, the most important of which is a national identity. Thus nationalism grows out of a new identification with others as members of a more inclusive ethnic or national community.

This process of developing a national identity is promoted, in general, by nationalist movements, their leaders, and promotional literature, all of which articulate and magnify the commonalities of a large number of people. But acquiring a national identity, in the modernization perspective, is generally considered a finite stage in the overall modernization process, akin to a "growth stage" through which collectivities of people learn to think about one another in more universalistic terms. Thus the phenomenon of nationalism is the means to an end, a stage in the modernization of systems of rule. It is like scaffolding in the long, incremental process of building modern nation-states out of traditional societies. It is assumed by modernization theorists that like scaffolding, nationalist movements and their accompanying structural supports—e.g., promotional literature and nationalist leadership—will disappear once the edifice of the nation-state stands on its own. Nationalism from this perspective is a natural extension of the progressive and universal broadening of people's self-consciousness anticipated by Enlightenment thought.

As a stage of growth, nationalism is a precondition for economic and political development in general, and capitalism and democracy in particular. In the first instance, one cannot promote a modern economy without first developing a national state capable of securing the rules that enable a free market to operate over a substantial territory. In the second instance, universal literacy and the other modern social skills and values that are required for people to work in industrially productive enterprises depend on the political development not only of a highly institutionalized state but of a democratically organized one. So, if nationalism is the resource that galvanizes people in support of a state of their own, then it is also the foundation for people to ensure that the state is limited and responsive to their needs and demands. From this theoretical perspective, nationalism can be said to be the first step in the evolution of a civil society and a political democracy within the modern nation-state.

Nationalism, however, differs somewhat in each country and sometimes it can go awry, as in the case of Germany or Japan in the period prior to World War II. In general, however, both the substance and the sequence of stages through which the movement to acquire a modern, national identity passes are similar everywhere.

Although latecomers to the process need to catch up with the nations that matured earlier, in the end the development of a national consciousness among all people of various states will even out.

World System Theory.   Nationalism, from the world system perspective, is more complex and contradictory in its functions as well as its consequences. It is not a "natural" concomitant of a universal development by which all peoples, going through various stages of growth at different times, eventually become organized into equal nation-states. Rather, nationalism is part of the specific historical process of a capitalist world system operating within and beyond one or more nation-states in which a few are always on the top (at the core) while a great many are on the bottom (at the periphery). In this evolving world system composed of vastly unequal nation-states, nationalism necessarily plays out differently in nation-states occupying different positions in the global system. For the populations of the few nation-states at the top, nationalism justifies why they are on top while for the many at the periphery it justifies their need to promote nationalism in the struggle for a place of their own in the sun.

As the global market economy grows beyond the institutional framework of the individual nation-states that pioneered it, the core nation-states find themselves managing not only their own domestic, national affairs but the increasingly complicated global affairs of the new international order. When the pioneer nation-states become settled custodians of this new international order, nationalism becomes as much of an international problem for them as it has always been a national solution for the difficulties within their territorial borders. Just as modern nationalism in Europe emerged out of the competition among nation-states on their long road to capitalist success, nationalism remains an important tool for the new core of nation-states in their competition to retain preeminence in the capitalist world system they have created. In the process of adapting to the expansion and internationalization of capital markets, core nation-states rely on nationalism to resolve the internal economic and political conflicts among social classes and clashing economic interests that accompany the changes demanded by a new global economic and political order. These include international as well as intra-national wars, massive migrations of labor and capital, and the continual restructuring of the technological, organizational, and political reforms necessary to preserve existing and create new comparative advantages.

In the case of peripheral states, nationalism has different functions and few if any resources with which to carry them out in the struggle to survive in the new global order. Nationalism is a necessary tool for colonized peoples to shake off foreign control. But in the enormous expenditure of human and emotional resources required to achieve liberation from foreign oppression, nationalist movements succeed only by raising people's expectations of what they will receive in the wake of national independence and a government of their own. Thus, when political independence is successfully negotiated and implemented, a fledgling nation-state finds itself poorer and weaker than it was under colonial protection. Unable to provide its people with even the material prosperity and physical protection that their former imperial patrons had furnished, the new governments in peripheral states turn for assistance either to their old colonial masters or the new masters represented by international banks, thus resuming informally a neocolonial dependence on the "core" of the world system. The resulting economic linkages tying the new states to powerful international patrons after they have achieved formal political independence enfeeble rather than strengthen their capabilities to pursue autonomous economic development. Unfortunately, nationalism in the service of a state incapable of delivering authentic economic progress can become a seriously destabilizing force.

Developmental State or Statist Theory.   The developmental state or statist perspective on nationalism and its relationship to the nation-state straddles modernization and world system theories. On the one hand, the statist perspective displays two readily apparent similarities with modernization theory. Both view nationalism as a necessary adjunct to the formation of territorially sovereign states. Both also understand nationalism as an internally generated consciousness of their collective identity among people who occupy both a territory and a state in common. On the other hand, statist theory also shares common ground with the world system's perspective on nationalism. Nationalism for both these theoretical approaches is part of a historical process. This means that neither nationalism nor the particular stages of growth of nation-states occurring at any one point in time can ever be repeated or duplicated. There is, however, a definitional stipulation that permits statist theory this straddle position which is that a moment in time is measured by generations rather than days, years, or even decades.

The differences between statist theory and the modernization and world system perspectives may be less obvious. One is that statist theory itself emerges in the context and for the express purpose of understanding those countries that it calls "late industrializers." These are countries that have for one reason or another been left out of the first two rounds of industrialization, those of the pioneer nation-states whose earliest industrial development was predicated on inventions (England, for example), and those of the second generation of industrializers whose development was built on innovation (the United States or Germany, for example). When the third generation of nation-states, dubbed "late industrializers," embark on their industrial growth, therefore, they cannot avoid being affected by the already crowded arena of already industrialized countries that jockey for position in international market. Not only well-established, powerful nation-states but also multinational corporations compete in this arena posing a variety of obstacles and complicating the endeavors of "late industrializers."

From the statist point of view, there is at least one constant in an otherwise historical outlook: Nationalism is an effective political force only as an adjunct of a strong developmental state. The elements of nationalism may be present in a society with a weak or nonexistent state but under these conditions they are ineffectual for the purpose of promoting industrial growth. Only developmental states possess the capacity to harness the potential of nationalist fervor to bring about effective development among "late industrializers." Nationalism in the service of a strong, developmental state, however, is an indispensable asset for achieving successful economic growth in late industrializing countries. It assists in this endeavor by consolidating popular support for the strong developmental state, enabling it to protect the frail edifice of infant industry as it attempts to catch up with the high competitive standards of the international market.

There are a number of interrelated ways in which developmental states make practical use of nationalism in the struggle to compensate for the disadvantages of being a latecomer to industrialization. The delayed launching of industrial development by latecomers caused by colonization means they are prohibited from using the comparative advantages forged by the first and second generation of industrializers that preceded them. That possibility is foreclosed by the futility of competing with already industrialized nations on their own turf, so to speak. Late industrializers, therefore, are denied both invention and innovation as premises on which to build an internationally competitive advantage. The first step in the direction of forging their own foundation for competing with the more powerful players in the international market was the discovery on the part of third-generation countries like South Korea and Taiwan of the developmental state. As described in Chapter 1, the developmental state was a departure, if not an aberration, from the perspective of early industrializers like England and the United States. This enabled the third generation of industrializing countries to forge a visible and well-articulated cooperation between the state and private enterprise sectors that brought planning back into the capitalist equation.

Subsequent steps in forging *learning* as a novel and effective basis for these late industrializers to carve a comparative advantage for themselves in the international market included the discovery of a number of ways to increase labor productivity without the benefit of costly labor-saving technology and to reduce costs of production through disciplined management-labor cooperation. The mobilization of nationalist sentiment among all the participants in production played a decisive role in implementing these strategies for reducing the production costs in order to export higher-quality goods at internationally competitive prices. From a statist perspective, then, nationalism is a significant force in industrial production geared to rapid economic growth and technical development without involving a nationalist movement, charismatic leaders, or a coherent ideology. This will be discussed in greater detail in Chapter 5.

Characteristics of Asian Pacific Nationalism

In its overall appearance, nationalism in the Asian Pacific exhibited characteristics of nationalism elsewhere. It was a reaction to regimes that did not represent or "belong to" the people they governed. Articulated first by intellectuals and espoused by the educated young, nationalism in the Asian Pacific followed the same evolutionary pattern found in other parts of the world. Beginning modestly, the first stage of nationalism expressed cultural claims to a collective identity distinguished by its language, art, religion, or other common bonds. In its second stage, this cultural identity assumed political form in demands for representation in government. In the third stage, cultural nationalism and representation became an overt struggle to replace the government in power.

Asian nationalism, like European nationalism, emerged as a full-fledged political force at different times among different people with varying degrees of intensity. In Japan and Thailand nationalism was promoted by ruling elites in the nineteenth century as a way of perpetuating themselves in power and in the twentieth century as a way of expanding Japanese power abroad. Malayan nationalism, in contrast, did not materialize until after World War II, when it erupted in conflicts between the Malays and the Chinese—separating rather than uniting them.

The final characteristic of Asian Pacific nationalism was that the external links of nationalist movements made them susceptible to changes in the international arena. World-shaking events, such as the World War I, the Bolshevik Revolution of 1917, the Great Depression in the 1930s, the Japanese invasion of East and Southeast Asia on the eve of World War II, and the cold war that followed in 1947, all left their imprint on the evolution of nationalism in the Asian Pacific.

In two important ways, however, nationalism in Asia was different from its predecessors in Europe. Unlike European nations whose identities emerged in relation to other Europeans in a regional context, Asian national identities emerged in opposition to Western imperialism and in a world context. Nationalist movements in Asia reacted against the existing Eurocentric international system and contributed to the creation of an evolving global community. Further, Asians formed their identity in terms of a dichotomy between Eastern and Western people based on profound religious differences and the invidious racial distinction between white people and people of color.

The Rise of Nationalist Movements

Nationalist movements in Asia did not spring full-blown from the head of Zeus. With some exceptions, nationalist organizations took shape gradually, evolving from obscure peasant revolts against the changes imposed by colonial administrations, moving from specific complaints against foreign rule to a generalized awakening of the national character of their purpose. Western imperialists and their Japanese counterparts each contributed to the process by training a select number of "natives" to assist in their colonial administration. In this way a leadership corps for nationalist movements was recruited and trained by the colonizers, often in the language and in the image of the oppressor himself. When this indigenous elite group found itself excluded from the Westerners' charmed circle of power, it also found itself isolated from its own people. Out of this dilemma was forged both the consciousness of a common opposition toward foreign rule and a strategy for bridging the gap between the educated and the uneducated in colonial society.

This strategy and the vision that instructed it will be covered in a series of illustrative comparisons of four pairs of countries: (1) China and Indonesia, where communism became embroiled in the nationalist struggle leading to violent confrontations; (2) Cambodia and the Philippines, where the movement for independence from France and the United States was nonviolent and encountered little resistance; (3) Burma and Malaya, where the development of a national consciousness was impeded by a deeply divisive ethnic pluralism; and (4) Thailand and Japan, where the nationalist revolution was launched from the top down by the government in a successful effort to fend off colonization by the Western powers.

THE EVOLUTION OF THE NATIONALIST MISSION IN CHINA AND INDONESIA

Expressions of nationalism emerged in Indonesia and China just after World War I, when the rallying cry of self-determination reverberated around the world. It struck a responsive chord among Western-educated professionals—doctors, teachers, and in the case of Indonesia government administrators—for whom the colonial experience was both promising and frustrating. As beneficiaries of a modern education that opened their eyes to the potentialities for improvement of their people, these professionals saw foreigners everywhere in control. The very nations that had gone to war for freedom and self-determination in Europe were running the affairs of Asians. How could the people of China and the Indies effectively assert *their* right to be masters of their own destiny?

Early Stages of Nationalism in China

Answers to this question had been sought by Chinese intellectuals for about 50 years. But until 1911 they had been framed by the teetering existence of an "alien" Manchu dynasty the Chinese blamed for permitting Westerners to overrun their country. With the monarchy toppled and China in disarray, intellectuals focused on the backwardness of Confucian culture as the source of weakness. Sun Yatsen, the Western-trained doctor and spiritual father of the National People's Party, the Guomindang, who became president of the new Republic of China, was enormously influential in spreading nationalist ideals. China's 400 million people, in his view, were just "a heap of loose sand." His answer was to create new bonds among Chinese dedicated to building China into a modern nation. Intellectuals, merchants, workers, and students were drawn to the party by the hope that China would be reunified under a government strong enough to eliminate both the foreigners and the warlords who controlled large areas of the country. But only this vague hope united members of the Guomindang. There was no agreement on what kind of state China should have, nor was there a strategy for retaking the provinces from the hands of warlords. Most important of all, the party had no military force to accomplish the reunification of China.

The agreements reached among the victors at the conclusion of World War I to deliver the German-held province of Shandong to Japan rather than return it to China provoked widespread boycotts and demonstrations. This outburst of nationalist energy, known as the May Fourth Movement, generated new organizations in two directions: toward Western individualism and Russian communism. Although the ideas of Western individualism were extremely popular among intellectuals and young people because to them it meant the freedom to choose one's wife, one's occupation, and one's government, the overwhelming fact remained that China was politically weak and divided. The awareness that no number of individual rights would bring about a strong, nationally united China led some intellectuals in the direction of communism.

The communism toward which nationalist Chinese gravitated in the aftermath of May Fourth came from the Soviet Union, where under the leadership of Lenin in 1917, a revolutionary movement had overthrown a culture and an authoritarianism as backward and entrenched as that in China. The idea that peasants in backward countries could join with workers in the Communist Party to overthrow Western imperialists and embark on a program of state-guided modernization offered a powerful solution to China's problem. Lenin's version of communism provided a vision of nationalism tied to social justice and a strategy based on anti-imperialism. It was not just a theory; it had worked in practice, a point that was brought home by the Soviet Union's unsolicited renunciation of the special rights the tsarist government had in Manchuria, as well as the remaining Boxer indemnity payments.

The first meeting of the Chinese Communist Party was attended by only 12 members representing 57 people. The party's survival was bolstered by Sun Yatsen's appeal to the Soviet Union for assistance in reorganizing and militarizing his own party, the National People's Party (Guomindang). From its 1894 objective of supporting the overthrow of the Manchu dynasty, the Guomindang had moved first to a cultural critique of China's weakness, then to a political program for nationalist rejuvenation with Western assistance, and, when that was not forthcoming, to an appeal to the Soviet Union for assistance. The result was a merging of the forces of the Guomindang and Communist parties. Under the stewardship of Soviet advisers, the Guomindang was reorganized along Leninist lines, a military academy was set up, and members of the Communist Party as individuals joined Sun's party in order to unify China militarily under the banner of a united nationalist front.

Early Stages of Nationalism in the East Indies

For the people of the East Indies, the answers to why they were powerless subjects of the Dutch and what needed to be done were somewhat different. In contrast to China, where colonialism contributed to disunity, the Dutch in a sense "invented" Indonesia by uniting the islands for the first time as their colony. The problem confronting Western-educated protégés of the colonial regime was how to find a single voice for the complex ethnic mosaic of peoples inhabiting the region: Islamic, Hindu-Buddhist, Confucian-Taoist, Christian, and animist; rice cultivators and traders; kingships and kin groups; Javanese and outer-islanders; literate and illiterate. The Western-educated secular elite that had emerged on Java in the 45 years preceding World War I, though light years apart from the traditional Islamic communities of the outer islands, recognized the need to bridge that distance. And the impact of the war produced the occasion for the first nationalist coalescence of an emerging Indonesia: the mass political organization of Sarekat Islam.

Sarekat Islam.   Founded in 1912 by Javanese traders fearing Chinese penetration of their enterprise, Sarekat Islam (SI) brought together the Islamic outer-islander and the secular Javanese strains of nationalist thinking into a broadly based nationalist objective similar to that of the National People's Party under Sun Yatsen: a commitment to carrying out social and economic development. Its popularity spread under the leadership of an aristocratic Moslem civil servant who affirmed national independence as its ultimate aim in 1917; by 1919 it claimed to have a membership of 2.5 million, made up of both rural and urban followers, religious and reformist Moslems, Social Democrats and Communists. But SI was affected by the proliferation of other nationalist organizations, the Indies Party led by a Eurasian,

Sun Yatsen

Sun Yatsen
© ChinaStock Photo Library

Sun Yatsen is considered the father of modern China by all Chinese and his mausoleum in Nanjing is visited by Chinese from all over the world, whatever their political persuasion. Sun's persistent efforts to free China from the rapaciousness of warlords and the exploitation of foreigners illuminate the darkness of China's humiliation at the hands of Western imperialist powers. His aspirations for China remain those of Chinese today: nationalism, democracy, and socialism at home and a position of strength, independence, and equality among the nations of the world.

Born to a peasant family in 1866 in Guangdong Province on China's southeastern coast, Sun at the age of 13 followed many others from that region by emigrating overseas. Joining his eldest brother, a successful businessman in Hawaii, he was educated at a conservative, British-run mission school where he excelled at English and developed an avid interest in Western learning. In 1883, discovering that Sun was about to be baptized, his brother sent him home to China, where his ridicule of local village gods resulted in banishment from his village. Continuing his studies in Hong Kong, Sun became a Christian, went home for a marriage his family had arranged for him, and left his bride to return first to Hong Kong and then back to Hawaii. Rather than work in his brother's business, Sun used the occasion to engage in his first fund-raising, enlisting the help of an American missionary and businessmen to raise $300 to return to Hong Kong where he decided to pursue a medical profession.

In 1885, while attending medical school in Canton, Sun befriended a member of a secret society dedicated to the overthrow of the Manchu dynasty, rekindling a childhood fascination with the Christian Taiping rebel leader, Hung Hsiuchuan. He completed medical training in Hong Kong but was not permitted to practice there, establishing himself in Macao instead. There he became drawn to the idea of contributing his knowledge of the English language and Western science to the reform of the Chinese empire. In 1894, at age 28, he traveled to Beijing to offer his services to Li Hung Chang, the principal adviser to the emperor. Arriving in the capital on the eve of China's war with Japan over Korea, Sun never even obtained an audience with Li, and the rebuff, the first of many in his life, prompted him to embark on an independent quest to revolutionize China.

Between 1894 and 1911, Sun traveled from one overseas community to another, using his charisma, self-assurance, and consummate rhetorical skills to raise funds among overseas businessmen in Europe, the United States, Hawaii, Singapore, Vietnam, and Japan to support the formation and activities of an anti-Manchu political organization. With munitions smuggled into southern coastal China, Sun and his supporters attempted ten uprisings, none of which succeeded. Meanwhile, revolutionary groups had sprung up throughout the coastal regions of China, and when a mutiny among imperial soldiers started a chain reaction that resulted in the overthrow of the Manchus in 1911, Sun read about it in a Denver newspaper.

Though he was by then the most widely known Chinese revolutionary, and the only leader capable of holding the disparate groups of Chinese revolutionaries together, Sun had no base of support within China and little credibility among Western heads of State. On his return home, he stopped in Washington, London, and Paris, hoping to obtain the stamp of approval of foreign governments and loans for his party. With neither in hand, he returned to China to a hero's welcome, was elected provisional president of the Chinese Republic but held office just long enough to hand power over to General Yuan Shihkai.

The years between 1911 and his death in 1925 were a difficult period of international turmoil and intense warlord rivalry within China. Impassioned and imaginative but impractical and politically naive, Sun Yatsen spent most of those years in futile attempts to play off warlords and international powers against one another in order to unify China and throw the foreigners out. After 1919, when urban Chinese erupted in mass nationalistic protest against the Western sellout of Chinese territory to Japan, Sun Yatsen's political connections with Japan and the Western powers became liabilities. Increasingly disillusioned with the prospects of gaining Western support for China's territorial integrity, Sun gravitated towards the Soviet Union for assistance in forging a military and political organization powerful enough to capture power from the warlords and declare China's independence from Western domination. He died without seeing his dream of a strong and unified China achieved.

Douwes Dekker, and the Indies Social Democratic Association (ISDA) founded by Hendrik Sneevliet, a Dutch Communist who later became the first Soviet-sponsored Comintern agent in China. SI's broad appeal and its policy of permitting members of other parties to join it created serious inner tensions between its radical and more conservative elements. At the core of these tensions was the ISDA, which later became the Communist Party.

Social Democrat and Communist Parties.   Like the Communist Party in China, ISDA was an ideologically coherent and organizationally sophisticated party whose members filled official positions in SI, exerting an influence on policy similar to the Chinese Communists in the National People's Party of China. By 1921, a year after ISDA became the Indies Communist Party (PKI), Sarekat Islam stopped allowing members to belong to other parties, effectively ousting the Communist Party from its midst, the parallel of events in China in 1927. After that, the PKI expanded as an independent rival, attracting members away from SI, which began to decline.

Communism in Indonesia was a pervasive element of the nationalist movement, its anti-imperialist analysis carrying a broad appeal for all nationalists. Its social and economic program was more inclusive than the Moslems' goal of an Islamic state and more focused than the vague solidarity of the secular nationalists' state. As a political party, however, Communists in Indonesia as in China faced the problem of steering a hazardous course between socialist revolution and nationalist accommodation. The PKI, after expanding its membership in the mid-1920s, led a series of disastrous revolts in 1926 and 1927. That independent bid for power ended with the Dutch rounding up "13,000 subversives, exiling 1,000 to the malarial swamps of New Guinea,"[2] and crippling the PKI for a generation. Reemerging after World War II, the PKI again rose, hitching its star to Sukarno's charismatic leadership of the nation of Indonesia.

Sukarno's Indonesian Nationalist Party.   More than any other individual, Sukarno gave the nation of Indonesia its distinctive spirit or "soul." With the assistance of students returning from Holland and a younger generation of more militantly nationalist youth, Sukarno founded a new, more assertive Indonesian Nationalist Party (PNI) in 1927. A new flag, a national anthem, and a transcendent purpose— "one nation–Indonesia, one people–Indonesian, one language–Indonesian"[3]—reflected Sukarno's flamboyant style, providing the PNI with powerful symbols to appeal to all shades of nationalist thinking. But functioning in an atmosphere of police surveillance and periodic repression that precluded mass political activity, the PNI was only able to project a solidly united Indonesian identity among the urban, educated elite. Actually mobilizing masses of people to act in concert as Indonesians was accomplished later, as a consequence of the Japanese occupation.

The Impact of the Japanese Occupation on the East Indies

When the Japanese took over the Dutch government in 1942, they added their own coercive techniques for actively enlisting the population in the war effort. By whipping up popular participation in support of "Asia for the Asians," they unwittingly supplied Indonesian nationalists with the mass base they needed to wrest independence from the Dutch after 1945. Sukarno and Mohammed Hatta, by collaborating with the Japanese, availed themselves of the Japanese communication apparatus to convey their nationalist message to a vastly expanded audience of Indonesians across the islands. An Indonesian army was raised with the assistance of the Japanese, who also enabled Indonesians to acquire higher-level administrative experience for the first time. Consequently, when in 1945 the Japanese suddenly withdrew in anticipation of an Allied offensive, the nationalist leadership of Indonesia was poised to declare independence from the Dutch. Sukarno and Hatta assumed the presidency and vice presidency and a constitution was drawn up for the new Indonesian state.

But the British landed troops in Jakarta to support the Dutch determination to reimpose colonial rule. The outburst of nationalist opposition this instigated swept Indonesians into the maelstrom of social revolution while negotiations between the nationalist politicians and the Dutch dragged on for four years. A mass uprising—called the *pemuda* (meaning "youth") movement in reference to the revolutionary youths who led it—erupted in response to the absence of any effective machinery of government under the new republic. Youth from all social classes, highly critical of the older political leaders' reliance on negotiations to settle the question of independence, believed that only force could bring the Dutch to accept Indonesia's independence. These youthful revolutionaries banded together around charismatic leaders, put together a nationalist army out of the disbanded Japanese-led youth and militia units, and discredited all groups and individuals who had demonstrated any support for the Dutch. The Chinese, Eurasians, and traditional elites were particularly vulnerable to abuse.

The violence unleashed by this movement was a double-edged sword for the new Indonesian government. On the one hand, it threatened negotiations with the Dutch as successive cabinets fell in the wake of criticism for having "sold out." On the other, it provided the mass base and military power the new government needed to establish national as well as international credibility for independence. The fruits of this revolutionary nationalist upheaval came when the United Nations and the United States intervened against the Dutch on the side of the nationalists; the Hague Agreement in November 1949 led to political independence for the Republic of Indonesia with guarantees for Dutch investments.

The Impact of the Japanese Occupation on China

The Japanese played an equally decisive role in determining winners and losers among the Chinese nationalist contenders for power in the postwar world. Foreshadowing the military's decimation of the Communists in Indonesia in 1965, the reorganized Leninist-style Guomindang under the leadership of Sun Yatsen's successor, Chiang Kaishek, had massacred thousands of Communists in 1927, thereby consolidating his government's control over the region along China's east coast, which remained a citadel of foreign influence. The Communist Party, virtually abandoned by the Soviet Union, went underground and dispersed to the countryside, where the handful of Communists we have come to identify as the founders of the People's Republic of China—Mao Zedong, Zhou Enlai, Zhu De, and Deng Xiaoping—reorganized the communist movement as a peasant-based nationalist force.

Sukarno

Sukarno

United Nations photo 49998 AF/pcd

One of the most colorful of the Asian Pacific nationalist leaders, Sukarno earned an international reputation for impassioned promotion of the cause of a united, independent Indonesia, for swaying crowds with his oratory and winning the adulation of the common people, for his charismatic personality and his love of life's pleasures, including the company of women. He was also criticized for his excesses, for collaborating with the Japanese during World War II, for being too willing to negotiate with rather than fight against the Dutch when they returned to the Indies, for being a poor administrator, for decreeing the end of constitutional government and instituting autocratic Guided Democracy, and for thinking that he could by sheer personal magnetism keep the antagonism between the PKI and the army in some kind of balance with him as the balancer. But whatever the assessment, no one can deny that he was the most beloved of the Indonesian nationalist leaders.

Sukarno was born in Java in 1901 to a Javanese Moslem father and a Balinese Hindu mother at a time when such "mixed" marriages were uncommon. Raised in modest circumstances in a small town where his father was an elementary school teacher, as a boy Sukarno absorbed the moral lessons of the *wayang* or shadow puppet plays of traditional Javanese culture to which he often referred in the public speeches for which he later became famous.

In 1916 he left home for a Dutch language secondary school in Surabaja where he boarded with the family of the leader of the early mass-based nationalist organization, Sarekat Islam. While there he met many of an eclectic mixture of nationalists in SI and had access to a library of the works of various Western political philosophers, whom he later quoted as inspiration for his own ideas. After graduation in 1921, he moved to Bandung to study engineering at the newly founded technical college there, leaving behind the young girl he had married in name only in 1920 and whom he later divorced to marry an older woman in whose home he boarded. His political involvement and education deepened in Bandung as he came to know more of the nationalist leaders and began to form his own adaptation of Marxism to agrarian Indonesian society, emphasizing anti-imperialism and downplaying the idea of class warfare.

After graduating as an engineer-architect in 1926, he taught briefly and opened an engineering business, but soon became involved in a political study club, meeting with Indonesian students returning from study in Europe and writing articles advocating the unification of Marxist and Islamic elements in a broad-based nationalist ideology. One of the founders in 1927 of the PNI, a political organization devoted to independence and building an Indonesian national consciousness, he became its chairman and tried to form a united front of all nationalist groups. Arrested by the colonial authorities in 1929 for making inflammatory speeches, he was imprisoned for two years, during which he studied Islam but never became a devout practitioner.

After release from prison he tried without success to unite the two political organizations that had been established in the wake of the dissolution of PNI after his arrest. Arrested again in 1933, Sukarno was exiled first to a remote island and later to Sumatra, where he worked as a schoolteacher and met the woman who became the third of his seven wives. During the years between his first arrest and the Japanese takeover of the East Indies, Sukarno spent all but 20 months either in jail or in exile away from Java.

Like nationalists in other Southeast Asian colonies, Sukarno cooperated with the Japanese, seeing them as part of the struggle of Asians against Western imperialism and as supporters of the idea of an independent Indonesia. In 1943 Sukarno went with a delegation to Japan, his first trip abroad and his first view of an industrialized country. While working with the Japanese occupiers, he strengthened his ties with the people and established himself as the symbol of national unity, which carried over into the postwar period. Sukarno's record as president after independence was finally won in 1949 is discussed in Chapter 4.

Settling in remote peasant villages often located on the border between provinces, the communist leadership joined forces with local "bandits" to strengthen their forces and build armed revolutionary base areas in the countryside. They gained popular support among poorer and landless peasants by pursuing land redistribution policies and addressing peasants' economic grievances against landlords and tax collectors. When the first base area in the Jinggang

Mao Zedong

Mao Zedong

AP/Wide World Photo

Mao Zedong was a man of epic proportions. He was loved and feared as if he were an emperor or a god but his own wish was to be remembered as a teacher. Self taught and college educated, versed in Western thought and Chinese classics, an accomplished military strategist and a poet, Mao Zedong combined the flexibility and tenacity of a politician with the inspiration of a visionary.

Born in 1893 in Shaoshan, a village in Hunan province, Mao was the eldest son of a poor peasant who worked his way to prosperity. From his tyrannical father, Mao learned his first lesson in the efficacy of rebellion. Having rebuked his father for insulting him in front of guests, Mao threatened to drown himself rather than kowtow in apology. To his surprise, his father relented. "I learned that when I defended my rights by open rebellion my father relented, but when I remained weak and submissive he only cursed and beat me more."

In the autumn of 1911, after refusing to acquiesce to an arranged marriage, Mao left his village to attend school in the provincial capital. There he found himself in the middle of the upheaval to overthrow the Manchus. Convinced of the necessity for reform in China, Mao threw himself into the fray, writing a revolutionary manifesto that he posted on the school wall and joining the revolutionary army. He returned to civilian life when the volunteers were not called into action and embarked on a period of voracious reading on his own. Then in 1913 he enrolled in a teachers' college, where he was exposed to a progressive faculty and students fired up by patriotism and enthusiasm for the New Culture movement. Schoolwork became framed in the context of an active political life: Mao participated in street demonstrations against Japanese expansionism, organized guerrilla warfare against warlord soldiers billeted at the school, and published revolutionary articles for *New Youth* magazine; his first was an article that promoted physical exercise as an essential step for the self-strengthening of the nation.

After graduating in 1918, Mao chose to remain in China rather than accompany his classmates abroad on government-sponsored work-study programs. He worked in the Beijing University library, joined a Marxist discussion circle, and fell in love with the daughter of his old philosophy professor. In the tumultuous years that ensued, Mao alternately taught school in Changsha, engaging in radical activity against the local warlord and fleeing back and forth to Beijing, Wuhan, and Shanghai in order to escape arrest. In the summer of 1921, Mao was one of the 12 delegates meeting secretly in Shanghai to found the Communist Party of China. As part of the United Front between the Guomindang and the Communists, he engaged in organizational activities in Shanghai, Canton, and Hunan, finally going underground and retreating to the countryside when Chiang Kaishek turned against the Communists in the Shanghai massacre of April 1927.

Throughout the years of revolutionary struggle Mao endured personal losses—his second wife and his brother were executed by the Guomindang, a son was later killed in the Korean War—continual bouts with malaria, and contention among his comrades over his last marriage to Jiang Qing, a Shanghai movie actress who unsuccessfully attempted to assume power after Mao died.

Mao ascended to power in the Communist Party by insisting on an independent course for the Chinese revolution. Repeatedly contradicting party directives from Moscow, Mao waited for the practical success of his ideas to win him the leadership of the party. In 1935, on the Long March, Mao's conception of a protracted guerrilla war based on organizing peasant communities into armed revolutionary bases became the accepted strategy for rebuilding the communist movement after its retreat from encirclement by the Guomindang. Reduced after the Long March from ruling over 19,000 square miles, encompassing a population of 3 million, to a single base in China's barren northwest, the Communists in Yanan adopted Mao Zedong's program for a second united front against the Japanese. On this foundation they swept to power.

During the period of relative seclusion in Yanan, Mao articulated his ideas in writing, yielding a body of work that has come to be known as Mao Zedong Thought. The theme of Mao's pursuit of nationalist revolution was one of "people's war." For revolution to succeed in China required a "mass undertaking" demanding that the party serve the people. To adequately prepare party members for this type of leadership, "rectification campaigns" were instituted for which Mao Zedong Thought provided the material. In the end, for better or worse, Mao's life and the people's China are inextricably bound to each other.

Mountains came under heavy Guomindang attack at the end of 1928, they moved eastward to a new location between the Jiangxi and Fujian provinces, which they set up as the center of a new regime, the Jiangxi Soviet. Learning from their earlier mistakes, the Communists refined their land-reform policies on the basis of a better understanding of the subtle gradations of class structure among China's peasantry. They consolidated and trained a fast-moving guerrilla force, the Red Army, and fostered social change by outlawing arranged marriages, promoting equality for women, and teaching literacy.

Though there were at least a dozen regions in which such base areas were established after 1927, they were unable to withstand the economic blockade and military encirclement of the Guomindang. In 1934, after a series of extermination campaigns waged by Chiang Kaishek's forces, intent on eliminating their Communist competitors once and for all, the Communists were finally routed from their rural strongholds. They embarked on the epic Long March, marching 6,000 miles west and north to Yenan, on foot and under fire for more than a year while the Japanese planned their conquest of all of China.

As the Japanese advanced through China inciting fierce nationalist opposition, the two rival political parties were tested in the crucible of the anti-Japanese struggle. The Communists behind enemy lines in the rural north gained a national reputation for guerrilla warfare against the Japanese. The Guomindang, retreating from the urban east coast areas where the Japanese concentrated their troops, conserved their military forces for a final showdown with the Communists after the war. In this critical stage, the Communist Party of China became identified as the symbol of nationalist opposition to the Japanese enemy while the Guomindang forfeited its nationalist credentials in the eyes of countless Chinese. While Chiang Kaishek was correct in his prediction that it would take the United States to defeat Japan, he did not foresee the decisive impact his party's failure to oppose the Japanese and support land reform for the peasants would have on his claim to inherit the nationalist mantle of legitimacy.

This became readily apparent in the civil war between the forces of the Guomindang Republican government and the Communist Party of China, which resumed in 1946. The military and logistical support Chiang Kaishek's forces received from the United States was insufficient to compensate for the popular sentiment favoring the Communists. With military hardware captured from their opponents, the Communists marched into the capital and, on October 1, 1949, proclaimed the establishment of the People's Republic of China. The significance of the event, aptly described by Mao Zedong, captures the essence of the nationalist purpose in Asia: "Our nation will never again be an insulted nation. We have stood up."[4]

Although China had stood up under the leadership of the Communist Party, the flag of the Republic of China was not hauled down for the last time as were the British, Dutch, French, American, and Japanese flags over Burma, Malaysia, Indonesia, Vietnam, the Philippines, and Korea. Chiang Kaishek, defeated on the mainland, retreated to the island of Taiwan, a province of China since the eighteenth century and a colony of Japan from 1895 to 1945. There, under the gathering clouds of the cold war, Chiang refused to acknowledge that the communist People's Republic had succeeded the Nationalists as China's government, claiming that the Republic of China was still the only legitimate government of all of China. The island-born population on Taiwan, already unhappy with their treatment by the Nationalists after the province was restored to Chinese rule after 1945, resented the influx of Chiang's officials and army in 1949. The subsequent history of Taiwan's nationalist evolution will be described in Chapter 4.

NATIONALISM AND THE MOVEMENT FOR INDEPENDENCE IN THE PHILIPPINES AND CAMBODIA

Unlike the experience in China and Indonesia, where the anticolonial movement faced formidable opposition, in the Philippines and Cambodia nationalist leaders achieved political independence with little resistance from the United States and France. The Americans early on had declared that the objective of their presence in the islands was to prepare the people of the Philippines for self-government and eventual independence. In 1934 the U.S. Congress set 1946 as the date for independence, and that date was kept despite the occupation of the islands by the Japanese from 1942 to 1945. In Cambodia's case France had not anticipated nor had Cambodians asked for an end to the 1863 French protectorate over the kingdom until the end of World War II, and by 1953 the French were ready to concede independence.

But apart from the relative ease with which political independence was achieved in Cambodia and the Philippines, the two countries (shown in Figure 3.1, the map of Southeast Asia) are quite different in the extent to which nationalism spread and in the form their nationalist movements took in the years leading up to independence. Cambodia had existed as a political entity before the Western colonialists arrived; the Philippines had not. Spain's rule over those islands provided their first experience of a common political identity and had much more intrusive economic and cultural effects on the indigenous society than did French rule in Cambodia. The symbolic form of the Cambodian monarchy was not disturbed under the protectorate nor did the French have much impact on the culture outside the capital city, Phnom Penh, nor on the traditional Cambodian economy. In the Philippines the sense of national identity developed and was expressed in nationalist organizations in the nineteenth century, earlier than elsewhere in Southeast Asia. In Cambodia nationalist sentiments appeared in the 1930s among Buddhist intellectuals, and anticolonialism was expressed by the small number of Vietnamese residents of Cambodia who were members of Ho Chi Minh's new Indochinese Communist Party. During the Japanese occupation armed groups opposed to the French formed, and after the war came political parties advocating Cambodian independence or at least greater autonomy.

The Philippines

The idea of a Filipino identity was created in reaction to Spanish exclusionist policies, spread by American educational policies, and reinforced by Japan's conquest and occupation; it found expression in the late nineteenth century in the formation of nationalist organizations and in the twentieth century in political parties, divided from the beginning along class and ideological lines.

FIGURE 3.1 Southeast Asia

88

The Spanish Period. The unwillingness of the Spanish-born officials to welcome island-born people into the government and ecclesiastical bureaucracies aroused antagonism among the *creoles,* people of Spanish ancestry born in the Philippines, and the *mestizos,* people of mixed Spanish, Chinese, and *indio* ancestry. Many of them were members of the emerging local elite of wealthy landowners whose sons came to resent the Iberian Spanish domination not only of the civil service but also of the parish priesthood and the monastic orders, which wielded important economic and political power through their ownership of large estates. In opposition to the Spaniards, the creoles and mestizos found a common identity as Filipinos, and that identity spread to other segments of the population.

Criticism of Spanish rule came from three groups expressing cultural, religious, and political nationalism. The first of these, the *ilustrados*, were the educated sons of the landowning class, many of whom went abroad to escape repression by the Spanish authorities and formed the émigré Propaganda Movement. The objective of that organization was to improve the status of Filipinos in the colony; it advocated equality for them, representation in the Spanish legislature, freedom of speech and assembly, less burdensome taxes, Filipinization of the clergy, and the promotion of a distinctive national cultural identity in literature, the arts, and pre-Hispanic history.[5] One of the leading *ilustrados* was Jose Rizal, a Chinese mestizo who returned home from exile in 1892 and founded La Liga Filipina to promote a modest program of economic and educational improvements; even that was too much for the Spanish, who promptly arrested him and deported him to the southern island of Mindanao.

The second strain of the nationalist movement involved Filipino clergy who wanted equal opportunity in appointments as parish priests and in the monastic orders. Suppressed by the execution of its leaders in 1872, the movement regained momentum at the end of the Spanish period when Father Gregorio Aglipay established the Independent Filipino Church. The Aglipayans took over churches and lands vacated by the departing Spaniards and at its peak attracted as members a quarter of Filipino Christians.

The third element of the nationalist movement was Katipunan (a Tagalog abbreviation for the highest and most respectable association of the Sons of the People), and its aims were more revolutionary than the other two. Founded by Andres Bonifacio, a Manila clerk, Katipunan advocated political independence from Spain, social revolution to benefit the common people, and seizure of the church-owned estates. Aware of his own limited education and the need to enlarge his base of support, Bonifacio tried unsuccessfully to persuade the *ilustrados* to join him. A Katipunan-organized rebellion was launched in 1896, and the Spanish authorities rounded up persons suspected of participating, including the *ilustrado* Jose Rizal. Mistakenly assumed to be the leader of the rebellion, Rizal was executed, providing a martyr for the nationalist cause and radicalizing *ilustrados* to switch from pressing for more participation in colonial government to pursuing the goal of independence. Leadership of the anti-Spanish revolt was taken over by Emilio Aguinaldo, a local official of Chinese-mestizo stock. But in the face of superior force Aguinaldo negotiated with the Spanish in 1897 for amnesty for his followers and an indemnity and exile for himself, only to be brought back from exile by the U.S. Navy when it arrived in 1898 to pursue the war with Spain. The struggle for independence resumed, this time with *ilustrado* support. Radical Katipunan economic and social goals were set aside in favor of nationalist political goals, and when the rebels declared the independence of the Philippine Republic on June 12, 1898, the *ilustrados* exerted the major influence in drafting a constitution for the new government.

The American Period.   The prize of independence was soon snatched from Filipino hands by the Americans, alongside whom they had been fighting. President McKinley decided to keep the islands after the Spanish surrendered, and by early 1899 the forces of the new Philippine Republic were waging guerrilla warfare against the Americans. The unity between Aguinaldo's followers and the *ilustrados* broke down when the Americans offered to involve educated Filipinos in the shaping of a new government, an offer with great appeal to many *ilustrados* but unacceptable to others in the resistance. The division was

> not simply a class struggle. It was, among other things, a contest between two world views—the urban, cosmopolitan, and educated versus the rural, unsophisticated, and innocent.... The *ilustrados* ... thought it foolish to continue struggling against the Americans when the opportunities were so great not only for themselves but for what they saw as the best interests of the country. In effect, the Americans made a deal with the *ilustrados*. At the price of collaboration and allegiance, they were offered the chance to fill the vacuum created by the Spanish withdrawal.[6]

The result was that many *ilustrados* withdrew from the Philippine Republic government that they had cooperated in creating and began to participate in the political institutions of the new colonial government. The independence forces were eventually defeated and the short life of the first republic ended.

The Philippine nationalist movement during the American period operated under conditions quite different from those in the Spanish period. Most important was that by 1900 the U.S. government had declared that its policy was to prepare the colony for self-government and independence, so for the Nationalists the question was no longer *whether* but *when* the United States could be persuaded that their wards were ready to stand on their own. Further, the Americans encouraged the formation of political parties, enabling the Nationalists to organize and operate openly. The first parties formed around leading personalities, all committed to political independence and to the forms of U.S.-style government and representing the landed and nascent industrial elites. Parties on the left, committed to social justice for the lower classes, emerged somewhat later and included the Communist and Labor parties and Sakdal, created in response to adverse conditions caused by the Great Depression in the 1930s. But the conservative parties favored by the United States dominated elections and the institutions of self-government; the most influential of these was the Nacionalista Party, led by Sergio Osmena and Manuel Quezon.

American-initiated policies concerning the church and education also affected Filipino nationalism. To counter the appeal of Father Aglipay's Independent Filipino Church, the Vatican acquiesced in the separation of church and state and moved to put more Filipinos into Roman Catholic Church positions and to reduce the church's large landholdings by selling some of them to the colonial government for resale to tenant farmers. Land reform, incomplete though it turned out to be, and the Filipinization of the clergy removed the principal objections of the Nationalists to the Catholic Church and undermined the influence of the breakaway Aglipayans.

In the field of education, American policy was to extend educational opportunities to a broader segment of the population by setting up more schools, staffing them as early as possible with indigenous teachers, and encouraging the teaching of Filipino history. The result was that the sense of belonging to the Filipino nation, which in the nineteenth century had gripped only a small minority, spread widely among the people and gave them a common bond of loyalty, despite the persistence of deep divisions between rich and poor, city and country.

The Japanese occupation during World War II opened up some fissures in the nationalist movement; while Quezon and Osmena left to run the government in exile, others stayed and collaborated with Japan, declaring an "independent" republic in 1943. Armed resistance to the occupation was widespread, led by the leftist People's Anti-Japanese Army, the Hukbalahaps. Both nationalism and pro-Americanism were strengthened by the occupation and the battle to drive the Japanese out.

After the war, Philippine independence was granted on schedule in 1946 and power transferred to the centrists and the leading personalities among them, representing the wealthy and middle classes, while the interests of the masses in countryside and cities remained unarticulated. This class division has continued to haunt postindependence politics, as we shall see in Chapter 4.

Cambodia

The story of the rise of nationalism and the nationalist movement in Cambodia can be told much more briefly because, in contrast to the Philippines, Cambodian nationalism did not really become visible until World War II, just a decade before independence. Such a delayed development might be considered surprising, since the Cambodian kingdom had long existed, and at its zenith in the twelfth and thirteenth centuries the Khmer empire extended over much of Southeast Asia. But the glories of the past had been largely forgotten by the eighteenth century, and Cambodia was dominated by its neighbors to the west and east, Siam and Vietnam, until France imposed a protectorate in 1863.

It was not until 1930 that two organizations were founded that became significant in the nationalist movement. One was the Buddhist Institute in Phnom Penh, established by the kings of Cambodia and Laos and the French, with the purpose of fostering Buddhist studies. In fact, it strengthened the ties between the Cambodian king and his people and awakened a sense of national identity among the groups of intellectuals that the institute brought together. These included Son Ngoc Thanh, a Vietnamese-Cambodian who started a Cambodian-language newspaper and later became a major figure in the anti-French movement.

The second organization founded in 1930 was a cell of the new Indochinese Communist Party in Cambodia. Its founders were Vietnamese residents of Cambodia rather than Cambodians, initiating a pattern of Vietnamese domination of the communist movement in Cambodia that persisted even after the ICP disbanded in 1951 and a separate Cambodian party took shape.

These two embryonic nationalist movements—one communist, the other not— were encouraged by the Japanese to mount demonstrations against the French administration, which Japan left in place to run the daily affairs of the colony. Armed groups under the banner of Khmer Issarak (Khmer Independence) formed in the countryside. In the last months of the war, the Japanese removed the French officials and told the young King Norodom Sihanouk, whom the French had crowned in 1941, that Cambodia was independent. For a seven-month interval from March until October 1945, when the French returned, Cambodians ran their own government. Son Ngoc Thanh, who had fled to Japan in 1942 after an anti-French demonstration, came back to serve first as foreign minister and then as prime minister in Sihanouk's government, only to be arrested and exiled again by the French. Khmer Issarak bands continued their resistance in the countryside and managed to take the town of Siem Reap for a brief time in 1946.

Faced with nationalist pressures, the French made some concessions. They gave Cambodia "autonomy" within the French Union, keeping for themselves control of two significant levers of power, the army and the police. They arranged for the election of a constituent assembly to draft a constitution and authorized the formation of political parties. Two were formed: (1) the pro-independence Democratic Party representing the middle bureaucracy, educated youth, and Buddhist monks, many of them supporters of Son Ngoc Thanh; and (2) the more conservative pro-French Liberal Party, toward which the king was inclined. The Democratic Party won elections to the constituent assembly and to the National Assembly that followed, but neither the French nor the king was willing to see the Democratic majority exercise effective control over the government.

Tensions between Cambodian political factions increased in 1951. Thanh returned to a huge welcoming crowd estimated at over 100,000, only to flee to the countryside a few months later. There, refusing to join forces with the Communist-led United Issarak Front formed in 1948, Thanh started his own anti-French, anti-Sihanouk resistance group. That same year the Cambodian Communists established their own party, the Khmer People's Revolutionary Party (KPRP), and Sihanouk began a campaign of his own to mobilize international support for his country's independence. By 1953 the French, preoccupied with holding on in Vietnam against the Viet Minh's struggle to evict them and facing not only pressure from their one-time protégé Sihanouk but also an insurgent movement that controlled large areas of the country, were ready to concede independence to Sihanouk's government. Cambodia's political history since 1953 is traced in Chapter 4.

NATIONALISM AND ETHNIC SEPARATISM IN MALAYA AND BURMA

The British colonies of Malaya and Burma faced formidable obstacles to developing a coherent, inclusive nationalism both before and after independence. Under colonial rule, both countries became plural societies, a result of large numbers of Indians and Chinese being brought into Malaya and Burma to serve British economic interests. Furnivall's description of multiethnic Burma, equally apt for Malaysia, captures the dilemma of colonized people in a plural society:

> Each group holds by its own religion, its own culture and language, its own ideas and ways. As individuals they meet, but only in the market-place, in buying and selling. There is plural society, with different segments of the community living side by side, but separately, within the same political unit.[7]

Held together by force of the centralized colonial administration of the British, these segregated ethnic communities were often more wary of one another than they were of their European rulers. When nationalist opposition to British rule did emerge, it was the parochial nationalism of the dominant ethnic group in each colony—the Malays in Malaya and the Burmans in Burma[8]—that defined the nationalist cause, lumping together all individuals of foreign descent—Chinese and Indians along with the British—as targets of their opposition. Japanese occupation during World War II exacerbated this interethnic animosity, ensuring that once the British left, the ethnic separatism both colonial powers had fostered would remain an enduring problem for postindependence governments to contend with in Burma and Malaysia.

Although ethnic pluralism was common to both societies, there were significant differences between them that affected the course of developing a national identity in Burma and Malaya. The principal religion in Burma was Theravada Buddhism while in Malaya it was Islam. Nationalism emerged early in the twentieth century in Burma and not until after World War II in Malaya. In Burma nationalism exhibited a revolutionary ethos, manifested in a broadly based demand for social and economic change along with a complete break with Britain. In contrast, nationalism in Malaya was conservative and accommodationist, reflecting the politically privileged position of the Malays encouraged by the British. After independence, Malaya remained a member of the British Commonwealth while Burma refused to join.

For Malays the racial understanding of their own ethnicity played a far greater role than either class or religion in defining their communal interests. Malay nationalism, therefore, was content to restrict the substance of its nationalist demands to the preservation of Malay privileges vis-à-vis non-Malays. In Burma nationalism may have been advocated principally by the Burmans, but the substance of its claims covered an entire spectrum of social and economic changes for a new nation. For them, the goal of nationalism was to create a state at least the equal of its precolonial state under the Buddhist monarchy, while for Malays nationalism had no unified state to look back on, only the feudal rights of the nine sultans who had ruled the region prior to the British colonial administration.

Early Nationalism in Burma

In Burma, as was true throughout Asia, organized nationalism began among an educated elite of Burmans and was initially expressed as a movement to reform or modernize their religion, Buddhism. The events of World War I, as elsewhere, politicized this cultural nationalist movement, the Young Men's Buddhist Association (YMBA), splitting it into pro-British and proactivist organizations. The proactivists who called themselves the General Council of Buddhist (later, Burmese) Associations (GCBA) were centered in the university and promoted village-level nationalist organizations ("own-race societies") in rural areas. But as these village-based nationalist organizations came under the leadership of young Buddhist monks, they became more militantly anti-British, creating a breach between the rural and urban segments of nationalist leadership. The rural Buddhist leadership sought to eliminate the colonial government in its entirety while the urban secularist leadership sought just to oust the British while preserving their administrative structure as the foundation of a new nation.

This split within the ethnic Burman community, however, must be placed in the larger context of a Burma traditionally divided between the dominant Burmans and the ethnic minorities, which include Chin, Kachin, Shan, Karen, Kayah, and other smaller groups. Relations between them and the Burmans had been troubled since precolonial times, when Burman monarchs on several occasions subdued the peoples on their border, ruling over them for relatively brief periods before their power declined and the conquered areas slipped from their control.

During the colonial period, the division between Burmans and others continued under the British policy of separate administrations for Burma "proper"—the lowland areas where many Burmans lived—and the "frontier areas"—the mountainous regions inhabited by the minorities along the country's western, northern, and eastern borders, as shown in Figure 3.2. The ethnic cleavage between Burmans and the minorities was reinforced by heavily recruiting minorities into the colonial armed forces, by introducing communal representation in the colonial legislature as a form of special protection for minority communities, by the success of Baptist missionaries in converting Karens to Christianity, and by the migration of Indians into the colony.

The picture was further complicated by the fact that politically Burma was administered as a province of India—in effect, a "colony of a colony"—while economically it was exposed to the vagaries of the international market. Using credit provided by Indian immigrants, Burmans expanded their rice cultivation for a booming export economy. But when the rice market collapsed the Indians, who were already in control of commerce, also acquired, along with a few fortunate Burmans, the bulk of the land. Thus by 1938, the largest landowners in the Irawaddy River delta owned 2.5 million acres or about 27 percent of all the land in lower Burma.[9] The majority of Burman peasants, on the other hand, fell into debt, foreclosure, and financial ruin, which led to anti-Indian riots and rebellions against colonial taxation and widespread impoverishment. These Burmans supplied a mass base for the radical leadership of the nationalist movement that coalesced just prior to and during World War II.

Two major issues divided the urban nationalist leadership in the lively political atmosphere of the 1920s and 1930s: One was whether or not to collaborate with the British-controlled constitutional government introduced in 1923; the other was the question of separation from India. The majority of the GCBA boycotted elections under the new constitution and favored direct action to oust the British, while traditional ethnic minorities who benefited from special representation in the legisla-

Tibeto-Burman

Burman

Chin

Kachin

Other
1. Lahu 2. Lisu
3. Naga 4. Akha

**Burman and
Mon-Khmer**

Karen

Karen

Kayah

Karen and Burman

Tai

Shan

Mon-Khmer

5. Mon 6. Wa 7. Palaung

Burman and Shan

△ Indians and Bangladeshi*

□ Chinese*

*Other Indians, Bangladeshi, and Chinese
are found mainly in the cities

FIGURE 3.2 Ethnic Groups of Burma

Source: From *Burmese Politics* by Josef Silverstein, copyright 1980 by Rutgers, The State University.

tive council formed an electoral majority against those Burmans who did enter party politics. Whether or not to separate from India in the struggle against colonial rule was equally divisive, some nationalists favoring freedom from India to obtain home rule on the best possible terms, while others sought alliance with the Indian nationalist movement to hasten the ouster of the British.

When the British decided in favor of separation, granting Burma a more democratic constitution in 1935, the urban nationalist movement split along generational lines. The older politicians formed new parties to seek office in the

Legislative Council while the militant university students set up their own revolutionary nationalist organizations among workers and peasants. The We Burmese Association, formally organized in 1933, rose to prominence under the leadership of the charismatic Aung San and the All Burma Students' Union after 1938. Calling themselves Thakins ("masters") to suggest they rather than the British were the rulers of Burma, these sons and daughters of the Burmese middle class included the future leaders of independent Burma. They applied Marxist ideas to Burma's colonial situation, organizing labor strikes among the mostly Indian factory workers and encouraging peasant unions with the goal of forcing the British out.

The electoral politics of the older generation of nationalist leaders held little interest for the vast majority of Burmese, whose participation in voting never exceeded 18 percent. The more youthful Thakins with their Marxist orientation, on the other hand, succeeded in arousing popular support from both peasants and workers for a broad range of antigovernment campaigns in the late 1930s. Although these two branches of the nationalist movement differed in principle on the issue of collaboration versus subversion, and in rhetoric between a more British-Labor and a more Marxist class orientation, their broad policy goals were substantially the same: independence, self-determination, and anti-imperialism. These goals were rooted in the question of land for the peasantry, an issue both sides were forced to address.

Thus nationalism in Burma prior to the Japanese occupation was composed of a number of distinct elements: the professional politicians for whom nationalism became a fight over perks and position in the British-controlled legislature that they hoped to inherit at independence; the youthful, revolutionary Thakins with a strategy for mobilizing the masses of downtrodden for noncooperation with the British; the Burman peasants who violently rebelled against the loss of their land, income, and traditional supports, for which they held both the Indians and the British responsible; and the various groups of ethnic hill people, each protective of their special privileges under the British.

The Impact of the Japanese Occupation on Burma

The Japanese occupation introduced yet another divisive and bewildering dimension to the uncertainties among the diverse Burmese nationalists. A small group of Burmese, including Thakin Aung San, had been trained by the Japanese as an officer corps of a new Burma Independence Army (BIA). As it passed through Burma, the BIA grew in size as politically inspired youth joined its ranks. The sight of Burmese participating in the defeat of British colonial rule immeasurably enhanced the power and prestige of the BIA, the more so as its members filled positions of local administration vacated by the mass exodus of British and Indians. Under Japanese control, a government of prewar Burmese politicians was installed and granted nominal independence in 1943.

But it was impossible for the quasi-independent Burmese government to replace the power of the British colonial state and the neutrality of its civil service. When, in addition, the brutality of the Japanese occupation began to cost the Burmese Independence Army (BIA) its popular support, Thakin Aung San, minister of war in the Japanese-sponsored government, astutely engineered an about-face and joined the Allies to form the Anti-Fascist People's Freedom League (AFPFL).

As in the case of China, the numerous nationalist organizations that cooperated in the struggle against the Japanese in Burma made strange bedfellows: the Communists and Socialists along with the Burmese Independence Army and the AFPFL joined with the Karen National Association, Burma's earliest modern political organization. This brought together Marxist-oriented students, peasants, and Burmese nationalists who sought to *throw out* the British in favor of an indigenously managed independent Burma with the Christian Karen and other ethnic leaders who sought to *bring back* the British to regain and protect their privileged position.

But these coalitions broke apart when the British were dissuaded from reimposing colonial rule by the league's effective organization of popular strikes and demonstrations between 1945 and 1948. When in the interest of achieving independence Aung San, the league's popular leader, demonstrated a willingness to negotiate compromises with the British, the increased likelihood that conservative politicians would be brought back into power alienated the Communists. This in turn caused severe strains in the league, culminating in Aung San's assassination by followers of a former premier, U Saw, some six months before independence in 1948. Thus the one figure capable of uniting the warring political factions in Burma was removed from the political scene. As a result, independence embroiled the new Burmese state in a civil war that echoed the tensions of the international cold war as the two factions of the Communist Party went underground to avoid arrest and pursue through insurrection what had eluded them through the electoral process.

Early Nationalism in Malaya

Colonialism stimulated nationalist sentiment by making Malays aware of themselves as a distinct ethnic group. The new forms of economic activity, urban life, and secular education that non-Malays enjoyed awakened Malays to the realization of their own backwardness. Three strains of nationalist consciousness emerged in the 1920s and 1930s, each appealing to different elements among the elites and with different aims. The first was a group of Islamic reformers, inspired by contact with the progressive religious movement in the Middle East. They emphasized the need to purge Malay Moslem practices of their un-Islamic beliefs in magic, superstition, and spirit worship, so that Islam could be a force for modernization among Malays. With that objective, the Islamic reformers ran into opposition from traditional religious leaders and were unable to win over the Malay masses to their cause.

A second group, equally unable to gain a following among the peasant class from which many of them came, was composed of secular intellectuals, mostly teachers and writers. Their radical views included the notion of a pan-Indonesian nationalism uniting Malay people in both British Malaya and the Dutch East Indies. On the eve of World War II they formed the Young Malay Union, a political organization kept under close watch by the colonial authorities.

The third group was conservative in outlook, drawn mainly from British-educated sons of the traditional elite class who had been recruited for administrative positions in the colonial service. Alarmed by the demographic trend that by 1931 showed non-Malays outnumbering Malays, they sought to protect the privileged position accorded Malays by British policy and to increase civil service opportunities, the amount of land reserved for Malays and immigration by their fellow Malays from Java to offset the size of the non-Malay population. Avoiding any undue criticism of their British patrons, they created Malay associations in the separate states, with strong links to the local sultans. These conservatively oriented associations multiplied throughout the Malay Peninsula, extolling the virtues of ethnic Malay consciousness with distinctly hostile overtones toward non-Malays, even those who were Moslem.

While Malays organized in a conservative direction to defend their rights as *bumiputra* ("sons of the soil"), urban Chinese nationalists pursued progressive politics related to their homeland, identifying either with Chiang Kaishek's Guomindang or with the Chinese Communist Party. The Malayan Communist Party, formed in 1930, was active among the mostly Chinese industrial labor force and closely identified with the Chinese community. It had links also to the communist movements in Indonesia and Vietnam. So when the Japanese invaded Malaya in 1941, the Chinese in the colony were obvious targets of suspicion.

The Impact of the Japanese Occupation on Malaya

Under Japanese occupation, the Chinese bore the brunt of Japanese brutality not only because of their support for the anti-Japanese struggle in China but also because they soon became involved in organizing resistance to the occupiers. Because of their early and militant opposition to the Japanese occupation of China, the leaders of the Malayan Communist Party were encouraged by retreating British military officers to organize the Malayan People's Anti-Japanese Army (MPAJA). After receiving training in Singapore, the Communists constituted the core of the MPAJA, which employed the same guerrilla tactics against the Japanese that they were later to use against the British.

In contrast to the Chinese resistance, the Malays were either passive or active collaborators with the Japanese, whose conciliatory policy toward them included promoting them to civil service positions vacated by the British. An interesting question is raised by a former Malay civil servant in his study of communalism in Malaysia:

> It is significant that while collaborating with the MPAJA, the British made little attempt to mobilize the Malays as allies against the Japanese.... As one Malay, who was trained as a radio operator before the Japanese Occupation, posed the matter, "Why were not the Malays told to form resistance groups, as the MPAJA were, by the British?"[10]

Thus Japanese occupation of Malaya increased the tensions among the communal groups, hardening the nationalist rivalries into mutual antagonisms. After the Japanese left, a settling of scores between the pro-Japanese and the resistance took place, with Malay collaborators subject to reprisals by the MPAJA.

After the War: The "Emergency"

In 1946 the British announced their postwar plans for a "Malayan Union." In an effort to consolidate the patchwork of political arrangements that the British had made with local rulers a century earlier, the sultans were to relinquish their sovereignty to the British Crown, and citizenship would be granted to persons born in, or long-term residents of, Malaya. Announcement of the British plan mobilized a storm of Malay nationalist feeling far exceeding any demonstration of national feeling manifested before the war. Within a few weeks a mass Malay movement, the United Malays National Organization (UMNO), had galvanized Malays into action against the British plan, which was hastily abandoned in favor of a return to a federal system recognizing Malay privileges and restricting citizenship.

But independence for the Federation of Malaya was delayed until 1957 by the "Emergency," precipitated by British military action against the Malayan Communist Party (MCP) and the struggle of its Malayan Races Liberation Army (MRLA) to oust the British. The "Emergency" illustrates the conjuncture of international and domestic affairs in the determination of nationalist policy in the postwar world and requires some recapitulation of events.

After the defeat of the Japanese, which they brought about in collaboration with the British, the Communists disarmed and embarked on a pursuit of their objective of independence through legal means.

The MCP's efforts to organize the industrial workers, most of whom were Chinese, met with considerable success, and the British began to clamp down on labor unions. By mid-1948 the Malay Communist Party decided to give up constitutional means to achieve power and reverted to armed struggle aimed at interrupting production in the rubber plantations and tin mines.

The "Emergency" was the British military and political war to prevent the Communists from obtaining power. Militarily, the British forced the Communists into the jungle by 1949, while politically they benefited from Malay support, since "most Malays saw the war as preeminently a Chinese attempt to gain control of the state and not only remained loyal to the colonial power but fought actively against the MRLA."[11] Employing pacification techniques that the United States later used during the Vietnam War, the British resettled 500,000 Chinese in more than 400 "new villages" between 1950 and 1952 and deported some 10,000 Chinese to China.

While they were attempting to rout the Communists militarily, the British were preparing for their withdrawal as early as 1949 by encouraging the formation of the noncommunist Malay Chinese Association (MCA) as the Chinese counterpart to the United Malays National Organization (UMNO). Ironically, closer cooperation between the Malay elite of the UMNO and the wealthy Chinese businessmen of the MCA was brought about (again with British encouragement) in an electoral pact to defeat the Independence of Malaya Party, a noncommunal party formed by Onn b. Jaafar, a founder of UMNO who had left that organization because of its Malay exclusivity. The informal alliance between the two communally oriented organizations, UMNO and MCA, was so successful in gaining the vast majority of seats in Malay's first democratic elections under the new federal constitution in 1952 that the Alliance was formalized in August 1953. When the Malayan Indian Congress agreed to join the Alliance, completing the representation for a stable electoral spectrum established along communal lines, the British felt secure in granting independence to the Federation of Malaya in 1957.

In both Malaya and Burma ethnic pluralism contributed to civil war between the government and its political opponents. In Burma the insurgency came after independence was granted; in Malaya the "Emergency" came before independence and was dealt with by the colonial government. Nationalist movements evolved differently in the two countries. In Burma, the special relationship of the British was with the Karen and Shan minorities rather than with the dominant Burmans, who were hostile to the British. In Malaya, it was the majority Malays whose status and traditions were protected by the British, resulting in an accommodationist form of nationalism. In Burma those who had been thrown onto the mercy of market forces mobilized in support of revolutionary nationalism. In Malaya the Malays, having been shielded from participating in the modern export sector, became proponents of a conservative ethnic nationalism, its principal purpose being to preserve their political privileges from encroachment by non-Malays, in particular the Chinese. Independence was demanded by the majority in Burma and conceded by the British soon after their return at the end of World War II. For the Malay majority, independence from colonial rule was a less pressing goal, and it took more than a decade for a bargain to be struck that enabled the British to turn power over to a conservative coalition dominated by Malays.

NATIONALISM FROM ABOVE IN THAILAND AND JAPAN

As in other Asian countries, Western imperialism stimulated the rise of modern nationalism in Thailand and Japan, even though both of them managed to remain independent. But rather than welling up from below in opposition to government by a colonial power, nationalism in those countries flowed from the top down. The Thai monarchs and the Meiji reformers acting in the name of the emperor undertook a process of self-modernization aimed at strengthening their countries' capacity to resist the threat of forced incorporation into the colonial empires and at reclaiming the sovereignty lost in the unequal treaties. The sacrifices required for modernization were made more palatable to the people by fostering a strong attachment to the nation, by putting loyalty to the monarch above loyalty to the local lord or to one's family, by creating national solidarity in support of the elite's domestic and foreign policy agendas. In both Thailand and Japan, education and religion were enlisted in the service of the nationalist cause. And in both, the ultra-Nationalists gained control of the government in the 1930s, only to lose it when their expansionist mission ended in failure at the end of World War II.

Nation Building by Siamese Monarchs

The integration of Thailand (then called Siam) into the Western-dominated world system began in 1855 with the negotiation of the first of the unequal treaties conceding to Western governments extraterritorial rights for their citizens, unrestricted trade, and low tariffs. The economic and social effects of being swept into the international trading networks were considerable. Siamese peasants began expanding production of rice for export, which gave them income to buy goods imported from the West. Exports of teak, tin, and rubber as well as rice transformed Bangkok into a major trade center. Chinese immigrants came to fill jobs opening up in construction, stevedoring, mills, banks, and offices, creating an ethnic division in Thai society along occupational lines similar to that in other plural societies in Southeast Asia.

Integration into the world system also stimulated the king and court to inaugurate other changes to create a modern nation-state. Governmental reforms were made with an eye to the ever present threat of foreign, particularly British, intervention. The British were on the move in the Malay states to the south and in Burma to the west, and the French were encroaching from the east into areas of traditional Siamese influence in Cambodia and Laos. King Mongkut (1851–1869) and his son and successor Chulalongkorn (1869–1910) assiduously tried to avoid giving the foreigners any justification for taking over their country and at the same time took steps to strengthen the power of the central government over the outlying areas vulnerable to foreign penetration.

Mongkut's initiatives were in the fields of education and religion. Realizing that to deal effectively with the Westerners, the royal family and the nobles needed to learn Western languages and something of Western science and technology, he hired foreign tutors for their children and brought in foreign technical experts to improve the military, the police, and the diplomatic service. Mongkut's influence in the religious sphere stemmed from the quarter of a century he had spent as a Buddhist monk before ascending to the throne; during that period he founded a new Buddhist sect, stripped of the local accretions that had accumulated in Siamese Buddhism over the centuries. Closer to the orthodoxy of early Buddhism, the practices of his Thammayut order were made by his son and grandson the basis for national norms in the selection and training of the Buddhist clergy, becoming one of the unifying elements for Thai nationalism.

During the reign of King Chulalongkorn major reforms were undertaken to strengthen the authority and capacity of the central government. Traditional king-vassal relationships between Bangkok and the outlying areas were replaced by provincial governments under the administrative authority of the national government. The power of the local lords was taken away, and they were either appointed by the central government to positions in the provincial governments or replaced by new officials responsive to Bangkok. The central government itself underwent renovation; functional ministries for interior and defense replaced earlier geographically organized ministries, and the tax system was restructured to bring in more revenue for the expanding bureaucracy and for public works programs such as the extensive railroad network linking parts of the country to each other and to neighboring countries.

Expansion of the power of the central government over the provinces was met with resistance in outlying areas where Siamese rule had previously been indirect and where the people were of different ethnic stock. Rebellions were suppressed by military force, but it was clear that for the newly centralized Siamese state to survive, all the people within its borders would need to be given a sense of membership in the Siamese nation. And this sense of nationhood, as Chulalongkorn, his advisers, and successors saw it, would be fostered by the new form of Buddhism, by extending education to the common people, and by promoting the king as the symbol of national unity. So the Buddhist priesthood was unified under the authority of a supreme patriarch appointed by the king. A state-controlled school system (although not fully in place until the 1930s) began to teach a standard version of the Thai language and a history of Siam stressing the king's rather than local rulers' role, as well as "modern" subjects such as science and math. Chulalongkorn's son Vajiravudh (1910–1925) expanded on his father's efforts to make the monarch more visible to the people. He appeared often in public in the uniform of the Wild Tiger Corps, a paramilitary group he founded, open to commoner and noble alike. The corps and a parallel Village Scout movement for children directed their members' loyalty upward to the monarch as the head of the nation. It was toward the end of Vajiravudh's reign that the Western powers, sufficiently convinced of Siam's modernity, agreed to end most of the restrictions imposed in the unequal treaties.

National Leadership by the Promoters

The Siamese revolution from above produced some remarkable achievements in the nineteenth and early twentieth centuries, but it had left the political core, the absolute monarchy, unreformed. It was not surprising, therefore, that the monarchy itself would be challenged by a new wave of nationalists in the modernized civil and military service the kings themselves had established. Recruited for their ability rather than their connections to the nobility, well educated, often with experience abroad, these people (whom today we would label "technocrats") knew that in the rest of the world absolute monarchies were becoming obsolete. They wanted to further their country's modernization, and expand their own influence, by curbing the power of the king. Under the pressure of a deteriorating national and personal financial situation caused by the Great Depression, a group of antiroyalist civil servants and military called the Promoters staged a bloodless coup in 1932, forcing Vajiravudh's successor King Prajadhipok (1925–1935) to accept the idea of a limited monarchy. From then on, the responsibility for nation building and national development passed from the hands of royalty to the new elite.

The Promoters and their supporters formed the People's Party and took their place in the government, successfully resisting a royalist countercoup in 1933. They soon split into a liberal civilian faction and a conservative military faction, and the leaders of the two factions, Pridi and Phibun, became rivals for influence in the government for the next two decades. Each man represented a different vision of modern statehood under a limited monarchy. Pridi's goal was to create a liberal constitutional system with the government chosen by and responsible to the electorate. Phibun, in contrast, emphasized the need for a strong state with decisive leadership at the center to direct the process of modernization. Pridi proposed a major role for government in economic planning and the establishment of cooperatives as the preferred form of private ownership. To the conservatives this smacked of communism and they ousted Pridi from the government and forced him into exile. Phibun, an army officer, became prime minister in 1938 and served until 1944. Pridi returned to hold a cabinet position briefly and then became regent for young King Ananda, who was in school in Switzerland until the end of World War II.

Ultranationalism Ascendant in Thailand

The years leading up to and during the war enhanced the influence of the military; ultranationalist ideas, in vogue in Japan and Europe, gained appeal in Siam. Resident Chinese, whose economic power made them visible and vulnerable to nationalist resentment, were restricted from engaging in certain enterprises, and the government created state enterprises to carry on activities formerly conducted by Chinese-owned enterprises. Limits were set on further Chinese immigration and Chinese-language instruction was prohibited. Symbolic of the desire to bring together all Thai-speaking people, including those beyond Siam's borders, Phibun had the country's name changed to Thailand. He followed up on this pan-Thai aspiration with a foreign policy aimed at taking advantage of the European powers' preoccupation with war in Europe to regain territories given up under duress in the late nineteenth century. Incidents along the border with Laos and Cambodia in between 1940 and 1941 led to war with the French colonial government. Japanese mediation resulted in the return of those lands to Thailand, a victory against colonialism that enhanced the prestige of the Thai military.

When the Japanese made their push into Southeast Asia in December 1941, Phibun's government acceded to their demand for passage en route to the conquest of British Malaya and Burma. Riding the wave of Japanese victories, Thailand allied itself with Japan and declared war on the Allies. This move brought short-term territorial and economic gains; Thailand retook areas in Burma and Malaya that it had given up to the British in the nineteenth century, and its economy benefited from increased trade with Japan and provisioning Japanese troops stationed in the country.

But these gains were lost with the Allied victory in 1945. Thailand was forced to return the territories taken from the French and British colonies, and Pridi, who had cooperated with the Allies during the war through the Free Thai underground, was elected prime minister in 1946. The military, temporarily eclipsed as a result of its collaboration with the Japanese, ousted Pridi in a coup in 1947, and he went into exile again. Phibun became prime minister once more in 1948, thwarting a coup attempt the following year by Pridi, who then left the country for good. Phibun remained in office until 1957, when a rival military officer overthrew him and he too went into exile, where he died.

The ouster of Pridi in 1947 marked not only the end of his career in government but the eclipse of the liberal element of modernizing nationalists that he exemplified and the ascendancy of the authoritarian element and military domination of Thai politics. The liberal view did not disappear, but its supporters over the years suffered repression in various degrees of severity at the hands of the military, most recently in 1992, as will be described in Chapter 4.

Nation Building by the Meiji Reformers

In Japan the process of modernization was undertaken from above, by the young samurai who had seized control from the shogunate and ruled in the name of the Emperor Meiji as the symbol of national unity. The nationalism that inspired the creation of a modern state had its foundation in a society more racially and culturally

FIGURE 3.3   Japan—Principal Islands and Cities

homogeneous than Thailand's, cemented by a confident ethnocentrism and reinforced by national myths about the divine origin of the emperor and his people.

As in Thailand, the stimulus for self-modernization was the need to become
strong enough to resist further Western encroachment and eventually to press for
termination of the unequal treaties exacted by the imperial powers in the waning
years of the Tokugawa. And as in Thailand, the modernizers recognized that national
strength required asserting the central government's political, fiscal, and military
dominance over the local clans and fostering a sense of national loyalty among all
classes of the Japanese people. The Meiji reformers moved quickly to bring the feudal domains under central control. Title to the land was given to the peasants who
worked it, and they were required to pay taxes based on the value of the property, in
cash directly to the central government, rather than, as before, paying a share of the
rice crop to the local ruler. This change assured the central government a predictable
revenue source for the increased expenses of modernizing the military and pension-
ing off the feudal class. The samurai as a fighting force were replaced with a national
army recruited by conscription. Although there was some peasant resistance to the

draft because it took sons away from work on the farm, military service became a way of forging consciousness of national identity and bonds of loyalty to the emperor and the central government rather than to the local lord.

Religion was also used in building a modern state. From 1868 to 1945, the Japanese government was the patron and advocate of Shinto, whose symbols and practices the state took over and adapted to bolster loyalty to the emperor and the nation. As one scholar puts it, "Shinto, as adopted by the modern Japanese state, was largely an invented tradition . . . to unite disparate elements into a modern nation."[12] Prior to the Meiji period, Shinto was a locally organized religion devoted to worship of many native deities at shrines throughout the country. Its ceremonies were closely intertwined with those of Buddhism, which had higher status during the Tokugawa era. After 1868, the Meiji leaders withdrew state patronage from Buddhism and ordered the separation of the two religions, creating a Department of Divinity to administer national religious affairs and conduct state religious observances. From 1870 to 1884, the government carried on a Great Promulgation Campaign to spread an official creed, teaching respect for the gods, reverence for the emperor, love of country, and obedience to the government. State sponsorship of the campaign "indicates that politicians believed Shinto would be useful in uniting the populace in a common creed that would transcend regional loyalties and differences of class."[13]

While the early Meiji era was a time of extensive borrowing from the West, perhaps excessively emulating Western dress, art, education, and technology to the neglect of Japanese traditions, by the late 1880s the time was ripe for a reassertion of Japanese identity and a renewed interest in Japanese culture. A movement to reverse what the cultural nationalists saw as a decline in morality due to Western influence led in 1890 to the promulgation of the Imperial Rescript on Education, which became the guiding principle for educational institutions. It exhorted the emperor's subjects to maintain harmonious relations with family and friends, to "develop intellectual faculties and perfect moral powers," to be law-abiding, and "should emergency arise, offer yourselves courageously to the State; and thus guard and maintain the prosperity of Our Imperial Throne coeval with heaven and earth." The Rescript concludes, "The Way here set forth is indeed the teaching bequeathed by Our Imperial Ancestors, . . . infallible for all ages and true in all places."[14] These universal values of loyalty and piety were inculcated in generations of Japanese children who participated in ceremonial readings and recited the text from memory, much as American children recite the Pledge of Allegiance. Shinto priests supported the promulgation of the Rescript, benefiting from the popular perception that all Japanese were obligated to observe rites associated with the Rescript and Shinto rites as well.

In the 1890s Japanese nationalism turned outward to the mission of expansion into continental Asia. War with China in 1894, intervention in Korea, and war with Russia in 1904 all elicited wide and fervent support. National pride suffered a series of injuries at the hands of the Western powers. Japan was forced to back down first on its claims to Siberian territory at the end of the Russo-Japanese War and then on some of its 21 demands on China during World War I. Its request for the adoption of a clause on racial equality at the Paris Peace Conference was rejected. It was assigned a position in naval power subordinate to England and the United States under the terms of the Washington Naval Disarmament Treaty. Having joined with the United States in sending an expeditionary force to Siberia to rescue anti-Bolshevik Czech military units there, Japan was pressured by the American government into removing its troops, which remained there after the mission was accomplished. Another cause of resentment was American immigration and local laws that discriminated against citizens of Japan.

The almost unanimous support for nationalist goals (dissent was expressed by some Christians, Socialists, and antinationalist Marxist intellectuals) may have obscured the growing differences between the moderate and the radical nationalists over both foreign and domestic policies. Hane characterizes the split as being between the bourgeoisie and liberal intellectuals on one side and the militarists and radical nationalists on the other, between city and country, between Tokyo and the provinces, between the Western-oriented culture and the traditional culture.[15] The radicals gained ascendancy in the 1930s, resorting to political assassination, book banning, textbook revision, compulsory attendance at Shinto services, and other measures to foster national unity and suppress opposition to their actions. Their success can be measured by the enthusiastic support for the decision to go to war in 1941. Japanese nationalism merged with militarism and imperialism to produce Japan's disastrous involvement in World War II.

INDEPENDENCE AND THE PROBLEMS OF NATION BUILDING

The surrender of Japan in August 1945 abruptly terminated its colonial rule over Korea and Taiwan; its wartime occupation of coastal and northeast China, the Philippines, the Dutch East Indies, French Indochina, British Malaya, and Burma; and its presence in nominally neutral Thailand. In Southeast Asia, Japan's defeat opened the way for the return of the Western powers to the colonies from which they had been evicted between 1940 and 1942. In China, the special privileges accorded foreigners by treaty had been abolished, but the Europeans and Americans returned to resume their commercial and missionary activities in that country.

During the last phase of the occupation and with Japanese encouragement, the Southeast Asian colonies had declared their independence in an abortive move to forestall the return of the former colonial masters. But the latter's military forces soon arrived to reassert control, the question being for how long. The United States and the United Kingdom were anticipating independence for the Philippines within a year and for Burma and Malaya somewhat later. The concern was to transfer the reins of government to local people of moderate political persuasion who could be trusted to pursue foreign and domestic policies compatible with the interests of their colonial "tutors" in the art of self-government. Independence came for the Philippines in 1946 and for Burma in 1948 but, for reasons explained above, was delayed for Malaya until 1957. Singapore was granted self-rule in 1959, and in 1963, along with the British-controlled states of Sabah and Sarawak on the island of Borneo, united with Malaya to form the Federation of Malaysia. Singapore left the federation under pressure in 1965 and became an independent state. Brunei, the last British colony on Borneo, became self-governing in 1957 and independent in 1984.

The French and Dutch took a different approach. Perhaps to compensate for the ignominy of being occupied by the Germans during World War II, they were determined to regain control of Indochina and the East Indies. Resistance was strong in both cases. The Dutch conceded independence to Indonesia in 1949 but kept the western part of New Guinea until 1962, and the Portuguese remained in East Timor until forced out in 1975. Cambodia and Laos became independent of France in 1953, and Vietnam became independent in 1954, with recognition of the existence of two governments, the Democratic Republic of Vietnam in the north and the Republic of Vietnam in the south.

The postwar fates of Japan's two long-term colonies, Formosa and Korea, were determined by three victorious Allied powers. Formosa, the Chinese province of Taiwan given up under duress in 1895, was rejoined to the Republic of China and in 1949 became the site of that government when the Guomindang lost control of the mainland to the Chinese Communists. In Korea, by mutual agreement between the Soviet Union and the United States, American forces entered to accept the Japanese surrender in the southern half of the peninsula, and the Soviet forces did the same north of the thirty-eighth parallel. This division of Korea formed the basis for separate military governments in the north and south, which in 1948 were terminated in favor of formal independence for the Democratic People's Republic of Korea in the north and the Republic of Korea in the south.

The fate of these two ex-colonies of Japan remains unresolved, with the issue of "independence" for the three territories—North Korea, South Korea, and Taiwan—shrouded in the unfinished aftermath of the cold war. Although technically still at war in 2000, the two Koreas seem propelled toward reunification by an enduring nationalist sentiment. And the force of Chinese nationalism, most adamantly in the People's Republic, continues to captivate the domestic politics of China on both sides of the straits.

Japan itself was subjected to American military occupation from 1945 to 1952. During that time, under the direction of the military government with General Douglas MacArthur as supreme commander, constitutional and land reforms were adopted and economic reconstruction from wartime damage begun. But despite Japan's phenomenal economic recovery, issues of Japanese nationalism and independence (given the enduring ties to the United States) continue to bedevil Japanese domestic politics and international relations in the postwar and post–cold war world.

As they enter the twenty-first century, all of the former East and Southeast Asian colonies (including Hong Kong, Macau, and the colonized territory of East Timor) have achieved the nationalist goal of political independence; their own flags fly over the capitals, their own compatriots occupy the desks in the government buildings, and the leaders of their independence movements have become the presidents and the prime ministers of the new states. But for many of them, the tasks of statecraft, of economic development, of political and social modernization, of solidifying a national identity have just begun. And these tasks have been complicated not only by internal conditions but also by pressures from beyond their borders.

Foreigners might no longer occupy the government positions, but they still have interests they want to promote and the political, economic, and military means to promote them. An important aspect of defining those interests was the cold war, which began to chill relations among the major powers almost immediately after the guns of World War II fell silent. That was a major complication, though by no means the only one, facing the governments and the people of the new states.

SUMMARY

The defining attribute of nationalism in the Asian Pacific is that it developed in opposition to Western imperialism. Nationalism, an emotional attachment to the "nation," originated in Europe, and colonialism brought to Asians its message of the right to national self-determination, inspiring demand for independence from foreign rule. In both Europe and Asia, nationalism spread from the top down, combining with a variety of ideologies that offered alternative paths to modernization, forging bonds of unity among members of the nation and becoming a potent source of conflict between nations.

In Japan and Thailand nationalism was promoted by the government as a means to prevent the imposition of colonialism by strengthening the state through a process of self-modernization. Their success in escaping colonization was not matched by China, where the inability of the imperial government to resist foreign encroachment led to its overthrow by republican Nationalists.

Beginning among the Western-educated intellectuals, nationalist sentiments in the colonies moved from cultivating recognition of their national cultural identity to demands for political representation in colonial institutions to insistence on complete independence from foreign rule. Nationalist political movements were affected by both domestic circumstances and international events, most notably the Bolshevik Revolution and World War II. Within each country, nationalists were often divided among themselves ideologically and organizationally between Communists and noncommunists, between religious and secular elements, and along ethnic lines, affected by colonial policies and precolonial traditions.

In China, the split between Mao's Communist Party and the Guomindang founded by Sun Yatsen resulted in civil war between the two nationalist movements, ending in communist victory in 1949. Rivalry between secular and religious nationalists, added to communist-noncommunist differences, delayed independence for Malaya, and resulted in postindependence civil war in Burma and Indonesia. Nationalists in Malaya and Burma also divided along ethnic lines, the majority Malays resisting and the majority Burmans leading the move for independence. Cambodian nationalism was slow to develop and also split along ideological lines. In the Philippines, class divisions surfaced in the opposition to Spanish rule; suppression of the populist insurgency in the American period opened the way for co-optation of the Filipino elites and to the peaceful transition from colony to political independence by mutual agreement.

The interval of Japanese dominance during World War II, which demonstrated to Asians the vulnerability of the European imperial powers, had different effects on the nationalist movements. In China, Communists and anticommunists partially and temporarily set aside their differences to fight the common enemy. The Thais, Malays (but not the Chinese in Malaya), and Indonesians collaborated with the Japanese, as did the Burmans initially, later organizing resistance. In the Philippines, some leaders collaborated with the Japanese and others fought them.

The end of World War II accelerated the process of decolonization, and in the decades that followed the nationalists' goal of political independence was achieved. How they managed the tasks of governing is the subject of Chapter 4.

QUESTIONS FOR DISCUSSION

1. What signs of nationalism do you see at work in politics today? Are its effects good or bad?
2. How effectively did leaders in Asian Pacific countries use nationalism in their struggle against colonialism?
3. What was there in the lives of Sun, Mao, and Sukarno that moved them to become leaders of the nationalist movement in their countries?
4. How did World War II accelerate the process of decolonization?

NOTES

1. Robert H. Taylor, *The State in Burma* (Honolulu: University of Hawaii Press, 1987), p. 67.
2. David Joel Steinberg, ed., *In Search of Southeast Asia: A Modern History*, rev. ed. (Honolulu: University of Hawaii Press, 1987), p. 307.
3. Ibid.
4. Quoted in Orville Schell and Joseph Esherick, *Modern China: The Making of a New Society from 1839 to the Present* (New York: Random House, 1972), p. 125.
5. Steinberg, *In Search of Southeast Asia*, p. 269.
6. Ibid., p. 276.
7. Quoted in Taylor, *The State in Burma*, p. 77.
8. *Burmans* is the term generally used to refer to the dominant nationality group in Burma.
9. Steinberg, *In Search of Southeast Asia*, p. 234.
10. James P. Ongkili, *Nation-building in Malaysia 1946–1974* (Singapore: Oxford University Press, 1985), pp. 23–24.
11. Steinberg, *In Search of Southeast Asia*, p. 407.
12. Helen Hardacre, *Shinto and the State, 1868–1988* (Princeton, NJ: Princeton University Press, 1989), pp. 3–4.
13. Ibid., p. 59.
14. Ibid., p. 122.
15. Mikiso Hane, *Modern Japan: A Historical Survey* (Boulder, CO: Westview, 1986), p. 249.

FOR FURTHER READING

Nationalism

Birch, Anthony H. *Nationalism and National Integration*. London: Unwin Hyman, 1989, part 1, pp. 3–74. Includes definitions and a general discussion of nationalism.
Breuilly, John. *Nationalism and the State,* 2nd ed. Chicago: University of Chicago Press, 1993. A systematic description of nationalism as a form of politics especially attuned to the modern state and the objectives of obtaining and using state power.
Emerson, Rupert. *From Empire to Nation.* Cambridge: Harvard University Press, 1960, chs. 1–4, 10.

Hutchinson, John, and Anthony D. Smith, eds. *Nationalism*. New York: Oxford University Press, 1994.

Palumbo, Michael, and William O. Shanahan, eds. *Nationalism: Essays in Honor of Louis L. Snyder*. Westport, CT: Greenwood Press, 1981, pp. 3–32. Considers the origins of nationalism in Europe.

Nationalist Movements

Drake, Christine. *National Integration in Indonesia*. Honolulu: University of Hawaii Press, 1989, pp. 16–44.

Hane, Mikiso. *Modern Japan: A Historical Survey*. Boulder: Westview, 1986, chs. 4–9.

Keyes, Charles F. *Thailand: Buddhist Kingdom as Modern Nation-State*. Boulder, CO: Westview, 1987, chs. 3–4.

Ongkili, James. *Nation-building in Malaysia 1946–1974*. Singapore: Oxford University Press, 1985, chs. 1–4.

Osborne, Milton E. *The French Presence in Cochinchina and Cambodia: Rule and Response (1859–1905)*. Ithaca, NY: Cornell University Press, 1969, pp. 175–258.

Sathyanurthy, T. V. *Nationalism in the Contemporary World: Political and Sociological Perspectives*. London: Frances Pinter, 1983, pp. 149–66 ("Anti-Colonialism and the National Movement: the Case of Burma").

Schirokauer, Conrad. *A Brief History of Chinese and Japanese Civilizations*. New York: Harcourt Brace Jovanovich, 1982, pp. 430–97.

Spence, Jonathan D. *The Search for Modern China*. London: W. W. Norton, 1990, chs. 10–16.

Steinberg, David Joel, ed. *In Search of Southeast Asia: A Modern History*, rev. ed. Honolulu: University of Hawaii Press, 1987, part 4, chs. 23–33.

Wurfel, David. *Filipino Politics*. Ithaca, NY: Cornell University Press, 1988, chs. 1–2.

Biographies

Legge, J. D. *Sukarno: A Political Biography*. New York: Praeger, 1972.

Schiffrin, Harold Z. *Sun Yat-sen: A Reluctant Revolutionary*. Boston: Little, Brown, 1980.

Schram, Stuart R. *Mao ZeDong: A Preliminary Reassessment*. Hong Kong: Chinese University Press, 1983.

Terrill, Ross. *Mao: A Biography*. New York: Harper and Row, 1980.

Wilson, Dick, ed. *Mao Tse-Tung in the Scales of History*. Cambridge, England: Cambridge University Press, 1977.

4

Asian Pacific Governments and Politics in Transition

In the decades since the end of World War II, governments in East and Southeast Asia have had to wrestle with a formidable array of internal and external challenges. For the leaders of countries freed from colonial control, the central challenges were to inaugurate self-government, to resist unwelcome interference in their affairs by the former imperial power or other foreign states, to win and hold the loyalty of often ethnically diverse people, to meet popular expectations of improved living conditions, and—like incumbents everywhere—to keep themselves in office. Given the potential for political disarray, it is not surprising that some degree of authoritarianism has been characteristic of each of them, whatever outward form the government has adopted or official ideology it has proclaimed.

To the countries that had not been colonies—Thailand, Japan, and semicolonial China—the end of World War II also brought challenges. Thailand's government needed to recover internationally from the burden of having sided with the loser in the war; Japan faced the suspension of its sovereignty during six years of American occupation as well as the economic devastation caused both by Allied bombing and the loss of its empire. China underwent political and economic revolution beginning in 1949, and the new communist government had the job of building socialism on the ruins left by the anti-Japanese and civil wars and in a largely hostile international environment. Reunification became a goal for China as for the other divided states, Korea and Vietnam, partitioned as a consequence of the U. S.–Soviet conflict.

If we fast-forward through the years since independence, three images of government and politics in East and Southeast Asia stand out clearly. The first is that modern Western-style institutions appear to have been adopted by most of the countries; the governmental structures of legislature, presidents and prime ministers, cabinets, bureaucracy, and judiciary exist, and elections, political parties, interest groups, and media, which in the West serve as the vehicles for popular participation in the political process, also exist. But—and here is the paradox—the second image is that all of the postcolonial political systems remain to some degree authoritarian, whether under civilian or military rule, communist or noncommunist or anticommunist. The third image is a recent one, reflecting authoritarian institutions besieged, in some cases toppled, by the effects of severe economic recession and pressures to reform.

So the central premise of this chapter is that, despite the early appearance of modern institutions of democratic government among post-independence Asian Pacific states, in reality these institutions, until very recently, have functioned *in practice* as a facade behind which the few control the levers of power over the many, and the many lack the will or the political experience to hold the rulers accountable. Authoritarian rule, like democratic rule, lacks a precise, widely agreed-upon definition. In this book the terms *democratic* and *authoritarian* will be used in an idiosyncratic manner to describe two countervailing forces at work concurrently in all forms of political rule. Viewed from this perspective, authoritarianism and democracy are not mutually exclusive political *systems* but tendencies (forces) that coexist in all modern nation-states. The authoritarian element refers to the necessary component of a state's power (sovereignty) that enables it to exercise effective rule, while the democratic element refers to the ways a modern nation state actualizes universal popular participation in the process of selecting and making governments accountable to the people they rule. In this framework of analysis, all modern polities exhibit both democratic and authoritarian elements in differing proportions.

The authoritarian element of a state, therefore, is *not* presumed to be a priori evidence of megalomania on the part of a leader or leaders. Whether it is or not is part of a larger question that is beyond the scope of this book. The working hypothesis for this chapter is that authoritarian tendencies overwhelm democratic forces in Asian Pacific countries as a necessary antidote to the threat of disunity and political dissolution. These new states in the Asian Pacific assert their authority in societies that to one degree or another are beset by disintegrative tendencies. Those tendencies, coming from divisions along ethnic, class, regional, sectional, or ideological lines, impede national unity and perhaps even jeopardize the survival of the nation-state itself. Thus, asserting the primacy of the state over all competing claims for obedience has been a necessary precondition of the development of capitalist economic development under circumstances in which feudal conditions of one sort or another still obtain. Authoritarian rule, in this sense, is understood in the Hobbesian conception of the state (see discussion in Chapter 1), as the only alternative to the total breakdown of civil order in a period of economic development from feudal-type socioeconomic systems into modern capitalist economic systems of production and distribution.

We begin with a discussion of what modernization theory, world system theory, and statist theory have to say about the kinds of governments likely to have emerged after independence. In the sections that follow, six different dimensions of state authority are described in the case of individual countries. We conclude by raising the explanatory question of why postcolonial governments in the Asian Pacific are authoritarian and the extent to which recent events have demonstrated a trend toward democratization.

THREE DISTINCT THEORETICAL PERSPECTIVES ON POSTINDEPENDENCE

As we saw in Chapter 1, all three theoretical approaches agree that government or the state plays a role in economic development. Not just the neutral "keep order, protect private property, and let the free market drive the economy" state of laissez-faire proponents like Adam Smith, nor just the "tool of the capitalists to keep the workers under their thumb" of Marx, the state itself is seen as an active promoter of development, and its policies are understood in fact to benefit the workers as well as the property-owning class, although disproportionately favoring the latter.

Modernization Theory

Initially, modernization theory made the assumption that liberal democratic political institutions are the most appropriate ones to foster development, but this view has been revised in light of a more careful reading of European history and of the phenomenal economic success of the NICs. Early capitalist mercantilism emerged in Europe under authoritarian regimes, and in Asia similarly undemocratic governments such as those in South Korea and Taiwan have presided over the period of rapid development. Accordingly, modernization theorists now take the position that some degree of authoritarianism may be better able in the early stages of development to provide the continuity of direction and the social controls necessary for the massive changes from preindustrial to industrial production.

So while the *form* of liberal politics may exist (legislatures, chief executives, bureaucracy, courts, parties, interest groups, elections), it is likely that full popular participation will initially be curbed by various restrictions on liberties, allowing the modernizing elite to direct the show and to prepare the masses for the responsibilities of eventual self-government. The first stage of rolling back the curbs on popular participation in incipient democracies is *liberalization* by which the state sheds its responsibilities for managing and supervising the economic affairs of the country. As the state extricates itself from intervening directly in decisions better left to the operations of the market, its exercise of power narrows and diminishes while its citizens become economically empowered. This then unlocks the door to democratizing their political institutions because citizens will recognize the significance of exercising political power once they have the economic interests to further.

The expectation is that, as in the historical evolution of the West, the trend will be toward democratization. In Britain and France, the legislature began as a concession forced from a reluctant king by representatives of the aristocracy, who formed political parties; then the middle class, creators of and created by the industrial revolution, demanded representation in parliament; and the middle class was followed by the working class, which expanded the electorate still further. In short, as the economy advances, society modernizes and authoritarianism is expected to give way to democracy.

World System Theory

World system theorists have fewer explicit expectations about the role of the state in the development of peripheral countries, in part because the level of analysis they consider crucial to focus on is the world system of international and transnational relationships, rather than on the nation-state and intranational relationships. From a bird's-eye perspective of the expanding and evolving world system that now covers the entire span of the globe, the specifics or details of individual states are less distinguishable or notable. Differences are apparent between core and peripheral nations but they are differences in degree rather than kind. In general, the world system perspective is skeptical about the notion that government of, by, and for the people has any real meaning in a global capitalist system.

States in core countries have evolved over a relatively long period of time and have therefore incorporated a large majority of their people into the electoral system. This makes their representative institutions more vibrant because they reflect a broad spectrum of social classes with their divergent interests. On the other hand, the economic institutions in core countries have for the most part become so massive and international in both structure and functions that they are no longer subject to control by the sovereign institutions of their country of origin.

To the extent that these large corporate private enterprises are the source of domestic problems within core countries, the fallout is borne entirely by the representative governments, not the economic corporations, which are unaccountable to people unless they are shareholders. As a result, governments become bigger and more powerful among core countries as they are forced to resolve an increasing number of social and economic conflicts to retain the allegiance of a substantial portion of their populations.

Looking at what has happened in the colonial periphery since formal independence, world system theorists see governments run by a minority of people linked in one way or another to foreign capitalists; they are the owners of large landed estates raising primary products for export, they own or manage foreign-financed manufacturing enterprises and export-import businesses, or they provide various services to foreign and domestic capitalists. Whether the government in the peripheral country is civilian or military, with one party or many parties or no parties, does not matter. Whatever the specifics, the general picture is of a "client" regime, serving the interests of foreign capitalists and their local collaborators. Where development takes place, it benefits the elite and impoverishes the majority of the population. Efforts by the poor to contest this increasing inequality and to demand a larger share of wealth and political power lead to repression by the ruling class in the name of preserving order. External forces and internal interests thus tend to favor authoritarianism.

Developmental State or Statist Theory

The major shortcoming of both modernization and world system theories from the statist point of view is their neglect of the state's critical role as an *independent agent* of development. Like modernization theory, statist theory credits the governments of individual countries with assisting in the formation of the market, and like world system theory, it sees the state and development as (parallel) historical trajectories. But unlike both modernization and world system theories, statist theory places government itself, over and above the market, at the center of its analysis of economic growth and development. Not only is the state essential to the creation of the market, it becomes bigger and more complicated and consequential for the market economy of a nation-state as time passes. "One of the few universals in the history of the twentieth century," from the statist perspective, "is the increasingly pervasive influence of the state as an institution and social actor."[1]

The state is a compulsory association claiming control over a given territory and its people by a monopoly on the legitimate use (and threat of use) of force. What a state *does*, however, from this unique perch is different from, and, for statist theory, far more important than what it *is*. Prior to the modern age, the state performed two major functions: (1) making war and (2) ensuring internal order. Even then, the state had an interest in economic intervention to ensure the means to carry out these objectives. But since the advent of modern times the state's economic role has expanded far beyond being the means to military ends. In today's world, seeking prosperity through economic growth becomes an end in itself and an essential justification for the state in its own right. This is especially the case for late industrializing countries trying to "catch up"; for them the creation of wealth cannot possibly be left to "nature" and "markets" (the components of classical Smithian comparative advantage) but can only be the result of active and astute statecraft.

To overcome the disadvantages of having to compete with technologically advanced players on the international market, "late industrializers" tend to develop institutions in response to the handicaps and advantages of lateness. From their studies of Japan, South Korea, and Taiwan, a group of scholars have drawn a profile of the "developmental state" that is at the heart of this approach to understanding development. The "developmental state," which is actually a set of institutions (see Chapter 1), enables a late industrializing country to *invent* a comparative advantage for itself by effectively orchestrating its own national strengths to take advantage of shifting opportunities in the international market. To accomplish this, the state must act as entrepreneur, banker, and industrial planner all rolled into one. Its partners in carrying out the various specialized tasks involved in such an undertaking are the large diversified business groups with whom the specialized bureaucratic officials of state have a symbiotic relationship.

The integrated circuitry of this network gives the developmental state a paternalistic command of the economy as a whole. It uses subsidies and protectionist devices to offset the disadvantages faced by national firms in international competition and to move the present industrial structure toward one with higher value-added, more technologically dynamic activities. The technology is borrowed and bought from abroad and used to promote both exports and learning. The emphasis of developmental states is on education, research for development, and exacting high performance standards from all the participants in production, managers included. Organizationally, the state must have the capacity to recruit "the best and the brightest" into the civil service, providing them with the structural, professional, and informational means of linking internal investment decisions with the opportunities offered by the global economy at different points in time. Internationally, the state must navigate its way assertively but carefully through the turbulent waters and shifting shoals of interstate politics and commerce. The various facets of the developmental state will be discussed in greater detail in Chapter 5.

We turn now from theory to practice and look at politics as it is carried on in Asian Pacific countries. While all of them exhibit some form and degree of authoritarianism, many of them have taken significant steps toward democracy; there is considerable variation from country to country, each country having features unique to it. No single pattern typifies the ways by which rulers install and maintain their monopoly of power. Some are civilian regimes and others military, in strong or weak states. Some have revolutionary goals, some reformist goals, and some the goal of preserving the status quo. Some operate through a single-party system, others a one-party-dominant system; others have many parties, and one has no parties at all. There are Leninist-style parties, mass parties, ethnically based parties, and religious parties, to identify some of the varieties. Authoritarianism may be brutal and repressive, relying on force to compel submission, or it may be more gentle and permissive, using subtle pressure and rewards to win compliance. But fear of disunity, insecurity in the face of internal centrifugal tendencies, or vulnerability to outside pressures underlies these regimes.

To organize our comparisons of the diverse forms and degrees of authoritarianism and democracy, we have singled out six prominent features of state authority shared by two or more of the countries in the region: (1) the anomalous authoritarianism of an unlimited monarchy in Brunei and the ex-colonial, regime-in-transit of Hong Kong; (2) systems in which Leninist-style parties dominate government and politics, with examples from both communist and noncommunist states; (3) rule by what we call military developers—in recognition of the prominent role of the military whose power has been used to promote economic development in a number of countries; (4) systems of "ethnic" authoritarianism, so-called because they keep at bay the disintegrative ethnic forces at work in the society; (5) rule by democratizing polities in the Asian Pacific, as represented by Japan and South Korea; (6) strong-state and weak-state authoritarian forms of rule.

Cambodia is presented as a special case where, as of this writing, the coalition government that resulted from the July 1999 election can best be described as still in formation.

These categories are neither the only way of classifying political systems, nor are they mutually exclusive. A country might fit into more than one of the varieties (Singapore, for example, fits into the category of countries with a Leninist-style party and into the strong rather than weak type of state), and a country might move over time from one variety to another (South Korea, for example, from civilian to military rule and back toward civilian government again and from an authoritarian to a democratic form of rule). But we think you will find the distinctions among different kinds of authoritarian governments a useful device for organizing the descriptions and analysis of countries in the Asian Pacific region.

"ANOMALOUS" AUTHORITARIANISM

The governments of Brunei and Hong Kong are survivors from an earlier era when unlimited monarchies and colonies were the common forms of government in most of the world. Brunei remains a family-based monarchy but shows some strains of its

---

Suggestion to Readers

To update the information about contemporary governments and politics provided in this chapter, you may find it useful to consult sources published after this book was completed in mid-2000. Changes in officeholders and recent developments in domestic and foreign affairs are reported in such sources as the *Statesmen's Yearbook*, the *International Yearbook and Statesmen's Who's Who*, the scholarly journals *Current History* and *Asian Survey*, and news magazines and newspapers, such as the *Far Eastern Economic Review* (which, despite its name, covers political events), the *New York Times*, *Los Angeles Times*, *Christian Science Monitor*, and *Asian Wall Street Journal*.

---

accommodations to the modern world. Hong Kong has returned to China but under the policy of "one country, two systems" will retain its political, economic, and social system for 50 years.

Brunei

The most recently independent of the Asian colonial possessions, Brunei, is an Islamic monarchy whose hereditary sultan, Sir Muda Hassanal Bolkiah, also holds the post of prime minister. He rules without the restraints of a legislature or political parties.

A colony of Britain from 1888, Brunei became self-governing in internal affairs in 1957, but independence was delayed until 1984 because of the sultan's reluctance to lose the support of the British presence. Under colonial rule, the Malay elite—the royal family and court—with the collaboration of resident Chinese entrepreneurs dominated political life, purposefully insulating the population of Malay peasants and fishermen from the modern oil-producing sector employing foreign personnel.

The traditional elite's dominant position was challenged in the mid-1950s by the formation of the anticolonial socialist Brunei People's Party, representing nontraditional interests and favoring independence and popular participation in government. When the first elections under the 1959 constitution were held in 1962, the People's Party won all the elected seats in a new Legislative Council, and the division between the traditional elite and the challengers deepened. A major policy difference between them concerned the relationship of Brunei with the other British colonies on the island of Borneo, Sarawak, and North Borneo, also known as Sabah. While the sultan favored unification of all three territories with Malaya, the other side advocated instead the unification of Brunei with Sarawak and Sabah. An armed rebellion against the sultan broke out in December 1962 and was quickly suppressed with the help of British forces. The Legislative Council was dissolved, party leaders were arrested or fled, and the movement lost its following.

Since then, the monarchy has kept tight control of the reins of government, the sultan holding the post of prime minister and ruling by decree. Public welfare measures, including free education and medical care, were initiated after the 1962 rebellion and help to keep the general population quiescent.

Elections were held in 1970 for a new Legislative Council, and again the opposition won and again the monarch dissolved the Council. In 1988 he banned the latest opposition, the small business-backed Brunei National Democratic Party, after it called for him to step down as prime minister. A decade later, after a public split with his youngest brother, he proclaimed his oldest son, 24, as next in line to become the thirtieth ruler of the 500-year-old Malay Islamic Kingdom. The only form of protest the sultan endures are *surat layang* or poison-pen letters, which have apparently increased in number since the fall of President Suharto in May 1998, some even demanding the resignation of certain members of the royal family.

So, despite fitful efforts to open up the traditional elite's monopoly of political power to participation by other segments of society, Brunei is still under the rule of an absolute monarch.

Hong Kong, China

After a century and a half of colonial autocracy as a British Crown Colony, Hong Kong returned to Chinese control as a Special Administrative Region (SAR) on July 1, 1997. It was an emotional occasion for Chinese all over the world, presided over by President Jiang Zemin and Britain's heir to the throne, Prince Charles. Just six years before, the residents of the colony had belatedly been given the right to vote for 18 of the 60-member Legislative Council (Legco) for the first time; the remaining members were chosen as their representatives by various "functional" occupational groups such as businesspeople, lawyers, and doctors. These modest electoral reforms had stimulated the formation of political parties: the United Democrats of Hong Kong, headed by Martin Lee and known today as the *Democratic Party* and the pro-business Liberal Democratic Federation, currently known simply as the *Liberal Party*.

Hong Kong, China's first legislative elections took place on May 24, 1998 with a record number of voters turning out; 53 percent of the registered voters compared with the 36 percent of registered voters that had turned out in the 1995 elections under British rule. The Democratic Party under Martin Lee received the largest number of seats, 9 of the 20 popularly elected seats and 4 of the remaining 40 seats set aside for professional and business groups. The avowedly pro-Beijing Democratic Alliance for the Betterment of Hong Kong won 5 of the popularly elected and 4 of the remaining 40 seats representing the occupational and professional associations. The pro-business Liberal Party were conspicuous losers in this first election considered by many a "dry run" for the next legislative election to be held in 2000. Given Hong Kong's long history as an executive-led government, which has been continued under the system laid out by the 1984 Basic Law, political parties may become much more vocal and discursive but they are likely to remain weak relative to the strong chief executive.

During Hong Kong's first full year under Chinese rule, there were major problems, none of which were related to the change of sovereignty. The economy was hit by the economic crisis sweeping through the Asian Pacific after the summer of 1997, an outbreak of the virulent strain of influenza known as "bird flu" which killed six people between April and January 1998, prompting the government to slaughter the territory's entire stock of 1.4 million chickens, and the onslaught of a red tide which wiped out most of the area's fish farms. Throughout these disasters, the PRC left the Special Administrative Region (SAR) government to handle each issue as it emerged except to offer support. On June 4, 1998, 40,000 people crowded into Victoria Park to commemorate the "Tiananmen massacre" of 1989 in what the foreign press dubbed as the first such memorial on Chinese soil.

LENINIST-STYLE PARTIES ADAPTED TO THE ASIAN CONTEXT

The Leninist-style party, which originated in the Soviet Union, has been the proto-type not only for communist parties in China, North Korea, Vietnam, and Laos, but also for the Guomindang in Taiwan and the People's Action Party in Singapore. These parties provided the leadership that created their newly formed states and presided over their survival into the post–cold war era.

Designed as an efficient and disciplined instrument for taking power at a time of social disorder, the Leninist-style political party is organized for the express pur-pose of establishing a new political order and bringing about revolutionary changes in society. As such, the Leninist party, which has commonly come to be known as the Communist Party, was admirably suited to conditions at the chaotic end of colonialism in the Asian Pacific. In China, both the Communist Party and the Guomindang were organized along Leninist lines to unify the country politi-cally and to transform its institutions economically and socially. When the Commu-nist Party emerged victorious in 1949, the Guomindang fled to Taiwan. There it uti-lized the party's tight-knit organization to transform the island into a modern industrial economy with the eventual goal of returning to power on the mainland. In North Korea, it was the Korean Workers' Party that successfully guided the di-vided country through the Korean War and the cold war years, only to find itself increasingly isolated after the demise of the Soviet Union. In Singapore, Lee Kuan Yew fashioned the People's Action Party along communist lines to transform that backward and vulnerable Chinese enclave in the Malay Sea into a rich and power-ful modern state.

While there are variations from country to country, all share the basic distinc-tive forms and functions of the Leninist party. The party dominates the state and is organized hierarchically, with decisions coming from the top and followed by the rank and file. These are "cadre" parties, not mass membership organizations; mem-bers are screened before admission and expected to accept the discipline necessary to lead the masses in the direction the party has chosen. The Chinese Communist Party and the Guomindang, both heavily influenced by Soviet advisers in their early years, the Communist Party in Vietnam, and the Communist Korean Workers Party of North Korea are the examples chosen to illustrate this variety of state authority.

Party and Government in Communist China: Parallel and Interlocking Hierarchies

China is essentially a one-party state; although eight "democratic parties" exist and are represented in the national legislature, they are not "opposition" parties, having accepted the leadership role of the Communist Party of China (CPC). The party structure of the CPC parallels the governmental structure, as shown in Figure 4.1; both are hierarchies of assemblies with the basic-level assemblies electing the next higher level and so on to the highest level. At the top, the party and state hierarchies are interlocked in the persons of leaders who simultaneously hold party and state positions. The major officials are President and General Secretary of the CPC Jiang Zemin, Premier Zhu Rongji, and Vice President Hu Jintao. The most powerful political body in China is the Party's 22-member Politburo and its 7-member Standing Committee.

Party Membership.   Unlike political parties in the United States, for example, where anyone can "join" simply by declaring a party preference when registering to vote, membership in the Communist Party is selective. Applicants must be recommended by two party members, investigated and accepted by the local party branch, and approved by the next higher party committee. A member is expected to work for the good of the people rather than for private gain, to follow party discipline, to avoid involvement in factionalism, to study the writings of Mao, Lenin, and Marx, and to set an example for others to emulate. In 1997 there were 60 million members, between 4 to 5 percent of the population.

As the sole conduit to high political office, the Communist Party has been the major path by which ordinary Chinese move up in the political world. In the first 30 years following the Communist victory in 1949, the level of education and administrative skill of the rank and file was low. This reflected the heavily peasant composition of a party that had spent the previous 20 years engaged in revolutionary warfare in the countryside. Since 1979, however, strenuous efforts have been under-

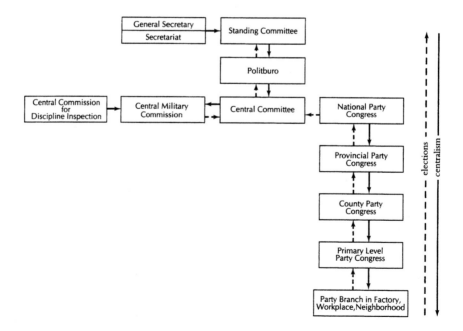

FIGURE 4.1   CPC and PRC: Principal Party and State Organs

taken to upgrade the caliber of party members by providing training at party schools, by recruiting more educated people, and by expelling the unfit as well as the ideologically suspect and those guilty of corruption or other economic crimes. The Fifteenth National Party Congress that met in 1997 is younger, better educated and more technocratic than any of its predecessors.

The party's role as central source of authority in society entitles all its members to be considered cadre, a term applied to individuals in positions of leadership in other organizations as well. The party is known as a cadre party, indicating that as an elite leadership corps, its members are expected to live up to the highest standards in society. But the term *cadre* (*ganbu*, in Chinese) is widely used in China to refer to people in positions of responsibility or authority. Generically, it can apply to all functionaries who have subordinates subject to their supervision. Prior to the 1990s, this would have included the local party official in a village, the accountant in a factory, or a general in the Army. Referring specifically to the political system, a cadre is anyone holding a crucial (though not necessarily high) position in the chain of authority linking policymakers at the center to persons at lower levels who have the responsibility for policy implementation. Those in positions of authority—whether in the military, for example, or in a university—are not necessarily Communist Party members.

Since the emergence of a substantial private sector under the Reform policy, however, the term is more often reserved for government employees; this would include the accountant in a state-owned enterprise but not one in either the private or joint-venture sectors. The term has a significance in China that "official" does not quite capture because the quality of the functionaries in the party, central

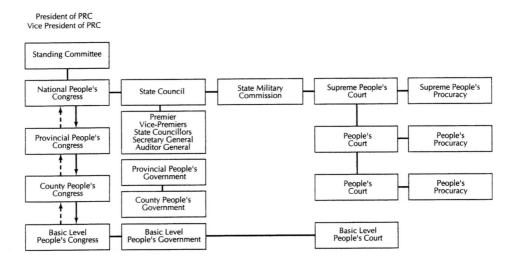

government, provincial and local government, and the military affects the quality of government in China to a degree not equaled in countries where policymaking is more widely dispersed among levels of government and between public and private sectors.

Party Structures and Functions.   At the lowest level is the party branch, organized in such places as factories, stores, schools, neighborhoods, farms, and units of the People's Liberation Army (PLA). Led by a branch secretary, the unit's job is to recruit members, maintain party discipline, educate the public about party policies, and provide face-to-face linkage between the CPC and the people.

At each of the higher levels of party organization (see again Figure 4.1), there is a congress, a large representative assembly chosen by the level below; the congress meets infrequently for brief sessions, delegating day-to-day supervision of party business to a smaller committee and a party secretary. At the national level are the National Party Congress, the Central Committee, the Political Bureau (Politburo), its Standing Committee, the Central Secretariat, and in addition the Military Affairs Committee and the Central Commission for Discipline Inspection, national organs for which there are no counterparts at lower levels.

The National Party Congress (NPC) is in principle the highest organ in the party, but since it meets only briefly every five years and is quite large (2,048 delegates at the Fifteenth Party Congress in 1997) its supremacy is more formal than real. Its principal functions are to summarize achievements since the last congress, establish the party line and elect the Central Committee for the following period, and listen to and approve proposals for revision of the Party Constitution. Although the National Party Congress does not actively debate policies or overturn what the Politburo has decided, it is an important forum for announcing new policies and directions. For example, the policy goal announced by the Fifteenth National Party Congress was to sell market shares in more than 100,000 ailing, inefficient State-Owned Enterprises (SOEs) to promote economic reform in the state sector.

When the Party Congress is not in session, its elected smaller body, the 344-member Central Committee (CC) decides party affairs. It usually meets annually in plenary sessions to discuss and approve party and state policies. These sessions, called Plenums, often arrive at momentous decisions that significantly alter the future of both the party and the country. The Third Plenum of the Eleventh Central Committee which met in December 1978, for example, adopted the Reform Policies that continue to profoundly affect China's development. Since the 1980s, older and less-educated Central Committee incumbents have been replaced by more highly trained younger members better qualified to preside over economic modernization. The current Central Committee, elected by the Fifteenth NPC in 1997, is composed of 193 full and 151 alternate members. Sixty percent of its members are new to the position, almost three-quarters have some college education, and about one-fifth have specialized postsecondary training; their average age is 55 and the single largest group (43 percent) is from local and provincial government, the next (31.4 percent) from the central government and party, and 19 percent from the military.

At the summit of power over party and government is the 22-member Political Bureau or *Politburo* for short, and its seven-member Standing Committee headed by the General Secretary of the Party; This small group conducts the party's day-today business when the Central Committee Plenum is not in session, making personnel and policy decisions for all of China. The Politburo meets often and, after reportedly lively discussion, reaches decisions by consensus. As with the Central Committee, the Communist Party has systematically retired the oldest Politburo members, replacing them with a younger generation of technocrats. Of the 22 full members chosen to the Politburo in 1997, five are under the age of 60 and Vice President Hu Jintao, who joined the Standing Committee of the Politburo in 1992 was 49 at the time. The Standing Committee is the top executive committee ruling China continuously.

Administration of party affairs and oversight of policy execution are the responsibility of the Central Secretariat, organized into departments and run by the General Secretary. Jiang Zemin, who is one of the seven members of the Politburo Standing Committee, succeeded Deng Xiaoping as State President, General Secretary, and Chairman of the Central Military Commission of the Communist Party when he died in February 1997. The Central Military Commission exercises party control over the People's Liberation Army (PLA) and reports to the Politburo. Finally, the Central Commission for Discipline Inspection investigates charges of breaches of party rules and misconduct by members.

Democratic Centralism.   The party operates according to the Leninist principle of "democratic centralism." The democratic component comes in the form of participation by the rank and file in electing delegates to party congresses and in their discussion of policy proposals initiated above and sent down for deliberation before a decision is made. Centralism lies in the top-down screening of candidates to weed out untested or distrusted party members from serving in higher positions and in the fact that central bodies, especially the Politburo, have the final power to make decisions. While consultations down through the ranks precede decisions and are designed to maximize the likelihood that policies will be carried out at the grassroots level, once decisions are made at the top all party members are expected to accept the outcome and work unreservedly to implement the decisions. Differences of opinion are not, in principle, to be allowed to solidify into permanent factions; "splittism" is deplored. (Nonetheless, as we shall see below, the CPC leadership has been and still is divided over important issues of policy and organization.)

The party, especially the top echelon, serves as the executive leadership for the whole country, setting the "general line" that provides the policy framework for state officials to make their plans and carry them out.

Government Structures and Functions.   The state hierarchy parallels that of the party, extending from local people's congresses to provincial congresses to the National People's Congress. The delegates at each of the higher levels are elected by and from the next lower level. Thus there are no general, nation-wide elections for top government positions. Elections occur instead over a period and people vote within each province in a tiered system. At the lowest level, people vote for their representatives to the local people's congresses which vote for their representatives to the provincial congresses, reaching finally to the National People's Congress. Anybody may stand for election and be elected according to the Electoral Law of 1979. Although the largest number of those elected are in fact members of the

Communist Party, it is possible for members of other parties or of no party to run for office.

The National People's Congress (NPC, which in English has the same abbreviation as National Party Congress), the legislature, meets annually for several weeks to enact laws, adopt constitutional amendments, approve the state budget, and elect a number of executive and judicial officials, including the president, vice president, premier, and other officers of the State Council, or cabinet. The Ninth National People's Congress, which began its five-year term in March 1998, is the counterpart of the Fifteenth National Party Congress and consists of just under 3,000 members, with 40 percent comprising workers, peasants, and intellectuals; the rest are officials from state and party bureaucracies, soldiers, and representatives of minor parties. Hong Kong participated for the first time, sending a delegation of 36 deputies.

Such a large body meeting briefly once a year clearly does not function like the smaller full-time legislatures in Britain or the United States, but the NPC does use the occasions afforded by its scrutiny of reports from the government to ask hard questions about policies and performance and to criticize and make recommendations. Between sessions, the NPC Standing Committee acts on its behalf. The Chairman of the National People's Congress Standing Committee is always one of the highest government and party members in the country. Former Premier Li Peng is currently serving in this position. In the early 1990s when Li Peng was still premier and closely identified with the 1989 military crackdown on Tiananmen demonstrators, the National People's Congress began to exhibit clear signs of a transformation. Up until that time, it had been regarded as merely a rubber stamp of the top Communist Party leadership. But at the Opening Session of the Eighth National People's Congress, when Premier Li Peng gave his report to that body, it evoked intense discussion and the addition of quite a few amendments before it passed. This marks the beginning of a more active National People's Congress characterized by more open debate than ever before.

The Ninth National People's Congress, meeting in 1998, highlighted the growing importance of political reform on the government's agenda. In summing up the Eighth NPC's achievements in reforming the political system, three areas were singled out: (1) establishing China as a system based on law, (2) downsizing the government bureaucracy, and (3) upgrading the participation of the noncommunist parties in government deliberations. Over the five-year span of its term, the Eighth NPC set up the legal framework for a socialist market economy by passing over one hundred laws and regulations, half of which dealt directly with issues of standardizing a market exchange system: a Corporate Law, Business Parnership Law, Commercial Banking Law, Foreign Trade Law, Real Estate Law, and Advertising Law to govern market relationships; a Budget Law and Central Bank Law to strengthen state macro-controls; and a law to govern social security among others. Also undertaken by the Eighth NPC was a streamlining of government ministries, trimming them from 40 to 29. The third area of political reform was to upgrade the importance of a second national deliberative body for China's democratic parties.

The Chinese People's Political Consultative Conference (CPPCC) is a holdover from the early years after liberation before the first state constitution was adopted and the NPC created. The CPPCC is a pluralist organization consisting of delegates representing all the groups outside the Communist Party: the eight democratic political parties, various interest groups, including for the first time 40 members from non–publicly owned businesses, and mass organizations such as the All-China Federation of Trade unions and the Women's Federation. Serving as a link between those groups and the Communist Party of China (CPC), the CPPCC functions as a consultative body to the National People's Congress. In this advisory capacity, its visibility and importance have increased markedly since the beginning of the Reform era, as indicated in two subtle but significant ways. One was a 1993 elaboration of the CPPCC's internal organization, which added 14 subcommittees and lower-level representatives at the provincial and county levels in order to facilitate its greater participation in evaluating legislation and drafting suggestions. Its function was changed from "participation in deliberation and administration of state affairs" to "political consultation and democratic supervision." The second was a constitutional revision acknowledging the change in a new description of the form of state of the PRC as a system of "multiparty cooperation and political consultation under the leadership of the CPC." This was formally adopted by the Ninth National People's Congress. The 2,196 members of the Ninth CPPCC met in Beijing concurrently with the Ninth People's Congress in March 1998 to mark China's transcentury leadership.

The State Council is the central executive body that is the state counterpart of the Secretariat at the top of the party hierarchy. As voted into office by the Ninth NPC in 1998, the state council consists of the premier, Zhu Rongji, (at 56, the youngest premier in the history of the PRC), four vice premiers whose average age is 62, five state councillors, and 29 ministers, many of whom have functions relating to the economy, such as planning, finance, agriculture, construction, and various other industries. This is the second downsizing of the cabinet; the outgoing one was composed of six vice ministers and 40 ministers. Even so, the State Council is too large to function as a cabinet, a role performed by an inner group of some 15 Council members.

So in the division of labor between party and state, party members provide leadership for the government, setting the policy course for the whole society every five years. The State Council at the pinnacle of the government structure translates "the party line" into a legislative/executive agenda that the ministries then implement. Although those serving in the state legislative bodies and bureaucracy are by no means all CPC members, the party's influence permeates the state apparatus and the armed forces all the way from the lowest level to the top government positions held by Politburo and Central Committee members. The greatest overlap is at the top where the premier and vice premiers are also members of the Politburo of the CPC.

The Maoist Era. Since liberation, the CPC's goal has been to transform all of China into a modern socialist state, promoting economic and social development within the broad framework of Marxism-Leninism. But that destination was a distant star in China's future compared to the immediate political problems facing the leadership after assuming power: creating a new social order, promoting agricultural growth, developing an industrial productive system, providing food, housing, education, and health care to more than 700 million people, building and training a regular army, forming a government, writing laws and dispensing justice in a society that had been torn asunder for over a hundred years. The communists had only their political experience in governing the areas under their control during the 1930s and 1940s and the expertise of "retained personnel" from the old regime to compensate for the absence of capital and wealthy friends with which to begin these formidable tasks.

The initial period under Mao Zedong's leadership was characterized by sharp divisions within the party between those who favored emphasizing and rewarding technical proficiency (being "expert") and those who endorsed the primacy of loyalty to the values of the revolution (being "red"). Promoting experts to achieve more productive economic organization meant favoring the sons and daughters of the already privileged educated class over ordinary people for whom the revolution had ostensibly been made.

The struggles among party members over policy were fierce and resulted in frequent policy fluctuations with sharp swings of the pendulum affecting the entire population. Mistrustful of intellectuals' revolutionary capabilities, Mao's inclination was to stir up masses of people through campaigns to achieve socialist political goals, favoring the majority of less-educated people but in the process disrupting the orderly economic progress engineered by the experts. His opponents preferred the bureaucratically ordered and politically stable party leadership of centrally planned economic change.

Between 1958 and 1960 and again between 1966 and 1976, the Maoists gained the upper hand and swept the whole country through two major social experiments known as the *Great Leap Forward* and the *Cultural Revolution.* The Great Leap Forward was aimed at finding an alternative to Soviet-style development and narrowing the gap between workers and the masses of peasants for whom the revolution was fought. The objective was to boost stagnating agricultural production while maintaining high industrial output, both without substantial government investment. The engine to accomplish this was mass enthusiasm unleashed in the countryside by consolidating the small parcels of household-owned land into collectivities called *communes.* Mass campaigns were launched to utilize the labor freed up by collectivized activities—everything from work, child-care, and food preparation—for deep ploughing, building dams, producing steel in "backyard furnaces," and constructing roads. When the Soviet government suddenly withdrew all its advisers and canceled 257 scientific and technical cooperation projects in July 1960, the Great Leap's disastrous consequences became apparent. Mao stepped down and the opposition moved in to put economic development back on an orderly, Soviet-style track once again.

For a second time, in 1966, Mao stepped forward to preside over the Cultural Revolution, an urban campaign to revolutionize popular culture. Urban youths were mobilized into bands of Red Guards to criticize and eliminate Confucian and other "feudal" ideas of the older, more educated generation of urban Chinese. Waving Red Guard banners and "little red books" containing Mao's sayings, competing groups of Red guards, each claiming superior loyalty to Mao's writings, stormed people's homes confiscating books, paintings, jewelry, and other symbols of "bourgeois decadence." They arrested and tortured local party officials, disrupted social services, and generally wreaked havoc in China's cities. Factories were reorganized and run by Revolutionary Committees representing workers, technicians, and managers disrupting and in some cases stopping economic production.

When turmoil in the streets escalated into civil strife, the Peoples' Liberation Army was called in to reestablish order. Millions of young people were sent "down to the countryside" to "exchange experiences and knowledge with the peasants," thus spreading the damage of the Cultural Revolution into the surrounding countryside. Though the campaign was officially terminated in 1969, the CR was dragged out until Mao's death in 1976 first by the army's intervention and then by the political uncertainty left in the wake of an unresolved struggle among party leaders. After Mao's death his widow, Jiang Qing, and three other radical leaders, known as the "Gang of Four," were arrested and eventually convicted of plotting against the party's choice of a new chairman.

The Deng Era and Beyond.   Following Mao's death, the anti-Maoists gradually succeeded in wresting control from, though not eliminating, their opponents in the party. Under Deng Xiaoping's leadership, the Maoist practice of instigating periodic episodes of mass political turmoil was put aside. Economic policies originally initiated to restore production after the failure of the Great Leap Forward and resumed after the Cultural Revolution became the basis for the Four Modernizations program to modernize agriculture, industry, science and technology, and the armed forces. Self-correcting pragmatism, expressed as "Seek truth from facts," was to guide economic development rather than ideological preconceptions. "Redness" alone was not to be valued above "expertness"; the test would be performance. As Deng put it, "Black cat, white cat, what does it matter as long as it catches mice?"

Deng Xiaoping persistently pursued a course of economic growth while carefully preserving the supremacy of the party. He reversed Mao's priorities by promoting economic reform at the expense of political reform. And the further he pushed economic reform in the direction of a market economy, the more steadfast he became in defense of firm party control as the necessary ballast to assure political stability. But orthodox elements in the party remained, people commonly identified as "hard-liners" or "conservatives" who feared the effects of loosening controls over the economy and increasing contacts with foreigners. Their fears of "cultural pollution" seemed justified when student demonstrations broke out in 1986 and 1987 at universities in various cities, calling for reforms in higher education and for political reforms as well.

The demonstrations were put down, only to erupt again in May 1989 in Tiananmen Square. Initiated by students at prestigious Beijing University and joined by workers and ordinary citizens in the capital, the movement spread to cities throughout China, coalescing around a multitude of grievances over inflation, job insecurity, and other economic issues, as well as aspirations for more popular participation in government and a loosening of the party's grip on society. The government's response was slow in coming, reflecting deep divisions over whether to negotiate with the movement's spokespersons or to clamp down forcibly. The latter course prevailed. Martial law was declared and, with the world watching on TV, tanks moved into the city and cleared the square, with considerable loss of life. Many of the activists were arrested, went underground, or fled the country. These "dissidents," both inside and outside the country, continue to be vocal and visible in their demands for greater political reform.

Since Tiananmen in 1989, the leadership has moved deliberately in the direction of promoting technocrats into leading positions. Deng was influential in easing his successor, Jiang Zemin, into the top leadership position before he died in February 1997. While Deng's program of economic reform has moved into high gear, his wariness of political reform has endured among the younger generation of political leaders. They exercise extreme caution in liberalizing Communist Party control over political life for fear of inviting political instability. Political parties that seek to overthrow the leading position of the CCP are not tolerated, nor are movements and organizations that owe their allegiance to some external authority like the Pope or the spiritual leader of Falun Gong. (See Chapter 6, p. 275.) Though by all appearances, the reins of power seem to be securely in the hands of the residents of Zhongnanhai—the walled quarter next to the imperial palace grounds in Beijing where the leaders live and work—their panic response in the summer of 1999 to the 10,000 followers of the Falun Gong spiritual movement who suddenly emerged out of nowhere to wage a peaceful protest suggests that a degree of political reform has already occurred.

And indeed, political reform has been a byproduct of successful economic reform in China. But it was a result of necessity not choice. As the state retreated from central planning and micromanaging the economy, large sectors of economic production were freed to operate in the market. This created a major fiscal crisis because the old Soviet-type fiscal system was incompatible with a decentralized market economy. The central government's solution was to incrementally delegate more and more of its fiscal responsibilities to regional and local governments, in the process transforming a centralized fiscal system into a system of self-financing at each level. The political decentralization this brought about hastened rapid economic growth in coastal regions but also raised the specter of political fragmentation, with the powers of rich provinces like Guangdong, eluding control of the center. Though the central government has since taken steps to restore some of its fiscal control, it has found it difficult to address local problems like corruption, crime, and tax gouging that undermine the regime's legitimacy. Perhaps as an attempt to address these problems of localities "going off on their own," a new policy was proposed by President Jiang Zemin in a speech he made to party cadres in May 2000 in which he directed that party members be attached to all enterprises in the private sector. Their function would be to ensure that enterprises abided by the laws established by the central government.

In other areas, the central government has moved towards political reform in the direction of democratization, i.e. increasing the accountability of leadership. Gradual but systematic institutional restructuring of the government (including the state-owned enterprises) was made the main agenda item of the Ninth NPC. This included streamlining the central government, raising the qualifications for civil service, using qualifying exams to increase the educational level of political officials, and promoting grassroots democracy at the village level. The impetus for adopting competitive elections of village leaders throughout the country came from the top in response to the political vacuum created by decollectivization. When economic decision making reverted to individual households leaving the county as the lowest level of government, each county governed thousands of villages under its jurisdiction. In the 1982 Constitution, therefore, the central government had instituted "autonomous village committees" to assume the political management of basic level rural village communities. Within a few years it became apparent that village leadership was not functioning: peasants resisted the implementation of onerous directives by village leaders, meetings were rarely convened, conflicts between villagers and village leaders were not only endemic but occasionally turned violent, and many a village leader used his position to enrich himself as an entrepreneur or specialized producer.

In response to this problem, the central government adopted the Law on the Organization of Villagers' Committees in November 1987. The law abolished the long practice of village officials being handpicked by governments at higher levels, requiring instead that all members of village committees (defined as mass organizations of self-government at the grass roots) be directly elected by the villagers and accountable to a village council comprised of all adult villagers. The law thus established the framework for conducting direct committee elections by secret ballot with multiple candidates and three-year terms for the positions of chairman, vice chairman and members of village committees. During the past decade, most villages across China have held two or three election cycles in which village committees of three to seven members were elected for three-year terms. Though not all villages actually provide a choice of candidates, most hold semicompetitive elections featuring one or two more candidates than positions. Some villages experiment with fully competitive elections, running twice the number of candidates as positions. There are even instances reported of village candidates using television speeches to oust their competitors in a rudimentary form of campaigning. In her empirical study of 56 villages surveyed in 1990, Melanie Manion documented evidence to indicate that there was voter choice and that it made village leaders responsive to their constituents. "The 'mundane revolution' of voter choice," she concluded, "is catching on in the countryside of one of the world's few remaining communist powers."[2]

This is in stark contrast to North Korea, which remains the most isolated and backward of the world's remaining communist powers. It is to North Korea's quixotic attempts to join the world of modern politics that we now turn our attention.

North Korea: The Risks of Coming Out from Under

The Democratic People's Republic of Korea (DPRK) is a socialist state that, since its establishment in 1948, has been ruled by the Communist Korean Workers' Party (KWP). Leadership of government and party was in the hands of President Kim Il Sung until his death in July 1994. His son, Kim Jong Il, was groomed as his political heir and became General Secretary of the KWP in October 1997 after a three-year self-imposed period of mourning for his father. Kim Jong Il is currently North Korea's head of state despite his deceased father's appointment to "state president in perpetuity" in September 1998. The prime minister is Hong Song Nam.

Party institutions follow the familiar Leninist pattern: The National Party Congress, which is elected by Provincial Party Assemblies, chooses the Central Committee, which elects the Politburo and general secretary. The KWP's organization parallels and penetrates the governmental institutions. At the national level, the Supreme People's Assembly chooses the president and members of the Central People's Committee, which oversees the National Defense Commission and the

Administration Council. Local and provincial governments follow a similar organizational pattern. Party control is exerted over the courts, the media, and mass organizations of youth, women, workers, and farmers, coordinated by the Democratic Front for the Reunification of the Fatherland.

The most salient influences on postindependence North Korean politics have been the domination of party and government by Kim Il Sung and the existence of the "other" Korea, protégé of the United States and perceived threat to the survival of socialism in the North. The torturous, conflict-ridden course of relations between the two Korean governments erupted into a three-year war soon after the establishment of the two states. That war will be discussed in Chapter 7.

Kim's rise to power after returning to Korea in 1945 from exile in Manchuria and Siberia was supported by the Soviets. He first had to establish his primacy not only over the noncommunist Nationalists but also over other Communists who, like him, came home from exile or who came up from the underground in Korea. Working at first through the North Korean Bureau of the Korean Communist Party headquartered in Seoul, the northern Communists created a united front to carry through the "bourgeois revolution." In 1946 they detached themselves from southern authority and launched the Korean Workers' Party. Party membership expanded and subsidiary organizations of labor, young people, and women were created. Governmental institutions were set up and elections held (with underground southern participation), culminating in the end of Soviet occupation and in independence in 1948, following a similar step in the South.

Both governments espoused the goal of Korean unification, and in June 1950 war broke out between them, each side accusing the other of having initiated hostilities. The United States immediately joined on the side of South Korea, and China entered later on the side of the North. Battle raged up and down the peninsula, causing loss of life and widespread devastation on both sides of the thirty-eighth parallel. Military stalemate led finally to an armistice agreement in July 1953 that is still in effect. There have been four-power discussions about the prospects of a peace treaty (see Chapter 7 for details) but no agreements have been reached, and the unravelling of the North Korean economy has further complicated the entire issue of reunification of the Korean peninsula.

After consolidating his control over the party and the state in 1958, Kim Il Sung pursued the Soviet economic pattern of development, expanding heavy industry at the expense of raising living standards. Ideologically, however, Kim parted company with the Soviet Union, stressing the need for Korea to follow an independent path based on its own revolutionary experiences. This ideological "distancing" from the Soviet pattern signaled also a movement away from Soviet party influence over the Korean party. His argument was similar to that of Mao in China: that Marxist-Leninist principles had to be applied to the particular conditions existing in Korea. And just as Mao had done for the Communists leading China's revolutionary transformation, Kim elaborated his own doctrine of *juche,* or self-reliance to strengthen the party and the military in North Korea's bid for independence from Soviet control. This self-reliance was embodied in a new Korean revolutionary tradition which he elaborated, again along the lines of the Chinese Communists' legendary "Long March," by combining reality and myth in a description of the struggle of the Korean guerrillas (he had been one) against the Japanese in Manchuria in the 1930s.

To further solidify the independent path of Korean development, Kim identified Korea's mission with a personality cult built around himself as the "Great Leader." This cult extended also to his parents, siblings, and his son, who moved up through the ranks of government and party to succeed his father. According to Hwang Jang Yop, a high-ranking North Korean defector who had worked alongside Kim Il Sung and his son, Kim Jong Il has been in command in North Korea, for all intents and purposes, since 1974.[3] In the capacity of military dictator, Kim Jong Il is reputed by this North Korean defector as strengthening the military, marginalizing the leadership of the ruling Workers' Party and in recent years using his absolute control of military and party elites to keep the system afloat in the face of massive starvation.

After a self-proclaimed three-year period of mourning for his father, Kim Jong Il became the general secretary of the Korean Workers' Party in October 1997. On September 5, 1998 the first session of the 10th Supreme People's Assembly (SPA) confirmed the younger Kim's status within the structure of the state. In a series of amendments to the 1972 constitution, the SPA abolished the state presidency, presumably to honor Kim Il Sung by leaving the older Kim as the first and only state president. The Chairman of the National Defense Committee (NDC), a position held by Kim Jong Il since 1993, was declared head of state and a civilian technocrat, Yon Hyong Muk, was added to the NDC. Kim Il Chol was appointed Korean Peoples Armed Forces Minister, Kim Yong Nam became SPA chairman, and Hong Song Nam was named prime minister. All four had served the regime for decades. The only acknowledged structure of the Party was the Politburo which consisted of Kim Jong Il, Hong Song Nam, and four cadres of long standing. The absence of any mention of other Party structures or activities was notably accompanied by the visibility of military leaders on all public occasions. The inference generally drawn is that Kim Jong Il has adopted the position of supreme leader along with a strengthened military chain of command.

In the last decade the economic accomplishments of the past have been undone; foreign debt has mounted, the loss of Soviet aid has left North Korea completely isolated, and responses to efforts to attract foreign capital are slow in coming. Although economic collapse has been predicted for a number of years already, the regime still seems to be in control. It has made repeated attempts to use its nuclear capacities and missile-firings as "threats" with which to "negotiate," some might say extort, favorable deals for oil, food, and other concessions from the custodian of the international order, the United States, and the regional powers affecting its destiny: South Korea, Japan, and China. Arguably, Korea's successive reversals between belligerence and accommodation can be interpreted as the initial steps to gain entrance into the world community on its own terms. Only a few months after threatening yet another test launch of a long-range ballistic missile over East Asia, North Korea dramatically switched course once again in December 1999, agreeing to resume talks on establishing diplomatic relations with Japan that had been suspended since 1992.

The on-again, off-again pattern of negotiations between North and South Korea—with China and the United States participating as "big brothers"—is likely to continue into the future. Agreements to increase cultural and athletic exchanges between the North and South, two countries technically still at war, and a growing South Korean tourist trade to the North guardedly promote interest in expanding

Jiang Zemin, President of the People's Republic of China, succeeded Deng Xiapong in 1997.

Source: R. Ellis-Sygma.

mutual understanding. More dramatic steps have included North Korean permission for American entertainers to participate in a "Year 2000 Peace and Friendship Concert" in Pyongyang on the eve of the new millennium, and North Korea's opening of a consulate in Hong Kong in February 2000. But having opened the door a couple of inches, North Korea seems determined to keep the latchkey firmly locked against any outside pressure to open it wider or faster than the North Korean government approves. The extreme caution and apprehension with which North Korea advances toward joining the outside world is likely to continue even after President Clinton's momentous visit to North Korea in November 2000. Clearly, however, the door to the outside can no longer be shut.

Vietnam: War and Unification Under the Communist Party

The Socialist Republic of Vietnam, as it has been called since 1976 after the communist Democratic Republic of (North) Vietnam defeated the Republic of (South) Vietnam in 1975 and unified the country, is governed by the Vietnam Communist Party. With a parallel structure of party and state similar to that of China, Vietnam began political reforms only two years after embarking on economic reform in 1986. The pattern of political reform in general displays marked similarities to that of China: it is limited, gradual, and cautious in preserving one-party leadership while shifting more real legislative responsibility to the assembly and supervisory powers to the councils. In September 1998, a younger generation of leaders assumed the top political positions: Phan Van Khai, a reform-minded southerner who had not joined the party until 1959 when he was 26 years old, became prime minister; Tran Duc Luong, a compromise candidate, ascended to the presidency; and General Le Kha Phieu, a general and army political commissar, moved into the most powerful position of General Secretary of the Party.

From 1945 to 1975.   Vietnam's socialist system was developed under Ho Chi Minh's leadership after defeating the French in 1954. At that time France and other states acknowledged Vietnam's independence and gave de facto recognition to two governments, the Democratic Republic of Vietnam (DRV) in the area north of the seventeenth parallel and the government headed by Emperor Bao Dai in the south. The division was to be temporary, until a nationwide election could be held to determine the country's future government; for reasons described in Chapter 7, that election did not occur. Although, the Vietnamese celebrate September 2, as their National Day—the day in 1945 when Ho Chi Minh declared the independence of the Democratic Republic of Vietnam—it was 30 years before the DRV actually achieved control over the whole country. This prolonged and painful rite of passage from French colony to unified independent state was so inextricably bound up with the cold war division of the world between the United States and the Soviet Union that the intervening story of war in divided Vietnam will be reserved for fuller treatment later in Chapter 7 on international relations. Here we briefly summarize events that occurred between 1945 and 1975 as an introduction to the subject of political developments in the years since unification.

In the years after 1954 Vietnam's division into North and South, the DRV established the full panoply of state institutions in the northern part of the country and launched a program of socialist transformation through land redistribution followed by collectivization of agriculture and the development of heavy industry. Peasant objections to land reform and antiparty resistance by Catholics, ethnic minorities in the mountains, and intellectuals all were overcome in this period, and party-state control was consolidated. In the south, Bao Dai was ousted in 1955 by the U. S.-backed anticommunist Catholic Ngo Dinh Diem, whose government received economic and military aid and diplomatic support from the United States. When Diem moved to eliminate Viet Minh and other opponents of his government, many went underground to escape arrest.

The war of liberation resumed in 1959 when Viet Minh partisans in the south finally persuaded the leaders in the north, who until then had been counseling them to engage only in political activities, to approve the southerners' use of armed resistance against the government there. War between the Viet Minh and the South Vietnamese army intensified in 1964, when American military and the North Vietnamese army joined in the combat. By 1973, U.S. ground troops were withdrawn. The South Vietnamese government fought on until the spring of 1975, when the country was finally reunited under the Hanoi government. Liberation, as in China, came out of bitter struggle, not just against foreigners, but against compatriots.

After Unification.   Political and economic integration of the two parts of the country has not been an easy task. Economic development in the north suffered a severe setback as a result of the material and human costs of the war effort and U.S. bombing. In the south, years of battle raging through the countryside had disrupted the lives of the peasants, bloated the population in the cities, and produced feverish economic activity artificially stimulated by foreign aid and geared to military needs. An ill-conceived effort following unification to collectivize agriculture in the south and the costs of occupying Cambodia and war with China in 1979 also retarded economic progress. Soviet financial aid, given after the termination of Chinese economic assistance in 1978 and the signing of a treaty of friendship between Vietnam and the Soviet Union, became a major source of funds until 1990.

Political unification also posed problems. In addition to the task of "reeducating" officials and supporters of the RVN who had not fled the country, there was the task of reuniting the northern and southern branches of the party into one national body, renamed the Vietnam Communist Party at the Fourth Party Congress in 1976. The government structures of the DRV, Provisional Revolutionary Government (PRG), and the Republic of Vietnam were absorbed into the Socialist Republic of Vietnam. The National Liberation Front (NLF) joined the Fatherland Front, and southern liberation forces merged with the north's People's Army of Vietnam.

Party leadership since unification survived the passing of the older generation of wartime leaders, and a younger, better-educated generation has been gradually taking their place. In 1995, a year after the United States lifted its 19-year embargo against Vietnam, the two countries normalized relations. In 1996, Nguyen Van Linh further opened Vietnam to economic reform. But by 1998, Linh had died and the full consequences of economic disaster throughout the region were being felt in Vietnam. In 1997 widespread peasant protests in the north were followed in 1998 by attacks on party corruption by the party's own senior members. The selection of a member of the military, Le Ka Phieu, as General Secretary in December 1997 can be seen as a move to balance the reformers and contain the discontent. Again, as in China, the generational shift from 1930s revolutionaries to the post-1945 communist generation was accomplished smoothly. This was facilitated by retaining the "retired" top leaders, Muoi, Anh, and Kiet, as honorary advisers to the 19-member Politburo after they (and Nguyen Dinh Tu, who had died in 1996) were officially replaced by four new members.

Since embarking on economic reform, therefore, widespread agreement appears to have been reached on the ends or goals of economic and political development though serious differences remain over the means. The central question dividing the leadership is whether and to what extent democratic political reforms are required by the economic reform program known as *doi moi,* "renovation" (described in Chapter 5). In Vietnam as in China, Communist Party leaders know, from the long years of revolutionary warfare that propelled them into power, that without popular support their hold on power is always vulnerable. But the mass mobilizational politics that had enabled the party to channel popular political participation into the war effort, no longer served the party well in implementing its peacetime policy of promoting economic growth. Once having aroused popular participation, however, the Communist Party, organized along authoritarian lines, could no longer confine popular demands for political participation to party wishes.

The problem is how to maintain this "democratization" after the Communist Party consolidates its power, and the common enemy—backwardness, outdated economic institutions, and lack of modern skills—no longer has a recognizable face. The 1992 constitution defines the Vietnamese political system as one in which "the party is the leader, the people the master, and the state the manager." In a "democracy *under one party leadership,*" however, the party, the people, and the state are not equal partners. How, then, can democracy be implemented and the legitimacy of the party preserved when economic reforms mandate unpopular decisions?

A case in point occurred in 1998 when the party attempted to promote agricultural development by increasing farm sizes and extending rural leases to achieve economies of scale in agricultural production. After intense debate in the

Politburo, which ended in lack of consensus, an unprecedented recommendation in the form of the question itself—"whether or not to amend the 1993 law to permit larger landholdings and longer leases"—was sent to the Central Committee. The Central Committee decided, after equally vehement debate, to propose that the law be changed to eliminate the 3-hectare cap on farm sizes and extend the 20-year leases on household landholdings to 50-year leases. When it was sent to the National Assembly, however, the 450-member body voted against extending leases but did allow for some larger farms—subject to conditions. Whether this outcome was a result of a democratically representative body being more conservative than the authoritarian party or merely the indecisiveness of the top party leadership, the consequence was construed by agronomists as an impediment to agricultural development.

Modest political reform in Vietnam, as in China, has succeeded in other areas as well. In the 1992 elections to the National Assembly, candidates not screened by the Communist Party were allowed to run as independents, though they were required to get approval from neighbors, coworkers, and the Fatherland Front. The rule of law, given explicit support in the 1992 Constitution, has been strengthened along with the competitiveness of elections at the grassroots level. In 1998, in response to peasant protests throughout 1997 against corruption among local officials and a public campaign waged by intellectuals against corruption in the party, the government launched a campaign which led to massive indictments in 1999. The reforms notwithstanding, political power in Vietnam by and large continues to be monopolized by the Communist Party working through the state, and mass organizations to make, carry out, and mobilize popular support for policies arrived at by an authoritarian party.

Underlying the issue of political reform in China and the other communist states—North Korea, Vietnam, Laos—are fundamental questions about the role of a revolutionary party after the revolution is won. Once the antirevolutionaries have been eliminated, cowed, converted, or outlived, and restoration of the old regime is no longer conceivable, what purpose does the party serve? Is it needed to keep alive the revolutionary vision, to "re-revolutionize" the masses from time to time lest they sink back into privatism and indifference to the collective good? Or, when the goal of society is to modernize and develop, which requires rational and efficient allocation of human, material, and financial resources, is the duplication of party and state hierarchies an unnecessarily cumbersome waste of talent and energy? If some decentralization of decision making is desirable, how much can be allowed without risking descent into anarchy? Would the process of economic and social modernization be better served by opening up more positions in government, and even the party, to direct election by the people? Should the leading role of the Communist Party be open to challenge by other organized parties and interest groups? These questions strike at the heart of the system and are not amenable to facile answers, to simple advocacy of "democracy" or other bumper sticker slogan solutions. Nor are they likely to be avoided indefinitely or to go away.

Some of these questions are also relevant to the future of the two anticommunist Leninist style party states, the Republic of China on Taiwan and Singapore, to which we now turn.

The Guomindang: Leninist Party without Lenin

The Guomindang (KMT), which in Chinese means "national people's party," has been the ruling party of the Republic of China (ROC) for most of the twentieth century. Its Leninist structure dates to the 1920s, when Sun Yatsen invited Soviet help in whipping the party into shape for the task of unifying and modernizing China.[5] With the communist victory on the mainland in 1949, the defeated Republic of China (ROC) government, led by General Chiang Kaishek, moved its seat of government to the province of Taiwan, bringing with it the mainland party and governmental structures, the nationalist army, and civilian officials. In May 2000, the first opposition party candidate for president was voted into office: Chen Shiu-bian of the Democratic Progressive Party (DPP); the Vice President is Annette Lu and the Premier is Tang Fei.

The Party.   Like the CPC, the Guomindang (KMT) is organized hierarchically, with the National Party Congress electing the party chairman and the 180-member Central Committee; it in turn approves the chairman's nominees for the Central Standing Committee. Provincial party structures follow a similar pattern. By the early 1980s party membership had grown to some 2 million, larger in proportion to the total population (20 million) than the CPC, making it—in the words of one observer—"somewhere between a small, tightly organized 'cadre' party and a 'mass' electoral party."[6] The large majority of the members are Taiwan-born, and even in the Central Standing Committee mainlanders were in a minority (15 of 32 seats) in 1988. Business leaders, technocrats, and local government officials of a younger generation have gradually been brought in as aging mainlanders died or retired.

Factionalism within the ranks of the KMT has some similarity to the divisions within the CPC. In Taiwan a central conflict is between old-guard "conservatives"— often older and mainland-born, who resist significant political change within the party and government that might loosen the party's traditional power position— and the "moderates," often younger, better-educated people with technical expertise who support gradual adaptation to changes in society that in their view will strengthen support for the party among the voters. Divisions within the KMT also surface among the military, the technocrats, and personalist factions organized around leading contenders for top positions. In 1993 a rift opened up over policy toward China, and a group of party members, mostly of mainland origin, who felt the government was not pursuing reunification vigorously enough left the Guomindang and formed the Chinese New Party. In the May 1998 legislative elections, both the New Party and the opposition pro-independence Democratic Progressive Party (DPP) lost seats while the Guomindang was swept solidly back into its position of dominance with more than two-thirds of all the seats. But the Presidency fell to the DPP in 2000.

Like the Communist Party in the PRC, the Guomindang on Taiwan maintains its leadership role for the rest of society through its control over nominations for public office, through youth and farmers' organizations, through ownership (though not monopoly) of the media. And, like the mainland, its management of the state has been assured by top-level party officials holding prominent positions in government. Chiang Kaishek held both the party chairmanship and the presidency until his death in 1975; his son Chiang Chingkuo succeeded him in the top party post and three years later became president; at his death in 1988, the U.S.-educated Taiwanese Lee Tenghui took over both positions. After 12 years in office, President Lee stepped down after the presidential elections in 2000. Despite or perhaps because of its position as ruling party, however, the KMT has been undergoing a basic transition in order to maintain itself in power, a story to be told below.

Government Structures.   The governmental apparatus of Taiwan is an archaic five-branch structure inherited from the party's founding father, Sun Yatsen. It was outlined in the 1947 Constitution that the party adopted while its government on the mainland was in a total state of collapse and its generals were preparing the KMT's retreat-in-defeat by ruthlessly suppressing popular independence movements on Taiwan. To maintain the nationalist government's claim to represent all of China (although its effective jurisdiction extended only to Taiwan and a few islands near the mainland), the government consisted of both the national government (presumably, in temporary exile) and the provincial government. For close to 50 years, these two governments coexisted in order to sustain the myth that the Republic of China also represented the people on the mainland.

As forces favoring independence for Taiwan gained in strength after 1990, the KMT was finally forced to address the reality of its permanent exile. In 1998 the national government abolished the offices of the provincial government—the provincial governor, a 79-member assembly, and its administration—absorbing its powers into the central government. Opposition members, younger Guomindang members and President Lee Teng-hui had supported this move earlier but it took the large margin with which the KMT reestablished its ruling majority in 1998 to obtain the necessary three-quarters vote of the National Assembly.

The national government consists of the 334-member *National Assembly,* which until 1996 selected the president but since then has responsibility only for amending the constitution and confirming presidential appointments; the 225-member *Legislative Assembly* that was relatively weak until 1990, for the most part endorsing policies initiated in the party and the executive; the *Executive Assembly,* which consists of the president, vice president, and premier, appointed by the president, who also chooses the cabinet; the *Examination Yuan,* which consists of a judiciary and an agency that supervises civil service exams, appointed by the president; and the *Control Yuan,* which monitors the other branches of government through its power to audit their accounts and to censure government officials.

As the older generation of KMT mainlanders passed on, both the government and the ruling party have embarked on the process of democratization. It began with the lifting of martial law in 1987. Opposition parties were legalized in 1990 and by the following year constitutional rule was fully restored. Subsequent political reforms sought to democratize the institutions of a government originally created to serve the authoritarian purposes of one-party rule. By 1996, not only the national and legislative assemblies but the presidency as well were elected by direct popular vote. From a relatively passive body that merely rubber-stamped the ruling party's decisions, Taiwan's legislature soon gained the reputation as a boisterous often rowdy gathering of highly partisan legislators intent on affecting policy. But

corruption within the ruling party and its failure to accomplish meaningful constitutional reform heightened public disenchantment with the KMT.

There were calls to eliminate the National Assembly as an outdated sinecure
for senior KMT officials, which originally met once every six years only to elect the
president. Having been stripped of its power to elect the president, the National Assembly today still has 334 members who, like the Legislative Assembly, are popularly elected and meet once a year, with each member receiving an annual salary of
$43,000 plus daily allowances of up to $250 a day during the two months each year
that it is convened. It is considered by many to be merely a showcase for ambitious
political novices seeking a higher position in the Legislative Assembly. When the
National Assembly managed to pass a constitutional amendment in 1999, after an
extended stalemate, it was opposed by the leaders of all political parties. The
amendment, which remained in force despite the disciplinary action taken against
the speaker of the National Assembly, reduced the number of seats in the assembly
by more than half, extended deputies' terms for two more years, and introduced a
proportional representation system for choosing future assemblies.

Political Evolution Since 1949.   Taiwan began its postwar history as an authoritarian regime forcefully imposed on a Taiwanese population that had lived under
Japanese rule. The experience of colonialism had resulted neither in the emergence
of an active movement for reunification with China, nor in a movement for Taiwan
independence. Instead, the Taiwanese political groups that had formed advocated
either integration with Japan or autonomy within the Japanese empire. Two principal factors may explain this. First, from 1895 on, the colonial authorities severed
contact between Taiwan and China, cutting off further immigration from and restricting travel to the mainland. For the next 50 years the islanders were insulated
from the experiences that were shaping Chinese national identity on the mainland.
This isolation increased receptivity to Japanese influence and may also have contributed to mainland Chinese suspicions about the islanders' loyalty when Taiwan
was returned to China at the end of World War II. And the initial contact between
Taiwanese and the mainland generals sent to prepare the island for KMT rule in
1947 ended in disaster: the massacre of thousands of Taiwanese.

Initially faced with a perceived threat from Communist China and widespread
hostility toward the "carpetbagging" mainlanders among the islanders, some of
whom actively supported the Taiwanese Independence Movement, Chiang Kaishek
imposed martial law, driving the independence movement underground, suppressing other critics of the regime, curbing the exercise of political rights, and prohibiting the formation of new parties. But the government instituted elections to local
assemblies, allowing non-KMT "independent" candidates to run, though party members held a large majority of provincial and local positions, except for the lowest-
level village assemblies.

Chiang's son and successor, Chiang Chingkuo—who took a position against
continuing opposition from the old guard mainlanders and brought more young
professionals and Taiwanese into the government and party—expanded the significance of local and provincial elections, and tolerated some political activity by "outside the party" (*dangwai*) groups. Political reforms reached a crescendo between

1986 and 1988 in the Democratic Revolution, which in 1987 ended martial law and allowed demonstrations to occur and the opposition Democratic Progressive Party (DPP) to organize officially. The trend toward liberalization and "Taiwanization" survived Chiang Chingkuo's death in 1988 when Vice President Lee Tenghui succeeded to the presidency and, despite opposition from the conservative faction of the party, to the chairmanship of the KMT. The old guard still asserted its influence but by 1994 the party's Central Committee endorsed a proposal by President Lee for direct popular election of the president, following the trend set for the selection of the provincial governor and mayors.

During the 1991 campaign, the DPP raised the issue of independence for Taiwan—that is, seeking international and PRC recognition as a separate state entity—and a sizable pro-independence demonstration was allowed to occur early in 1992. The government, fearful that agitation for such a step would provoke China to a preemptive seizure of the island, was cautious and warned against too vocal an advocacy of independence by DPP. But by 1998, the KMT faced a number of severe challenges to its stable ruling majority: a steadily *decreasing* percentage of the popular vote, *widening* support for the DPP's pro-independence platform as reflected in its garnering 31 percent of the popular vote in the 1992 elections, doubling its representation in the legislature to 50 seats, and the surprising setback for the KMT in local elections in 1997.

Faced with the possibility of losing its majority status in 2000, the KMT modified its course assisted by two fortuitous events. One was the surprise electoral victory of the KMT nominee for mayor of Taipei: a young, articulate and good looking lawyer, Ma Ying-jeou. Personally sponsored by President Lee, Ma Ying-jeou won 51 percent of the votes to oust his popular DPP incumbent in the March 1998 election. A second fortuitous event aiding the KMT's electoral prospects for the year 2000 was the formation of a new centrist coalition among the younger generation of both native Taiwanese and children of mainlanders. Drawn together by support for a more pragmatic approach to relations with the mainland, this coalition of youthful supporters of Hsu Hsin-liang, a DPP candidate for the presidency in the 2000 elections, appealed to a growing number of voters in the middle of the political spectrum. For the KMT, it created the opportunity for expanding its electoral base by moving the party away from its mainland roots and identity, closer to its youthful Taiwanese constituency.

The opportunity was irresistible for President Lee and the campaign for the mayoral position in Taipei proved the perfect venue for reorienting the KMT's identity to transcend the polarizing divisiveness between "mainlander" and "native Taiwanese." And Ma Ying-jeou was the perfect candidate to serve as "poster-boy" for a "new Taiwanese" identity. Born in Hong Kong to parents who had migrated from the mainland, Mao Ying-jeou grew up in Taiwan and identified himself as a Taiwanese: "I eat Taiwanese rice. I drink Taiwanese water. I'm a new Taiwanese." Used initially as an effective election ploy, this "new Taiwanese" identity was parlayed into a new strategy with which to confront the mainland and win an overwhelming majority in the election of 2000. President Lee obliquely referred to the new strategy in an interview with a German newspaper in August 1999, when he asserted that Taiwanese sovereignty meant that any negotiations on unification held with the mainland had to be based on "a special kind of state to state relationship" between Taiwan and China. The scathing rhetoric with which the PRC leadership attacked President Lee ensured an escalation of tension between Taiwan and the mainland that is likely to continue through the election year 2000.

Although mainlander-islander antagonisms persist, it would be an oversimplification to regard the KMT as the party of the mainlanders and the DPP as the islanders' party; islanders are a majority in both parties. Nor would it be correct to imply that islanders are all pro-independence and all mainlanders opposed. Though the KMT majority shows no signs of abandoning its official "one China" stand in favor of explicit support of Taiwanese separatism, it remains wary of unification with a communist mainland, insisting instead that ultimate unification can come about only when democracy exists on both sides of the straits. The internal political transition of Taiwan toward an institutionalization of stable party pluralism is likely to strengthen Taiwan's ultimate negotiating position with the mainland in any future discussions on unification. And by redefining a new centrist position, the KMT unwittingly may have prepared the way for the opposition DPP's victory in the 2000 presidential elections (discussed further in Chapter 7).

The Party System in Singapore and in Other Asian Pacific Countries

In Singapore the pattern of a Leninist party seems to have been established in the 1950s when People's Action Party (PAP) founder and long-time leader Lee Kuan Yew, a British-educated lawyer, joined forces with Communists in Singapore to press for independence from Britain. Although Lee cut ties with the Communists and became a firm anticommunist once independence was won, the organization and function of the PAP closely parallel the CPC. It is described as "a tightly disciplined elitist party, monitored by a small authoritarian leadership and supervised through a cadre system, the identity of whose members is kept a close secret."[7] From the time of independence until 1991, when the opposition won four of the 81 seats, PAP was the only party represented in parliament. The power of the state is skillfully used to carry out programs decided on by PAP leadership and to keep the party firmly in control of agenda setting. Its pervasive influence over government, the economy, and the private lives of Singapore's citizens is legendary.

Party systems in other Asian Pacific countries are varied. As noted previously, Brunei bans parties and Hong Kong's fledgling parties play an increasingly visible but not very powerful role in policymaking. In Myanmar the proliferation of insignificant parties contributes to their inability to wrest control from the military. Malaysia's communally based parties reinforce the separation of the Malays, the Chinese, and the Indians, although the parties affiliated with the three ethnic groups are linked in the ruling coalition and in the opposition. Thailand and the Philippines have fluid multiparty systems, organized around leading personalities, mainly civilian in the Philippines and mainly military and former military in Thailand.

In the one-party-dominant systems of Singapore and Taiwan, opposition parties exist but are eclipsed by the brilliant sun of the government party. That observation was also true of Japan, South Korea, and Indonesia until more recently when these one-party-dominant systems became more genuinely pluralistic. In Japan, this happened when defections from the dominant Liberal Democratic Party lost the party its control of the government and a coalition of opponents came into power in mid-1993. In South Korea, the long-time dissident, Kim Dae Jung, won the presidency in December 1997 by only 1.4 percent of the vote. Two contributing factors may have helped: the looming economic crisis and formation of a coalition between Kim Dae Jung's party, the National Congress for New Politics, and a conservative party, the United Liberal Democrats. The economic crisis also toppled Suharto from power, bringing Vice President Habibie to power. In the first democratic elections in over 40 years, held in June 1999, the party headed by Megawati Sukarnoputri, Sukarno's daughter, received the largest number of votes in a contest among a huge number of political parties. In a complex electoral system, Abdurrahman ("Gus Dur") Wahid of the National Awakening Party was chosen as Indonesia's fourth president and Megawati became vice president. With internal ethnic and religious conflicts raging throughout the archipelago—from Aceh in the west to Ambon, the Moluccas, and East Timor in the east—and a military that is heavily implicated in human rights violations, the political situation in Indonesia remains unstable.

Nowhere in the Asian Pacific do parties, whether organized around ideology, class, ethnicity, personalities, or some mix of those factors, effectively serve to unite the ordinary citizens into political action groups, articulating alternative programs and influencing the making of public policy by electing officials and holding them accountable. The liberal and socialist vision of authentic government of, by, and for the people remains unrealized everywhere. In a number of countries the military is, or until recently has been, the core element of authoritarian regimes, commonly defining their missions as defense of the state against external enemies and/or internal chaos. Some of them have also successfully pursued the goal of national economic development.

RULE BY MILITARY "DEVELOPERS"

Indonesia, Thailand, and South Korea are the leading examples of development-driven military regimes. The first two will be examined in this section. South Korea, where the military since the late 1980s has been relinquishing its hitherto visible control to civilian leaders, will be discussed in a later section on democratizing systems. The economic development programs and achievements of these military regimes are discussed in Chapter 5.

Indonesia's "New Order"

Governing a chain of islands stretching 3,000 miles from Sumatra to New Guinea and with a large, ethnically diverse population is no easy task. It requires some strong cement—perhaps a charismatic leader or a compelling ideology or coercion—to hold the pieces together. Since its independence in 1950, Indonesia has had the first and last, and it is currently embarking on a period of reform in an effort to devise institutions capable of countering the centrifugal forces that threaten the state's existence.

The Sukarno Era.   During the first phase (1950–1957), parliamentary democracy with Sukarno as president was tried, but even his considerable political clout as the charismatic independence leader was not able to get enough cooperation among political parties deeply divided along ideological, religious, and regional lines to make the parliamentary system work. In Indonesia's first election in 1953, four major political parties together garnered 78 percent of the parliamentary vote: the big Muslim parties of Masyumi and Nahdlatul Ulama received 20.9 percent and 18.4 percent respectively, Sukarno's Nationalist Party (PNI) captured 22.3 percent and the Indonesian Communist Party (PKI) received 16.4 percent of the vote. But the issues dividing the parties—the question of an Islamic state, whether a secularist state should pursue Nationalist or Communist goals—were too contentious to make viable coalitions possible and the country slid toward disintegration.

During the second phase (1957–1965), Sukarno improvised an authoritarian system he called Guided Democracy. Instituting martial law, he suspended parliament, dissolved opposition parties, and tried desperately to balance the growing power of the military by bringing the Indonesian Communist Party into his government. But if balancing two such irreconcilable enemies was not enough to destabilize Sukarno's government, there was concerted opposition to his non-Islamic state by the otherwise fractious Muslim parties and intervention by the U.S. CIA in support of a rebel government in West Sumatra. Finally, the armed forces was itself divided over the issue of Sukarno's militant "Confrontation" with Malaysia over the latter's incorporation of British colonies on Borneo. The showdown came in 1965 when leftist army officers attempted a coup, which was averted by the military forces under General Suharto's control. When Suharto took over, he set about eliminating the communists (PKI) as a political force. What followed was an orgy of killings carried out by vigilante mobs with army collaboration that whittled away Sukarno's authority until, in 1967, he agreed to turn over presidential functions to Suharto. Banished from taking part in politics, Sukarno died in 1970.

The Suharto Era.   First as acting president and then in 1968 as president, Suharto inaugurated the New Order. It was a continuation of the authoritarianism of Guided Democracy, except that the military now wielded undisputed power. Suharto retained the trappings of democracy, including Sukarno's strategy of enlisting the support of functional organizations such as labor unions and peasant and other associations. To counter the influence of the old political parties, Suharto brought together several hundred such groups in a government-sponsored coalition called *Golkar.* This umbrella organization became in effect the government's own political party, running candidates and controlling its representatives in parliament. Although most of Golkar's constituent groups were civilian organizations, the military dominated the party's central secretariat and held the top party post until 1993 when, under pressure from Suharto to "civilianize" Golkar, a nonmilitary chairman was chosen to head the party.

Between 1971, when elections were reinstated in Indonesia, and 1998, when Suharto was forced to resign, Golkar won substantial majorities in every election. In 1973, having infiltrated the ranks and reduced the activities of the remaining old political parties, Suharto finally forced all of them to merge into two faction-ridden

Indonesian President Wahid, second from left stands with his wife, far left and vice president Megawati Sukarnoputri, second from right, with her husband far right after the swearing in of the Cabinet during a group photo at the state palace in Jakarto, Indonesia, Friday, October 29, 1999.

Source: Photo by Kemal Jufri/Corbis Sygma.

coalitions, the secular nationalist Indonesian Democratic Party (PDI) and the Islamic United Development Party (PPP). Their function as "opposition" party coalitions was severely curtailed by their acceptance of government subsidies and by limitations that restricted their campaigning in the villages to a few weeks before elections. In this manner, like the puppet theater of Javanese tradition, the shadow play of competitive elections was acted out for the benefit of audiences at home and abroad.

In the government of the New Order, the executive held the reins of power and the legislature was weak. The president was chosen, not by the voters or by parliament, but by a 1,000-member People's Consultative Assembly (MPR), which met briefly every five years for that purpose. Neither the president nor his cabinet were in effect accountable to parliament, the People's Representative Council (DPR). The reverse was the case with 100 of parliament's 500 members appointed by the president, practically assuring him a pro-government majority in that body. Throughout Suharto's rule, parliament was a compliant partner, neither making legislation nor rejecting any submitted by the president. "The running joke about the parliament is that its activities can be summarized by the five D's: *datang, duduk, dengar, diam, duit,* which roughly translated, means 'show up, sit down, listen, shut up, and collect your paycheck.'"[8]

In the person of Suharto, the military (*Abri*) dominated Indonesian politics, finding its justification in the Doctrine of the Dual Function (*dwifungsi*), according to which the armed forces not only have responsibility for internal and external security but also have a legitimate part to play in political and economic life. In 1983, the Abri held 13 out of the 32 cabinet positions, a decade later it held 10 out of the 41 cabinet posts. Military officers also held key positions at all levels and in all branches of the government—as ambassadors, provincial governors, and city mayors as well as in regional bureaucracies, state-owned enterprises, the judiciary, the government sanctioned labor union, and Golkar. The military foreclosed possible challenges to its rule from nongovernmental groups by incorporating them into Golkar and by selecting party candidates and running their campaigns. It controlled the civilian bureaucracy first by purging it of hostile elements and then by requiring civil servants to support Golkar. Additional levers of power were the central security agency, *Kopkamtib* (Operations Command to Restore Order and Security), with extensive powers to arrest persons suspected of threatening the New Order, and the territorial military units, based throughout the country and paralleling the civil administrative structure. Although the government retained civilians in positions of authority, the military was clearly dominant in this civilian-military partnership.

For the first 20 years of the New Order, Suharto and the military were for all intents and purposes synonymous. Military officers were also significant actors in the economy through their administration of public enterprises and through appointment to the boards of private corporations. These connections generated income free of legislative scrutiny for both the armed services and individual officers. Suharto managed to keep the armed forces under his control by advancing the careers of his "political" and "financial" generals, by providing ample funds for the military as well as indirect financial advantages. Military as well as civilian officials received payments for providing protection to Indonesian-Chinese entrepreneurs who were always vulnerable to nationalist reprisals, especially so since they benefited greatly from the economic successes of the New Order. By the mid-1980s, however, Suharto was exercising power independently and to the economic detriment of the military. Competing intermediaries had emerged, among them an affluent middle class of professionals and, most prominently, Suharto's children who had displaced the military in a number of businesses that had previously filled the military's coffers: notably in oil-trading, timber, and the airlines. By 1993, therefore, there were military officers that were anxious to see Suharto's tenure come to an end.

If rival commanders in the armed forces were vying for position in the inevitable succession scramble, the discontent below was reaching critical proportions heightened by the visibility of corruption and excessive profiteering by Suharto's "cronies," especially his children. The preeminent position of Chinese business leaders who flourished under Suharto's rule made them convenient targets of hostility. The voices of discontent became more audible from a number of directions: the growing middle class, the Islamic opposition to the secular nature of the state, regional pressures for decentralization of authority, the separatist movement among the Acehnese on Sumatra, resistance by the Papuan natives in Irian Jaya to the government's program of relocating large numbers of Javanese there, and the independence movement in predominantly Catholic East Timor, the former Portuguese colony taken by force in 1975.

Suharto's departure was imminent; what finally brought it about was the economic crisis that swept through the Asian Pacific in 1997 and 1998. As long as economic growth had accompanied New Order politics, winning the approval of the United States with its avowed anticommunism, the visible apparatus of representative institutions—parliament, elections, parties—provided a convenient cover for Suharto's rule, one that was, in the words of one observer, "strictly for show."[9] Once the economy collapsed, however, the stark reality of rule by a group of military oligarchs claiming to act in the interests of the people while enriching themselves, dissipated whatever remaining support Suharto could muster to stay in power. On May 21, 1998, just two months after being rubber-stamped for a seventh term, President Suharto was literally forced to resign by Vice President Habibie's public disavowal of the Suharto presidency. With the support of other members of Suharto's own government, Habibie became President.

Despite his attempts at damage control, however, Habibie, was too closely tied to the Suharto dynasty to be anything other than an interim leader. Suharto's delayed departure after 32 years of military rule exposed the depth of the underlying fault lines embedded in the foundation of Indonesia as a nation-state. The mosaic of ethnic, religious, and ideological groupings and islands that made up Indonesia after independence became unglued after Suharto's departure. The long-festering rebellion in East Timor picked up momentum, demonstrating the desperation of a military loosened from its political moorings. The result was civil strife throughout the length and breadth of the archipelago. President Habibie's reform agenda, instead of bolstering his own presidency, paved the way for a new, more democratic regime combining moderate Muslims and nationalist supporters of a secular state.

The legislation passed under Habibie's brief tenure established new election procedures and a plan for regional autonomy that included free elections to determine the political fate of East Timor. The People's Consultative Assembly (MPR), akin to an electoral college, that actually elected the president was reduced from 1,000 to 700 members. Originally composed mostly of presidential appointees whose sole function was to rubber-stamp past achievements and reanoint the president for another term, the Consultative Assembly now was to consist of the People's Representative Council (DPR), which was expanded from 500 to 550 representatives, plus 81 elected representatives from provincial parliaments and 69 members appointed by social and community groups. The DPR was in turn made up of 420 representatives elected from districts under a first-past-the-post system, 75 members drawn from a national list to ensure small-party representation and, controversially, 55 military appointees. The new laws also allowed for an unlimited number of political parties to replace the two-coalition "parties" that were allowed to supplement the ruling Golkar "party."

On June 7, 1999 Indonesian voters went to the polls in what was hailed as the country's first democratic elections in four decades. They elected 462 representatives to the People's Representative Council (DPR) which constituted the largest segment of the 700 member Consultative Assembly that would chose the new president in November. The Indonesian Democratic Party for Struggle (PDI-P) led by Megawati Sukarnoputri (the daughter of Sukarno) received 34 percent of the parliamentary vote, with Golkar placing only second with 22 percent. Despite receiving a plurality, however, the presidency eluded Megawati who, as a woman, did not meet with the approval of the more orthodox Muslim constituency. She became vice president in November, the result of a partnership she forged with Abdurrahman Wahid, the 59-year-old Muslim cleric, who headed Nahdlatul Ulama (NU), the country's largest Muslim organization and the only one of the four largest parties in the 1955 elections to remain intact over the years.

The new cabinet named by President Wahid (widely known as Gus Dur, Old Brother Dur) is an all-inclusive coalition drawn from the entire spectrum of Indonesian politics. It includes former Golkar party loyalists, bureaucrats, military reformers, a navy admiral as armed forces chief, orthodox Muslim politicians, civilian progressives, two ministers of Chinese descent, a dynastic Balinese ruler, and even a Catholic philosopher.[10] The rainbow nature of this cabinet confirms President Wahid's reputation as a pragmatist adept at compromise and reconciliation. A human rights portfolio has been created in the cabinet and the armed-forces chief is now rotated among the three main services to dilute the army's influence and restore faith in the military's capacity to avoid human rights abuses. Questions that remain to be answered are whether the new government can successfully address the large problems facing the country: economic and political reform, reining in the military while cleansing it of an atrocious human rights record and mending the ethnic conflicts that threaten to pull Indonesia apart.

The prognosis for Indonesia is mixed; there are strengths and weaknesses built into this post-Suharto regime. Economic recovery may be assisted by President Wahid's conservative approach to change if he exercises strong leadership. He has the tentative backing of the business community and has reassured the IMF about Indonesia's intention to stand by its international commitments. His economic adviser, on the other hand, hints at adjustments in Indonesia's relationship to international lending institutions whose conditions create hardships for ordinary citizens. Probably Gus Dur's greatest assets as president of Indonesia at this moment in its history is his unpredictability, candor, and sense of humor.

The weaknesses of the new government, on the other hand, derive from the political uncertainty inherent in balancing acts. President Wahid is an accommodationist leader whose attempts at restoring peace in the wake of riots, demonstrations, civil insurrections, and separatist demands that have been brewing for years under the Suharto regime may founder on the perception of weak leadership. This raises the question of where the military stands in the face of such political instability. Discredited abroad and at home by its human rights abuses, the military appears to be disunified. But if religious conflicts and secessionist strife continue to threaten Indonesian sovereignty, will the military be able to intervene, toppling the newborn civilian government "to save" the country from unravelling? The *coup de grâce* may well be the fragile health of a nearly blind president who has suffered a major stroke. Although the popular vice president, Megawati Sukarnoputri—who actually received the plurality of votes in the last election—would succeed the president in the event of his death, a woman as president—even if she is the daughter of the founding father and first ruler—in a predominantly Muslim country carries its own risks and uncertainties.

This is a critical time in the evolution of Indonesia's political development. The multiple tasks confronting the newly elected civilian government, even taken one at a time, are daunting. Together they seem insurmountable. In the final analysis, it may be that economic adviser Yusuf Faishal is correct when he says that everything will depend upon the new government's capacity to nurture institutions necessary for a system based on law: an active parliament, an independent judiciary, and a chastened, unified military.

Thailand's Military Bureaucracy

Never a colony, Thailand escaped both the exposure to Western institutions by a colonial administration and a struggle for independence that might have stimulated the formation of political parties and a mass nationalist movement. Instead its traditional institutions—the monarchy, the Buddhist clergy, the military, and civilian bureaucracies—continued to function without interruption. Comfortable with a centralized hierarchy, no one had any particular motivation for challenging the monopoly of power held by the elite. Even the coup of 1932 by progressive modernizing civilians and military officers was aimed at putting the unlimited powers of the king under constitutional limitations. They did not challenge either the principle of monarchy or elite rule; rather, they asked for, and got, an expansion of their share in the elite ranks.

Bureaucratic Dominance. Since 1932, Thai politics has been "a matter of competition between bureaucratic cliques for the benefits of government. In this competition the army—the best organized, most concentrated, and most powerful of the branches of the bureaucracy—has come out on top."[11] (And a top-heavy "branch" the army is, with more than 600 generals, one for every 300 to 350 troops; in Western armies the average is one general to between 3,000 and 4,000 troops.) Competition among bureaucratic cliques—civilian and military—has played itself out in frequent coups (at the end of 1992, 19 had been attempted or succeeded) and alternation between military and civilians as prime minister; civilians held the position only one-fourth of the time from 1932 to 1991, and some of them were "simply fronts for the military."[12] Justification for autocratic rule by the bureaucracy is that it alone can provide the stability and other requisites for economic development.

The degree of autocracy practiced by the bureaucracy varies over time. When disorder and corruption mount, the reins of control are grasped tightly; elections, parties, and legislatures are suspended. When order and cleaner government are restored, there then comes a loosening of control; elected legislatures resume and parties are once again tolerated. But the reins remain in bureaucratic, intermittently military, hands. Since the 1992 violence that resulted in the downfall of General Suchinda Kraprayoon—who ruled as nonelected premier—the Thai military has kept a low political profile. When the financial crisis, which began in Thailand in the summer of 1997, brought down the economy, the military was one of the first victims when it was forced to cancel an aircraft order from the United States, forfeiting the down payment of $74.5 million. Further support for a weakened political role for the military in the future came in 1998 when then prime minister and defense minister Chuan Leekpai was credited for the appointment as army commander (the most powerful position in the military) of a general who is considered a professional in favor of an all-volunteer military.

Party Weakness. Political parties were viewed with suspicion by the first generation of military rulers, and subsequent experience confirmed their view that parties are troublesome and destabilizing. Thai military leaders have not chosen—or been able—to create a single government-sponsored party, as their Indonesian counterparts have done. Individual officers and factions have formed separate parties to further their special interests. Given legal status only in 1955, parties have at times been prohibited, and they are weak, fragmented, and without mass followings. Bureaucratic hostility and government control of radio and television keep them weak, which in turn weakens the elected legislature. Such weaknesses further undermine the parties while strengthening the military's contention that democratic party government is incapable of serving the national interest.

The potential of private associations and other interest groups as vehicles for popular participation is limited. The few independent nongovernmental organizations that exist are in the main centered in Bangkok. Out in the countryside, the Ministry of the Interior controls the village headmen and councils, and the army's civilian affairs branch has managed to take over existing interest groups, limiting their capacity to act as independent agents on behalf of their members and as challengers of the status quo.

Civilian Interludes.   At only two junctures between 1932 and 1991 was military rule temporarily eclipsed. The first such period was in 1944, when the government of Field Marshal Phibun collapsed because it had backed the losing side in World War II. He was succeeded by civilian Prime Minister Pridi until a coup in 1947 brought him back. A second interruption in military rule came in 1973, when a student-sponsored movement for political reform led to clashes between the police and hundreds of thousands of demonstrators on the streets of Bangkok. With the military divided over the question of further repression, a civilian government took over until 1976, when the military returned to power after violent confrontations with students at Thammasat University. In each case the civilian interlude was brief. New constitutions were adopted, and an array of left, right, and center parties contested elections for parliament and formed transitory coalitions leading to unstable, weak governments and growing ideological polarization. Finally, charging corruption and an impending descent into chaos, the military intervened to bring back order (if not law), and most people seemed at least at first to welcome their return.

Events Since 1992.   A civilian government came to power when voters took to the streets to oppose the election results in 1992. Pro-military parties who had won a majority in parliament had named a prime minister, General Suchinda Krapayoon, who was not an elected member of parliament. Opposition to Suchinda as prime minister triggered large-scale demonstrations in Bangkok, reminiscent of those in 1973 that led to the temporary ousting of the military. Some of the demonstrators in 1992 were former activists from that era.[13] The crisis deepened when the military fired on the demonstrators, killing several hundred people, injuring and arresting others. Amidst the rising anger against the military, the king intervened, persuading General Suchinda to resign, in favor of a caretaker government until elections could be held in September 1992. In that election, a coalition of antimilitary parties won a small majority in the House of Representatives and Chuan Leekpai, head of the centrist Democracy Party, was named prime minister.

Despite the discord among coalition partners, Chuan Leekpai's administration managed to survive for two years and eight months, longer than any civilian govern-

Chuan Leekpai, elected prime minister
of Thailand in 1992.

Sources: United Nations photo 184272/J. Issac.

ment in Thai history. Finally brought down by scandal, it was followed by two short-lived administrations, one headed by a provincial politician, Banharn Silpa-archa, from July 1995 to September 1996, the second led by General Chavalit Yongchaiyudh, who resigned when he was accused of having brought on the financial crash in November 1997. Chuan Leekpai then came back into office with high hopes of being able to turn Thailand's economy around. But by August 1998, Chuan was increasingly under fire as the economic crisis worsened, prompting an unprecedented public statement by the queen in support of Chuan's economic policies. In September, with only a slim majority in parliament, Chuan bolstered his precarious government by inviting the Chart Pattana Party from the opposition to join the ruling coalition. Thus Chatichai Choonhavan, another old face, returned to government—he was prime minister before but was ousted in Thailand's last military coup in February 1991—as head of a newly renovated political party. If Chuan Leekpai's "new" government serves its full term, elections must take place by November 2000.

It remains to be seen whether the 1992 election was a watershed marking the beginning of the end of military domination of Thai politics or is just a temporary setback. Some observers believe that corruption is endemic to Thai politics and therefore requires periodic military takeovers to clean up the mess. This is in line with scholars like Karl Jackson who talk about Indonesia as "a presidential variation of a bureaucratic polity."[14] In the same vein, Duncan McCargo argues that the bureaucratic polity in Southeast Asia "can be understood as the counterpart or a variation of the Northeast Asian developmental state."[15] There are others who agree with the new Thai Army secretary, the highest administrative position in the force, when he claims the army has "a new face." They point to the army's strict new code for soldiers to stay out of politics, its efforts to get out of business by selling off their enterprises, its cutting of troop numbers, especially at the top by reducing the number of generals, admirals, and air field-marshals—going within a ten year period from more than 1,600 to 1,000—and to the army's role in the peacekeeping force in East Timor. If this professionalization of the military in Thailand comes to pass, it will be a major testament to the positive impact of the economic crisis on political reform in Southeast Asia.

Military participation in politics takes different forms in different countries; Hernandez distinguishes three kinds of roles: control, participation, and influence.[16] Control may mean intervention by an openly military junta or with a front of civilian "partners," as in Indonesia between 1965 and 1998, Thailand between 1932 and 1992, South Korea between 1964 and 1988, and Myanmar since 1962. Or the military may play a participatory role in a "dual-power" relationship where both military and civilian leaders are decision makers, the military having an autonomous sphere and a potential veto over the civilians' moves; this seems to be the situation in the Philippines since martial law in 1972 and in the communist governments and Taiwan, whose ruling parties had military origins. In Japan, Singapore, Malaysia, and Brunei, the military has influence on the political leadership, but the distinction between the military and the political role is clear and the military accept that distinction, the senior military officers working through channels to provide expert advice to the political authorities and lobbying for their share of the national budget.

While providing leadership and stability for economic development may help explain some cases of military or civilian authoritarianism, in others a more compelling explanation is the need for "glue" to hold together ethnically divided societies. In the next section we look at three examples of "ethnic" authoritarianism.

"ETHNIC" AUTHORITARIANISM

Ethnic minorities are present even in the homogeneous societies of East Asia (Koreans in Japan, Koreans and other nationalities in China), and overseas Chinese are scattered in larger or smaller proportions throughout Southeast Asia. In Malaysia, Myanmar, Laos, and to a lesser degree in Singapore, deep divisions between communal groups in these heterogeneous societies contribute heavily to the authoritarian character of their governments. In Malaysia, people of Chinese and Indian ancestry constitute over 40 percent of the population; the rest are Malay or non-Malay indigenes in the Borneo states. In Myanmar, a third of the people are minorities (Shan, Karen, Chinese, Mon, Indian, and others) and the rest Burman; the Karen have been waging guerrilla warfare against the government for decades. Laos, as the result of boundaries drawn to suit the purposes of the colonial powers, has some 40 ethnic groups, with the lowland Lao accounting for a little less than half the population; contacts among groups are limited by language, poverty, and the mountainous terrain. Singapore's Chinese are about three-fourths of the total, the rest mainly

Malay and Indian; government policy is to create a "nonracial" Singaporean identity and to ensure minority representation in the legislature.

In this section we will look more closely at Malaysia, Myanmar, and Laos as examples of "ethnic" authoritarianism.

Malaysia

A federation of 13 states incorporating former British territories on the Malay Peninsula (except Singapore) and Sabah and Sarawak on the island of Borneo, Malaysia is a constitutional monarchy. The position of head of state rotates among the sultans of the nine traditional states. The monarch and the state legislatures select members of the upper house of the federal legislature; the lower house is directly elected by the voters, and it chooses the prime minister. Dr. Mahathir bin Mohamad has held that position since 1981. The ruling political group is the Barisan Nasional (National Front), a coalition of the United Malays' National Organization (UMNO), the Malaysian Chinese Association, the Malaysian Indian Congress, and other minor parties. This multiethnic coalition, in which UMNO is dominant, has been in power since independence in 1957. Other parties exist but are weak, except in the states of Sabah and Kelantan.

The Ethnic "Bargain."   The most salient feature of Malaysian politics since independence has been an explicit ethnic bargain between the state bureaucracy dominated by Malays and the private economic sector dominated by the Chinese and Indian minorities. Ethnic tensions between the Malay majority, considered the indigenous population, and the Chinese and Indian minorities, considered "immigrants," dates back to the British colonial policy of keeping the ethnic communities separate geographically and occupationally. Chinese and Indians worked their way into an economically advantaged position while the majority of Malays remained in their traditional occupations of subsistence farming and fishing. At the time of independence, a bargain was struck: In return for granting the "immigrants" the right to become citizens and tacitly accepting their dominance in the economy, the Malays were given control of politics. Their privileged status as the *bumiputra*, or "sons of the soil," is protected in the constitution. Malay is the official language, Islam the state religion, and Malays have preferential treatment in government jobs, business licenses, educational assistance, and landownership.

Ethnic separateness is preserved in communally based political parties and interest groups: the United Malays National Organization (UMNO), the Malaysian Chinese Association, and the Malaysian Indian Congress (MIC). Any advocacy by non-Malays of a nonracial Malaysian identity is considered suspect, particularly by the Malay majority. Malay apprehension in part accounts for the ejection in 1965 of predominantly Chinese Singapore from the Malaysian Federation (which it joined in 1963) after the Singapore majority party campaigned for a "Malaysian Malaysia" policy of multiracialism without special privilege for any group. Even the Communist Party, which from 1948 to 1960 had waged armed struggle against the Malay-privileged federation and continues to exist though fragmented and diminished in support, is predominantly Chinese.

Dr. Mahathir bin Mohamad, prime minister of
Malaysia since 1981.

Sources: United Nations photo 178196/E. Debebe.

Communal Riots, 1969.   The political alliance among the Malaysian Chinese Association (MCA), the Malaysian Indian Congress (MIC), and the senior partner, the United Malays' National Organization (UMNO), under the leadership of Tunku Abdul Rahman, the first prime minister, managed in the main to keep intercommunal strife under control from independence in 1957 until 1969. Elections that year were preceded by particularly acrimonious campaigning by the alliance parties and their opponents. The latter were split among five principal parties, like the Alliance organized along ethnic lines. Three of them stressed communal differences in their platforms: the Pan Malaysian Islamic Party, which felt UMNO had sold out Malay interests to its partners, the MCA, and MIC; the Democratic Action Party, mainly Chinese who rejected MCA as too closely tied to the Malay elite; and the People's Progressive Party, a predominantly Indian party. The other two opposition groups, the radical Malay Partai and the Partai Gerakan Rakyat, nonracial but with a membership mainly of British-educated Chinese and Indian professionals, tried to avoid communal issues and instead focus on corruption in the ruling alliance.

In the election, the opposition won more than half of the popular vote, but because of electoral districting that favored rural constituencies the Alliance kept nearly two-thirds of the seats in parliament. Rioting broke out in the capital, Kuala Lumpur, between Malays and the other ethnic communities and took a serious toll of lives and property, especially among the Chinese and Indians, before being put down by the army. The government suspended parliament, ruling for nearly two years by decree through a National Operations Council. It reasserted Malay political dominance, arresting many of the non-Malay opposition parties' leaders, and put through a constitutional prohibition on public discussion of racially sensitive issues, such as the special position of the Malays.

The New Economic Policy.   Tun Abdul Razak, who became prime minister in 1970, reconstituted the alliance as the National Front, adding by 1973 some of the former opposition parties to its ranks. Recognizing that Malay dominance in politics had not resulted in improved economic status, he reneged on the earlier bargain and inaugurated a New Economic Policy (NEP) of active state intervention to reduce Chinese economic power and to increase *bumiputra* ownership of businesses, as well as raise living standards in rural areas where most Malays live.

In the next decades Malaysia's economic progress moved it into the second tier of NICs, with light manufacturing joining commodity production as a leading generator of wealth. The consequent economic changes brought both social and political repercussions in the form of greater diversity in society beyond the stereotype of rich Chinese versus poor Malay and in the form of challenges to the traditional National Front–UMNO dominance. NEP had the effect of differentiating Malay interests, raising some to the status of small businesspeople, incorporating others into the industrial working class, recruiting some as settlers on state-sponsored farms, allocating agricultural development projects to political allies in the countryside, leaving others behind still in the ranks of the rural poor. Principal beneficiaries of NEP were government officials charged with the establishment of state enterprises, often large-scale joint ventures with foreign investors. These enterprises reduced opportunities for small local entrepreneurs while creating opportunities for officials to line their own pockets and gave this new class of state business leaders a strong voice in the UMNO power structure.

Challenges to UMNO.   Although UMNO remains today as the dominant party in the 14-member, ruling National Front coalition, it has been facing steadily increasing criticism and opposition. There have been two serious challenges to UMNO rule that Mahathir with characteristic boldness and persistence has managed to weather. The first grew out of mounting discontent with the political status quo that began in the 1980s. Civil servants were unhappy over the freezing of their salaries, settlers on state farms wanted title to the land, industrial workers chafed under the prohibition of unionization, environmentalists objected to the rapacious exploitation of natural resources, and support grew for the opposition Pan Malaysian Islamic Party (PAS). To these strands of discontent was added the erosion of Malay loyalty to UMNO, caused by the diversification of Malay economic interests.

All these elements converged in 1987 to split the UMNO into two factions, divided over the prime minister's leadership style and allegations of corruption and "money politics." Mahathir barely escaped being ousted as party president and quickly put in place policies to solidify bourgeois support by privatizing some state enterprises and cracking down on reformists and labor strikes and protests. The dissidents in UMNO who lost the intraparty power struggle broke away in 1989 to form an opposition party, Semangat 46. In the 1990 elections, Semangat 46 allied with two other opposition parties, the multiracial but still predominantly Chinese Democratic Action Party (DAP) and the Islamic PAS. Thus, as one observer put it, "For the first time in Malaysia's electoral history, the ruling Barisan Nasional (national front) was challenged by another Malay-led multiracial opposition that projected itself as a viable alternative to the present government."[17] But despite the fact that the opposition won a third of the seats in the national parliament, the National Front, with about 52 percent of the popular vote, held onto its two-thirds majority.

The second attempt to forge a viable opposition to unseat Mahathir and UMNO arose out of the financial crisis that spread throughout Southeast Asia after the summer of 1997. Mahathir, characteristically unlike other Southeast Asian leaders, went on the offensive, faulting Western capitalists for precipitating the financial crisis by their speculative practices. Following a dispute over Mahathir's plan to adopt capital controls, he fired his deputy and self-appointed successor, Anwar Ibrahim, who was charged on criminal offenses (sodomy and corruption) for which he was later tried and given a six-year jail sentence. Out of the furor that emerged, especially among Malay youth, against Mahathir and the ruthless manner in which he had crushed his political opponent and erstwhile successor, an opposition coalition emerged to contest Mahathir in general elections mandated to occur prior to the spring of 2000.

Rather than wait for the discontent to subside, Mahathir and UMNO embarked on a successful campaign of damage control, appealing especially to Malay university students and relying on the traditional fear of ethnic violence on the part of older Malay voters. What Mahathir may not have known with certainty but certainly banked on was economic recovery, which in fact had made considerable strides by the time of the November 1999 general election. When the vote was tallied, Mahathir and UMNO had demonstrated once again the efficacy of the old UMNO patronage network which, helped by government control of the press, won the National Front its traditional two-thirds majority of parliament for another five years.

For now, UMNO remains the dominant party in the 14-member, ruling National Front coalition and Mahathir will serve his fifth term as prime minister. A number of factors explain UMNO's and in particular Mahathir's staying power. Several have already been mentioned: the economic recovery Mahathir promised and delivered against the advice of most western economists, the well-organized patronage network that UMNO has built up to get out the vote, government control over the press, the charismatic personality and political skills of Mahathir, and the voters' ever-present fear of ethnic conflict tearing the fragile social fabric that holds Malaysia together. Mahathir is seen as a strong leader with both the courage and capacity to effectually stand up against fundamentalist Moslems on the one side and sectarian demands by non-Malay minorities on the other. His authoritarian style of leadership and outspoken criticism of Western goliaths may be controversial but it is also a source of nationalist pride. It has put Malaysia on the map in the same way that Lee Kuanyew did for Singapore, an analogy that has particular resonance for Malays who feel Singapore belittles them.

But there is an unspoken awareness on the part of Mahathir and in public sentiments that he may have reached the end of his prime ministership. Although Mahathir and UMNO retained their two-thirds majority in Malaysia's tenth general elections in 1999, it was largely with the support of the Chinese and Indian voters who form about 38 percent of the population while large numbers of Malays deserted their party to vote for the Islamic party, PAS. UMNO also benefited from its partners in the eastern states of Sabah and Sarawak. Two factors explain UMNO's loss of support from their traditional Malay constituency. One is Mahathir's treatment of his erstwhile chosen successor, Anwar Ibrahim. The other is the changing political landscape brought about by rapid economic growth. To the degree that all Malaysians have participated in the increased standard of living, a greater social and economic pluralism regardless of ethnic identity has evolved in Malaysian society. Accompanying this growth of social and economic pluralism is an accumulating discontent with the closely controlled nature of political life under Mahathir's monopoly of political power. In the context of similar changes throughout the region, Malaysians are developing a significant momentum for Malaysia to move on toward a new, more democratic stage of political development.

In contrast, the Burman majority in Myanmar has had more difficulty in establishing and keeping control of the state against centrifugal forces at work in that country.

Myanmar/Burma

A British colony from 1885 until 1948, Burma (its official name is now Myanmar) has been bedeviled since independence by ideological differences and also by divisions between the Burman majority and Karen, Shan, Kachin, and other ethnic groups. The Anti-Fascist People's Freedom League (AFPFL), which had organized the resistance to Japanese occupation during World War II and successfully pressured the returning British into granting Burma's independence, became the government party, with U Nu as prime minister.

Control of the state by U Nu's secular civilian government was immediately challenged by left factions within AFPFL and by the army, the Communist Party, Buddhist clergy, the Karen National Union, and other groups who wanted local autonomy in a Burma federation. The army, charged with putting down insurrections, became increasingly Burmanized as minority officers and civilians left its ranks to join the insurgents. The government was unable to maintain law and order or to carry out economic development plans. Conditions deteriorated rapidly until 1958 when the civilian government temporarily turned power over to a caretaker military regime to restore order. In 1960, U Nu returned as prime minister, but renewed internal disorder, expressing peasant and minority dissatisfaction with the government, led to a military coup under General Ne Win in March 1962. Unable to engender a viable political order for Burma, the 14-year-old experiment with democracy culminated in military rule.

Exercising state power through a Revolutionary Council, the military sought but failed to gain the cooperation of civilian political leaders. The council then formed its own political party, the Burma Socialist Program Party (BSPP, or Lansin Party), and consolidated control by rejecting the minorities' demand for political autonomy and repressing all political opposition. Policies to improve the lot of the peasants were instituted, and BSPP party membership was expanded because it provided a vehicle for obtaining government employment. But nationalization failed to ignite economic growth, and in 1974 a new constitution was adopted that reverted land to private ownership and replaced local governments run by military commanders with elected People's Councils run by BSPP members. Formally re-named the Socialist Republic of the Union of Burma, the country was a socialist one-party state under the sole leadership of the BSPP. By 1981, BSPP had 1.5 million members, about 5 percent of the total population.

Burma's policy of self-imposed isolation and the government's inability either to improve economic conditions or to resolve the insurrections of ethnic minorities and political opponents left the military in a political quagmire. Students without prospects of employment, workers seeking higher wages, and dissident army officers all wanted to oust the leadership. In 1981 the army, by its own account, fought four major and 11 minor armed opposition groups, both ethnic and communist. The breaking point came in 1988 when brutal military suppression of student demonstrations provoked a widespread hostile reaction which led to General Ne Win's retirement from official position and the resumption of direct military rule in a reconstituted leadership body known as the State Law and Order Restoration Council (SLORC). With a new National Unity Party to replace the discredited BSPP, SLORC abandoned the socialist rhetoric, changed Burma's name to Myanmar, and began to encourage foreign investments and a free-market economy while assuring itself of income by asserting its right to a share in the profits of the drug trafficking between Myanmar and its neighbors, China and Thailand.

In an apparent attempt to break out of the destructive circle of self-imposed isolation, SLORC organized a general election for the national legislature in May 1990. Despite the restrictions on voting in a number of minority areas said to be under heavy security threat, several hundred parties sponsored candidates for the People's Assembly. The result was an overwhelming victory for the leading opposition party, the National League for Democracy (NLD), which received 80 percent of the seats, vastly outnumbering the government-backed National Unity Party. SLORC never allowed the assembly to convene; instead, many members of the NLD were arrested while others fled into exile. The league's General-Secretary Aung San Suu Kyi, daughter of the leader of the Burmese independence movement, was kept under house arrest for six years and prevented from going abroad to accept the Nobel Peace Prize awarded her in 1991.

Faced with many challenges—from pro-democracy forces, from the fragmented communist guerrilla movement, from Karen and other minority separatist forces, from Bangladesh to protect the rights of the Moslem minority, and from a broad array of international pressures to end the Burmese civil war—the military government in 1992 moved to strike some form of bargain with its ethnic opponents. Rather than negotiating with the Democratic Alliance of Burma, the front organization of ethnic and other political opposition groups, SLORC chose to negotiate with each of them separately. Cease-fires were reached with the Shan, Wa, Pa-O, and Palaung rebel armies, with the four communist insurgent forces, and in late 1993 with the Kachin Independence Army. Peace talks began early in 1994 between SLORC and the Karens, Karenni, and Mons leaders, against the opposition of Burma pro-democracy activists whose bases of operations up to then had been in minority-controlled areas of the country.

Burmese Prime Minister Than Shwe at the National Holiday
Golden Jubilee.
Source:
D. Aubert/Corbis Sygma.

Over the past decade, the military junta has reached cease-fire agreements
with over two dozen ethnic rebel armies, permitting them to engage in any kind of
business (including opium production) as long as they refrain from fighting the government's forces. The SLORC strategy of offering separate deals to each of the various ethnic groups has precluded coordinated actions among its various geographically dispersed opponents. By defeating or marginalizing ethnic resistance against
the regime, SLORC has strengthened its hand against the pro-democracy opposition led by Aung San Suu Kyi in the towns and cities of Myanmar's heartland. Not
only has the military been able to concentrate its efforts against the pro-democracy
NLD by withdrawing from frontier areas, it has also expanded its forces both in
numbers and weaponry as a result of trade with China.

On November 15, 1997, the authorities announced that SLORC—the 21 generals who had ruled since 1988—had been disbanded, 14 of the officers pensioned
off and several placed under temporary house arrest on charges of corruption. In
what has been dubbed "a quiet coup," a new 19-member leadership body called the
State Peace and Development Council (SPDC) took its place. The chairman of
SPDC, General Than Shwe, is also prime minister and minister of defense but he is
the only SPDC member to hold cabinet office. Lieutenant-General Khin Nyunt, reported to be the strongman of the junta, is chief of military intelligence and heads a
think tank called the Office of Strategic Services (OSS), which brings together the
best educated among the new generation of Myanmar's army officers to provide information to the junta, to establish links with intelligence groups in Thailand,
Malaysia, Indonesia, China and Pakistan, and to advise the Foreign Ministry on
Myanmar's relations with its neighbors. The OSS has become influential in a wide

area of policymaking, from ethnic affairs and the country's drug policy to mapping out economic policies and hiring two Washington lobbying firms—Bain & Associates and Jefferson Waterman International—to improve the junta's image abroad.

To sustain the momentum of the democratic movement, Aung San Suu Kyi called a "people's parliament," made up of the winners of the 1990 election, to convene in Yangon in mid-1998. The military's response was immediate and forceful: students were arrested and an estimated 800 elected NLD parliamentarians and other organizers were rounded up for questioning and "accommodation in government guest houses." The military would not brook opposition. By the following year, when a mass uprising was widely anticipated on the auspicious date of September 9, 1999, none materialized. Utilizing more sophisticated techniques, the military has effectively stymied the NLD from either strengthening party organization or furthering its cause of democracy. Because of Aung San Suu Kyi's stature and reputation, NLD leadership is still able to mobilize international sentiment but cannot translate that into effective opposition on the ground.

To date, the military regime of Myanmar has had only limited success in gaining international recognition and opening the country to economic investments. Lieutenant-General Khin Nyunt, Myanmar's strongman, successfully engineered Myanmar's acceptance into the Association of Southeast Asian Nations (ASEAN). But just two months after joining, together with Laos, on July 23, 1997, the entire region was thrown into economic turmoil. Watching the fate of Suharto and the military in the wake of Indonesia's economic recession must have made Myanmar's hard-line military officers wonder if membership in ASEAN may be more of a liability than an economic asset. ASEAN for its part became jittery at the prospect that Myanmar's internal problems would spill over into the region, becoming a problem for ASEAN with its tradition of noninterference in the internal affairs of member states.

The likelihood of regional spillover was precisely the result Myanmar's rulers achieved by pursuing their policy of extricating the military from the wars against Myanmar's ethnic minorities. They left minorities to solve their own problems, virtually consigning them to disaster, deterioration, and desperation. In ending the regime's burden of fighting against a mulitiplicity of ethnic insurrections, Myanmar's military created new problems not merely for its own people but also for the region and the international community. Opium production as well as the number of addicts has escalated sharply in Myanmar's "frontier regions," (areas inhabited by minorities). Hundreds of thousands of people have been driven from their homes in the process of the many years of warfare. In the case of the southwestern Shan state, in particular, many have fled into refugee camps in Thailand, creating problems in the relations between Thailand and Myanmar. Estimates put the number of internally displaced people within the border areas at close to one million. In many cases, the social fabric of entire communities in a region has been destroyed, leaving thousands of children to either join up with the remaining insurgents or wander into neighboring countries.

A number of incidents have highlighted the potential for increased tension in the region as a result of the corner into which Myanmar's rulers have boxed the country. In one incident that occurred in October 1998, Myanmar's Embassy in

Thailand was captured by Burmese dissidents who were later released and escorted by helicopter back into the jungle along the Thai-Burmese border, prompting Myanmar to close its borders with Thailand. In a second incident in January 2000, a group of ten Karen rebels—the ragtag remnants of insurgents who call themselves God's Army took over a hospital in Ratchaburi Province west of Bangkok holding patients and personnel hostage, killing one and wounding others. In this instance the military pursued a hard-line course, killing all ten after a 24-hour stand-off.

All of these incidents serve as reminders that the unresolved problems confronting Myanmar not only impede its own economic progress but easily become regional and international issues.

Laos, to which we now turn, has a similarly diverse ethnic population but a distinctly different set of political circumstances.

Laos

Laotian politics since independence in 1953 has been significantly affected by three factors: (1) lowland Lao constitute only one-half of the country's small and diverse population, which includes more than 40 other ethnic groups living in the uplands and mountainous areas; (2) the development of Lao nationalism has been retarded partially as a consequence of this ethnic mixture, brought together within borders arbitrarily drawn by the French during the colonial period; and (3) foreign influence in Laotian affairs, especially Communist Vietnamese influence, has been marked through ties to Laotian Communists and U.S. political intervention and extensive bombing during the Vietnam War.

From independence until the peaceful takeover by the Communists in 1975, the government (ostensibly a monarchy) was caught up in cold war politics. The United States, in an effort to create a noncommunist regime, supported the rightist faction of Lao princes against the Pathet Lao, which was supported by China and North Vietnam. Two efforts at a coalition government under Prime Minister Souvanna Phouma, who attempted to steer a neutralist foreign policy course, fell apart into factional warfare because neither the United States nor the government of North Vietnam were going to allow Laotian neutrality to interfere with the resolution of their conflict in South Vietnam. As the war in Indochina wound down, Pathet Lao and North Vietnamese military victories mounted, and in 1974 a new coalition, the Provisional Government of National Union, was formed with the Pathet Lao in the dominant position. The provisional government lasted until the end of 1975, when the monarchy was abolished and the People's Democratic Republic was inaugurated in a peaceful transition. In 1988 elections to the National Assembly were held for the first time since the Communists came to power and a new constitution was adopted in 1991, recognizing the leading role of the communist Lao People's Revolutionary Party.

In the early 1990s, economic reforms, stimulated by the loss of financial support from the Soviet Union and Vietnam, opened the way to increased trade and investment, mainly involving Thailand. But opening the door to increased private enterprise and foreign investment brought its own political problems for the ruling Lao People's Revolutionary Party (LPRP). The first, expressed at the sixth congress of the LPRP in March 1996, was the increase in corruption, prostitution, gambling, and drug abuse that accompanied greater liberalization. The second problem was the increased intertribal tensions brought about by resentments that reform had benefited the Lao Loum-dominated lowlands more than minority regions. The third problem involved the sudden and severe impact of the regional economic crisis on the Laotian economy. Although still by and large agrarian, the Laotian *kip* was particularly vulnerable to the collapse of the Thai *baht* because so much of the economic reform in Laos was dependent on foreign investment from Thailand. A plummeting currency, soaring inflation and capital flight were almost immediately registered in the December 1997 elections for the 99-member assembly of Laos.

Although there is only one party, the LPRP, the 99 seats in the national assembly are selected from a list of candidates, all of which have to be approved by the party's mass organization, the Lao Front for National Construction. When the 1997 list was announced, there were 160 competitors, of which only 41 were recognizably "technocratic" in training, like those who had been elected in 1993. The rest of the candidates were party veterans more like those who had ruled in pre-reform days. In selecting from these 160 candidates, the Front gave greater representation to the two smallest of the three broad ethnic groups into which the government divides the Laotian population. As a result, the Lao Loum—Thai-speaking Buddhists of the lowlands who constitute 50 to 60 percent of the 4.8 million people—received 64 of the 99 seats. Another 26 went to Lao Theung tribes, a group representing one-third of the population, mostly those of Mon-Khmer origin, animists, and uplanders. The Lao Song, the 10 percent of the population the Front was most eager to placate, received the remaining nine seats. They are highlanders like the opium-growing Hmongs in the north, suspected by the government of having instigated the violence in late 1997.

In the first session of the newly elected national assembly, held in February 1998, Prime Minister Khantay Siphandone was made the new president, replacing the ailing President Nouhak Phoumsavanh, and Vice President Sisavath Keobounpanh was appointed prime minister. There were two vice–prime ministers, one of whom with a decidedly liberal perspective who had disappeared for a number of years, was also appointed Finance Minister. Choummaly Sayasone was appointed Defense Minister and Somsavat Lensavad became Foreign Minister. In general, the government created in 1998 has pursued a policy quite similar to that in China: they have persisted in promoting economic reform but retain a tight grip on party control of the state.

Next, in recognition that at least in two cases authoritarian regimes have made significant progress in breathing life into their formal democratic constitutions, we look at Japan and South Korea as democratizing political systems.

AUTHORITARIAN PLURALISM AND THE TRANSITION TO DEMOCRACY

In authoritarian pluralist systems, politics is not broadly participatory and competitive. Elections may be held, but who runs the government and sets policy is predetermined by the reality that one group has an effective monopoly on political power. Opposition candidates and parties, where they exist, lack the strength to pose a real challenge to those in power. The "ins" use the "stick" of repressive measures and the "carrot" of positive inducements to keep themselves in power and keep the "outs" out of power. Japan and South Korea as they evolved in the period after World War II, roughly between 1950 and 1993, are examples of authoritarian pluralist systems.

Both Japan and South Korea began their postwar development under U.S. military occupation (the details of which will be covered in Chapter 7). Thus, the United States played an instrumental role in refashioning the political life of these two defeated states. This may be one factor that explains distinct similarities in their postwar political systems. Two other factors are equally important, especially in comparing their current transitions from what we have called authoritarian pluralism to democratic pluralism. One is the 35 years prior to World War II that Korea was a colony of Japan, tightly integrated into the larger Japanese East Asian empire. The second is a profound difference in the U.S. military's conception of its responsibilities as an occupying power in these two countries. The United States viewed its military occupation of Japan in the context of guiding a defeated imperial power in the direction of preventing it from ever waging war again. In Korea, by contrast, the United States viewed its military presence as part of waging a war, the war against communism. These factors constitute the historical backdrop for understanding the similarities and differences in the postwar political development of Japan and South Korea as authoritarian pluralist systems.

Authoritarian Pluralism in Japan

Authoritarian pluralism in Japan has relied principally on the carrot rather than the stick, although the ultimate power of the state is always there to break up unruly demonstrations, for example, and to set limits on permissible dissent. Opponents are allowed to organize, speak, run for election, and serve in the legislature and as local officials. Citizens may join parties and form pressure groups, civil and political rights are protected, the press is reasonably free, the judiciary reasonably independent. Co-optation rather than confrontation is the preferred style. But the paramount position of the dominant party remained effectively unchallenged in Japan until 1993, when the Liberal Democratic Party was driven from office for the first time in 38 years.

The rise of Japan—like the legendary phoenix from the ashes of its own destruction, to become the world's second economic power—is well known, and the government's role in that "miracle" will be analyzed in Chapter 5. What is striking about Japanese politics in the decades from the end of the American occupation in 1952 until mid-1993 is the continuity in leadership provided by the durable coalition of party, government, and business. Except for a brief stretch of Socialist Party government in 1947, the Liberal Democratic Party (LDP) and its predecessors, the Liberal and Democratic Parties, controlled all postwar governments until it lost a vote of confidence in June 1993 and failed to win in the elections that followed in July 1993. A new coalition of parties then took over the government with the LDP in opposition. That coalition disintegrated in June 1994 and the LDP, in an unprecedented alliance with the Social Democratic Party of Japan, returned to power in a new government headed by a socialist prime minister. That improbable partnership lasted until the election in October 1996 when the LDP gained the largest number of votes of all the parties but still short a majority, requiring another coalition. It was this coalition that in the summer of 1997 confronted the financial meltdown of almost the entire region as a result of which Prime Minister Hashimoto resigned and Keizo Obuchi took his place. Keizo Obuchi died suddenly in May 2000 and was succeeded as prime minster by Yoshiro Mori. In June 2000 elections for the lower house of the Diet, the LDP, hung onto a slender majority, the opposition made some gains and over a third of the voters did not vote. It is still too early to predict if and when the chaotic political maneuvering that began in 1993 will lead to a permanent reshaping of Japanese party politics.

We will look first at the period of LDP dominance and at the circumstances that led to its loss of control in 1993, then at the formation and re-formation of coalitions that succeeded the LDP loss of its monopoly on power, during which Japan had five different prime ministers in six years. The section concludes with an analysis of the complex forces in contention at this juncture in Japan's postwar history.

Party-Bureaucracy-Business Collaboration in the Period of LDP Dominance. United in a shared devotion to maximizing their own interests by promoting economic growth, the LDP, the bureaucracy, and big business produced the stability and predictability needed for postwar economic recovery and expansion. In the political or electoral sector, the LDP maintained its dominance without formal legal restrictions on or covert interference with the opposition parties' right to organize and compete for voter approval. The opposition parties included the Social Democratic Party of Japan (SDPJ), the United Social Democratic Party (USDP), the Democratic Socialist Party (DSP), the Komei ("Clean Government") Party, loosely affiliated with a Buddhist sect, Soka Gakkai, and the Japan Communist Party (JCP). The two centrist parties, Komei and DSP, cooperated with the LDP to give it control in the upper House of Councillors when the LDP lost its majority there in 1989.

LDP's share of the popular vote fluctuated and its cohesiveness at times seemed on the verge of being blown away in the heat of ferocious fights between organized factions in the party, loyal to leading members of parliament. But LDP kept voters' support by using pork barrel enticements, by an electoral districting system that overrepresented rural constituents who are staunchly pro-LDP, and by co-opting issues raised by critics (such as environmental deterioration) and adopting programs to correct the problems. But above all, its appeal came from the country's phenomenal economic success, which brought benefits to almost everyone. Also contributing to LDP dominance was the inability of the other parties to form a united opposition and to project to the voters the image of people capable of actually running the government. In the Kabuki drama of politics, they seemed destined to be cast as minor players, never as principal actors.

The LDP's role was to elect members of parliament and to name the prime minister but to leave the initiation of public policy, especially in matters of trade, finance, business, and other economic affairs, in the hands of the highly professional and prestigious bureaucracy, particularly the Ministry of International Trade and Industry (MITI) and the Ministry of Finance. License to formulate policies without legislative and partisan "meddling" allowed the ministries to do long-term planning and to involve big business, especially Keidanren, the Federation of Economic Organizations, in the process of policymaking and implementation. Since government relies more on persuasion than on compulsion to get private sector compliance with its plans, much depended on the maintenance of a working relationship between the bureaucrats and the businesspeople. As its part of the bargain, business provided campaign funds to LDP candidates and positions as corporate managers and members of the board to officials when they decided to retire from public service. The LDP gave legislative approval to the ministry-initiated policies and opened up seats in the Diet for bureaucrats ready for a career change.

For decades, LDP dominance and the three-way collaboration with big business and the bureaucracy survived the tremendous changes that affluence wrought in Japanese society. But the sense of national crisis that had brought them together in the early postwar period had faded, social and economic interests had become more diverse, factional and generational differences within the LDP had begun to weaken it, and campaign financing scandals eroded the party's appeal to voters. An economic recession in the early 1990s precipitated by the bursting of the speculative "real estate bubble" finally ended the political dominance of the LDP as linchpin of the triumvirate. The rash of business bankruptcies, layoffs, and bank failures that drove down the annual economic growth rate from 3 percent to almost zero intensified public reaction to the corruption and scandals that loomed like a black cloud over the fortunes of the LDP.

The Fall of the LDP Government.   All those factors converged in the summer of 1993 to bring down the government, but it was the defection of leading members of the LDP, more than a sudden rise in popularity of the traditional opposition parties, that dealt the final blow. Revelations about the acceptance of millions in illegal campaign funds by Shin Kanemaru, head of the LDP's largest faction, led to demands by voters and within the party for the government of Prime Minister Kiichi Miyazawa to undertake reforms of election-financing laws and of the election-districting system. When Miyazawa failed to act, a number of LDP legislators led by Ichiro Ozawa and Tsutomu Hata voted against him in a no-confidence vote and formed Shinseito (Japan Renewal Party), a new party joining two earlier LDP-breakaway groups, the Japan New Party of Morihiro Hosokawa and the Sakigake (New Party Harbinger) of Masayoshi Takemura.

In the elections called by Miyazawa in July 1993, the LDP failed to win the 256 of 511 seats needed for a majority, although it still held the largest number of seats, 223, plus the support of five independents. This opened the way for the three LDP-defector parties and the centrist Komei to join with the Social Democratic Party of Japan (holding 70 seats, the second largest number) and other socialist parties in a diverse multiparty coalition barely large enough to form a new government. Hosokawa became prime minister, Hata became foreign minister, and Takako Doi of the SDPJ became speaker of the lower house, leaving the LDP and the Communist Party as the opposition.

The Hosokawa and Hata Governments.   Upon taking office in August 1993, the new prime minister faced a formidable array of domestic and foreign policy problems, the key one being to live up to his promise of electoral reform. The initial proposal was to ban cash donations to individual candidates, to require public disclosure of business and organization contributions, and to switch the majority of parliamentary seats from multimember constituencies to single-member districts, redrawing districts to reduce the disproportionate weight given to rural areas. Among opposition party members, the LDP opposed finance reform while some of the Socialists were reluctant to support the creation of single-member districts, which tend to disadvantage smaller parties that have a greater chance of winning seats in proportionally represented multimember districts.

Though the government's reform proposal passed the lower house, it was defeated in the upper house. Forced by lack of unanimous support from his coalition partners, Hosokawa negotiated with the new LDP head, Yohei Kono, to reach a compromise that met LDP objections and allowed passage of a modified reform bill in late January 1994. The total ban on cash contributions was abandoned in favor of a limitation on the amount. The new electoral system combined smaller, single-member, winner-take-all districts to fill 300 of the 500 seats with the remaining 200 elected from larger regional constituencies on the basis of party proportional representation. After the LDP came back into power as the ruling party in 1997, the upper house defied a boycott by the smaller opposition parties to further political reform by reducing from 200 to 180 the districts in the lower house based on proportional representation. In 1994, however, this reform of the electoral districts exhausted Hosokawa's political capital, and his remaining reform agenda to revive the country's sluggish economy and to deal with Japanese–U. S. trade issues was stalemated by policy differences between right and left elements of the governing coalition.

Two events finally led to Hosokawa's resignation in April 1994: (1) his lifting of Japan's long-standing ban on rice imports, which further raised the ire of rural voters, and (2) disclosure of questionable campaign and personal financial dealings, which seemed to make a mockery of political reform. His political ally, Foreign Minister Hata took over as prime minister for a brief stint that was taken up entirely by political maneuvering. By June 1994, he was turned out of office by a surprising coalition of Liberal Democrats and their traditional Socialist opponents, whose leader, Tomiichi Murayama, became prime minister first, to be succeeded by the Liberal Democratic leader, Ryutaro Hashimoto. By 1997, the Liberal Democrats resumed their position as ruling party and by mid-1999 they were in control of the upper house as well.

The Liberal-Democratic Return to Power: Hashimoto and Obuchi.   The general election called by Prime Minister Hashimoto in 1996 came on the heels of a disastrous year (1995) that began with a massive earthquake in the port city of Kobe that killed 5,500 people, leaving more than 300,000 homeless. Three months later, sarin nerve gas was unleashed in a Tokyo subway station, an apparent terrorist attack by a religious cult, Aum Shinrikyo, which killed 12 people and injured more than 5,000. Coupled with a lingering flat economy, popular anxieties concerning the government's capacity to solve Japan's problems resulted in a low voter turnout on October 20, 1996. Although the Liberal Democrats received 239 of the

500 seats in the lower house, returning Hashimoto to the position of prime minister, they failed to get the majority that would have enabled them to rule without a coalition. The Social Democrats lost half their previous 30 seats along with defectors from the party who had joined the new Democratic Party, which received 52 seats in the house. This new LDP-led coalition was pledged to undertake radical reform of Japan's ministries. But before the year was out, Japan found itself in the direct path of the regional economic storm that had its origins in the financial collapse of the Thai baht in the summer of 1997.

By March 1998, the Japanese economy had not only stopped growing, it shrank for the first time in 23 years. Although Hashimoto tried backtracking from his austerity program of seeking budget-deficit reductions to putting together a 16 trillion yen stimulus package to turn the toppling markets around, it was too late to save the LDP from losing its majority in the upper house of parliament in July 1998. Hashimoto's subsequent resignation led to factional disputes within the LDP in a struggle for the position of party president. (This person was automatically certain to become the new prime minister because the LDP still retained its majority in the lower house, which elects the prime minister.) Two of the three candidates vying for the position had the greatest popular support, but the third, Finance Minister Obuchi who was the leader of the biggest faction in the LDP, was assured victory in the race.

A slow but cautious consensus builder, Obuchi managed to stay in power longer (and shorter) than anyone could have predicted. He pursued what he called the "Third Way" to reform—not following the pattern of either the United States or Europe—hoping to retain "the strengths of Japanese-style management . . . while new business practices from abroad are incorporated."[18] The 99 percent of all businesses that are small and medium-sized enterprises in Japan were supported by a 3 trillion yen government loan-guarantee program to minimize bankruptcies. Large Japanese corporations were urged to make unprecedented job cuts, plant shutdowns, and mergers while the government used billions of yen in public works appropriations and bank bailouts to preserve the Japanese system, details of which will be covered in more detail in Chapter 5. But Obuchi's tenure was cut short by a stroke in April 2000 that left him in a coma until his death in May. Unlike the United States where a constitutionally stipulated line of succession exists, in a Cabinet system like Japan's, the choice of a successor has to be "situational" because a cabinet may be a coalition of parties. In Obuchi's situation, Chief Cabinet Secretary Mikio Aoki served as interim Prime Minister until a successor was chosen a few days later. The new prime minister, Yoshiro Mori, was from a rival faction *within* the LDP. New elections for the lower house of the Diet were called for June, the results of which will determine the next prime minister.

The LDP and its leadership were beneficiaries of the economic upturn in the region that occurred in 1999. But what impact this will have on Japan's political restructuring remains to be seen. The problems that continue to haunt Japan's political transition to a leaner, more competitive economic system are dazzlingly complex, involving not only fissures between the old-style parties and the breakaway ex-LDP, ex-Social Democratic, and other reformist parties and within both sets of parties, but also questions about the relationship between the bureaucracy and business and the international role of Japan in the post–cold war. Important policies that in the past had been settled by agreement within the LDP-bureaucracy-business triad are now open for contention and are the subject of a new activism among voters, notably consumer and environmental groups. There are indications of an increasing separation between the business and the political worlds in the direction of those business and consumer advocates that favor reducing government controls over the economy. But politicians who seek greater leverage to modify the conservative fiscal and trade policies promoted by the bureaucrats still face huge hurdles.

In the arena of foreign policy, Japan's postwar reliance on the security treaty with the United States, long denounced by the Socialists who until recently advocated a neutralist foreign policy and the end of American bases in Japan, has shown only small signs of changing under fire from nationalists like Ozawa and the newly elected governor of Tokyo, Shintaro Ishihara. They want the country to take a more active and independent role in global affairs. To offset an increasingly assertive China and an unpredictably belligerent North Korea, Obuchi reaffirmed Japan's commitment to the U.S.-Japan security pact but also demonstrated Japan's intention to pursue an independent foreign policy by meeting with Burma's leaders and indicating a readiness for "constructive engagement."

How Japan will pursue a more active and independent role in global affairs with an unsettled internal political situation will depend to a great degree on whether the electoral reforms adopted under the Hosokawa government are put into effect and how candidates and parties adapt to the changed rules of the election game. The redrawing of electoral districts will give greater clout to urban voters; the reliance on single-member constituencies for 300 of the seats in the lower house will presumably favor the larger parties and encourage consolidation among the smaller ones; changes in campaign financing, if they actually yield the intended results, may affect the influence of special interests in election outcomes, continuing the trend toward reduced business contributions to LDP and its allies since 1993. But who will gain and who will lose as a consequence of these changes is unclear, as is the longer-term question of how quickly or slowly Japan will move away from the authoritarian pluralism of its past toward a more competitive two- or multiparty system.

South Korea: The Long Road to Democracy

As with North Korea, the division of the country and the goal of reunification have been major factors in the politics of South Korea, but the political history of the two Koreas since 1948 has been strikingly different. In contrast to the apparent stability and continuity of the government in the North, southern politics have been marked by instability and conflict. The founding president, Syngman Rhee (1948–1960), resigned from office under popular pressure, and since then presidential succession on three occasions has been determined extraconstitutionally. Coups brought two military men, Park Chung Hee (1964–1979) and Chun Doo Hwan (1981–1987) to the presidency, and Park was removed from office by assassination.

The Republic of Korea has a presidential form of government that, since 1992, has been moving away from authoritarian rule, which characterized previous governments, toward greater democracy. President Kim Young Sam, elected in December 1992 to succeed General Roh Tae Woo, was the first civilian president in over 30 years. An even more decisive break with authoritarian rule occurred in 1997 when longtime dissident leader, Kim Dae Jung, was elected president. This marked the first real change of government since 1948. What is notably different about South Korea's transition from authoritarian to democratic pluralism is that it was not the top-down, elite-initiated process characteristic of the other three "tigers," Taiwan, Hong Kong and Singapore. For this reason and because it raises critical questions about developmental state theory, the following section will outline the dynamic conflict between civil society and the authoritarian state that brought about the transition to greater democracy in South Korea.

Syngman Rhee's Republic.   South Koreans staged a nationwide uprising in October and November 1946 to demonstrate their overwhelming opposition to both the creation of a separate regime in the South and an internationally imposed division between North and South. Despite this popular resistance to establishing a separate South Korean government, the United States designed and promoted the Republic of Korea as an anticommunist state under Syngman Rhee's leadership. "Thus while publicly championing the ideals of democracy, the occupation forces crushed popular democratic demands and helped Syngman Rhee establish autocratic power over a forcibly depoliticized society."[19] A series of revolts in the south followed the creation of the First Republic. The government's response was to expand its police force and to enact the National Security Law that gave the state complete freedom in the use of coercive powers against "subversive" opposition. This began a cyclical pattern of direct, violent conflict between the popular forces in civil society and the authoritarian state in South Korea.

The Rhee regime, though democratic in form, institutionalized the use of coercive power to exterminate its leftist opponents and silence its conservative critics. But it lacked a popular base of support and was widely perceived by South Koreans as a puppet of its U.S. benefactor. The Korean War (1950–1953) decisively changed that by providing the South Korean state with a rationale for its existence. The horrendous devastation and human suffering caused by Koreans at war with one another could only be comprehended as an apocalyptic struggle against evil, the evil in this case was communism. The South Korean government existed as a defense against the evil of communism.

If the Korean War supplied the Rhee regime with an unassailable ideology, it also produced more tangible benefits. The weak institutional framework of government originally designed by the United States was transformed in the course of the war into a powerful bureaucratic organization equipped with a large military force. Financially supported by the United States, the South Korean army had to be maintained in a continual state of military preparedness. The ceasefire, which brought neither peace nor reconciliation, not only guaranteed the continued division of the country but also a climate of fear that became an integral part of South Korea's political culture: fear of communism and of being labeled a communist.[20] So long as the North Korean regime existed, the authoritarian South Korean state had both a reason for existence and the requisite power to sustain itself.

From the Rhee period on, however, the power of government was used against domestic opposition. Peasant and army rebellions in the early years and student-worker demonstrations in the late 1980s and 1990s were forcibly suppressed. Elections were punctuated by demonstrations, violence, and charges of fraud. Legislative vote buying, surveillance by internal security police, control of and pressure on the media and labor unions were employed by the government to tame and undermine opposition. But as the government increased its repression, it also strengthened the commitment of the opposition which grew increasingly sophisticated and militant. The student uprising on April 19, 1960, ignited by Rhee's attempt to prolong his rule through rigged elections, effectively challenged the legitimacy of the Rhee regime, culminating in his fall from power. The democratic government that followed, unable to quell the demonstrations and economic turmoil, barely survived one year before Park Chung Hee assumed power in a bloodless coup. Under his leadership, the military used its coercive might to suppress all opposition and consolidate a stable political base in support of a high-speed pursuit of economic prosperity. A state-fostered program of rapid industrialization made use of foreign capital and relied heavily on a domestic political alliance of civilian bureaucrats, technocrats, and industrialists.

Though Park was acclaimed in Western circles for bringing about a "Korean miracle," his regime was never able to eliminate dissident movements, grass-roots labor protests, and student demonstrations.

Park Chung Hee's Developmental State.   During the 1960s and 1970s, rapid economic growth drastically changed the socioeconomic landscape in South Korea. In a population shift even greater than that which took place during the course of the Korean War, the bulk of South Korea's people migrated to the cities to seek employment, thus accelerating the process of occupational differentiation and the diversification of economic interests. Though denied political expression, these new economic interests formed the social basis for an expanded civil society. Almost in tandem, Park reinforced the coercive apparatus of the state by adopting the Yushun constitution in 1972 by which all semblance of democracy was obliterated from Korean politics. Opposition parties were suppressed, civil rights restricted, the National Assembly's role in politics diminished, effectively denying the wider public any access to the political process. Economic growth required order and stability.

Though students have traditionally played a major role in Korean politics as critics of and mobilizers of demonstrations against government policies, prior to the 1970s their activism had been confined to the campus, precluding any cooperation with labor strikes or opposition parties. Under Yushun rule, however, dissidents began forming a network of groups that included students, intellectuals, urban industrial workers, and a radical wing of the Korean church. By the end of the 1970s, this loose political alliance was joined by two opposition parties that merged in the New Democratic Party under the joint leadership of Kim Dae Jung and Kim Young Sam. The common cause of this broad coalition of forces was to turn South Korea into a democratic state.

When Park's assassination by his own intelligence chief in October 1979 temporarily paralyzed the state and its coercive apparatus, strikes and demonstrations broke out almost immediately. This was a repeat of what had happened in 1960 when President Rhee was toppled, but this time the organized protests were larger in number and broader in scope. On May 17, 1980, the entire population of Kwangju, a city of one million in Cholla province, rose up en masse to protest government policy. The military under General Chun Doo Hwan was responsible for suppressing the uprising. The bloody massacre that followed reinforced the perception that the ruling party, whose members were mostly from Park Hung Chee's home province of Kyongsang, systematically discriminated against Cholla province. Situated in southwestern Korea, Cholla province had also been largely excluded from the program of rapid industrialization under Park Chung Hee.

Chun Doo Hwan assumed state power after the Kwangju rebellion in 1980, forcing the interim president, Choi Kyu Hah, to resign. But by June 1987, he faced a mass campaign for constitutional revision. The urban middle class, disgruntled by government corruption and meddling in business, had joined the students' and dissidents' demands for democratic accountability. The magnitude of the opposition to Chun Doo Hwan provoked a split in the military command between Chun and Roh Tae Woo, who was worried that the mass campaign would end in another Kwangju-like massacre. Unwilling to risk a showdown of such major proportions, Roh Tae Woo reached a compromise with the moderate middle-class supporters of direct presidential elections in return for their abandoning the rest of the movement's (maximalist) objectives—i.e., for economic justice. Chun then bowed to public pressure and agreed to democratic elections, which were held in December 1987. Roh Tae Woo was elected president with only 36 percent of the popular vote and the three opposition parties formed the majority in the National Assembly.

In the first few years of his presidency, Roh Tae Woo made efforts to curb the undemocratic features of Korean politics and promote a more open, competitive system as he had promised in his presidential campaign. By marginalizing the more militant demands of labor and students, Roh was able to contain the conflict, stabilize the political situation, and preserve the advantage of big business (the *chaebols*) over labor while reaping the benefits of being a proponent of democracy. Students, in the meantime, gravitated toward a more fundamental challenge to the regime: reunification. They propagandized a renewed image of North Korea as kin rather than enemy, emphasizing the common bonds of Koreans, North and South, while reproaching the United States for its interference in Korean history for its own purposes. Roh responded to the challenge with another compromise. He issued a Declaration on July 7, 1988 which changed the guidelines for the state's reunification policy, making North Korea a part of one "national community."

A year later, however, under pressure from opposition lawmakers to account for abuses occurring under Chun's leadership, Roh's Sixth Republic began to retreat from its reform agenda. Considering its minority position in the legislature, and an economic downturn that threatened to undermine economic prosperity,[21] the ruling Democratic Justice Party shook up the economic bureaucracy and merged its party with two opposition parties—Kim Young Sam's Reunification Democratic Party and Kim Jong Pil's New Democratic Republican Party—to form the new Democratic Liberal Party (DLP), modeled on Japan's LDP. A shaky coalition at first, the DLP failed to win control of the legislature in the March 1992 elections. But it rallied in the presidential race at the end of the year by running Kim Young Sam, who had run *against* Roh in 1987, as its candidate. His electoral victory, won in a three-man race against Kim Dae Jung of the Democratic Party and Hyundai founder Chung Ju Yung of the new United People's Party, made him the first civilian president in 31 years.

The Democratization Process.   Although there was evidence that intelligence agents and military officers had engaged in clandestine tactics to achieve the DLP electoral victory, when Kim took office he moved ahead with political reform measures. Legislation was passed to curb the Agency for National Security Planning's notorious penchant for activities aimed at stifling political dissent. The judiciary, long accustomed to being under government control, was encouraged to assert its independence and to purge itself of corrupt judges. Widespread political corruption among other officials was a particular target of President Kim's administration; it brought charges against politicians, former military, and businesspeople for tax evasion and bribery and pushed through legislation requiring officials to disclose their financial assets. Most notable among President Kim's targets were former presidents Chun Doo Hwan and Roh Tae Woo. Their successful prosecution and conviction to life sentences for treason and corruption, however, was also the turning point of President Kim's fortunes.

The anti-corruption campaign President Kim had initiated came back to haunt his administration. He had to dismiss his own Defense Minister, Lee Yang Ho, on corruption charges and was himself implicated in obtaining lighter sentences for his party associates than his political opponents received. Political and economic events in 1996 did not help his popularity either. When a North Korean submarine ran aground on South Korean territory, President Kim endorsed expanding defense spending. When the students began street demonstrations in opposition to increased defense spending, President Kim recommended restoring the broad internal investigative powers of the Korean CIA, which he himself had helped to dismantle in 1994. And the economic slowdown that enabled him to get into office in 1992 collapsed under the impact of the regional financial meltdown in the summer of 1997.

In 1996, for the first time in South Korean history two long-time antagonistic political parties had joined forces to dislodge the DLP, which under various names had ruled the country since 1948, from the Blue House (South Korea's "White House"). Kim Dae Jung and his progressive National Congress for New Politics forged a political partnership with Kim Jong Pil and his conservative United Liberal Democrats (ULD), previously a junior partner in Kim Young Sam's government. Kim Dae Jung whose political career began as a student activist frequently jailed for his militant opposition to government policies, thus allied himself with the retired Army general, who as founder of the Korean CIA under Park Chung Hee had arrested the young Kim on one such occasion. This unlikely coalition forged a common program to restructure politics. They pledged to work on a new constitution for the government that would diminish the power of the president, and make the prime minister the effective leader of government. Kim Dae Jung was to rule as president until the year 2000 when the prime minister, to come from the ULD, would take over under the new governmental charter.

Kim Dae Jung's historic victory in December 1997 by a mere 1.4 percent of the vote was quickly overshadowed by the economic calamity which, as it happened, also provided the crucial swing vote against Lee Hoi Chang of the Grand National Party (GNP) that made President Kim's victory possible. His first priority as president was to restructure the private sector, enabling producers to be more competitive in the global economy. Kim Dae Jung referred to the task as "opening Korea a second time," the first having been the opening of the hermit kingdom in the nineteenth century. Even before he was sworn into office in February 1998, President Kim had dispatched a government delegation to New York to discuss a debt-rollover agreement with international banks to halt the plummeting *won*. By September, President Kim had managed to stabilize the exchange rate and replenish South Korea's foreign-exchange reserves. Politically, however, the obstacles were more difficult to overcome. In the National Assembly the previous ruling party still held 171 of the 299 seats, with Kim's new coalition holding only 120 seats. Using the threat of anti-corruption investigations against individual lawmakers, Kim cajoled enough defections to reverse the balance in favor of his coalition.

But the ousted Grand National Party resisted the reform package, refusing to confirm Kim Jong Pil as prime minister on grounds that he had been a leader of Park Chung Hee's army coup in 1961. By the end of 1998, none of President Kim's reform agenda items—restructuring the *chaebols*, laying off workers, reforming the bank sector, among others—had made any progress despite the fact that almost the entire Grand National Party (GNP) was under investigation for a variety of allegations of corruption. In the parliamentary by-elections in July, the GNP had actually gained ground, winning four of the seven seats that were contested. The *chaebols*, however, had begun restructuring on their own, prompting strikes and shut-downs in which workers even won substantial concessions. In the extended strike against the Hyundai Motor Company, for example, workers forced the company to limit job reductions from the proposed 8,000 to 260 workers.

But with a long-time dissident in the Blue House, outrage was now directed at the National Assembly. In the first half of 1999, citizens' groups and other non-governmental organizations (NGOs) began making demands for downsizing parliament. They sought to link MPs pay with performance, to make policymaking more transparent, to increase citizens' participation in policy discussions. There were calls for citizens to nominate candidates (traditionally the bailiwick of party bosses in Seoul), and recall MPs convicted of criminal offenses or of defecting to another party or otherwise committing a breach of trust. In anticipation of legislative elections, more than 400 NGOs joined together in a Citizens' Coalition for General Election 2000 to systematically collect, evaluate, and publicize the background records of hundreds of politicians. They concluded that 299 members of South Korea's legislature—including prominent figures like Kim Jong Pil the recent prime minister and head of the President's minority party in government—should not hold public office. As part of their anticorruption drive, they blacklisted "rejected" and "undesirable" candidates and publicized their status by organizing citizens to send these politicians hundreds of thousands of red and yellow cards to indicate the degree of their disapproval.

For Kim Dae Jung, this pressure for political reform is both welcome and problematical, presenting him with the conflict between satisfying the public's expectations of fundamental democratic political reforms and bolstering his own party's strength against the opposition in parliament. To achieve the latter goal, he must exercise control over the party, particularly in the area of leadership selection. Publicly, however, he applauded the activities of the Citizens' Coalition as well as its campaign for the general election, vowing to take their complaints into consideration in the process of nominating his party's candidates.[22] Although the cycle of conflict between the state and civil society in South Korea will undoubtedly continue, democratic reform has taken a major step forward in the last decade.

South Korean political development in the last half of the twentieth century is quite different than what might be expected from the literature on the developmental state. The dominant theme of developmental state theory suggests that a strong state coincides with a docile and quiescent society apolitically engaged in the pursuit of economic prosperity. Contemporary Korean politics, however, demonstrates that a weak civil society is not necessarily a correlate of a strong state. South Korea as an authoritarian state has generated active and effective grass-roots political participation in shaping the evolution of a modern democratic system. Even under military rule, the government in South Korea has had to take into account the most radical and militant elements of the population, specifically students and industrial workers, both of whom have a history that lends them credibility.

The military that set the stage and made the rules for South Korea's postwar drive to industrialize has been discredited in many peoples' eyes by its past abuses of power. But it has also spawned a worthy adversary capable of sustaining the long-run struggle to democratize. The biggest challenge, that of reunification, lies ahead. The bumps on that road will be covered in Chapter 7. Although Kim Dae Jung has conceded that reunification of Korea is beyond the possibility of achievement in his term of office, he has taken the historic step of meeting with North Korea's Kim Jong Il in June 2000. Acknowledgment of President Kim Dae Jung's contribution to this historic achievement came in October of that year when he was awarded the Nobel Peace Prize, the first such honor for Korea.

The final category of authoritarian pluralist systems we will use in our comparisons of Asian Pacific governments looks at the strength of the state in different countries.

STRONG STATE–WEAK STATE

As with authoritarian and democratic elements of the state, the distinction between strong and weak states is more impressionistic, even subjective, than precisely measurable. But states do differ in their capacity to handle the pressures put on them by the effects of modernization. A strong state has political institutions sufficiently cohesive, flexible, and independent of other forces in society to prevail over challengers to its authority, whether from outside the country (from, for example, multinational corporations and foreign governments) or from inside (for example, from insurgent groups and separatist movements). A weak state lacks that capacity and is therefore liable to manipulation by foreign or domestic forces, or both.[22] Singapore and the Philippines are the examples we have chosen to illustrate this aspect of authoritarian rule.

Strong State: Singapore

Although diminutive (only three times larger than Washington, D.C.), this island ministate located at the juncture of peninsular Malaysia and Indonesia survived incorporation into the Malaysian Federation in 1963 and expulsion in 1965 to become a wealthy commercial, financial, and industrial center. Under the leadership of Lee Kuan Yew's People's Action Party (PAP), which has dominated the government since the beginning, Singapore's "administrative state," as a Singaporean political scientist calls it,[23] has managed to invite foreign investment without becoming its captive, to mute Chinese-Malay antagonisms, to keep the rising middle class quiescent, to control labor unions, and to keep political opponents incapable of challenging PAP's dominance.

The government's success in promoting economic development and maintaining stability and order in a previously volatile multiethnic society has been achieved by the benevolent paternalism of Lee's tightly run political party working through a highly competent and uncorrupted bureaucracy, and by manipulating the institutions of democratic participation by use of rewards for acquiescence and punishment for opposition. The major themes in Singaporean political discourse are three: (1) national interests must always be put ahead of sectoral interest; (2) strength must be planned for in the long-run, not the short-term; (3) and setbacks must be used as opportunities to calmly and quietly forge ahead.

In the social sphere, government has actively tried through media campaigns, integrated housing, and education to create a "Singaporean" identity above the separate ethnic identities of Chinese, Malay, and Indian. Recognizing that the Malays as a group are at a disadvantage in this society committed to the principle and practice of meritocracy, the government has tried to wean at least some Malays away from traditional habits that impede their adaptation to "modern" society. An important aspect of a Singaporean identity is well-being that begins not only with good health and housing but a good education.

In the political sphere, the outward appearance of democracy is preserved. Elections to parliament are held, following brief campaigns in which minor parties run candidates against those of the PAP. The legislature meets and selects the prime minister according to majority rule. But the reality behind the appearance is different. Electoral districts are drawn to perpetuate PAP's success, and opposition leaders are kept under surveillance by internal security police, frequently harassed by such actions as libel suits by government officials, sometimes arrested, and generally neglected by the government-controlled media. One of just two opposition MPs, whose first term was served in 1991, was reelected in the 1997 elections. He survives by avoiding expensive lawsuits and by directing his criticism at government policies rather than government officials. In his words, "I'm a watchdog, not a mad dog." Freedom of speech, the press, and assembly is restricted, and unions are either government controlled or kept under close surveillance. Parliament's role is to rubber-stamp policies coming from the executive, and the real locus of power is in the PAP-dominated bureaucracy.

In addition to political controls, the government's paternalistic intrusions into other aspects of people's lives are notorious and to outsiders seem to go beyond the usual requirements for a civil and modern society. Campaigns are waged to curb such undesired behavior as speeding, smoking, gum-chewing, and failure to flush public toilets, and severe fines are imposed on offenders. In an interview in 1992, Lee (now retired from the prime ministership) attributed the need for such regulations of personal behavior to Singapore's rapid transformation from a poor, slum-ridden backwater village to a modern metropolis with cars, high-rise apartments, and other appurtenances of affluence. Asked about the fines for failure to flush public toilets, he said, "Perhaps the reason why they don't flush is because . . . only day before yesterday they were using a hole in the ground, and it really doesn't matter whether you flush it or you don't. It didn't matter."[24]

In recent years, the government has survived without visible difficulty the transition from its larger-than-life founding prime minister to his successor, Goh Chok Tong, who took the top government post in 1990 and the party secretary-generalship in 1992. Singapore has also weathered the economic storm with its usual aplomb. The government announced that the budget would run a deficit and people had to tighten their belts. Lee Kuan Yew remains very much involved in politics as senior government minister, and recently provoked a great deal of controversy in Malaysia with the publication of the first volume of his memoirs. His son Lee Hsien Loong is deputy prime minister and presumably next in line for the top position. PAP's effective monopoly on power seems unshakable.

Weak State: The Philippines

Philippine politics since independence in 1946 has been heavily influenced by American economic and strategic concerns and dominated by Filipino economic elites. For the first two-and-a-half decades the institutions of representative government laid down in the 1935 constitution were maintained, and two major parties, both essentially creations of the wealthy, competed for office. Behind the appearance of Western-style liberal democracy, the political-economic oligarchy controlled not only the political parties but the legislature, the bureaucracy, and elections by the power of money and, where required, by their private armies as well as the military and police. The Filipino state was kept weak and incapable of responding positively to the rising demands of the masses in the cities and the countryside, though not so feeble that it would be unable to serve elite purposes.

While the connection between wealth and political influence is not unique to the Philippines, income and property ownership and consequently political power are highly concentrated in the upper and upper-middle classes, which are estimated to constitute about 10 percent of the population.[25] Elite control of politics was reinforced by the persistence of traditional patron-client relations, which in precolonial times filled the gap left by the absence of a unified state. The pattern of reciprocal trust and obligation between patron and client served as the model for political parties and leaders. Votes, jobs in government, favoritism in getting licenses and gov-

Goh Chok Tong, who succeeded Lee Kuan Yew as
prime minister of Singapore in 1990.

Source: Photo from the Prime Minister's Office, Singapore.

ernment contracts were all part of the "currency" exchanged, seen as honorable fulfillment of one's obligations rather than flagrant corruption.

Family ties are important among the rich, whose wealth often came from
landownership but who after World War II went into industry and commerce. Kinship networks mute the phenomenon found in other developing countries of conflict between the export agricultural sector tied to and dependent on the world economic system and the emerging "national bourgeoisie." Although tensions between
the two have surfaced over trade and foreign investment policy issues, they have
closed ranks when mass mobilization under the banner of reform or revolution appeared to threaten their privileged economic and political position. This was the situation on the eve of martial law in 1972.

With the support of most of the elite and the military, who had lost confidence
in constitutional government's ability to preserve order against rising demands for
social and political change, President Ferdinand Marcos imposed martial law that
year and remained in office beyond the constitutional limit of two four-year terms.
He dissolved congress, suspended elections, intimidated the press, and cowed his
opponents, relying increasingly on the military, whom he rewarded with appointments to government posts and expanded scope for the practice of violence against
insurgents and dissidents (including the assassination of his leading opponent, Be-
nigno Aquino Jr.).

Domestic and international criticism of Marcos's government gathered momentum in the early 1980s. The mainly middle-class reformist opposition gained mass support after Aquino's death and the Roman Catholic Church under the leadership of Jaime Cardinal Sin lent its influence to the reformist cause. Even worse for Marcos, his base of support in the business community and the armed forces began to erode. Disenchantment among one-time Marcos boosters accelerated as his declining health raised unsettling questions about a potential succession struggle. The destabilizing effects on the economy of such a crisis were feared both by international investors and domestic economic interests, as well as by the technocrats brought into government to promote development. Fissures appeared between the old oligarchy and the newly rich Marcos cronies, between the cronies and the technocrats, between the military and the civilian bureaucracy, and within the military between the Reform the Armed Forces Movement (RAM) group of graduates of the Philippine Military Academy and other officers. Worsening economic conditions adversely affected the business community, farmers, and workers, and contributed to growing support for the radical New People's Army, despite counterinsurgency campaigns against it.

When Marcos ran for reelection in 1986, he was challenged by Aquino's widow, backed by a united opposition. The president's claim to have won was denounced as fraudulent, and the defection of some of the military, combined with mass demonstrations of support for Corazon Aquino on the streets of Manila, brought her into office.

The triumph of Aquino's People Power Revolution over Marcos's authoritarianism did not signal the inauguration of a new, truly democratic order. Instead, the traditional elites (of which she is a member) continued to control the political processes and the use of repression against those who would challenge the status quo, as evidenced by the outcome of land-reform efforts and the record on human rights during the Aquino period. Her agrarian reform program was delayed, whittled down in the legislature, and hampered in implementation by opposition from sugar plantation and mill owners. And despite efforts of the Aquino government to curb them, human rights abuses continued because the Philippine state is too weak to prevail over challenges to its authority from the elites who resist efforts to ameliorate the grinding poverty in which most Filipinos live.

Another factor was military resistance to civilian efforts to curb their operational autonomy and put limits on their extraconstitutional techniques for combating insurgents and other politically suspect individuals and groups. The pro-reform group within the military (RAM) was behind six coup attempts against Aquino's government and sabotaged efforts to negotiate an end to the insurgency of the Communist Party's New People's Army and to accommodate the demands for autonomy of the Mindanao-based Moslem Moro National Liberation Front. Furthermore, the antigovernment insurgents were themselves guilty of abuses and by their very existence created a climate in which violations of rights appear to some to be justified.[26]

The significance of Aquino's years as president is assessed by one observer in these words:

In the end, the transition from authoritarian rule in the Philippines ushered in a political restoration, rather than a revolution.... There has been
a return to a brand of democratic governance characterized by weak parties, factionalism based primarily on personalities rather than ideology,
and the dominance of the traditional, provincial elites. Important elements
of the military have resisted a return to a less political role and a nationwide insurgent movement continues to threaten the foundations of the
Philippine state.[27]

These problems were inherited by Aquino's successor, retired General Fidel
Ramos, who took office in June 1992. A West Point graduate, former head of the
constabulary, armed forces chief of staff, and defense secretary, Ramos was elected
by less than a quarter of the votes in a contest against candidates of six other parties. His own party, Lakas-NUCD, with the help of allies elected by other parties,
had a majority in the lower house of the legislature, but the senate was controlled
by the LDP, the party of traditional provincial politicians. So Ramos's power base,
like the state itself, was weak.

Ramos undertook some initiatives toward reconciliation with the rebel military and the Communist and Moslem insurgents. Amnesty for political crimes was
offered and talks with the Moro Islamic Liberation Front (MILF) culminated in an
agreement early in 1994 to give more autonomy to Moslem provinces on the islands
of Mindanao and Palawan. In the economic sphere, Ramos launched an "anti-
monopoly" campaign in 1993 to dislodge certain Marcos cronies from controlling
interest in several corporations and replacing them with directors favorable to the
government. A Protestant, Ramos also challenged the church hierarchy by supporting family planning aimed at curbing the high population growth that adds to the
country's deep economic problems.

Perhaps the best news about the Philippines' enduring economic difficulties,
which were exacerbated by a crushing foreign debt, and the effects of natural disasters, was that its economy was not as devastated by the regional economic crisis as
the high-growth performers among Asian Pacific countries. Although the stock
market and the value of the peso dropped sharply in the fall of 1997, the usual
Christmas increase in overseas workers' remittances and $500 million in loans from
the IMF, World Bank, and Asian Development Bank buffered the fall. The bad
news about the Philippine economy is its perennial economic sluggishness and foreign indebtedness, aggravated by corruption, a bloated bureaucracy, weak political
parties, and an oligarchy unwilling to risk its privileged position by accepting state
action to get at the roots of poverty. All these factors contribute to the continued
weakness of the Philippine state.

Although the state remains weak, it is taking decisive strides toward greater
democracy. In 1998, Fidel Ramos gave up his plans to seek a constitutional amendment enabling him to serve a second term. He supported Jose de Venecia as his
party's presidential candidate but Venecia, along with five other even less successful presidential aspirants, came in a distant second to Joseph Estrada, a popular
movie star in the 1960s and 1970s who had gone on to serve for 16 years as mayor

of San Juan township in greater Manila. Opposed by the establishment elite, Estrada appealed to the masses of ordinary Filipinos as a champion of their cause. He surrounded himself with supporters from the entire political spectrum, which helped him gain a slim majority in the Senate, with the assistance of three independent senators.

When he came into office, Estrada removed the military men his predecessor had placed in key government offices and corporations, and appointed an eclectic cabinet which included representatives of big business in the departments of Finance and Trade and Industry, academics in the departments of the Budget and Economic Planning and social activists in the departments of Agrarian Reform and Energy. Besides civilianizing the government, Estrada brought a change of leadership style to the presidency. Befitting both a movie star and a political populist, Estrada's performance is continuously being monitored by ratings. His popularity among the business community was high when he resolved the labor disputes between Philippine Airlines (PAL) and PAL unions; Estrada was seen as resisting both the demands of strikers and legislative advocates for a government takeover of the financially ailing airlines. From his populist constituency, however, he won kudos for patriotism; they saw him safeguarding the airlines for the sake of national pride. For PAL's owner, Lucio Tan, Estrada was repaying a debt; Lucio Tan had financially supported Estrada's presidential campaign; he was also a former Marcos supporter.

By September 1999, however, Estrada's ratings fell sharply. Having run for office on an anticorruption plank that promised to return government to the people, Estrada was increasingly perceived as merely substituting his own "cronies" for those of Ramos and Aquino, the Marcos family most notably among them. Two of Marcos' children were among the substantial number of politicians' offspring gaining elective office in 1998. Moreover, Chinese-Filipino businessmen were suspected of receiving lucrative government contracts in return for their support. Estrada's populist constituency accused him of forsaking his poverty program, the business community was frustrated by his inability to promote greater economic growth and most Filipinos were opposed to his promoting a constitutional amendment that would permit foreign ownership of land and utility companies. The one area in which the president could claim a measure of success was in challenging the Moro Islamic Liberation Front to end their armed insurgency and taking a forceful position against the communist insurgents.

With several years of his presidential term ahead of him, President Estrada is trying to confront these criticisms. He has dropped his advocacy of the highly contentious constitutional amendment, fired a number of his appointees, and announced specific resolutions for furthering economic reform. Instrumental in assisting the president in achieving his objectives has been his vice president, Gloria Macapagal-Arroyo—a member of the opposition Lakas Party and the daughter of the late President Diosdado Macapagal. With a Ph.D. in economics and impressive political skills, the vice president has earned the respect of both the business community and the populist constituency that catapulted Estrada to power. Above all, her loyalty to President Estrada displays the political acumen that may place Vice President Gloria Macapagal-Arroyo in the position of heir apparent to the presidency.

THE SPECIAL CASE OF CAMBODIA

The weakest of all Asian Pacific states is Cambodia. Fought over by Thailand and Vietnam before being taken over by the French, Cambodia, after independence, became a battlefield for global contestants in the cold war. When the cold war ended, Cambodia was finally abandoned for the Cambodians to fight over, with interested participation of their neighbors, Vietnam and Thailand. In 1993, amidst a civil war between the Kingdom of Cambodia and Khmer Rouge (KR) insurgents, a UN-sponsored election set the stage for a compromise merger between the Cambodia People's Party's (CPP) state apparatus and the United Front for an Independent, Neutral and Free Cambodia (FUNCINPEC), the royalist political organization that had waged war against it for years. In 2000, following another internationally supervised election in 1998, the same two party organizations are still attempting to consolidate the sovereign state of Cambodia.

Like its neighbors in other parts of what was French Indochina, Cambodia's political history since independence in 1953 has been greatly influenced by external actors, especially communist Vietnam, Thailand, the United States, and China. Like Laos and in contrast to Vietnam, the end of French colonialism came relatively peacefully for Cambodia, but since then its fate has been extremely troubled; in the course of one tumultuous decade its government underwent four abrupt changes.

Sihanouk to Lon Nol

From 1953 to 1970, Cambodia was a constitutional monarchy under Prince Norodom Sihanouk, who in 1955 abdicated the throne to become prime minister. Sihanouk pursued a foreign policy of nonalignment, accepting aid from both East and West, trying to foster national unity and maintain the country's independence by accommodation with China and North Vietnam as counterweights to Cambodia's historical enemies, Thailand and South Vietnam, then allied with and armed by the United States.

The Sihanouk government gradually lost support of the civil service, the middle class, and, most important, the army, which objected to Sihanouk's toleration of the presence of Vietnamese Communist forces on Cambodian territory. In 1970 a rightist military group overthrew him, abolished the monarchy, and put in power the U.S.-backed anticommunist Marshal Lon Nol. Spillover into Cambodia from both sides in the war in Vietnam brought heavy American bombing and invasion by ground forces to root out the Vietnamese enemy. The consequences were severe economic disruption, corruption stimulated by massive American aid to the Lon Nol government, and an increase in popular support for the antigovernment communist insurgent Khmer Rouge, backed by China.

Pol Pot to Hun Sen

The Khmer Rouge in turn ousted Lon Nol in 1975 and established Democratic Kampuchea, led by Pol Pot. During the next four years the Khmer Rouge government pushed through radical measures to reorganize society, hunting down foreign-educated people to eradicate foreign influences, abolishing private property and communizing the peasants, forcibly depopulating the cities to which many had fled to escape the bombings and civil war in the countryside, and attempting to eliminate religious institutions through attacks on the Buddhist clergy. More than a million of the country's five million people are estimated to have died as a result of these government actions.

Not only did Pol Pot's government turn on its own people, but it turned against its neighbors and historical enemies, the Vietnamese, refusing to negotiate a dispute over territory along their common border. Charging provocation, the Vietnamese, supported by the Soviet Union, invaded in December 1978 to remove Pol Pot and put a more moderate ex–Khmer Rouge group of Communists in his place. The ousted Khmer Rouge, led by Pol Pot and Khieu Samphan and supported by the Chinese, remained an active force, in effective control of areas along the Thai border and carrying on insurgent operations against the Vietnamese-sponsored government in Phnom Penh.

Renamed the People's Republic of Kampuchea and later the State of Cambodia, that government was led by the People's Revolutionary Party (now the Cambodian People's Party) with Hun Sen as prime minister and Heng Samrin as president. Facing almost unanimous international condemnation as a puppet of the Vietnamese, whose troops remained until 1989, the government's legitimacy was challenged internally by the Khmer Rouge and by two Western-supported noncommunist insurgent groups, one headed by Sihanouk and the other by Son Sann, all three of them in 1982 forming a coalition government-in-exile. Finally in 1991, the outside backers of the various Cambodian political groups decided it was in their interest to push for some sort of accommodation. The opposition groups and the government agreed to a cease-fire, to transitional arrangements leading to elections in 1993, and to a new government able to restore peace to this troubled land.

A Period of Transitional Authority

Under a transitional agreement, the United Nations Transitional Authority in Cambodia (UNTAC), with some 22,000 military and civilian personnel, monitored the cease-fire and tried with only limited success to arrange for the partial disarmament of the insurgent forces and the State of Cambodia (SOC) army. Taking over temporary responsibility for running five key government ministries, UNTAC made preparations for the election of a national assembly, registering voters and arranging for repatriation of Cambodians from refugee camps along the Thai border. A Cambodian consultative group, the Supreme National Council, was set up with six representatives from SOC and two from each of the three oppositional groups; Sihanouk, veteran politician and durable symbol of national unity, was chosen president. Contending that SOC control of the army and the bureaucracy would give it an advantage in the elections, the Khmer Rouge refused to participate. UNTAC decided to go ahead without them.

Election and the New Government

The election was held under close UN supervision in May 1993, the Cambodian People's Party coming in second with 38 percent of the vote behind Prince

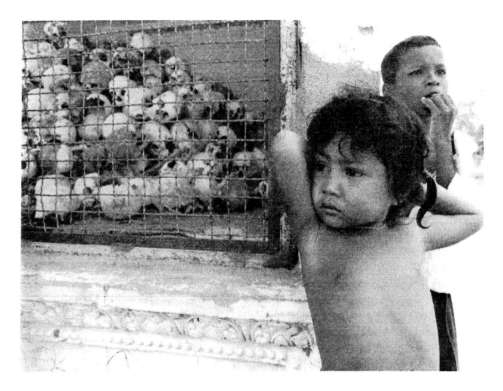

Children play near the memorial at Choeung Ek where bones of Cambodians executed by the Pol Pot government are displayed.

Source: United Nations photo 159733/J. Isaac.

Norodom Ranariddh's FUNCINPEC, which won 46 percent. The assembly met and drew up a new constitution, restoring a constitutional monarchy with Sihanouk as king. Compromise between Sihanouk's son Ranariddh and Hun Sen led to an unusual power-sharing arrangement, under which the prince became first prime minister and Hun Sen, the Vietnam-backed ex-Khmer Rouge commander, second prime minister, serving together as coministers of defense, interior, and public security with the other ministries divided between the two parties. Its mission accomplished, UNTAC departed.

The government attempted but failed to eliminate the Khmer Rouge on the battlefield while the KR, for its part, resisted power-sharing. Legislation was passed by parliament in 1994 outlawing the KR, after which an increasing number of top KR leaders led mass defections in return for pardon or amnesty for themselves. But relations between the two coalition partners deteriorated, abetted by the prolonged absence for health reasons of King Sihanouk, who had provided a tenuous bridge between them. With the national army, police, provincial heads, and much of the bureaucracy under Cambodian People's Party (CPP) control, Hun Sen seized control of the government in 1997 forcing Prince Ranariddh into exile and prompting international condemnation, especially by the United States, which suspended all project aid. With bloody street battles between the royalists and Hun Sen's troops and the onset of financial meltdown in the region, the Japanese intervened to broker a peace plan that would enable Ranariddh to return and pull together his shattered party for new internationally sponsored national elections to be held on July 26, 1998.

Thirty-nine political parties registered candidates to run for 122 national assembly seats in the July 1998 election, but the campaign boiled down to a three-cornered contest between CPP, FUNCINPEC, and the Sam Rainsy Party. Though the opposition parties disputed the outcome and some members of the international community were skeptical, CPP was said to have won 64 seats with 41.4 percent of the vote, while 43 seats with 31.7 percent of the vote went to FUNCINPEC and 15 seats with 14.3 percent of the vote went to the Sam Rainsy Party. While France and Thailand urged all parties to accept the election results, violence broke out again in Cambodia with incidents of Vietnamese being targeted and recriminations all around. By the end of the year, an agreement was reached between the two main political parties for Prime Minister Hun Sen to assume leadership of a coalition government. The CPP would be in charge of finance, industry, commerce, agriculture, planning, public works, and foreign affairs ministries while FUNCINPEC party members would head the ministries of justice, tourism, information, health, rural development, and education. Sam Rainsy who had gone into self-imposed exile was left out of the coalition.

With the Khmer Rouge decimated and several of its leaders living freely in Cambodia,[28] a single state appears to be in control of the entire country for the first time. But old political conflicts remain just beneath the surface of the fragile peace. Large areas of northern and northwestern Cambodia are still strongholds of Khmer Rouge support and thousands of soldiers are still loyal to the cause, even though their leaders have defected. This also may be why Prime Minister Hun Sen resists demands for an international tribunal to try Khmer Rouge leaders on charges of crimes against humanity. The dilemma for Cambodia is how to restore international confidence in the viability of the regime so it can get on with the economic development of the country. Holding public trials, especially in an international forum, threatens to reopen wounds that could easily shatter the delicate national reconciliation that is still more of a hope than a reality.

Having looked at manifestations of authoritarianism in each of the countries, we are now ready in the concluding section of this chapter to offer some explanation for the persistence of authoritarianism and to speculate on the prospects for democracy in the Asian Pacific.

WHY AUTHORITARIANISM? IS THE TREND TOWARD DEMOCRACY?

To people who expected and hoped that liberal democracy would take root in the Asian Pacific after independence and create the conditions of stability and free choice considered necessary for rapid economic and social development, the record thus far is disappointing. To others who expected that Marxist socialist democracy would be the chosen route to liberation from colonialism and to rapid development under a centrally planned command economy, the record is equally disappointing.

Liberal democracy has been short-lived and where tried did not produce much economic progress. Instead, those countries where economic progress has been most remarkable have had authoritarian political systems, and government has played a much more intrusive role in the economy than expected. In countries where Marxists have come to power, the record in economic development has been considerably less spectacular than hoped for, at least until economic "reforms" began to depart from the orthodoxy of central planning and allow market forces in some sections of the economy to drive growth. There has not yet, however, been a comparable loosening of Communist Party political control.

What accounts for the persistence of authoritarianism in these countries? One explanation is that the attitudes toward authority and patterns of relationships between the ruler and the ruled that existed in the traditional precolonial societies are still powerful influences. In them the norm was a hierarchical social order, presided over by a monarch or a village chief, who was expected to take responsibility for the well-being of his subjects; they in turn owed him obedience and respect for his exalted status. Such norms are clearly not compatible with the modern democratic notions of the accountability of rulers to the ruled and the ruled's right and even responsibility to participate in the selection of rulers and in making policy choices.

Another explanation is that the experience of colonial rule further reinforced the traditions of the precolonial political order. Rather than effectively shouldering the "white man's burden" of preparing the subject peoples for the responsibilities of self-government, colonialism not only encouraged the pattern of "top-down" rule by an alien bureaucracy unaccountable to those governed, but in some colonies propped up local sultans, kings, and emperors as convenient instruments for indirect rule. In some cases, the imperial power made efforts, usually modest and belated, to indigenize the bureaucracy and to involve a select segment of the colonials in appointive or elective positions. But this was far from providing experience in running a modern nation-state. Another legacy of colonial rule that has created a further impediment to democracy was the differential treatment of various national or ethnic groups that created or exacerbated intercommunal hostility and retarded the development of a sense of *national* identity.

Another explanation for authoritarianism is that it is better suited than liberal democracy for handling the difficult transition from a traditional economic and social order to a modern dynamic economy and society. Rather than relying on the invisible hand of the free market to allocate capital and human resources for economic development, it is argued, in the early stages at least government must provide the leadership and coherent view of the course of action the nation needs to take to launch it on the road to a productive modern industrial economy.

In a curious way, both the modernization theorists and the Marxist practitioners in China and the Soviet Union have similarly repudiated the views of their intellectual progenitors. The former, inspired largely by the experience of Japan and the NICs, have departed from the theories of Adam Smith, recognizing the necessity of authoritarian governments in the early stages of economic development. The Marxist practitioners in communist states have diverged from Karl Marx, whose position was that capitalism is well suited for making the painful transition from feudalism to industrialism and expanding the society's productive capacity to the point where it can provide the affluence needed for an egalitarian socialist democracy. Rather than wait through the capitalist accumulation process, Lenin, Mao, and other Communist revolutionaries decided not to let pass the opportunity to seize power, and assigned to the Communist Party as trustees for the working class the job of handling the transition from feudalism to industrialism and then to socialism. At that point, according to Lenin, the need for the state as the instrument of the ruling class would vanish and the state itself would wither away.

Of course, as Lenin pointed out and as world system theorists emphasize, the transition to socialism and a stateless society is likely to be delayed, and the need for dictatorial rule continued, by the persistent opposition of international capitalism with its imperialist designs on the rest of the world. Another curious change in communist practice has come in recent years with the introduction of market-oriented policies, reducing the role of government as the sole manager of the economy; this might be interpreted as at least a partial return to the original view of Marx about capitalism's unique capacity for laying the foundation of a modern economy. By whatever route they use to reach it, most observers and practitioners of modernization and development seem to agree that authoritarianism in some degree is either desirable or unavoidable to achieve the conditions of rapid economic growth.

What are the prospects for "democratization" in these authoritarian regimes? One commonly held view is that economic development itself sets in motion social and political changes that lead to demands for more popular control over government. Affluence, diversification of economic interests, education, and the rise of a middle class are all thought to contribute to the trend toward democratization.

But if affluence, or at least progress toward it, is provided by the authoritarian state, why would its beneficiaries want to rock the boat by demanding political change, the initial effect of which is bound to be destabilizing? That runs the risk of killing the goose that lays the golden eggs. And diversification of economic interests from a predominantly agricultural base to a variety of industrial, commercial, and service industries does not necessarily produce political pluralism manifested in parties and pressure groups speaking for those interests. Nor is a growing middle class necessarily an agent of political change.[29] Its potential for challenging the authoritarian status quo is limited in many Asian Pacific countries by its dependence on the state for employment; it is rarely an autonomous class like the property-owning bourgeoisie that pushed through political reforms in Western Europe.

Another view is that, however modest the capacity for and commitment to democratization and however necessary authoritarianism may be to launch economic development, at some point preservation of the status quo becomes an impediment to continued economic advancement; democratic change, however unsettling its initial effects, is a necessity for the long-term stability and legitimacy of the political order.

Others, world system theorists included, are less sanguine about the prospects for democratization, because governments responsive to popular pressure might embark on economic reform programs threatening to powerful domestic and foreign interests, which would by overt or covert means engineer a reversal of the democratic trend, if they allowed it to get underway at all. Even a country that be-

comes strong enough and determined enough to break out of neocolonial subordination to outside influences is in this view likely to need an authoritarian political
system to accomplish this feat and successfully resist pressures to restore the old
relationship.

Another perspective on the "democratization" issue raises the question of
whether the Western vision of what democracy is might be too ethnocentric, constrained by European political philosophers and institutions and practices that grew
out of Graeco-Roman traditions. It is certainly possible to consider that the different cultural grounds of Asia might produce new and different forms of political participation, whether hybrids springing from the contact between indigenous and outside traditions or uniquely Asian varieties.

It is probably too early to hazard a guess whether the trends toward "soften-
ing" authoritarianism in Taiwan, South Korea, and Thailand and toward economic
liberalization in China, Vietnam, and Laos are harbingers of a democratic "spring"
in the Asian Pacific. People outside the region may hope for and support progress
toward greater opportunity for political participation and for material well-being,
but they should not be demoralized if that progress is fitful, slow, and at times
reversed.

SUMMARY

All the Asian Pacific governments remain authoritarian, but the degree of control
varies from country to country, as do the political structures and the techniques by
which elites maintain their dominant position in society. Nonetheless, with the exception of Brunei, where old-style authoritarianism in the form of unlimited monarchy persists, dramatic political reforms have occurred in all Asian Pacific countries.
While Communist parties that came to power with the aim of revolutionary transformation still effectively monopolize politics in China, North Korea, Vietnam, and
Laos, they have already embarked on economic reforms that make political reform
inevitable. In Cambodia one communist regime was ousted by another, which now
shares power with noncommunists. In Indonesia, South Korea, and Burma the
fragility of postindependence civilian governments led to military takeover, but the
recent economic crisis has created a new impetus for political reform. In Indonesia,
Thailand, and South Korea, the armed forces successfully carried out substantial
economic development and in Thailand and South Korea at least, civilian governments for the first time appear to be on solid enough ground to resist a military
takeover. Indonesia, however, faces daunting obstacles, even to its survival as a unified state.

Civilian governments under the dominance of a single ethnically based party
have ruled multiethnic Malaysia and Singapore since independence. Taiwan's dominant party, transplanted from the mainland, only recently elected its first opposition
president. In Japan, the one-party dominant system that lasted until defections from
the government party forced it out in 1993 may be restored, or it may be replaced
with a new system, the features of which are unclear as of this writing. In the Philippines electoral competition among multiple personalist political parties, a weak

state, and politicized armed forces constitute a system suited to the purposes of the economic and local political elites.

The widespread existence of authoritarian rule is variously explained as a continuation of traditional precolonial times, as the reinforcement of those patterns by colonial rule, and as a requirement of nation building and economic development. Progress, however, if it is measured in real rather than virtual time, is clearly visible in the reasonable certainty that authoritarianism in the Asian Pacific, despite its persistence, is a temporary phase, to be followed by movement toward more democratic competitive political systems. In the next chapter, we turn our attention to the connection between politics and economics, in particular to the preeminent role of the state in cases of successful economic development.

QUESTIONS FOR DISCUSSION

1. What are the distinguishing features of authoritarianism? Do you think that the label fits the governments of Asian Pacific countries? Why?
2. Do you agree with those who argue that some type of authoritarianism is necessary to guide a country through the processes of modernization and development? Why?
3. Why has the military played such a major role in Indonesia, South Korea, Myanmar, and Thailand? What positive and negative effects do you see in military rule?
4. How durable do you think the trend away from authoritarianism is likely to be in such countries as South Korea, Taiwan, Thailand, and the Philippines? What forces might be working in that direction, or counter to it, in China, Vietnam, North Korea, and Myanmar?

NOTES

1. Peter Evans, *Embedded Autonomy: States and Industrial Transformation* (Princeton, NJ: Princeton University Press, 1995), p. 4.
2. Melanie Manion, "The Electoral Connection in the Chinese Countryside" (paper presented at the 1996 annual meeting of the American Political Science Association, San Francisco), p. 15.
3. Far Eastern Economic Review, *"North Korea: Running Against History: Hwang Jang Yop interview with Olaf Jahn,"* October 15, 1998. pp. 30–31.
4. *New York Times,* December 4, 1999, p. A8.
5. Although *Kuomintang,* the earlier romanization, is still used in Taiwan, we use *Guomindang* throughout the book.
6. Cal Clark, *Taiwan's Political Development: Implications for Contending Political Economy Paradigms* (New York: Greenwood Press, 1989), p. 121.
7. Stanley S. Bedlington, *Malaysia and Singapore* (Ithaca, NY: Cornell University Press, 1978), p. 228.
8. Adam Schwarz, *A Nation in Waiting: Indonesia's Search for Stability*, 2nd ed. (Boulder, CO: Westview Press, 2000), p. 272.
9. David J. Steinberg, ed., *In Search of Southeast Asia: A Modern History*, rev. ed. (Honolulu: University of Hawaii Press, 1987), p. 426.
10. *Far Eastern Economic Review*, McBeth and Murphy, "Indonesia: Balancing Act," November 4, 1999, p. 18.
11. David Wilson, *Politics in Thailand* (Ithaca, NY: Cornell University Press, 1962), p. 277.
12. Chai-Anan Samudavanija, "Thailand: A Stable Semi-Democracy," in *Democracy in Developing Countries: Asia,* ed. Larry Diamond et al. (Boulder, CO: Lynne Rienner Publishers, 1989), p. 320.

13. Paul Handley, "People's Wrath," *Far Eastern Economic Review*, May 28, 1992, p. 10.
14. Quoted in Richard Maidment, David Goldblatt and Jeremy Mitchell, eds., *Governance in the Asian-Pacific* (London: Routledge and the Open University, 1998), p. 138.
15. Ibid.
16. The distinction among control, participation, and influence is made in Carolina G. Hernandez, "The Philippines," in *Military-Civilian Relations in South-East Asia*, eds. Z. H. Ahmad and H. Crouch (New York: Oxford University Press, 1985), pp. 157–58.
17. Hari Singh, "Political Change in Malaysia," *Asian Survey* 31, no. 6 (August 1991): 712.
18. "Interview with Obuchi," in *Far Eastern Economic Review,* December 2, 1999, p. 12.
19. Jang Jip Choi, "Political Cleavages in South Korea," in *State and Society in Contemporary Korea,* ed. Hagen Koo (Ithaca: Cornell University Press, 1993), p. 20.
20. Ibid., pp. 21–23.
21. In 1989 annual economic growth had plunged from a previous 12 percent to 6.5 percent while land prices continued escalating at a rate of over 30 percent a year.
22. For a discussion of the distinction between strong and weak states, see Joel S. Migdal, *Strong Societies and Weak States* (Princeton: Princeton University Press, 1988), pp. 4–5.
23. Chan Heng-chee, "Politics in an Administrative State: Where Has the Politics Gone?" cited in Bedlington, *Malaysia and Singapore*, p. 228.
24. Charles P. Wallace, "Making a Case for Kinder, Gentler 'Big Brother,' *The Los Angeles Times*, May 19, 1992, p. H15.
25. David Wurfel, *Filipino Politics* (Ithaca: Cornell Press, 1988), p. 62.
26. G. Sidney Silliman, "Human Rights Under the Marcos and Aquino Regimes" (paper presented at the meeting of the Association for Asian Studies, Washington, D.C., April 2–5, 1992).
27. Jeffrey Riedinger, "Everyday Resistance to Redistributive Reform: Agrarian Reform in the Philippines" (paper presented at the meeting of the Association for Asian Studies, Washington, D.C., April 2–5, 1992), p. 19.
28. The city of Pailin in western Cambodia is said to be controlled by former Khmer Rouge officials.
29. Tun-jen Cheng, "Is the Dog Barking? The Middle Class and Democratic Movements in the East Asian NICs," *International Studies* Notes 15, no. 1 (Winter 1990): pp. 10–17.

FOR FURTHER READING

See the periodicals suggested on page 117 for current information.

Multicountry Studies

Ahmad, Zakaria Haji, and Harold Crouch, eds. *Military-Civilian Relations in South-East Asia.* Oxford, England: Oxford University Press, 1985.
Bauer, Joanne R. and Bell, Daniel A., eds. *The East Asian Challenge for Human Rights.* Cambridge: Cambridge University Press, 1999.
Diamond, Larry, Juan J. Linz, and Seymour Martin Lipset, eds. *Democracy in Developing Countries.* Vol. 3, *Asia.* Boulder, CO: Lynne Rienner Publishers, 1989, chs. 1, 6–9, 11.
Sachsenroder, Wolfgang and Frings, Ulrike E. *Political Party Systems and Democratic Development in East and Southeast Asia,* Vol. I: *Southeast Asia,* Vol II: *East Asia.* Brookfield, VT: Ashgate, 1998.

Individual Country Studies

Brown, MacAlister, and Joseph J. Zasloff. *Apprentice Revolutionaries: The Communist Movement in Laos, 1930–1985.* Stanford, CA: Hoover Institution Press, 1986.

Calder, Kent E. *Crisis and Compensation: Public Policy and Political Stability in Japan, 1949–1986.* Princeton, NJ: Princeton University Press, 1988.

Clark, Cal. *Taiwan's Political Development: Implications for Contending Political Economy Paradigms.* New York: Greenwood Press, 1989, ch. 5.

Crouch, Harold. *The Army and Politics in Indonesia,* rev. ed. Ithaca, NY: Cornell University Press, 1988.

Dreyer, June Teufel. *China's Political System: Modernization and Tradition.* Boston, MA: Allyn and Bacon, 1996.

Kerbo, Harold R. and John A. McKinstry. *Who Rules Japan? The Inner Circles of Economic and Political Power.* Westport, CN, London: Praeger, 1995.

Keyes, Charles F. *Thailand: Buddhist Kingdom as a Modern Nation-State.* Boulder, CO: Westview, 1987, chs. 4–6.

Koo, Hagen, ed. *State and Society in Contemporary Korea.* Ithaca, NY: Cornell University Press, 1993.

Lee, Chong-Sik, and Se-Hee Yoo, eds. *North Korea in Transition.* Berkeley: University of California Institute of East Asian Studies, 1991.

Ongkili, James P. *Nation-building in Malaysia 1946–1974.* Singapore: Oxford University Press, 1985, chs. 5–7.

Parnwell, Michael J. G. *Uneven Development in Thailand.* Brookfield, VT: Ashgate, 1996.

Pike, Douglas. *History of Vietnamese Communism, 1925–1976.* Stanford, CA: Hoover Institution Press, 1978.

Rodan, Garry, ed. *Singapore Changes Guard: Social, Political and Economic Directions in the 1990s.* New York: St. Martin's, 1993, part I.

Steinberg, David I. *The Republic of Korea: Economic Transformation and Social Change.* Boulder, CO: Westview, 1989, chs. 6, 8, 9.

Steinberg, David Joel. *The Philippines: A Singular and a Plural Place.* Boulder, CO: Westview, 2000.

Taylor, Robert H. *The State in Burma.* Honolulu: University of Hawaii Press, 1987.

Wurfel, David. *Filipino Politics.* Ithaca, NY: Cornell University Press, 1988.

5

Political Economy
and Development

As varied as national states in the Asian Pacific are—the subject of the preceding chapter—they all share a common objective: to promote the economic growth and prosperity of the people living within their borders. How well or how poorly states carry out this task is what confers or revokes legitimacy on them in the eyes of both their own and the world's population. The fate of the Soviet Union and its Eastern European satellites is a compelling reminder of how a state can fall victim to its own economic failures. Closer to hand, the 1997 collapse of Asian Pacific economies demonstrated the vulnerability of these states to their own political mortality at a time of economic contraction. These post–Cold War, international as well as national economic disasters have drawn attention to the significance of political economy, of understanding the variety of ways in which state and economy depend on one another not merely within the boundaries of any single nation-state but internationally as members of a global community. The relationship between politics and economics at the juncture where national states intersect with the international order is the subject of this chapter.

The astounding economic development of the Asian Pacific since World War II has focused special attention on the role of the state in bringing about economic expansion and successful integration into the global economy. From the devastation of defeat in war, the small island nation of Japan has emerged as the second largest economy in the world, rivaled only by the United States. Following Japan's example, South Korea, Taiwan, Singapore, and Hong Kong have successfully transformed themselves into vibrant capitalist economies contributing to the region's reputation for "economic miracles." Even the economy of the People's Republic of China—opened to the international market only since 1978—has become the second largest industrial producer in the world today, registering an impressive 9 percent economic growth rate in 1991 after averaging an industrial growth rate of 10 percent annually since 1953. None of these countries is either a democracy or a "free enterprise" system as generally understood in the West; authoritarian politics and an interventionist state are more often the rule either formally or informally. Yet they are at the forefront of the fastest growing region in the world, challenging a broad range of Western ideas and practices concerning the role of the state in the economy.

In an equally stunning economic downturn in the summer of 1997, these vibrant capitalist economies with their directorial governments once again startled the world, this time challenging their own elites with a financial disaster of world-class proportions. Beginning with the sudden collapse of Thailand's currency, one after another of the Asian Pacific countries from Indonesia to South Korea (with the exception of China, Taiwan, and Singapore) sank into economic recession, this time provoking questions about how such economically interventionist states might have fostered the vulnerabilities that invited economic catastrophe. Accusations flew in both directions. Some Asian Pacific statesmen blamed irresponsible speculation on the part of international capital investors for their misfortune while western leaders pointed their fingers at the "crony capitalism" characteristic of Asian Pacific economic development. At the heart of this contention is the fundamental issue of political economy: what is the proper relationship of government to the economic policy making that either ensures or undermines economic development?

A comparative analysis of political economy in the Asian Pacific raises practical as well as theoretical questions about where global development is headed. Does the state's activist role as manager of the market account for the prodigious productivity and economic success of East Asian national economies? Or is the state's intervention in the economy an equation for economic disaster that imperils the entire global economy? Is the East Asian export-oriented strategy a universally applicable model or is it a unique product of its time and place? If it is universally applicable, is there room for all countries to pursue successfully an export-oriented strategy of development or are there inevitably losers in the zero-sum competition of a finite international market? Is there emerging in the Asian Pacific a form of mixed economy distinct from others, possibly a model for global convergence? Through their own developmental achievements and failures, the nations of the Asian Pacific have placed their experiences at the center of the answers to these questions.

We begin with a consideration of the ways in which the political economy of development in the Asian Pacific experience differs from its Western counterpart, both in its successes and its failures. We then describe four models of political economy and how they relate to the theoretical perspectives through which development has been viewed in the West. The third section consists of a comparison between the Japanese and the Maoist patterns of political economy, inviting the reader to assess their similarities and differences. The developmental strategy of the "four little tigers"—South Korea, Taiwan, Hong Kong, and Singapore—is examined in the fourth section, followed by a discussion of the market reforms in China, Vietnam, and Laos. Finally, the achievements of the newly exporting countries, the NEC's—Malaysia, Thailand, and Indonesia—will be compared and contrasted with the failures of Myanmar and the Philippines to break out of the cycle of Third World underdevelopment.

DISTINCTIVE FEATURES OF DEVELOPMENT IN THE ASIAN PACIFIC

Development is a difficult term to circumscribe. Generally it includes the totality of changes that accompany the process of industrialization: mechanization, urbanization, commercialization, and democratization. In those countries that pioneered industrialization between the sixteenth and nineteenth centuries—the Western European nations and the United States—the process unfolded in a spontaneous manner we call capitalism. Increasingly, however, this process has become more deliberate and planned. Beginning with economic growth in the form of commodity production for an international market, capitalist development was pursued in Western countries by a new class of businesspeople whose activities were supported but not directed by a centralized political order, a national state. As the market expanded in response to the application of new technology, self-generating economies reshaped the social and political institutions of national life. The entirety of these remarkable transformations ushered in the irresistible modern world.

But time warps occur globally as peoples originally left out of this modernizing process are engulfed by its awesome powers. They encounter the modern world as a *fait accompli*: a delicate filigree of interrelated institutions and beliefs that appear to have neither beginning nor end. Peoples who overnight discover that they are "backward" are compelled to master a bewildering complex of new survival skills or be reduced to permanent bondage. This process of large national communities learning to act as one in order to reshape their economic, social, and political destiny is known in social science circles as *development*. It requires self-consciously untangling the complicated strands of a modern way of life that presents itself as a finished product with few clues as to how or where to begin to duplicate it and which elements to omit. In the Asian Pacific, this process of development has differed in three major ways from the experience of the "early developers," and those differences have contributed to the greater role of the state in development.

Late Developers

Historically, all Asian societies are "late developers," a concept widely identified with Alexander Gerschenkron, who noted the special characteristics of countries, like Germany and the Soviet Union, that joined the global tide of development when it was already in rapid motion. Gerschenkron's hypothesis is that the later a country industrializes the greater will be the role of the state in compensating for the "missing prerequisites" that enabled earlier developers to industrialize.[1] Thus when Japan embarked on modernizing its government and economy in the 1880s, the Japanese had the advantage of learning from a second generation of developers—Germany and France. This meant starting with a more advanced and foreign machine technology that required the superior resources of the state to acquire. For countries like China, South Korea, and Malaysia, which commenced the process even later, the scope and cost of launching economic development meant an even greater role for the state. Time, therefore, is one factor in understanding the expanded intervention of the state in the economic planning of Asian Pacific development.

Imperialism

Another factor is imperialism, the forceful imposition of modernity by foreign rule. Asian Pacific countries are not merely "late developers" in the manner of Germany or the Soviet Union but share the experience of colonization (either directly or indirectly) by members of a foreign civilization, an experience unlike any in Europe or the United States, except that of the Native Americans. Wresting independence from colonial rule requires replacing the colonial government with a state powerful enough not only to maintain order but to generate massive social and economic change. Among Asian Pacific peoples, therefore, there is a shared legacy of strong, legitimately interventionist government with sufficient power to secure the economic livelihood of its people.

Cultural Collectivism

A third factor distinguishing political economies of Asian Pacific countries from those in the West is cultural: the shared emphasis placed on the collective good, whether of the family or the state, over and above the individual. The primacy of the common good requires collective restraints to curb the selfish, narrower pursuit of short-term, partisan interests. And in the Asian cultural context, this is expressed in the acceptance of a state as authoritarian in its preeminence. It is more like an extended family than it is an association of unrelated adults who compete with one another for the acquisition of wealth. The role of the state is not simply to regulate conflicts among individuals but to nuture harmony and conformity with proper conduct.

The political ramifications of this preference for harmony have already been evidenced in the pervasiveness of one-party-dominant political systems described in Chapter 4. In this chapter, the widespread acceptance of the state's leadership role in determining the collective economic interest will be discussed as an essential characteristic of successful Asian Pacific political economies. This is as true for the communist command economies of China, North Korea, and Vietnam as it is for the "developmental" states of Japan, Taiwan, South Korea, Malaysia, Singapore, Thailand, and Indonesia.

FOUR MODELS OF POLITICAL ECONOMY

Three models, often with different labels, have been used by Western social scientists to delineate the broad spectrum of political economies in the post–World War II world. At one end is a model or ideal type of capitalist *market economy* culled from the 18th century experiences of Western European states; at the other end is a model of the communist *planned economy* extrapolated from the experiences of the Soviet Union and other communist states since 1917; and in between are two clearly distinguishable mixtures or combinations of the two. One form of *mixed economy* became clearly identifiable in the political economies of Western Europe after W.W.II. and this became known as a "mixed economy." A different type of mixed economy became apparent in the common developmental experiences of Asian Pacific countries in the last quarter of the 20th century which we will specify as a fourth model of political economy, the *developmental state political economy.*

Capitalist or Market Economy

In the capitalist or market model of development, economics and politics comprise separate spheres of activity in modern society. Adam Smith, as we recall from Chapter 1, prescribed that the economy should be governed by its own rules unfettered by the artificial constraints of the state. Total private control by individuals (usually referring to firms or households) of the factors of production (land, labor, factories, resources) enables the market through principles of competition, supply, and demand to determine what gets produced, at what value goods and resources are exchanged, and how individuals can optimally increase their accumulated value (profit). Thus the market economy is demand oriented, each actor making decisions on what to produce and/or exchange on the basis of the demand for various goods. The "invisible hand" automatically converts the sum of profit-seeking individuals into the common good of the whole society.

How, then, is government connected with the economy? It creates and preserves the context within which the market operates and provides for the national defense. Examples of legitimate state policies are protecting private ownership of property, guaranteeing the inviolability of contracts, implementing the use of a common currency and uniform weights and measures. Although even Smith recognized a larger role for the state—for example, in providing welfare—to create and maintain the "free" market system than did some of his latter-day acolytes, he nonetheless bequeathed a legacy of reverence for the virtues of an economy completely owned and controlled by private individuals free from state intervention. Is it legitimate for the state to regulate the economy in order to protect competition? To safeguard individuals' rights? Should the state monitor and control consumer goods so individuals are protected from harmful products? Is it also appropriate for the state to correct other flaws of the market as they become apparent? These questions provide great latitude for controversy. It is clear, nonetheless, that the state's role in the market model is both modest and in accordance with the decisions of individuals taking part in the market.

This market model is at the core of modernization theory. Its proponents assume that each developing country will find its interests best served by promoting a free market internally and free trade with the other members of the international community. Whatever assets a state has can thus be transformed into a comparative advantage in trade with others and the earnings used to purchase the advanced technology needed to develop. This is the basis for an export-led strategy of development. The exigencies of late development may require a greater role for the state in protecting the market, perhaps even regulating trade to protect infant indigenous industry, but there is never any doubt that the state plays a secondary role, depending upon the market to provide the impetus and mechanics of production and distribution.

Planned Economy

A second, alternative model of modern political economy arises out of the experience of the Soviet Union after 1917. In this model, the state takes over total control of all factors of production, determining what goods will be produced and how they will be distributed to the population. The state draws up a detailed plan specifying what amounts of each good will be produced from what combination of resources and at what prices the goods will be bought and sold. The plan indicates that a dress manufacturing factory, for example, will receive a certain amount of fabric, thread, buttons, and other items to produce a certain number of dresses. From whom the requisite materials will be obtained and to whom the dresses will be distributed are also designated by the plan along with the size, composition, and wages of the labor force. In contrast to the market economy, the planned economy is supply oriented: The state makes production decisions on the basis of supplying citizens with goods and services appropriate to their needs and the state's budget and priorities. All these considerations are guided by a broad social and political vision of the society's destination: a time when all citizens' needs and aspirations can be provided for by a technically sophisticated and prosperous productive system.

The state's role in a planned economy is overwhelming, requiring the central direction of a highly organized and disciplined political party. The Communist Party has performed this function as leader of the state and guardian of its economic goals and socialist aspirations. In their capacity as public officials, high-ranking party members make a staggering number of production decisions that affect the livelihood of the entire population and the fortunes of the country as a whole. The rationale for the party-state's exercise of such extensive economic control is twofold: to catch up rapidly with the already powerful and industrialized nations in the world and to substitute for the weakness of an entrepreneurial class historically charged with carrying out the tasks of capitalist development.

From the world system perspective, the model of a planned economy provides an alternative to the foreign domination brought about by incorporation into the global capitalist economy. Adherents of world system theory argue that underdeveloped peoples are too weak to resist external encroachment by industrialized nations without a revolutionary party capable of establishing a strong, highly centralized state. A planned economy, presumably in the context of a socialist revolution, allows a developing country to concentrate its resources, thereby strengthening the autonomy of its state and raising the revenue to pursue an independent economic course of action. With this model of development, an import-substitution strategy is employed by the state to protect the domestic economy from external competition, enabling it to grow in a self-reliant manner. The state plays the principal role in this approach to economic development by acting as a substitute for the market.

Mixed Economies

The mixed economy is a hybrid model that combines the strengths and avoids the weaknesses of the market model on the one hand and the planned economy on the other. It is a system in which there is a significant sector of state planning to serve the common good while retaining the privately owned market free from state control. The usual examples of this model are Western European states in which a substantial percentage of industries like banking, telecommunications, utilities, and transportation are owned and operated by the state while most other industries remain in the hands of private entrepreneurs and investors. The state engages in economic oversight, making recommendations to private sector industries as well; this is referred to as indicative planning in the case of France. Market mechanisms in general determine production decisions in a mixed system because nationalized industries operate within a market context, competing with private industry for resources and markets. But the state can place constraints on the behavior of private enterprises, deciding minimum wages, for example, and in some cases establishing overall guidelines for the economy as a whole.

In the Cold War context that followed World War II, it was generally assumed that market and mixed systems fostered democratic political institutions while planned economies invited totalitarian control. In the first two decades after the war, the political map of the Asian Pacific seemed to corroborate this view: China, North Korea, and North Vietnam were planned economies with communist states presumed to exercise totalitarian control while Japan, South Korea, Taiwan, and Singapore were pro-Western and market-oriented states with what appeared to be democratic institutions. By the 1980s, however, the extraordinary economic growth of Japan and the NICs began to appear in a new light. The Cold War adversaries, the United States and the Soviet Union, were entering a period of economic decline and international political retrenchment while the Asian Pacific emerged as a new, vibrant center of economic expansion. This prompted closer scrutiny of how Japan and the NICs had achieved their dramatic economic ascendance, revealing a pattern of development quite different in some respects from the one suggested by any of the prevailing models of political economy. This second type of mixed economy—the developmental state-centered model—constitutes the fourth type of political economy.

The Developmental State-Centered Model

Chalmers Johnson, in his influential book, *MITI and the Japanese Miracle,*[2] introduced the model of a developmental state as a corrective to the misperception that Japan was following Adam Smith's recipe of the market economy as the way to develop. Johnson demonstrated that Japanese economic development was the consequence not of a democratic state's benign neglect of the market but of an authoritarian state's active intervention in shaping business decisions. From the beginning of the Meiji era, according to Johnson, Japan has followed a unique pattern in which a market economy has benefited from self-conscious direction by a bureaucratic authoritarian state. Although the political sphere is formally organized as a representative democracy, it has actually contained all along two institutionally segregated functions: *ruling,* which is the authoritarian decision making of the bureaucracy, and *reigning,* which is the political give-and-take of competing partisan interests in a parliamentary forum. Reigning is the domain of democratically elected "politicians," while ruling, the orchestration and guidance of the national economy, is carried out by technocratic civil servants in government agencies.

The developmental state that Johnson extrapolates from the Japanese experience applies equally well to the newly industrializing countries of Singapore, Taiwan, and South Korea. Economic growth in these countries has followed the same pattern: a market that is the engine of economic growth and an authoritarian state as the driver of the engine. For this reason, developmental states have been dubbed BAIRs by Cumings: bureaucratic authoritarian industrializing regimes.[3] However, to distinguish Japan's postwar democratic system from more blatantly authoritarian regimes (like South Korea under Park, for example) Chalmers Johnson uses the term *soft authoritarianism* to describe a regime in which persuasion and negotiation rather than command and coercion are used by the governmental bureaucracy to achieve market compliance. Although it is not clear whether this is a matter of style or substance, the distinction between soft and hard authoritarianism is subsidiary in any event to the category of developmental state.

Four structural elements are identified as characteristic of the political economy of developmental states:

1. Bureaucratic autonomy from politics that protects the developmental state from bowing to partial and competing political demands and pressures that might undermine long-term national economic growth;
2. Close collaboration of public and private sectors directed by a powerful planning agency or board;
3. Heavy and continuing investment in education for everyone and policies to ensure equitable distribution of the wealth gained through high-speed growth; and
4. The use of incentives and persuasion rather than commands so that the state's economic intervention is based on the price mechanism of the market rather than administratively assigned prices.[4]

Other aspects of this model of political economy have drawn considerable attention: its pragmatic, nonideological character, its suppression of independent labor unions and populist groups, its reliance on paternalistic corporate structures modeled on the family, its role as mediator between the opportunities and dangers of the international market, and the benefit of the domestic national economy. Some of these will be discussed more fully in our comparisons of the political economy of Japan and the NICs.

The significance of this developmental model of political economy is its deviation from both the classical laissez-faire Western model of the market economy and the model of economic planning associated with the command economies of socialist states. Though similar in some respects to the mixed economy of Western European countries, which combines substantial sectors of state-owned property with the productive resources and mechanisms of a market economy, the developmental model combines state direction of a market economy without the state owning any significant portion of the productive resources.

The defining characteristic of the developmental model is not the amount of industry owned and controlled by the state but the degree, scope, and direction of the state's management of the market as a whole. In fact, the state in Japan "is actually smaller in terms of revenues, outlays, and equity ownership than most capitalist countries in the West."[5] Yet the state's role in orchestrating the Japanese, South Korean, and Taiwanese economies is greater than in any of the mixed economies of Western Europe. The developmental state intervenes in the market not only to remove serious obstacles to national economic development and dilute the effects of market failures but to direct the nation's economic growth and ensure its international competitiveness. Primary responsibility for determining national economic priorities is not left to the market but is assumed by a state with sufficient autonomy to pursue developmentally desirable national economic policies. Does this signify that the developmental model is a distinctive type of political economy? If so, is it a unique invention peculiar to the Asian Pacific or is it similar to the earliest period of capitalist development in Western Europe as suggested by Sandra Halperin?[6]

The practical ramifications attending these as yet unanswered questions are critical: Is it possible for other regimes to duplicate the strategic role of the state in "taming domestic and international market forces and harnessing them to a national economic interest"?[7] Is the developmental state an enduring model, let alone one that other countries can adopt? If it is an enduring model, is it one toward which both command economies and market economies will gravitate? Or with the passage of time will Japan and its acolytes, the NICs and the NECs, begin to behave more like the classical market economies of capitalism? In the wake of the economic catastrophe of 1997 that bore down hardest on Japan, South Korea, Indonesia, and Thailand, the collaboration between large corporate enterprises and state bureaucracies was widely blamed by international financial institutions for inviting the disaster. Indeed, the advice administered by those who interpreted the "Asian flu" as a result of "crony capitalism" was that only by liberalizing the market economy and extricating the state from involvement in its business could good economic health could be restored. Is it possible that the developmental "model" is an obstacle rather than a spur to continued economic growth among Asian Pacific states?

These tantalizing questions have theoretical implications as well as practical ones. If, as some scholars believe, the developmental state model of political economy is essentially distinct from the market, command, or mixed economy models, then the experiences of developmental states are anomalies from both the modernization (liberalization) and world system theoretical perspectives. Both modernization and world system theories minimize the significance of the state's role in bringing about modern capitalist development among late developers. The developmental state theory, on the other hand, views the state as indispensable for late developers to industrialize by joining the global economy. This enhances the significance of high economic growth rates among the Asian Pacific political economies; they constitute important evidence corroborating one or another theoretical and ideological perspective. The reform policies pursued by Communist parties in China, Vietnam, and Laos, and to a lesser extent in North Korea, can be interpreted in three distinct ways: (1) as a movement in the direction of convergence with the developmental states in the rest of the Asian Pacific, (2) as an independent mixture of capitalism and socialism captured by the term *market socialism*, or as a step on the road to a full-fledged market economy.

A central issue at the heart of all the questions is the claim that Japan's "developmental state" model is actually closer to the experience of the centrally planned economies than it is to the classical market model of the West, which, except perhaps in Hong Kong prior to its reversion to China, is nowhere approximated in the

Asian Pacific. The implication of this claim, made by Chalmers Johnson,[8] is that only the planned economy and the developmental state economy are pertinent to the examination of political economies in the Asian Pacific. This is explored in the next section in a comparison of the political economies of Japan from its Meiji roots to the present and Communist China from its inception in 1949 through its Maoist phase, which ended in 1978. It should be noted that, although China has systematically abandoned central planning in favor of "socialist markets" since 1982, this has transpired in the context of China's earlier planned economy which is the subject of discussion in this next section.

CONTRASTING THE POLITICAL ECONOMY OF JAPAN AND PRE-REFORM CHINA

Among late developers in Asia, Japan and China offer a striking contrast. Japan has a market economy guided by a highly professional government bureaucracy within a parliamentary system; China, has had a centrally planned economy governed by the Communist Party in a socialist state structure. But neither political economy is quite what it appears to be. Japan's economy has actually been a collaborative enterprise among government bureaucracy, big business, and (until mid-1993) the Liberal Democratic Party; China's centrally planned economy, in operation from 1949 to 1978, was neither as centralized nor as planned as it claimed. Since adoption of the Reform policy (to be discussed in conjunction with the NICs), China's planned economy has moved more self-consciously in the direction of the Japanese model. The initial conditions under which China and Japan embarked on the road to a modern political economy, however, presented different opportunities.

China's Political Economy: Surviving a Transplant

The kind of development a country follows is never a wide open choice among all rational possibilities, but it is decisively influenced by which models are available and acceptable to political leaders at any particular point in time. Marxism gained a following in China during the 1920s because it appealed to Chinese nationalism; it offered a successful anti-imperialist alternative to Western models of modernization, a perception the Soviet Union sought to bolster by proposing to return the Chinese Eastern Railway. But the initial allure of Soviet Marxism waned when Soviet advice came into conflict with the needs of the Chinese Communists after 1927. Subsequent events widened the gulf of experience between them and the Stalinist leadership, so that by 1949 their ideas of "revolution" and "communism" were no longer congruent. Nonetheless, faced with an embargo imposed by Western nations, Mao Zedong left China for the first time in his life, traveling to Moscow in 1950 to negotiate a treaty of friendship with Stalin.

The treaty provided China with economic development aid and technical assistance: 156 complete heavy industrial plants accompanied by blueprints, technicians, and a model of the planned economy with which to begin industrialization. With this limited but decisive Soviet assistance, the Chinese began the serious task of large-scale industrial development within a framework of building a new socialist society. The dilemma was how to raise the level of agricultural output high enough to support both an enormous population and the burden of financing a modern industrial sector. Utilizing the Soviet experience as a model, the Chinese adopted a command economy governed by a five-year plan that concentrated on heavy industry directed from the center. Investment in agriculture was kept to a minimum, emphasizing gradual collectivization and projects such as land reclamation that required no financial outlays. It took only two years of applying Soviet practices under the First Five-Year Plan (1953–1957) for the Chinese to show signs of rejecting the transplant.

Beginning in the winter of 1957, Mao Zedong introduced the Great Leap Forward, the first of China's attempts to innovate a self-reliant alternative to the highly bureaucratized system of central planning inherited from the Soviet Union. The Great Leap Forward swung the national economy away from sober economic rationality toward experimentation with spontaneous and unconventional means of organizing economic production. Decentralized responsibility for drastically increasing agricultural and industrial production replaced the top-down, orderly management of Soviet-style economic planning. Agriculture took precedence over industry and small- and medium-scale industries were developed in the countryside as part of a new form of social organization, the *commune,* modeled on China's revolutionary base areas. The essential characteristics of the Great Leap Forward were a heady optimism that sought to restore the revolutionary ardor and egalitarian ethic of earlier days, the preference for ideologically minded political activists over technical experts as leaders, and the idea of substituting local initiative and ingenuity for scarce capital and remote planners.

Disastrous harvests, mismanagement, and starvation brought back into power the party advocates of Soviet-style planning, who proceeded to restore an economy in shambles. Mao's solution had turned out to be worse than the problem. A scant six years later in 1966 the Cultural Revolution, a second, nationwide experimental campaign, was launched in the factories and schools of urban China (discussed further in Chapter 6). From 1953 until Mao's death, Chinese policy oscillated between the two competing conceptions of development: Soviet-style centralized economic planning and Mao's periodic experiments with decentralized antibureaucratic mass politics. The developmental pattern of the Maoist period is thus a zigzag fluctuation that includes both Mao's antibureaucratic and antimarket economics and the return to Soviet-style bureaucratic planning that followed. The common denominator distinguishing both aspects of Maoist development strategy from the Japanese model was the absence of a market economy.

Japan's Political Economy: Transplanting the Past

In contrast to the peripatetic fluctuations of Maoist development, the structure of Japanese development has remained remarkably stable since Meiji times despite catastrophic defeat in war and an American-imposed set of reforms. A market economy has been in place since the nineteenth century, but unlike the Western model it has been governed by close collaboration between state officials and the business elite. This partnership between government and business (described in

Chapter 2) began with the modernization of the samurai class, one part of which entered government service while the other became a modern business class. Borrowing heavily from German experience, the Meiji state set up an authoritarian and nationalistic political system based on a powerful bureaucracy and military dedicated to achieving international status. Heavy industrial enterprises thought to be essential for military defense and international competitiveness—steel, shipbuilding, railways, telegraphic communications, and armaments—were initiated by the government and were auctioned off to favored capitalists at a loss when they became a financial burden.[9] Thus like Germany, Japan developed a market economy closely but informally nurtured by its association with government in the form of a strong, bureaucratic authoritarian state.

Government collaboration with industry became even more intense in the late 1920s and 1930s in response to various economic crises: The state assumed powers to forge cartels, approve investments that would expand facilities, or persuade cartel members to curtail production. Thus Japan's postwar governmental authority in the area of licensing and administrative guidance of investments has its origins in policies pursued by the Ministry of Commerce and Industry (the predecessor of MITI, the Ministry of International Trade and Industry) in conjunction with the military's expansionist program before the Second World War. "Unlike other nations defeated in World War II or torn by revolution in the wake of World War II, Japan did not experience a radical discontinuity in its civilian bureaucratic and economic elites."[10] The same "economic general staff" in charge of industrial planning for purposes of military expansion in the 1930s resumed its position after the war, this time in pursuit of an economic "miracle." The planners' restoration was made possible by a shift in U.S. policy away from its immediate postwar preoccupation with democratizing Japanese institutions.

Shortly after Japan's recovery had commenced under American tutelage, Cold War pressures led the U.S. government to reverse its earlier policy of dismantling the prewar bureaucratic-industrial complex, thought to have been responsible for bringing about the war. Instead, faced with union unrest, Communist Party activities, and potential instability, the United States sought to restore the strength of prewar institutions as a bulwark against Asian communism. To achieve this aim, the state bureaucracy was given free rein to rebuild the private sector corporate giants, the *zaibatsu*, into new forms of concentrated economic power, the *keiretsu*. These provided the engine of Japan's postwar economic miracle, updating their physical plants, diversifying their holdings, and honing their competitive international edge. The driver of the engine was the state bureaucracy, which had ironically benefited from the one reform that remained intact from the early days of U.S. occupation, the constitutional renunciation of war as an instrument of national policy. Limited to a self-defense role, the military was thus eliminated as the only rival strong enough to check the Ministries of Commerce and Industry and of Finance.

Similarities in the Political Economies of Japan and China

By the late 1950s, when former colonies in the rest of the Asian Pacific were prepared to launch their own programs of modernization, the Japanese and the Maoist-

Chinese models of political economy offered alternative paths of development. Different from one another in fundamental ways to be discussed in the following section, they nonetheless share some broad underlying similarities that require mentioning. For both countries, modernization first appeared as an external threat, stimulating an intense nationalism that has accompanied the relentless drive of both governments to seek national economic growth and international recognition. In pursuit of their overriding national purpose of catching up with the highly industrialized nations, both China and Japan prized political stability over individual rights. Japanese "exponents of *national* betterment and [national] rights"[11] have accentuated the obligations of Japanese citizens to their state in the same manner as their Communist counterparts in the People's Republic of China. Both stress national unity at the expense of social and individual diversity, relying on authoritarianism—"soft" in Japan, "hard" in China—to ensure political stability.

Strong government has been the result in both Japan and China. A ruling party's dominant faction has acted as a compression chamber to consolidate the diversity of pluralistic demands into a nationally integrated policy. The outcome is two variants of economic planning. In the case of Japan, incremental industrial planning by the state has relied on a private sector market economy to achieve rapid and sustained economic growth *and* a high per capita income. In the case of Maoist China, a centrally administered plan covering every facet of China's economy has relied on political leadership to obtain high industrial growth rates at the expense of producing ample goods and services for consumption.

Different Forms of Property Ownership

While both China and Japan share strong governments with a self-conscious determination to promote industrialization, they have pursued that end by fundamentally different means. The Japanese state from Meiji times to the present has followed a Western European model of a market economy, maintaining a separation between privately owned productive property and the public responsibility for national economic growth and prosperity. The Chinese regime under Mao followed the socialist principle of the Soviet Union that productive property belongs to all the people and government is responsible for its management. Stalin's formula for a socialist political economy provided the basis for comprehensive administrative planning in virtually every socialist country. In North Korea and Vietnam as well as in China the proletarian party-state substituted for the capitalist entrepreneurial class to pursue economic development on the basis of self-sufficiency, investment in large-scale heavy industry, the legal elimination of markets (black markets resisted elimination), and collectivized agriculture. These policies were geared toward achieving economies of scale, a sustained high rate of savings, investment, and growth, and the elimination of capitalist inequality and waste.

China.   Since 90 percent of the Chinese population lived in the countryside in 1949, the first task of the Communists was to reorganize agricultural production. The initial stage was to provide every Chinese household with title to a piece of land, eliminating the despotic power of the landlords in the process. With land reform completed, the government proceeded to collectivize all the land, integrating

An urban "Free Market" in northeast China.

Source: Photo by Vera Simone.

the tiny, isolated parcels belonging to individual households into successively larger agricultural cooperatives. During the Great Leap Forward, cooperatives were urged to form gigantic communes in the hopes that the economies of scale thereby created would free labor from its household moorings to engage in large-scale irrigation works, construction, and land improvement projects and to begin industrializing the countryside, even building backyard steel furnaces. Despite the rapidity with which these profound social changes were undertaken, they were heralded, much to the chagrin of the Soviet leadership, as "true communism."

In the urban areas, which provided a livelihood for only 20 percent of the population as late as 1980,[12] large, medium, and small industrial enterprises were nationalized in stages. Thus by 1958 two forms of property generally prevailed in the cities: the state-owned industrial sector (a significant portion of which—34.7 percent of total industrial output value—had been inherited from foreign owners and bureaucratic capitalists)[13] and the collectively owned light industrial workshops. There were also a small number of privately owned service businesses carried out by tradespeople who repaired pots, sharpened knives, and reconditioned furnishings. The effect of both rural collectivization and urban nationalization was to take investment decisions out of private hands, conferring on government the sole responsibility for centrally administering the country's economy. With total state revenues during the Maoist period constituting about 30 percent of the gross domestic product, the government was able to invest a substantial proportion of national income in the further construction of heavy industry.

Thus property ownership in Maoist China constituted a three-tiered hierarchical system with state-owned urban property at the top, collectively owned rural and urban property beneath it, and private plots and small-scale urban enterprises on the very bottom. Despite official homage paid to the importance of agriculture and peasants, state-owned industries received the lion's share of investment funds from the government, and workers in state-owned factories enjoyed full-time employment at fixed and generally higher wages *regardless of productivity*, with extensive benefits including housing, health care, food subsidies, pensions, and education for their children. Peasants, on the other hand, received only their share of whatever their collective or commune was able to produce in any one year. If the harvest was dismal, either as a result of government policy or natural disaster, the peasants' standard of living plunged. They had to build their own homes, fund the commune's clinics, schools, and industries, and pay out of their collective earnings for any goods and services required from the outside. Private enterprise, which in the countryside meant selling produce from one's private plots on the open market, though constitutionally recognized for most of the Maoist period, was ideologically suspect and intermittently vulnerable to curtailment whenever a campaign to put "politics in command" was launched.

Japan.   Private property carried no such stigma in Japan, where productive property had been owned by individual families since Meiji times. The Land Tax Revision of 1873–1876 transformed feudal estates into cash-producing commodity enterprises by converting farmers' payments-in-kind to fixed cash sums based on the value of the property. Farmers unable to support themselves on the land under these new conditions were forced into urban factories while successful farmers increased their landholdings. Land eventually became concentrated in the hands of absentee landlords and rich peasants. To rectify this, democratize the country, and neutralize the Communists' demands for a comprehensive rural revolution, the U.S. military government after World War II assisted the Japanese in implementing a land-reform program. The policy succeeded in producing an agricultural sector of small-scale family-owned farms that, with the help of the government, revitalized domestic agricultural production.

The government increased its role in agricultural production to furnish rural investment funds formerly provided by the landlords and wealthy farmers. It invested heavily in land improvement (reclamation, irrigation, and drainage), price supports, and subsidies in the form of low interest rates. But the accelerated economic growth in agriculture that resulted from these farm supports did not resolve the problem of income disparities between farmers and their urban counterparts, the industrial workers. When farmers organized themselves into powerful associations to pressure the government for a fair return for their labor, the government responded by adopting a formula that tied the price of rice to increases in *non*agricultural wages. Thus the government paid the price of supporting highly capitalized, small, family-owned farms when agriculture, unable to benefit from the economy of scale, lost its developmental role in the economy.

Like land, industrial property in Japan has been privately owned since the Meiji state sold off its industrial holdings to private entrepreneurs in the late nineteenth century. But unlike the agricultural sector, where postwar land reform succeeded in breaking up the large concentrations of land, the attempt to break up the concentrated industrial holdings, the *zaibatsu,* was jettisoned by the U.S. military government in response to the exigencies of the Cold War. Instead, the U.S. occupation administration sanctioned the restoration of the two-tiered system of property ownership that had characterized prewar Japan. On the lower level, the small- and medium-sized enterprises, which date back to Admiral Perry's forced opening of Japan to the outside world, are today the labor-intensive suppliers of goods and services to the huge modern, capital-intensive corporate conglomerates. This higher level of extremely large, family-based corporate cartels sprang up out of the successful partnership between early "political merchants" and the Meiji state.

These *zaibatsu*, known since their postwar reorganization as *keiretsu* (Mitsui, Sumitomo, Mitsubishi, and Yasuda are the "Big Four"[14]) are typically diversified holdings under tightly interlocking ownership. Each group is a network of corporate alliances among diverse manufacturers organized around a common bank and trading company and exercising direct control of their subsidiaries through their monopoly of credit. Sumitomo, for example, is not a single manufacturer but a group of distinct companies, each of which owns parts of the others. Constituent members of a *kereitsu* do business with one another rather than with outsiders. And their relations with subcontractors (the suppliers of components) are not strictly contractual, calculated on cost-benefit comparisons among competing suppliers. Instead, the individual enterprises of a *kereitsu* incorporate suppliers into a quasi-permanent network based on personal loyalty and protection. Suppliers are flexible in rendering services to their corporate "patrons" on short notice and providing them with customized components—for example, different grades of plastic for seats and dashboards in the case of an automobile company. In return, the automobile manufacturer guarantees its loyalty as a buyer of its client's suppliers, regardless of competition, the state of the market, or the lure of higher profits with alternative suppliers. A similar pattern of "relational contracting" has evolved between state-owned enterprises in China and their small-scale collective rather than state-owned suppliers.[15]

The reciprocal nature of hierarchical relationships between employers and workers within large corporations and between large corporations and their small family-sized subcontractors is not unlike the situation of large state-owned enterprises in China. In both cases, large enterprises offer workers lifetime employment, retirement and health benefits, and bonuses for high productivity (the latter only adopted in China since the reforms of 1984). Promotion is on the basis of seniority, and one is expected to carry out whatever job the firm may need. In China, for example, teachers of Russian in the Institute of Technology, for which the author worked in 1984 and 1985, were required to teach English because of the shift in national language priorities. Both in Japan and China, one's firm is not simply a workplace but an identity; one's "danwei" is where one is somebody. A casual question about what you do, among strangers, is likely to elicit the name of your firm, an indication of the importance of "company culture" as a source of identity. In the United States, by contrast, one's identity is more likely to be expressed in terms of one's individual skill or occupation. The company, in Japan and China, is also the source of one's friends, with social activities revolving around company affairs. But in Japanese companies (and here they differ markedly from Chinese *danwei*) all workers, including managers, are motivated to work long, extra hours without additional pay.

Loyalty to one's company is akin to belonging to a family in Japan; it precludes changing employers on the basis of market opportunities or organizing against employers to obtain higher salaries. In China, until recently, the same result was achieved by the state assigning individuals their jobs. The interests of "company unions" in Japan and trade unions in China, unlike those in the West, are identical with those of management. In Japan, and in China since the reforms, they meet annually with management to fix salaries and bonuses. Since executive salaries are directly tied to the salaries of other workers, with both determined by the profits of the firm as a whole, the company avoids an adversarial zero-sum relationship between labor and capital. Unlike China, however, management in Japan actively seeks to maximize the profits of the enterprise by providing every worker with an opportunity for promotion, even if that means proliferating the hierarchy of job gradations. In China, the tendency is still to reward workers collectively. This was demonstrated in the way the reform policy of bonuses was handled: Instead of rewarding workers individually, bonuses were often used to reward everyone equally for contributing to a factory's increased productivity.

The comparison between businesses and workers at the lower end of the property hierarchy in China and Japan is also instructive. In both Japan and China, workers hired by small-business subcontractors receive lower wages, have less job security, and depend for their livelihood on the vagaries of the market. In recessionary periods, therefore, these small-scale enterprises can fire their own workers. Though they are more dependent on the market for profits, they are under ordinary circumstances protected from going under by the "relational contracting" mentioned above. As a whole, this two-tiered organization of private property in Japan, though it defies some of the rudimentary "laws" of supply and demand, acts as a flexible and stable system in which predictability is maximized for both business, large and small, and the market as a whole. As we have tried to show in the comparison with China's two-tiered arrangement between large state-owned and small non-state or "private" businesses, the conception of property ownership implied by this organization of production is quite different from the Anglo-American institutionalization of property ownership.

Planning in China's Socialist and Japan's Developmental State

At the beginning of this chapter, the issue of who *plans* economic growth, second only to who *owns* productive property, was identified as the central distinguishing factor between a planned and a market economy. In a mixed economy, according to that discussion, one would expect state planning to be limited to the productive property owned by the state, which could vary between all and none. Japan, however, does not fit this category of a "mixed economy": The state owns virtually no productive property yet is heavily engaged in quite extensive planning. In China, public ownership of industrial and agricultural property put the state directly in the business of running the economy. In Japan it was the imperfection of the capitalist market that brought the government indirectly into the business of planning, not to *replace* the market but to *improve upon* its performance by compensating for its weaknesses and enhancing its capabilities.

How Are the Plans Carried Out?   The imperfections of the market that require state planning include its narrow short-term pursuit of profit, its concern for individual company interests at the expense of the national interest, its encouragement of opportunistic rather than collectively responsible behavior, its obliviousness to structural changes and social dislocations, and its potential for subordinating national to foreign commercial interests.[16] To counteract these market flaws, the government anticipates the shortcomings of the market and plans a specific course of action to remedy them. Known as an industrial policy, the government's plan determines the parameters within which corporations compete, thereby removing some of the uncertainties and undesirable outcomes of market forces for the best interests of the nation.

The government in Japan alters the expansion, contraction, and direction of corporate investments through a "discriminating use of administrative guidance."[17] This form of "preventive intervention" (as distinct from retrospective or regulatory intercession) requires neither the big government nor the coercive power of a command economy. It achieves maximum economic results with a minimum of public participation, although government intervention in the economy is far greater than in any of the Western capitalist market systems. To some observers it is the source of dynamism and flexibility that has enabled Japan to become an economic superpower. In the aftermath of Japan's first major postwar recession, it is blamed by many for the country's inability to dig itself out.

The key difference between government planning in Japan and pre-Reform China is that in the latter it was centralized, direct, and comprehensive in scope, covering the entire gamut of human activities from economic production to marriage and population growth, while in Japan state planning has never been either comprehensive or compulsory. In industry as well as agriculture the Japanese government deftly mimics Adam Smith's invisible hand. It seeks indirectly and subtly to orchestrate the actions of private entrepreneurs so as to guide the market in a particular direction. Signals are sent by government bureaucrats to private entrepreneurs, indicating specific industries that need to either increase or decrease production in order to enhance Japan's competitiveness in the international market.

Businesses that follow the advice of the Ministry of International Trade and Industry (MITI, the central governmental organ responsible for drawing up industrial policy) are rewarded with easy access to capital, tax breaks, and approval of their plans to establish joint ventures or import foreign technology. With some exceptions, most firms abide by government guidelines because the government's control over credit and licensing can be decisive. Although the extent of the state's power over economic decisions remains controversial, the scope of its planning covers a considerable range, from control of electric power rates and bike racing to how much research and development will take place in different product lines.

By contrast, China's economic planning has been characterized by bureaucratic heavy-handedness. In part this is a function of the sheer magnitude of China's economy, but more essentially it results from the centralized structure of micro- as well as macro-economic planning in such a vast country. By its nature, planning the total economy of China is a multifaceted and complex undertaking in which hundreds of millions of people participate. The comprehensive nature of such planning requires marshaling an extraordinary amount of information from all levels in every sector of economic production. The organization that makes this feasible, by its thoroughgoing penetration of society down to the lowest level, is the Communist Party of China. Economic policy is decided at the top of both the party and the state pyramids (with their overlapping memberships), followed by a complex process of negotiation and accommodation down the ranks. Even today, when Reform policy has structurally decentralized decision making and responsibility, overall planning of the entire economy remains a central function of the state, which retains legal ownership of the productive property.

Who Makes the Plans?   In China long-range 20-year goals of the nation and a strategy for achieving them are formulated by the Politburo, whose Standing Committee represents the prevailing consensus among the top leaders of the Communist Party. Called the *General Line of the Party,* this overarching program of long-run projections sets the parameters within which medium-term (five-year) and annual plans are drawn up, principally by the State Planning Commission (SPC) in conjunction with the State Statistical Bureau and the functional ministries. In addition, the SPC determines the money supply, draws up the budget, and effects the nation's balance of payments, akin in some respects to the U.S. Office of Management and Budget, though on a vaster scale.[18] The State Economic Commission (SEC), immediately below the SPC, assumes responsibility for implementing the shorter-term (one-year) plans by directing the ministries and provinces (and so on down the administrative ladder) to fill in the details relevant for production at each of their levels. All government planning agencies are under the jurisdiction of the State Council, which coordinates all the government's economic work and is formally accountable to the National People's Congress, the highest sovereign body.

In Japan, national economic policy is formulated by the ministerial bureaucracy and centers on industrial policy. Agriculture, by now a small and shrinking sector, is protected by the Ministry of Agriculture. And in the legislative or "political" sphere where until recently it has been overrepresented, agriculture had a disproportionate electoral influence. If agriculture has its special voice in the Diet, the Japanese parliament, big industry has its mainstay in the bureaucracy, most powerfully in the Ministry of International Trade and Industry. Industrial policy is fashioned by MITI and enjoys relative immunity from the pressures of partisan politics. Deriving from wartime planning and continued under postwar conditions of privation and disorganization, MITI's authority to plan for Japan's industrial development was strengthened rather than weakened by American-imposed postwar reforms. In its role as "economic general staff," MITI is assisted by the Ministry of Finance along with other ministries and the Economic Planning Board, and its broad policy mandate for industry requires approval by the legislature.

In contrast, industrial planning in Communist China has from the start been buffeted by tidal waves of political change. The preponderantly peasant composition of the Communist Party that assumed power in 1949 poorly qualified it for the specialized economic task of industrial planning. Compounding the problems of this rural-based leadership in implementing Soviet-style planning were the repeated Maoist campaigns, which disrupted the orderly planning process. They increased the participation of large numbers of peasants and workers in production decisions and injected "mass politics" into the planning process. During the Cultural Revolution, for example, newly founded revolutionary committees at all levels, from provincial government down to the factory floor, were empowered to engage in planning activities: to set quotas and determine the resources needed to meet various targets. Final plans specifying production quotas were then negotiated between the enterprises or communes and the planning officials from the center.

But the Maoist attempts at decentralizing economic decision making, represented by the Great Leap Forward and the Cultural Revolution, were only temporary departures from the Soviet planning model, which, when they failed, delivered the economic system back into the hands of the Soviet-type planners. In this zigzag pattern, the Chinese Communist Party throughout the Maoist era found itself struggling to define a strategy that synthesized its own distinctive revolutionary experience with the professionally rigorous bureaucratic demands made by the Soviet system of central planning. A resolution to this tension was brought about only with the Reform policy, which after 1978 pursued the Maoist goal of decentralization using Western-type market devices in place of the collective or mass politics preferred by the founder of new China.

Comparative Strategies for National Development

The question of which economic strategy a country uses to promote its national economic goals is closely linked to historical contingencies. China's Maoist strategy embracing self-sufficiency evolved in response to a hostile capitalist world economy, while Japan's export-led strategy unfolded in response to international economic opportunities (see box). Beginning with a fortunate coincidence, Japan evolved an outward-looking strategy of manufacturing. By producing for export, private industries acquired both the revenue and the upgraded technology to manufacture successively more sophisticated exports. In this fashion, a virtuous spiral of export-led and import-protected growth was set into motion. The contribution of the Japanese state to this product-cycle sequence of development has been fourfold:

1. It balances the need for exports, which require *low* tariffs or a free trade policy, against the need for imports, which require *high* tariffs to protect new domestic technologies.
2. It acts as a scout for international opportunities, canvassing the world's "technology shelf" for industries "which appear to have future potential

Development by Accident

Japan was launched on an export-led course by an infection that destroyed all Italian and French silkworm eggs in the 1860s, creating an instant market for its profitable and labor-intensive silk industry. Japan's response to this opportunity resulted in the formation of an internationally oriented entrepreneurial class and the accumulation of valuable export revenue for a government attempting to strengthen its autonomy against the demands of the United States.

By the time the European silk industry had recovered, Japan had a thriving silk-export industry that grew exponentially in subsequent years. Thus began Japan's industrial growth in a sequence of stages that looked to the outside world for clues to its direction. While revenues were raised by exporting resources (silkworm eggs), the Japanese state facilitated the technology transfer and investments necessary to produce labor-intensive light industrial exports (silk and cotton textiles). The state then utilized a system of taxes, subsidies, and direct controls to steer production toward higher-growth industries such as shipbuilding, iron and steel machinery, and chemicals in the second stage, knowledge-based industries in the third stage, and high-tech industries at the cutting edge of world technology in more recent decades.

for achieving an advantageous position over the next decade, *despite a comparatively disadvantageous position at the time.*"[19]

3. It functions as a gatekeeper for the protection of domestic industries against their more advanced foreign competitors.
4. It administratively sets industrial priorities for curtailing some and expanding other investments.

Maoist strategy moved in the opposite direction, turning its back on a hostile international community to concentrate on the country's internal transformation into an industrial socialist state. In the late 1960s, at the pinnacle of Maoist influence, China was being assailed by both the United States and the Soviet Union. Mao pointed to self-reliance—in particular, to the self-sustained communes—as illustrations of how the country could defend itself from outside attack and build socialism at the same time. But after Mao died, and the damage was surveyed, the cost for China of adopting Maoist strategy was high. By reinforcing the age-old inclination to cut itself off from the rest of the world, China's leadership had lost valuable time in building an infrastructure of roads, transport, and communications to provide the foundation for a modern interdependent economy. The sum of China's immense population, scarcity of arable land, and economic insularity was shared poverty, not socialism.

What is remarkable about the Maoist strategy, however, is its unflinching embrace of experimentation. Its combination of opposites was bold in conception and startling in execution, punctuating the rigidity of a highly centralized planning system with periodic outbursts of mass political participation. The turmoil, uncertainty, and precariousness of life for people faced with an entire society oscillating between two such extremes are almost unfathomable. Two results, however, have been both fortuitous and ironic. Despite all the disruptions, China was able to maintain annual average industrial and agricultural growth rates of 11 and 2.5 percent, respectively, throughout this period; and because of the disastrous economic consequences of these experimental disruptions, the Chinese people were more prepared to energetically embrace economic reforms in 1978 than they might otherwise have been.

Patterns of Securing Compliance

Implementation of government strategies in both China and Japan is a top-down process that involves aggregating information, negotiating differences, making compromises, and persuading opponents to comply with policies deemed by centralized elites to be in the best interests of the nation. In China, the elite Communist Party runs like a spinal cord down the center of the entire body politic, providing coherence and backbone to the task of securing compliance with government policy. In Japan, on the other hand, MITI operates more loosely, exercising its muscle through a complex network of cultural ligaments connecting the corporate economy to the state bureaucracy. Although it may appear in the abstract that the Communist Party, with the full weight of its centralized power reaching directly down through the ranks, would be more effective than MITI in implementing its recommendations, this is not necessarily the case. A great deal depends on the resources of those in command and the willingness of those whose compliance is sought.

Securing Compliance in Japan's Market System.   The Japanese bureaucracy has a combination of resources at its disposal to obtain compliance with its planning priorities. The most widely touted is the high individual and corporate savings rate of the Japanese. Through its postal savings system, the Japanese government has access to extensive financial resources with which to offer subsidies, loans, and credits to industries. Household and firm savings thus accumulated provide 40 to 50 percent of the General Accounting Budget, which together with postal life insurance and pensions constitute a valuable source of capital for the government clearly distinct from tax revenues. MITI also uses its authority to set exchange rates, interest rates, taxes, and the prices of selected factors of production to obtain private sector compliance with its economic policies. Most important, however, is MITI's authority to negotiate, persuade, and arbitrate consensus among private sector enterprises to go along with the government's national economic objectives. As explained by Chalmers Johnson, "With its self-assertiveness, its strong native nationalism, its loyalist posture, . . . and its 'workism,' MITI reminds us of the General Staff Office of the defunct army."[20]

MITI's clout is evidenced in the weight its stamp of approval carries: a virtual guarantee that a corporation will have access to private loans. The nature of this partnership between government bureaucracy and private enterprise sets the Japanese developmental state apart from the Anglo-American form of capitalism. What is the source of cohesion in this partnership? Two aspects will be briefly re-

viewed: the institutional interlocking of government, financial, and production organizations; and the cultural interlocking of lifetime employment, the organization
of the educational system, and the social conception of "the market" in the Japanese understanding.

Industries in Japan are commonly observed to be in collusion with one another. Research has suggested, however, that rather than being a matter of conspir-
atorial behavior, this collusion results from the way industrial institutions are organized. The industrial group or *keiretsu*, as discussed above, arranges a diversified
group of industries under one roof, so to speak, in an interlocking financial arrangement by which each owns a significant portion of the others' stocks and all are tied
closely to a single bank. This manner of financing one another's productive enterprises has three important functions: (1) it creates a measure of certainty in supply
and demand when members buy and sell among themselves; (2) it counteracts hostile takeovers when substantial blocs of each industry's stock are held by loyal partners in the *keiretsu*; and (3) it precludes pressure for short-term high dividends on
the part of absentee owners from interfering with management of the long-term interests of the corporation.

Similarly, there is collaboration between private enterprise and the government bureaucracy in the form of an intricate web of personal and informal connections. Personal relationships may be the result of marriage or of having attended the
same school or the same class at school. Informal contacts that members of MITI
have with businesspeople are extensive and ongoing throughout the lifetime of a
civil servant's career. The anticipated outcome of these informal connections is "descent from heaven" (*amakudari*), retirement to a comfortable position in one of the
private corporations with which one has worked in the Ministry. From this corporate position one is expected to use one's expertise and connections in the ministry
to help the company secure licenses and approval for projects. The Japanese refer
to the relationship between a senior ex-bureaucrat and his or her successor in
the bureaucracy as "digging around the roots"—preparing the groundwork for a
government-business decision.[21] Altogether these relationships cement the bonds
that expedite government's continuous consultations, negotiations, and consensus
building with private enterprise.

The same group loyalty that binds companies of a *keiretsu* together also works
to forge industrywide cooperation. National trade associations such as the Association of Electric Companies and Keidanren, the Federation of Economic Organizations, which promotes the collective interests of large business enterprises, play
an important role in securing industrywide cooperation and sectoral economic
management. Though they operate as interest groups, trade associations enjoy
quasi-public status among Japanese. They negotiate with MITI to shape official
government-approved industrywide policies on the basis of which informal agreements are worked out among individual firms to balance government (cost-based)
pricing at the apex of the industry with market pressures that operate at the lower
end. MITI's role in the entire process is to settle specific disputes between industries (sometimes sending their representatives on a holiday together to foster trust
and cooperation) and provide, in general, the disciplined leadership to spur members of an industry to reach an agreement they fundamentally desire but lack the
capacity to bring about.

The extraordinary influence MITI exercises in the economic realm is related to the nature of the educational system and its ties to government. Japan's modern educational system from its origins has been designed to grade abilities for employment, with the effect that it reinforces the "company culture" of corporate employment. Each university (and high school) has a fixed number of entrants solely determined on the basis of performance on nationally standardized exams. Students who rank in the highest percentile of exams upon high school graduation go to the top-ranking Tokyo University, with each next lower percentile going to the next lower-ranking university. Educational background based on a two-track system—university graduate track and high school career track—is therefore the basis for entry level into the corporate world. The top percentage of the most prestigious Tokyo University graduates join MITI, with successively lower ranks of graduates recruited by the other ministries and by corporations. Thus standardized nationwide testing determines who gets to go to college and who, therefore, gets which jobs in the government and corporate hierarchy; it is an open system permitting upward mobility.

Implementing Plans in Communist China.   In pre-Reform China, compliance with the dictates of central planning was secured by the Communist Party through a combination of ideology and organization. The party, reaching down to the village and enterprise level, used "mass line" techniques to ensure widespread familiarity with the ideological requirements of government policy. Everyone studied the documents in political study groups, a compulsory activity attached to every work unit (factory, school, mine, retail shop, or residential neighborhood); they were also discussed in mass organizations, like the trade unions or the Women's Federation, and became the subject of mass campaigns. Thus the Chinese to a much larger extent than the Japanese, used mobilizational techniques to substitute for market incentives. Production decisions in Japan may be shaped by government planning, but they are implemented by the individual company whose effectiveness is measured by market forces and the monetary rewards of workers. In China, though production decisions were similarly shaped by consultations between party officials and economic managers, during the Maoist period their implementation was effected through involuntary political participation and measured by political rewards.

Unlike Japan, where economic decision makers in administrative positions were shielded from the political conflicts within the ruling party, compliance with the economic policy of the Chinese state inextricably became enmeshed with the political wrangling among factions of the Communist Party. Economic performance in China, therefore, reflected the succession of winners and losers in the political infighting among party factions with contradictory visions of *how* China could best accomplish its economic ends. Party advocates of Soviet-style rapid industrialization favored material incentives to promote workers with greater technical competence. When Maoists came to power, however, political criteria were used to discredit the technically proficient, rewarding those who excelled at political mobilization. Throughout the pre-Reform period, these contradictory approaches alternated with economic production plagued by unpredictable shifts in economic policy.

Thus economic development in China after 1949 continued to feel the reverberations of the revolution that had ushered in modernization on a nationwide and systematic basis. What in Japan was an orderly administrative process of strengthening the entrepreneurial activities in the private sector was in China a turbulent oscillation between a centrally administered economy and its nemesis, the politics of mass participation. Given this marked contrast between the continuity of Japan's nationalistic political economy and the vicissitudes of China's ideologically driven political economy, it is noteworthy that in both countries it was a strong state that facilitated rapid and impressive economic growth. Equally notable, however, was the subsequent weakening of the Japanese state as a consequence first, of deregulation and second, of the real-estate bubble that burst in the 1980s after which Japan suffered an extended period of low economic growth. By 1997 an already weakened Japanese state was faced with economic recession in the wake of the Asian financial crisis which, ironically, China with its strong state intact weathered with relative ease. This question of the relationship of a strong state to economic growth assumed even greater significance when, beginning in the 1970s, the newly industrializing economies (NICs) of the Asian Pacific made their dramatic entry onto the world stage.

THE NICS' DEVELOPMENTAL PATTERN

The unexpected ascendance of the NICs into the world of rapidly industrializing countries led to a reexamination of Japan's development. The NICs, like Japan, employed exports to finance industrialization in a product-cycle sequence of stages (as described earlier). Taiwan and South Korea, as colonies, had been exploited for their comparative advantage as part of Japan's regional development of a coprosperity sphere. Similarly, Manchuria in northeast China had initially been industrialized by the Japanese in this manner. This has led Bruce Cumings to stress the regional nature of industrialization in Northeast Asia: "A country-by-country approach is incapable of accounting for the remarkably similar trajectories of Korea and Taiwan."[22] If, as he suggests, Korean and Taiwanese development occurred within an essentially Japanese context, it may be possible to understand China's reform in 1978 as a similar, if long-delayed, resort to the Japanese model of development to rectify its problems with a command system of planning. To pursue this line of discourse, we will juxtapose discussion of the reform program which began in China in 1978 with the NICs' pattern of industrialization to explore the possibility that China's opening to the international economy represents a regional convergence of political economies.

With what appeared like startling speed, Taiwan, South Korea, Singapore, and Hong Kong had emerged from Third World poverty and "backwardness" into the front ranks of industrializing countries. In contrast to other developing countries around the world, East Asian NICs exhibited sustained high growth rates (see Table 5.1), a relatively equitable distribution of the product of development, a continuing capability to alter domestic economic structures in alignment with changing international circumstances, and a powerful state capable of mobilizing and deploying domestic economic resources. The question for both scholars and political leaders is how to explain this winning combination of characteristics. Four possibilities have been suggested:[23]

TABLE 5.1   GDP Average Annual Growth Rate (Percentage)

Country	1980–1990	1990–1997
China	10.2	11.9
Hong Kong	6.9	5.3
Indonesia	6.1	7.5
Japan	4.0	1.4
Malaysia	5.2	8.7
Philippines	1.0	3.3
Singapore	6.6	8.5
South Korea	9.5	7.2
Taiwan	7.9	6.5
Thailand	7.6	7.5

Sources: World Development Report 1998/99, table 11, Oxford University Press, pp. 210–121. *Taiwan Statistical Data Book, 1999,* table 3-2a/2b, Council for Economic Planning and Development, Republic of China, pp. 42–43.

1. It is a result of embracing a market economy with a free trade policy.
2. It is a consequence of "special circumstances" unlikely to be easily duplicated.
3. It is attributable to a shared Confucian heritage emphasizing hard work, frugality, hierarchy, and harmony.
4. It is the consequence of economic planning by a strong state in close collaboration with a market-driven, export-oriented economy.

After examining the ways in which the political economies of the NICs differ among themselves and from the Chinese or Japanese experience, the reader should be able to determine which of these explanations, and in what combination, is most helpful to understand the dynamics of economic development in the Asian Pacific.

Embracing the Market Economy and Free Trade

That Hong Kong, Singapore, South Korea, and Taiwan are all market economies pursuing an open policy of international trade is indisputable. As a British colony (until 1997), Hong Kong was closest among the NICs to the Western market model of a political economy: The government followed a hands-off policy, leaving economic affairs to the international and Chinese business communities. Although highly diversified business groups had existed since the early days of British rule, the preponderance of business enterprises consisted of small- and medium-sized manufacturing companies dependent on the flow of refugee labor from mainland China. Adhering for the most part to its British colonial role as entrepôt, Hong Kong was industrialized alongside the NICs while remaining atypical by comparison. This means that many of the observations below about the role of the state are not applicable to Hong Kong.

The controversies among observers center on the deviations in the other three NICs from the Western prototypes of a market economy: the substantial state-owned sector in the case of Taiwan, the concentration of economic power in huge conglomerates in the case of South Korea, the heavy reliance on multinational capital in the case of Singapore, and the extensive state intervention in the economies of all three of these NICs. These departures from the Western model raise questions about what a market economy means in the context of Asian Pacific economic development.

Singapore, a city-state like Hong Kong, has a highly internationalized economy, 70 percent of which is owned by multinationals. The shortage of local entrepreneurs, most of whom are in small-scale business, contrasts with the mainly foreign-dominated sector of Singapore's large industrial, export-oriented, high-tech private enterprises, attracted to the island by a highly educated workforce and a modern, sophisticated infrastructure.[24] In both South Korea and Taiwan, on the other hand, state-owned enterprises have played a pivotal role in economic development. The South Korean government, through its state-controlled banks, has exercised a decisive control in shaping the contours of economic growth. In industry as well as external trade, a few very large, privately owned industrial groups called *chaebol*, such as Samsung, Daewoo, and Hyundai, exhibit a remarkable resemblance to the Japanese giants, the *keiretsu* described earlier. At present, the Korean economy is controlled by 30 to 50 of these conglomerate business groups, each owned and managed by a single family. Although the *chaebol* have tended to be more dependent on the Korean state for credit and access to foreign capital than their Japanese counterparts, they have increasingly demonstrated an inclination toward independence from the South Korean state bureaucracy.[25]

In contrast to South Korea, Taiwan has the largest sector of state-owned corporations of all the NICs, and they are disproportionately represented among Taiwan's largest corporations in key industrial sectors. They tend also to be controlled by mainlanders who monopolize government office, while the privately owned sector is composed mostly of small- and medium-sized enterprises predominantly owned by Taiwanese. Based on the criterion of private ownership of property, there is little doubt that the NICs, like Japan, qualify as market economies. Yet there is the separate question: Is it the market forces in these East Asian countries that have driven economic growth, or has the market been propelled, as in Japan, by the state?

Some have argued that trade itself, the adoption of an export-oriented industrialization (EOI) policy, ignited the explosion of industrial activity in the NICs during the 1960s. This line of reasoning suggests that it was the early switch of the "little tigers" to an export-led development that triggered their impressive growth rates. With fewer natural resources than Japan, the NICs had no choice but to export manufactured goods if they were to develop at all. They shifted away from the high tariffs of earlier import-substitution policies to lower tariffs that would promote exports of labor-intensive manufactured goods. The sequence was the same as Japan's, except that the NICs followed one step behind in the product cycle: As

Japan moved on to high-tech information equipment, the NICs moved into the production of electronic equipment. However, the successful economic ascent of the NICs left them with a far higher trade dependence than Japan, as shown in Table 5.2. The NICs' dependence on Japanese imports (both of technology and capital) has increased as Japan has surpassed the United States as an exporter of intermediate goods and technology. As a result South Korea, Taiwan, Hong Kong, and Singapore are import-dependent on Japan and export-dependent on the United States.

"Special Circumstances"

But the virtuous spiral of economic development created by trade requires an initial outlay of substantial amounts of capital as well as accessible markets capable of absorbing the exports. How did the NICs satisfy these preconditions? One of the explanations for the NICs' unusually rapid development is offered by those who argue that "special circumstances" existed early in their development and gave them a nonreplicable advantage.

Unlike China or Japan, the NICs are creatures of unusual circumstance. Two are ministates; two are fragments of countries produced by the international rivalry between the United States and the former Soviet Union. As frontline states in the war against communism, South Korea received an annual average of $270 million in economic aid from the United States between 1953 and 1958, and Taiwan received $100 million annually between 1951 and 1965. Military assistance was twice that amount. Singapore and Hong Kong enjoyed advantages from their earlier status as entrepôts: an urbanized population, high literacy rates, a skilled workforce, and long experience in trading internationally. Taiwan and South Korea acquired many of their infrastructural foundations under Japanese colonial rule: a modernized agricultural system, a network of roads and communications, high literacy rates, and linkages with the international economy. American advisers after World War II assisted in land reform (as they did in Japan), thus completing the modernization of agriculture begun under the Japanese. As a result of these historical "special circumstances," the NICs were all well located for international trade and ready to "take off" economically at a time of expanding world markets.[26]

TABLE 5.2   Ratios of Foreign Trade Turnover to GNP

Country	Percentage
Japan	20
South Korea	54
Taiwan	83
Hong Kong	160
Singapore	189

Source: William Nester, *Japan's Growing Power Over East Asia and the World Economy* (New York: St. Martin's, 1990), p. 86.

Confucian Values

A variation of the "special circumstances" perspective on the economic success of the NICs is rooted in the observation of their common Confucian background. As Chinese-based communities, it is argued, Singapore, Hong Kong, Taiwan, and South Korea share cultural values and traditions that have contributed substantially to their rapid industrialization. Hard work, frugality, the paternalistic family, education, and the ethical responsibilities of political leaders are values that have conditioned Asians growing up in a Chinese cultural setting. It is suggested that "entrepreneurial familism" has provided an economic motor for capitalist development in Confucian-based NICs, particularly in Taiwan and Hong Kong. The paternalistic management of family-owned enterprises fosters the flexibility and inventiveness that enables them to be competitive in a high-risk, rapidly changing international market. And a high level of trust among family members permits cost-cutting financial and labor arrangements, a centralized form of decision making, and informal mechanisms of control and accountability that promote secrecy and preserve entrepreneurial autonomy.[27]

Though it is difficult to measure the extent to which these values have contributed to such factors of development as universally high savings rates, the absence of unionization, and compliance with the authority of the state, they undoubtedly have played a role in laying the foundation for a strong authoritarian state that is expected to actively intervene in the economy. Certainly, the belief that a state should be strong and exercise sufficient authority to administer a well-managed economy is widespread in East Asia.

The Role of the State in Economic Planning

The single most compelling factor in the economic development of South Korea, Taiwan, and Singapore is the extensive and intensive ways in which government has pushed economic levers and pulled financial strings to accomplish economic development. The prominence of the state in promoting, financing, shaping, and nudging the economy toward economic growth places the NICs in the same category as Japan and China. All have strong authoritarian regimes aware of the necessity of modern economic growth for their national strength and survival. Among the conditions provided by the governments of the NICs to promote economic growth are land reform, a literate labor force, capital for investments, raw materials, a strong industrialization ideology on the part of the government, a well-trained, efficient, and relatively incorrupt bureaucracy, and institutions for linking the public and private sectors.

Land Reform.   As we have already seen in the case of Japan and China, the initial task of the state in fortifying itself and laying the groundwork for a modern productive system is land reform. For the entrepôts, Hong Kong and Singapore, this was not a problem, but in Taiwan and South Korea, where land was the primary source of wealth, it was essential. Land provides not only food to support a growing nonagricultural sector but raw materials for industry, commodities for export, surplus capital for investment, and labor to fill the nonagricultural jobs.

Though in both Taiwan and South Korea the Japanese had already modernized agricultural production for their home consumption, tenancy rates remained high after the war, with an elite in each case inheriting the greatest proportion of land from the Japanese. The Guomindang leaders who fled to Taiwan in 1949, realizing the significance of land reform as a factor that cost them control of the mainland and in any event not landowners themselves, were eager not to make the same mistake. With the help of American advisers, therefore, they redistributed the land to create a nation of smallholders eager to invest and innovate. This eliminated a powerful internal source of resistance to industrial development and redirected idle capital away from land speculation into manufacturing and commercial enterprises. South Korea, also on the advice of the United States, undertook land reform with similar results. Though land reform did not make the peasantry rich, it did create a more equitable income distribution, which additionally strengthened the centralized authority of the state.[28]

Labor Force.   Another benefit of land reform in South Korea and Taiwan was that it made available a disciplined and low-cost labor force, an advantage that Singapore and Hong Kong had by virtue of being urban centers that attracted a large inflow of refugees. The NICs were in fact unique, as Alice Amsden points out, in garnering world markets "on the almost exclusive basis of low wage rates . . . a truly new international division of labor."[29] The Korean government, building on what the Japanese had begun, invested heavily in education, reducing illiteracy, defined as the absence of any schooling whatever, from 40 percent of the workforce in 1946 to virtually nil by 1963.[30] It is not only the level but the content of education that has contributed to the NICs' comparative advantage, as Robert Wade points out.[31] In Taiwan and South Korea an increase in the ratios of skilled to unskilled or only basically skilled people in the labor force over the past 40 years has enabled their economies to sustain a comparative advantage in progressively more skill-intensive, higher-wage productive enterprises. By ensuring an influx of higher-skilled people into the workforce, government policy in these countries lowers the relative cost of skilled labor, promoting investments in industries that require shifting combinations of skill levels.

Capital.   In the area of capital formation for business investment the government has played an equally activist role in the NICs (with the exception of Hong Kong). The governments of South Korea and Taiwan received massive amounts of foreign aid and military assistance from the United States, providing them with both money and know-how with which to powerfully influence the market. South Korea also received American surplus products under very favorable terms. In addition, the governments of Korea, Taiwan, and Singapore promoted domestic savings and the inflow of foreign capital in a number of important ways. Singapore, for example, introduced the Central Provident Fund (CPF), a new financial institution to mobilize private sector savings. The CPF is a means of obtaining forced savings that, while designed to secure economic provisions for old age and health care, is also used by the government to provide housing and other investments for the private sector. Taiwan invested in public sector industries and facilitated the transfer of financial resources from informal (gray) underground networks to legitimate, aboveboard financial institutions. And the government of South Korea owns and controls the banks that, through discriminating lending policies, exercise a considerable influence over investment decisions. Thus government in the NICs, even more than in Japan, has played a dominant role in shaping the nature and direction of economic expansion through its privileged access to domestic savings and foreign investments.

Industrialization Ideology and Efficient Bureaucracy.   Critical to the activist role of government in promoting savings, obtaining resources, and attracting foreign capital are a strong industrialization ideology and a well-trained, efficient, and relatively incorrupt bureaucracy. The core of these officials in the case of South Korea and Taiwan has been American-educated economists, technocrats, aid administrators, and foreign experts working for such organizations as the World Bank, the International Monetary Fund, and the U.S. Agency for International Development. Singapore, reflecting its origins as a British imperial outpost, along with the British colony of Hong Kong, tend to have British-educated economists and experts both as officials and as advisers. Taiwan is noted for a concentration of engineers among its administrators.

The common denominator of these technocrats, reflective of both their training and the policies of the lending institutions from which they obtain investment funds, is a commitment to investing for economic growth as an end in itself. We call this *industrialization ideology* to differentiate it from liberal, socialist, or communist ideology, according to which there is an end quite distinct from the pragmatic considerations of how best to promote economic growth. Liberal ideology, for example, indicates that free markets and free trade are ends in themselves that ought not to be sacrificed at the altar of growth for growth's sake. Industrialization ideology, however, is a pragmatic adherence to whatever achieves economic growth as measured by the quantities of goods and services produced, labor productivity, and the like.

Public-Private Sector Linkages.   The major way in which governments in South Korea, Taiwan, and Singapore promote economic growth is by linking their public sector policies with those of the private sector. Financially, this is done in a number of different ways. In Singapore the government has established control over savings, which the private sector has responsibility for investing. Thus the government is an intermediary between savers and investors, effectively forging a collaboration with substantial power for the public sector.[32] In South Korea the government achieves this "merging" somewhat more coercively through its state-owned banks, which are the major source of loans for the private sector. But on the positive side, the South Korean government has also monetarily compensated firms for financial losses incurred as a result of exporting commodities at the government's suggestion.[33] In Taiwan private and public sectors are intermeshed through the government's ownership of large corporations in such basic industries as petroleum, steel, and electric power.

Other mechanisms utilized by government in all three NICs include providing an array of incentives for investment in specific areas, control of prices (which in the case of South Korea begins with the price of money), and informal pressures put on manufacturers to procure a larger share of their inputs domestically. The overall principle of public-private relationships is one of cooperation among management, labor, and government in the formulation of plans, much as it is in Japan. In Singapore and Taiwan, the cooperative alliance is among government, foreign enterprises, and local business.

Assessing the NICs' Development

The pattern of economic development in the NICs (with the exception of Hong Kong) is broadly similar to the Japanese model of political economy. The government in each case assumed initiative for creating and has continued to pilot industrial market economies dependent almost entirely upon trade with the outside world, most importantly with Japan and the Western industrialized nations but increasingly with the remaining Asian Pacific nations. By targeting exports that take advantage of a disciplined labor force and by selectively promoting imports that drive the economy up the product-cycle ladder, the government engineers a dynamic market relationship between international demand and domestic supply. A local entrepreneurial class has been strengthened in Taiwan and South Korea, though in Singapore it is the community of international entrepreneurs that has benefited.

"Special circumstances" have played an important role in the development of NICs. In South Korea, for example, a strong military, built up by U.S. aid and training, took over the government in 1961 and systematically engineered economic growth. Under military rule, the windfall profits made by some under the corrupt Rhee regime were used in a new, more growth-oriented direction, giving rise to an entrepreneurial class.[34] In Taiwan the National People's Party, motivated by its defeat on the mainland, embraced land reform, purged its military of corruption, and used martial law to strengthen the state in all areas of life. The role of Confucianism in the development of the NICs has been to preclude any independent opposition on the part of either organized labor or organized interest groups that might fragment the "grand alliance." Thus strong states bolstered by an anticommunist mission, a well-trained military, and Confucian values of hard work, frugality, discipline, and authority undertook planned economic modernization in collaboration with the "free world."

The intriguing aspect of the NICs' political economy is the combination of an authoritarian political regime, government planning of the national economy, and a market system closely integrated in the global economy. The difference between this developmental pattern and China's command political economy is its reliance on the free market. Put into place and assisted by government bureaucrats who intermediate between national interests and international opportunities, the market provides the basis of exchange. Indeed, the performance of the market as an indispensable stimulant for economic growth among the NICs was not lost on the socialist countries of East Asia. The declining efficiencies and low returns on capital investments of their planned economies led China and Vietnam in the late 1970s, and North Korea more recently, to move in the direction of opening their economies to world trade and absorbing market mechanisms to spur economic growth.

Two decades later when command economies in China and Vietnam had already embarked on marketization to emulate the rapid economic growth of the NICs, the financial crisis that swept through East and Southeast Asia raised new questions about the structural viability of the developmental model so closely associated with NIC "miracle economies." The lessons, once again, were not lost on China's leadership. We turn now to China's economic reform, which to a considerable extent has benefited from the developmental experiences of the NICs.

THE SEARCH FOR A SOCIALIST GUIDED MARKET

In the decades between 1978 and the present, a series of policies have been adopted in China and Vietnam to reform the Soviet-style or Stalinist model of political economy. Although many of these problems had been recognized all along, they assumed critical importance in the changed international circumstances of the late 1970s. The retreat from Vietnam by first the United States and then the Soviet Union drew attention to Japan's position as economic superpower and the impressive strides of the NICs following closely in its footsteps. Though it was not a question of copying either Japan or the NICs, their experiences provided the socialist countries with an Asian alternative to Western-type capitalism and its liberal democratic politics. Looked at from the perspective of this "Japanese model," the socialist or Stalinist pattern of development revealed not merely the full extent of its flaws but a viable direction in which to move to eliminate them. What the Japanese model demonstrated and the NICs confirmed about a successful pattern of development for late industrializers was the efficacy of a market economy guided by government planning.

Reform Policy in China

Although the Maoist regime had delivered on some of its promises—an average annual industrial growth rate of 11 percent, full employment, an impressive array of widely distributed social services—the economic system was unable to increase either the standard of living or the labor productivity of its people. The reform policy unveiled at the Third Plenum of the Eleventh Party Congress in 1978 envisioned a revitalization of the economy by opening up to the outside world, emphasizing light and consumer industries, decentralizing production decisions, introducing market mechanisms to determine prices, and separating political power from economic decision making.

Just over two decades later, these reform policies have transformed China into the second largest industrial producer in the world (after the United States) with a GDP as measured in purchasing power parity (PPP) that ranks third in the world behind the United States and Japan. Goods in all sectors of China's economy are now basically allocated through market transactions, and most prices have been liberalized. State-owned enterprises have retained their importance in such core heavy industries as coal mining, petroleum extraction, metallurgy and machine building, and they remain primary sources of tax revenue for government at all levels. But they produce a much smaller share of China's total national industrial output and are currently the target of aggressive restructuring to prevent the bank failures that resulted elsewhere in the region following the economic collapse of 1997. The nonstate sector, by contrast, has become a dynamic engine of growth, dominating the export and infant high-tech sector.

Perhaps the most remarkable aspect of China's metamorphosis from a centrally planned economy into a "socialist" free market economy is the gradual manner in which it has transpired. For 20 years prior to the advent of Reform, largely without the assistance of outside capital and despite the repeated disruptions of political campaigns, the communist regime had accumulated capital in the state-owned heavy industrial sector by transferring the agricultural surplus produced by 80 percent of the population working in agricultural collectives. Utilizing "an extremely complex, integrated bureaucratic network developed to achieve macroeconomic planning through micro management of the individual firm,"[35] this state-owned sector produced over 75 percent of China's industrial output in 1978. By 1995, as a *result* of economic reforms, this figure had dropped to under 35 percent. The remaining two-thirds of China's industrial output in 1995 was produced by a nonstate sector that grew incrementally from a series of experimental economic reforms.

Though no longer controversial in principle, economic reform in practice has created staggering problems of its own and generated a wide range of new questions among China scholars and Chinese alike: How will economic reforms be extended to the more backward areas of the country and to all its citizens? What impact will economic reforms have on the political and social fabric of an avowedly communist country? Are the enormous inequities that have accompanied China's switch from a planned to a market economy an inevitable concomitant of becoming highly developed? Does China's successful accommodation to capitalist markets portend an inevitable abandonment of socialist principles? Or is it merely, as the leadership still contends, a necessary intermediate step called "market socialism" on the road to communism?

The Household Contract System.   Economic reform made its debut in the countryside. Referred to as a "household responsibility" system, the policy reversed collectivization by dividing up the land belonging to the production teams (the lowest rung of a commune) and leasing it back to individual households. The land was as meticulously and equitably parceled out as it had been under land reform: Each household received some of the best-, medium-, and worst-quality land of the team. Leases at first were limited to 15 years but later extended to 50, with the right of children to inherit their parents' land. Each household decided what and how much to produce on the basis of a contract system. The household had a base contract with the state, a tax, to provide a specified quota of a particular crop at a fixed price; anything produced over and beyond that could be sold to the state at a higher (closer to the market) price or to any private party. Each household was thus rewarded on the basis of its work.

Township Industry and Rural Markets.   By the end of 1983, China had reverted to full-scale family farming, with 94 percent of peasant households operating within the system of household responsibility.[36] The range of choices for rural households widened as the government permitted peasants to sublease their land and take up new occupations—providing transport, for example, or starting a new business in the township. As households that excelled at commodity agriculture leased more land from others who gave up farming and moved off into townships, the rural economy diversified and large numbers of people migrated off the land into the townships, the old seats of commune government. *Specialized households* were promoted by the government to concentrate on a narrow range of farm or nonfarm production, raising their level of technical expertise in a single area. In some cases entire rural areas turned into rural commodity markets, specializing in one commodity—all the varieties of buttons, for example, or electrical appliances—and selling wholesale across the nation through the services of peasants-turned-traders.[37]

While some farmers became "10,000-yuan farmers," the equivalent of millionaires, the townships became thriving centers of rural industry. At the core were the industrial collectives that had prospered under the commune system and now operated under contract to the village or township to which they formerly belonged. Industries like cement and fertilizer, already producing large shares of total national output by the early 1970s, were now joined by a wide range of industries producing goods and services for rural and urban households. There were small individual entrepreneurs, larger private entrepreneurs who employed eight or more workers, and township and village owned enterprises (TVEs) that collaborated with foreign investors of capital and technology to venture into the global market. Thus returning economic decision making to family initiative and local incentives produced a lively agricultural and industrial rural economy, at least in those areas well endowed with factors of production.

Urban Economic Reform.   In 1984, economic reform in the urban areas received the green light in a set of directives described as "socialism with Chinese characteristics." The major problems that inspired reform were the declining efficiency and poor quality of production in state-owned enterprises (SOEs), the procurement bottlenecks that resulted in underutilization of capacity, the slow pace of innovation, and the lack of separation between governmental functions and enterprise management that stifled worker productivity. Three solutions were envisioned: one was managerial autonomy for enterprises, the second was an industrial contract responsibility system, and the third was price reform. By divesting government of its management role in the economy, making enterprise managers responsible for their profits and losses free from party interference, gradually eliminating mandatory planning, and expanding the role of the market correspondingly, reformers sought to combine the vigor of the market with the promise of socialism. *Guided Planning* was the term used to describe the government's function vis-à-vis a productive system that produced goods and services in accordance with market forces.

SOE Reform: Managerial Autonomy.   Reforming the 400,000 state-owned industrial enterprises that employed about 80 million people at the onset of economic reform was at the heart of urban economic reform. The initial phase was to separate ownership from management of the day-to-day control of a plant's operations. The owners—theoretically the state as representative of all the Chinese people but actually the party officials—were to remove themselves from managerial decision making, allowing enterprises to become "independent economic entities," with enterprise managers responsible for the profits and losses of their firms, for determining job descriptions and performance criteria for workers, and for hiring and firing employees. Laws were passed to convert individual enterprises into "legal persons with certain rights and duties." Party officials, who for almost 30 years had been in the driver's seat of these state-owned enterprises, were now to retreat to the caboose, from where they were to "provide active support" without interfering in the enterprise manager's job.

Industrial Contract Responsibility.   As with households in the countryside, workers and their factory director contracted with the state to turn over a specified amount of taxes and profits, keeping for their own use "any or almost any amount above the set quota."[38] Under this contract system, applicable in particular to the larger state-owned enterprises, factory managers would be competitively selected through a system of public bidding. Entire enterprises would also be subject to evaluation: If they could not turn out inexpensively priced commodities of good quality, they would be eliminated. But by 1986, although 75 percent, or 9,270 of the 12,380 larger state-owned industrial enterprises, had introduced the contract responsibility system, there were few, if any, enterprises going bankrupt.[39] Large-scale state-owned enterprises engaged in nonvital productive activities were urged to transform themselves into joint-stock companies with limited liability. They would thus become shareholding enterprises with stocks purchased by workers as well as individuals outside the enterprise, though the government initially retained 51 percent of the stock. Management was to be in the hands of a board of directors, an arrangement that was equally applicable to joint ventures of Chinese enterprises with foreign investors.[40]

A Two-Tiered Ownership Structure.   Decentralized management control over state enterprises was calculated to preserve the best of the large SOEs at the core of market socialism. The hope was that factory directors, freed from the constraints of central planning, would be inspired to make their enterprises more competitive and profitable. At the same time, economic reform did promote experimentation with diverse, flexible forms of cooperative management and economic associations among state-owned, collective, and individual sectors of the economy. Between 1985 and 1987, all small-sized state-owned enterprises with fixed assets of less than U.S. $400,000 were leased out under contract to individuals or cooperatives for a period of five years in the hopes of loosening up the rigidities of production in the state-owned sector. In this category is the vast array of small retail services, repair, light industry, catering businesses, transportation, and construction. These private businesses made their own contractual arrangements independently of state supervision, paying only rent and taxes to the state. According to one estimate, this sector of private business accounted for half of the value of total gross industrial output in China in 1985.[41]

These reforms have in effect created in China a two-tiered ownership structure similar to the one existing in Japan. The upper tier consists of large, key enterprises akin to trusts or industrial combines, while the lower tier consists of massive numbers of small enterprises privately run by cooperatives, individual households, or some mixed form of ownership. The private sector does not require state financing yet produces supplies for the large, state-owned enterprises on a more flexible basis than central planning could ever do. It fills the perennial gaps produced by shortages in the planned economy and also absorbs some of the growing number of workers no longer guaranteed or assigned jobs by the state. The hope was that by creating space for worker initiative, economic reform would enable nonstate mostly small enterprises to inject innovation and resourcefulness into the top-heavy state-owned enterprise system. Workers in small private businesses were free to manage their affairs through the market and workers in large, state-owned enterprises producing nonessential commodities were now free to own shares in their enterprises, presumably enhancing their stake and initiative in the enterprise.

Price Reform.   Decontrolling prices was both an essential and nettlesome part of "growing out of the plan" and into a market economy.[42] When the prices of products are fixed according to plan they reflect political considerations rather than economic costs. Price reform, therefore, entailed reducing the number of products controlled by centralized planning, freeing their prices to rise to a level dictated by the market, while prices of key commodities were kept artificially low by mandatory state controls. In the mid-1980s hundreds of commodity prices were still set by the State Council. By 1994, according to the World Bank, China conducted "more than half (perhaps two-thirds) of all transactions at market prices."[43] The inevitable corollary of deregulating these prices was the pressure of demand on available supply. As investment expanded and economic growth accelerated in the private sector, consumers with expanded buying power faced the lack of available goods and spiraling inflation.

The repercussions of price reform were politically volatile: Runaway inflation, increased inequality, a frenzy of investment activity, speculative ventures, bad investments, duplication of efforts, and fraudulent deals accompanied the spurt of economic growth in the private sector. The government's response to these problems of an overheated economy and the discontent they aroused among people was periodically to apply the brakes to economic expansion, attempting to reimpose administrative controls, raise interest rates, and reassert its political clout in the public arena. But it met with only partial success because economic decentralization had granted individuals and enterprises sufficient autonomy and managerial control over production decisions to undermine the central government's control over such critical elements as the growth of the money supply. In command of only half of the nation's GNP in 1995, the central government found itself with fewer levers to compel compliance on the part of enterprises at provincial, local, and municipal levels. These enterprises could ignore the government's directives and entreaties to cut back their investments because alternative sources of funds were now available to them.

New decentralized financial institutions created by the State Council in its implementation of market-oriented financial reform could extend credit and make loans without approval from the higher-ups, depriving the central government of its control over investment priorities. Thus enterprises at the local and regional levels were able to collude with private financial sources other than banks to bypass the policies and authority of the central government. As a result the central bank, the People's Bank of China, was incapable of controlling the money supply in the manner of the Federal Reserve Bank in the United States. Even its authority over the specialized state banks, like the People's Construction Bank of China or the People's Agricultural Bank of China, was limited. These state banks, like the central bank, are primarily intermediaries, cashiers that allocate funds largely to insolvent state enterprises according to state plan. If the central government were to raise interest rates to reflect the true cost of money the way the informal money market does, it would either have to let firms go bankrupt or increase their subsidies to keep them afloat. Thus the central leadership was caught between a rock and a hard place: inflation on the one hand or mass unemployment on the other.

Financial Reform.   The twin issues of mass unemployment and bankruptcy have been at the center of the government's problem in administering economic reform. Although a bankruptcy law had been passed in 1986, the number of bankruptcies was minuscule until 1993. In 1994, when the government expanded its experimental bankruptcy program from an initial three major cities to 76, the number of bankruptcies increased almost ninefold within three years. However, this still represented only .6 percent of the total number of SOEs.[44] Yet the number of applications for bankruptcy far exceeded the number approved. Among firms that did go bankrupt, the vast majority (80 percent) consisted of small and medium SOEs engaged in light manufacturing that were edged out by the rapidly growing rural nonstate enterprises (TVEs). Large SOEs were structurally insulated from bankruptcy by the "soft budget constraints" of the government which used state-owned banks to grant these SOEs "policy loans." In effect, the government was endorsing an unlimited expansion of nonperforming loans. "By the mid-1990s, government estimates placed the level of nonperforming loans in the state banking system at approximately 20 percent of all assets."[45] Not only did the government forfeit substantial tax revenue by continuing to sustain unprofitable SOEs, it opened the entire banking system to the risk of insolvency.

Although actively promoting bankruptcies would have speeded up the restructuring of heavily indebted SOEs, the government lacked the revenue to fund unemployment compensation to the massive numbers of urban unemployed who would be entitled to it if they lost their jobs. Instead, by keeping afloat large, loss-making SOEs through unrestricted state-bank loans, the government compelled the SOEs to retain idled workers on their own payrolls. Because these "laid off" workers, unlike "unemployed workers," still received an array of social services provided for by their enterprises, the government avoided the political costs accompanying extremely high urban unemployment.[46] Thus, although the government supported *both* SOEs *and* their workers indirectly, the revenue actually came from peoples' savings while the government gained time to make its embryonic social security system fully operative. But government awareness that time was running out was expressed at the Fifteenth National Party Congress in 1997 when Premier Zhu Rongji set a three-year time limit for completing SOE restructuring. And in the aftermath of the Asian economic collapse in which similarly vulnerable banking systems threw entire economies into recession in Indonesia, Malaysia, Japan, South Korea, and

Hong Kong, China signaled its resolve to finally permit the destruction of the state sector by meeting all the conditions for WTO membership.

Contrasting Purpose and Performance.   Immense obstacles notwithstanding, economic reform has successfully transformed China's command economy into a capitalist-type market system by the year 2000. In China, it is referred to as "market socialism," suggesting that markets operating in a socialist framework are distinct from capitalist markets. Though it is probably not clear to anyone precisely what "a socialist framework" denotes, it does suggest that the Chinese state expects to remain an active participant in macromanaging China's economy as it becomes more deeply integrated into the global economy. According to Gordon White, three elements are required to find a more productive balance between state control and decentralized initiative and flexibility:

1. the capacity to strengthen technical and institutional information-gathering and communication as well as upgrade new skills;
2. the facility to restructure the overly bureaucratized management system, recruiting and promoting cadres on the basis of technical skills; and
3. the capacity to establish a more rational, less competitive relationship between central and local governments and between different layers of local government.[47]

Though it is too early to assess the degree to which economic reform in China has achieved these goals, it seems clear that economic reform is also a profoundly political and social process bound to encounter technical problems, institutional resistance, political challenges, and the cultural persistence of older social attitudes and ideological predispositions. In her study of urban reform and relational contracting in post-Mao China, Dorothy Solinger observes that, despite the formal organizational changes brought about by the reforms, the underlying patterns that were built up among bureaucrats and businesspeople under the old party-state system still persist.[48] In ways strikingly similar to Japan, there is relational contracting between firms based on the loyalty and mutual trust of a long-term commitment that is sheltered from market forces. As in Japan, these relationships, usually between large firms and their smaller suppliers, are appropriate to "transactions of a recurring and nonstandardized kind," in which specific readjustments can be made on short notice and short-term losses can be sustained in exchange for certainty and predictability. Thus the "'marketizing' of the Chinese economy has resulted in a market system wherein economic exchange paradoxically continues to be structured along lines very similar to those that existed under a more centrally-planned economy."

China's Open Policy and Special Economic Zones (SEZs).   The overall context for China's economic reforms is the opening of the country to the outside world. China's Open Door policy has differed from liberalization in its piecemeal allocation of territories—initially there were 14 coastal cities plus the island of Hainan—as specialized autonomous zones to attract and absorb foreign technology and capital. These zones are like gigantic industrial parks the government equips with infrastructure and special laws to facilitate international commerce. Their short-term purpose is to exploit their coastal advantages to compete actively in the global marketplace. Foreign direct investment is enticed by the availability of cheap labor and advantageous tax and trade regulations to develop export-oriented industries utilizing imported technology and raw materials. The foreign exchange China earns from its export-led growth can then be used to buy technology for development of capital-intensive heavy industry and mechanized agriculture. The technique is identical to that used by the NICs, though the long-term objective is singularly Chinese: to link the country's vast rural interior with its urban sector in the process of entering into the competition of the global marketplace.

Reform Policy in Vietnam

Establishing a modern political economy in Vietnam has been complicated by both its colonial heritage and the protracted war that further split the country in two until 1975. Vietnam inherited three distinct regional political economies from the French, each separately linked to the international market. The South specialized in rice and rubber production, mostly based on plantation agriculture, while the North was dominated by mining. Trade between North and South was limited under the French, each region oriented toward export commodities, with the railroad, which was to link the two, remaining incomplete until 1936. The only functioning trade link between North and South was coastal shipping.

The Impact of the United States.   This split between North and South was exacerbated by the United States, which supported an economy in the South heavily dependent on military aid and imported goods. The inequities in the land tenure system that led South Vietnamese peasants to support the Communists did finally prompt the United States to undertake land reform in the South, accompanied by a "green revolution" with its application of chemical fertilizers and new seed strains. By 1973, one-third of the cultivated area in the South had been mechanized and modernized. Thus while North Vietnam's development followed a course similar to China's, from land reform to collectivization, which brought with it increased yields, in South Vietnam the beneficiary of land reform (paid for by the United States) was a strong, privately based, highly capitalized agricultural system.

After unification in 1975, therefore, the North faced innumerable problems attempting to extend collectivization and Soviet-style central planning to the South. The withdrawal of American aid to the South and winding down of Chinese aid to the North combined with resistance to collectivization in the South to reduce farm output in both parts of the country. The economic situation deteriorated further under the impact of Vietnam's intervention in Cambodia in 1978 and war with China in 1979. To punish Vietnam for the Cambodian invasion, the United States imposed an embargo on all trade and financial relations and opposed any aid from the World Bank, IMF, and other international lending agencies. American allies followed the U.S. move, further limiting Vietnam's access to the world market, foreign aid, and investment. With the economy in crisis, the government responded by making modest moves toward reform that eventually were incorporated into a more comprehensive program of "renovation" known as *doi moi.*

Economic Reforms.   The general direction of reform in Vietnam is the same as in China: to make the transition from a centrally planned economy to a market economy under state direction. In the early phase of piecemeal reform from 1979 to 1981, collectivization was put on hold, and practices that had sprung up at the grass roots as unauthorized ways of coping with the economic crisis were legitimized and extended. After 1981 the contract system was instituted, allowing individual households to lease land from the cooperatives in return for delivering a fixed quota of their crop and selling the rest on the open market. These measures stimulated economic recovery but also contributed to inflation and, especially in Saigon (renamed Ho Chi Minh City), to smuggling and speculation.

Following a brief period of conservative retrenchment between 1982 and 1985, the party adopted *doi moi* in 1986. A more thorough but flexible approach to devising new forms of ownership and management under the leadership of the Communist Party, *doi moi* involves three related elements: (1) expanding the private sector and the market, (2) decentralizing managerial authority, and (3) cultivating connections to the world economy. Private enterprise was extended to crafts and small industry, and businesses in the South that had been nationalized after unification were returned to their former owners. Lengthened terms for land usage contracts meant de facto family ownership of land. The national currency was allowed to float, and adjustment in interest rates brought inflation under control. Policies were adopted to phase out state subsidies, lift price controls, and require state enterprises to base prices on the cost of production. Privatization of state enterprises was delayed until early 1994, when the first sales of shares in a few companies began.

The enactment of a foreign investment law brought in capital from Europe, other Asian countries, and Vietnamese expatriates. The state monopoly on foreign trade was ended, exporting enterprises were allowed to enter contracts directly with foreign importers, and four cities were authorized to establish their own export-import corporations. Foreign governments gradually ceased to follow the U.S. embargo and the United States finally lifted its embargo on American business dealings with Vietnam in February 1994. Diplomatic relations between the United States and Vietnam were restored the following year.

In 1998 as the economic crisis spread through the region, Vietnam was in the midst of negotiating a number of foreign investment plans to "build-operate-transfer" infrastructural projects—a power plant, a telephone system, and a pipeline to pump natural gas from the Nam Con Son basin—that would provide the foundation for further foreign direct investments. Vietnam, like China, was expected to escape the full brunt of the financial storm that devastated Thailand and Indonesia because it still had a nonconvertible currency and tight controls on capital flows. But the consequences of regional economic collapse were nonetheless severe on Vietnam's reform plans. With two-thirds of Vietnam's exports targeted for the Asian regional market, export growth stagnated; new foreign investments dropped almost 50 percent from the previous year; foreign investment disbursements declined over

23 percent as a result of the collapse of previously approved deals; and the big-ticket infrastructural projects foundered on the shoals of low investor confidence.

Discord resulting from disputes between foreign owners and their local joint-venture partners over profit losses forced a great many of the Vietnamese partners to sell out, creating a trend toward more 100 percent foreign-owned investments. But the biggest obstacle to Vietnam's economic growth has been the state-owned enterprise sector that confronts the Vietnamese government with the same dilemmas described above in the case of China. Since the inception of Vietnam's restructuring program in 1992, only 150 state firms have been selected for selling their shares to the public. The opening date of a securities market was postponed several times with a less enthusiastic than anticipated debut in 2000. The state-owned banks, which account for 80 percent of Vietnam's lending, lack the rudiments of regulation for independent audits, credit-risk management, and bad-loan provisos. But in contrast to China, the Vietnamese have not yet developed sufficient trust in banks to cease sleeping on their savings.

The good news for Vietnam has been a bumper rice crop and higher crude oil prices, both of which promise increased exports as well as foreign exchange earnings. Of course, economic renovation, as in China, has brought costs as well as benefits, among them increased unemployment, greater inequalities in income and regional differences, corruption, and environmental deterioration. But the reformists seem to have successfully fended off objections from the conservatives in the party and to be proceeding on the course they have chosen to raise the living standard of their country.

Laos Embarks on Economic Reform

Somewhat later than Vietnam, and in response to similar problems, the communist government of Laos has also embarked on a course of economic reform. Beginning in 1986, controls on the price of rice and other foods were ended, the currency allowed to float, and trade freed. Some state enterprises have been sold, and aid and guidance has been solicited from the World Bank, IMF, UN Development Program, the Asian Development Bank, and foreign governments.

The results are a 6 to 7 percent GDP growth rate, rising export earnings, currency stability, reduced inflation, and a degree of prosperity in the capital, Vientiane. But the potential for sustained growth is limited by lack of roads and other communications within Laos and to neighboring countries and a shortage of educated people with technical and managerial skills. For many of these reasons, businesspeople in Thailand are better positioned than Laotians to take advantage of trade and investment opportunities, including expansion of hydroelectric power that it already buys and exploitation of coal and other mineral resources.

As in the other areas in Laos marked out for development—like raising cattle and pigs for export and upgrading forestry exports from raw timber to processed wood products of greater value—there is a heavy reliance on foreign money and know-how since the internal sources of both are inadequate to the tasks. Imports are always higher than exports for Laos, which has not registered a trade surplus since 1928. For the decade prior to the crisis of 1997, however, the deficit was covered by the donor financing of foreign investors, which enabled the government to build up bank deposits that could be used by other sectors. But the crisis dried up foreign investments and sharply reduced capital inflows, with Thailand heading the list. Particularly hard hit among Laos's exports were wood and forestry products and the export of electricity. To offset heavy dependence of Laos on Thailand, two of Laos' neighbors came to the rescue of the cash-strapped country. China provided a grant of 10 million renminbi ($1.21 million) for development and Vietnam signed a treaty to further barter trade between the two countries, lessening for both their dependence on foreign hard currencies.

With few tools at its disposal, the Laotian government attempted to lessen the impact of the crisis by selling bonds to the public to raise cash reserves, merging three state-owned banks into one and discouraging the consumption of increasingly expensive Thai consumer goods. To acquire foreign exchange, the government promoted tourism, hailing 2000 as "Visit Laos Year." Despite a shortage of hotel rooms and other facilities, Laos did enjoy some gains in this area. The National Tourism Authority announced in April 1999, that tourism had surpassed the exports of textiles to become the country's highest revenue-earner in the preceding year. Tourism has also provided an opening to the last of the communist-led countries of East Asia to seek entry to the global economy: the Democratic People's Republic of Korea—North Korea.

Incentives for Reform in North Korea

Like China, North Korea adhered to a centrally planned economy supervised by a powerful bureaucracy on the Soviet model. Also like China, it followed a course of development that stressed heavy industry and self-reliance. More than 30 percent of its budget was spent on capital construction, with over a third of its import bill going toward the acquisition of capital goods. In the mid-1980s, therefore, despite all the drawbacks and rigidities of this type of development, North Korea had made substantial progress toward becoming an industrialized country. It was not one of the star players but it shared a spot on the stage. In the words of observers at the time: "the North Korean economy has performed better than that of any other Asian state outside Eastasia, except possibly Malaysia."[49] In part because of this achievement, which is reason enough to insulate itself from any comparison with South Korea, and in part because of the absence of domestic political turmoil, North Korea has effectively averted stirring up internal pressures to reform. The pressures for change have come from without.

When the Soviet bloc collapsed, North Korea's economy suffered a severe decline. As long as the Soviet Union and Eastern European countries had functioned as a trading bloc, North Korea was able to exchange its exports at favorable rates for petroleum and other industrial inputs.[50] After the demise of the Soviet Union and the Eastern bloc, however, North Korea was left high and dry, without either a market for its exports or any access to foreign exchange with which to acquire needed imports. The dilemma posed by North Korea's isolation became total when Russia and China adopted economic reform and began insisting on foreign exchange as the currency of trade. With no empathetic trading partners and no hard (internationally acceptable) currency, North Korea was forced to realign itself with the international economy. Predictably, invitations to join the global economy were not forthcoming and North Korea was on its own to figure out how to gain entry into the global economy.

The first steps in the direction of economic reform occurred in the early 1990s when North Korea established the Rajin-Sonbong area as a free-trade zone where tax cuts and other incentives were designed to attract foreign investors to help reconstruct the country's economy following the pattern of China and Vietnam.

As North Korea struggled with the predicament of precisely how and on what terms to break out of its debilitating isolation, it was hard hit by a series of natural disasters that combined with lack of fertilizer and industrial inputs to create extreme hardship, even severe famine in parts of the country. Faced with human catastrophe on an unprecedented scale for peacetime, North Korea opened its borders just enough to accept international humanitarian assistance from South Korea, the United States and the European Union. But the difficulties North Korea faced in finding the "right terms" on which to gain acceptance by global investors became clear in a series of military confrontations initiated by North Korea (see Chapter 7 for details). These hostile maneuvers suggested that further economic reform awaits some definitive movement toward a peace treaty between North and South Korea. A big first step in that direction has been taken at the historic summit meeting in Pyongyang between South Korean President Kim Dae Jung and North Korea's supreme leader Kim Jong Il, of June 12–14, 2000.

The exuberance and exhilaration that enveloped every aspect of this summit were amplified by their unexpectedness. The two leaders exhibited a personal chemistry that evoked a celebratory spirit of peace and cooperation on both sides of the parallel that divides the two countries. An accord was signed that set a common agenda for national reconciliation and reunification beginning with three major agreements: to facilitate a finite number of North-South family reunions, to repatriate Communist prisoners and to pledge not to engage in offensive military operations against each other. Arrangements were also agreed to covering rail connections, hot lines between the leaders, offices in each other's capitals and joint economic projects. Clearly, the terms of the accord had been worked out in draft form at secret meetings prior to the summit, testimony that the meeting of the two Kims was more than ceremonial. And as if the historic occasion called for some international approval, President Vladimir V. Putin paid a visit to North Korea in July, 2000.

The groundwork for the summit goes back to April 1998, when the two Koreas met in Beijing for their first substantive discussions since 1994. It was not auspicious: the two sides deadlocked, the North refusing to permit home visits for divided families in exchange for the 200,000 tons of fertilizer it sought from South Korea. Two further events that year afforded North Korea its only good economic news. One was that its autarkic economic policy insulated North Korea from the disastrous effects of the 1997 regional crisis; the other was the gift of 1,000 head of cattle by the South Korean patriarch of the Hyundai Group to his home village in the North. This merited a meeting with Kim Jong Il in which an agreement was reached between the Hyundai Group and the North Korean government to spend $940 million in return for exclusive tourist and commercial rights to build a resort area in the Kumgang Mountains. Since November 1998, thousands of South Koreans have spent three nights on a luxury cruise ship docked in a North Korean port to be taken by bus on day hikes to the scenic mountains.

In January 1999, a separate enterprise, Asan Corporation, was set up by seven of Hyundai's affiliates to further develop the resort. And in August of the same year a Hong Kong investor, the Emperor Group, opened the doors to a $180 million Seaview Casino Hotel in the Rajin-Sonbong free-trade zone. Although visa restrictions still limited visitors to citizens of communist countries, the Hong Kong investors are targeting northern Chinese and Russians to patronize the casino, which will be off limits to the North Koreans except of course for the 70 percent of its staff who work there.

For countries as remote from the rest of the world and as lacking in infrastructure as North Korea (and Laos), tourism thus provides an avenue for luring East Asian foreign investors and bringing desperately needed foreign currency into the country. A natural advantage of tourism as a means of edging toward global integration is that it can function as a buffer cushioning the shock of the hurly-burly "free market" on a population sheltered by the discipline of tradition and authoritarian rule.

The decade of the 1980s has witnessed a convergence of sorts between the NICs, which began as weakly dependent appendages of Britain, Japan, or the United States, and the communist countries, which began as fiercely independent revolutionary upstarts opposed to the international capitalist market. The NICs engineered successful industrialization by taking advantage of their political embeddedness in the "free world" to transform their economies into productive links in the global capitalist market. At about the time the NICs were reaping their first rewards, China and Vietnam were acknowledging the limitations of a planned self-reliant development completely cut off from the global economy. Their reforms, decentralizing and "privatizing" agricultural and industrial ownership, have moved them in the direction of the East Asian NICs. After the dissipation of the Cold War, which had separated the NICs and the communist countries from each other, there emerged in its place an expanded international market to which all nations of the Asian Pacific, without exception, wanted entry, regardless of the ideological underpinnings of their particular form of nationalist government.

SOUTHEAST ASIA: THE NECS AND THE EXCEPTIONS

Among the Southeast Asian countries that were neither NICs nor communist countries, Thailand, Malaysia, and Indonesia not only jumped on the bandwagon of export-led development but managed to hang on, joining the magic circle of states with high economic growth rates. Because they achieved middle-income status among developing nations by adopting export-led growth strategies under circumstances quite distinct from the NICs, these three countries will be referred to as newly exporting countries (NECs). Similar to the NICs in combining authoritarian

Rapidly modernizing downtown Kuala Lampur, Malaysia.

Source: Photo taken in 1996 by Vera Simone.

regimes with market economies, the NECs are in three other respects quite different. We will examine the similarities and differences that might account for their status just behind the NICs in the "flying geese" formation.

The two remaining Southeast Asian countries—Myanmar and the Philippines—are exceptions to the Asian Pacific success story on opposing ends of an "openness-to-the-world" continuum. The Philippines' attempt to sustain high economic growth rates using an export-led strategy has failed, in part because of a weak state that has made the Philippines too open to international forces and too resistant to the need for fundamental internal changes. Myanmar, on the other hand, is only just pulling up to the starting line in the industrialization process, in part because it has been too closed, until recently shunning interaction with the international community, except for the illicit heroin trade. The Philippines and Myanmar share a handicap that may have contributed to their problem: Neither has achieved the kind of political integration required to pursue truly national economic growth, the Philippines because its economic elite identifies itself too closely with the international community, Myanmar because its military elite has persisted in distancing itself from the international community.

If it appeared that modern economic prosperity for Asian Pacific countries was contingent on being moored to the world capitalist economy, this in no way prepared any of them for the hardships and risks of undertaking the journey of "liberalization." The three-year "Asian" economic collapse beginning in Thailand in 1997, dramatically demonstrated the magnitude of unknown costs attached to membership in the global economy. A brief discussion of the origins and possible impact of the Asian economic crisis on the future of the region is the third strand of the following discussion.

Thailand, Malaysia, and Indonesia

Like the NICs, the NECs are privately based market economies with bureaucratic authoritarian states. As in South Korea and Taiwan, the military has played a prominent role in Thailand and Indonesia, related in part to U.S. security interests in the area. And in all three of the NECs, state intervention in the economy has been a noteworthy aspect of their economic development. But three characteristics distinguish the political economies of the NECs from the NICs: (1) abundant natural resources of a wide variety; (2) ethnic pluralism, particularly the presence of Chinese, who have dominated the economic arena in Thailand, Malaysia, and Indonesia; (3) a heavy and enduring dependence on international, increasingly Japanese investment capital, technology, and organizational skills. The governments of Thailand, Malaysia, and Indonesia have accelerated their countries' economic development by luring international capital from production locations where labor costs are rising, in particular the NICs. The opportunity presents itself as a result of the jockeying among the world's leading capitalist states to advance or maintain their relative positions in a rapidly changing international division of labor. For Japan, the region provides a natural location for dispersing its production sites to offset factors like currency appreciation and tariff barriers.

Resource-Intensive Development.   Thailand, Malaysia, and Indonesia have large amounts of rubber, rice, palm oil, tin, petroleum, natural gas, and teak and other timber. Since colonization of the region, they have therefore relied on exporting their primary products to generate foreign exchange and investments. In the 1960s, after serious internal conflicts had been settled, the governments of Thailand, Malaysia, and Indonesia, on the advice of international lending institutions, pursued import substitution policies to strengthen domestic production capabilities and the power of the state. By the 1970s, again on the advice of international monetary agencies, the NECs' strategy of development shifted to a policy of export promotion. Following the NICs was a conscious element in the policy of increasing the manufacturing component of their exports. Although the NECs were slower to succeed and their growth rates have not quite reached the level of the NICs, they did dramatically increase the industrial proportion of their exports. Nonetheless, primary products still comprise a significant component of their exports.

Ethnic Pluralism: The Role of the Chinese.   The second element the NECs have in common is the vital yet equivocal role the Chinese have played in their economic development. Under colonial rule, the Chinese were merchants, tax collectors, and operators of state trading monopolies. This provided a springboard for Chinese in Thailand, Malaysia, and Indonesia to become the driving force of capitalist development. Because of their position as "outsiders," however, the Chinese were forced to ally themselves with indigenous ruling elites, agreeing to a subordinate political role in return for protection and enhancement of their economic positions. In Malaysia, the wealthy Chinese elites allied themselves with the politically powerful, traditional Malay aristocrats who monopolized government positions despite continuous ethnic rivalries. In Thailand it was the upper ranks of the *sakdina* class and in Indonesia the ruling Javanese with whom the economically powerful Chinese cooperated.

As the immigrant communities of ethnic Chinese came to dominate the business world in all three countries, they aroused the resentment of increasingly nationalistic indigenous populations. In Thailand they faced discrimination after 1945 when the state attempted to force Chinese to assimilate; in Indonesia they were massacred after the unsuccessful coup attempt of the PKI (Indonesian Communist Party) in 1965; and in Malaysia they were embroiled in the race riots of 1969. To differing degrees, the singular success of Chinese in the commercial world remains a problem for these three Southeast Asian countries.

Thailand has made the most progress toward integrating the Chinese middle class and business community into mainstream Thai society. A reversal of the anti-Chinese nationalism of the earlier period began between 1957 and 1973 during the rapid economic expansion that occurred under authoritarian military rule. By the 1980s, economic growth had given rise to a more open political environment in which substantial numbers of Chinese business people had become not only Thai citizens but parliamentarians and cabinet members. The assimilation of ethnic Chinese into Thai society also contributed to a significant number of independently organized business associations with an effective public voice in the economic policy-making process.

In contrast the business class in Indonesia remains widely stigmatized as a Chinese enclave, which despite its considerable financial resources is unable openly to secure a significant share of political power. This is part of a deep-seated anti-Chinese sentiment that has been endemic, especially among Javanese, for over 30 years. From the 1965 massacre of Chinese to the anti-Chinese riots that resulted from Indonesia's economic collapse and brought about Suharto's fall from power in 1998, the government consistently pursued policies that fueled hostility, even overt violence, against the Chinese minority: ethnic Chinese citizens were forced to adopt Indonesian names, not permitted to use their own language or celebrate their holidays in public and virtually barred from politics, the military, and government service.

Generally fearful of publicly asserting their interests in face of government opposition, Chinese business people have preferred to work through personal relationships with patrons among senior military and civilian officials. This subordination of the Chinese-dominated business sector to the Javanese-run state in Indonesia reflects the relatively small scale of the private sector compared to the state-owned enterprises that dominate key sectors of industry, notably oil and gas. With two-thirds of its revenue coming from these sources, the government has been able to prevent the private business sector from using its economic power as leverage to increase its share of public political power. It should be noted, however, that far from precluding private access to the powerful heads of state on the part of the few extremely successful and wealthy Chinese magnates, it mandates it, reinforcing a political climate of "cronyism" that breeds anti-Chinese discrimination.

With the demise of Suharto and a new popularly elected president, Abdurrahman Wahid, who subscribes to religious and ethnic inclusivity, there is reason to believe that the largely Javanese-controlled government may pursue a more liberal policy toward its Chinese minority. A small sign of the government's greater willingness to acknowledge the rights of its ethnic minorities was observed in February 2000 when for the first time in more than 30 years, the Chinese were permitted to celebrate Chinese New Year in public. Given the large number of Indonesia's ethnic minorities, the tensions among them—often exacerbated by internal migration—as well as the persistent threat to Indonesian unity posed by separatist movements, greater equality for Indonesia's ethnic communities, and "outer islands" is likely to take a rather long time.

Malaysia occupies a middle ground between Indonesia and Thailand, promoting the ideal of an ethnic balance among social and ethnic groups; but to achieve that balance, *bumiputra* have been given preferential access to higher education and employment in business and the professions, to the detriment of Chinese. This will be expanded upon in the following section.

Foreign Capital and State Intervention.   A third similarity of the political economies of Thailand, Malaysia, and Indonesia is their extensive reliance on direct foreign investments by multi- or transnational corporations to advance their economies. A high percentage of each country's manufacturing and extractive industries is controlled and owned by foreign corporations, which carries with it somewhat higher social costs and political vulnerabilities than is the case in the NICs. Some differences both in the degree of foreign capital and domestic state intervention between Thailand's and Indonesia's political economy will be roughly sketched, as well as the manner in which ethnicity and class intersect in the Malaysian political economy.

The Thai economy, despite sizable U.S. foreign aid and investments, has been most successful in financing important industrial sectors with domestic capital. Among industries promoted by the Board of Investment, Thai capital accounts for 75 percent of total registered capital. In the textile industry, although the percentage of foreign-owned registered capital appears to be higher, it is estimated that the Bangkok Bank alone finances 70 percent of the industry. Thus while foreign companies are a major force in the Thai economy—75 percent of the investment projects approved by the Thai Board of Investments in the late 1980s were from foreign firms[51]—certain key sectors remain dominated by Thai capital. There is in addition a wariness of extending the state too far into the business of investing in the economy itself. After 1958, both Thai business and international advisers pushed to confine the government to new investment promotion and infrastructural development and away from state business partnerships like the National Economic Development Corporation Limited, whose crash had left the government greatly in debt.[52]

Indonesia is at the other end of the spectrum, with international capital extensively involved in its economic development along with a major role of the government as an investor and financier of business enterprises. Under Sukarno, the inability of the state and the national bourgeoisie to generate effective economic development left the generals little choice but to reintegrate Indonesia with the international capitalist economy.[53] Employing American advisers known as the Berkeley technocrats, the New Order regime offered funds for projects, loans, and inducements to new foreign investors in the form of tax holidays and guarantees of profit repatriation. The state has also invested directly in production and economic organization through state-owned corporations: banks; state corporations supervising concessions in the resources sector; joint ventures in property, construction, resources, cement, and petrochemicals; and state organizations that organize distribution and pricing of certain procurements, like rice and other basic necessities.[54]

Malaysia began its development with a laissez-faire economic policy that applied equally to domestic and foreign capital. The state provided only infrastructure to facilitate capital accumulation, while foreign and domestic capital was permitted a free hand. On the surface, the alliance between landed, aristocratic Malays who monopolized political bureaucracy and the Chinese who monopolized the urban economy worked smoothly. But beneath the surface Malay resentments against the Chinese mounted: The Malay elites wanted economic control commensurate with their political power, while the Malay peasants were dissatisfied with the class polarization fostered by laissez-faire capitalism in the rural areas. The racial contention came to a head in May 1969. One result was a shift in the role of the state toward greater intervention in economic development and the aggrandizement of the mostly Malay bureaucratic class.

Adoption of the New Economic Policy (NEP) in the early 1970s had a two-pronged purpose: to alleviate the poverty of rural Malay peasants by providing them with access to more land and modern training and to spawn a new Malay capitalist class by supplying urban Malays with a 30 percent share in modern economic enterprises. The objective was to shift 30 percent of the wealth to the Malay community by 1990, decreasing the foreigners' share from 63.3 to 30 percent and increasing the non-Malay share from 34.3 to 40 percent. Redistribution was to come from economic growth rather than existing GNP, making it more palatable for the Chinese, who were understandably worried about losing a share of their wealth. A series of four-year plans detailed the process. The idea was that Malays were not being given but would work for their 30 percent share of corporate capital by expanding the total output through their participation. And in fact, NEP was vigorously pressed by the government, with the major impetus for growth coming from public investment and consumption in areas like manufacturing, utilities, public administration and transport.

NEP's difficulties, however, stemmed from the underlying economic nature of what the government defined as a racial problem. One difficulty was that the eradication of rural poverty envisioned in NEP failed to address the structural source of rural poverty: landlessness that resulted from a feudal land tenure system. The uneconomic size of most farm holdings and the large numbers of farmers who did not own the land they worked meant that only the already well-to-do rural Malays could avail themselves of the land and infrastructural supports provided by the government. Thus NEP contributed to the rural problem by further increasing income inequality between rich and poor Malays in the rural sector.

A similar difficulty arose from the government's role in expanding the Malay ownership and management of urban corporate wealth. The discretionary power of the government entrusted with the "management shares" allowed it to obtain control of companies, through the use of statutory bodies, with a minimum outlay of cash. The majority of the shares reserved for the Malay community were then purchased by those who could afford them: the small number of richer members of the Malay community who were often politicians, civil servants, and their patrons. Thus by increasing the concentration of economic power under bureaucratic control, NEP further increased the inequality of income and wealth within the urban Malay community and in the process adversely affected both private, mainly Chinese, investment and public support for the ruling governmental elite.[55]

The NECs clearly learned some of their lessons in development strategy from the NICs—i.e., moving up the product cycle from natural resource exports to manufacturing and higher value-added exports, employing government incentives to encourage domestic capitalist expansion, restricting labor. But the close, personal nexus of political, financial and entrepreneurial institutions that typified economic development in the NECs—referred to as "cronyism" or "crony capitalism"—as well as their heavy dependence on foreign capital raised questions about the long-run viability of their export-driven formula for high economic growth. These questions came to the fore suddenly when Thailand's financial system collapsed in the summer of 1997 and economic failures spread rapidly through the region.

The Asian Financial Crisis.   With the liberalization of capital accounts in Malaysia and Thailand in the early 1990s and the exceptional success of most of the economies in the region—"emerging markets" they were called—the area became an attractive venue for bankers and money managers in the United States, Japan, and Europe. Especially in small countries like Thailand and others in Southeast Asia, where stock markets were relatively undeveloped, it was possible to bid up prices with modest investments thereby attracting more and more investors. Once a few prestigious investors began betting on the profitability of Thai stocks, bonds, and currency, the "herd" followed the trail, creating a huge influx of capital into these markets.

Three aspects of this capital inflow leading up to the 1997 financial crisis in Thailand were new. One was the sheer quantity of "stateless wealth" circulating the globe in search of the best return. In the decades between 1970 and 1997 spending by investors had increased 197-fold, which meant that by 1995 mutual funds, pension funds, and institutional investors controlled $20 trillion, ten times the figure for 1980.[56] The second new element was the composition of this vastly increased capital inflow. In the 1980s much of the capital flow into Thailand (as elsewhere in Southeast Asia) had been in the form of foreign direct investments; these tended to be long-term commitments. In the 1990s, however, capital inflows shifted toward more liquid portfolios that were more often short-term rather than long-term investments.[57] The third new element of the capital flow into Southeast Asian markets was provided by changes taking place in the exchange rates among various currencies after 1995. Like other developing countries, Thailand's currency was pegged to the U.S. dollar, which meant that as the dollar's value increased against the yen and major European currencies, Thailand's exports became more expensive, thus eroding their competitiveness in the international market.

As Thai exports fell off in the mid-nineties, the traded-goods sector within Thailand contracted, and available capital was channeled by local banks and non-bank financial institutions into the nontraded sector: land, real estate, and the construction of high-rise "monuments" to modernity in Bangkok: the 63-story World Trade Tower, the 3.6 million-square-foot Royal Charoen Krung Tower, the 550 room Hotel Sofitel Riverside. A self-reinforcing upward spiral was created as the increasing values of the collateral (land, real estate, and financial assets) were used to borrow more externally-sourced capital which, reinvested in the same areas once again, increased still further the value of the very same assets. This is what is generally known as a "bubble" because the values of the same assets are inflated over and over again without any increase in actual wealth production. Thus a conjunction of factors—lower interest rates internationally, declining exports, and long-standing exchange rate pegs conspired to encourage financial institutions in the "emerging markets" of Southeast Asia to borrow foreign exchange abroad, convert it into domestic currency, and lend it domestically, assuming the exchange risk. Since such conditions are not indefinitely sustainable, at some point the entire upward spiral goes into reverse, the process feeding on itself in a downward plunge.

Ignited by massive capital flight, the financial crisis in Thailand resulted in loan defaults, illiquidity, bank closures, a rapid pileup of nonperforming loans, corporate bankruptcies, escalating unemployment, and the varied ills that accompany economic recession. The entire downward cycle quickly spread throughout East Asia—Malaysia, Indonesia, the Philippines, Hong Kong, Taiwan, Japan and South Korea—evoking the term "contagion" and raising fears that the entire global economy would be "infected." This mobilized the IMF and the World Bank which came to the immediate rescue of some of the countries—Thailand, Indonesia, the Philippines, and South Korea—in the form of negotiated bail-out loans with the usual structural adjustment conditions. Japan, the one country that might have been able to assist the collapsing economies of its regional trade partners in 1997 had already fallen into a quagmire of economic stagnation in the early 1990s when its own land prices had collapsed. All countries in the region were affected by the crisis to one degree or another. Indonesia was the hardest hit; China stoically absorbed punishment without devaluing its currency; Vietnam, North Korea and Myanmar though troubled by severe problems of their own, bore less of the brunt of the regional economic crisis.

By February 2000 the Asian financial crisis was over. The impact on the political economies of the area, though difficult to evaluate, dispels one of the widely circulated beliefs: that the crisis reflected the flawed path of development of the Asian Pacific "model." For the most part, the structure of political economies, as described in this chapter, have picked up where they left off when the crisis began. Economically, there has been restructuring of insolvent financial and productive institutions through mergers, acquisitions, and auctions. New regulations have been adopted governing loan policies, bankruptcies, and disposing of non-performing loans, which together with new auditing and more stringent monitoring procedures move in the

Selling vegetables at an open-air market in Jakarta, Indonesia.

Source: United Nations photo 122601/Wolff.

direction of obtaining greater transparency in financial transactions. Politically, with the exception of Indonesia—the only Asian Pacific country where unemployment and inflation reached double-digits—there have been no major structural upheavals despite currency depreciations of up to 40 percent and recessions that reached nearly 10 percent of GDP in 1998.[58]

Among noncommunist Southeast Asian states, two never experienced the full brunt of the Asian crisis because they had not yet achieved successful growth. Chronically subject to debilitating centrifugal pressures with roots in their earlier integration in the international political economy, the Philippines and Myanmar have lacked the dynamic qualities of developmental states elsewhere in the Asian Pacific. They are exceptions to the patterns of development that have become so closely identified with the Asian Pacific region.

The Southeast Asian Exceptions

Philippines.   Politics in the Philippines is like a pair of mirrors facing one another in an infinite regression of images. One mirror is corruption, the other is political violence. As Emmanuel S. de Dios observes, "politics, in an underdeveloped context, is itself a major form of organization of the economy. Political violence may be viewed simply as one form of investment, and corruption as a form of return."[59] Viewed in this way, the scale of venality that occurs routinely in the Philippine political economy becomes at least more understandable, if not more tolerable. The continuity in policies between Marcos and Aquino, for example, can be understood if one sees the installation of the Aquino regime as a return to the political practices and rules prevailing before martial law was declared by Marcos. The split in the ruling elite at that time gave rise to dictatorship, and the schism continues as an unresolved problem today. But that schism highlighted a deeper problem.

From 1946 until the declaration of martial law in 1972, the dominant elites, divided into two political parties, took turns filling elected offices on the basis of their varying public positions on corruption and political violence. This "elite democracy," a combination of landowning, business, and financial interests, was made up of vertical dyadic relationships between powerful and wealthy patrons and their poor and dependent clients. The political elite was drawn from those who could afford to be patrons: landowners, employers, professionals—people whose occupations permit them to do favors for large numbers of ordinary voters. Once in office, these patrons used their political connections to further their business interests, which also enabled them to contribute to the welfare of their clients. Thus political economy in the Philippines has been a vicious circle among elites whose wealth positions them in politics and whose politics in office furthers their accumulation of wealth.

When Marcos illegally extended his political career as president, he adopted populist rhetoric against the "oligarchs"—the older established political clans such as the Lopezes, Osmenas, Aquino-Cojuangcos, and Jacintos—to justify expropriating their holdings and politically persecuting them. But the logic of his regime was an extension of everything that had preceded it. Up until the 1940s the Philippines had a typical colonial pattern of political economy: It exported mineral and agricultural resources in exchange for imported manufactures. In the second phase, beginning in 1948, national policy shifted to an import-substitution strategy to counteract the large balance of payments problem. This gave rise to a manufacturing class that was largely composed of branches of the old landed elite, with the result that no clear line distinguishes the manufacturing interests from the landed aristocracy; both are segments of the same social and economic class with a common interest in preventing any redistribution of the wealth. By the early 1960s, when the Philippine economy had exhausted the benefits from ISS, further industrialization was stymied by the narrow base of incomes constituting the domestic market. Industries were unable to produce on a large enough scale to permit export competitiveness. At the root of this problem of a narrow domestic market was the skewed distribution of land. But to date, land reform has never seriously been implemented because of the identity of interests between manufacturing and landholding factions of the elite who dominate the political arena.

Marcos prevailed under martial law as long as export prices remained high, interest rates low, and international capital continued to flow into the Philippines sufficient to placate the displaced "oligarchs" as well as enrich his "crony capitalists." The expanding role of government under martial law facilitated this process. Government guarantees on foreign loans profited those businesses with ties to the Marcos regime. When, however, these highly leveraged projects failed—because of corruption, incompetence, and/or adverse external circumstances—the government assumed their debts. The government's role in financing these investments and projects, therefore, accounts for the magnitude of the external debt accumulated during the Marcos regime. The bubble broke as a consequence of the international recession of 1980–1981, which threw the Philippines into economic crisis. When in October 1983 a moratorium was declared on debt payments that had skyrocketed as a result of Marcos's attempt to cover the bad investments of previous years, international loans evaporated, and the United States withdrew its support of the Marcos regime. With Aquino's reelection, the older elite, the "oligarchs," came back into power, although in order to win the elections, they had initially to enter an uneasy alliance with populist forces making more radical demands.

Structurally the political economy of the Philippines has remained the same under Aquino, Ramos, and Estrada. The central problem that underlines the regime's crisis of development is the conflict between growth and debt service. And it is perpetuated by the dynamics of politics as a symbiosis between national and local elites for which Carl Lande's description of premartial law politics remains apt:

> Candidates for national offices need votes, which local leaders with their primary hold upon the loyalty of the rural electorate can deliver. Local leaders in turn need money to do favors for their followers, and this the candidates for high offices can supply. Local leaders also need a constant supply of public works projects and services for their localities. Holders of high elective offices such as senators and congressmen, from whence come most such benefits in the Philippines, can affect the supply of projects and services. The result is a functional interdependence of local, provincial, and national leaders.[60]

The primacy of localism that predates both the Spanish and the American conquest of the Philippines has endured, providing the straitjacket within which the Philippines' development is arrested.

Burma/Myanmar.   The political economy of Myanmar illustrates the complexity and contradictoriness of development. Burma is richly endowed with natural resources—abundant arable land, fertile soil, fish, the best jade in the world, precious gems, water power, timber, gas, coal, and oil—yet it is today the poorest country in the region. At one time the world's largest exporter of rice and considered the "Golden Land" by its Southeast Asian neighbors, Myanmar today has barely enough food to feed its 42 million people. After the military coup in 1988 by General Saw Maung, the State Law and Order Restoration Council (SLORC) ruled Myanmar. The new military regime abolished the old socialist system and began to encourage a free-market economy and foreign investment.

With two-thirds of its population Buddhist Burmans, the government under a military dictatorship has been at war with its ethnically diverse minority nationalities since independence. And since 1988, when a popular movement for democracy was brutally suppressed, the government has been at war with almost its entire population, leaving a political economy dependent upon selling its natural resources, everything from drugs to timber.

Socialism was adopted in principle as an alternative to both capitalism and communism, each of which was unacceptable. Capitalism was associated with colonial Burma, when Indian moneylenders had dispossessed Burmese cultivators, and under British auspices large-scale rice cultivation for export subjected the entire country to the whims of international commodity prices. Communism, on the other hand, was fundamentally incompatible with Buddhist values. The alternative was some form of democratic socialism adapted to Burmese cultural values. Aung San's commitment to socialism was tempered, as he explained at an AFPFL convention in 1947, by the realization that moving directly to socialism was impossible for precapitalist Burma and that the country would first have to go through a controlled capitalist stage of private enterprise, but without the "old evils of monopoly and exploitation."[61] Landlordism would be ended by giving the land to those who cultivate it, though ultimately it would be nationalized and the central government would own transport, natural resources, communications, and the principal means of production. This stage of economic development was, he said, neither capitalism nor socialism, but something in between.

U Nu was similarly committed to the goal of socialism wedded to the cooperative spirit of Buddhist teachings. During his prime ministership, many enterprises formerly in private British hands were nationalized and run as state enterprises and the foreign-owned oil and other industries converted to joint ventures of government and private owners. Logging and export companies were nationalized and the purchase and export of rice were monopolized by a state marketing board. Capital was invested in import-substitution industries and in power generation capacity for industrial growth. Despite these measures, the restructuring of the economy did not proceed very far; "only in the sphere of government expenditure itself was there a significant change in the state's share of the economy from before the war to the end of the 1950s. Even in the state marketing and transportation sectors, the independent nationalist state had control over a smaller proportion of all activity than had the colonial laissez-faire state."[62]

When the military Revolutionary Council came to power, the founding generation's commitment to socialism was reaffirmed in the "Burmese Way to Socialism," which combined Marxist economic rhetoric, Buddhist ideas about human greed, and the need for strong one-party rule. Initially, the military pursued a radical program of nationalizing banks and all foreign and large local businesses and establishing a government monopoly on both internal commodity and foreign trade. The goal was to liberate the country from dependence on foreign goods, foreign capital, and outside markets. But in the late 1970s economic stagnation led to a change of policy under the Burma Socialist Program Party, which sought limited external aid and allowed the private sector more latitude. Further policy changes in the late 1980s and early 1990s liberalized the grain trade, regularized the lucrative smuggling trade, and increased government revenues by imposing a tax on that trade and creating the Burma Holdings Corporation with capital equal to 20 percent of the country's GNP. State monopoly of banking and natural resources other than agriculture continues. These changes, according to David I. Steinberg, are signs that "Myanmar is moving, hesitatingly, from state socialism to a modified state capitalism, not economic pluralism as understood in the United States."[63]

Recognizing the role that a deteriorating productive sector played in triggering the urban-based mass uprising in 1988, SLORC abandoned the "Burmese Way to Socialism," promoted free enterprise, and courted foreign investments. And despite continued international condemnation of the regime's repression of political opposition, foreign capital responded to the invitation with expanded private investments in Myanmar. By 1992, U.S. companies actually headed the list of foreign investors, with U.S. $163.7 million, mainly in oil, gas, and fisheries; Japan, the Netherlands, South Korea, and France also were actively investing in development of Myanmar's natural resources. In 1994, the Burmese government proposed a project to build a dam on the Salween River, diverting water from Myanmar to Thailand and generating hydroelectric power for both countries. A feasibility study was undertaken in November 1998 by consultants from Thai and Burmese power companies along with experts from a Japanese utility. According to initial results reported by a coalition of Thai nongovernmental organizations (NGOs) who oppose the project for environmental reasons, it would cost $4 billion to $7 billion and provide an estimated 3,700 megawatts of electricity for Thailand as well as Burma. There have been protests in Thailand opposing the project even before it has begun.

Problems also surround Burma's biggest foreign investment project to date, a joint venture between the Burmese government's Myanmar Oil and Gas Enterprise, France's Total, and Unocal of the United States. The first field was the offshore Yadana oil field in the Gulf of Martaban, a project costing $1.2 billion from which the Burmese government hoped to receive an estimated $400 million per year in sales to the Petroleum Authority of Thailand. Unfortunately, the contract with Thailand was signed in 1996 shortly before the onset of its financial crash. In the course of the ensuing economic crisis, Thailand found it had neither the capital nor the energy needs for the oil. In addition, it appeared that the pricing formula to be used made the imported gas more expensive than the gas produced from domestic sources in Thailand. This may have accounted for the delays in constructing the power plant in Ratchaburi on the Thai side of the border, which had been designed to receive and process the gas. In the interim Unocal came under fire in the United States for its involvement with business that benefited Burma's military regime.

If Myanmar's attempts to generate foreign exchange have met with limited success to date, its attempts to resolve the country's longstanding civil war against diverse insurgent groups have fared somewhat better. Since 1994 when one of the largest rebel armies, the Kachin Independence Army, signed a peace treaty with Rangoon (now Yangon), the government has signed cease-fire agreements with about two dozen ethnic rebel groups permitting their members to engage in business of any kind as long as it does not involve fighting the government. As a result commercial activities have markedly increased in the northern towns of Myanmar with the centrally located city of Mandalay overtaking the capital city of Yangon as an economic center of the country. Unfortunately, much of the country's commerce relies on the opium production and trade which has more than doubled over the past decade.

In an effort to reduce the country's dependence on the drug trade and use land reclaimed from insurgency warfare, the government promoted raising agricultural output both for export and internal consumption. In the state of Shan, where hundreds of thousands of farmers had already been displaced to isolate them from insurgent guerrillas, remaining small farmers were uprooted to enable the government to expropriate their small plots and consolidate them into massive land holdings. These were then put up for sale to big investors to grow cash crops like tobacco, corn, fruit, and potatoes. Although these "agro-industrial farms" have not materialized to date, the number of internally displaced people has continued to escalate, with estimates varying between 500,000 to one million. More than 100,000 of these dislocated people have escaped into refugee camps in Thailand while an estimated half million Shans have left for Thailand without going into the camps. They attempt to survive as farmhands, construction workers, domestic helpers, and prostitutes.[64]

Among ASEAN nations, there is increased interest in drawing Myanmar closer into the orbit of the Southeast Asian organization's regional concerns, because of both the country's lucrative investment opportunities and its strategic significance on China's border. Singapore, now Myanmar's largest trading partner after China and among its top ten foreign investors, is the first noncommunist government to send its top political leader, Prime Minister Goh, on an official visit to Myanmar. This followed Indonesia's invitation to Myanmar's powerful intelligence chief Khin Nyunt to meet with President Suharto, whose principal concern is countering the great weight of China's historical influence over Burma. Khin Nyunt is said to have remarked to Suharto that Myanmar would like to emulate Indonesia's dual military and civilian political framework for development. And mutual interest seems to transcend individual leaders as evidenced by the newly elected Indonesian President Abdurrahman Wahid's visit to Myanmar on November 8, 1999, not long after taking office. There is, however, a reluctance among some ASEAN members to move too quickly in embracing Myanmar into their midst without first satisfying their Western partners' objections to Myanmar's human rights violations.

SUMMARY

As latecomers to the process of modernization, Asian Pacific countries share certain cultural and historical experiences that differ from those in the West. Central among these has been the greater dependence on the state as navigator of national economic development.

As the analysis of political economy in Japan and China also demonstrates, however, employing one or another type of political economy is not an open-ended choice on the part of political leaders but a complex, historical response to different circumstances and opportunities. The Soviet-style political economies of China, North Korea, Taiwan, Vietnam, and Laos were as determined by the constraints of the Cold War and their internal dynamics as were the developmental state patterns of Japan, South Korea, and Singapore. More recently, with dramatic changes occurring in the post–Cold War world, China, Vietnam, and Laos have introduced market reforms that move their political economies closer to those pioneered by Japan and then emulated by the NICs and the NECs. Furthermore, they have done so retaining their authoritarian political structures more or less intact. The Philippines and

Myanmar are special cases, the former illustrating the drawbacks of being too completely embraced by the international market, the latter illustrating the price of shunning the world economy altogether.

One question to ponder is whether the developmental state that seems to characterize so many Asian Pacific political economies is a distinctive political economy or merely a transitory stage toward a more classically structured market model of political economy. It may be that as these countries develop further, they will converge toward a singular new model of political economy. But whether or not this is the case, the Asian Pacific experience suggests that certain forms of state intervention in the market produce dramatic results in economic growth. When governments in the Asian Pacific underwrite pilot agencies, like MITI in Japan or the Economic Planning Board in South Korea, they insulate them from shareholders or constituents, allowing them to authorize and implement long-term strategies for realizing national economic priorities. Examples might be subsidizing specific industries to make them more internationally competitive, investing in research and development with no immediate prospect of profit, increasing the level of skills of the labor force, or restricting foreign direct investments to serve national economic priorities.

There is another generalization that is warranted by our explorations into the political economy of the Asian Pacific countries. It is that political economy is not something that occurs within the territorial boundaries of nations. It is a global phenomenon that often creates these national boundaries to begin with, boundaries that divide real estate and people's allegiances but do not bar capital, labor, or technology. As international capital, which is the currency of development, continues to roam the world in search of the most cost-effective way of combining factors of production, it confronts and interacts with the political dynamics of nation-states. The results, as we are witnessing in today's world, are unsettling and bewildering. This will be the focus of the remaining chapters.

QUESTIONS FOR DISCUSSION

1. What factors distinguish development in the Asian Pacific from development in the West?
2. How do the four models of political economy differ from one another?
3. Why did Soviet-style Marxism appeal to Chinese revolutionaries in search of a development strategy?
4. How was the political economy of Maoist China different from the political economy in modern Japan? How does Reform policy in China compare to development elsewhere in the Asian Pacific?
5. Which factors do you think are persuasive in explaining the NICs' successful economic growth?

NOTES

1. Alexander Gerschenkron, *Economic Backwardness in Historical Perspective* (Cambridge, MA: Harvard University Press, 1962).
2. Chalmers Johnson, *MITI and the Japanese Miracle: The Growth of Industrial Policy, 1925–1975* (Stanford, CA: Stanford University Press, 1982).

3. Bruce Cumings, "The Origins and Development of the Northeast Asian Political Economy: Industrial Sectors, Product Cycles, and Political Consequences," in *The Political Economy of the New Asian Industrialism,* ed. Frederic C. Deyo (Ithaca, NY: Cornell University Press, 1987), pp. 44–83.

4. The characterization of the developmental state used here is based on Chalmers Johnson, "Political Institutions and Economic Performance: The Government-Business Relationship in Japan, South Korea, and Taiwan," in *Asian Economic Development-Present and Future,* ed. Robert A. Scalapino, Seizaburo Sato, and Jusuf Wanandi (Berkeley: University of California, Institute of East Asian Studies, 1985), p. 71.

5. Daniel I. Okimoto, *Between MITI and the Market: Japanese Industrial Policy for High Technology* (Stanford, CA: Stanford University Press, 1989), p. 2.

6. Sandra Halperin, *In the Mirror of the World: Capitalist Development in Modern Europe* (Ithaca, NY: Cornell University Press, 1997).

7. Gordon White and Robert Wade, "Developmental States and Markets in East Asia: An Introduction," in *Developmental States in East Asia,* ed. Gordon White (New York: St. Martin's, 1988), p. 1.

8. Johnson, *MITI and the Japanese Miracle,* p. 31.

9. "By 1912 only 12 per cent of 'factory' operatives were employed in government establishments." W. J. Macpherson, *The Economic Development of Japan c. 1868–1941* (London: Macmillan, 1987), p. 38.

10. Johnson, *MITI and the Japanese Miracle,* pp. 110, 113.

11. From J. W. Hall, "Changing Conceptions of the Modernization of Japan," quoted in H. W. Arndt, *Economic Development: The History of an Idea* (Chicago: University of Chicago Press, 1987), p. 66.

12. Only within the last decade has the state-owned industrial sector reached more than 40 percent of GDP to become the dominant productive sector of the economy.

13. Victor D. Lippit, *The Economic Development of China* (Armonk, NY: M. E. Sharpe, 1987), p. 135.

14. Two of the "Big Four"—Mitsui and Sumitomo—existed before the Meiji period, during the Tokugawa period.

15. Dorothy J. Solinger, "Urban Reform and Relational Contracting in Post-Mao China: An Interpretation of the Transition from Plan to Market" (paper presented at UCLA Center for Chinese Studies and Southern California China Colloquium, June 3, 1989), p. 3.

16. Okimoto, *Between MITI and the Market,* p. 12.

17. Ibid., p. 1.

18. Michel Oksenberg, "China's Economic Bureaucracy," in *The Challenge of China and Japan: Politics and Development in East Asia,* ed. Susan Shirk (New York: Praeger, 1985), pp. 220–21.

19. Miyohei Shinohara, *Industrial Growth, Trade, and Dynamic Patterns in the Japanese Economy* (Tokyo: University of Tokyo Press, 1982), p. 24.

20. Johnson, *MITI and the Japanese Miracle,* p. 154.

21. Chalmers Johnson, "Japan's Economic Bureaucracy," in *The Challenge of China and Japan,* ed. Susan Shirk, p. 229.

22. Bruce Cumings, "The Origins and Development of the Northeast Asian Political Economy: Industrial Sectors, Product Cycles, and Political Consequences," in *The Political Economy of the New Asian Industrialism,* ed. Frederic C. Deyo (Ithaca, NY: Cornell University Press, 1987), pp. 46–47.

23. The following scholars represent each of the four perspectives: (1) free trade: Bela Balassa; (2) "special circumstances": Paul Streeten; (3) Confucian values: Hung-chao Tai; (4) developmental state: Chalmers Johnson.

24. Lawrence B. Krause, Koh Ai Tee, and Lee (Tsao) Yuan, *The Singapore Economy Reconsidered* (Singapore: Institute of Southeast Asian Studies, 1987), pp. 8, 92.

25. An indication of this may be the independent electoral bid launched by the head of the Hyundai group in the 1992 elections.

26. Peter Nolan, "Assessing Economic Growth in the Asian NICs," *Journal of Contemporary Asia* 20, no.1 (1990): 41–85.

27. Siu-Lun Wong, "The Applicability of Asian Family Values to Other Sociocultural Settings," in *In Search of an East Asian Development Model,* ed. Peter L. Berger and Hsin-Huang Michael Hsiao (New Brunswick, NJ: Transaction Books, 1988).

28. Alice H. Amsden, *Asia's Next Giant: South Korea and Industrialization* (New York: Oxford University Press, 1989), p. 37.

29. Ibid., pp. 18–19.

30. Ibid., pp. 221–22.

31. Robert Wade, "The Visible Hand: The State and East Asia's Economic Growth," *Current History* 92, no. 578 (December 1993): 433.

32. Koh Ai Tee, "Saving Investment and Entrepreneurship," in Krause, *The Singapore Economy Reconsidered,* p. 100.

33. Amsden, *Asia's Next Giant,* p. 70.

34. Ibid., p. 39.

35. Edward S. Steinfeld, *Forging Reform in China: The Fate of State-Owned Industry* (Cambridge: Cambridge University Press, 1998), p. 59.

36. Peter Nolan, "Petty Commodity Production in a Socialist Economy: Chinese Rural Development Post-Mao," in *Market Forces in China: Competition and Small Business—the Wenzhou Debate,* ed. Peter Nolan and Dong Fureng (London: Zed Books, 1990), p. 8.

37. Zhang Lin, "Developing the Commodity Economy in the Rural Areas," in Nolan, *Market Forces in China,* pp. 97–107.

38. *Beijing Review* 34 (August 24, 1987): 4, quoted in James C.F. Wang, *Contemporary Chinese Politics,* 4th ed. (Englewood Cliffs, NJ: Prentice-Hall, 1992), p. 266.

39. Wang, *Contemporary Chinese Politics,* p. 266.

40. Ibid.

41. Ibid.

42. The term is from Barry Naughton, *Growing Out of the Plan: Chinese Economic Reform 1978–1993* (Cambridge: Cambridge University Press, 1996).

43. Quoted in Lincoln Kaye, "Policies Too Hot to Handle," *Far Eastern Economic Review,* January 28, 1994, p. 37.

44. Nicholas R. Lardy, *China's Unfinished Economic Revolution,* Washington, DC. Brookings Institution Press, 1998, pp. 36–38.

45. Edward S. Steinfeld, "Beyond the Transition: China's Economy at Century's End," in *Current History* 98, No. 629 (September 1999): 275.

46. Nicholas R. Lardy, *China's Unfinished Economic Revolution,* pp. 3–6.

47. Gordon White and Robert Wade, "Developmental States and Markets in East Asia: An Introduction," in *Developmental States in East Asia,* ed. Gordon White (New York: St. Martin's, 1988), pp. 13–22.

48. Dorothy Solinger, "Urban Reform and Relational Contracting in Post-Mao China," p. 3.

49. Roy Hofheinz Jr. and Kent E. Calder, *The Eastasia Edge* (New York: Basic Books, 1982), pp. 62–63.

50. Bruce Cumings, "Toward a Comprehensive Settlement of the Korea Problem," *Current History* 98, No. 632 (December 1999): 404.

51. Kevin J. Hewison, "The State and Capitalist Development in Thailand," in *Southeast Asia: Essays in the Political Economy of Structural Change,* ed. Richard Higgott and Richard Robison (London: Routledge and Kegan Paul, 1985), pp. 273–75.

52. Hewison, "The State and Capitalist Development in Thailand," p. 277.

53. Richard Robison, "Class, Capital, and the State in New Order Indonesia," in Higgott and Robison, *Southeast Asia,* p. 308.

54. Ibid., pp. 310–11.
55. David Lim, "The Political Economy of the New Economic Policy in Malaysia," in *Further Readings on Malaysian Economic Development* (Kuala Lumpur: Oxford University Press, 1983), pp. 10, 12.
56. "Global Contagion: A Narrative, Networked Economies," first in a 4-part series, February 15, 1999, *New York Times* online www.nytimes.com/library/world/global/021699global-econ.html)
57. Marcus Noland, Li-Gang Liu, Sherman Robinson, and Zhi Wang, *Global Economic Effects of the Asian Currency Devaluations* (Washington, DC: Institute for International Economics, 1998), pp. 3–29.
58. Linda Lim, "Globalization Is the Best Welfare," *Far Eastern Economic Review,* 163 No. 16 (April 20, 2000): 36.
59. For most of this section on the Philippines, we have relied on the article by Emmanuel S. de Dios, "A Political Economy of Philippine Policy-Making," in *Economic Policy-Making in the Asia-Pacific Region,* ed. John W. Langford and K. Lorne Brownsey (Halifax: Institute for Research on Public Policy, 1990), pp. 109–45.
60. Quoted in de Dios, "A Political Economy," p. 145.
61. Aung San, *Burma's Challenge* 1946, p. 4, quoted in Josef Silverstein, *Burmese Politics* (New Brunswick, NJ: Rutgers University Press, 1980), p. 143.
62. Robert H. Taylor, *The State in Burma* (Honolulu: University of Hawaii Press, 1987), pp. 259–60.
63. David I. Steinberg, "Democracy, Power and the Economy in Myanmar," *Asian Survey* 31, no. 8 (August 1991): 735.
64. Most of the information on this contemporary situation comes from the *Far Eastern Economic Review, Asia 2000 Yearbook,* pp. 89–93.

FOR FURTHER READING

Theoretical Perspectives

Berger, Peter L., and Hsin-Huang Michael Hsiao, eds. *In Search of an East Asian Development Model.* New Brunswick, NJ: Transaction Books, 1988, pp. 3–23.
Black, Jan Knippers. *Development in Theory and Practice: Bridging the Gap.* Boulder, CO: Westview Press, 1991, pp. 15–44.
Gereffi, Gary, and Donald L. Wyman, eds. *Manufacturing Miracles: Paths of Industrialization in Latin America and East Asia.* Princeton, NJ: Princeton University Press, 1992, pp. 323–52 and 368–403.
Scalapino, Robert A., Sato Seizaburo, and Jusuf Wanandi, eds. *Asian Economic Development: Present and Future.* Berkeley: University of California Press, 1985, pp. 63–89.
Streeten, Paul, ed. *Beyond Adjustment: The Asian Experience.* Washington, DC: International Monetary Fund, 1988, pp. 68–105.
Wade, Robert. *Governing the Market: Economic Theory and the Role of Government in East Asian Industrialization.* Princeton, NJ: Princeton University Press, 1990.

Multicountry Studies

Appelbaum, Richard P., and Jeffrey Henderson, eds. *States and Development in the Asian Pacific Rim.* Newbury Park, CA: Sage, 1992.
Brown, Richard Harvey, and William T. Liu, eds. *Modernization in East Asia: Political, Economic, and Social Perspectives.* Westport, CT: Praeger, 1992.
Deyo, Frederic C., ed. *The Political Economy of the New Asian Industrialism.* Ithaca, NY: Cornell University Press, 1987.

Higgott, Richard, and Richard Robison, eds. *Southeast Asia: Essays in the Political Economy of Structural Change.* London: Routledge and Kegan Paul, 1985.

Langford, John W., and K. Lorne Brownsey, eds. *Economic Policy-Making in the Asia-Pacific Region.* Halifax: Institute for Research on Public Policy, 1990.

Lee, Chung H., and Ippei Yamazawa, eds. *The Economic Development of Japan and Korea: A Parallel with Lessons.* New York: Praeger, 1990.

White, Gordon, ed. *Developmental States in East Asia.* New York: St. Martin's, 1988.

Single-Country Studies

Amsden, Alice. *Asia's Next Giant: South Korea and Late Industrialization.* New York: Oxford University Press, 1989, chs. 3–6.

Bowie, Alasdair. *Crossing the Industrial Divide.* New York: Columbia University Press, 1991.

Clark, Cal. *Taiwan's Political Development: Implications for Contending Political Economy Paradigms.* New York: Greenwood Press, 1989.

Krause, Lawrence B., Koh Ai Tee, and Lee (Tsao) Yuan, eds. *The Singapore Economy Reconsidered.* Singapore: Institute of Southeast Asian Studies, 1987, chs. 3–6.

MacIntyre, Andrew. *Business and Politics in Indonesia.* AAS of Australia and Allen and Unwin: 1991.

MacKerras, Colin, Pradeep Taneja and Graham Young. *China Since 1978: Reform, Modernisation and Socialism With Chinese Characteristics.* New York: St. Martin's Press, 1994.

Okimoto, Daniel I. *Between MITI and the Market: Japanese Industrial Policy for High Technology.* Stanford, CA: Stanford University Press, 1989.

Pearson, Margaret M. *China's New Business Elite: The Political Consequences of Economic Reform.* Berkeley: University of California Press, 1997.

Posen, Adam S. *Restoring Japan's Economic Growth.* Washington D.C.: Institute for National Economics, 1998.

Riskin, Carl. *China's Political Economy: The Quest for Development Since 1949.* Oxford, England: Oxford University Press, 1987, chs. 3–5, 7–10, 12–14.

6

Culture and Ideology

I deas of who we are as human beings are embedded in two types of *worldview,* one called *culture,* the other *ideology.* Culture is the intricate set of habits (customs), values, beliefs, and attitudes we inherit from those who nurture us in early life. In countless different cultural settings, we learn the elements of behavior, speech, and thought that shape our conduct and govern the way we relate to one another. Like nature, culture is taken for granted and remains unexamined unless we encounter others differently endowed. Yet it is essential to how we find our way around in the world, providing a "pictionary" of symbols and images against which we match our perceptions of reality. Thus culture is more than ideas: It is a symbolic map with which we learn to determine who we are, where we are going, and how to get there. In all its many forms, culture is a constant, a necessary complement to the indefinite and diffuse nature of human genetic inheritance.

Ideologies, by contrast, are ideas that are precipitated by and respond to radical political and social change. When we no longer recognize the social terrain using the habitual language of culture, we find ourselves unable to make appropriate judgments and take effective action. With the advent of modern structures of relations between people, a new set of symbols is required for us to understand how to think, talk, and act in a new environment. Ideologies provide self-conscious patterns of ideas and images that redefine human beings' relationships to one another in terms of the modern state or body politic. Each new ideology describes, explains, and justifies a set of goals and means for social action to either preserve, reform, uproot, or rebuild our social order. As the symbolism of modern ideologies joins that of culture, therefore, it acts as a counterculture, criticizing aspects of political life in need of change and mobilizing people to bring it about.

In individual as well as social life in modern times, there is always tension in the interaction between culture and ideology. The nature of this interaction as it has occurred among the peoples of the Asian Pacific since their encounter with the modern world is the subject of this chapter. What are the similarities and differences among the various cultures in the region? How have those cultures influenced and been influenced by the ideologies imported from the modern West? The subject is elaborate and imprecise, encompassing not only a large number of distinct cultures in East and Southeast Asia but their interactions with various European ideologies. The complexities are compounded by variations within a single cultural matrix, such as Confucianism, and in various belief systems; there are not only different sects of Buddhism, Islam, and Hinduism and variations within socialist, communist, and liberal doctrines but also mixtures resulting in distinctive blendings of cultural and ideological influences that have traveled throughout the region.

By the mid-nineteenth century, three ideologies destined to have a major impact on the rest of the world—liberalism, conservatism, and socialism—had made their appearance in Western Europe and begun their dispersion abroad. As these ideologies spread throughout the colonial world, they lost their original contexts, changing in curious ways by interacting with cultures and circumstances vastly different from those in the West. When refracted through the prism of Asian nationalism and culture, therefore, they were no longer recognizably Western ideologies; they emerged as distinctively Asian ideologies. All reflected the strong sense of nationalism aroused in Asians by Western imperialism. Thus, although nationalism has already been discussed in Chapter 3, it inevitably permeates much of the analysis in this chapter.

We begin with a summary of how each of our development theories deals with the question of culture and ideology and then consider the argument that culture itself is the decisive factor explaining the extraordinary development among East Asian NICs. We then briefly describe the elements of Western ideologies that appealed to nationalist leaders in their search for a model of modernity and then discuss Asian cultural traditions that have endured in the postcolonial era. The remainder of the chapter considers the outcome of the confrontation between Western ideologies and the Asian Pacific cultures they encountered.

CULTURE AND IDEOLOGY IN THE THEORIES OF DEVELOPMENT

Modernization Theory

According to modernization theory, nations that pursue modernization undergo a gradual process of substituting modern scientific ideas for their traditional cultural beliefs, duplicating, with local variations, the original experiences of Western countries. As people learn more advanced ways of cultivating the soil and manufacturing goods, rationality and scientific attitudes are expected to incrementally replace religion and superstition; a progressive linear conception of time and change displaces the relatively static idea of change based on a cyclical conception of time; in addition, individual achievement gradually prevails over the family and socially assigned positions as the determining element of success. This modern substitute for traditional culture is not ideology, however, but a scientific, pragmatic, and presumably universal outlook.

The cultural evolution from "traditional" to "modern" ways of thinking and acting is assumed to follow automatically as a result of the economic and technological changes that spearhead modernization. Yet even in the most advanced modern societies, religion and superstition continue to coexist with science and rationality. And in the most successful examples of late modernization, Japan and the East Asian NICs, the family rather than the individual has remained the prototype for modern industrial organization. This raises two questions left unanswered from the perspective of modernization theory: Why do traditional cultural traits persist alongside modern ideological divisions? What combination of cultural attributes constitutes a "truly" modern culture?

World System Theory

From the world system/dependency perspective, it is ideology, not culture, that is considered significant for the capacity of developing countries to industrialize on their own terms, without incurring crippling indebtedness to outside interests. For example, communism, by which is meant the ideology of Marxist-inspired party regimes, was assumed until recently to be an asset to late-developing nations because it empowered governments to resist the economic and political stranglehold of neoimperialist forces. The problem for adherents of world system theory, however, was that communist countries were not able to join the world system; they had to develop an alternative "economic world system" which came to be known as the communist bloc. Unfortunately this ersatz world system did not generate either the capital or the dynamism of the capitalist world system which was, in the end, the reason for its collapse. This left countries like China, Vietnam, Laos, Cambodia, and more tentatively North Korea, to seek the rewards of economic liberalization only attainable by joining the capitalist world economy.

Since communism, which continues to recede from the political agenda of countries, did not provide the beliefs that enable peripheral countries to join the global economy *on their own terms,* the world system/dependency perspective is left with unanswered key questions. Is it ever possible for peripheral countries to resist incorporation into the world system in some way that does *not* subject them to the dominance of the capitalist world system's core players? What beliefs *might* empower the government of a peripheral state to join the global economy without losing its national autonomy?

If modernization theory fails to answer the question of what inspires people to adopt the cultural ideas of "modernity," and world system theory has no answer for how and why any particular ideology can empower the government of a vulnerable peripheral country to join the world system on its own terms, developmental state theory does have an answer.

Developmental State Theory

In the thinking of most adherents of developmental state theory, culture not ideology is decisive for how a society adapts to the exigencies of industrialization. In contrast to the world system approach which emphasizes the *vulnerabilities* of peripheral countries seeking to develop in a world system already dominated by rich and powerful players, developmental state theorists emphasize the compensatory advantages of latecomers to the task of development. Their greatest asset in pursuing a developmental agenda is an autonomous state that is deeply embedded in the Asian culture. This autonomy to govern relatively unimpeded by the partisan political demands of diverse constituencies is what enables the developmental state to effectively orchestrate the national will in the direction of "catching up" with the highly industrialized powers of the world. Support for such an authoritarian state derives from the high esteem and benevolent status that the state enjoys in a traditional Asian setting.

Thus culture rather than ideology provides the underpinnings of the developmental state. It derives not only its legitimacy but its manner of rule, its *modus operandi,* from its embeddedness in the culture of a nation. East Asian developmental states have been able to utilize high savings rates, a strong belief in the virtues of education, discipline and hard work to mobilize the nation's resources toward the goal of rapid industrialization. The state relies on its moral and material support from the population to maintain legitimate informal linkages between specialized governmental agencies and privately owned industrial enterprises. These informal linkages make it possible for the state to rely on the price mechanisms of the market rather than administratively assigned prices to carry out its will. Through the close collaboration of public and private sectors, therefore, the sum of market decisions is not left to the vagaries of an "invisible hand" but is guided by the hand of presumably benevolent rulers.

Although the "statist" approach builds on an appreciation for the virtues of culture, its central focus is the state itself for which culture only provides the setting. If politics is the protagonist of the developmental story according to the "statist" perspective and economics plays the lead role in both the modernization and world system explanations, it is from anthropology that a distinctively cultural explanation for development in the Asian Pacific has emerged.

Cultural Theory

The cultural approach views the "habits of the heart," which distinguish one culture from another, as the determining factor in how ably a society adapts to the opportunities of modern capitalist development. Following the lead of Max Weber, the German sociologist who argued that Protestantism was the essential factor in molding Western capitalist thinking, some proponents of the cultural approach suggest that culture shapes attitudes toward time, money, work, saving, and success in ways that either promote or discourage development. It is argued, for example, that Confucian cultural beliefs, which like Protestantism extol the virtues of hard work, frugality, and piety, are uniquely suited to achieving modernization. Some scholars even credit Confucianism with the rise of a singularly effective "oriental model of economic development,"[1] explaining the remarkable economic success of South Korea, Taiwan, Hong Kong, and Singapore. At least one scholar, on the other hand, suggests that the ethical principles of Buddhism may be impediments to industrialization, accounting for Burma's *failure* to develop.[2]

Other advocates of the cultural approach confine themselves to analyzing the impact of a variety of cultural understandings of power and authority on the style and substance of different cultures' adaptation to modernization. Lucian Pye, for instance, claims that Asian cultural traditions of paternalistic authority not only lead these nations along dissimilar routes toward modernization but will result in modern societies that are distinctively different from those in the West. As Asian cultural traditions adapt to modernization, they necessarily shed some of their traditional differences, developing characteristics common to all modern societies. Yet their distinctive underlying cultural patterns persist, resulting in modern societies unlike those in the West.

Each of the above theories has a different take on the elements of culture and ideology. Modernization theory emphasizes the universality of modern Western culture. World system theory stresses the role of ideology in enabling newly developing countries to modernize on their own rather than Western terms. Cultural theory asserts the primacy of indigenous culture as decisive for Asian patterns of development.

THE APPEAL OF WESTERN IDEOLOGIES

Western ideologies have held different and often overlapping appeals to modernizers in the Asian Pacific, depending on the time and circumstances of their nationalist movements for independence, described in Chapter 3.

Liberalism

In general, the appeal of liberalism to nationalists in Asia was its suggestion of liberation, the right to free oneself from the external bullying of foreign powers and from the constraints of antiquated ideas and institutions. Liberalism appeared as a promise of science, progress, power, and prosperity. It signified the choices that exist for individuals, for movements, for countries, to choose an independent path to becoming modern. Often identified with the institution of privately owned property and a free-market system of exchange, liberalism was the antithesis of old feudal forms of bondage. In this vague condemnation of all that is old and confining, however, liberalism contained a number of quite different implications.

In early twentieth-century China, liberalism had led intellectuals to embrace the necessity of a revolutionary break with the Confucian past. By contrast, liberalism in Japan and Thailand had resulted in a conception of modernization that emphasized conserving cultural traditions as a veneer for industrialism managed by a state bureaucracy. Among nationalists in British colonies, like Malaya, Burma, and even Singapore, liberalism was understood to mean a bureaucratically organized government capable of providing professional leadership by a political elite based upon merit. In French Indochina, liberalism was identified with an expanded cultural and intellectual freedom to explore new horizons, a trait that continued to characterize revolutionaries when they adopted socialism. Liberalism for the Filipinos had a distinctively American flavor, stamped by the period of tutelage under the United States. And for all the colonies, liberalism meant freedom from foreign rule, the right to self-determination.

Conspicuous by their absence in this list of various appeals that liberalism held out for Asian nationalists are the elements Westerners often assume are its defining features: the human rights of individuals independent of the state and the idea that governments derive their legitimacy from the people. Wherever elements of it were embraced in the Asian Pacific, liberalism seems to have omitted the legalistic, individualistic, and contractual aspects of the ideology considered so essential by its adherents in the West. This raises interesting questions about the nature of Western ideologies commonly identified as liberal, conservative, and socialist. Are they mutually incompatible belief systems based on distinctive premises and principles, or can their component elements be combined in unpredictable ways? Do ideologies constitute timeless and universally valid models for social action regardless of cultural context? Or are they moving targets that serve the shifting interests of different cultural groups and social classes?

Conservatism

The values associated with conservatism in the West are more consistently appealing to Asian Pacific peoples than are those of liberalism. Its emphasis on authority as commanding the obedience of individuals is as central to the communist worldview as it is to the official tenets of government in all the noncommunist systems. Throughout the Asian Pacific region, even in Japan, a country generally considered to have a democratic ethos, the state's authority is based on the paternalistic model of family life: Just as the father carries the obligation to provide for the welfare of his family, the government has the responsibility to secure the well-being of its citizens. Individuals have determinate duties rather than abstract rights, and power is required by the state to carry out its commitments. All social relations are predicated on the authority of those who are superior over those who are inferior, even when positions are filled on the basis of merit or virtue rather than heredity.

The values identified with conservative ideology in the West, such as loyalty, discipline, and patriotism, are commonplace themes in the culture and rhetoric of politics in all Asian Pacific countries, perhaps with the exception of the Philippines. This is also the case with community, which is so universally considered as taking precedence over individuals in Asian Pacific societies that it hardly merits the description of ideology. There is among belief systems in all Asian countries, both traditional and modern, a broad agreement that to live in society requires discipline, obedience to authority, and loyalty to the state, without which neither order nor the graces of civilization are possible. But in Asia these beliefs are part of an age-old cultural legacy rather than an embattled ideological alternative to mainstream liberal beliefs in individual rights, as is the case in the West.

Socialism

If the appeal of an ideology were judged by how frequently its label is invoked, socialism in all its varieties (especially Marxist socialism and democratic socialism) might be considered a top contender. Not only China, North Korea, Vietnam, and Laos but also Burma, Singapore, and Indonesia employ socialist rhetoric in justifying public policies. And in Japan, it must be remembered, the socialists constitute the second largest party. The attraction of socialism for Asian Pacific peoples is its unequivocal commitment to economic and social equality, achieved through the power of collective action rather than by individual effort. In most of these countries, an enormous gulf separates the governing elites from the vast majority of people, who remain very poor. The compelling nature of socialist symbolism for leaders in this situation is its combination of dedication to material prosperity with the promise of social equality in its vision of all citizens sharing in the economic benefits of a modern economy.

An additional element of socialism that has made it appealing to Asian Pacific leaders is its opposition to exploitation and oppression in all forms. It is explicitly anti-imperialist, enabling leaders of ex-colonies to deflect internal discontent over the sluggish pace of progress under postindependence rule. And as a critique of inequality, domestically as well as internationally, socialism addresses continuing imbalances in all Asian Pacific societies between the rich and the poor, urban workers and rural laborers, the politically privileged and the politically underprivileged. Thus for Asian Pacific countries socialism has offered a compelling model of progress, bridging the gap between their tradition-bound way of life and their modern aspirations, with a program for non-Western people to become prosperous and modern without becoming Western and capitalist. In the current transition toward greater liberalization of political discourse in Asia, however, the kind of socialism that is likely to be embraced is more akin to that of Sweden than that of the former communist countries.

DISTINCTIVE FEATURES OF ASIAN CULTURES

"East is East and West is West, and never the twain shall meet" was Kipling's characterization of a supposedly unbridgeable chasm between European and Asian cultures. To many on each side of the divide, the "Other" seemed strange, exotic, inscrutable, even perverse and wrong. But the two sides *did* meet and out of that meeting have come changes in both East and West. Yet even the changes brought by political modernization and economic development in Asia have not eradicated the features of Asian cultures that distinguish them from European and other Western cultures. That distinctiveness persists and strongly influences the political and economic course of contemporary Asian states.

In this section we identify those "Eastern" cultural characteristics that contrast with "Western" views, particularly as they concern attitudes toward political authority; those characteristics have profoundly affected the reception given in Asia to the array of modern secular ideologies of European origin and have shaped the reconstruction of those ideologies in adapting to the Asian context. Certainly there are important differences between the Confucian and Mahayana Buddhist-influenced cultures (China, Japan, Korea, Vietnam, Taiwan, Singapore, Hong Kong), the Theravada Buddhist cultures (Myanmar, Thailand, Cambodia, Laos), the predominantly Moslem Malay cultures (Malaysia, Indonesia, Brunei, and the southern Philippines), and among the countries in each of those groupings.

Still, they have some features in common. These include *collectivism,* a strong identification as members of groups and the expectation that people will subordinate their individual interests to those of the collective; *consensus,* a high value placed on sustaining the harmony of group life by avoiding contentiousness and

Buddhism has been a major influence on the cultures of East and Southeast Asia, spreading outward from India and reaching as far as Japan. Shown here is the Great Buddha at Kamakura, Japan.

Source: Photo by Arthur Feraru.

overt confrontation; *hierarchy,* acceptance of a paternalist pattern of authority and a social order based on superior-inferior rankings in human relationships from husband-wife to emperor-subject; and *power as status,* a traditional reverence toward power as the necessary component for generating order and civilization out of chaos and barbarism.

Collectivism: Loyalty to the Group a Prime Virtue

The solidarity of the stereotypical Asian family is often the object of praise and even envy among non-Asians. It exemplifies the cultural tradition of giving higher priority to the family, the village, the workplace, and the nation, rather than to the individual members of those groups. Responsibility to the "collective" takes precedence over the individual's self- (or selfish) interest, and individual pursuits defer to cooperation with other group members.

Putting a higher value on group solidarity, loyalty, and cooperation than on individual freedom of action is not seen as a starkly simple situation of the group against the individual. Rather, it reflects a more "organic" view of the intimate relationship between human beings and the social networks into which they are born. Much like the nested doll of Russian folk art, the individual is the smallest figure encapsulated in successively larger figures—the family, the town, the province, the country—each serving as a protective shell around the smaller figures inside it. Belonging to groups is, in this view, not an option we choose but a necessary condition of being human; our identity is embedded in and defined by the groups to which we belong and our individual well-being depends on the well-being of those groups. The implicit assumption is, "What's good for my family (or my company or my country) is good for me, and in working for its good I am working for my own good."

Indication that group membership is still a higher priority in Asian cultures is found in a study of preschools in China, Japan, and the United States.[3] When teachers, parents, and other adults were asked to name the most important things for children to learn in preschool, the Chinese gave first place (37 percent) to "cooperation and how to be a member of a group," with "creativity" (17 percent) and "perseverance" (13 percent) the next most-favored choices. Almost two-thirds of the Japanese selected cooperation and group membership (30 percent) or another group-oriented objective, "sympathy/empathy/concern for others" (31 percent). The top choice for Americans was the individualist virtue of "self-reliance" (34 percent), with (surprisingly?) cooperation and group membership in second place (32 percent).

The expectation that individual interests must be compatible with, and in fact are best served by, loyalty to the group contrasts sharply with the modern Western assumption that the needs of the individual and the group often conflict with each other. The emphasis on individual rights—to "life, liberty and the pursuit of happiness," as Thomas Jefferson put it—derives from an image that is basic to modern Western political and legal thought: that prior to the existence of governments, individuals lived as solitary beings in a "state of nature" and that they set up government by agreement with others for the limited purpose of protecting their individual interests.

The atomistic Western view that humans are naturally unconnected to other humans and the contract theory of the origin of the state are quite alien to Asian cultures. Indeed, their acceptance in the West is neither complete nor without strain. Collectivism still has a hold on Westerners, as witnessed by the willingness of most of them to put their lives on the line for their nation, the ultimate expression of self-abnegation to the "collective." The endemic popularity of "cults" is a similar expression of deep-seated yearning for submerging the individual to a group will to achieve meaning as part of a collective endeavor. Modern society's emphasis on individualism and competition puts strains on people. Substance abuse, violence, suicide, and other forms of antisocial behavior are interpreted as evidence that the stress on individualism overlooks a deep-rooted human need to belong, to be part of a community. While individualism frees people to "do their own thing," to be innovative and creative agents of change, it has its dark side too: depriving people of the close bonds of mutual support, leaving them with feelings of detachment, of rootlessness, facing alone the blame for the consequences of failure.

On the face of it, the Asian emphasis on the group seems to be an asset in the process of economic and political modernization. The habit of loyalty to the collective is an advantage to modern enterprises, as demonstrated by the legendary company loyalty of Japanese workers and managers. And, if extended upward to the modern state, it enables government to mobilize its citizens in the task of nation building. But this is true only when a state, as the legitimate power representing all people under its jurisdiction, already exists. Until such a nation-state has established its credibility, loyalty to particularist local, ethnic, religious, and regional groups often produces intergroup conflict and feuds, weakening or impeding attachment to a larger national community. This has certainly been the case in Myanmar and to a significant degree in Indonesia, where ethnic particularism has been detrimental to the formation of a truly integrated, legitimate national power.

The resilience of group loyalties at the local level and (when it exists) the national level in Asian cultures has been promoted by the process of decision making based on consensus building.

Consensus: Harmonious Unity a Desired Goal

The secular Confucian tradition as well as the sacred traditions of Hinduism, Buddhism, and Taoism place a high value on the achievement of harmony. The Confucian ideal of the good society is a pyramid of harmonious interpersonal and intergroup relations from family compounds to palace grounds, while the religions adjure believers to attune themselves to supernatural forces and a cosmic order. With the acknowledgment that it may not always be possible to attain and maintain such a demanding level of correct behavior, it is expected that at least the outward appearance of harmony will be preserved. Even though the members of a group may be locked in bitter disputes, good manners require that the disagreement be masked in a formal show of unanimity. Open expression of dissent is considered at minimum in poor taste and at worst high treason. This preoccupation with preserving at least the appearance of unity is attributed by Lucian Pye to a deeply rooted fear of the ever-present threat that any significant diminution of civilized authority will open the gates to a takeover by "primitive power," the fang-and-claw rule of the jungle.[4] In short, harmony preserves order and unity keeps anarchy at bay.

The cultural preference for decision making by consensus has its roots in traditional practices at the village level, where the inhabitants gathered to discuss and reach agreement on matters of common importance. Although the village headman may in fact exert the guiding role in determining what is acceptable to all, the appearance of equality in participation to reach agreement is not only preserved but accorded great value. Decisions may benefit some and not others, but the essential objective is the preservation of the group itself. While in Indonesia, consensus has long been a tradition at the village level, in China and Japan the appearance if not the reality of consensus has been a conspicuous aspect of party politics at the highest level. Although to Westerners this may seem an expedient to avoid the onus of individual responsibility, it is in Asia a culturally prescribed way of reaffirming harmony among constituents with diverse views or sharp disagreements over policy. Adherence to consensus as the formal basis for expressing group decisions, even when it is widely speculated that sharp disagreements exist among participants, secures perpetuation of the group by including everyone in the decision and in the responsibility for implementing it.

The priority given in Asian cultures to the value of harmony and consensus is not found in Western liberalism; not that the West courts *dis*harmony and *dis*-sensus, but rather that differences of interests and viewpoints are *expected* and can be openly advocated without breaching the etiquette of private or public discourse. Confrontation is neither impolite nor treasonous. Out of the rough-and-tumble conflict of ideas and objectives, conducted within the bounds of accepted "rules of the game," come pragmatic or workable decisions for the group or the government. The decision is what the majority of the participants want, although it is acknowledged that some people carry more weight in the process of decision making than others.

In contrast to the idea that political decisions express group preferences, Asian cultural traditions suggest that group decisions reflect a cosmic order. Truth is not arrived at by contention among rival conceptions but a pattern of righteousness arrived at by everyone through a process of reaching consensus. In this cultural conception, a "loyal opposition" is an oxymoron and majority rule a threat both to continued elite dominance and to the position of ethnic, political, or religious minorities. But as Asian societies are transformed into dynamic modern systems with a complexity of varied, often dissonant, interests, it may no longer be either feasible or desirable simply to declare harmonious assent by fiat from above. Under these circumstances, majority rule as a populist egalitarian form of participation in politics directly challenges another feature of Asian cultures—the assumption that hierarchy is natural in all human relations.

Hierarchy: Reciprocal Obligations of Superior and Inferior

Basic to the traditional Asian concept of authority is the notion of superior-inferior status in all relationships, derived from the model of the father's position in the most basic social unit, the family. This paternalist pattern involves reciprocal obligations between superior and inferior partners in the relationship, the specifics of which may vary as do the roles fathers play in different societies. But the underlying assumption that hierarchy is the natural, legitimate order of things was and is still quite widely held.

At the top of the pecking order in Confucian China was the emperor and his scholar-officials; ideally, farmers ranked below them but still higher than soldiers and merchants. In two other Confucian societies, Vietnam and Japan, the military were accorded more respect than in China, and the emperor's divine lineage received more credence in Japan than in secularized Confucian China. The Chinese model of a centralized merit-based bureaucracy was more closely followed in Vietnam than in Korea or Japan. In pre-Meiji Japan officialdom was more decentralized, and the Chinese practice of recruitment by examination never really caught on. In Korea, the principle of meritocracy was somewhat diluted when the landed aristocracy laid exclusive claim to eligibility for the examinations to become officials; competition among them for the limited number of available positions and land reached intense levels, contrary to the Confucian ideal of harmonious cooperation. But all the Confucian-influenced countries subscribed to the hierarchical model of a benevolent father-figure monarch, assisted by meritorious officials, ruling over loyal and obedient subjects, setting an example for them of virtue and upholding the moral order so fundamental to a civil society.

In Southeast Asian cultures under the influence of Hinduism and Buddhism, the "god-king" occupied the pinnacle of the hierarchy; his responsibility was to use his divine connection and the power of rituals carefully performed to protect his subjects from the whim of supernatural forces, to keep the society in harmony with the cosmic order. At lower levels of society, superiority-inferiority took the form of more voluntaristic and personalist patron-client relationships, in which the patron provides protection and favors to his clients, who in turn give him loyalty and services. So in all these hierarchical relationships in East and Southeast Asia, the superior and the inferior both had obligations to each other and expected benefits in return; they were linked in a form of mutual dependence, of *inter*dependence presumably satisfying to both partners.

This traditional pattern of hierarchical relationships was reinforced by the experience under colonialism and was continued or revived after independence as a means of attaching legitimacy to the new governments and gathering support for the tasks of modernization. The pattern is only now being challenged by people dissatisfied with their own ranking in the hierarchy or with the hierarchical system in principle. Egalitarianism, for several centuries now in the West a symbolic though incompletely realized goal, is gaining adherents among Asians. Still, hierarchy remains the dominant pattern in political as well as social relations.

Power: The "Antipolitics" of Status and Ritual

The traditional concept of power as responsibility for setting an example of virtue and performing rituals, in return for which the ruler enjoyed the "perks" associated with status, is quite unlike the modern Western notion of power as responsibility for proposing policies and making decisions. To us, the traditional Asian idea of power is profoundly antipolitical, accustomed as we are to expecting that political leaders will use their position to promote change, to carry out programs, to demonstrate their power to *do* things.

But the concept of power as status, rather than as policymaking, seems on reflection to be eminently suited to static societies where change is neither rapid nor a particularly sought-after objective and where the capacity of the state to mobilize resources for major ventures is quite modest. The limited power at the disposal of the rulers and officials fits very nicely with the expectation that the ruler will be free of responsibilities for decision making and that the bureaucracy will handle whatever decisions are required to preserve the status quo. Ritual and administration are the stuff of power, and when used well the outcome is more of the same—that is, the perpetuation of a stable society in which people are given some measure of protection from natural disasters and the wrath of supernatural forces. Pye sums up the historic concepts of power in Asian cultures in these words:

> Power had little to do with the concepts of utility, efficiency, and representation which have been central to understanding power in the Western experience. Power as ritual or status was an end value, not to be debased for utilitarian purposes. Since the goals of action were stylized acts performed

in support of the collective well-being and not to promote specific policies, there was little sense that more efficient application of power would be desirable or even possible. Those with power tended to conceive of themselves as embodying the collectivity, defending a consensus, rather than representing particular interests. People tried to avoid adopting partisan positions on public "issues," but instead they generally preferred the techniques of intrigue and personalized tactical maneuvering, which were more compatible with conflict in stable hierarchical arrangements.[5]

Such an approach to the uses and management of power would seem to be incompatible with the premises underlying the Western ideologies that were embraced to some degree in all of Asia. In fact, a major dilemma for the postindependence power-holders has been whether to try to plant in Asian soil one or another of the "alien" Western ideologies (much as the "miracle" strains of rice were imported in the "Green Revolution") or to try to graft the "modern" idea of politics as policy-making onto the rootstock of status politics or to cultivate a new variety of politics, grown in Asian soil and well adapted to the new tasks of economic development and social and political modernization. Which choices were made in the various Asian countries, and with what outcomes, are the subject of the next two sections.

EVOLUTION OF IDEOLOGIES IN CONFUCIAN SOCIETIES

East Asian ideologies are indelibly marked by their common Confucian ancestry, some elements of which have been discussed above. Our task now is to describe how Western ideas have been recast to explain and direct the course of modern development in the Confucian-based societies of Japan, China, North and South Korea, Vietnam, Taiwan, Singapore, and Hong Kong. As each country (excepting Hong Kong, of course, which officially rejoined China in 1997) gained its independence, the ideas designed by its nationalist leaders in the course of coming to power became enshrined as the common outlook of the new social order. There were, of course, a great many contending ideas throughout this period, but we will limit discussion to the dominant worldviews that have prevailed in these countries since independence.

Among the views held in these countries, there are marked differences in attitude toward the function of ideology. In countries adopting the Marxist variety of socialism, ideology is viewed positively, its function being the systematic instruction of people into a modern, revolutionary way of understanding and promoting political change. In China, North Korea, and Vietnam, therefore, the ideas of Soviet Marxism were embraced and energetically incorporated into political life as the emblem of orthodoxy and righteousness. In this sense the ideas Westerners identify as "communism" have served in these countries as a substitute or replacement for Confucian orthodoxy. Marxism-Leninism, like Confucianism, is broad and all-encompassing. It relies heavily upon repetition of standardized formulas to provide the correct guide to thought and behavior. Similarly, the concepts of communist ideology in these countries, although derived from the same Marxist orthodoxy, are subject to divergent interpretations, frequently evoking intense public discussion and private individual scrutiny for signs of the official political disposition.

In Japan, South Korea, and Taiwan, by contrast, ideology has assumed a negative symbolic connotation, one that implies radical change, a sharp break with the past. This has not prevented the actual dissemination of ideas to impart new ways of thinking and acting in these countries. Rather, it has encouraged retention of older cultural ideas, while changing their symbolic significance to adapt to new circumstances. In this manner, progress—the central concept of liberalism—was adopted by making it, in the case of Japan, an essential component of loyalty to the emperor. Leaders in all three of these countries have subliminally if not self-consciously invoked a Confucian heritage to bolster political authoritarianism while selectively appropriating liberal concepts to champion a market economy. But the eclectic combination of Confucian attitudes toward status, hierarchy, and the moral authority of the state with liberal ideas of progress, economic growth, and freedom to defend one's way of life has enabled these countries with an avowedly noncommunist identity and affiliation to evade the "nasty" symbol of ideology.

With this introduction to the political ambiguities of the uses of ideology, we now address the ways in which Western ideas have intermingled with traditional cultural presuppositions in Japan.

Japan: The Meiji Mystique

The dominant belief system in Japan today is still at heart the Meiji amalgam of traditional and modern ideas, minus the militarism and chauvinism that led to defeat in 1945, plus the pacifism and liberal democratic elements introduced by the American occupation.

Meiji Era.   The nineteenth-century samurai-turned-modernizers promoted their program of national renovation by retaining feudal values, expanding on popular attachment to national symbols, and introducing selected elements of conservatism and liberalism that seemed congruent with traditional values and stimulants to the process of modernization. But they deftly disguised their indebtedness to Western ideas by dressing them in traditional clothes. By explaining their reforms as part of the "restoration of imperial rule," the samurai-statesmen were able, in the name of obedience to the will of the emperor, to promote ideas that would otherwise have been branded unpatriotic, if not treasonous.

Rather than beginning with a systematized ideology, Meiji leaders evolved a national ideology built around the core feudal values of family, social hierarchy, and communal harmony. Novel elements were gradually added, not displacing the older values but fitting themselves into and expanding earlier rules. Loyalty to the emperor and allegiance to the state were among the earliest political precepts to be added to the feudal core in fashioning an ideology for modern Japan. Symbols that glorified the tribal nation were promoted: the emperor as descendant of the sun goddess, the Japanese as the chosen people, and the honor of the nation, which required outperforming the industrial and military might of the Western imperialist powers.

Empress Nagako and the late Emperor Hirohito of Japan, whose
reign from 1926 to 1989 spanned the rise of the Japanese empire,
defeat in World War II, and postwar recovery to become the
world's number two economic power.

Source: UN photo 129292/T. Chen.

As Carol Gluck points out in her study, *Japan's Modern Myths,*[6] the Meiji oligarchs tailored specific versions of a national ideology to target particular audiences
to be transformed from subjects into citizens of a modern monarchy. To farmers being conscripted for military service, the emperor was presented as a majestic object
of the spirit of loyalty and *Bushido,* that is, the code of honor of traditional Japanese
warriors, depending on the virtues of the village as the bedrock of national integrity.
Urban folk, on the other hand, were reminded of the obligations of social equality
"now that all men are samurai." Whether directed to farmers, artisans, housewives,
students, schoolteachers, or local officials, these different versions of the nationalistic
message were sent in a "dialect" designed for that particular audience.

Nonetheless, the themes of the ideological messages overlapped, reinforcing
one another: the emperor as the embodiment of Japan's uniqueness; allegiance to
him as the source of national unity and social order; the glory of Japan's empire in
the East as proof of Japan's status as a first-class nation; loyalty and patriotism as
ideals to which everyone conformed. The result was not only a sense of the nation
but a set of ideas delineating the national purposes for which people labored and
for which the nation stood. Symbols like loyalty and patriotism, in addition to providing the general civic content of moral education in the schools, were applied to a
wide array of worthy causes such as "party loyalty, the entrepreneurial imperative
to rise in the world, or the promotion of the sales of domestic—rather than imported—beer."[7]

To these adaptations of feudal and imperial traditions were added Western concepts like progress, liberalism, constitutionalism, and representative government, which at the start of the Meiji period were considered alien in form and meaning, but by the end of that era were accepted as natural elements of the Japanese way of life. Among noted intellectuals exposed to Western ideas, many of whom had close associations with or were themselves members of the Meiji government, liberal ideas were enthusiastically espoused as the means by which Japan would "attain an equal footing with the other powers."[8] In the belief that government had to be broadly representative, Okuma Shigenobu, a senior member of government (later prime minister and founder of Tokyo College), proposed establishing a parliamentary system based on elections contested by political parties. Freedom of speech and the press and the right to hold public meetings were endorsed.[9]

But Japan's traditions favored adopting the "enlightened conservatism" of late-nineteenth-century Germany rather than the individualism of classical liberalism, and it was this ideological route that provided the business class an escape from the inferior rank assigned it by Confucianism to high status in Meiji times, as today. At the beginning of the reform period, Japanese merchants still suffered from a generally contemptuous attitude toward their activities, especially on the part of Meiji officials. They were suspected of the stereotypical sins of merchants: being greedy, corrupt, fraudulent, dishonest, and likely as not unpatriotic. A newspaper editorial in 1895 exhibited Confucian scorn for merchants as a way of mustering patriotic support behind the Meiji oligarchs:

> Examine the speech, appearance, attitudes, character, spirit, and habits of our merchants—all are shameful. They fight over trivial sums and short-range profits, and their only ambition is to feed themselves and their families. They know nothing of sovereign or country, nor are they concerned with the prosperity of the people or the good of society.[10]

The response of businesspeople was to deny that pursuit of profit was their motivation, insisting that national greatness rather than narrow self-interest was what drove business enterprise to succeed. Thus, contrary to the advice of Adam Smith, Japanese business developed an identity of self-sacrifice: to overcome adversity and be successful through dedication to the nation, a sense of duty, and patriotism. They became "warriors armed with an abacus,"[11] upholding principles of honor, integrity, and fidelity to one's word.

Thus, starting from a position of inferiority, the business class in Japan evolved an ideology quite distinct from that of its counterpart in the West, fitting itself into rather than rejecting traditions of subservience and loyalty to the state. The Meiji oligarchs, for their part, using a combination of nationalism and Confucian traditionalism to promote industrialization, enhanced the power of government rather than the independent power of the business class. Nationalism served as a rationale both for government aid to private business and for the rejection of the laissez-faire idea of Western liberalism as formulated by Adam Smith. Government accepted private enterprise without reservation and businesspeople for their part accepted the leadership role of the government in the interests of the nation as a whole.

After World War II.   Much of the Meiji ideology of "enlightened conservatism" has survived both defeat in war and economic prosperity in peace. Business resumed its relationship with the state after the war—with U.S. blessing—but rather than the military, the Liberal Democratic Party (until 1993) occupied the third side of the triangle. In close collaboration and unchecked by a powerful military, big business and the state bureaucracy today once again steer Japan's course in pursuit of international greatness, this time in the direction of conquering foreign markets rather than territory.

Japan's defeat in World War II brought a new ideological direction dictated by the United States. In place of the discredited symbols of Japanese nationalism and militarism, the United States substituted an ideology of peace and freedom for the Japanese people. Peace is symbolized by Article 9 of the new constitution adopted in 1947, which renounces the sovereign right to engage in war. Freedom is symbolized by the full range of civil rights found in the U.S. Constitution, to which were added the rights to collective bargaining, full employment, free choice of residence and occupation, and equality, which specified sexual equality and "the right to maintain the minimum standard of wholesome and cultured living."[12] Therefore, Japan today is committed to democracy as the means by which to determine its national purpose and has transferred its former reliance on the military to economic competition as the way to secure Japan's status as a world power.

At the core of Japan's present-day ideology is a self-image of the nation as a corporate entity whose members are involved domestically (as *insiders*) in maintaining economic growth, social harmony, and political stability, while internationally engaging (as *outsiders*) in fierce competition with other businesses and states for increased market shares, global economic penetration, international prestige, and recognition for their nation. This distinction between "insiders" and "outsiders"—an enduring legacy of an earlier cultural pattern—is an important element in understanding what often appears to non-Japanese as a double standard of behavior. In their bid to attain equal status with other powers, Japanese adopt the behavior of outsiders as a means perceived necessary to protect the realm of the "inside." Accompanying this tribal sense of devotion to Japan's self-preservation is the racist aspect—generally unacknowledged—of its nationalism. This aspect of Japanese ideology has implications for Japan's assuming a larger political role as a leader of the world community, a topic to be touched on in Chapter 8.

China: Maoism Eclipsed

Whereas the ideology accompanying modernization in Japan was a reconstructed form of traditionalism, the ideology embraced by Chinese revolutionaries on their ascent to power was decidedly modern and Western. Marxism was adopted by revolutionary intellectuals seeking a new China precisely because it was opposed to Confucian culture, a mental straitjacket they viewed as responsible for keeping China weak and backward for over a century.

It is difficult to describe Confucianism as a way of life. For thousands of years, the cultural pattern that most closely embodies the ideals of Confucianism actually governed the behavior of only a small minority of the population of China. The more than 85 percent of people who lived in rural China have always believed in an eclectic blend of ritual, ancestor worship, *qigong* (physical exercise regimen), and superstition that has a closer affinity to folk religion than it does to Confucianism. But Confucian values in a loose sense have permeated the entire society since ancient times. Its most palpable trait is a belief in, for lack of a better term, the humanness of life. In contrast to the absolute and wrathful supernatural being of monotheism that pervades Western sensibilities, Confucianism is infused with a belief in man as part of a natural world that is composed of opposites that require balancing. Human perfection or the fulfillment of human life, therefore, is to be found in human understanding, harmony, and gentility.

Because so much of Chinese culture was imbued with this stress on mutual regard and composure, Chinese revolutionaries believed it was largely responsible for China's weakness in defending itself against the intrusion of the West. For the communist leadership, ideology was the modern alternative to displace traditional Chinese cultural beliefs. Unlike the Meiji "reformers" in Japan, therefore, the communist revolutionaries who took over power in 1949 could not utilize Chinese traditions as a vehicle for modernizing the cultural habits of the Chinese people. An ideology derived from Marxism via Lenin became the replacement for what has very loosely been called Confucianism.

Three questions will be explored in an attempt to understand how and why the Chinese adapted Marxism for their new symbolic framework: Why did Marxism resonate with Confucianism to become the vehicle for transforming China? In what ways did Mao Zedong elaborate and apply communist ideology in the process of fitting it to the framework of Chinese culture? In what ways do the Deng era reforms continue or depart from Maoism?

Affinities Between Confucianism and Marxism.   Of all the ideas to engage the minds of Chinese in their long struggle to reunify the country, Marxism succeeded because of its remarkable similarities to traditional Chinese culture. If we were to try to construct a modern counterpart to Confucianism, we could hardly improve upon Marxism-Leninism-Mao Zedong Thought, as it is officially called. Like Confucianism, Marxism is both empirical and normative, realistic and idealistic. Like Confucianism, Marxism is comprehensive, all-encompassing, secular, and historical. Both have a cosmic vision, but the Marxist vision is of *change,* looking toward the future for its ideal of perfection, not to the idyllic past of Confucianism. Like Confucianism, Marxism assumes the best, not the worst, about human nature; the difference is the promise it holds for all human beings, not merely an educated elite, to fulfill their potential. And like Confucianism, Marxism views the material world as made up of opposite or contradictory forces; the difference is that Marxism looks for their resolution through struggle, at least in human history, rather than accepting them as given elements of the human condition.

Human history, according to Marxist analysis, is a process in which societies pass through successive stages distinguished by how they produce the material things people need to survive and prosper. From low-tech agricultural production dependent on human and animal labor, societies move to vastly more productive industrial technology, using machines of ever-increasing sophistication, eventually reaching the stage we now call "postindustrial." At each stage the people who own the means of production—in feudal times the landowning class, in the industrial age the capitalists—dominate political life as well as economic, using the power of the state to protect their privileged position.

For Chinese revolutionaries, this analysis fit Chinese reality: Landlords exploited peasants with the connivance of the imperial mandarins; foreign capitalists and their Chinese collaborators exploited workers and undermined the government's limited capacity and will to resist. But Marxism also held out hope, with the assertion that each stage gives rise by its own inner contradictions to the class struggle that ushers in its successor. Marx predicted that the capitalist stage of production would be succeeded, through the efforts of the more numerous industrial workers, by the communist stage, in which control of the government and of the means of production would pass from the capitalist class to their rightful owners, the working class.

When the transition that Marx had predicted failed to materialize in the most advanced capitalist societies of Western Europe, Lenin modified the theory to fit the opportunity for bringing about revolutionary change in underdeveloped and still largely feudal Russia. Even without a sizable industrial working class or a capital-rich business class, Lenin demonstrated, backward feudal societies could industrialize using the Communist Party as the engine of change. For countries lacking the prerequisites for Western capitalist development, such as China, Lenin's theory, and its successful application in Russia, offered a compelling alternative route to development.

These changes in both theory and historical reality have generated considerable confusion over the term *communism*, which can usefully be clarified here. It is used rather indiscriminately to describe three different things: First, communism is used as the name of the future society that Marxist-Leninists believe will emerge out of the contradictions inherent in the fully developed form of international capitalism. According to Lenin's vision, communism will be a classless society in which, because there is no longer an exploited class to be suppressed, the need for a coercive government disappears and the state will wither away. Nowhere has this stage yet been reached. Instead, countries like China describe themselves as having reached an intermediate stage, "socialism," in which class differences (though no longer exploitation) remain, and government is still needed to complete the process of development and for protection against the outside world.

A second usage of the term *communism*, almost always by noncommunists, is to describe the regimes led by the Communist parties in the former Soviet Union and Eastern Europe as well as in China, North Korea, Laos, Cambodia, and Vietnam. Note that these governments do not call themselves "communist"; Vietnam alone uses the term socialist in its name and the others variously identify themselves as "people's" and/or "democratic" republics.

A third usage of *communist*, by both Communists and noncommunists, applies to parties and political movements that derive their purpose and their destination from Marxist theory (but curiously, no specifics on how to accomplish that purpose and reach that promised land). Thus in China, the ambiguity of communist ideology stems from its justifying a modern revolution in the name of a mythological future, while in Japan the ambiguity of Meiji ideology resulted from making modern revolutionary changes in the name of a mythological past.

Mao's Contributions to China's Ideology.   The communists in China embraced the ideology of Marxism as a means for turning around China's humiliating defeat and depredation at the hands of the Western powers. Central to the success of this venture was Mao Zedong's effective conversion of Marxist-Leninist ideology to accommodate China's cultural and historical circumstances. To his credit and discredit, it was Mao's ideology that set the unique course of China's modern destiny. But the enormity of Mao's accomplishments in redefining the way Chinese think and behave, for better and for worse, defies summary. So just four aspects of Mao's contribution to the ideology that guided China's development will be discussed: (1) the rural revolution, (2) the role of the Communist Party, (3) thought reform, and (4) "putting politics in command."

The Rural Revolution.   To throw out the foreigners and set China on an independent course required strength and vision. By 1927 Mao had decided that the peasants alone could provide the strength to bring about revolution in China. The idea of a "rural revolution" was not original with Mao; peasant rebellions were abundant throughout Chinese history and Soviet advisers had counseled their Chinese protégés to take the peasants and their problems seriously. But there was a new element in Mao's formulation, one that was repeatedly to bring the Communist Party into conflict with the traditional elite of China, the intelligentsia, throughout the period of Mao's leadership. His novel suggestion was that China's intellectual elite *follow* the peasants, joining them, working among them, learning from them in order to become a part of that China from which they had always remained aloof. This belief of Mao's in the revolutionary leadership potential of the peasantry was the foundation of the People's Republic of China.

In 1927 the question Mao posed was whether Chinese intellectuals who had set themselves up as leaders of a Chinese revolution were willing to recognize the masses of illiterate peasants as true revolutionary forces capable of challenging traditional Chinese institutions. In Mao's eyes, this was not only necessary given their numbers and the Communists' base of operations in the countryside but a virtue, enabling them and China to have a "blank page" on which to write China's destiny.[13] It is interesting to note, therefore, that Mao Zedong never actually substituted the peasantry for the working class as "vanguard of the revolution." The party, he carefully reiterated time and again, must be a working-class party. How, then, does one reconcile a hypothetical working-class party with the fact that its membership is constituted of peasants? One answer is that Mao always exhibited a capacity to play revolution as much by "ear" as by doctrine. Another clue, one that credits Mao with greater theoretical acumen, is his conception of the party as an instrument for the socialization of peasants into revolutionary proletarians.

The Role of the Communist Party.   "Rural revolution" as a means for setting China on a revolutionary course toward communism required redefining the Communist Party's relationship to its followers. Faced with a party that was working class in name only, Mao sought to expand its educational role. Ideology was used to create a curriculum for the mass education of peasant recruits into the party, teaching them everything from literacy and self-discipline to organizational skills and principles of guerrilla warfare. Many of Mao's writings address this task of turning the ideological principles and precepts of Marxist thinking into educational materials to train party recruits from increasingly varied backgrounds. When large numbers of intellectuals climbed aboard during the Yanan period, the "rectification campaign" became the prototype for building "a unified party with common ideals, ideology and goals."[14] Mao's concern was that party cadres understand his ideas about party leadership and how to put them into practice; this was the core of "mass line" politics, a unique result of the party's rural roots.

The idea of the mass line was to ensure that party leaders would serve the interests of the people they led. Among the various techniques of Mao's mass line politics, which included small study groups, criticism/self-criticism sessions, struggle sessions, and mass campaigns covering a range of targets, rectification campaigns were the most unusual. They focused on cadres and how they could improve their work styles. In this process, cadres, or leaders, were expected to criticize their own errors (for example, commanding people with a high-handed attitude). If the criticism was deemed inadequate by other people attending the meeting, additional criticism was invited from the audience. During the Cultural Revolution, rectification campaigns turned into direct attacks on party leaders, even the elite of the elite who ran the country, a phenomenon unheard of elsewhere in the world and directly in conflict with the Confucian culture that still influences people 50 years after the communists came to power.

Thought Reform.   Much of Chinese communist ideology in the Maoist period, both in word and deed, centered around the question of creating the socialist human being. *Thought reform,* the core of Mao's strategy for confronting this question, illustrates the singular way in which communist ideology tapped traditional aspects of Chinese culture, creating a novel practice aimed at changing undesirable and misguided behavior among the Chinese citizenry. Regardless of one's feelings about the political use of thought reform, its bad connotation in the West is in large part derived from a misunderstanding of what it is and how it works. It is an approach to dealing with behavior that is much like childhood socialization. It addresses the question of how one gets people to "behave in a particular way when either they disagree with you or they have been ignorant of your wishes."[15] Whatever the standards may be for correct socialist behavior (and they change, sometimes radically, over time), they are communicated and implemented by people with whom one works and lives.

When an individual displays antisocial behavior, as defined at a given point in time by prevailing party policy, it is brought up for criticism by one's peers in the small group at work, at school, or, in the case of a youngster stealing a bike, in the residential neighborhood committee. The individual is persuaded to change that behavior because of the "law" (the expected norm of behavior), exploring the causes of the behavior, and explaining its consequences. If the behavior recurs, one's immediate peers and/or boss increase the pressure to change in an attempt to raise the

School children engaged in manual labor as part of their education during the
Cultural Revolution.

Source: Photo taken in February 1976 by Vera Simone.

discomfort level sufficiently to obtain compliance. Although the method is used systematically in penal institutions, it is more importantly a widespread method for
teaching the "law" and ensuring compliance with it. Mass campaigns of thought reform can target a wide assortment of activities to which people must comply, ranging from public sanitation and physical fitness to birth control and increasing out-
puts of a particular crop.

"Putting Politics in Command" and the Politics of Morality.   Mao's belief in the
salutary effects of applying ideology to the task of revolutionizing China extended
to all realms. During the Great Leap Forward, when China was short of capital and
expertise to increase people's productivity, Mao substituted organizational and ideological measures to reach the same objective. There were two interrelated aspects
to this. First, organizationally, people's lives were radically reoriented as households
joined into large communes the size of several villages. Second, ideological resources were applied by exhorting people to put all their hopes for a better future
into working harder to increase agricultural output. The belief behind "putting politics in command" appears to be that untapped energies would be unleashed by liberating women from household work, collectivizing the burdens of child rearing, increasing the efficiency of labor management, providing equal pay for equal work,

and by community construction of schools, health clinics, and rudimentary backyard steel furnaces.

The Cultural Revolution was, like the Great Leap Forward, presented as "putting politics in command." During this extended campaign, between 1966 and 1976, it was the culture rather than the economy that was the target of change. All symbols of either old Chinese or modern Western civilization were defined as "bourgeois" objects, reflecting the decadence and dissipation of a ruling rather than a proletarian class. Young Red Guards were mobilized to raid the homes of those suspected of harboring old paintings, Western books, expensive jewelry, and Ming vases. Proletarian morality was exhibited by austerity in dress, rudeness in manner, the exaltation of manual labor, and confrontational politics between political factions, both on the street and in the government. In schools children did manual labor for half the school day while in factories engineers were required to work on the shop floor. And in the most glaring affront to Confucian values, urban-educated youth were sent to the countryside to labor in the fields along with intellectuals and "capped" party officials who were assigned to do the most menial jobs. The disasters that resulted from this application of Mao's notion of "politics in command" have been amply documented and contributed in no small degree to the ease with which the policy changes known as the Reforms were embraced in China after the Cultural Revolution.

Despite his avowed antitraditionalism, his fervent attempts to undermine Confucian culture in refashioning a modern, proletarian way of thinking, Mao employed ideology in a traditional Confucian manner, as a modeling device for behavior. Ideology, for Mao, was not merely the justification of a preference in policymaking, one side winning an argument over another, but a method or guide for determining the morally correct position. His juxtaposition of politics and expertise, "red versus expert," insisted that expertise does not automatically confer on those who possess it a sense of right and wrong; it may, in fact, obstruct the sense of what is moral. Mao's belief that morality could be embedded in politics is like the Confucian cultural adage that politics consists of setting the proper moral example so that people are inspired to do the right thing for its own sake. It is precisely this moral conception of politics that would be rejected in the pragmatism of Reform ideology espoused by Mao's successors.

Reform Ideology after Mao.   Few elements of Reform ideology are entirely new, but the paradigm that has emerged from their combination provides a new ideological perspective, frequently called "market socialism" or "the socialist market." In principle, capitalism and bourgeois pollution are still rejected. The underlying shift has been away from the idea that politics, the will of politically correct leaders, can bring about fundamental economic changes. Reformers substitute the notion that economic progress is governed by its own laws. The activities of political leaders, therefore, have to be limited to ensure that socialist economics operate in accordance with objective economic laws. The politics of the Communist Party is necessary but economists rather than political pacesetters need to be in charge of making economic decisions.

Reform ideas have advocated correcting the imbalances that resulted from the Maoist strategy of combining politics and economics. The arena of production and distribution needs to be clearly distinguished from the political responsibilities of the party.

The party's responsibility, according to Reform ideology, is to lead the entire society on its march toward socialist prosperity. This can best be accomplished if the state removes itself entirely from micromanaging production and turns its full attention to exercising the skills of macroeconomic management of a complex modern political economy as it negotiates its passage through the international market. Thus the central principle and foundation of the Reform outlook has been the reintroduction of markets and the operation of the laws of supply and demand to determine which commodities are produced, at what prices they sell, and how profits are reinvested.

This has amounted to a reversal of the entire edifice of Maoist ideology. In place of state planning, socialist commodity production is to follow market dictates for an indeterminate period, providing the flexibility and dynamism associated with the capitalist state of development. For individual entrepreneurs, directors of factories, households, and cooperatives, this means pursuing profit rather than depending upon state allocations and rewards for fulfilling state targets.

In place of Maoist egalitarianism, getting rich individually is the new first commandment of China's socialist market economy. State planning is reduced to a more selective and restrained intervention in the economic sphere designed to complement market forces. Economic enterprises, though not entirely freed from the pressures of state planning, have greatly expanded operational independence from bureaucratic management. They are responsible for making their own contracts with other enterprises to procure resources and markets for their products.

The responsibilities of the state for which the Communist Party provides leadership are numerous and diverse: to create and enforce an appropriate system of laws so that China's political economy can be synchronized with the principles governing the international capitalist political economy; to coordinate the balanced economic growth of all sectors and segments of society in the interests of internal unity and harmony; to establish a nationwide social net providing Chinese with unemployment and health insurance, education and social security; to regulate the entire process of modernization for the maintenance of of the economic prosperity, political stability, and military security of a "spiritual civilization."

The ideological ramifications of the Reform model—of "socialism with Chinese characteristics"—are momentous and unpredictable. Although the party through the state is clearly in control, economic imperatives will more than likely place constraints on anyone with an ideological agenda, even if it appears in traditional cultural guise. This was the case with Falun Gong, a movement based on the mixture of ancient breathing exercises, philosophical beliefs, and the ideas of its exiled founder, Li Hongzhi. Stunned by the sudden appearance of an ideological mass movement in April 1999 with such traditional cultural appeal, the government reacted swiftly and forcefully to ban the movement and jail its public adherents. Whether it is a pro-democracy movement or a movement to promote traditional ideas about physical and spiritual health, the state will not tolerate any ideological interference with the economic goals of institutionalizing "socialist prosperity."

Reform ideology also raises questions concerning the continued ideological viability of the Communist Party. What kind of leadership can the Communist Party possibly provide for a China based on market principles? How compatible is the notion of getting rich with the party's original goals of selfless service? On what other ideological grounds can the party address the widespread corruption among its members that is the principal target of much of the public discontent? How compatible is the growing income gap between the rich and the poor with the socialist egalitarian expectations still fostered by ideological training in the schools?

Reformers differ among themselves about how best to achieve an effective interface between a state that calls itself socialist and market processes that promote inequality, "selfish" individualism, and the pursuit of materialistic wealth and ostentatious consumption. But whatever the differences among reform groups that may continue to contend over their disagreements, they will recur within the narrowed range of a fundamental commitment to rapid economic development. Even when they are as economically successful as they have been in China, economic reforms once launched are like a vehicle sent into outer space, subject to unanticipated forces increasingly remote and beyond the ideological control of the political planners.

Taiwan: Familism and Statism

Ideology in Taiwan is composed of two elements that roughly correspond to the age-old split in traditional China between society—life governed by the family— and the state. Among the native Taiwanese, who had emigrated from China centuries earlier, a family-centered commercial orientation flourished under Japanese rule, stimulated by the island's exposure to the international economy. Contained within the social sphere by a repressive Japanese state, this lively market orientation has provided the dynamism and flexibility unique to Taiwanese *guerrilla capitalism*. The term refers to a cultural characteristic of Taiwanese small business strategy: selecting a product the firm is capable of manufacturing, making it quickly, saturating the market with it, and moving on as the price of the product drops in response to increased competition.[16] Familism is the ideology of this small-scale commercial capitalism distinctive of local society in Taiwan.

When the mainlanders arrived in Taiwan after 1945, they brought with them the ideas of Sun Yatsen and enthusiasm for a second chance at implementing them. The ruling party of the mainlanders, the Guomindang (National People's Party), took over from the Japanese both the reins of state power and the large public industrial sector. And by carrying out land reform in the rural areas, the Guomindang laid the groundwork for their own legitimacy and an effective development strategy based on family use of small-scale private property. With islanders pursuing business in the private sphere, mainlanders proceeded on a state-directed or statist course of promoting economic growth, which accorded with both Sun Yatsen's doctrine and the realities of the public ownership of basic industries.[17] Statism is the ideology the mainlanders used to justify an extensive role for the state in redistributing national assets, setting economic objectives, regulating foreign transactions, providing an effective national defense, and directing the national development effort.

Native Taiwanese familism and the statism of the mainlanders have converged to provide the ideological basis for rapid industrialization of the island nation. There is both tension and complementarity in this combination of familism and statism. Familism opposes state regulation, closely guarding traditional family financing from outside scrutiny. It values close competition based upon labor-intensive, low-wage employment, and it is generally sensitive to speculative opportunities for increasing profits. Statism, on the other hand, is an ideology that equates progress with capital accumulation on a scale only government can undertake. Expressing disapproval of the "negative economic effects of private property, particularly speculation in money, commodities, land, and other assets,"[18] mainlanders champion the public enterprises of the state, mismanaged though they may be, as the backbone of state capitalism. It is the form of development prescribed for late-developing countries by Sun Yatsen in the *San Min Chu I* (Three Principles of the People).

Despite Sun's adherence to a form of social democracy, the *San Min Chu I* have provided a perfect ideological instrument for the Guomindang's program in Taiwan. Politically, Sun's first principle, nationalism, acts as a justification for the Republic of China's insistence that Taiwan is an inextricable part of China, an idea that has stirred the opposition of native Taiwanese. Sun's second principle, tutelary democracy, a long period during which people unaccustomed to self-rule learn the culture of democracy, has justified the authoritarian one-party rule exercised by the Guomindang, the mainlanders' party, over Taiwan. But in response to persistent pressure by Taiwanese for a more autonomous state for Taiwan, the ruling party in 1994 acknowledged that the last stage of constitutional democracy had arrived, when competitive electoral politics previously confined to the local level would be institutionalized at the national level. The third principle is the people's livelihood.

With the people's livelihood secure and the aging of the mainlanders under whose rule prosperity and military security were attained, the Taiwanese have stepped up to the batter's plate. President Lee Teng Hui—the first Taiwanese to occupy the position—not only espoused democracy but attempted to move the ruling party, the Guomindang, closer to the Taiwanese goal of independence by equating "statism" with the independence of Taiwan. In conjunction with the first direct election for president, this resulted in the first presidential victory for the opposition party candidate running on a platform of independence for Taiwan. For the first time, therefore, the "familism" of the Taiwanese population has come into open conflict with the "statism" of the mainlanders. How this ideological conflict will resolve itself in the international context of China's resolute commitment to returning Taiwan to the fold of the motherland remains to be seen. The ideological battleground on which the struggle is being waged, however, is Sun Yatsen's idea of democracy.

The most intriguing aspect of Sun Yatsen's conception of democratic government is its Confucian paternalism, manifested in the claim that government power and popular sovereignty are always two separate aspects of government. Justification for separating the two is based on his observation that just when modern civilization requires a powerful government to administer the complex affairs of a nation, its people, incapable of understanding the work of government, distrust all political power because the government cannot be held accountable. Sun's solution is to give the operation of government to "the qualified, who must not be hampered by constant interference by the people or representatives of the people."[19] In a democracy, however, since government must be subject to control by the people, sovereign rights must be retained by citizens. Sun "compared government to modern industries, and the president and his staff to experts who know how to manage the company, while the people were like shareholders, retaining control over the president but in general not interfering with the management."[20] Democracy can function in the modern world only in the Confucian spirit of benevolent paternalism on the part of able leaders and deferential consent on the part of subjects who value negotiation and accommodation over confrontation. This Chinese conception of democracy is one with which the founder of the modern city-state of Singapore can heartily agree.

Singapore: Music by a One-Man Band

Some years ago British Foreign Minister George Brown said approvingly to the British-educated prime minister of Singapore (known in his youth as "Harry" Lee), "Harry, you're the best bloody Englishman east of Suez!"[21] No doubt Brown thought he was paying Lee Kuan Yew the highest compliment, and perhaps the prime minister regarded it as such at the time. But in the years since "Harry" returned home from England in 1950 to join the struggle for independence, his ideas may have become less English and more attuned to the cultures of his Asian constituents.

One of the last surviving members of the "first generation" of nationalist leaders, Lee has been a veritable "one-man band" as composer and performer of the sweet music of success during his 30-year tenure as prime minister and in his current post as senior minister. Although not without critics, he has demonstrated an apparent genius for selecting and adapting Western political values and institutions to harmonize with the multicultural traditions of the people of Singapore and with the twin objectives of political stability and economic development. Having earned the reputation of elder statesman, Lee is now invited to other Asian countries to share his formula for success and offer advice on how to proceed in their own situation.

At the time of independence in 1965 Singapore looked quite unpromising, lacking as it did the conventionally accepted ingredients for survival as a state and for economic viability. The country was small in land and population, ethnically divided, poor, lacking in both natural resources and capital, and the object of suspicion, even hostility, on the part of its neighbors.

Lee's Blend of Confucianism and Western Ideologies.   Out of these inauspicious ingredients and drawing upon ideas from his upbringing in a Chinese family that had been in Singapore for four generations, his education in British schools in the colony and at Cambridge University, living under the Japanese occupation, his training and practice as a lawyer, his experiences in the united front with communists in the anticolonial nationalist movement, and elements of the cultures of his three Asian constituencies, Lee gradually put together the recipe for success that still seems palatable to most (though not all) Singaporeans. It is a concoction of Confucian principles of collectivism, consensus, and hierarchy and Western notions of individual freedom and political participation. It combines democratic socialist attachment to realizing the goal of equal opportunity and conservative insistence on the need for discipline and order, free market economics, and state intervention-

Lee Kuan Yew in his youth. After three decades
as Prime Minister of Singapore, he remains active
in government as Senior Minister.

Source: United Nations/T. Chen.

ism. Lee's ideas constitute the reigning ideology of Singapore and have been implemented through government policies and programs.

To create a Singaporean identity in this multiracial and multicultural society,
the national ideology promotes the shared values of "Nation before [ethnic] community and society above self; Family as the basic unit of society; Regard and community support for the individual; Consensus instead of contention; Racial and religious harmony."[22] Acceptance of these shared values, it is hoped, will be the glue
that holds Singaporeans together while at the same time allowing each group to
keep its own cultural heritage.

Government's "4Ms" Policy.   Harmony among the diverse "racial," religious,
linguistic, and cultural groups to which Singaporeans belong is the objective of the
government's "4Ms" policy of "multiracialism, multilingualism, multiculturalism
and multireligiosity."[23] Chinese, Malays, Indians, and the 2 percent of the population who are none of those are to be treated equally and allowed, even encouraged,
to keep their identification as members of different groups. The constitution recognizes four official languages—Mandarin Chinese, Malay, Tamil, and English—and
bilingualism (English and one of the three Asian languages) is fostered through the
education system, although mastery of English confers special advantage. Unlike
Malaysia, where Islam has official support as the state religion, Singapore is a secular state, allowing the practice of all religions but favoring none above the others.

The equality of treatment that the 4Ms policy endorses provides justification for insistence on individual merit as the criterion for success. Meritocracy, which was the principle underlying the mandarinate in imperial China, has its modern incarnation in the concept of a civil service recruited on the basis of skills and performance, not on ethnicity or personal connections, and in public sector employment Singapore has recruited the brightest of its technologically qualified university graduates. The combination of equal access to education and employment based on merit is intended to produce a "natural" hierarchy, reflecting differences in individual talent and effort.

Respect for cultural differences, educational opportunity, and nondiscriminatory employment practices have not, however, produced equally successful results for Singapore's Malay minority as for the Chinese majority and the Indian minority. The most cohesive of the ethnic groups, Malays lag behind in education and in business; consequently, since the 1980s the government has encouraged special "affirmative action" programs to raise the school performance of Malay students and self-help projects for Malay entrepreneurs. Still, the government violates its own equal opportunity policy by restricting the numbers of Malays in the Singapore Armed Forces, reflecting doubts about Malay loyalty and evidencing the incompleteness of national integration. The "mixed salad" metaphor for Singaporean society fits the hyphenated identity of Chinese-, Malay-, Indian-Singaporeans better than the "melting pot" of a nonethnic collective Singaporean identity.

Fundamental Concern for Political Order.   The quest for social harmony among Singapore's heterogeneous people has its parallel in the political sphere, where Confucian distaste for overt expression of dissent has combined with a conservative fear of disorder to produce an authoritarian regime where political opposition is suppressed and individual freedoms of expression and organization are curtailed. The People's Action Party's official ideology, proclaimed at its founding, is "democratic socialism." The appearance of Western-style democracy—elections, opposition parties, and so on—exists but, as described in Chapter 4, the reality is otherwise. Some aspects of socialism are retained: the commitment to equality of opportunity, the welfare state programs of social services for its citizens, and government ownership of some enterprises and guidance of the economy, described in Chapter 5.

Lee explains his views on democracy in the Asian context in a way that underlines his overriding concern for order:

> I do not believe that democracy necessarily leads to development. I believe that what a country needs to develop is discipline more than democracy. Democracy leads to undisciplined and disorderly conditions which are inimical to development. The ultimate test of the value of a political system is whether it helps that society to establish conditions which improve the standard of living for the majority of its people, plus enabling the maximum of personal freedoms compatible with the freedom of others in society.[24]

Lee's own political style is notoriously paternalist, even domineering. To behave with the authority and responsibility of a father toward his family is in the Confucian tradition, as is being a model of virtue for others to emulate. But quite unConfucian is Lee's approach to power, eschewing the ritual and trappings traditionally associated with power holding; he travels on regularly scheduled Singapore Airline flights for his official trips, and his tastes in personal attire, government office, and residence are simple, even austere. Unlike the Chinese emperors' preoccupation with ceremony and the mandarins' preoccupation with status over policymaking, Lee's idea of power is utilitarian: What use can be made of it to bring about changes in conformity with his vision of what is good for the people of Singapore? Those uses range all the way from government actions to stimulate economic growth and attract foreign capital (described in Chapter 5) to regulating the citizens' personal behavior in the interest of health, safety, and private morality (for example, the ban on spitting and on smoking in public places, the installation of devices on trucks and taxis to warn the driver when the vehicle is exceeding the speed limit, and censorship of "morally offensive"—to officials' tastes—foreign books, periodicals, films).

Some Singaporeans find these and other restrictions intolerable and exercise the option of moving to another country. Others deplore the "cult of materialism"[25] that seems to be the central value driving the citizens of "Singapore, Inc." to conspicuous and competitive consumption, to evaluating themselves and others by their wealth, and to holding a vision of the future as more wealth through high technology and job-related technical education, rather than nonmaterialist "liberal" values in education and in personal and social goals.

Lee Kuan Yew's contribution to the economic development and political stability of Singapore is clear. Whether his particular mix of Asian cultural heritage and imported Western ideologies offers a durable pattern, transferable to other Asian societies, is not so clear. But there is no doubt that Lee has put his personal imprint on the encounter between culture and ideology in the spin-off Confucian society that is modern Singapore.

North Korea: Another Solo Performer

The similarities between Lee Kuan Yew and North Korea's President Kim Il Sung are numerous: Both are "Founding Fathers" and each has been the principal composer and conductor of the ideological themes that have guided and legitimized his particular brand of postindependence politics. Both have ruled through a Leninist-style party, prevailing over opponents by autocratic means; both have groomed a son as successor; and both have given the state a major role in economic development.

But there are differences too. While Lee began with an affinity for democratic socialism as he had observed it in England, Kim's political upbringing was, of course, in Marxism-Leninism. Lee is well educated, and his professional experience as a British-trained lawyer is quite different from Kim's limited education and his experiences as an anti-Japanese guerrilla fighter in Manchuria before returning from exile with the Soviet Army after the Japanese surrender in 1945.

Kim's goal when he came to power was the revolutionary overthrow of the old order, and the political institutions he created followed the Soviet style in both government and party; Lee, with less-than-revolutionary objectives, emulated Western-style governmental institutions. Kim's commitments to command socialism and to a Stalinist emphasis on heavy industry and agricultural collectivization remain unaltered, despite the changes that have occurred in both China and the Soviet Union/Russia; Lee's policies have certainly not displayed any special devotion to socialism. While his road to development led to Singapore's integration into the world capitalist system, Kim's policy was to develop without dependence on foreign capitalists (a policy that has shifted somewhat in the last few years toward efforts to attract foreign capital). Lee has long sought to bring into government and politics the most highly qualified technocrats, a class of people only now beginning to replace the aging guerrilla-fighter generation of political elites in North Korea.

Juche.   Kim Il Sung's contribution to the pantheon of ideologies in the communist world can be pictured as a troika, harnessing a breed of Soviet Marxist-Leninist orthodoxy together with a Stalinist-Maoist-demigod cult of personality behind a lead horse, the doctrine known as *Juche*. Juche, translated roughly as "self-reliance," was explained by Kim in a speech in Jakarta in 1965:

> Juche means holding fast to the principle of solving for oneself all the problems of the revolution and construction in conformity with the actual conditions of one's country, mainly by one's own efforts. This is the realistic and creative stand, opposing dogmatism and applying the universal truth of Marxism-Leninism and the experiences of the international revolutionary movement to one's country in conformity with its historical conditions and national peculiarities. This is an independent stand of discarding the spirit of dependence on others, displaying the spirit of self-reliance, and solving one's own affairs on one's own responsibility under all circumstances.[26]

Juche's premise that one must fit Marxism-Leninism to the particular conditions in one's own country serves less as specific guidance for devising policies and programs (what "fits" is largely a matter of subjective choice, in principle testable by trial and error) than as justification for not slavishly following other communist countries' revolutionary patterns. As Kim put it in that same 1965 speech:

> It is self-evident that we cannot make a revolution by relying on others, and that others cannot make the Korean revolution in our stead. . . . While resolutely fighting in defense of the purity of Marxism-Leninism against revisionism, our Party has made every effort to establish Juche in opposition to dogmatism and flunkyism towards great powers. Juche is ideology, independence in politics, self-sustenance in the economy, and self-defense in national defense—this is the stand our Party has consistently adhered to.[27]

Kim's repeated exhortations to avoid the three cardinal sins of "dogmatism," "revisionism," and "flunkyism" were as much for external as internal consumption. A simple, even simplistic, formula, "self-reliance" was in a sense forced upon North Korea, located as it is between two rival fraternal communist "protectors" and an array of capitalist "enemies"—South Korea and the U.S. forces there as well as ex-occupier Japan. Juche put China and the Soviet Union on notice that North Korea was determined not to become a "flunky" of either of them, nor to become too dependent on what North Korea sees as unreliable sources of support. The doctrine has served as "an instrumental principle ... in coping with the twin alliance security dilemmas of abandonment and entrapment—maximizing allied support in the face of a perceived threat from the South and minimizing the dysfunctional and delegitimizing input of allied control and/or interference."[28] The impact of Juche on the people of North Korea probably can best be understood by the people of Israel, for whom the necessity of self-reliance held a similar life and death message.

Although Juche has functioned for over 40 years as the ideological backbone of North Korea's fierce determination to survive on its own, in today's world it has rapidly become archaic, even self-destructive. The irony for North Koreans is that the very quality of Juche—its rigidity—that made it successful in bolstering national resilience against extreme hardship and isolation makes it extremely difficult for the nation to "open up" to the outside world.

The Cult of Personality.   As with the doctrine of Juche, nationalist pride and discipline is at the core of North Korea's idolatry of its leadership. What is generally called "the cult of personality" has been cultivated around the persons of Kim Il Sung and his son, Kim Jong Il. Kim Il Sung was a dedicated nationalist who fought as part of a coherent and sustained political and military war first against the Japanese and later against the powerful landlord class in a thorough-going program of land and social reform. His image was one of a great, fatherly figure whose paternalistic care for his "children" was made possible by his enormous power. The state, which provided everyone with free health care, education, extremely low-cost housing and an excellent pension system, was viewed as the head of the family and inseparable from the founding father of North Korea.

As with traditional fathers of every kind, there is room for only one and he brooks no interference, opposition, or criticism from either inside or outside the "family." Kim's prescription for the Korean Workers' Party illustrates the sentiment: "iron discipline should be established in the Party, the unity of its ranks defended, the slightest factionalist tendency not tolerated, and the Party should be firmly protected from infiltration of bourgeois ideas."[29] Undoubtedly, this belief in paternalistic authoritarianism was as solidly embedded in Kim Il Sung's personality as it was in the Confucian ideological firmament. It was the basis of his sharp criticism of Mao Zedong's Cultural Revolution though it never reached the level of an open disagreement.

Ruling over North Korea in what were, relatively speaking, good times, Kim Il Sung can be considered a great leader in the traditional, imperial context of politics: As supreme ruler, there was no challenge too great for him to overcome; he was successful in war and in peace; and he ruled for almost half a century in which Korea had more than its share of exceptional challenges. He did this, in part, by establishing a personality cult of such extreme proportions as to offend many, if not most, people outside North Korea. No matter how offensive this personality cult, however, it must be recognized as having inculcated in people the spectacular strength, endurance, discipline, and resilience of Kim's own leadership. Although the elder Kim was able to pass the rule of North Korea to his son, Kim Jong Il, before his death in 1994, the conditions of the world on the eve of the twenty-first century were no longer hospitable to leaders of this kind. And Kim Jong Il seems to have understood this, judging by the summit accord he agreed to with President Kim Dae Jung of South Korea in June 2000.

Other Confucian Societies

South Korea.   The reigning ideology has been a combination of several factors: influences from Korea's political past under the monarchy and then under Japanese colonialism; the contemporary influence of the United States, first as occupier and then as military ally; and the ominous presence of the "Other" Korea, the communist regime in the North. From the monarchical period came the lesson that a strong center is necessary insurance against enemies, both internal and external. From the Japanese came training in "thought police" and other techniques of political repression, and the crippling effect of being denied experience in open political organization and activity. From the West, particularly from the United States, came the idea of constitutionalism, which in South Korea became a ritual exercise intended to legitimize successive authoritarian governments, all operating under the banner of republicanism. Frequent rewriting and amending of constitutions (currently the sixth since 1948) became the tool by which politicians manipulated the structures and powers of government to serve their own purposes. From the looming presence of the North, reinforced by the experience of the Korean War and by the Cold War policy of the South's American ally, came an implacable anticommunism that provided justification for repression of dissent, including the use of armed force by the police and the military against civilians.

In recent years, the ruling elite has modified its ideological stance and its practices, allowing space for opposition parties to operate and admitting into its own ranks a leading opponent, Kim Young Sam, who won the presidency in 1992. These changes, described in Chapter 4, have been heralded as evidence that political democracy is being incorporated into the Korean political culture. There is some support for that perception: In a 1991 public opinion survey three out of five respondents expressed a preference for democracy over authoritarianism (but two out of five did not see democracy as the best system of government);[30] there were important variations by class, age, and region, with greater support for democracy among the better-educated, more affluent younger people and in Cholla Province, long a center of opposition to the military regimes. The election of Kim Dae Jung, a venerable veteran of the war against military rule, to the presidency in December 1997, has moved the ideological center of national politics one step further toward democratic rule and peace with the North. It was President Kim Dae Jung's persistent advocacy of his "Sunshine Policy" that gave voice to the political aspirations of South Korea's grassroots democratic opposition and culminated in the summit meeting between the leaders of North and South.

Vietnam.   Unlike other societies in Southeast Asia, Vietnamese culture became Confucianized during a millennium of intermittent Chinese rule. Although Buddhism remained the dominant religion even after French missionaries enjoyed some success in converting a sizable minority to Catholicism, the prevailing model was the Confucian tradition of a secular state, headed by the emperor and administered by a meritocracy of mandarin scholars. Adoption of Confucianism under the influence of the high culture of China endowed Vietnamese with a sense of superiority over their non-Confucian Southeast Asian neighbors. This is manifest in rivalry with Thailand and competition for influence in Laos and Cambodia, both of which have more cultural affinity with (as well as geographical accessibility to) Thailand than Vietnam.

Like Korea, the division of Vietnam into two states after World War II produced a bifurcation in the ideological development of the country that ended with Vietnam's unification in 1975. In the North Marxist-Leninism, as interpreted and adapted to local conditions by Ho Chi Minh and other leaders, prevailed. In the South no coherent ideology emerged to guide successive governments. Nor did American pressure to create at least the appearance of a liberal democracy in South Vietnam succeed in producing commitment in theory or in practice to such a political vision. With unification under the Communists in 1975, the North's ideology became the orthodoxy for the whole country.

As mentioned in Chapter 4, there has been no modification of the principle of the leading role of the Communist Party in the political life of the state, although there has been some opening up of the political process to popular participation through direct elections to the national legislature and through some relaxation of party screening of candidates for public office. Religion, though not part of official party and government ideology, continues to influence popular attitudes and the clergy.

Government policy toward religion is that religious freedom is to be respected, but relations between the state and religious organizations have not been untroubled. The churches fear government restrictions on their activities and the government fears that foreign and internal opponents will use the Catholic and Buddhist churches as vehicles for antigovernment activities. The arrest and detention of Buddhist monks in Hue is explained by the government as the consequence of their antigovernment political acts, not because of their religious beliefs or observances.

To Buddhists, the distinction between political and religious action is blurred by the long tradition of the "god-king" and of religious involvement in government. The concept of a secular state and the principle of the separation of church and state are unfamiliar, contrary to historical and recent experience.

Hong Kong.   Under British colonial rule, there was no room for direct political participation in the affairs of the territory. This has left a legacy of indifference toward politics among a substantial portion of the population. The British government's rather last-minute conversion to the notion that the residents of the colony have some right to participate in their governance was an attempt to change this. Nonetheless, opinion surveys in the early nineties show a high degree of distrust of leaders and the many groups that were active in local politics.[31] They were seen more often than not as excessively concerned with political issues to the neglect of economic and social issues. Yet at the same time the respondents indicated high expectations of what political parties could or should do. Finally, although there was support in principle for democratization, people still expressed satisfaction with rule from above because it produced stability. One can only speculate whether the high value placed on stability is attributable to a persistent Confucian cultural bias toward order and predictability or to business preference for stable conditions or to a happy conjunction of both factors.

But if public attitudes were a hindrance to the emergence of strong democratic sentiment among Hong Kong citizens before 1997, it has since then been strengthened only among the opposition to mainland rule. The return of Hong Kong to China in a peaceful fashion may be attributable to three factors: the high level of comfort with the notion of "rule from above," the lack of conspicuous interference in local political affairs—with the exception of the dispute over which Chinese mainlanders could be considered eligible for settling in Hong Kong—and the Chinese government's positive support for business concerns over the impact of the regional economic crisis on the Hong Kong economy.

Having looked at Confucian societies, we now turn to societies in Southeast Asia where the influences of Buddhism, Islam, and Christianity are strong.

EVOLUTION OF IDEOLOGIES IN OTHER ASIAN SOCIETIES

The predominantly Buddhist countries (Burma,[32] Thailand, Laos, and Cambodia), the predominantly Islamic countries (Malaysia, Indonesia, and Brunei), and the Christianized Philippines each have responded in somewhat different ways to the challenge of incorporating traditional values and practices into postindependence efforts to create or preserve national unity and promote economic development. In this section Burma, Malaysia, Indonesia, and the Philippines have been chosen for examination.

Burma: Socialism, Buddhism, and Nationalism

Burma, like the Philippines, as noted in Chapter 5, is an exception to the economic success story of other Asian Pacific countries. One factor frequently cited to explain Burma's relatively retarded economic growth is its self-isolation from the world economy, a policy at the opposite extreme from that of the Philippines. A second factor often mentioned as responsible for Burma's inability to spur economic growth and development is the government's difficulty in forging national unity out of an ethnically and religiously divided population. Attempts to cobble together an ideology out of elements of nationalism, socialism, and Buddhism have met with little success in achieving either national unity or economic growth. An explanation that has intrigued scholars is the possibility that Burma's attempt to mesh Buddhism with nationalism and socialism has constituted part of the problem. To consider this question, we turn to the cultural and ideological contributions of its four prominent leaders: Aung San, U Nu, Ne Win, and Aung San Suu Kyi.

Socialism was embraced by the first generation of nationalist leaders exposed to Western ideas and has retained a certain appeal among a broad segment of the population. Even the rulers of SLORC relied on the rhetoric of socialism inherited from the military junta's official embrace of "The Burmese Way to Socialism." But continuity in the use of "socialism" as an ideological plank in the platform of Burma's various governments obscures significant differences in the mix of traditional Buddhism, nationalism, socialism, democracy and sheer opportunism that has characterized Burmese leadership since independence.

Aung San, U Nu, and Ne Win shared the same purpose: to provide a common moral identity for the new Burmese state, one that would ensure popular support for the new government and political unity for both Burmans and the splintered minority populations. Capitalism and communism were equally objectionable to these Burmese leaders though for different reasons: capitalism because it had been discredited as the vehicle used by the British to exploit and subjugate Burma; Marxism because it was materialistic and justified the use of violence; and the Leninist one-party system of the Soviet Union because it contradicted their notion of democracy. Democratic socialism provided the alternative. After taking power in 1962, the military dropped the term "democratic" but retained "socialism" to legitimize its regime. As a consequence of its association with military rule for over two decades, the term "socialism" has been abandoned by Aung San Suu Kyi, the daughter of Aung San—Burma's founding father—who continues at the start of the twenty-first century to do battle with the government in the name of "Buddhism" and "democracy."

Aung San's Secular Socialism.   Aung San's understanding of democratic socialism was secular, addressing itself to Burma's economic plight.[33] His vague idea of Burmese socialism as "something in between" capitalism and socialism was never elaborated as a practical ideology but served as an empty receptacle into which the purposes of successive leaders and the underlying patterns of Burmese culture have flowed. For Aung San, Buddhism, because it was a religion, belonged in the private sphere of civil society; Buddhist faith and the power of the monks needed to be disengaged from politics, not only to promote freedom of religious worship among people with differing faiths but to foster the purity of religious beliefs. "We must draw a clear line between politics and religion, because the two are not one and the same thing. If we mix religion with politics, then we offend the spirit of religion itself."[34] Economic rather than spiritual principles are the underpinning of government in the modern world, which for Aung San meant two things: that the separation of church and state as practiced in the United States was the appropriate model for Burma to follow, and that traditional Buddhist philosophical principles, if they were to become compatible with modern economic institutions and democratic ideas, had to be cleansed of their superstitious beliefs and rituals.

U Nu's Buddhist Socialism.   But this changed under U Nu's political leadership in 1960 when the idea of socialism became equated with the traditional Buddhist rejection of Western materialism. U Nu embraced socialism out of a profoundly religious Buddhist conviction that it offered a substitute for the evils of

U Nu, devout Buddhist, a leader of Burma's nationalist movement and first prime minister.

Source: United Nations photo 46405 MB/pcd.

capitalism, which was rooted in human greed and selfishness. This led him to espouse a form of religious revivalism "reminiscent of the Buddhist kings of old."[35] Buddhism, in this tradition, is an integral part of Burmese politics and the backbone of an identifiable Burmese state. Propagating Buddhist faith, therefore, was a way of strengthening Burma's national identity, the power of the state, and the spirituality of its people. To this end, U Nu sponsored ritual efforts to propitiate evil spirits and the construction of 60,000 sand pagodas throughout Burma, further aggravating the economic situation and digressing markedly from Aung San's idea of democratic socialism in Burma. But while U Nu's nationalist-religious resurgence appealed to members of the Burmese urban elite who had been "'culturally disinherited by colonial acculturation' . . . [having] succumbed to western values and ways of life,"[36] it alienated the sizable and varied minority of ethnic nationalities for whom Buddhism as a state religion had historically meant a state controlled by and for the Burman majority.

Military Socialism. When the military under General Ne Win came to power in 1962, the "Burmese Way to Socialism" took another turn. A more secularized rhetoric of socialism stressing the importance of a rational, scientific worldview replaced the religious denial of the importance of this world and the belief that one's fate depended on the whim of supernatural forces. Monks were out, technocrats were in. The Revolutionary Council, through which the military ruled, ended the privileged position of Buddhism and financial support for it, viewing the clergy as parasitic and opposed to their socialist program. Though Buddhism was relegated to the private sphere, the military regime nevertheless tried to win popular support by espousing as one of its goals the spiritual, as well as material, happiness of the people. While religion might be a private matter, the state had responsibility for improving the people's spiritual life, for promoting Buddhist moral values as the ethical foundation of socialism.

Aung San Suu Kyi and Buddhist Democracy.   Unlike U Nu and Ne Win, Aung San Suu Kyi was educated abroad, returning from exile much as her father had at the end of World War II, to inspire a democratic movement against military rule. Placed under house arrest by the military junta, she nonetheless led the party she had formed, the National League for Democracy (NLD), to electoral victory in 1990. But the military having been forced to agree to holding democratic elections, refused to convene the new assembly, launching a systematic campaign to decimate the NLD instead. Leaders and followers alike were jailed, harassed and intimidated, sowing the seeds of internal dissension within the NLD. After six years, Aung San Suu Kyu was released from house arrest in 1995 and continued to promote democratic change even though the organization she founded was being destroyed by the regime. In 1999 when the government felt it had succeeded in destroying its opposition, the NLD, it changed the name of its governing body from the State Law and Order Restoration Council (SLORC) to the State Peace and Development Council.

Today Aung San Suu Kyi espouses liberal democracy in the language of Buddhism. Her appeal is for an open, free, democratic process that will secure the physical safety, material well-being and spiritual fulfillment of all the Burmese people. She refers to the military regime that has cloaked itself in socialist rhetoric as "totalitarian socialism."[37] Accusing the military leadership of feeding the people "a pabulum of shallow, negative dogma" designed to create "rice-eating robots," Aung San Suu Kyi descries the government's attempts to discredit the idea of democracy as a Western idea that is incompatible with Burmese Buddhism. She has countered the military's interpretation of Buddhism as irreconcilable with Western democracy, demonstrating in deed as well as word that Buddhism not only is congruent with democracy but mandates it.

Her argument reclaims Buddhism as a moral force for democracy. In the Buddhist view of world history, "when society fell from its original state of purity into moral and social chaos, a king was elected to restore peace and justice." This ruler was known by three titles that illuminate his purpose of restoring peace and justice: Mahasammata because he is named ruler by the unanimous consent of the people; Khattiya because he has dominion over agricultural land; and Raja because he wins the people's affection through observance of virtue, justice, and the law. "The agreement by which their [the people's] first monarch undertakes to rule righteously in return for a portion of the rice crop represents the Buddhist version of government by social contract." In this way, the daughter reverses her father's politically suspect insistence on separating a too-superstitious Buddhism from the "idea of the modern state." In a simple, straightforward manner, Aung San Suu Kyi reunites Buddhism with the idea of a democratic state: "because the Mahasammata was chosen by popular consent and required to govern in accordance with just laws," the concept of elective government is *not* alien to traditional Burmese thought.

Buddhism and National Development.   It is not clear what capacity Buddhism, the religious anchor of most Burmese, retains to lend or deny political legitimacy, to promote or retard national integration and economic development. The anthropologist Edmund Leach suggests "that there is something about the Ethic of Buddhism which is fundamentally at variance with the Spirit of Capitalism."[38] Wealth that a person accumulates is to be given to support the clergy and build temples, bringing religious "credit" to the donor but making that capital unavailable for materially productive purposes, such as building factories. As Medford Spiro observes, Burmans are culturally predisposed to use wealth in ways that assure them a more pleasurable rebirth rather than investing in economic enterprises destined to decay in this material world in which one is only a transient.[39] It is not, according to the noted scholar, Mya Maung, a question of whether the Burmese want to improve their living conditions but the absence in Buddhist culture of attitudinal incentives to work and its opposition to acquisitiveness.[40]

In the years since independence in 1948, Burma has undergone several metamorphoses. In each of the earlier ones, leaders claimed to be pursuing socialism while actually pursuing an essentially nonideological and opportunist agenda. Whether Aung San Suu Kyi's appeals for democratic government will prove effective in peacefully ousting the military-backed government or not, remains to be seen. But in a society ethnically fragmented into rival groups, each with its own banner of nationalism, in the absence of an overriding sense of collective identity and minimal consensus to hold the country together as a political community, the military can always be counted upon to save Myanmar from a fate like that of the Soviet Union or—worse—Yugoslavia.

Malaysia: Affirmative Action for the Malay Majority

In contrast to China, where Maoist ideology directly challenges both the traditional Confucian hierarchy and Western liberalism, Malaysian ideology encourages both Malay cultural values and elements of British liberalism. Unlike Japan, however, where traditional culture was systematically integrated with German conservatism to form a modern corporate ideology, Malaysia's strategy has been to preserve Malay culture intact while adopting a liberal commitment to representative government and economic progress. This formal endorsement of liberal values makes it possible for non-Malays to acquiesce in the Malay political elite's position as senior partner in the coalition of communal parties that have dominated Malaysian politics since preindependence days and in the special rights accorded to Malays in the constitution.

In the years leading to independence, Malaysian political elites shaped the nationalist ideology to fit certain inescapable realities inherited from precolonial and colonial days: an ethnically and culturally divided population in which Malays had a shaky majority; the influence of Islam, especially among the indigenous rural masses; the territorial division of the country into sultanates; and the acceptance by the Western-educated class of British liberalism as the legitimate model for a modern political system. Ethnic division produced *bumiputerism*, continuing and expanding on the British practice of preferential treatment for Malays; Islam became the state religion; the sultans accepted federalism as the formula for national unification; and liberalism was interpreted as representative government, majority rule, and laissez-faire in economic matters. In the decades since independence, each of those realities has undergone changes, effecting adaptation in the dominant ideology and in government policies.

Bumiputerism.   At the core of national ideology in Malaysia today is the concept of *bumiputerism*. Derived from *bumiputra,* meaning "sons of the soil," it refers to the special rights of Malays (and other non-Malay indigenous people in Sabah and Sarawak) as distinguished from the "immigrant" Chinese and Indians, descendants of laborers the British encouraged to come to extract tin and rubber for the world market. Preferential treatment for Malays in access to higher education and civil service positions had begun as British colonial policy and was incorporated in the constitution drawn up at the time of independence. The tacit agreement then between Malay and Chinese leaders was that politics and economics would be kept separate, with the Malays dominating the former and the Chinese the latter.

But this compact proved less than satisfactory to the Malays, as Chinese wealth brought with it political clout and as the income gap between the Malay masses and the Chinese and Indians widened. The slowness of Malays to move up economically was at least in part the result of British policy encouraging them to preserve their traditional way of life, protected from the inroads of commercialism and urbanization. Tensions between Malays and Chinese increased in the decade after independence, resulting in riots in 1969 and in an expansion of bumiputerism in the New Economic Policy (NEP). A form of "affirmative action" for the benefit of the disadvantaged majority, NEP involved government action to increase the Malay share in business and to improve the lives of rural Malays.

Ethnic separation, which had originated in the alliance between British colonial rulers and the Malay aristocracy, was reinforced during the Japanese occupation, when Malays collaborated with the occupiers while the Chinese waged armed struggle against them. The separatism thus magnified between ethnic Chinese and Malays was further solidified by the postwar "Emergency," pitting mainly Chinese Communist insurgents against the British authorities. Today, it is continued by bumiputerism and inhibits the formation of a national ideology integrating all the citizens of Malaysia.

However, the bonds linking bumiputra may come under pressures generated by economic development, which differentiates interests along occupational, class, and rural-urban lines. And fissures are opening up between Malays and the indigenous people in Sabah who, although they are not Malay and many are Christian, were accorded bumiputra status at the time of joining the union in 1963. Political disagreements between the central government and UMNO on the one hand and the Sabah chief minister and the mainly Christian opposition party in control there have erupted in disputes over logging regulations and in federal prosecution of the chief minister on charges of corruption. These fissures in the bumiputra community further complicate the ethnic impediments to a truly national Malaysian identity.

Federalism.   The British first introduced the concept of federation as a way of bringing the separate sultanates under a common colonial administration without disturbing the traditional relationship between sultans and subjects. However, upon returning to Malaysia at the end of World War II, the British proposed as a step toward independence the creation of a unified state as well as the abolition of special privileges for Malays and the granting of citizenship to all long-term residents and all those born in the colony. This proposal aroused vociferous opposition among the Malay community; peasants united behind their aristocratic leaders to fight this threat to their dominant position. They forced the British government to back down on the idea of a Malay Union with equal citizenship for Malays and non-Malays alike. So the constitution was drawn up for an independent Federation of Malaya (renamed the Federation of Malaysia at the time of the addition of Singapore, Sabah, and Sarawak in 1963). Sultans kept their thrones and state governments share power with the central government.

In recent years, Prime Minister Mahathir has come into conflict with the sultans, succeeding in reducing their privilege of immunity from prosecution, publicizing their expenditures for luxuries such as palace renovations and racehorses, and backing a rival claimant to the Kelantan throne. His objective is seen as increasing the power of the central government over the states, a modification of the original federal compact, perhaps signifying a trend toward the unitary state proposed by the British in 1946 and rejected by the Malay majority. Now, in a curious twist, the non-Malay non-Moslem minorities tend to support states' rights against centralization of power because they feel their chances for protecting their rights are greater in a decentralized federal system.

Liberalism.   The alliance between the British colonial authorities and the Malay aristocracy contributed to the latter's embracing British liberalism as the favored ideological orientation. Liberal principles and institutions, including representative government, majority rule, and protection of individual rights, were incorporated in the constitution, and the liberal policy of minimal government intervention in the economy was continued.

With the passage of time, however, adherence to those principles suffered some erosion. The interethnic riots in 1969, in which the police were unable to protect Chinese and Indians from heavy casualties at the hands of Malay mobs, led to a period of suspension of the parliament and rule by decree. Restoration of constitutional government was followed by the adoption of constitutional amendments prohibiting public discussion of sensitive racial issues that might cause social unrest and assigning quotas for bumiputra in universities.

Another sequel to the 1969 riots was the adoption of the New Economic Policy, signaling departure from the principle of laissez-faire in economic affairs. Since "direct government involvement in the economy was associated with socialism, a political ideology that was anathema to the existing leadership,"[41] the shift away from a laissez-faire system was justified by citing the stellar case of Japan as proof that government intervention in a nonsocialist state could be beneficial in obtaining specific economic results. More recently, Prime Minister Mahathir has denounced the laissez-faire development models promoted by the World Bank and International Monetary Fund.

So the commitment to liberalism made by the early leaders has been modified over time to advance the cause of Malay progress and to defuse the volatile issue of interethnic relations by muzzling public discussion.

Islam. The final element of Malaysian ideology is Islam. Schooled in British liberalism, the secular-oriented political elite has not only recognized Islam as the state religion but moved in the direction of "Islamization." In order to strengthen its primarily rural political base among conservative Malay Muslims and to counter the appeal of the Islamic opposition party, PAS, UMNO has increasingly incorporated spiritual elements representing the perspective of more orthodox Moslems. This may account for some of the rhetoric of Dr. Mahathir: "Our concept of being developed does not simply focus on per-capita income, but on the quality of life and morality as well. The hedonistic materialism of present [Western] models is not for us. We hope the rest of the world will give us this freedom of choice and not harass us into conformity in the name of freedom."[42]

Still, the prime minister aims at transforming the influence of Islamic beliefs from conservative resistance to the government's goals of economic and social modernization into a moderate progressive force. In 1992 the government created the Malaysian Institute for Islamic Understanding, described by its director as "a policy study body which will offer Islamic interpretations of government policy."[43] Its agenda seems to be to formulate and publicize a Moslem "work ethic," convincing the faithful that hard work and material success are compatible with fidelity to Islamic beliefs and practices. "The idea," according to the head of a nongovernmental youth organization, "is to refocus the ethos of Islam and give progressive principles embodied in the religion more attention."[44] A balance must be struck, in Mahathir's words, "between spiritual attainment and material development."[45]

Vision 2020. The most current expression of national purpose is the prime minister's projection of what Malaysia will become by the year 2020, called "Vision 2020." Having moved in the years since independence from an economy based almost solely on the export of raw materials to an exporter of light industrial goods as well, Malaysia now aims at reaching the pinnacle of "full development" by 2020. The prime minister's vision is described by Kamal Salih, the executive director of the Malaysian Institute of Economic Research, an influential think tank: "The details are still very sketchy on what it means to become fully developed. But the country closest to what we want to achieve would probably be Sweden. We like their high level of education, their solid industrial base, their advanced technology and their strong social system."[46]

The goal of economic progress may have a broad appeal to all Malaysians sufficiently compelling to diminish the majority-minority differences that have troubled the society and shaped political discourse for more than a century. An expanding "pie" of wealth certainly opens the way to making the bumiputra richer without making the Chinese and Indians poorer. But whether Vision 2020 will hold the center against the challenge of Islamic fundamentalism, the resistance of the sultans to inroads on their prerogatives, the inertia of rural Malay society, the tensions between peninsular and insular states, and the long-standing animosities between the indigenous and "immigrant" communities is impossible to predict.

Indonesia: Industrialization Ideology Holds It Together

In Indonesia as in Malaysia, modern ideology grows out of the nationalist opposition to foreign rule. But unlike Malaysian nationalism, which settled into a moderate blend of Malay culturalism and British liberalism in the context of an amicable transfer of power, Indonesian nationalism has been volatile, shifting from socialist radicalism to military-sponsored industrialization ideology in response to a complicated intermeshing of national and international forces. In the aftermath of a revolutionary struggle for independence against the Dutch, nationalist sentiment was militant. But it was divided both culturally and ideologically.

Cultural Divisions.   Culturally, nationalist sentiment in Indonesia inherited a threefold division among animist, Hindu-Buddhist, and Islamic "layers," each representing the dominant thinking among people in the archipelago at successive periods in time. Though the majority of Indonesians are Moslem, comprising the largest Muslim population of any nation, this common denominator masks a diversity of religious outlooks deriving from earlier influences that swept across these islands at the crossroads between the Indian and Pacific Oceans. As each "layer" has historically settled on top of the influences of its predecessor, considerable mixing of elements of all three occurred. Islam spread slowly throughout the archipelago between the thirteenth and sixteenth centuries, eroding the institutional structures of the earlier religions, animist and Hindu-Buddhist, incorporating some elements and replacing others with Islamic institutions. But for people whose spiritual symbolism had for centuries been shaped by the earlier Hindu-Buddhist and animist beliefs, Islam provided more of a veneer, beneath which the older symbols continued to hold sway, than a substitute for older beliefs.

In Java especially, each of the three "layers" has remained the particular identity of a singular social class that has evolved its own distinct ideological response to the challenge of modernization. Since Javanese are the largest of Indonesia's 300 distinct ethnolinguistic cultures, making up almost half the country's population, and have provided the core of political leadership in modern Indonesia, this tripartite division of Javanese by class and culture has played a significant role in the formation of a dominant ideology for the country. There is an upper class (*prijaji*), with its roots in the court cultures of the great Hindu-Buddhist states; a lower peasant class (*abangan*), with roots in the ancient animist world of spirits, magic, and communal rituals; and a merchant class (*santri*) of coastal traders with a staunch faith in Islam. *Santri* is a term that has come to identify Moslems, both in villages and in towns, whose strict observance of daily prayer and close attachment to the other institutions of Islam are marked off from the rest of Javanese society.[47]

The peasant class was able to adopt Islamic practices without rejecting animist beliefs. The result was the "statistical Moslem,"

> the man who was circumcised, married, and buried by Muslim rites, because there was no institutionalized alternative, but who ate pork, fasted not during Ramadan but on moonless nights, placed trust in magical daggers, took wives and concubines as often as he pleased, and worshipped the spirits of his ancestors and a plurality of gods as much as Allah.[48]

In somewhat different fashion, members of the upper class became secularized Moslems, retaining their Hindu-Buddhist belief in social refinement and self-control as signs of their status as spiritual superiors. But to the more orthodox Moslem religious community of merchants, students, and scholars, the characteristic Javanese pattern of inclusivism, which permitted people to embrace Islam in addition to their other beliefs, was a perversion of the Moslem religion. Thus, accompanying the cultural tolerance of the Javanese tradition for including Islam into the house of Gods, there is the tension between the devout Moslem on the one hand and the "statistical Moslem" on the other.

Ideological Divisions.   The underlying conflicts among these disparate cultural strains found expression in three contending ideological movements. The *prijaji* had formed the Nationalist Party (PNI), the *abangan* peasants had found political representation in the Communist Party (PKI), and the *santri* merchants, the devout Moslems, joined forces with the reformist Moslems in the Masyumi Party. The Nationalists occupied a broadly defined ideological center between the revolutionary social and economic agenda of the Communists on the left and the religious Moslem agenda associated with an Islamic state on the right. Some Nationalists were adherents of Liberalism, advocating science and progress as the foundation of a cosmopolitan Indonesian state; others gravitated more toward either a socialist idea of economic justice or a religious idea of social justice. Sukarno took these traditional cultural strands and modern ideological ideas and wove them into a symbolic design for the new Indonesian state.

Pantja Sila.   First articulated during the latter days of the Japanese occupation, Sukarno's vision of the new republic's symbolic framework was composed of five principles, the Pantja Sila. It was designed as a "sacred" but nonsectarian ideological foundation for rival political forces to live together under the same national roof. As a statement of principles, the Pantja Sila is "short, ambiguous, and impeccably high-minded, the five points being 'nationalism,' 'humanitarianism,' 'democracy,' 'social welfare,' and (pluralistic) 'monotheism.'"[49] While in the Javanese tradition of syncretic inclusivism, Pantja Sila provided no clear direction for concrete social and political action and became, in the end, little more than a nationalist slogan for whatever government ruled Indonesia. As such it remained the official ideology of Suharto's New Order military regime.

Sukarno's "Guided Democracy." During the period of constitutional democracy that followed independence, Indonesia descended toward political chaos under a proliferation of parties and factions within parties. Only the Communists and the religious Moslems formed ideologically driven movements, but neither they nor the military had sufficient power to rule Indonesia. Sukarno, by virtue of his charisma the only person commanding enough to contain all these segments within one regime, imposed authoritarian rule, calling it Guided Democracy.

Like the Pantja Sila, though somewhat more programmatic, Guided Democracy was made up of five elements: the 1945 constitution, Indonesian-style socialism, Guided Democracy, Guided Economy, and Indonesian personality. Couched in an increasingly strident anti-Western and anti-imperialist rhetoric, this program intimated that authoritarianism today would bring about a system of collective production and distribution gradually and without class struggle sometime in the distant future. All groups were to work together as the "people," a concept that became mystically embodied in Sukarno himself. In his words:

> It is because of this that I always urge: unity, unity, and again unity. And we must understand that our revolution can only exert its maximum power when it is truly a national revolution, national and aligned. The revolution of a *people*. And *not* the revolution of one or another class. How often is the word "people" misused. It is used as a mask to camouflage the interests of a particular class. . . . All social and religious sections of our people are without exception revolutionary, because the purpose of the struggle is to annihilate imperialism and the old order, and to accelerate the advent of a new order in the form of national freedom.[50]

While publicly supporting the Communist Party, prohibiting opposition parties, and promoting socialism, Sukarno attempted to retain the loyalty of the military by entrusting it with management of the nationalized Dutch corporate assets in Indonesia. This placed the military in an unusual position. Since 1955 it had received material support and technical training from the United States. Thus military officers were increasingly subject to influence by technocratic ideas of the military-as-modernizers just as they found themselves gaining experience in running the nationalized economic enterprises of Indonesia. In the years that followed, as the army was called on to suppress the protests, plots, and rebellions (including one instigated by the CIA) precipitated by deteriorating conditions under Sukarno's rule, it strengthened an identity of itself as the only salvation of Indonesian unity with the promise of economic development. Lacking a mass base of his own, Sukarno by 1965 found himself powerless to prevent the squaring off of the two antagonists, the Communists and the military, that he had hoped to balance but who were vying with each other for control of Indonesia's destiny.

Suharto's New Order.   The New Order ushered in by General Suharto was heavily indebted ideologically to the patronage of the United States. It was based on an ethos of staunch anticommunism and modern military professionalism. A thoroughgoing purge of Communists was carried out with the complicity of militant Moslems in the wake of the military "countercoup" of October 1, 1965. One and a half million Indonesians suspected of communist sympathies were massacred and a permanent legal ban was placed on any form of Marxism. Having eliminated the Communists, the military regime used the Pantja Sila as a political weapon against militant Moslems by making it official state doctrine to be adhered to by all organizations. With its stress on a nonsectarian secular state, the Pantja Sila was a convenient device for neutralizing Moslem demands for an Islamic state. In this way, the New Order nullified radical demands from both the left and the right, setting the parameters for a politically stable, secular state that offered appropriate safeguards to acquire loans from international lending institutions and assure foreign capital a safe environment for its investments.

The ideological achievement of the New Order was to substitute pragmatic policymaking on the part of the military for futile ideological conflict among contending parties. What justified the military as the appropriate political actor to carry out this pragmatic policymaking was the doctrine of Dual Function, a constitutional principle that sanctioned the military's carrying out a dual role in both security/political and social/economic affairs. This doctrine was supplemented with the New Order insistence on "monoloyalty," a policy that strictly forbade civil servants (including teachers and faculty members of state universities) from any political affiliation other than absolute loyalty to the government. As the military transformed itself into a civilian party, the general population was forced to abstain from political activity except during elections. This created the political ambiance for the task at hand: "accelerated modernization," a program for rapid industrialization to be carried out with the technical assistance of "international lending institutions, friendly foreign governments, and private foreign capital."[51]

With the inflow of foreign capital assured by antilabor, anticommunist government policies, military officials of the New Order were able to build a political coalition as a base of internal support. Middle-class beneficiaries of successful development policies were willing to trade their political rights for economic gain. Catholic and Protestant minorities, alarmed by Moslem "extremism," joined civil servants and military officers to suppress Moslem activism. And traditionalist aristocrats, who had fallen from favor in the heyday of the nationalist struggle for independence, made a political comeback, their conservatism bolstering the regime and adding ethnic color for a growing tourist industry. Thus, "industrialization ideology," adopted on the advice of U.S. technocrats in conjunction with the World Bank and other international lending agencies, was successful at holding Indonesia together. But this lasted only as long as economic growth kept the economic pie expanding.

With the Asian financial crisis and the forced resignation of Suharto, all the latent religious, ethnic, and separatist conflicts, exacerbated by extensive migration, flared into the open. Long contained by a combination of military repression and economic opportunity, these conflicts quickly unravelled the loosely knit fabric of Indonesian nationalism. Faced with the potential disintegration of Indonesia,

President Abdurrahman Wahid (known as Gus Dur) who was democratically elected into office in November 1999, 17 months after the departure of Suharto, brings to his task a number of strengths. A Muslim cleric who believes fervently in religious inclusivity, ethnic fairness, the rule of law, and the healing power of laughter, he has moved swiftly to calm tensions and reassure all ethnic groups of their rights and the justice of their cause. But in order to undertake the overhaul of Indonesia's corruption-riddled political and economic institutions, he must first contend with a military whose loyalty he has to win while purging it of corruption.

The Philippines: Patron-Clientism in American-Style Politics

In the Philippines more than anywhere else in the Asian Pacific, liberalism in its classical sense provided the modern symbolism for the nation-state. Though usually attributed to American influence, popular sentiment for liberal principles of government in the Philippines has its roots in Spanish colonialism. Starting in the 1870s and culminating in the Filipino revolution in 1896, an educated class of Filipinos demanded the same political rights enjoyed by Spaniards under the monarchy. Jose Rizal, the fifth-generation Chinese mestizo novelist, poet, and physician who had studied in Spain and later became a martyr to the cause of Filipino nationalism, advocated elite participation in self-government under Spanish colonial rule. As part of the reform movement of the educated class, the *ilustrados,* Rizal had based his claims for Filipino rights on the Enlightenment principles of natural law.

Thus, in 1899, when the United States annexed the Philippines rather than granting its independence, Americans aborted a revolution committed to liberal principles of the natural rights of individuals. Although the United States suppressed the revolution, it confirmed Rizal's reputation as a national hero in the American-run educational system. This served the purpose of diverting attention from more radical nationalists by ensuring the dissemination of a moderate rather than a revolutionary liberal ideology among Filipinos. As a result, by 1935, when the Philippines was preparing for its promised independence from the United States, the economically and politically powerful Filipino elite that was poised to take control of the country identified ideologically with the liberalism of Woodrow Wilson and Franklin Roosevelt.[52]

The Tradition of Patron-Client Relationships.   Another element of Rizal's nationalist contribution was the rediscovery of Filipinos' Malay heritage. At the core of this traditional indigenous culture, submerged beneath layers of Spanish and American influence, is the mutual trust that grows out of the debt of gratitude one owes to "someone who has given selfless aid in time of crisis."[53] The prototype for this kind of enduring trust is the relationship between father and son. But in Philippine society it expands beyond the family into "fictive kinship" relationships between individuals occupying unequal positions of wealth and power. The *compadre* system, for example, consists of choosing high-status sponsors for the baptism or wedding of one's children, the choice based on the sponsor's social standing and financial capacity to care for and promote the weaker, more vulnerable "family" charges. In this manner a network of dyadic patron-client relationships is the basis for vertically cementing all social relationships.

The political ramifications of a patron-client system are visible even today in the Philippines. One is the relationship between a politician and the constituents he has assisted in some way (with cash, a job, or a license). They repay their debt by loyally voting for him when he runs for office. Unlike the traditional forms of mutual trust typifying families of old, however, political loyalties are implicit bargains based on expedience and subject to recalculation. Just as ordinary individuals seek the patronage of a politician to solve personal problems, the politician seeks out yet more powerful sponsors, expanding his own fictive kin to assist him with greater resources. In this way limitless patron-client relationships constitute the social and political bonds that tie the weaker to the stronger in vertical networks of dependence. In the Philippines, where neither nationalism nor the state has been strong enough to foster "public trust," this patron-client pattern of personal ties still dominates rural political and, although to a declining degree, urban life.

How does this culturally inherited pattern of face-to-face ties connect with the liberal ideology that emerges from Western rule in the Philippines? First, by defining individuals' "rights" in concrete (rather than abstract) terms as depending on *who* rather than *what* one knows, traditional culture makes the democratic electoral framework a captive of traditional purposes. The demands placed upon democratic political institutions reflect the interests of those with personal connections both in electoral and bureaucratic positions. Such preferential treatment for friends and family on the part of politicians might easily be mistaken for "corrupt" behavior in an American cultural context. Second, the patron-client system in the Philippines promotes political parties that are indistinguishable from one another by ideological principles or programmatic agendas for action. If one's electoral loyalty is governed by calculations of who is wealthy and powerful enough to repay a favor, then switching parties to support an incumbent is a pragmatic, even rational response to political options. If and when bargaining fails to deliver benefits, however, ideologies become important. Discontent with the political system's capacity to function can lead to ideological critique. Ideologies, therefore, are more often invoked by parties in opposition to the government, particularly leftist insurgents.

The Role of Ideology and the Supernatural.   The relative irrelevance of ideologies as a basis for politics is reinforced by the mix of sacred and secular elements in Philippine political culture. A religious conception of politics is, of course, central to Moslem and some Christian communities in the Philippines. But outside the religious communities, a widespread belief among peasants that magic and luck, or *suerte,* determine why people acquire wealth and power discourages more rational explanations of political authority. This sacred element in Filipino attitudes toward political events (for example, the overthrow of Marcos was widely attributed to divine intervention) frequently coexists with attitudes and values of Western origin, like individual rights to freedom of expression and assembly.[54] Filipinos turn out in great numbers for political rallies and express great interest in elections, without necessarily eschewing supernatural ideas about what affects political outcomes.

Thus while Philippine society is observed by many to be both highly democratic and highly politicized as measured by voting turnout and participation in political rallies, its democratic institutions are permeated by older traditional patterns of patron-client relations and sacred (sometimes magical) notions attached to worldly success that impede an identification of politics with public trust and justice for all. In this respect the Philippines is similar to other Asian Pacific nations, which exhibit a unique mixture of Western ideas and Asian cultural precepts carried into the modern age.

SUMMARY

The ways in which Asian nations have borrowed and transformed Western ideologies to express their modern aspirations defy easy generalizations. Countries that were colonized were influenced by the ideology of their rulers: Malaysia absorbed liberalism from the British while the Philippines learned liberalism from the Americans. In practice, then, there were varieties of liberalism as there were of the other Western ideologies introduced to the Asian colonies by imperialist powers. When alternative ideologies were available to modernizers, the particular ideology a country settled on was influenced by such factors as its own cultural heritage, the ethnic homogeneity or diversity of its population, and the "fit" between its own political goals and those favored by the particular ideologies in circulation at the time.

Ideologies were important in shaping the new structures and institutions with which a country began its economic modernization and political development. For Japan, a mixture of conservative ideas from Germany and liberal ideas from England, France, and the United States molded the institutions of government and the economy under Meiji rule, with equal rights and constitutional guarantees of freedom added by the U.S.-imposed constitution after World War II. In China, Vietnam, and North Korea, communism meant the institutionalization of economic equality under the dictatorship of the Communist Party. And in the ethnically and religiously pluralist societies of Myanmar, Malaysia, and Indonesia, syncretic ideologies were fashioned to obtain consensus under the leadership of the dominant ethnic group.

But ideologies alone provide only the skeletal outlines of modern political structures; the persistence of inherited cultural ideas flesh out how these structures actually work. Thus, in Asian Pacific countries, cultural values of power-as-status, collectivism, hierarchy, and the harmony produced by consensus continue to define how the new ideas and the structures in which they are embedded actually function. Just as patron-client relationships give substance to the idea of "people power" in the Philippines, the corporate harmony of respected leaders and loyal followers provides the substance of "enlightened conservatism" in Japan and the paternalism of Communist Party functionaries dispenses the justice of "socialism with Chinese characteristics" in China. In the Asian Pacific in general, Western ideological influences have thus been modified in practice by the cultural inheritance of one or more groups of people inhabiting the modern state.

The distinctive blending of Western ideological principles with Asian cultural beliefs and practices has yielded in all these countries a continuing tension between ideology and culture, between the ideals of a modern system of justice and the cultural expectations of equity and fairness. The fulcrum at which these unevenly matched partners balance one another on the scales of justice shifts imperceptibly as states succeed or fail in delivering on their promises.

QUESTIONS FOR DISCUSSION

1. In what significant ways do you see Asian Pacific cultures as similar to and different from your own?
2. How have Asian Pacific leaders adapted Western ideologies to suit the cultural circumstances and practical needs of their people?
3. What similarities and differences do you see between Marxism as a philosophical outlook and Confucianism?
4. What were Mao's contributions to Marxist thought? How do you think they reflected Mao's personal background and/or the cultural fabric of Chinese civilization?
5. What, if any, similarities do you see in the ruling ideas championed in China, Taiwan, Singapore, North Korea, and Vietnam?
6. How do you think religion has influenced the formation of ideologies in Myanmar, Malaysia, Indonesia, and the Philippines?

NOTES

1. Hung-chao Tai, ed., *Confucianism and Economic Development: An Oriental Alternative?* (Washington, DC: Washington Institute Press, 1989), p. 7. A more widely known example of the cultural approach is Lucian Pye, *Asian Power and Politics: The Cultural Dimensions of Authority* (Cambridge, MA: Belknap Press of Harvard University Press, 1985).
2. David I. Steinberg, *Burma's Road Toward Development: Growth and Ideology Under Military Rule* (Boulder, CO: Westview, 1981), p. 176.
3. Joseph J. Tobin, David Y. H. Wu, and Dana H. Davidson, "How Three Key Countries Shape Their Children," *World Monitor* (April 1989): 36–45.
4. Pye, *Asian Power and Politics*, pp. 32–38.
5. Ibid., p. 53.
6. Carol Gluck, *Japan's Modern Myths: Ideology in the Late Meiji Period* (Princeton, NJ: Princeton University Press, 1985), p. 248.
7. The material in this section comes from Gluck, *Japan's Modern Myths*, pp. 248–51; the quotation is found on p. 250.
8. Robert T. Oliver, *Leadership in Asia: Persuasive Communication in the Making of Nations, 1850–1950* (Newark, DE: University of Delaware Press, 1989), p. 30.
9. See Oliver, *Leadership in Asia*, pp. 36–45, for a biographical sketch of Okuma Shigenobu.
10. From an editorial in the *Toyo Keizai Shimpo*, December 25, 1895, quoted in Byron K. Marshall, *Capitalism and Nationalism in Prewar Japan: The Ideology of the Business Elite, 1868–1941* (Stanford, CA: Stanford University Press, 1967), p. 11.
11. Marshall, *Capitalism and Nationalism*, p. 97.
12. Found in Chapter 3 of the Japanese constitution, full English text reproduced in Robert E. Ward, *Japan's Political System* (Englewood Cliffs, NJ: Prentice-Hall, 1978).
13. "We are first "poor" and second "blank." . . . By "blank" I mean we are like a blank sheet of paper . . . which is good for writing on." From "On the Ten Major Relationships," in *Selected Works of Mao TseTung*, vol. 5 (Peking: Foreign Languages Press, 1977), p. 306.
14. Mark Selden, "The Yenan Legacy: The Mass Line," in *Chinese Communist Politics in Action*, ed. A. Doak Barnett (Seattle: University of Washington Press, 1970), p. 104.
15. Victor Li, "Law and Penology: Systems of Reform and Correction," in *Deviance and Social Control in Chinese Society*, ed. Amy Auerbacher Wilson et al. (New York: Praeger, 1977), p. 148; see also Victor Li, *Law Without Lawyers* (Boulder, CO: Westview, 1978).

16. Danny Kin-Kong Lam and Ian Lee, "Guerrilla Capitalism and the Limits of Statist Theory: Comparing the Chinese NICs," in *The Evolving Pacific Basin,* ed. Cal Clark and Steve Chan (Boulder, CO: Lynne Rienner, 1992), p. 120.

17. Edwin A. Winckler, "Statism and Familism on Taiwan," in *Ideology and National Competitiveness: An Analysis of Nine Countries,* ed. George C. Lodge and Ezra F. Vogel (Boston, MA: Harvard Business School Press, 1987), p. 180.

18. Ibid., p. 183.

19. Quoted in Chester C. Tan, *Chinese Political Thought in the Twentieth Century* (Garden City, NY: Anchor Books, 1971), p. 129.

20. Ibid.

21. Stan Sesser, "A Nation of Contradictions," *New Yorker,* January 13, 1992, p. 46.

22. John Andrews, *The Asian Challenge* (Hong Kong: Longman Group Far East Limited, 1991), p. 144.

23. Sharon Siddique, "Singaporean Identity," in *Management of Success: The Moulding of Modern Singapore,* ed. Kernial Singh and Paul Wheatley (Boulder, CO: Westview, 1990), p. 563.

24. Lee Kuan Yew, quoted in "Discipline vs. Democracy," *Far Eastern Economic Review* (December 10, 1992): 29.

25. Ho Wing Men, "Value Premises Underlying the Transformation of Singapore," in Singh and Wheatley, *Management of Success,* pp. 671–91.

26. Yuk-sa Li, ed., *Juche! The Speeches and Writings of Kim Il Sung* (New York: Grossman Publishers, 1972), p. 45.

27. Ibid., pp. 45–46.

28. Samuel S. Kim, "North Korea and the Non-Communist World: The Quest for National Identity," in *North Korea in Transition,* ed. Chong-Sik Lee and Se-Hee Yoo (Berkeley: University of California Institute of East Asian Studies, 1991), p. 27.

29. Li, *Juche!,* p. 15.

30. Myung Chey, "Democratization in Korea as Perceived by Its Mass Public" (paper delivered at the annual meeting of the Association for Asian Studies, Los Angeles, March 27, 1993).

31. Siu-kai Lau, "Hong Kong Chinese Attitude Toward Political Leadership" (paper presented at the annual meeting of the Association for Asian Studies, Los Angeles, March 27, 1993).

32. In this chapter "Burma" is used rather than "Myanmar" because that was the country's name during most of the period under discussion.

33. Aung San, *Burma's Challenge* 1946, p. 4, cited in Josef Silverstein, *Burmese Politics* (New Brunswick, NJ: Rutgers University Press, 1980), p. 143.

34. Donald Eugene Smith, *Religion and Politics in Burma* (Princeton, NJ: Princeton University Press, 1965), p. 118.

35. John F. Cady, "Religion and Politics in Modern Burma," in *Far Eastern Quarterly* 12 (1953): 161.

36. Smith, *Religion and Politics in Burma,* p. 124.

37. The quotes in this entire section are from "In Quest of Democracy," in Aung San Suu Ky *Freedom from Fear* (London: Penguin Books, 1995) pp. 168–78.

38. Quoted in David I. Steinberg, *Burma's Road Toward Development* (Boulder, CO: Westview, 1981), p. 176.

39. Quoted in Steinberg, *Burma's Road Toward Development,* p. 178.

40. Steinberg, *Burma's Road Toward Development,* p. 177.

41. Mavis Puthucheary, "The Shaping of Economic Policy in a Multi-Ethnic Environment: The Malaysian Experience," in *Economic Policy-Making in the Asia-Pacific Region,* ed. John W. Langford and K. Lorne Brownsey (Halifax, Nova Scotia: Institute for Research on Public Policy, 1988), p. 282.

42. Quoted in Karl Schoenberger, "Column One: The Model Here Isn't America," *Los Angeles Times,* January 30, 1991, p. A1.

43. Michael Vatikiotis, "Hearts and Minds," *Far Eastern Economic Review* (May 20, 1993): 32.

44. Ibid.

45. Ibid.

46. Quoted in Schoenberger, "Column One," p. A9.
47. Sartono Kartodirdjo, "Agrarian Radicalism in Java: Its Setting and Development," in *Culture and Politics in Indonesia,* ed. Claire Holt (Ithaca, NY: Cornell University Press, 1972), p. 82.
48. Benedict R. O'G. Anderson, "Political Culture in Indonesia," in *Columbia Project on Asia in the Core Curriculum: Case Studies in the Social Sciences,* ed. Myron L. Cohen (Armonk, NY: M. E. Sharpe, 1992), p. 325.
49. Clifford Geertz, "Ideology as a Cultural System," *in Ideology and Its Discontents,* ed. David Apter (London: Free Press of Glencoe, 1964), p. 67.
50. From a booklet, *Sarinah,* that, though written by Sukarno in 1947, explicitly elaborates on the nature of the Indonesian revolution, quoted in C. L. M. Penders, *The Life and Times of Sukarno* (Teaneck, NJ: Fairleigh Dickinson University Press, 1974), p. 110.
51. Benedict R. O'G. Anderson, "Authoritarianism: Indonesia," in Cohen, *Columbia Project on Asia,* pp. 314–15.
52. David Wurfel, *Filipino Politics: Development and Decay* (Ithaca, NY: Cornell University Press, 1988), p. 10.
53. Ibid., p. 34.
54. Ibid., pp. 42, 43.

FOR FURTHER READING

Anderson, Benedict, and Audrey Kahin, eds. *Interpreting Indonesian Politics: Thirteen Contributions to the Debate.* Ithaca, NY: Cornell Modern Indonesia Project, Interim Reports Series, Publication No. 62, 1982, pp. 92–103, 117–130, and 131–148.

Apter, David, ed. *Ideology and Discontent.* Glencoe, IL: Free Press, 1964, pp. 47–76.

Brainard, Cecilia. *When the Rainbow Goddess Wept.* New York: E. P. Dutton, 1994.

Brook, Timothy, and Hy X. Luong, eds. *Culture and Economy: The Shaping of Capitalism in Eastern Asia.* Ann Arbor: The University of Michigan Press, 1999.

Cohen, Myron L., ed. *Columbia Project on Asia in the Core Curriculum: Case Studies in the Social Sciences.* Armonk, NY: M. E. Sharpe, 1992, pp. 91–104 and 323–35.

Dore, Ronald. *Taking Japan Seriously: A Confucian Perspective on Leading Economic Issues.* Stanford, CA: Stanford University Press, 1987, pp. 169–92.

Gluck, Carol. *Japan's Modern Myths.* Princeton, NJ: Princeton University Press, 1985, chs. 1, 2, 5, 8, 9.

Heywood, Andrew. *Political Ideologies: An Introduction.* New York: St. Martin's, 1992.

Kapp, Robert A., ed. *Communicating with China.* Chicago: Intercultural Press, 1983.

Kerkvliet, Benedict J. Tria. *Everyday Politics in the Philippines: Class and Status Relations in a Central Luzon Village.* Berkeley: University of California Press, 1990.

Mackerras, Colin, and Nick Knight. *Marxism in Asia.* New York: St. Martin's, 1985.

Milne, R. S., and Diane K. Mauzy. *Malaysia: Tradition, Modernity and Islam.* Boulder, CO: Westview, 1986, ch. 4.

Okimoto, Daniel I., and Thomas P. Rohlen, eds. *Inside the Japanese System: Readings on Contemporary Society and Political Economy.* Stanford, CA: Stanford University Press, 1988, pp. 1–38.

Pye, Lucian W. *Asian Power and Politics.* Cambridge, MA: Belknap Press of Harvard University Press, 1985, chs. 6–12.

———The Mandarin and the Cadre: China's Political Cultures. Ann Arbor: Center for Chinese Studies, Univeristy of Michigan, 1988, pp. 1–108.

Tai, Hung-chao, ed. *Confucianism and Economic Development: An Oriental Alternative?* Washington, DC: Washington Institute Press, 1989, chs. 8 and 9.

Walder, Andrew G. *Communist Neo-Traditionalism: Work and Authority in Chinese Industry.* Berkeley: University of California Press, 1986, chs. 4 and 5.

Wilson, Amy Auerbacher, Sidney Leonard Greenblatt, and Richard Whittingham Wilson, eds. *Deviance and Social Control in Chinese Society.* New York: Praeger, 1977, pp. 14–33.

7

The Global Context of Asian Pacific Development— The Cold War and After

During the second half of the twentieth century, the Asian Pacific region has moved from a peripheral to a central place in world politics. The region has ceased to be a minor player overshadowed in the drama of international relations by the "stars" in Europe and America and has become a central actor in the theater of global politics. Taking their place on the international stage in the years after World War II, Asian Pacific countries confronted difficult choices of great significance for their objectives of consolidating national independence and promoting economic growth. The complex course of their involvement in regional and global political, economic, and strategic relationships is the subject of this chapter and the next.

In this chapter, after first surveying the changes in the global political system in the more than five decades since World War II and suggesting some guidelines for the study of foreign policy, we then move on to the primary focus of the chapter: international politics in the Asian Pacific during the changing phases of the Cold War and in the years since it ended. In Chapter 8 the focus is on international political economy, on patterns of trade, aid, and investment, and on regional economic institutions.

THE CHANGING WORLD POLITICAL SYSTEM FROM THE 1940s TO THE NEW CENTURY

The process of decolonization that began at the end of World War II brought the former colonies in Asia new status as member states in the international political system. Not only was that system European in origin, but Western countries still dominated it. The modern international system, which emerged in Europe during the seventeenth century, is composed of states, each with a clearly demarcated territory and a population over which its government exercises the sovereign right to rule as it sees fit. International law—rules of behavior voluntarily agreed to by governments as binding on them—regulates relations between states; it rests on the principles of sovereignty, equality, and mutual respect for the territorial integrity and political independence of all states. While these principles are not always adhered to in practice, a fundamental assumption remains that within their own borders governments are supreme, subject to no outside authority without their acquiescence.

The notion of clearly defined territorial boundaries between states that are all legally equal (in principle at least) was alien to precolonial Asia. There, borders between kingdoms were often fluid and permeable, and empires rested on superior-subordinate relations between a central hierarch and less powerful local rulers. The experience of colonialism, when the outside powers imposed borders to define their respective possessions, converted Asian colonials to the European view of the significance of territoriality. Testimony to that significance is apparent in postindependence conflicts between neighbors on jurisdiction over land borders (for example, the Chinese-Soviet border) and over offshore islands (such as the Spratlys) that have strategic, economic, or symbolic significance to the parties.

Bipolarity and the Cold War

In addition to the need to become accustomed to the rules of the game of international relations in this Eurocentric interstate system, leaders of Asian Pacific states also had to make their way through the shoals of a postwar polarization of the world into hostile anticommunist and communist camps in what came to be known as the "cold war." The origin of the Cold War is too long a story to go into in detail here. It is sufficient to recall that hostility began as far back as 1917, when the Bolshevik Revolution in Russia and the establishment of a communist Soviet Union met with the antagonism of the capitalist powers. That antagonism was put aside temporarily to form the World War II alliance against Hitler, but it resurfaced after the war as a confrontation over the extent of Soviet influence in Eastern Europe.

What began as an intra-European conflict spread worldwide in the late 1940s as the United States, responding to what it and other Western powers saw as Soviet expansionism aiming at world domination, initiated the policy of "containment" of communism by diplomatic, economic, and military means. The "West"— the capitalist anticommunist bloc led by the United States—and the "East"—the anti-imperialist communist bloc led by the USSR—each lined up protégés among Asian governments, political parties, and insurgent movements, forming military alliances, providing arms, acquiring bases, and giving various forms of political and economic support and guidance.

The two superpowers took opposing sides in the civil war in China, in the Korean War, in the Vietnam War, and in a number of local insurgencies in Southeast Asian countries before and after independence. Asian states entering this bipolar world were confronted with the need to choose sides in the U.S.–Soviet conflict or to find an alternative to alignment with either side. Burma and Indonesia opted for nonalignment as their official policy, as did Malaysia and Singapore later on, when they became independent. Lined up on the American side in the early phase of the Cold War were the governments of Japan, South Korea, the Philippines, Taiwan, Thailand, the French and their supporters in Vietnam, Laos, and Cambodia, and the British in colonial Malaya and Singapore; on the other side were China (after 1949), North Korea, Ho Chi Minh's Democratic Republic of Vietnam, the Pathet Lao in Laos, and various other insurgent groups in Burma, Thailand, Malaya, and the Philippines. Many of the internal political and armed conflicts between Communists and anticommunists within nationalist movements before independence and between governments and political opponents after independence were at least in part an extension of the global contest between the two poles clustered around the superpowers.

Erosion of Bipolarity

The bipolar division that characterized the world political system in the late 1940s to the mid-1950s eroded somewhat in the late 1950s and the 1960s. The superpowers took modest steps toward détente in an effort to reduce tensions that might lead to catastrophic nuclear war between them, and centrifugal tendencies appeared in both the East and West camps. In Asia, the alliance between the Soviet Union and China deteriorated into mutual recriminations, and as the split between them came into the open it was mirrored in splits within communist movements in other countries. The Sino-Soviet breakup also confounded American preconceptions about the monolithic nature of the world communist movement and eventually raised questions among U.S. allies about the justification for the pursuit of containment in the war in Vietnam.

Bipolarity was further eroded by the growth of the nonaligned movement in what came to be known as the "Third World," the less-developed, mainly ex-colonial countries, many of which tried to remain outside the orbit of either superpower. Détente did not stop the United States and the USSR from competing for influence in Asia and other parts of the developing world. The Soviets and the Chinese proclaimed their support for wars of national liberation even where the liberation movement was noncommunist and the United States favored nationalists with sufficiently anticommunist credentials. East and West competed with each other in the use of inducements such as economic and military aid to win uncommitted governments to their side, or at least to prevent them from slipping into the other side's orbit. Competition between the superpowers for influence in the Third World provided some leverage for those countries to benefit from both sides.

Evolution Toward Polycentrism in the 1970s and 1980s

Although the Cold War confrontation between the United States and its allies and the Soviet Union and its allies continued to be a central reality in international politics until the disintegration of Soviet dominance in Eastern Europe in the late 1980s and of the Soviet Union itself in 1991, the world political system in the 1970s and 1980s became in many respects quite polycentric. Groupings of states formed around interests apart from the East-West division; OPEC, the European Community (EC), the League of Arab States, and the Association of Southeast Asian Nations (ASEAN) are some of the organizations that became important centers of attachment for their members and influence in international relations.

Arenas of international cooperation and conflict, such as international trade, aid, investment, the global environment, population growth, and human rights, took their place on the agenda of international relations formerly dominated by military and security issues. And the growing importance of actors other than states, such as multinational corporations, the United Nations, the World Bank, and international nongovernmental organizations, also contributed to the creation of networks of interaction at regional and global levels, which in many respects displaced Cold War antagonisms as the central focus of foreign policy and international relations. For Asian Pacific states, these changes created new opportunities and new uncertainties in their relations with each other and with extraregional powers.

Instability in the Global Political System in the 1990s

The decade of the 1990s began with a high degree of instability in the global political system. The end of the Cold War and the shrinking of Soviet power have contributed to uncertainty about the U.S. politico-strategic role in the world. Some would label post–Cold War global politics a "unipolar" system, since—in their view—only the United States has the economic and military capacity for a truly global reach. Others see American power as waning and already seriously challenged by the economic clout of Japan and the EC (now EU), by the proliferation of weapons of mass destruction as well as conventional weapons, and by the upsurge of intergroup violence within states.

None of these challenges is easily met by the application of American military force or economic power. Old political enemies in Asia have become economic partners, and long-time economic partners find themselves at odds over market competition and trade imbalances. The shifting security concerns of the United States and other countries in the post–Cold War era require important adjustments for the Asian Pacific region, as for the rest of the world, and the process of adjustment has already begun.

WHAT EXPLAINS FOREIGN POLICY BEHAVIOR?

Three "themes" are implicit in our analysis of international relations in the region and indeed in the whole world. One is that the distinction between "domestic" and "foreign" policies is an artificial abstraction, since in reality the two are inextricably intertwined. A change in Japanese electoral law, for example, that reduces the overrepresentation of rural areas is intimately connected to changes in foreign trade policy on rice imports.

A second theme is that all states in the world are inescapably interdependent, although the intensity and frequency of transactions and interactions among countries does vary considerably. Some states, like Singapore, are heavily enmeshed in global networks of international relationships, while others, like Myanmar, have fewer external ties and mainly with close neighbors. The interdependence may be

Chronology of Major Events in Asian Pacific Relations, 1945–2000

1945   Japanese surrender, ending World War II
1948   North and South Korean governments established
1949   People's Republic of China established
        Soviets test A-bomb
        NATO formed
1950   Sino-Soviet Alliance (expired 1980)
        Korean War begins
        Pro-French monarchies in Vietnam, Laos, and Cambodia given limited independence within the French Union
1951   Japan–United States peace treaty signed
        Philippines–United States Mutual Defense Treaty
1952   U.S. occupation of Japan ends
1953   Stalin dies
        Armistice in Korea
1954   First Geneva conference on Indochina; Vietnam divided
        SEATO established (dissolved 1977)
        Republic of Korea–United States alliance
        Republic of China (Taiwan)–United States alliance
1955   Bandung conference of Asian-African states
        Cambodia leaves French Union
1957   Soviets launch *Sputnik* orbiter
        Communist insurgency begins in South Vietnam
1960   Sino-Soviet split
1961   Non-Aligned Movement formed
1962   Sino-Indian border war
1963   Sukarno starts Konfrontasi against Malaysia
        South Vietnamese President Diem assassinated
1964   China detonates nuclear device
        U.S. air strikes against North Vietnam begin
        North Vietnamese army enters South Vietnam
1965   U.S. ground forces sent to Vietnam
        Cultural Revolution begins
        Asian Development Bank established
1967   ASEAN founded
1968   Tet offensive
        Peace talks begin in Paris
1969   Sino-Soviet border clashes
1971   Five-Power Defense Agreement (Australia, New Zealand, Malaysia, Singapore, UK)
1972   China-Japan establish diplomatic relations
        Nixon visits China; Shanghai Communique

	SALT I signed
	PRC takes China's seat in United Nations
	Okinawa returned to Japan
	North and South Korea open talks on normalizing relations
1973	Paris Accords on Indochina
	U.S. troops withdraw from Vietnam
1975	Indonesia annexes East Timor
	South Vietnam falls, Vietnam unified
1976	Mao dies
1978	Soviet-Vietnam Treaty of Friendship
	Vietnam invades Cambodia
	United States–China communique on Taiwan
	Japan-China peace treaty
1979	China invades Vietnam
	Soviets invade Afghanistan
	United States–China establish diplomatic relations
1980	United States–Taiwan treaty ends
1981	China proposes talks with Taiwan on reunification
1983	Soviets shoot down Korean Airlines plane
1984	UK–China agreement on return of Hong Kong
1986	Gorbachev speech in Vladivostok
1987	United States–Soviet Intermediate Nuclear Forces agreement
	Portugal-China agreement on return of Macau
	Taiwan lifts ban on travel to mainland
1988	Gorbachev Krasnoyarsk speech
	Seoul hosts Olympics
1989	Gorbachev visits Beijing; Tiananmen Square events
	Vietnamese withdraw from Cambodia
	End of Cold War?
1990	China-Indonesia restore diplomatic relations
	USSR–South Korea establish diplomatic relations
1991	Gorbachev visits Japan
	Gulf War
	Paris agreement on Cambodia
	President Bush visits Japan
	Breakup of the Soviet Union
	Philippine Senate ends U.S. bases lease
	North and South Korea admitted to the United Nations
	Taiwan and China establish unofficial bodies to handle contacts between them
1992	UN Transitional Authority in Cambodia (UNTAC) formed
	Non-Aligned Movement summit, Jakarta
	China–South Korea establish diplomatic ties
	Japanese emperor visits China

Chronology of Major Events in Asian Pacific Relations, 1945–2000 (continued)

1993	G-7 summit, Tokyo
	President Clinton visits South Korea
	UNTAC leaves Cambodia following election of new government
	LDP loses election; new Japanese government formed
	President Yeltsin visits Japan
	APEC summit, Seattle
	China issues policy paper on Taiwan
	Taiwan seeks membership in UN
1994	United States lifts economic embargo on Vietnam
	United States renews China's most favored nation trading status
	Japanese Emperor visits the United States
	North Korea and the United States hold talks on North Korean nuclear facilities
	North Korea, the United States, China, and South Korea sign the Geneva Framework Agreement (GFA)
	North and South Korea agree to hold summit meeting
	Kim Il Sung dies
1995	Vietnam becomes the seventh member of ASEAN
	Vietnam–United States relations normalized
	Kobe earthquake in Japan
	Okinawans resist signing lease documents for U.S. base
	Taiwan's President Lee on unofficial visit to United States
	PRC tests missile near Taiwan, test-launches first mobile ICBM and holds underground nuclear tests
	China agrees to multilateral talks with ASEAN to resolve dispute with Philippines over Spratly Islands
	Cambodia and Laos sign a treaty of friendship and assistance
	Taiwan offers UN $1 billion development fund for UN membership
1996	Cambodia establishes diplomatic relations with Burma and South Korea
	Cambodia receives MFN trading status from United States
	China launches surface-to-surface missiles near Taiwan's coast to influence Taiwanese elections; United States dispatches aircraft carrier Independence
	China announces moratorium on further nuclear testing
	North Korean "midget" submarine runs aground near South Korean coast
	Japan and China dispute territory named Senkakus by the Japanese and Diaoyu by the Chinese
	United States–Japan discussions on updating their security pact

1997   Deng Xiaoping dies
Kim Dae Jung, elected president of South Korea
Burma and Laos join ASEAN
First Prime Minister Prince Norodom Ranariddh of Cambodia ousted;
United States holds Hun Sen responsible for "coup" but Australia,
Japan, ASEAN, and EU claim action unavoidable
IMF multi-billion dollar bailout packages for Thailand and South
Korea
Brunei contributes $500 million towards the 17.2 billion IMF rescue
package for Thailand.
DPP makes spectacular electoral gains in local elections in Taiwan

1998   High-level talks between Taiwanese and PRC resume (under U.S.
pressure) after 5-year freeze
Provincial level government of Taiwan eliminated symbolizing
Taiwan's rejection of its provincial status as part of China
North Korean missile over Japan provokes United States–Japan joint
research on a theatre-missile defense shield (TMD)
Former Khmer Rouge leader Pol Pot dies
Brunei gives financial aid to Indonesia and Malaysia and shifts
investments to ASEAN region in the wake of the economic crisis.
Kim Jong Il becomes General-Secretary of Korean Workers Party
after 3-year period of mourning for his father
President Suharto is forced to resign after prolonged violent unrest
Joseph Estrada, former town mayor and actor, elected President of
Philippines
President Clinton visits China
Lt. General Prabowo, Suharto's son-in-law, is discharged from armed
forces over disappearance of pro-democratic activists
Japan brokers peace plan for Prince Norodom Ranariddh's return
from exile to run for office

1999   Taiwan's President Lee asserts that Taiwan and China must negotiate
on basis of "state to state" relations
Massive earthquake in Taiwan
Abdurrahman Wahid's (fourth Indonesian President) post-inaugural
visit to Singapore
Mahathir and UMNO win two-thirds majority in Malaysia's general
elections
Edmund Ho named Macau's Chief Executive after handover
Four-power security meeting about Korean peninsula issues
Outspoken nationalist, Shintaro Ishihara, elected governor of Tokyo
Legislation in Japan enshrining the Rising Sun flag and the Kimigayo
anthem as national symbols
Nuclear chain reaction in Japan contaminates dozens of people

Chronology of Major Events in Asian Pacific Relations, 1945–2000 (continued)

	Macau returns to Chinese rule on December 20th.
	10,000-strong, peaceful Falun Gong demonstration in front of Government compound in Beijing
	Japanese upgrade defense guidelines to United States–Japan security alliance
	NATO (United States) bombing of the Chinese Embassy in Belgrade
	East Timor placed under martial law after widespread burning, looting, and shooting of East Timorese by Indonesian militiamen
	Arrival of UN Assistance Mission in East Timor to supervise the independence or autonomy referendum
	PRC celebrates fiftieth anniversary of independence
	Washington pays China $4.5 million as compensation for victims of the embassy bombing
	Cambodia becomes tenth and final member (in the SEAsian region) of ASEAN
	Brunei establishes diplomatic relations with North Korea
2000	President Clinton scheduled to visit Vietnam and North Korea
	Vietnam receives so-called normal trading status by United States, subject to annual review
	China set to join WTO

Note: For events since mid-2000, see sources suggested on p. 117.

symmetrical, between states more or less mutually dependent, or it may be quite asymmetrical, with one partner dominant and the other subordinate.

The third theme is that the relationships of Asian Pacific states with each other and with non-Asian powers are characterized both by conflict and by cooperation, although the "mix" may vary between partners over time. The United States and Japan, for example, conflict over trade relations and cooperate in military security affairs; China and Taiwan allow person-to-person contacts and are in fundamental agreement that Taiwan is a province of China, while profoundly in conflict over who should govern China.

Explaining Foreign Policies: Three Levels of Analysis

What explains the choice of foreign policy goals and the actions taken by governments? Why, for example, did China respond positively to Nixon administration overtures toward establishing normal diplomatic relations after years of vilifying the United States as an enemy and even while the United States was waging war against communist Vietnam? Was it because Mao had become senile and lost his grip on power to other less doctrinaire leaders? Was it because popular weariness with the disruptions of the Cultural Revolution led to pressure for improving the standard of living, which could be helped by ties to the United States and Japan? Was it because China needed the "America card" to play against a closer enemy, the Soviet Union? Scholars in the field of international relations identify three clusters of factors that are likely to influence the foreign policy choices states make. Those clusters relate to three levels of analysis: (1) the level of the individual decision makers, (2) the level of the nation-state, and (3) the level of the international system in which the state is a participant.

At the individual level are such factors as the personality, the life experiences, the beliefs, the personal political goals, even the health of the decision makers. For example, his age might in part have made it possible for Japanese Prime Minister Hosokawa in 1993 to do what none of his older predecessors had done: to apologize for the terrible deeds done to the people of countries Japan subjugated in World War II.

At the nation-state level are the multiplicity of characteristics relating to the governmental system, the economy, military power, geographic location, topography, natural resources, the society as a whole, its traditions, its history, its people, their religion, their political beliefs. For example, the willingness of the Philippines to align itself with the United States and to have American bases on its soil for more than four decades after independence might be understood in part as a result of the economic benefits derived from U.S. military aid and expenditures in the islands, by the desire of its people to have privileged access to the U.S. market and to emigration to the United States, to the relatively benign historical experience under American colonialism, to goodwill generated by the willing acquiescence to the request for independence, and to the affinity of Filipino political institutions to the American model.

At the system level are such external factors as the configuration of power in the world system, whether it is a multipolar, bipolar, unipolar, or some other type of system; the relative weight of the state in that system, whether it is a small weak state or a major or middle power; the objectives of other states in the system that affect it, the history of relations with neighboring and more distant states; the significance of participation in alliances, in regional or global international organizations. For example, the foreign policy orientation of nonalignment chosen by Burma might be attributed to the fact that it is a small weak state located at the juncture of South, East, and Southeast Asia, bordering on five countries, including a powerful China and Thailand. Or the low-profile political role played by economically powerful Japan might in part have been chosen in recognition that bold initiatives might be resisted by other Asian countries as presaging a revival of Japan's earlier bid for hegemony.

Each level of analysis contributes something to our understanding of foreign policy behavior, although the influence of factors at different levels may vary depending on the characteristics of leaders, of the state, and of the international system. For example, the influence of individual leaders is thought to have greater weight in authoritarian systems than in those where decision making is subject to some degree of oversight by elected officials. In states where the bureaucracy is strong, the idiosyncratic characteristics of top leaders are thought to have less impact than in states where the institutionalization of the foreign policy bureaucracy is incomplete. Economically developed states are presumed to have more latitude in foreign policy choices than less-developed ones. However, it is also recognized that the multiplicity of economic interests in more developed economies may impose constraints on policymakers, as evidenced by the pull and tug of various segments of business and labor organizations over issues of free trade or protectionism in relations among major East Asian trading partners. Influences of actors and conditions outside a state's borders are considered to be greater for small states than for the "movers and shakers" in the international system, but even *they* are subject to pressures from outside as well as within.

Although the relative weight to be assigned to any one factor in explaining a particular foreign policy choice is far from certain, we can state with assurance that *many* influences enter into foreign policy decisions. Looking at causality from the three levels of analysis increases our chances of coming up with plausible explanations for past decisions and possibly some informed predictions about future behavior. Our three theories about development bear some relevance here, although they do not directly set out to explain or predict foreign policies of developing states.

Modernization, World System, Developmental State Theories, and Foreign Policy

Modernization theorists assume that newly independent states will take their place in the world political system as sovereign equals, responsible for making choices, as other states do, about what will best serve their national interests in development and security. Their options are to select and use the various instruments of international relations—diplomacy, participation in international organizations, alliances, trade agreements, aid, investments, propaganda, even the threat or use of force—to promote their objectives. Whether they succeed or not depends on individual and societal factors such as the decision makers' skill in choosing appropriate goals and strategies, in mobilizing resources, and in implementing policies. In short, modernization theory implicitly assumes that a developing state has equal opportunity to play the game of international politics to its advantage.

World system theorists, in contrast, warn that formal independence does not mean real independence for former colonies, unless they are able to break out of the invidious connections to the world economic system set up by the imperial powers for their own benefit. But the likelihood is that after formal independence is attained, "neocolonialism" will continue the dependent relationship with the former imperial power or with another advanced industrial patron as the controlling partner. For these "neocolonial" states, control over their own foreign policy is more apparent than real, subject as they are to external influences, whether of other states or nonstate actors such as multinational corporations and international lending agencies. So world system theory would place greater importance on systemic factors than on individual or societal influences on foreign policymaking.

If modernization theory views foreign policy in developing countries as the prerogative of independent states and world system theory sees it as constrained by the system as a whole, developmental state theory observes foreign policy from an institutional perspective. From the statist point of view any dichotomy between the nationstate on the one hand and the global system on the other is misplaced because a nationstate is inextricably embedded in and therefore interdependent with both the global system on the outside and the diverse social and economic institutions over which it governs. A state's foreign policy, therefore, will depend upon the kind of state it is and the institutional capabilities it displays. A developmental state is distinguished by its capacity to utilize the opportunities provided by the global or world capitalist economy to serve the interests of national economic growth.

Whichever theory you find more persuasive, the impact of the external reality of the Cold War on the foreign relations of the Asian Pacific states cannot be minimized. To that we now turn.

THE EFFECTS OF THE COLD WAR: WARS AND ALLIANCES

None of the Asian Pacific countries escaped providing the stage and a cast of actors for the dramatic contest being played out between the opposing sides in the Cold War. In Burma, Cambodia, Laos, Malaysia, Indonesia, and the Philippines, the struggles among political parties and between the government and insurgents in each country were battlefields connected to the global struggle between the "East" and the "West." But most profoundly affected by the Cold War were Korea, Vietnam, and China. It resulted in the division of each of those nations into two states, one communist and the other anticommunist. Korea and China remain divided and Vietnam, unified after a long and bitter war, still struggles to overcome the effects of partition from 1954 to 1975. The victory of the communists in China in 1949 and the signing of the Sino-Soviet treaty of mutual assistance early in 1950 appeared to the United States to signal an alarming extension of the "Red empire." Then came the outbreak of war in Korea in June 1950, seen as validation of the contention that the Soviets were militarily expansionist and as the first major test of the American policy of containment in Asia.

War in Korea: What Led to It and What Resulted from It

There was no reason in 1945 for the Koreans to anticipate that the arrival of Soviet and American troops to accept the surrender of the Japanese forces in Korea would mean the permanent division of their country. True, in Korea's history there had been rival kingdoms centered in the north and in the south, and under the Japanese the north's mineral and power resources had been developed and an industrial base established, while the more populous south remained largely agricultural. But it was also true that Koreans regarded themselves as one people, a sense of identity that had been strengthened and popularized by foreign occupation.

Yet nationalist opposition to Japanese rule, although in principle united behind the Provisional Government in Exile in Shanghai, was deeply divided ideologically and geographically. The movement included right-wing conservatives, propertied elements backed by the Chinese Nationalists, some moderates and noncommunist leftists, and communist elements that looked to the Soviet and Chinese communists. Many had gone into exile, dispersing to Siberia, Manchuria, Yanan, Shanghai, and the United States, and the ideological divisions among Koreans in exile were paralleled by divisions in the anti-Japanese resistance within Korea. However, as World War II drew to a close, the various factions inside the country agreed to establish a Preparatory Committee for Korean Independence under a leftist, Lyuh Woon Hyung. The committee proclaimed the independence of the People's Republic of Korea, formed local committees to take over government functions from the Japanese, and prepared to welcome the Allied forces.

Two Occupation Zones.   When the Americans arrived in September 1945 to take control of the southern half of the country below the thirty-eighth parallel, they refused to deal with the committees. Instead, the Japanese were put back in their jobs (including the police) until an American military government could begin to function. In the American zone Syngman Rhee, a leading conservative nationalist who had spent years of exile in the United States, succeeded in winning out over rival contenders in the competition leading to the creation of a civilian government in the south. In the north, the Soviets at first worked with local committees under a central committee headed by a noncommunist Christian until the return of anti-Japanese resistance forces from Manchuria, among them Kim Il Sung, who won Soviet support and displaced the early leadership.

The two occupying powers had agreed to work through a joint commission on the formation of a government for all of Korea, but they and various Korean leaders disagreed on which Korean political groups should be consulted on the process. The dividing line between the Soviet and American zones effectively curtailed political connections across the line, and the north and south under foreign occupation grew further apart. In each zone, Korean military forces were formed, land reform programs put through, parties organized, and local elections held. The leader and party favored by each occupying power grew stronger, squeezing out moderate elements that might have prevented polarization between Communists and right-wing anticommunists.

Two States Created.   With negotiations between the United States and the Soviets on reunification of Korea stalled, the United States in 1947 brought the problem to the United Nations General Assembly, in which the American-led bloc then had a controlling majority. The UN Temporary Commission on Korea (UNTCOK) was set up to oversee elections in all of Korea. When the Soviets objected to the conditions UNTCOK laid down for the voting and refused to allow the commission into its zone, the United States went ahead in May 1948 with elections to the National Assembly in the south under UNTCOK observation. In August the Republic of Korea was established with Syngman Rhee as president and the UN General Assembly in December 1948 declared it the legitimate government of South Korea. The United States withdrew its forces except for a small training mission. After the creation of the ROK government, the Soviets withdrew their military from the North and turned over the government to the Democratic People's Republic of Korea with Kim Il Sung as president.

Both North and South expected that the division would be temporary, each anticipating that reunification would soon come about with its side incorporating the other. True believers in the North were convinced that with the tide of history on their side the progressive forces of workers and peasants under communist leadership and with the support of the Soviets would inevitably triumph over reactionary capitalism represented by the United States and its protégé Rhee. In the South Rhee and his supporters were convinced that they could harness the power of the United States, which by then had decided on a course of active resistance to the spread of communism in Europe, to support Rhee's vision of a Korea unified under his regime. So in the months following the separation of Korea into two states, efforts by a new UN Commission on Korea (UNCOK) to bring the two governments into negotiations on unification came to nothing. Verbal volleys were fired from both sides and each built up its military forces with the help of its patron. Cross-border raids occurred frequently, UNCOK duly reporting those incidents back to UN headquarters.

War Between North and South.   On June 25, 1950, large-scale hostilities broke out. Each side accused the other of having started the fight. The extent of Soviet and American foreknowledge of or complicity in the launching of the war is still not clear. Some insist that Moscow must have ordered or at least ratified Kim's bid to reunify Korea by force; others suggest that Rhee was the initiator, possibly encouraged by the American diplomat John Foster Dulles to expect U.S. support after the fact for his anticommunist crusade; still others see the war as essentially a civil war, initiated by Koreans, into which the outside powers were drawn by the logic of their mutual suspicions and regional commitments.

Whatever the truth surrounding the initiation of the war, President Truman quickly committed the U.S. military to the South's side, despite the fact that the United States then had no military alliance with South Korea and had publicly announced in January 1950 that the American defense perimeter in East Asia excluded Korea. Truman took the matter to the UN Security Council, which the Soviets were boycotting in protest against the UN's failure to seat representatives of the People's Republic of China in place of the defeated Republic of China government on Taiwan. With the concurrence of all four Asian states then members of the UN (Burma, the Republic of China, the Philippines, and Thailand), the UN approved support for the South and set up a UN command, headed by General Douglas MacArthur, to coordinate military operations. Troops or logistical support were contributed by forty-five countries, including the Philippines, Thailand, Australia, and New Zealand. Still, nine out of ten of the foreign troops fighting on South Korea's side were American.

The battle raged down the peninsula and back up again in early fall 1950 as MacArthur crossed the thirty-eighth parallel with the objective of unifying the country by force. The UN General Assembly reaffirmed its desire for a unified, independent, and democratic Korea and set up the UN Commission for Unification and Rehabilitation of Korea (UNCURK). As UN and ROK forces drew closer to the border between Korea and China, Beijing sent warnings through neutral countries that China would intervene if UN troops continued to move north. MacArthur discounted the warnings, pressed on, and in late November the Chinese counterattacked with nearly a million men. UN forces were driven back deep into the South and then fought back up again to the thirty-eighth parallel, where the military situation stabilized by mid-1951. After two years of diplomatic effort, hampered somewhat by the General Assembly's condemnation of China as an "aggressor" and its refusal to allow the Beijing government to take China's seat in the UN, an armistice agreement was reached in July 1953 and prisoners of war exchanged. The armistice is still in effect but in the wake of the summit meeting in June 2000, a peace treaty could be signed by the time President Kim Dae Jung of South Korea leaves office in 2003.

Effects of the War.   The Korean War had significant long-term effects on Asian states and on relations between them and the United States. For China, it brought Chinese troops into hand-to-hand combat with Americans, confirming convictions on both sides that the other was implacably hostile and preventing the establishment of normal relations between the two countries for almost thirty years. The war moved China's nemesis, the government on Taiwan, more closely under American protection, which from Beijing's perspective signified continued U.S. interference in the Chinese civil war. Truman's decision to extend the U.S. defense perimeter to include Taiwan and to send the Seventh Fleet to patrol the Formosa Straits thwarted the Chinese Communists from completing their victory over the Guomindang by taking control of the island. Mao's government deeply resented the action but was powerless to prevent the United States from signing a security pact with Taiwan in 1954 and from supplying military and economic aid to Chiang, whose announced aim was to retake the mainland. Aid even included CIA backing for a remnant Guomindang army that had fled into Burma, from which it launched repeated but unsuccessful invasions into China. Another affront was U.S. use of the UN to condemn it as the aggressor and to block it from taking China's place in the organization until 1972.

Other Asian countries as well as Taiwan benefited from the intensification of the Cold War that the "hot" war in Korea brought. A major beneficiary was Japan. Its economy profited greatly from the stimulus of serving as a crucial staging point and supply source for the war, and its political status was rapidly elevated in 1952 from that of occupied ex-enemy to newly sovereign state and American ally. Over the objections of the Soviet Union, China, Burma, and other countries that had fought the Japanese in World War II, the United States concluded a peace treaty and a security pact that allowed it to continue to occupy bases in Japan in return for the promise of American protection.

The Republic of Korea, like the Republic of China, got a mutual security pact and economic and military aid from the United States, as did the Philippines, where American forces already were stationed. Australia and New Zealand joined the United States in the ANZUS pact—a mutual defense treaty signed in 1951—and in 1954 the web of military alliances along the periphery of the Asian mainland was completed with the creation of a regional security pact, the Southeast Asia Treaty Organization. SEATO linked the Philippines, Thailand, and Pakistan with the United States, Britain, France, Australia, and New Zealand, and its protection was extended to the nonsignatory states of Laos, Cambodia, and the Republic of (South) Vietnam.

Another effect of the Korean War was to raise the level of American involvement in the conflict between France and its former possessions in Indochina. Vietnam, Laos, and Cambodia, like Korea, became a local theater for the Cold War rivals to carry on their global struggle. What had in 1945 appeared to many Americans as an effort by France to reimpose colonialism now came to be perceived as an integral part of the "Free World" resistance to a worldwide communist conspiracy to seize all of Indochina. Accordingly, the United States began in the early 1950s to provide a generous financial subsidy to France for its military campaign against the Vietnamese independence movement, the Viet Minh. In both Vietnam and Korea, partition into two states was agreed to in recognition of the existence of communist and anticommunist spheres of influence, but each side expected eventual reunification on its terms. Koreans and Vietnamese suffered the agony of internecine war, with American forces heavily involved. War in Korea lasted three years, in Vietnam three decades.

War in Indochina

The Viet Minh, a coalition of various nationalist groups, had been formed on the initiative of the Indochinese Communist Party during World War II to fight against the Japanese occupation and the return of French colonialism. Partisans from the Viet Minh base in the northern part of the country had cooperated during the last months of the war with secret U.S. agents in gathering intelligence and rescuing American flyers who had crashed in Vietnam. In August 1945, in anticipation of the entry of Nationalist Chinese and British forces to accept the surrender of the Japanese, the Viet Minh organized mass demonstrations of popular support and persuaded Emperor Bao Dai to abdicate. On September 2 the Viet Minh leader and long-time Communist Ho Chi Minh declared the independence of the Democratic Republic of Vietnam. In his speech in Hanoi on that occasion, Ho invoked the words of the American Declaration of Independence to justify Vietnam's claim to self-determination and independence and appealed to President Truman for support of that cause.

When the British landed in southern Vietnam they ousted the Viet Minh committee functioning as the local government in Saigon and used Japanese troops to drive the Viet Minh into the countryside in preparation for the French return to the part of the country they called Cochin China. Meanwhile the DRV government in the north was coping with the presence of almost 200,000 ill-disciplined Nationalist Chinese troops who entered to disarm the Japanese and seized the opportunity to take whatever they could from the local population. Faced with the need for leverage to get the Chinese to withdraw, Ho's government decided to acquiesce in the return of French forces to the north in 1946.

The French Phase (1946–1954).   Once back in, the French rejected the Viet Minh's declaration of independence and for the next eight years the two antagonists were locked in combat on the battlefield and at the negotiating table. To

counter the DRV's ambition to liberate all of Vietnam, the French restored Bao Dai to his throne and threw their support in Cambodia and Laos behind monarchs sufficiently tractable to serve French interests. By 1950 France was ready to allow the establishment of three "Associated States" within the French Union, an arrangement giving France continued control of its finances and defense. Western governments accorded diplomatic recognition to those states, as did the communist governments to the Democratic Republic of Vietnam, whose cause had benefited from the Chinese Communist victory in 1949. The DRV backed communist independence movements, the Pathet Lao and the Khmer Issarak, in neighboring Laos and Cambodia.

So the foreign and indigenous players were now in place on the scene and had chosen their parts. To the French, the Americans, and the French puppet monarchs, the contest was a battle against communism, local and international. To China, the Soviets, the DRV government, the communist resistance in Laos and Cambodia, and to many noncommunist nationalists in Indochina, the contest was a struggle of nationalism and self-determination against colonialism. By 1954 the principal international actors were ready to attempt a negotiated settlement and agreed to meet at Geneva to discuss Indochina as well as other issues, including Korea.

The Geneva Conference, 1954.   The conference brought together representatives from the United States, France, the United Kingdom, the USSR, China, the Democratic Republic of Vietnam, and the three Associated States of Vietnam, Laos, and Cambodia. Although the major powers failed to resolve the problem of Korean reunification, the conference did produce agreement on the neutralization and demilitarization of Laos and Cambodia and an armistice between France and the DRV. Viet Minh forces were to withdraw north of the seventeenth parallel and French forces south of it, with all-Vietnam elections to be held within two years to determine the future of the country. An international commission of representatives of Canada, India, and Poland (Western, nonaligned, and Eastern) was created to oversee the armistice and the elections.

The Geneva meeting was significant in other ways. It coincided with the defeat of the French at Dien Bien Phu by Ho's forces. The loss convinced the French that although the enemy might not have the military power to oust them from Vietnam, neither did they themselves have the capacity to defeat the Viet Minh decisively. Facing a colonial struggle closer to home in Algeria, they opted out of Indochina and completed withdrawal of their armed forces in 1956, convinced that the United States could be counted on to continue the struggle against the Communists. President Eisenhower endorsed the "domino theory," according to which the "fall" of Vietnam would topple noncommunist governments in the rest of Southeast Asia and threaten Japan and the West's access to vital raw materials and markets.[1]

Geneva also signaled international acceptance of the PRC as a major participant in world affairs, although the United States still refused to recognize it as the government of China and Secretary of State Dulles declined to shake the hand of Prime Minister Zhou Enlai during the meetings. Neither the United States nor the Bao Dai government in southern Vietnam signed the agreements, objecting to any concession to the Viet Minh, and the United States was already at work on negotiations for SEATO to line up defenses against communist aggression and the alliances with Taiwan and South Korea. Nor was the DRV happy with the concessions it made under pressure from the Soviets and the Chinese in pursuit of their own agenda of "peaceful coexistence." It had agreed to withdraw from areas it controlled south of the seventeenth parallel, to the temporary division of the country at a line further north than seemed fair, and to de facto recognition of the French-created State of Vietnam as a partner in arranging countrywide elections. However, given their assessment of the limited popular appeal of Bao Dai's government even to noncommunists, the Viet Minh had reason to expect they would win those elections.

What was the outcome of the Geneva agreements? As one American journalist put it: "In the end, the Geneva Conference produced no durable solution to the Indochina conflict, only a military truce that awaited a political settlement, which never really happened. So the conference was merely an interlude between two wars—or, rather, a lull in the same war."[2]

The Lull Between Wars (1954–1957).   The "lull" after Geneva lasted until the end of the decade. During that time, Vietnamese leaders north and south of the armistice line worked at strengthening their political bases with the help of their chief outside patrons, China and the United States. In the south Ngo Dinh Diem, Bao Dai's prime minister, maneuvered against his political opponents with open and clandestine support from the United States. A Roman Catholic, Diem persuaded influential Americans, including then-Senator John F. Kennedy, that he was the Vietnamese political figure most capable of successful resistance to the communists. The exodus from the north of nearly a million Catholics, with American encouragement and transport, seemed to demonstrate the magnetism of their coreligionist's government. Again with U.S. support, Diem resisted entering into consultations for the all-Vietnam elections, arguing that fair and free elections would be impossible in areas controlled by the Viet Minh. Instead, he held a referendum in October 1955 to abolish the monarchy and establish the Republic of Vietnam with himself as president, winning more than 98 percent approval, a majority of dubious authenticity. The DRV government protested the South's failure to comply with the Geneva agreement on elections in the whole country, but the protest fell on deaf ears among the great powers, including the Soviet Union.

At that point the Diem government's effective control of the territory south of the seventeenth parallel was mainly limited to Saigon and other cities; much of the Mekong Delta and the rest of the countryside was beyond the reach of his officials and military. So Diem undertook a campaign to win over the peasants with a half-hearted land reform program and to eliminate other resistance by arresting and detaining supporters of the Viet Minh, Buddhists suspected of disloyalty to the regime, the Cao Dai, and other armed sect members. American-trained police and the Army of the Republic of Vietnam (ARVN) used intimidation, torture, and other terror tactics to coerce village chiefs to carry out government orders. One of Diem's projects was the forced creation of *agrovilles,* new rural settlements fortified against Viet Minh infiltration. They did not meet with much success initially, but the concept was revived later by enthusiastic American advisers as the "strategic hamlet" program. Based on the successful use of a similar program by the British in curbing the

Ho Chi Minh

Ho Chi Minh.

Source: Photo AP/Wide World.

The revered founding father whose portrait adorns offices and other public places in Vietnam, "Uncle" Ho was born in central Vietnam in 1890. His birth name was Nguyen Tat Thanh, Ho Chi Minh being one of several pseudonyms he used during his underground political career. His father was an educated man, a minor official until discharged for his anticolonial views. Ho received his secondary education at a *lycée* in Hue and taught in a village school before leaving for Saigon to learn a trade. In 1911 he shipped out as a messboy on a French ship and for the next thirty years did not return to Vietnam.

Ho's travels took him to Africa, Europe, perhaps the United States, in various jobs including restaurant worker in England and photo retoucher in Paris. There during World War I he joined the French Socialist Party and tried to get attention for the cause of Vietnamese independence at the Versailles Peace Conference. When the French socialist movement split, Ho sided with the leftists and became a founding member of the French Communist Party. From then on his time was spent in communist training and organizational activities for the international communist movement (the Comintern) in Paris, Moscow, China, Thailand, Singapore, and Indochina. He met many of the European Communist leaders and gradually fitted his understanding of communist doctrine to the situation in colonial Indochina. One of the founders of the Indochinese Communist Party in Hong Kong in 1930, he was jailed by British authorities in 1931 and deported. He spent most of World War II in China, returning briefly to Vietnam in 1941 with the support of the Chinese Nationalists to form a united front, the Viet Minh, of organizations committed to resisting Japanese and French imperialism. During the Japanese occupation Ho ordered the creation of military units inside Indochina to engage in the dual job of propagandizing among the people and (with less emphasis) in armed struggle against the Japanese, including assistance to downed Allied flyers and to the U.S. Office of Strategic Services' clandestine operations in occupied Indochina.

Ho finally returned to his native land on the eve of the Japanese defeat and proclaimed the establishment of an independent Vietnam in September 1945. Negotiations with the returning French for some degree of self-rule ended in failure and from 1946 to 1954 Ho, with a cadre of trusted associates, managed the war against the French and other affairs of the Viet Minh, the party, and the government from headquarters in a liberated base area north of Hanoi. When the 1954 Geneva conference brought international recognition of the Democratic Republic of Vietnam, the seat of government moved finally to Hanoi, and from then until Ho's death in 1969, he held various positions as president, prime minister, and party secretary.

The object of vituperation in the United States and among his political opponents in South Vietnam during the American phase of Vietnam's war of independence, Ho is venerated in his homeland as the consummate independence leader and founding father, a person who never married but was like a beloved uncle to many of his people. In life Ho lived simply, even austerely, shunning ostentation; it is ironic that his wish to be cremated and have his ashes scattered in various parts of Vietnam was overridden by his colleagues. Instead his body (like Lenin's and Mao's) was put on display in a huge stone mausoleum in the capital city and is visited by thousands each year.

communist insurgency in Malaya, the lesson turned out not to be transferable to Vietnam. Unlike Malaya, where the insurgents were mainly Chinese and easily distinguished from the Malay population, in Vietnam the insurgents were Vietnamese, indistinguishable from the rest of the population among whom they moved.

NLF Insurgency Begins.   During the early years after Geneva the DRV was concentrating on building up its strength in the North and embarking on socialist economic reconstruction. Its leaders strongly counseled the Viet Minh partisans in the South against initiating full-scale rebellion against Diem, arguing that such action was too risky and doomed to failure. But beginning in 1957 under the impact of Diem's campaign of terror against them, Viet Minh and other targets of RVN who managed to escape arrest reverted to tactics used in the anti-French struggle and went underground, forming guerrilla bases in the countryside and engaging in assassinations of village collaborators, hit-and-run attacks on ARVN and police, and various forms of armed resistance. By 1960 Hanoi conceded legitimacy to insurrection against Diem and authorized the organization of the National Liberation Front (NLF), a coalition of communists and noncommunists united by their opposition to Diem, with the objective of liberating the South. The NLF (called "Viet Cong" by its opponents) organized its military forces as the People's Liberation Armed Force

(PLAF) and in 1969 formed the Provisional Revolutionary Government (PRG), the counterpart of the RVN government in areas in the South under NLF control.

To the United States, the anti-Diem movement in the South was instigated by and directed by North Vietnam as part of the global communist campaign of subversion and aggression, a breach of the Cold War line drawn at the seventeenth parallel. The NLF maintained that it was of local southern origin, with little help initially from the North and that it included not just Communists but a broad spectrum of noncommunists opposed to Diem's regime.

In the next few years, Diem's popularity dwindled further despite continuing U.S. aid and advice from American military personnel, whose numbers increased from under 1,000 at the time Kennedy became president in 1961 to 11,000 in 1962 to 16,000 in 1963. The strategic hamlet rural pacification program failed to reduce NLF dominance in the countryside, and Buddhist monks led demonstrations in the cities, using self-immolation as a dramatic form of protest against Diem. Now disenchanted with their protégé, the Americans were willing to see him ousted in a military coup in November 1963, just weeks before President Kennedy's assassination. Unfortunately for the South's government and U.S. purposes, Diem was replaced by a succession of military officers none of whom was able to keep the situation from deteriorating further.

United States and North Vietnam at War (1964–1973).   The year 1964 saw an intensification of American involvement, as President Lyndon Johnson authorized support for South Vietnamese commando raids on the North Vietnamese coast. When two U.S. destroyers gathering intelligence in the Gulf of Tonkin reported being fired on by North Vietnamese patrol boats, Johnson asked for a Congressional resolution authorizing him to use force to repel armed attacks on American forces, and he ordered air strikes against North Vietnamese naval bases. Thus the United States moved beyond supplying South Vietnam with weapons, intelligence, and advice to overt military action by American forces, a fateful step further into the quagmire.

A flurry of efforts by third parties at diplomatic settlement met with failure. French President de Gaulle urged an end to foreign intervention and offered to serve as mediator. UN Secretary-General U Thant proposed a meeting in Rangoon, and Soviet Prime Minister Nikita Khrushchev pressured North Vietnam to agree to attend. The Soviets and North Vietnamese called for reconvening the Geneva conference. But the Americans, needing time to bolster the disintegrating government in South Vietnam, were not ready to negotiate, and North Vietnam was making preparations to send army units south. In October 1964 the first units of the North's People's Army of Vietnam (PAVN) went into South Vietnam. In December the United States began bombing the network of footpaths and dirt roads leading from the North through parts of eastern Laos and Cambodia that became known as the Ho Chi Minh Trail.

In 1965, faced with further deterioration in the political situation in South Vietnam and convinced that a strategy of mounting military pressure would convince Hanoi to stop its "aggression" against the South, President Johnson rapidly escalated U.S. military participation in the war. Ground combat forces were sent to fight in the South and naval and air forces struck the PLAF and PAVN in the South, the North, Laos, and Cambodia from bases in Thailand, South Vietnam, Guam, and the Philippines. The number of Americans involved rose from 23,000 at the beginning of 1965 to 540,000 in 1968, and they were joined by Thai, Filipino, and South Korean contingents paid for by the United States.

The fighting intensified, with heavy casualties on both sides, reaching an orgy of bloodletting early in 1968 at the time of the Vietnamese new year's holiday, Tet. Departing from their customary small-scale hit-and-run style of warfare, the PLAF and PAVN mounted a countrywide offensive against Saigon and other cities and towns throughout South Vietnam. They did not succeed in holding any of their conquests for long except Hue, which they occupied for nearly a month before American and ARVN troops retook the city in fierce street-by-street fighting. Tet cost both sides dearly. Communist casualties, estimated at 50,000,[3] hit the southerners especially hard, and the vacancies in the NLF organization left by their deaths were filled by northerners. But, while Tet was militarily a defeat for the Communists, it contributed to President Johnson's decision to make a serious offer of negotiation. As evidence of good faith, he stopped air and naval attacks on all except the southern part of the DRV and later in the year ordered a complete halt to bombing of the North.

Talks between the United States and Hanoi began in Paris in May 1968, joined in 1969 by the Provisional Revolutionary Government and a reluctant Saigon government that objected to giving the PRG status as an independent entity. While the war continued, negotiations dragged on for five years, at an impasse over American insistence that PAVN withdraw from the South and the Communists' insistence on PRG inclusion in a coalition government in Saigon. When Richard Nixon became president in 1969 (a year also marked by the death of Ho Chi Minh), he kept up military pressure on the North, bombing their supply lines in Laos and Cambodia and sending ground troops into Cambodia in 1970 to destroy the communist command center for South Vietnam. In 1972, after a new communist offensive, Nixon resumed bombing in the North and ordered the mining of Haiphong Harbor, through which Soviet and Chinese aid came. In the South, Nixon decided, the answer to mounting antiwar pressure at home was to accelerate "Vietnamization." That meant preparing ARVN to take over full responsibility for combat south of the seventeenth parallel, allowing the gradual withdrawal of U.S. ground forces. Nixon announced a new "doctrine" redefining the U.S. security role toward South Vietnam and other Asian countries: America would live up to its obligations to its allies by continuing to provide economic and military aid, but from then on those countries would have to rely on their own troops—not American troops—to defend themselves.

The Paris Accords of 1973 and After.   Finally in 1973 the negotiations reached a conclusion with the signing of the Paris accords. The agreement was for a cease-fire in place (leaving South Vietnam a patchwork of areas under communist and RVN control), for the withdrawal of all "foreign" (that is, U.S.) forces, and for the recognition of the PRG as one of two administrative entities in the South. Negotiations were to follow among representatives of those two and of other South Vietnamese not aligned with either, leading to the creation of a National Council of

Concord and Reconciliation and eventually to the peaceful reunification of the whole country at some unspecified future time. A secret commitment was made to North Vietnam for American help in its postwar reconstruction. South Vietnam's President Nguyen Van Thieu had adamantly refused to the terms of the Paris agreement, despite heavy pressure from Washington, until Nixon, in a secret letter, assured Thieu "of continued assistance in the post-settlement period and that we will respond with full force should the settlement be violated by North Vietnam."[4]

American troops withdrew, but the United States continued to be militarily involved, bombing Cambodia until Congress stopped it in August 1973. Although banning the use of U.S. funds for military action in Indochina, Congress did approve military aid to Thieu's government for the next two years. Reconciliation talks among the South Vietnamese never began and the cease-fire did not hold. A communist offensive early in 1975 led to the unexpectedly rapid disintegration of the more numerous and better equipped South Vietnamese military. The final collapse of RVN came with the fall of Saigon at the end of April 1975.

Laos fared somewhat better than Vietnam after the Paris accords. A cease-fire and new coalition government were agreed to between the Pathet Lao and the royalists, and the United States ordered an end to the bombing of Laos, begun in 1965 with the consent of the royalist government. When South Vietnam fell in 1975, the Pathet Lao took full control of the Laotian government, and in Cambodia the Khmer Rouge accepted the surrender of the U.S.–backed Lon Nol government. Three "dominoes" had finally fallen to the Communists.

But the "fall" produced fewer repercussions outside Indochina than had been expected when the contest between the communist and the "imperialist" camps began there thirty years earlier. During the intervening decades, alignments in world politics had shifted (as will be described later in this chapter), blurring the clarity of the sharp dividing lines of the early Cold War. In the increasingly complex game of global politics played by the two superpowers and the regional power, China, their protégés in Indochina were to be protected, but not at all cost, and expended when it served the big powers' interests. For them, the significance of the "fallen dominoes" was less strategic in the long run than hoped for or feared. But to the people of Indochina, the long struggle had incalculable and enduring significance.

Effects of the War.   Deaths and injuries took their highest toll among military and civilians in Vietnam. Bombing by the United States had stalled economic progress in the North, damaged towns, roads, and bridges, and caused evacuation of city-dwellers, but it had not destroyed the will to resist nor the apparatus of government and social order. The South was in much worse shape. Rural areas had suffered from years of American and RVN bombing and spraying forests and fields with 19 million gallons of herbicides[5] to destroy the enemy's cover and food supply, resulting in defoliated hardwood forests and unusable cropland. To destruction from the air were added the effects of ground combat. The American "search-and-destroy" sweeps through the countryside, the "free-fire zones," and the "pacification" program aimed at taking back the countryside from the NLF left bomb craters, unexploded ordnance, villages destroyed, and local leadership wiped out by one side or the other. Uprooted from their homes and livelihood, many peasants had fled into the towns and cities in search of some measure of safety. The population of Saigon and other urban areas ballooned; prostitution, black market thievery from the cornucopia of American supplies, drug trafficking, and widespread corruption among officials all contributed to demoralization in the South and to the destruction of the fabric of society.

The war accentuated historical differences between the northern and southern regions of the country. Thirty years of socialism in the North contrasted with the feverish parody of capitalism in the South, stimulated by the injection of large amounts of American money and matériel into an economy unable to put them to productive uses. Animosity was to be expected between the victors and those who had been officials and supporters of the losing side, but tensions existed too among the victorious communist comrades-in-arms. Disagreements had arisen during the war years between the PRG and DRV over military and political decisions. The southerners had of necessity accepted northern leadership in the contest on the battlefield and at the negotiating table. With victory in 1975 they found themselves pushed aside by northern "carpetbaggers," insensitive to southerners' expectation of equal partnership in shaping the future of their region.

In Cambodia, Khmer insurgents and NLF-DRV use of territory along the border with South Vietnam called down a torrent of American bombs from 1969 to 1973 (a quarter of a million tons from February to August 1973 alone[6]). As in South Vietnam, country people in the combat areas fled to the capital, Phnom Penh, which like Saigon became bloated beyond its capacity to provide housing, jobs, and services. When the Khmer Rouge took over in 1975, one of their major efforts was to force people back to the countryside. Laos too suffered U.S. bombing from 1965 to 1973, an invasion in 1971 by the South Vietnamese, as well as warfare between the government and Pathet Lao–North Vietnamese forces.

All three of the countries needed foreign assistance to rebuild, but the U.S. Congress in 1976 forbade government aid to them and in 1977 blocked funding from the World Bank and other international lending agencies to which the United States belonged. Negotiations in 1977 between Vietnam and the Carter administration on normalization of relations broke down over Hanoi's insistence that Washington honor the secret promise made by Nixon in 1973 to give aid for reconstruction. A U.S. trade embargo imposed on Vietnam in 1979 (and not lifted until 1994) cut off opportunities for private investment and commerce.

Other Asian countries benefited from the Indochina war. The economies of South Korea, Thailand, and the Philippines especially gained from military aid, bases, procurement, expenditures of American servicemen on R and R, and payments for their military's service in Vietnam. However, failure to keep South Vietnam from falling raised doubts about how far other countries could count on the United States to help them in a similar situation. Besides, the world had changed since the bipolarity of the 1950s. The Third World had emerged as a force in world politics, the communist camp was deeply split, and the East-West divide was being crossed in surprising ways, all of which had great significance for the Asian Pacific countries.

EROSION OF BIPOLARITY: NONALIGNMENT AND REALIGNMENTS

Centrifugal forces were at work in both blocs, most dramatically in the East, where the rift between the Soviet Union and China fractured the world communist movement irreparably. But in the West as well, America's dominant position changed with the recovery of Western Europe from the traumas of war and loss of empire and the phoenixlike rise of Japan from the ashes of defeat. The bloc leader's overwhelming preponderance of power diminished and its allies began to assert a degree of independence in foreign policy that was unthinkable in the early years of the Cold War. Global politics were also in the process of becoming less Eurocentric, with the rapid increase in the number of newly independent states in Asia, Africa, and the Middle East joining the older ex-colonies of Latin America in a loose affiliation as members of the "Third World." Although some Third World states were formally or informally aligned with the Western or the Eastern camps, they and their nonaligned cohorts shared a sense of themselves as distinct from the "First" and "Second" worlds. In those "worlds" industrialization had already brought the riches and the power to which the Third World aspired and the "developing" countries of the "South" (many of them being in the southern hemisphere) began to see the need for solidarity in dealing with the developed countries of the "North."

The Third World Emerges

In 1955, the year after the Geneva conference, the first meeting of leaders of ex-colonial countries took place in Bandung, Indonesia. Sukarno characterized the gathering as symbolizing "new forces" emerging to challenge the old order in world politics. Sponsored by Indonesia, Burma, and the South Asian countries of India, Pakistan, and Sri Lanka, invitations went to all independent governments in Asia and Africa except Israel, North and South Korea, Taiwan, South Africa, Australia, and New Zealand. Prime ministers and foreign ministers from twenty-nine governments attended; the East and Southeast Asians represented were Cambodia, the People's Republic of China, Japan, Laos, the Philippines, Thailand, both North and South Vietnam, and the cosponsors, Burma and Indonesia.

Discussions at the conference reflected their common concerns with maintaining their sovereignty and independence and with economic development. The final communique called for a speedy end to colonialism and pledged cooperation in development. Wide support was expressed for Chinese Prime Minister Zhou Enlai's articulation of five principles that should govern relations among countries: (1) mutual respect for sovereignty and territorial integrity, (2) nonaggression, (3) noninterference in the internal affairs of others, (4) equality and mutual benefit, and (5) peaceful coexistence. But opinion divided on the issue of alignment with either the Soviet or the American bloc. India's Prime Minister Nehru pushed for the principle of neutrality in the big power conflict. By not taking sides, the newly independent countries would serve their own interests and world peace, acting as a third-party mediator between the two opposing blocs. Some of the countries at Bandung had already chosen sides, so nonalignment failed of endorsement. The issue of alignment or nonalignment continued to divide African and Asian countries and prevented a second conference, planned for 1965, from being held.

However, representatives of twenty-five governments committed to staying out of military alliances with East or West met in Belgrade, Yugoslavia, in 1961, the first in a series of meetings of the Non-Aligned Movement (NAM). NAM membership grew over the years, and it became one of a number of regional and global groupings through which developing countries have exerted pressure on the developed world's governments and the UN and other international organizations. The criteria for qualifying as "nonaligned" are fuzzy. Some NAM members indisputably have had special ties to one side or the other. Singapore and Malaysia, while declaring commitment to nonalignment, have had security links to Britain and other Western countries since independence. Indonesia, which hosted the 1993 NAM summit meeting, also has had military ties to the United States since Suharto came to power, reversing Sukarno's tilt toward the communist side in the early 1960s. And Burma, which had scrupulously avoided foreign attachments, left the NAM at the Havana conference in 1979 on the grounds that the movement was tilting too much toward the Soviet Union.

Incentives for countries to opt for a nonaligned stance in foreign policy were heightened by the superpowers' shift in cold war rivalry from nuclear brinkmanship in central Europe to competition for influence in the uncommitted Third World. Nonalignment made countries eligible for wooing by Moscow and Washington. Governments skillful enough to encourage both suitors and avoid a firm commitment to either might manage to gain benefits from both sides, although détente between the superpowers did not rule out either side's support for antigovernment movements in Third World countries when it served their purposes.

External alignments of governments, communist parties, and insurgents in Asian Pacific countries became even more complicated with the fissure that began developing between China and the Soviet Union in the late 1950s and burst into the open in 1960.

The Sino-Soviet Split

From the Chinese perspective, there was ample reason to be wary of the Soviets, despite the shared bond of Marxism-Leninism and China's need for outside help in recovering from years of war and embarking on the task of development. Not only were the Soviets the inheritors of tsarist expansionism into Chinese territory and spheres of influence during the century of China's weakness but, after the 1927 disaster resulting from their advice to the young CPC, Moscow ceased to give aid to the Chinese communist movement. Having come to power in the world's most populous country by their own efforts, the Chinese leaders expected to be treated as equals in relations with their Soviet counterparts. Mao traveled to Moscow in 1950 to negotiate a thirty-year treaty of friendship and Soviet aid in the form of credits and technical assistance. But the seeds of conflict were already in place, finding fertile ground in disputes over their common border, in doctrinal disagreements, in contention over leadership in the communist bloc, and over policy toward the Third World. Abrupt termination of Soviet aid in 1960 signaled the chilling of relations between the two allies.

Border Issues.   After a century of vulnerability to foreign intervention and loss of territory, China's preoccupation with border security was understandable. In the decade following the Korean War, the primary enemy was, of course, America, encircling China through its alliances and bases in Korea, Japan, and Taiwan and its growing involvement in Vietnam. Still, China took issue with its ally over the frontier in the northeast along the Amur and Ussuri Rivers and in Xinjiang in the northwest. Soviet actions increased China's sense of insecurity: Moscow's pursuit of détente and arms control with the United States; Khrushchev's refusal of the Chinese request in 1958 for nuclear protection in the crisis over islands held by Taiwan; Soviet aid to India, with which China also had a border dispute; the buildup of forces along the Sino-Soviet frontier. Clashes between Chinese and Soviet forces erupted in the northeast, reaching a peak in 1969. Later, the 1978 Soviet-Vietnam treaty of friendship and the 1979 Soviet invasion of Afghanistan appeared to China as threats to its southern and western borders.

Doctrinal Disagreement.   Here the issue arose over which country had chosen the correct road to socialism. Mao's departure from the Soviet pattern to launch the Great Leap Forward and the Cultural Revolution was roundly criticized by Moscow. In response, Mao charged Khrushchev with "revisionism," with losing sight of revolutionary goals in pursuit of crass materialism. The exchange of verbal abuse reached amazing depths of vituperation and led to a rupture of party-to-party contacts between the CPC and the Communist Party of the Soviet Union (CPSU). State-to-state relations continued in chilly though correct fashion until Gorbachev's overtures in the 1980s began a slow warming process.

Bloc Leadership and Policy Toward the Third World.   Stalin's assumption and Khrushchev's insistence that Mao must acknowledge the leading role of the USSR in the communist camp galled the Chinese. Sensitive to issues of international status after the century of unequal treaties with Western powers, they refused to be treated as subordinate and charged the Soviets with the sin of "hegemonism." From that point on, China successfully challenged the CPSU for dominant influence in Vietnam and Korea and with nonruling Communist Parties in Indonesia, Malaysia, Thailand, and Japan. Policy toward noncommunist Third World governments was also in contention. At issue was whether to support local Communists in pushing for a socialist revolution in those countries (Mao's preference) or to cooperate with noncommunist but anti-imperialist, "bourgeois nationalist" leaders (Khrushchev's choice).

Repercussions of the Sino-Soviet Split.   The immediate effect of the rupture between the leader of the communist bloc and its Asian challenger was to confront ruling and nonruling communist parties around the world with a choice of siding with one of them, trying to stay on good terms with both, or splitting into rival Maoist and pro-Soviet parties. In Asia, China had the assets of proximity, of being Asian, and of experience in making a socialist revolution in an overwhelmingly agrarian society. To many Third World communists, Mao's revision of Marxism-Leninism fit their societies better than the Soviet pattern because they were, as

China had been, still preindustrial and lacked an urban working class to be the revolutionary base. But while China might be a more inspiring model than the Soviets to Asian revolutionaries, Moscow was richer and in a better position to give tangible assistance to communist governments and parties.

Longer-term effects on communist parties and states of rivalry between China and the Soviet Union were particularly visible in Vietnam and Cambodia after the Indochina War. Though Vietnam received help from both of them throughout the struggle for unification, when the war ended old enmity between China and Vietnam surfaced. It was triggered by Vietnam's refusal to join China in opposition to the Soviet Union, by rival claims to the Spratly and Paracel Islands, by Vietnam's treatment of its Chinese community, and by its assertion of a "special relationship" with Cambodia and Laos. The Khmer Rouge objected to the latter, resenting Vietnam's annexation in the nineteenth century of Cambodian territory in the lower Mekong Delta and the dominant role asserted by Vietnamese in the Indochina communist movement since its beginning in 1930. Pol Pot's Democratic Kampuchea government launched repeated attacks along the border with Vietnam and the Chinese provided him with aid, completing the triangle of tensions. Faced with hostility on two fronts, Vietnam sought assistance from the Soviets, signing a treaty of friendship in November 1978.

The next month Vietnam invaded Cambodia, ousted the Khmer Rouge, and replaced them with a new communist government of former Khmer Rouge more receptive to its interests. Vietnam's intervention and continued occupation of Cambodia met with almost universal condemnation as a violation of that country's territorial integrity and political independence and, despite Pol Pot's record of genocide against his people, Democratic Kampuchea was allowed to keep Cambodia's seat in the United Nations. China and Thailand threw their support behind Khmer Rouge guerrilla warfare against the new government of Heng Samrin, and China launched a brief punitive invasion into Vietnam in February 1979. The United States, by then having restored full diplomatic relations with China, indirectly supported the KR in giving aid to the two other resistance movements led by Prince Sihanouk and Son Sann, which joined with the KR in a coalition government-in-exile. All this produced the curious situation where the leader of the anticommunist bloc, its ally Thailand, and other ASEAN members were lined up on the same side with Communist China and Communist Khmer Rouge against the new communist government in Cambodia, Vietnam, and the Soviet Union. It is hard to imagine any clearer demonstration of the irrelevance of ideological bonds in determining international affiliations.

Finally, the split between China and the Soviet Union made it possible for a new triangular pattern eventually to emerge in Chinese-Soviet-American relations. It gave them room to maneuver in playing the old game of balance-of-power politics, each siding with one against the other to bring about some desired change in the latter's behavior and then switching sides for some other purpose. The guiding principle underlying this intricate improvisation was flexibility, meaning "no permanent allies, no permanent enemies, only permanent interests." Both of the others should be acceptable as a partner when partnership would serve one's national objectives, but no partnership should ever become so firm as to threaten the third power with permanent isolation. Clearly this new game was to be much more complex than the "us versus them" lineup of early cold war bipolarity, and it would require more sophistication and less messianic fervor on the part of foreign policymakers than before. Fortuitously, such men were on the scene in Beijing and Washington as the 1970s began.

Sino-American Accommodation

Recognition of the possibility of radical change in relations came slowly. The rupture between Beijing and Moscow meant that China now had two major enemies, America and the Soviet Union, and the abrupt termination of Soviet aid in 1960 forced it to take the path of self-reliance in foreign relations. Though deprived of help from Soviet weapons experts, Chinese scientists successfully tested a nuclear device in 1964, gaining China entry into the exclusive club of nuclear weapons states. The Cultural Revolution came the next year, turning attention inward and further isolating China from external affairs. America during that period was absorbed in the Vietnam War and in groping toward a redefined relationship with the Soviets that would allow them to compete with each other and at the same time reduce the risks of nuclear war. This trend toward superpower cooperation struck the Chinese as ominous. By the end of the decade, China was emerging from the Cultural Revolution and getting ready to resume contacts with the outside. Nixon and Henry Kissinger were in the White House, and conditions were auspicious for a new era in relations between the two countries. The process culminating in the establishment of formal diplomatic relations in January 1979 took almost eight years from Kissinger's secret visit to Beijing in 1971, the principal roadblock to normalization being each side's position on Taiwan.

Shanghai Communique, 1972.   Americans of the author's generation, who had followed Richard Nixon's career from his early days as a crusading anticommunist, found it hard to believe the spectacle of the president in Beijing chatting with Chairman Mao and in Shanghai signing the joint communique with Premier Zhou Enlai, the very same person Secretary of State Dulles had snubbed at Geneva two decades earlier. To Chinese who had fought Americans in Korea and who for years had regarded the United States as Enemy #1, the events must have been equally startling. But Nixon's acceptance of Premier Zhou's invitation to visit earned him a secure place in the "friends of China" club, a place that survived Watergate and his resignation in disgrace from the presidency.

The Shanghai Communique expressed the two countries' agreement on principles to govern the conduct of relations between them and named next steps to be taken in developing trade and person-to-person contacts.[7] The basic principles agreed on were the same five principles Zhou had presented at the Bandung conference; added to them were statements that "progress toward normalization of relations between China and the United States is in the interests of all countries," and that "neither should seek hegemony in the Asia-Pacific region" nor "enter into agreements . . . directed at other states" (the latter to allay possible Soviet fears of Sino-American collusion against the USSR).

The communique also contained a statement of each party's views on international affairs and on Taiwan. China expressed support for the "struggle of all the oppressed people and nations for freedom and liberation" and their "right to choose their social systems," while the United States expressed support for "individual freedom and social progress . . . free of outside pressure or intervention." On the subject of Indochina, China favored the PRG's proposal for peace, while the United States supported the Republic of Vietnam's plan. On Korea, China endorsed North Korea's program for peaceful unification, while the United States said it would "maintain its close ties with and support for" South Korea and its efforts "to seek a relaxation of tension and increased communication in the Korean peninsula." China expressed support for "an independent, democratic, peaceful, and neutral Japan" and opposition to "the revival and outward expansion of Japanese militarism." The U.S. statement placed "the highest value on its friendly relations with Japan" and the continued development of "close bonds."

The differences over Taiwan were most marked. China specifically rejected any idea of "two Chinas" or "one China, one Taiwan," which the United States had suggested in 1971 as a compromise on the question of Chinese representation in the United Nations. China's position was clearly stated: that it is the "sole legal government of China, that Taiwan is a province of China," that its "liberation" is "China's internal affair in which no other country has the right to interfere," and that "all U.S. forces and military installations must be withdrawn." The American position moved closer to Beijing's by declaring that the United States "acknowledges that all Chinese on either side of the Taiwan Strait maintain that there is but one China and that Taiwan is a part of China" and that the U.S. government "does not challenge that position." Affirming its interest in "a peaceful settlement of the Taiwan question by the Chinese themselves" and the "ultimate objective" of withdrawing all U.S. forces and installations, the United States stated it would progressively reduce those forces "as the tension in the area diminishes." Domestic matters in both countries stalled further moves until the impasse on United States–Taiwan ties was overcome in 1978.

Joint Communique on Establishing Diplomatic Relations, 1978.   By the agreement on establishing diplomatic relations beginning January 1, 1979, the United States recognized the PRC as the sole legal government of China but specified that cultural, trade, and other unofficial relations with Taiwan would be maintained. This arrangement was modeled on the formula agreed on by China and Japan when they established diplomatic relations in 1972: End official government-to-government ties with Taiwan, but conduct trade and other relations through "private" organizations set up for that purpose.

In statements issued separately from the communique, each government recorded its position on related issues. China reiterated the point that how to bring Taiwan "back to the embrace of the motherland . . . is entirely China's internal affair."[8] For its part, the United States announced that with the establishment of diplomatic relations with the PRC, it would end diplomatic relations with Taiwan, start withdrawing its forces, and terminate the 1954 defense treaty a year later. No explicit commitment was made by China to refrain from the use of force to regain

Taiwan nor by the United States to stop supplying arms to the island. The arms issue continues to be a bone of contention in Sino-American relations, as is the provision Congress wrote into the 1979 Taiwan Relations Act that the United States has the right to provide Taiwan with defensive armaments. Diplomatic ties between the United States and Taiwan are handled through the technically "private" American Institute in Taiwan and the Coordination Council for North American Affairs in Washington.

After 1979.   The establishment of diplomatic relations was followed by a gradual increase in trade and U.S. private investments and a period of close strategic cooperation in intelligence gathering and military consultations stimulated by the two countries' shared concern over the Soviet invasion of Afghanistan and its support of Vietnam's invasion of Cambodia. The "honeymoon" was marred by China's strong objections to a deal offered in 1981 by President Reagan to sell China high-tech arms it wanted and at the same time sell advanced fighter planes to Taiwan. China maintained that such arms sales were interference in its internal affairs contrary to the U.S. acknowledgment in the Shanghai communique that Taiwan is a part of China.

After long negotiations, another communique was agreed on in 1982 that mitigated, but did not really resolve, the differences on arms to Taiwan or the possibility of forceful unification. The communique referred to the Chinese government's "fundamental policy to strive for a peaceful solution to the Taiwan question" and to American intention to reduce arms sales and not to "exceed, either in qualitative or in quantitative terms, the level of those supplied" since 1979.[9] No date was set for ending arms sales, and the controversy flared up again in 1992 when President Bush decided to allow Taiwan to buy American fighter planes. But with the dissolution of the common enemy—the Soviet Union—relations between China and the U.S. deteriorated. By 1995 the issue of arms sales to Taiwan, rather than being resolved, had broadened into an entire "package" of issues. The United States was vociferous in its opposition to China's underground nuclear testing in early May 1995. In June, the United States permitted President Lee to visit as a "private" citizen which provoked an angry Chinese denunciation. In March of the following year, the Chinese apparently sought to influence the outcome of Taiwan's first direct presidential election by holding military exercises off its eastern coast facing Taiwan, even lobbing "dummy" missiles within 30 kilometers of the island's coast. This prompted the United States to send two aircraft carriers to the region in a show of support for Taiwan.

Despite this extravagant display of antipathy between China and the United States over Taiwan, hostilities between the two countries were actually quite clearly delimited and contained by each country's economic interests in the other. For China, the U.S. market is indispensable for its flourishing export trade while for the U.S. China continues to hold out the promise of one billion customers for U.S. products. An accommodation of this flareup, therefore, was reached in mid-1996 in the course of a few high-level meetings between U.S. and Chinese defense officials after which both sides described the Taiwan issue as "successfully resolved." The Clinton-Jiang summit in 1998 was cordial, with the Chinese displaying a surprising degree of candor in their live television coverage of exchanges between Presidents Clinton and Jiang and between Clinton and students at Beijing University. President Clinton affirmed U.S. support for China's "three no's policy"—not to support independence for Taiwan, a two-Chinas policy, or membership for Taiwan in any organization for which statehood is a requirement—and President Jiang offered "strong and quite unambiguous" commitment not to devalue China's currency in face of the regional economic crisis and a promise to refrain from exporting nuclear or missile technology to Pakistan.

All this did not preclude yet another serious deterioration of relations between the ascendant great power in Asia and the remaining superpower in 1999. First came a Pentagon report which concluded that China's military modernization posed a serious threat to U.S. strategic interests in East Asia; then the long awaited congressional (Cox) report was leaked to the press rife with allegations of Chinese spying and the culpability of a Taiwanese-born scientist at the nuclear weapons laboratory in Los Alamos; and finally, the most damaging of all to Sino–U.S. relations was the "accidental" U.S. bombing of the Chinese Embassy in Belgrade which took the lives of three people. This was sufficient to induce China's suspicions that "hostile forces were at work in the West to ruin China." After President Lee Teng-hui took advantage of this deterioration of relations between China and the U.S. to provoke the communist leadership even further, with his suggestion that Taiwan could only negotiate with China on a "special state-to-state" basis, the United States once again mollified the Chinese leadership by reiterating its support of the "one-China policy."

This on-again off-again pattern of conflict between China and the United States over Taiwan is likely to recur, though any improvement in the relationship between Taiwan and China may change the focus of disputes between China and the United States away from the issue of Taiwanese security to issues of Japanese security or the balance of trade. If the new pro-independence president of Taiwan, Chen Shui-bian, can ease cross-strait tensions with the mainland, for example, hostilities between the United States and China are much more likely to be redirected rather than reduced. Two such continental-sized, regional and global great powers as China and the United States facing one another across the Pacific are likely to find themselves in conflict with one another for as long as Russia remains relatively weak.

Sino-Japanese Relations

As a loyal ally, Japan's government had followed American policy by maintaining diplomatic relations with the Chinese Nationalist government to the exclusion of official ties to the communist government. Nevertheless, Japanese companies engaged in trade with the mainland and as that trade grew, so did their pressure on the Liberal Democratic Party (LDP) to distance itself from American policy toward China. When Nixon, without prior notice to the Japanese government, announced that he was going to China, Japan quickly moved ahead of its ally, extending full recognition to the Beijing government in 1972. With China's assent, under the "Japan formula" economic and cultural relations continued between Japan and Taiwan through unofficial associations.

It took six more years of negotiations, complicated by concurrent Japan-Soviet negotiations over fishing rights and over the islands taken from Japan at the end of

World War II, for China and Japan to reach agreement on the peace treaty of 1978, which officially ended the state of war between them. At China's insistence, an "antihegemony" pledge was written into the treaty, part of China's effort to secure itself against superpower ambitions. Although at times China suggested that Japan should beef up its military defenses against the Soviet threat, the lingering specter of revived Japanese militarism led it to accept continuation of the U.S.–Japan security relationship as a restraint on that occurring. Increased trade and Japanese loans and investments followed the signing of the peace treaty, all important to China's Four Modernizations program. Strains have appeared over Japan's trade surplus, the treatment in Japanese textbooks of the country's actions in the war in China, and a dispute over possession of Diaoyutai/Senkaku Island in the Yellow Sea.

To China's diplomatic successes in opening relations with the United States and Japan was added the signing in 1984 of the agreement with the United Kingdom for the transfer of Hong Kong to China in 1997 and a similar agreement on Macau with Portugal signed in 1987 to return Macau to China in 1999.

While bipolarity declined and contacts grew between communist and noncommunist countries, the first steps toward regional cooperation in Southeast Asia were being taken, resulting in the inauguration of ASEAN in 1967.

ASEAN's Role

The founding members of the Association of Southeast Asian Nations were the Philippines, Thailand, Indonesia, Malaysia, and Singapore (Brunei joined in 1985, after it became independent). More seemed to divide them than unite them. Two members were militarily allied with the United States and had American bases on their territory; the others were nonaligned, though Western-leaning, and professed resistance to the presence of foreign bases. Rule by three different colonial powers inhibited the development of ties among them, so that at the time of independence their ties with the United States, Britain, and the Netherlands were much closer than the ties with each other. Furthermore, their economies were competitive, not complementary, and the goal of development set them in competition with each other for external aid, trade, and investment. Finally, there were territorial disputes among them, most over colonial-imposed boundaries, that threatened amicable relations in the region. The most recent flare-up prior to ASEAN's founding had been over the proposal to incorporate the British colonies on the island of Borneo, along with Singapore and Malaya, in a new Federation of Malaysia. Objections were raised by Indonesia and the Philippines, which laid claim to Sabah as having belonged to the Sultan of Sulu. When Britain and Malaya went ahead with the Federation in 1963, Sukarno waged Konfrontasi, a propaganda barrage combined with sporadic raids against Malaysia, which only ended with his ouster in 1965.

The desire to settle future disputes such as these among themselves, thereby avoiding opportunity for outside powers such as China, the Soviet Union, and Japan to fish in troubled waters, was one motivation behind the establishment of ASEAN. The United States, according to David J. Steinberg,[10] was favorably inclined to closer ties among the anticommunist governments in the neighborhood of Vietnam, where the war was reaching a crescendo. And each of the member states saw that coordinating their foreign policies on specific issues and cooperation in economic, technical, and cultural matters might increase their international clout politically and economically. So they agreed to establish ASEAN, successor to two regional institutions: Maphilindo (Malaya-Philippines-Indonesia), set up in 1963 at Philippine initiative, and the Association of Southeast Asia (Thailand-Philippines-Malaysia), which had held ministerial-level sessions in 1966.

According to ASEAN's founding declaration, its purpose is cooperation to promote economic growth, peace, and stability in the region. The emphasis, in the words of Thanat Khoman, then foreign minister of Thailand and a leading figure in ASEAN's founding, "would be on economic and other nonmilitary activities," purposely excluding military matters "because of the unhappy experience with the Southeast Asia Treaty Organization (SEATO), which failed dismally because of divergent interests between the European and Southeast Asian members."[11] The declaration contained a reference to all foreign bases as "temporary," remaining only with the consent of the host countries, and not "to be used directly or indirectly to subvert" their national independence or the "orderly processes of their national development."[12] Membership was open to all states in the region and a modest institutional framework set up: annual meeting of foreign ministers, and later economic ministers, as needed, with a standing committee to function between those gatherings, and a national secretariat in each member state. A small central secretariat was later formed in Jakarta.

In the first two decades of its existence, ASEAN achieved some success in fostering cooperation on efforts to open markets, stabilize commodity prices, reform the international monetary and trading systems, and deal with extraregional powers on trade, aid, and investment matters. But no progress was made on regional economic integration, either in joint projects or on regional trade liberalization, and intra-ASEAN trade remained quite small. Political cooperation has come more easily since, as Evelyn Colbert points out,[13] the members' foreign policy goals—resist great power interference and get Western help for development—are harmonious and their elites have a similar conservative orientation, seeing political stability as a higher priority than democracy and, as a result of experience with insurgencies, strongly anticommunist and wary of China and the Soviet Union.

One foreign policy initiative taken collectively during this period was the endorsement of the principle of neutrality for the region, the goal being to gain big power acceptance of Southeast Asia as a zone of peace, freedom, and neutrality (ZOPFAN). ZOPFAN and ASEAN's nonalignment as an organization were not regarded as incompatible with existing security ties linking Thailand and the Philippines to the United States and Malaysia and Singapore to the Commonwealth countries. A second issue of more immediate collaborative action concerned Indochina after the end of war there and lessened American presence. At the first ASEAN summit meeting in 1976 in Bali, the leaders agreed that a U.S. "over-the-horizon" military presence was needed for regional stability and that friendly relations with newly unified Vietnam should be sought to wean it away from China and the Soviets and toward closer identification with Southeast Asian countries. Those hopes were dashed by the Vietnamese invasion of Cambodia. From 1979 on ASEAN played a major role in mobilizing international pressure on Hanoi to withdraw and on efforts to negotiate the formation of a representative government in Cambodia, which culminated in the 1991 Paris agreement. The Cambodian issue most directly concerned Thailand, the only "frontline" ASEAN state, while Indonesia, less ready than Bangkok to see Hanoi as China's successor in the role of chief regional threat, countered any anti-Hanoi ASEAN "tilt," keeping channels of communication open and sponsoring informal meetings of interested parties in Jakarta to explore possible ways of settling the Cambodian issue.

ASEAN's stature in international affairs has been enhanced with the waning of the Cold War, which opened up new opportunities for creative adaptation to the changing context of global and regional politics. That and other recent developments in international relations are the subject of the next section.

THE END OF THE COLD WAR:
NEW AFFINITIES, OLD ENMITIES

Like its beginning, the cold war's ending originated in events in Europe, and Asia felt the repercussions of the momentous changes in Eastern Europe in the late 1980s and the disintegration of the Soviet Union in 1991. As superpower hostility further abated, the international environment provided opportunities for initiatives toward the resolution of long-standing regional conflicts of Cold War origin.

The post–Cold War international system differs from the Cold War era in three major respects: (1) multipolarity is replacing bipolarity as the dominant pattern in world politics; (2) nuclear deterrence is being replaced by conventional deterrence, likely to be less stable than the "balance of terror"; and (3) national security is coming to depend more on a state's own economic power, as compared to the prior primacy of military power and the protective shield of a superpower ally.[14] In the Asian Pacific region multipolarity also prevails, the major powers being China, Japan, the United States, and Russia, with the NICs and ASEAN constituting two other power groupings. Hsiung foresees that South Korea, Taiwan, and Singapore "will most likely be drawn into the Japanese economic orbit."[15] With the second largest defense budget in the world, Japan has a combined economic and military power that means its influence in the region will increase and U.S. influence decline.[16] In both the Asian Pacific and the world generally, "geoeconomic" concerns will supplant geopolitics as the motivation of foreign policy. The region deviates from the global post–Cold War pattern in the continued presence of a group of communist states and the absence, with the possible exception of Indonesia, of a surge of ethnic nationalist conflict on a scale such as that seen in Yugoslavia and several former Soviet republics.

Responses to Moscow's Foreign Policy Initiatives

Initiatives undertaken by Soviet President Gorbachev in the last years before the dissolution of the Soviet Union offered to Asian Pacific countries (as well as to the United States) opportunities to break out of the confrontationist militarized situation that had characterized relations until then. The initiatives were inspired by Gorbachev's "new thinking" about foreign policy, in recognition that success in his program of economic and political reforms required reduction in military expenditures, which in turn required a lessening of international tensions. The development of Siberia and the Far Eastern maritime provinces of the USSR would benefit by more foreign trade and investments, and that required reaching out for new relationships, especially with China, Japan, and South Korea. Accordingly, in speeches at Vladivostok in 1986 and at Krasnoyarsk in 1988, Gorbachev expressed the desire to improve bilateral relations with all countries, to work toward negotiated settlement of regional conflicts such as in Cambodia, and to reverse the military buildup in the region. Asian reaction was generally positive but cautious, awaiting deeds to back up Moscow's words. And the deeds were not long in coming.

Responses from China.   From China's viewpoint, Soviet actions in 1988 went far toward meeting the three conditions Beijing had laid down for normalization of relations: withdrawal of Soviet troops from Afghanistan, withdrawal of Vietnamese troops from Cambodia, and reduction of Soviet troops along the Chinese border. Commitments were made on all three issues, paving the way for President Gorbachev to visit Beijing in May 1989, just as the "prodemocracy" movement took shape in Tiananmen Square. It was hardly an auspicious moment for a summit meeting. The Chinese leaders' reception of Gorbachev was cool, in part because of the distraction and embarrassment of the demonstrators' occupation of the historic center of the capital city, but also because of the Chinese leaders' negative opinion of Gorbachev's glasnost and perestroika policies. Economic restructuring they could accept, even endorse, since their own economic reforms predated and went beyond those of the Soviet Union. But what about the new political ideas of "openness" that were having such a destabilizing effect in Eastern Europe and might infect other communist countries? That risk had to be guarded against in China, lest the leadership role of the Communist Party be undermined by such challenges as the misguided, even subversive, students occupying Tiananmen Square. The summit concluded without too much loss of face, and afterward, when the Chinese government forcibly cleared the square, the Soviets refrained from joining international condemnation of the act.

Since then, relations between Beijing and Moscow have continued on a normal basis, even after the breakup of the USSR. Trade has grown and, reflecting its concern with upgrading its armed forces, China took advantage of Russia's sell-off of weapons at bargain prices to buy $1.8 billion's worth in 1992.[17] In November 1993 the two countries signed a five-year military cooperation agreement aimed at further modernization of the Chinese military through technology transfer from the Russians. The removal of intermediary nuclear forces from Soviet Asia, in accordance with a U.S.–Soviet agreement, as well as withdrawal of Russian military from Mongolia and Vietnam and reduction of troops along the Chinese frontier have done much to mitigate China's apprehensions about the security threat from its northern neighbor. The relationship with Russia and the newly independent Central Asian states improved even further as China's relations with the U.S. deteriorated after 1995. In April 1996 President Jiang Zemin met with President Boris Yeltsin in Moscow; they signed their third communique resolving to settle outstanding border disputes and they agreed to establish a direct hotline telephone link between the Kremlin and Zhongnanhai. Thereafter both met in Shanghai with the leaders of Kazakhstan, Kirgystan, and Tajikistan with whom China signed a series of "confidence-building measures" which included mutual notification of troop movements and a promise that the Central Asian states would not support Muslim separatists in the northwestern province of Xinjiang.

Japanese Response.   From Tokyo's viewpoint, Gorbachev's overtures for improved relations were less well received than in Beijing, the sticking point being the "Northern Territories," the four islands in the Kurile chain closest to Japan that the Soviets, in accordance with Allied agreement, occupied at the end of World War II. Although Moscow moved away from its past insistence that ownership of the islands is nonnegotiable and has ceased to condemn the U.S.-Japanese alliance, the official Japanese position is that satisfactory settlement of the territorial issue is a requisite for the signing of a peace treaty ending the state of war that has existed since 1945 and for the establishment of normal relations between the two countries. During a state visit to Tokyo in October 1993 Russian President Yeltsin assured his hosts that signing a peace treaty was his goal and that he would live up to past Soviet commitments (which include a 1956 Soviet promise to give back two of the islands). Yeltsin also apologized for the treatment of Japanese prisoners of war detained in Soviet labor camps after World War II. Prime Minister Hosokawa asserted, "This is a new page in Russo-Japanese relations."[18]

History, economic interests, and domestic politics are underlying impediments to such a qualitative improvement in relations between the two countries. They were rivals for influence in northeast Asia at the turn of the twentieth century, marked by the Russo-Japanese War of 1905, and relations after World War II were chilled by the Cold War. Its end, from the Japanese perspective, has not meant the end of the raison d'etre of the security treaty with the United States, and Japanese public opinion still regards Russia as hostile. Nor is potential profit from joint ventures in Siberia sufficiently appealing to lure Japanese capital away from more lucrative investment opportunities in other parts of Asia. Bilateral relations between Japan and Russia have improved somewhat since 1999 when Japan quietly dropped its insistence on settling the territorial question of the Kurile Islands as a precondition for reaching other agreements. Japan has also extended overseas development aid to Russia, financed feasibility studies for modernization of Russian Far Eastern electricity plants and backed commercial development of the oil and gas fields off Russia's Sakhalin Island.

Effects on Korea.   Gorbachev's initiatives got a positive reception in South Korea, fitting nicely with President Roh's "Northern Policy" of seeking full diplomatic relations with communist countries. Discussions about expanding trade between South Korea and the USSR were held in 1989 and diplomatic relations were established in 1990. The Soviets dropped their objection to the admission of the two Koreas to the United Nations and both joined that body in 1991. South Koreans were further reassured by statements from Soviet officials that North Korea had started the war in 1950 and later reports that Stalin had been involved in planning the operation.[19]

Trade has grown, but South Korean investment in Russia has been very limited and the government suspended economic aid because of Moscow's failure to keep up interest payments on earlier loans and to pay compensation for the shooting down of a Korean Air Lines plane that overflew Soviet territory in 1983.[20] The focus of South Korea's interest is in the Russian Far East where maintaining influence is important for the long-term, when a reunited Korea would be in a position to contribute toward development of the region. A bilateral intergovernmental agreement already has set up a project to build a Russian-Korean Industrial Land Park near the industrial port city of Nakhodka to create favorable customs and tax terms for Korean industrial enterprises to operate within Russia.

For North Korea the opening of diplomatic relations with Seoul by Moscow and Beijing and the breakup of the Soviet Union brought an increasing sense of isolation, of abandonment by its former protectors. Economic difficulties were exacerbated by Russia's insistence on payment in hard currency for the oil it had previously supplied on generous terms, resulting in shortage of power for industry, transport, and home use. By supporting the admission of both states to the United Nations and opening formal diplomatic relations with Seoul, the Soviets seemed to signal to the North Koreans their virtual abandonment. In 1995 Russia informed North Korea that the 1961 treaty on friendship, cooperation, and mutual assistance would not be renewed when it expired in September. Although North Korea anticipated negotiating a new friendship treaty without any defense provisions with Russia, it also intended to pursue negotiations for a peace treaty with the United States that would guarantee North Korea's survival. China's attitude toward Pyongyang remained supportive on the surface, though the Chinese made pointed suggestions about the need for North Korea to undertake economic reforms.

This succession of unwelcome events that the ending of the Cold War brought contributed to North Korea's sense of being under siege. On top of the experience of being isolated from the world's nations, North Korea suffered a series of devastating floods and crop failures leading to famine in parts of the country. This post–Cold War scenario lengthened the timetable for possible reunification.

The Divided States: Relations Across the Thirty-Eighth Parallel and the Taiwan Straits

Although ideological divisions between communists and noncommunists have become less salient as a consequence of the ousting of ruling communist parties in Eastern Europe and the Soviet Union, in Asia that split remains in two cases—Korea and China. Contacts—at first unofficial, now official for Korea and semiofficial for China—have been made between the two sides, but the end of the Cold War has not removed the obstacles to reunification of the divided states.

Relations Across the Thirty-Eighth Parallel.   In the decades since the armistice ending the Korean War in 1953, North and South moved fitfully away from their initial posture of implacable hostility and avowed intention of reunification by force to a grudging acceptance of the other's existence and to the beginning in 1972 of dialogue on peaceful reunification. The talks resulted in a joint communique on principles to guide the discussion but were broken off by the North in 1973. Resumed from 1984 to 1986, and again in 1991, negotiations at the prime ministerial level produced two important agreements signed in December 1991 and ratified by both governments in 1992.

The Agreement on Reconciliation, Nonaggression, Exchanges and Cooperation between the North and the South committed them to respect for each other's government, to refrain from the use of force against each other, to the creation of a joint commission to consider alleged violations of the armistice, to setting up a hotline between Pyongyang and Seoul, and to economic and other contacts across the thirty-eighth parallel. In the second agreement, a joint declaration on nuclear arms, the two sides agreed not to acquire nuclear arms, nuclear fuel reprocessing, or uranium-enrichment capabilities and to establish a joint commission to inspect sites in both countries. (The obstacle to agreement posed by the presence of nuclear weapons in the hands of U.S. armed forces stationed in South Korea had been removed by U.S. withdrawal of such weapons late in 1991.) North Korea agreed to inspection of its nuclear power and research facilities by the International Atomic Energy Agency (IAEA).

The optimism inspired by the signing and ratification of these two agreements between North and South Korea was not matched by forward movement in relations between them until late June 1994, just on the eve of President Kim Il Sung's death. At that time, a months-long impasse over suspicions that the North was engaged in nuclear weapons development was broken and agreement reached for a July summit meeting between the two Korean presidents. Though the summit between the two leaders was foreclosed by Kim Il Sung's death on July 8, 1994, an accord between the four signatories of the Armistice was signed in Geneva in October 1994. According to the Geneva Framework Agreement (GFA), the United States agreed to broker construction of two light-water reactors in North Korea to provide for that country's energy needs in return for its promise not to pursue a nuclear program of its own.

The Nuclear Issue.   Most troubling to North-South relations has been North Korea's resistance to permitting full international inspection of its nuclear facilities to determine whether fuel was diverted for weapons purposes. Having consented to IAEA monitoring of its nuclear power plants, the North resisted the agency's request for full inspection of research sites at Yongbyon, where it was suspected that a plant for reprocessing nuclear fuel was being constructed, a violation of the 1991 North-South agreement and of the North's obligations as a party to the Nuclear Non-Proliferation Treaty. The North Korean government maintained that the plant's purpose was peaceful and denied any intent to develop nuclear weapons. International pressure for inspection continued and in 1993 North Korea announced it would withdraw from the nonproliferation treaty but suspended carrying through on its threat after high-level talks with American officials. After repeated agreements that were repudiated, the IAEA concluded it was unable to certify North Korea's compliance with its treaty obligations. Declaring its intention to seek UN Security Council sanctions against North Korea, the United States in a last-ditch effort at diplomatic resolution scheduled a meeting between President Jimmy Carter and Kim Il Sung.

The meeting with President Carter succeeded in bringing North Korea back into separate talks with South Korea and the United States. Both sets of negotiation began but were interrupted by Kim Il Sung's death. After they resumed, the Geneva Framework Agreement was concluded and signed in October 1994 by the United States, North Korea, China, and South Korea. In subsequent years, negotiations inched along as differences in interpretation of the GFA were addressed. Internal circumstances in each of the four signatory powers contributed to the snail's pace at which the mountain of mistrust separating North Korea from both the United States and South Korea was whittled away. The course North Korea set for itself to terminate its self-imposed exile from the international community began by obtaining diplomatic recognition from the United States. Nothing, not even hunger on the part of its own population, would be permitted to stand in the way of gaining international respectability as a condition of rejoining the global community of nations.

North Korea, faced with severe floods and famine, was unable to buy fuel oil and fertilizer, which for a country based on the sanctity of self-reliance, constituted a serious national security dilemma as well as an economic catastrophe. North Korea's response was to assume a posture of defensive pride in its isolation. In June 1995 when Seoul shipped 150,000 tons of rice as part of its offer of $200 million worth of food aid, North Korea made a point of *not* backing down on its insistence that South Korea be excluded from any talks between the North and the United States on the question of diplomatic recognition. When the treaty on friendship, cooperation, and mutual assistance that North Korea had signed with the Soviet Union in 1961 expired in September 1995, North Korea found itself not only ostracized by the international community but abandoned by Russia. Left without any external assurance of support for its survival as a nation, North Korea refused to participate in the four-party peace talks jointly proposed by the United States and South Korea in 1996, until North Korea had been able to engage in bilateral negotiations with the United States over a range of issues revolving around diplomatic recognition.

Perhaps as a way of pushing for such bilateral talks with the United States, North Korea engaged in a number of provocations that raised the level of mistrust between North and South Korea and between the United States and North Korea. Perhaps the most bizarre of these incidents occurred in late 1996 when a North Korean submarine ran aground on South Korean territory. The surviving commandos from the grounded submarine escaped into South Korea fanning the anxieties of South Koreans that an imminent invasion of the South by the North posed a serious military threat. In similar fashion, whenever North Korea, for whatever reasons, reminded the world that it was waiting for recognition rather than "handouts," it increased the internal political difficulties for the remaining three signatories of the GFA to finding a peaceful resolution to the division of the Korean peninsula into two armed camps. South Korea under President Kim Young Sam shifted back and forth between wielding the stick and waving the carrot at North Korea, especially given his position in the polls and the immediacy of the public's perception of belligerence from the North. On the other hand, the South Korean *government* had to worry about the possibility of a total collapse in the North.

As the North's economic situation continued to deteriorate, therefore, the focus of negotiations shifted to an agreement to supply the North with 500,000 tons of fuel oil per year until the light-water nuclear reactors could be made operational, the required funds to be provided by the United States and the European Union. South Korea, in the meantime, had delayed the start of construction of the light-water reactors while the United States resisted any further lifting of economic sanctions as well as delaying the delivery of contracted amounts of heavy fuel under the GFA until it could be assured that North Korea was no longer pursuing its nuclear program. China, for its part, remained fearful of a massive influx of North Koreans into Northern China should starvation become more widespread. The election in 1997 of Kim Dae Jung as President of South Korea brought renewed hope for an easing of tensions between the North and South. Long an advocate of a "sunshine" policy of engagement by constructive dialogue, Kim Dae Jung set his sights on entering into direct negotiations with North Korea's leaders. But setbacks seemed to occur daily. On August 31, 1998 in the course of celebrating its fiftieth national anniversary, North Korea launched a rocket that flew over Japan before landing in the Pacific Ocean. But the United States later "assessed the firing as a failed satellite launching."[21]

In this tortuous manner, North Korea has inched its way closer to rejoining the community of nations. After a break of 25 years, North Korea restored diplomatic relations with Australia in May 2000, similar relations with Italy having been established in January. North Korea is in continuing talks to normalize relations with the United States and Japan. The first substantive meeting between North and South Korea following the GFA of 1994 took place in April 1998 in Beijing at the start of the Asian economic crisis. And a historic summit meeting between President Kim Dae Jung and Kim Jong Il, which was held in Pyongyang June 12–14, 2000, succeeded beyond all expectations yielding a signed accord dedicated to promoting a peaceful path to reunification.

Plans for Reunification.   Both North and South have offered plans for reunification. The North proposes the creation of a democratic confederal republic under the slogan "one nation, one state, two systems, two regional governments." It would be a unified state with a national council of representatives from South and North in equal numbers (though the South has twice the population of the North). The armed forces of the two sides would be merged, but the two existing governments would remain as "regional" governments, keeping their individual characteristics and conducting relations with other countries while the confederal government would act internationally on behalf of the whole country.[22]

South Korea's proposal, in contrast to the North's idea of unification from the top in one fell swoop, is for a gradual process of step-by-step measures leading eventually to the creation of a unitary democratic state. Articulated by President Roh in 1989, the "Korean National Community Unification Formula" calls for an interim Korean Commonwealth, based on a charter adopted at a summit meeting and approved by the legislatures of the South and North. The commonwealth structures would consist of a joint council of presidents as the supreme decision-making body, a council of ministers of cabinet-level officials from each side to discuss various economic, social, and cultural measures to integrate the two societies, a joint secretariat and liaison offices in each capital, and a council of representatives with equal numbers of legislators from North and South to draw up a constitution for a unified democratic republic. Once the constitution is accepted, general elections would be held to form a single legislature and government for the whole country.[23]

Although a momentum appears to be building toward reunification at the opening of the twenty-first century, it is likely to take time; the problems are formidable. With the experience of German unification as an example, South Korea is aware of the costs of unification with an economically disabled other half while North Korea is keenly sensitive to the pitfalls of capitulation. What can be observed, however, is a political climate—more so in South Korea but apparently also in North Korea—that is far more receptive toward a policy of cooperative engagement between the divided countries of Korea. In the parliamentary elections held in April 2000 in South Korea, immediately following the summit announcement, the opposition Grand National Party, which had lost the presidency to Kim Dae Jung in 1997, made an impressive comeback, winning four seats short of a majority. Even more conspicuous was the new cooperative and pro-Reform spirit expressed by the new opposition leader, Charles S. Lee—a former high-court judge, who is expected to run for president in 2002.

> We've become the No. 1 party. . . . This means people now expect us to not only check and criticize the government but also to actively lead the national agenda as the opposition party . . . in a country like ours where a political culture of cooperation and synergy between the ruling and opposition parties hasn't fully developed, we could be at a point of new departure. . . . The South-North summit must turn out to be a historic meeting. And I highly value the fact that this has come to pass, and believe it should take place with all citizens' agreement and support. In my meeting with President Kim, I proposed three principles to assuage concerns that some people might have about it.[24]

When the opposition leader in South Korea not only speaks of cooperation with the ruling party on a national agenda in support of the South-North summit meeting but can also praise his opponent, President Kim, for "his record of struggling for democracy," while pinpointing the strides toward democracy that still have to be made in South Korea, it augurs well for both political reform and a new cooperative relationship between South and North to replace almost half a century of mutual hostilities.

Relations Across the Taiwan Straits.   As with Korea, relations between the People's Republic and the Republic of China have moved from military clashes in the 1950s and 1960s to verbal fusillades in the 1970s and 1980s, to virtual fusillades in the 1990s, combining expressions of continued hostility with proposals on unification, to unofficial contacts and a growth in indirect trade beginning in the late 1980s. Those contacts never reached the official status that relations between the two Koreas have, each accepting the other as a separate state. Beijing has never retreated from its insistence that Taiwan is an inalienable province of China. And as long as the Guomindang—the Nationalist Party of Chiang Kai-shek who sought refuge in Taiwan after its defeat by the communists on the mainland—remained firmly in power on Taiwan, it shared the PRC contention: There is only one China and Taiwan is a province of China. This has changed gradually as Taiwan became economically prosperous and younger generations of Taiwanese came of age politically. In 1987 when martial law was lifted by Chiang Kai-shek's son, the ban on travel to mainland China was also removed, heightening the contentiousness of Taiwan's relations with mainland China.

When the younger Chiang died in 1988 and his vice-president, Lee Teng-hui, became the island's first native-born president, other political parties were legalized, constitutional rule was restored and by 1996 full popular elections for both the legislature and the presidency had been put into effect. Two opposing interests— the political interests of the staunchly pro-independence Democratic Progressive Party (DPP) and the economic interests of Taiwanese businessmen eager to expand their investments and production facilities on the mainland—benefited from these changes. In the 2000 elections, the DPP candidate for president, Chen Shui-bian, was victorious, defeating the Kuomintang for the first time and bringing the two opposing forces to a critical juncture. To be able to follow the course of events that transpire at this turning point in Taiwanese history, a brief recapitulation of what has transpired up until now follows.

PRC's Efforts to Isolate Taiwan.   In the 1970s, a series of changes in the external environment—the Sino-Soviet split, the opening of Sino-American contacts, the removal of the U.S. Seventh Fleet from the straits, which it had been patrolling since the beginning of the Korean War, and the decision at the UN to allow PRC representatives to take China's seat—combined to reshape relations between Beijing and Taipei. Beijing's strategy was first to isolate Taiwan by insisting that, as a condition of establishing diplomatic relations with PRC, other governments must break official relations with ROC and that Taiwan be denied membership in international intergovernmental organizations before PRC would join. Taipei's response was to counter that isolation and loss of official diplomatic recognition from most of the world's governments by strengthening its economic power and increasing foreign trade. It also set up, with China's tacit consent, "unofficial" trade/diplomatic missions in Japan, the United States, and other countries that had switched from official ties with Taiwan to recognition of the PRC.

PRC Proposal for Unification.   In 1981 Beijing proposed that talks on reunification be held between the ruling parties in the two governments and called for exchanges of mail, trade, and visitors. The terms of reunification, under Beijing's "one country, two systems" formula of 1981 and elaborated in later years, would allow Taiwan considerable autonomy and minimize changes in existing institutions and practices. The proposal was that Taiwan would keep its armed forces and that Beijing would not station PLA troops on the island. Taiwan's local government and socioeconomic system would continue, its officials would participate in national politics, and Beijing promised not to interfere with Taiwan's internal affairs. But it refused international pressure to commit itself unequivocally to using only peaceful means to bring about unification, taking the position that Taiwan's relationship to the mainland is an internal matter to be decided as a sovereign right by the Chinese government.

Taiwan's response to Beijing's proposal on reunification was the "three no's": no official contacts, no compromise, no direct negotiations. Unification would be possible only when Beijing gave up communism and accepted Sun Yatsen's Three Principles and when the Chinese people freely chose reunification. PRC's proposal was regarded as impractical while conditions on the two sides of the straits were so different, and it could have no significance other than an attempt by Beijing to project a favorable image abroad.

Taiwan's Shift on Relations with PRC.   In 1987 Taiwan's policy changed from the negativity of the "three no's" to a more positive mode, signaled by the lifting of the government's prohibition on travel to the mainland. Chang attributes the shift to President Chiang Chingkuo's personal initiative just prior to his death and to the need of Taiwan's small- and medium-sized export-oriented businesses for access to the mainland market.[25] Island entrepreneurs took advantage of the lifting of travel restrictions to increase indirect trade (usually through Hong Kong) with PRC, transferring labor-intensive production to the mainland and entering into joint-venture agreements with mainland enterprises.

In 1990 the government created a cabinet-level council to advise the president on unification policies. It drew up a set of guidelines on principles for unification: recognition that Taiwan and the mainland are parts of one China and that unification must come about by peaceful and democratic means and must serve the interests of the people of Taiwan. In 1991 the Straits Exchange Foundation (SEF), a semiofficial body, was established to handle contacts with mainlanders on cross-straits matters, and Beijing created a counterpart entity, the Association for Relations Across the Taiwan Straits (ARATS). Since then SEF and ARATS have served as the ostensibly nonofficial vehicles for contacts between the two governments, enabling both sides to maintain their mutual nonrecognition as the government of China. In August 1993, however, Beijing broke off talks begun earlier that year in Singapore as a demonstration of its displeasure with Taipei's campaign for admission as a UN member.

Taipei's vision of the unification process is similar to that of South Korea, favoring a phased process in three stages. The present stage of increasing unofficial contacts is the preliminary to a second phase of direct links, requiring as a precondition that Beijing renounce the use of force against Taiwan and end its opposition to Taiwan's membership in international organizations. The final stage would be official contacts and negotiations on unification.

The preconditions are unacceptable to the PRC, as was made clear in a policy paper, "The Taiwan Question and Reunification of China," issued on August 31, 1993. The paper reiterated the "one country, two systems" position, reviewed the basis for Chinese sovereignty over Taiwan, and stated Beijing's determination to block any efforts to divide that sovereignty by admitting Taiwan to UN membership.[26] This position was reiterated in another white paper released in 2000 in response to the presidential victory of the pro-independence candidate.

Taiwan's Bid for UN Membership.   Having been evicted from most global international intergovernmental organizations following PRC's seating in the UN in 1972—though the Asian Development Bank resisted Beijing pressure to oust Taiwan, which is still represented in the ADB and also in the Asian Pacific Economic Cooperation (APEC) forum—in recent years Taipei has campaigned for readmission to various international organizations. In 1993 a group of Central American states asked the UN General Assembly to consider membership for ROC. Although the PRC can stop positive action on admission by its veto power in the Security Council, by raising the issue Taiwan gets an international forum to present its viewpoint to the rest of the world.

The case for admission is "based on the principle of universality, and on the precedents of parallel representation for divided nations."[27] Universality of UN membership, it is argued, means that the 21 million inhabitants of Taiwan, who have not been represented in the UN since the seating of the PRC, should be given a voice by the admission of Taiwan as a member. There is the precedent of the representation of the two Koreas and the two Germanies, which did not prevent German unification. To avoid seeming, by seeking separate admission to the UN, to depart from the principle that there is only one China, Taipei points out that ROC has "coexisted with the PRC within China's borders for almost half a century."[28] A further inducement is that Taiwan is able and willing to make substantial financial contributions to the work of the UN. Beijing's 1993 policy paper labels Taiwan's bid for UN membership "an attempt to split state sovereignty" and blames foreign meddling for the continued division of China.[29]

The Movement for Taiwan Independence.   Despite its effort to gain entrance to international organizations, the Guomindang, which ruled Taiwan until recently, shares Beijing's objection to the notion of a declaration of independence by Taiwan. That is, however, a step advocated by the DPP, most of whose members are native Taiwanese and whose presidential candidate won the elections in 2000. Although the new president, Chen Shui-bian, has backtracked somewhat claiming that Taiwan need not declare independence since that is already an established political fact, Beijing has reinforced its warning that any attempt to indefinitely postpone acceptance of the "one China policy" will be countered, if necessary by force. This places President Chen in a delicate position. He has the daunting task of keeping advocacy of Taiwan independence alive but carefully harnessed to avoid aggravating the PRC's animosity and upsetting the status quo in cross-strait relations.

President Chen Shui-bian has the kind of nationalist, pro-Taiwanese credentials that could enable him to reach a long-term accommodation with the mainland that would ease tensions and facilitate cross-strait direct trade and investments. Though progress on political reunification seems at an impasse with irreconcilable demands on both sides—no incentive for Beijing to accept the costs of bringing about unification by force nor economic incentive for Taiwan to seek it voluntarily—the process of economic integration is well underway, notably between Taiwan and the mainland coastal provinces of Fujian and Guangdong. Trade, investment, and travel have boomed in the 1990s and those "nonpolitical" unofficial ties may in the long term overcome or outlive political obstacles to unity. President Chen has shown both strength and restraint in his policy statements, making no concessions on "the one China" principle which Beijing demands as a precondition for negotiations but raising expectations both at home and abroad that he will bring about a breakthrough.

The peaceful transition of Hong Kong's reversion to PRC control in 1997 is a precedent that the mainland points to as a model for Taiwan but the differences between the Hong Kong and Taiwan cases are great. Still, the colony's successful experience with reunification and the subsequent problems that have emerged may yield some lessons useful to both Beijing and Taipei in preparations for changing their relationship.

RETHINKING NATIONAL SECURITY IN THE POST–COLD WAR ERA

The perennial search for national "security" takes on different dimensions with the passing of the Soviet Union as a superpower and the end of communist insurgencies everywhere in the Asian Pacific except the Philippines. What are the current and possible future threats that Asian Pacific governments perceive as causes of insecurity? What means are they using to protect their countries and promote their interests? What role in regional security do they see for the United States now that the containment of communist expansionism no longer provides the rationale that it did in the region and globally for almost a half-century? Is Japan's political and military influence in the region likely to expand, commensurate with its preeminent economic position? Is some form of multilateral defense arrangement among the Asian Pacific countries a desirable successor to bilateral alliances with the United States or to the strategy of nonalignment followed by others? Should existing regional bodies, such as ASEAN or APEC, take on new or more responsibilities in conflict resolution and other politico-military matters? These and related issues shaping the post–Cold War perspectives and foreign policies of Asian Pacific states are raised in the final section of this chapter, starting with a review of actual and potential causes of apprehension.

Threats to Security—Causes of Insecurity

Traditional geopolitical/strategic concerns have not evaporated in the post–Cold War age, despite the reality of inescapable economic, environmental, and cultural interdependence. These include calculations of the "balance of power" and the possibility that some action by a major or middle power may upset the balance, thus putting others in jeopardy. Arms races in conventional weapons, as well as the specter of nuclear proliferation, are causes for alarm. Disputes over territory remain unresolved, some over the location of land borders and over rival claims to islands of strategic, economic, or symbolic significance, and they are potential causes of armed clashes, particularly the Spratly and Paracels Islands in the South China Sea.

Other matters of concern are the vulnerability of sea lanes to blockage, especially the narrow straits between Malaysia and Indonesia, and the difficulty of preventing spillover along land frontiers from turmoil in neighboring countries, such as antigovernment forces seeking haven in Thailand from Myanmar's military government. The dangers that the division of the Chinese and Korean nations will erupt into violence or that a declining U.S. military presence will be met with increased military influence on the part of China or Japan are troubling to some, even most, Asian Pacific governments. Uncertainties about Russia continue to be a source of disquiet. While only the most paranoid would assert that Moscow now has the intent or the political unity needed to threaten its neighbors militarily, it does still have the weapons; the disintegration of the Russian Federation or the rise to power of a xenophobic nationalist movement could have profound effects, especially on Northeast Asia. Finally, mention should be made of competition over spheres of influence and the revival of old hostilities that had been at least partially muted during the Cold War. Particularly in Southeast Asia, rivalries between China and Thailand over Myanmar, between Thailand and Vietnam over Cambodia and Laos, and between Indonesia and Malaysia over political leadership are sources of tension and concern among the parties and their neighbors.

To these traditional geopolitico-strategic security issues should be added new-style "geoeconomic" concerns, a reflection of the importance that a healthy economy has for a country's security and of the degree of integration into the world economy of Asian Pacific countries (with the possible exception of Myanmar). The significance of these geoeconomic concerns was dramatically underscored by the rapid spread of the "Asian flu" which devastated entire political economies throughout the region following Thailand's financial collapse in the summer of 1997. Geoeconomics involve such concerns as vulnerability to the loss of foreign markets resulting from competitors' successes or from unilateral or multilateral protectionism or from currency exchange speculations; the influx of foreign goods under free (or freer) trade conditions that affect domestic producers adversely; the loss of access to foreign supplies of oil and other vital raw materials; the loss of private foreign investment, perhaps resulting from political instability, environmental regulations, or other conditions in the host country that discourage investors, or from restraints imposed on investors by the home governments for political purposes; and the loss of bilateral or multilateral foreign aid because donors are cutting expenditures or are withholding aid to express displeasure with the recipient government's behavior.

Not all of these concerns apply to every country, of course, but they do show the range of matters that affect foreign policy perceptions in adjusting to changes in the environment of international relations in the post–Cold War era. The economic foundation of security may be regarded as more crucial than military capabilities, as Hsiung asserts: "A consequence of the end of the Cold War is the decline of nations' concern for military security in favor of economic security. Under the circumstances, former allies may turn out to be potential adversaries (such as in trade matters). . . . The lines between allies and adversaries are blurring."[30]

Post–Cold War Security: The View from Tokyo

Tokyo's recognition of the importance of economics to national security was expressed in the early 1970s in what came to be known as the policy of "comprehensive security." Having accepted the American-imposed constitutional prohibition on maintaining armed forces and on using war as an instrument of national policy, the Japanese had chosen at the end of the occupation in 1952 to serve as a forward base for the U.S. military and to shelter under the "umbrella" of American nuclear and conventional power for protection against Soviet or Chinese expansionism. Soon, giving in to American pressure to do so, the Japanese government undertook to build a modest army and navy, circumventing the constitutional prohibition by calling them the Self-Defense Forces. Freed of primary responsibility for its own safety by the alliance that committed the United States to Japan's defense (but did not oblige Japan to reciprocate) and assured of access to American markets for the output of its industries being rebuilt with American aid, Japan was able to pursue a pacifist neomercantilist external policy, concentrating on export-oriented growth and protecting its own domestic market from foreign competition.

"Comprehensive Security" Policy.   For the first two decades after regaining its independence, Japan usually followed the U.S. lead on foreign policy issues, notably on the policy of nonrecognition of PRC. But in the early 1970s a series of events (OPEC's quadrupling of oil prices and Nixon's decision to revalue the dollar and to go to China, decisions that directly affected Japan but were made without consulting or even notifying the Japanese government) jolted Tokyo into realization of the need for active pursuit of its own interests. The concept of "comprehensive security" was devised, defining security "in a broad sense of economic well-being and invulnerability to disruptions as well as traditional military security, and the active use of diplomatic, economic and cultural initiatives as well as a strong military defence."[31] Still under American protection, Japan could concentrate on strengthening its economic position by diversifying the external sources of oil and other raw materials on which it depends and diversifying its foreign markets so it would not be vulnerable to the loss of any one of them. It also aimed at increasing foreign dependence on Japanese capital through direct foreign investments and official development assistance, and on Japanese technology, goods, and services. Reparations to countries in Southeast Asia for damages suffered during the Japanese occupation have also tied the recipients to Japan's economy. Instrumental in the founding of the Asian Development Bank (ADB) and a major contributor of its capital, Japan actively supports other instruments of multilateral economic cooperation in the Pacific Basin.

With the economic influence it gained in South Korea, China, Taiwan, and the ASEAN countries as an asset, Japan also began to take a more active role in regional political matters. It has undertaken to act as a diplomatic intermediary in regional conflicts. It maintains relations with both PRC and ROC, tries to play a bridging role between South and North Korea and between ASEAN and Vietnam. It worked for a diplomatic resolution of the Cambodian civil war and sent troops abroad for the first time since World War II to serve with the UN Transitional Authority in Cambodia, headed by a Japanese UN official. Recognizing the legacy of anti-Japanese sentiment remaining from World War II, government officials have finally in recent years begun to make formal apologies for the treatment of citizens of occupied countries. In October 1998 Japan used the occasion of an official state visit of South Korea's President Kim Dae Jung to Japan to deliver a "heartfelt" Japanese apology for its brutal former occupation of Korea. A month later when

Chinese President Jiang Zemin visited Tokyo, however, the Japanese were on the receiving end of a stern lecture by the Chinese leader warning Japan not to support Taiwan, berating Japanese "in high positions" for distorting history and calling for Japan to make a full apology to China for atrocities committed in World War II.

Japan's foreign policies now extend beyond the Asian Pacific and are global in scope. It gives bilateral aid to countries in all regions and is now the world's leading provider of foreign aid. The second largest contributor to the UN budget, Japan is an increasingly active participant in the United Nations and affiliated organizations, building a case for a permanent seat on the UN Security Council and calling for reform of the world body. Its participation in UN peacekeeping operations extended to the Middle East when it dispatched military personnel to the Middle East in 1995 to assist with logistics on the Golan Heights, winning praise from both the Israelis and the Palestinians. Diplomatically as well, Japan increased its visibility beyond the region by supporting President Yasser Arafat in the areas of Palestinian self-rule, endorsing the U.S. decision to launch missile attacks on Iraq for its incursion into Kurdish safe havens in northern Iraq in 1996, sending prime ministers with offers of aid to Latin America, and promising a conference on African development in Tokyo.

An important element in Japan's security is maintaining good relations with China. Since Japan surged ahead of U.S. leadership and established formal diplomatic ties with Beijing in 1972, relations have been calm, surviving even the Tiananmen affair with only a brief suspension of Japanese aid. The Japanese government has refrained from joining in Western criticisms of Chinese human rights conditions. Prime Minister Kaifu visited China in 1991, and Emperor Akihito made a state visit in 1992. When President Jiang Zemin visited Tokyo in 1998, however, relations between the two powers exhibited signs of strain, as noted above. Security issues started to become problematical in 1995 when China resumed nuclear testing (along with France). Japan suspended its loans to China eliciting a strong response from China, charging Japan with its own U.S. nuclear umbrella of interfering in internal Chinese defense affairs. This tension over security between Japan and China has been exacerbated since then by Japan's reaffirmation and upgrading of its military security arrangements with the U.S. This did not, however, interfere with Japan's support for China's entry into the World Trade Organization (WTO).

Military Security.   The military aspect of national security is not neglected by any means, and Japan's military power is formidable, though limited in reach. Even the self-imposed budgetary limit on military expenditure of 1 percent of the GNP is a large amount, given that the GNP is the second largest in the world. It buys technologically advanced equipment for the quarter of a million members of the armed forces. Even so, Japan cannot expect to match either Russia or China in numbers, and so far it has kept to the post-Hiroshima determination not to acquire nuclear weapons, which both of its neighbors do possess, although that option is clearly available. The Japanese government in 1993 indicated reluctance, in light of the threat of North Korea going nuclear, to commit itself indefinitely to the Nuclear Non-Proliferation Treaty. The prospect of an extensive military buildup even in conventional weapons, which might extend Japan's reach beyond the present 1,000 miles from its shores, would clearly be disturbing to other Asian Pacific countries.

A key issue in the post–Cold War period is whether the security arrangement with the United States has outlived its usefulness now that communist expansionism is no longer a threat. So far the Japanese government seems reluctant to abandon the special relationship with the United States, despite obvious strains arising from American pressure for Japan to open up its domestic markets to U.S. goods and to share more of the cost of U.S. bases. Not only is there external opposition to such a move, especially among Southeast Asians who see the United States as a restraint against potential revival of a Japanese bid for regional hegemony, but there are also internal constraints on such a departure from traditional security policy. Public opinion in the postwar period has consistently opposed remilitarization and nuclear armaments and supported the alliance with the United States. While the LDP was in power, the opposition Socialist and Communist parties condemned the presence of American bases and the security treaty, but when the Socialists became members of the coalition government that replaced the LDP in 1993, their opposition to the security treaty was muted.

Several factors converged in 1996 to induce Japan to redefine its security alliance with the United States. One was the collapse of the coalition government. With the resignation of Tomiichi Murayama as prime minister in January, Ryutaro Hashimoto, a well-known proponent of projecting Japanese power beyond the limits set by Article 9 of the Constitution, ascended to the position. A second factor provided Prime Minister Hashimoto with the opportunity for redefining the U.S.–Japanese security pact. A serious impasse had developed between the people in Okinawa Prefecture and the central government over renewal of leases for U.S. military bases in Okinawa. Instigated by the rape of a 12-year-old girl by three U.S. servicemen in September 1995, the citizens of Okinawa Prefecture were galvanized into widespread protests to prevent the land from being leased to the United States for its military bases. A third factor adding weight to the argument in favor of upgrading the security pact with the United States was the deterioration of Sino-Japanese relations following disputes over the Senkaku or Daioyu Islands south of Okinawa.

Prime Minister Hashimoto began a four-year process of extending Japan's security pact with the United States that continued through Prime Minister Obuchi's term in office when the revised security guidelines were passed by the Japanese Diet. At the outset it was an agreement between the two sides to widen Japan's security responsibilities well beyond the country's main islands. In the event of a regional security threat, Japan was enabled to invoke U.S. cooperation even if the military conflict did not involve a direct attack on Japan. The United States, for its part, agreed to a reduction in the extraterritorial benefits accruing to its military personnel in Japan. This permitted Hashimoto to resolve the Okinawan impasse while increasing Japan's role in providing regional security in North Asia. In 1998 and 1999, under Prime Minister Obuchi, two incidents occurred that helped garner the necessary votes to get the "new guidelines" passed by the Japanese Diet. The first was the launching of what appeared at first to be a ballistic missile over Japan. It was later determined to be an unsuccessful rocket launching as the North Koreans had claimed. The second was when two ships suspected of spying were chased out of Japanese waters by a Japanese warship flanked by coast guard vessels. In their final form, the new guidelines governing Japanese and U.S. security cooperation provided for

1. a joint U.S.–Japanese research program to develop a missile-defense system for the region;
2. launching four spy satellites by 2003;
3. increasing Japanese military spending for the first time in three years;
4. granting greater access to American forces based in Japan to air and seaports in the country; and
5. authorization for Japan's Self-Defense Forces to back up U.S. troops by carrying out search-and-rescue missions, evacuations, and mine-sweeping.

This enhanced U.S.–Japanese security pact has been both positive and negative in its consequences for overall security in the region. A continued U.S. military presence in the Asian Pacific has been reassuring to those countries who want to counterbalance China's ambitions as a regional superpower. On the negative side, the extended scope of U.S.–Japanese military cooperation beyond the borders of Japan has intensified conflicts between China and Japan, Taiwan and the United States. It has already resulted in China's embarking on closer relations with Russia.

A Bigger Political Role?   There are those inside Japan and outside as well who advocate that Japan accept a political role commensurate with its economic clout. Japanese proponents of the "internationalist" position have in the last decades had some success in overcoming the reluctance of the "neomercantilists" to enlarge foreign policy objectives beyond economic matters, but some aspire to a greatly expanded and more visible political and security role for Japan in regional and global relations. The question is, for what purpose? If national security is protected by the present strategies, why take on more? Winning international recognition, perhaps symbolized by a permanent seat on the Security Council, might be appealing to national pride, but would it make Japan any more secure or the lives of the Japanese any more comfortable or meaningful? Taking on more global responsibilities and seeking to be in the global spotlight may be less beneficial than working quietly outside the spotlight to accomplish objectives that serve more modest national goals.

The View from Beijing After the Cold War

The receding of the Soviet threat to China's security has not been an unmitigated blessing, from Beijing's perspective. The breakup of the Soviet Union and the overthrow of the Communist Party in Russia leaves the United States as the sole survivor of the pair of "hegemony-seeking" superpowers and without a world-class rival to counterbalance its ambitions for a "New World Order." The American vision of making the world safe for its version of capitalist democracy conflicts with the worldview of China's leaders, who conclude that self-protection requires convincing other Third World states to join in resisting U.S. ambitions.

Deprived of the prominence it once enjoyed as the pivotal "switch" member of the Moscow-Washington-Beijing triangle, China is now laying the foundation for a new Sino-Japanese-American triangle, with China's influence enhanced by the opportunity to mediate in any rift between Washington and Tokyo. Relations with

Japan, already good, must be strengthened; the economies of the two countries are complementary and mutual interests in trade and investment are powerful enough to weigh against the lingering hostility felt by Chinese as the result of Japanese conquest in the 1930s and 1940s. The chill in relations with the United States since 1989 has not thawed out though there is a greater recognition on the part of President Clinton that the United States can neither ignore China's key position in Asia, nor cow it into submission to demands for compliance with foreign notions of "human rights" and curbs on China's legitimate arms sales to other countries.

Peaceful Coexistence.   The larger vision of security, of which China's manipulation of the China-Japan-United States triangle is a part, involves elevating the country's status economically, politically, and militarily. Continued economic progress requires internal stability and a benign external environment. To that end, peaceful coexistence with all its neighbors, whatever the past ideological differences, is the theme of Chinese diplomacy. Restoration of normal relations with Indonesia (suspended since 1965) and Vietnam (interrupted in 1979) and the opening of relations with Singapore occurred in the past few years, with the result that PRC now has formal diplomatic relations with all of the Asian Pacific countries. Contacts have been extended beyond the region, with a flurry of visits by top officials to Africa, Latin America, and Europe. The two Koreas and ASEAN are targeted for particular emphasis, not only for economic reasons but also to build up China's political "capital" in dealings with Japan and the United States. Efforts to rebuild ties to Indochina led to PRC's disengagement from the Khmer Rouge and to support for the international peace effort in Cambodia. Even PRC's long-standing antagonism toward India has been mollified by high-level visits between the two countries and by India's recognition of China's possession of Tibet.

Territorial Disputes and Military Modernization.   Territorial issues set China against a number of its neighbors and may at least in part account for efforts to upgrade the technological sophistication of the military. Defense of its claims to the Spratly and Paracels Islands in the South China Sea is thought to be behind the acquisition of airplanes with greater range and for the buildup of "blue seas" naval forces. The dispute over the Paracels pits China against Vietnam, and the Spratlys are claimed by both of them and Taiwan, the Philippines, Malaysia, and Brunei. Offshore oil deposits are a stake in the controversy, and China and Vietnam occupy some of the islands. The PRC National People's Congress in 1992 passed legislation formalizing China's claim and authorizing the use of force to protect areas within the country's territorial waters. The Taiwan government followed suit with similar legislation, though omitting mention of the use of force. (The PRC and ROC positions and the legal arguments on which they base their claims are identical, said to be the outcome of a conference held in 1991 between staff members of government "think-tanks" from Taipei, Shanghai, and Beijing.)

In its territorial disputes, China reserves a large part of its ire for the United States—because it is the global hegemon and because it retains a "special" security relationship to both Taiwan and Japan. The United States and to a lesser degree Japan, are viewed with a mixture of mistrust and awe. By contrast, China's posture toward its neighbors is far more accommodating. In 1994 the Philippines—having discovered a Chinese-built "military structure" on one of the Spratly reefs—accused China of being the biggest threat in the region, which prompted the ASEAN foreign ministers at their subsequent meeting in Manila to adopt a declaration calling for the peaceful solution of territorial disputes. The Chinese response was a proposal that all the claimants consider joint exploitation of the island resources. In March 2000, China and ASEAN agreed to frame a nonlegally binding common code of conduct for resolving claims to disputed areas in the South China Seas as a means of building trust. In 1996, by contrast, the Japanese asserted sovereignty over some rocky islands north of Taiwan eliciting such an outburst of antipathy by ordinary Chinese toward Japan that the government had to ban all anti-Japanese protests. Nothing worries and incites ordinary Chinese to often startling displays of anger and outrage like Japanese nationalistic militarism and expansionism. The vehement reaction of Chinese to the upgrading of the U.S.–Japanese security pact completed in 1999 was illustrative.

Modernization of the military has taken on additional significance with the recent escalation of tensions between the PRC and Taiwan. In addition to upgrading its hardware, the military has been ordered to professionalize its fighting forces by divesting itself of its sizable business empire. When economic reform was undertaken in the 1980s and early 1990s, the People's Liberation Army (PLA) became heavily involved in expanding its purely commercial enterprises that included giant trading companies, star-rated hotels, nightclubs, and telecommunications. In July 1998 President Jiang Zemin ordered the PLA and the militia or People's Armed Police (PAP) to divest themselves of all purely commercial enterprises. With certain exceptions—telecommunications industries—this has been largely accomplished. In March 1999, the PLA and PAP had transferred 2,937 businesses to the state and closed an additional 3,928 enterprises. Among those businesses were some of the most lucrative ventures like China's largest pharmaceutical company, 999, and the Xinxing Group whose core business is trade in military supplies such as uniforms, tents, and port equipment. Not included in the divestiture order were many not so purely commercial enterprises such as farms and factories employing soldiers' family members especially in the more remote areas of China and the less-lucrative businesses that existed prior to the economic reform era like its hospitals and research institutions. The aims of divestiture are to restore military discipline by eliminating the distractions of running businesses and recapture the loyalty of the public by removing opportunities for corruption.

In addition to modernizing its conventional forces, China maintains its nuclear weapons, testing nuclear devices in 1992, 1993, and 1995. Although the PRC's nuclear arsenal is small compared to that of the United States and Russia (along with several other members of the Confederation of Independent States), still it does constitute the key to membership in the exclusive club of nuclear weapons states and a modest deterrent to first use by others. While expressing support for international nuclear arms control measures, the Chinese government has taken the position that the nuclear "giants" must first make substantial reductions in their arsenals.

Regaining Lost Territories and Prestige.   China's perennial goals of regaining territories and prestige lost during its "Century of Humiliation" have made substantial headway with the rejoining to the motherland of Hong Kong in 1997 and Macau in 1999. Remaining on the agenda are the internationally more complex issues, principal among them the return of Taiwan to Chinese sovereignty, which was discussed earlier in this chapter.

National prestige is also at stake in U.S. actions that China regards as meddling in its internal affairs. From the Chinese leaders' perspective, their handling of political dissidents in Tiananmen Square in 1989 and antigovernment Tibetan demonstrations was necessary to protect domestic order and, in any case, not the business of outsiders to criticize. During the Bush administration such criticisms came more often from private organizations and members of Congress than from the Department of State. The Clinton administration, however, took actions in its first year in office that struck China as infringing on its sovereignty. Renewal of China's most favored nation trading status with the United States in 1993 was made conditional on demonstration of progress in human rights, a condition that was effectively dropped in the renewal of most favored nation status in 1994. Also in 1993, the United States charged China with exporting missile components to Pakistan in violation of an international agreement neither country had yet ratified. A few months later it asked for inspection of a Chinese ship bound for Iran carrying, according to U.S. information, substances to be used for manufacturing chemical weapons; inspection turned up no evidence to support that contention.

Following President Clinton's reelection campaign in 1996, criticism of China once again emanated from the U.S. Congress which more often than not painted the president as part of the problem. Accusations against China contained in congressional hearings and reports running the gamut from illegal presidential campaign contributions to spying on the part of a Taiwanese-born scientist working at Los Alamos nuclear laboratory received wide media coverage alongside the more customary charges of human rights violations. When, in 1997, the United States promoted the joint project to develop a missile defense system with Japan, the Chinese concluded that they were the intended target. But the crowning injury to Chinese national pride was the "accidental" U.S. bombing of the Chinese Embassy in Belgrade in May 1999 as part of the NATO peacekeeping mission in Kosovo. When widespread anti-American demonstrations occurred in China, even resulting in some damage to the U.S. Embassy, reports in the U.S. media that they were orchestrated by the government rather than spontaneous was taken by Chinese as adding insult to injury.

The bombing incident taken together with the upbeat Clinton-Jiang summit meeting that took place less than a year before in Beijing symbolize the contrary elements that characterize the uneasy transitional relations between an ascendant power's expectations for respect and recognition and a hegemonic power that resists the changing global configuration of power. Even when the U.S. House of Representatives voted in favor of granting China permanent normal trading relations in May 2000, it came with provisions in the legislation to establish a commission to monitor Beijing's record on labor and human rights. Lauding the vote, China denounced the provisions for monitoring China's internal affairs. Beijing's sensitivity to actions that seem insulting to its sovereignty and political independence does not, from its viewpoint, constitute an obstacle to the goal of improving relations with the United States. It is, rather, one element in the grand strategy of achieving for China the eminent place in world politics that it feels it deserves.

The Quest for Security by Other Asian Pacific States

The ending of the Cold War has affected superpower clients and even nonaligned states to varying degrees. Most adversely affected is North Korea, as discussed earlier in this chapter, and Taiwan—perhaps paradoxically—the least; its military security has been precarious since the U.S. protective shield was lifted. So, as a deterrent to possible attack from across the straits, Taipei beefs up its air force and surface fleet, spending a third more on defense in 1993 than the PRC, while pursuing the policy of increased unofficial economic, cultural, and family ties with the mainland and with other governments and international organizations. Though the 2000 presidential election results in Taiwan heightened global anxieties of a cross-strait military confrontation, the temperate inaugural speech delivered by the new Taiwanese president and a nonbelligerent response from Beijing's leadership suggest a new optimism about the probability of resolving (in President Chen's words) the "question of a possible future 'one China.'"

South Korea and the Philippines.   Both countries continue to be under the protection of security treaties with the United States. Despite student demonstrations calling for the removal of American bases, the South Korean government remains militarily dependent on Washington as the deterrent of last resort to military action by North Korea. Implicit also is the possibility that South Korea might exercise the option of acquiring nuclear weapons to balance such weapons in the North. The success of former President Roh's "Northern policy" in establishing diplomatic and economic relations with China and Russia removes them as serious military threats, and Seoul's "bridge-building" efforts toward Pyongyang, combined with Japanese and American contacts with the DPRK, are aimed at moderating the potential threat from the North. Economic security remains heavily dependent on Japan, on the American market, and on the ability to adjust to competition from the NECs.

Unlike South Korea, the Philippines has taken a step away from its accustomed status as a U.S. client state and toward greater identification with its Asian neighbors. Whether the Philippine Senate's refusal to extend the lease on the U.S. bases at Clark Field and Subic Bay signals the end of neocolonial dependence is not yet clear. Almost a century of the American military presence is over and American aid is drying up, though the security treaty is still alive and the Manila government concurs with other ASEAN members that a precipitous American withdrawal would have a destabilizing effect on the region. Although the Philippines faces no external security threat, economic difficulties have international dimensions. Creating internal conditions that will inspire confidence among private investors and bilateral and multilateral aid donors is imperative; the push is for more investments from overseas Chinese. Diversification of external economic partners may be a way of reducing the Philippines' economic dependence on the United States and Japan.

Other ASEAN States.   Indonesia, Malaysia, Singapore, and Thailand have their own security concerns and ways of managing them. Although none of the countries in Southeast Asia faces imminent *external* dangers, Indonesia, Malaysia, and Thailand are expanding their navies from "brown-water" coastal protection to "blue-water" capability. Speculation about the motivation behind those moves suggests a number of possibilities: to have the capacity to enforce control over the 200-mile extended economic zones recognized under the Law of the Sea treaty, to back up Malaysia's Spratly claim, to tighten Jakarta's control over its outer islands, and in anticipation of the vacuum resulting from the downsizing of American naval forces in the Western Pacific.

Singapore, nonaligned but pro-United States since independence (like Malaysia and Indonesia since the 1965 coup), took up some of the slack left by the closing of U.S. bases in the Philippines by providing alternative air and naval facilities (scrupulously not called "bases" to comply with ASEAN's declared opposition to foreign bases in the region). The most vulnerable of the ASEAN states, Singapore is also the most ardent advocate for keeping the United States engaged in the region, whether as insurance against the threat of a revived Japanese militarism or outward pressure from the mainland's "awakened giant" China or as an outsider capable of keeping simmering intraregional conflicts from erupting into violent confrontation. The first of those reasons for a continued American presence was expressed obliquely by Senior Minister Lee Kuan Yew, who said in an interview, "We'd all be happier if the American security alliance remains, leaving Japan to concentrate on high-definition television."[32]

Although other ASEAN governments also favor a continued American presence, there is rising sentiment, especially since the 1997 currency meltdown, in favor of greater regional cooperation to strengthen its comprehensive security. The most outspoken critic of the United States has been Malaysia's Prime Minister Mahathir. He has been vocal in his opposition to Western views on a range of issues from international currency trade and human rights to U.N. interference in the internal affairs of countries. His proposal for an East Asia Economic Group, without U.S. participation, is a would-be competitor to APEC of which the United States, Australia, New Zealand, and Canada are members. He refused to attend the 1993 APEC summit hosted by the United States. In 1999, having weathered the economic downturn in Malaysia without the help of the IMF, Mahathir spoke extensively at various international forums—in the United Nations and at the World Economic Forum—urging reform of the world's financial architecture to eliminate the "unnecessary, immoral and counter-productive" activity of currency speculators.[33] He defended Malaysia's use of capital controls to regulate the flow of money coming into and leaving the country, acknowledging that he was borrowing a page from China's economic textbook.

For the most part, Mahathir has looked to Japan as his favored candidate for a greater role in the region, but he frequently also aligns himself with China on international issues. On his fifth visit to China in August 1999, he was greeted as "an old friend of the Chinese people." But the prime minister's antipathies to the United States were not shared by Indonesia's former leader, ex-President Suharto, who viewed Mahathir as a brash rival for regional leadership in ASEAN. When Indonesia's economy was devastated by the Asian financial crisis, however, and Suharto was forced to resign, Malaysia responded to President Habibie's request for aid by shipping Indonesia over $60 million worth of rice. The cooperative gesture was reciprocated by President Abdurrahman Wahid ("Gus Dur") who lost no time paying Mahathir a courtesy call when he came into office, receiving an additional $100 million in food assistance and the promise of financial aid in turn. As the regionally divisive issue of Mahathir's political vendetta against his erstwhile heir apparent, Anwar Ibraham, was forgotten, Malaysia's relationship with Indonesia improved.

If Mahathir embraced a prominent, often contentious role for Malaysia as a regional power, Suharto attempted to keep Indonesia out of the international limelight. His annexation of East Timor in 1976 against Timorese and international opposition was possible only because the United States and Australia conveniently looked the other way in deference to a staunchly anticommunist ally. As the Cold War wound down in the 1990s, international support for the East Timorese struggle against military oppression became the focal point of increasing Western criticism of Indonesia. The financial collapse of the rupiah in 1998 provided the proverbial straw that broke the back of Suharto's hold on power, exposing long-suppressed ethnic fissures and religious animosities: between Christians and Muslims on the islands of Ambon, South Sulawesi, and the Moluccas; between Madurese settlers and both Dayak tribesmen and Melayu villagers in West Kalimantan; between the separatist movement in Aceh and the Indonesian military in northern Sumatra; between Chinese and Moslems in Java, and among all the outer islanders against the Javanese. With the fragile mosaic of Indonesian statehood crumbling, Suharto's successor President Habibie decided to sacrifice the nettlesome territory of East Timor in hopes of saving the body politic. On January 27, 1999, he offered the East Timorese an autonomy-or-independence referendum scheduled for the beginning of August 1999.

Within days of the announcement, the Indonesian military in East Timor were recruiting thousands of new pro-integration paramilitaries and organizing them alongside the militia—who were trained by the Indonesian Special Forces—to intimidate East Timorese from voting for independence. By June when the UN Assistance Mission on East Timor (UNAMET) arrived to supervise the referendum, there was little that could be done to stem the militia killings and dislocation of East Timorese suspected of pro-independence sympathies—virtually the entire lowland population. In light of violence that included attacks on UN workers, UN Secretary-General Kofi Annan postponed the referendum until the end of August. On the relatively peaceful day of the referendum, 439,000 East Timorese went to the 200 polling stations and 344,000 voted for independence. Notwithstanding Habibie's promise to Western ambassadors that Indonesia would not leave East Timor "like barbarians," the Indonesian soldiers and militiamen embarked on a burning and pillaging spree that left the capital city, Dili, and environs in ruins. Hundreds of thousands of East Timorese were forced to flee into the Indonesian West Timorese part of the island where they were held in closely guarded camps. The Indonesian government declared martial law in East Timor but that only intensified the violence, forcing UNAMET to abandon its compound in Dili.

When in September, 1999, at the APEC forum meeting in New Zealand, neither Indonesia nor ASEAN (of which Indonesia is the largest member) had taken any action to quell the disorder in East Timor, Indonesia—under threat of international war crimes—acquiesed to the Security Council authorization to send a 7,500-strong international force into the province to restore order. It was the first armed international intervention in the region since the Vietnam War; it was under Australian command and had a sizable contingent of 1,500 combat soldiers from only one of the region's major powers: Thailand. After restoring order, the international force withdrew, leaving East Timor under the administration of a UN mission until East Timorese society could be brought back to life. The ultimate failure of Indonesian rule in East Timor is obvious in the total absence of institutions on which to build a country that stands on its own. East Timor starts from "below zero." It must build homes, hospitals, schools, an electricity grid, a water system, a civil service, a police force, a central fiscal authority, a health and educational system but it must also nurture the institutional mores to make these structures work.

Two aspects of this human catastrophe in Indonesia have ongoing regional security implications. One is the continuing political instability in Indonesia as the civilian government attempts to rein in and exercise a modicum of control over an entrenched, once-glorious military that has ruled Indonesia for 30 years. While the military (and Suharto) are being questioned and their transgressions investigated, ethnic and religious conflicts throughout the Indonesian archipelago escalate. The separatist movement in Aceh, on the northern tip of the large, resource-rich island of Sumatra, is probably the oldest, most serious and contentious of these insurrections. With smuggled weapons from Thailand, the "Free Aceh" separatist movement that has been fighting "outside" centralized rule since *before* Indonesia became an independent state, was galvanized into energetic open rebellion by the success of East Timor's long and highly internationalized campaign for independence.

The second aspect of East Timor's plight has had an even more profound effect on Asian Pacific regional security: It took an international armed force under the non-Asian leadership of Australia to come into and restore order in a province of the largest member state of ASEAN. Not only was Indonesia incapable of stopping the violence of the pro-Jakarta militias against the East Timorese people, but the regional organization, ASEAN, was unable to garner the forces necessary to make it an Asian operation. The Australian-led force Indonesia was pressured into accepting on its soil made its share of mistakes as well, giving rise to resentments against "Westerners" coming in to straighten out the affairs of Asians. Watching as outsiders came into the largest sovereign nation-state in the Southeast Asian region to settle a "humanitarian crisis" must certainly accentuate the institutional weakness of its organizations to provide for their own regional security. It is probably scant consolation that this problem is not singularly Southeast Asian but an increasingly troublesome global occurrence with profound implications for the "new world order" that is evolving before our eyes.

Thailand, long a close American ally, has shifted from "client" to a more equal relationship with the United States, playing its "China card" of closer ties to the

PRC, long regarded as the nemesis to the north. Thailand's military purchases Chinese arms at prices so low as to constitute aid, and the two countries were allied in supporting the Khmer Rouge in Cambodia as an antidote to the Vietnam-Soviet alliance. In 1999, Thailand and China signed an unusual treaty pledging deeper bilateral trade relations in the twenty-first century. It is the first of its kind to be signed by China with any country. For *its* part, Thailand was also engaged in a "first" of another kind. Its dispatch of 1,500 troops to East Timor as part of the Australian-led peace operation was the start of a new program that commits the Thai military to future participation in UN-style missions in the region. In a similar bid to boost Thailand's image as part of the global community, the government dropped its long-standing opposition to Vietnam and the Vietnam-installed government of Cambodia, promoting Thai trade and investment opportunities in those countries as well as their admission to ASEAN.

Thailand's objective is to become the economic "core" of mainland Southeast Asia and to regain the political influence it once enjoyed in the region before the era of colonialism. Historically, Cambodia and Laos had been the objects of competition between Thailand and Vietnam, and that rivalry persists. At present, Thai influence is in ascendance, having the advantage of cultural and language affinities with Cambodia and economic assets of interest to Laos as well as the topography favorable to commerce with those neighbors. But an economically revitalized Vietnam will surely become a worthy competitor to Thailand for influence on the other two members of what was once French Indochina. Completing the roster of states toward which Thailand has turned its attention is Myanmar. The two countries share a history of armed conflict as well as a long land frontier permeable to drug traffickers and anti-Yangon insurgents in search of a haven from the Myanmar government's reach. In the past, the Thai government allowed the Myanmar military to enter Thai territory in pursuit of the insurgents. Currently, however, because of the increasing quantity of drugs and refugees entering Thailand from Myanmar, tensions between the two countries have escalated, although it was Thailand's initiative in ASEAN that led to Myanmar's admission to ASEAN (along with Laos) in 1997.

ASEAN.   Members of the Association of Southeast Asian Nations (ASEAN) have expanded not only in number (from six to ten) but also in the organization's agenda, which has moved beyond its initial focus on economic cooperation to include regional political and security matters. This trend, as seen above, has accelerated in the post–Cold War period. Consultations occur in the context of the "post-ministerial" conferences held immediately following the annual meetings of ASEAN foreign ministers. Those discussions bring together representatives of the ten ASEAN member states with their counterparts from the seven "dialogue partners"—Japan, South Korea, Australia, New Zealand, Canada, the United States, and EC. ASEAN thus serves an ad hoc role as the institutional core around which an informal structure of relationships has formed, linking Southeast Asia, other Asian countries, and outside states with interests in the larger pan-Pacific region. The network was expanded in 1993 at the ASEAN meeting in Singapore, to which China and Russia were invited as guests and Vietnam, Laos, and Papua New Guinea as observers. It was agreed there to set up the ASEAN Regional Forum through which the participating governments are to work on political and security cooperation. The form such cooperation might take is left open, but it seems clear that a NATO-like organization is light-years beyond the desires or capacities of the governments involved. The forum's first meeting took place in 1994 in Bangkok, with a representative of Myanmar present as a guest of Thailand. Of the Asian Pacific States, only North Korea, and Taiwan are not presently in the "loop" for political and security discussions, although Taiwan participates in the APEC gatherings.

Vietnam, Laos, Cambodia, and Myanmar.   The end of the Cold War has brought major changes in the external relations of the three former Indochinese states. Deprived of Soviet economic and military support, which it enjoyed from the late 1970s to the 1980s, Vietnam of necessity shelved the ambition to protect its western flank by keeping or putting cooperative communist governments in power in Phnom Penh and Vientiane. Dropping the ideological bent of its previous foreign policy, Hanoi moved to break out of the diplomatic and economic isolation imposed as punishment for the Cambodian intervention by withdrawing its forces and agreeing to the Paris accords on ending the civil war. Vietnam was admitted to ASEAN in 1995 and pushed hard to get Cambodia admitted. The thrust now is to reestablish good relations with China, Japan, the West and its ASEAN partners so as to build up its economic strength by inviting foreign investment, trade, and bilateral and multilateral economic aid.

International responses have been positive, particularly from Japan, the ASEAN states (Singapore and Japan are Vietnam's largest trade partners), Australia, and Western Europe. Even the United States, which withheld diplomatic recognition for a long time because of the MIA/POW (missing in action/prisoner of war) lobby, lifted its 19-year trade embargo in 1994, restored diplomatic relations in 1995, and signed a trade agreement in July 2000 (subject to Congressional approval) granting Vietnam normal trade relations. The millennia-old security problem of being one of the frontline states along China's southern border appears at present to pose no obstacle to closer relations between Vietnam and China. Normal relations with the PRC were reestablished in 1991, and Vietnamese officials have paid yearly visits to Beijing since 1997, making repeated pledges to resolve border disputes and boost trade. The only objects of dispute between the two governments are the islands in the South China Sea. Despite the demise of the Soviet Union, Vietnam maintains close ties with Russia from whom the Vietnamese still receive technical and military support as well as assistance with projects like the oil refinery the Russians are helping Vietnam to build.

For Laos, a bit player in the unfolding drama of world politics, security is always at risk on a regional stage dominated by China to the north, Thailand to the south, and Vietnam to the east. Laos has little choice but to accommodate to the ebb and flow of external influences. Relations with the PRC have improved since the period when the two countries backed opposing sides in Cambodia, China supporting the Khmer Rouge and Laos siding with the Vietnamese-installed government. China sees Laos as a potential outlet for the transit of goods from interior southern China and itself as a balance to Thai influence, which has increased with the end of the Cold War. As Thai investments and trade grew, and Bangkok dropped its aid to Lao insurgents operating along the Thai border, Laos became increasingly dependent on Thailand. In 1997 Laos was admitted to ASEAN and anticipated closer relations with the noncommunist economies. But ASEAN member states were hit by the Asian financial crisis that year and Laos found itself relying once again on its communist partners, China and Vietnam. In the early part of 1999 when Laos was hard-pressed for cash, China extended Laos a grant of $1.21 million for development projects and Vietnam pledged closer economic cooperation. A barter trade arrangement was signed later in the year to help Laos cope with the impact of the economic crisis and to lessen both countries' dependence on foreign hard currencies. Although Laos remains committed to its participation in ASEAN and moving closer to its noncommunist Southeast Asian neighbors, the withdrawal of Thai investments, an ailing economy, the continued withholding of normal trade relations by the United States and a resurgence of the Hmong insurgency—a vestige of the Vietnam War era—have moved Laos closer to Vietnam and China.

Cambodia, which was to have been admitted to ASEAN in 1997, became the last country of Southeast Asia to join ASEAN as its tenth member in 1999. Its membership plans had been put on hold in 1997 because the coalition government created in 1993 collapsed when Hun Sen ousted his co-premier, Norodom Ranariddh. When the coalition was patched together again and recognized internationally in December 1998, ASEAN finally admitted Cambodia. Its position in the Southeast Asian configuration, however, has not changed. As is the case with Laos, Cambodia is a minor power sandwiched between the larger and more dynamic Thailand and Vietnam. And its relationship with both these neighbors remains strained despite the fact that all three of them now participate in ASEAN. The antipathy toward Vietnam and Vietnamese residents in Cambodia is widespread among Cambodians and is likely to strain relations with Hanoi for some time. There is also a contentious issue of a stretch of land that Cambodia claims Vietnam appropriated when it changed the borders between them in the 1980s. Cambodia's relationship with Thailand is more ambivalent. Cambodians mistrust Thai business interests suspecting them of illegally logging and helping themselves to gems mined in the Cambodian border areas formerly occupied by the Khmer Rouge.

Cambodia's most powerful ally remains China. Leaders of both countries exchanged visits in 1999 and China gave Cambodia $220 million in interest-free loans and grants to improve its infrastructure and industrial base. Among the larger projects for which the money was earmarked were two dams. In contrast to the no-strings-attached money given to Cambodia by China, Western as well as Japanese donations are usually contingent on Cambodia's improvement of its human rights conduct, a difference not lost on the Cambodians. It is not surprising under the circumstances to see an increasing number of Chinese firms investing in Cambodia's garment industry, infrastructure projects, and the building of hotels, restaurants and private homes.

Finally, we move to Myanmar, the last of the three Southeast Asian "frontline" states on the Chinese border. "When China spits, we swim" is a Burmese saying that expresses graphically, if somewhat inelegantly, the core issue of the country's security: the need to keep on amicable terms with China. That has been accomplished by pursuing a policy of strict nonalignment, combined after 1962 with a degree of self-imposed isolation from which it is now emerging. It rejoined the Non-Aligned Movement in 1992 and was admitted into ASEAN in 1997. China is its main ally and supplier of military equipment. The armed forces has been strengthened since the 1988 popular uprising; it currently numbers 450,00 as compared to 195,000 in the late 1980s. Myanmar is also reputed to have built a modern, high-tech military-intelligence apparatus, the Directorate of the Defense Service Intelligence (DDSI), with equipment obtained from a Singapore-based company which also provides on-site training. Political support has also come from Singapore, whose senior minister, Lee Kuan Yew, said after one of the Burmese government's crackdowns on the National League for Democracy of Aung San Suu Kyi, "At the end of the day, the opposition in Burma has to face the realities of life. The one instrument of effective government there is the army."

Ties developed during World War II between Japan and the first generation of independence leaders, including Ne Win, were an asset in obtaining aid from Japan, which was Burma's biggest donor before 1988. When the Japanese government indicated in February 1998 that it would provide a $20 million loan to help Myanmar finance work on Rangoon's international airport, it emphasized that this did not mean a resumption of aid but a disbursement of 10-year-old commitments. In any event, it was accompanied by a warning that the Burmese junta needed to clean up its human rights violations. The Myanmar government ignores or rebuts U.S. and European criticisms of its human rights record and found support among ASEAN countries in rebuffing Western pressure for an international arms embargo against its military regime. Now as a member of ASEAN, however, and especially in light of the embarrassing outcome of the humanitarian crisis in East Timor, other ASEAN members may be rethinking one of the fundamental principles of the organization: noninterference in the internal affairs of any country.

Ten years after the government crushed the democracy movement in Myanmar, the SLORC leadership (of 21 generals) was disbanded and a new 19-member military junta, the State Peace and Development Council, took over. Composed of younger, lower-level officers, the new junta seems better equipped for Myanmar's move in the direction of closer relations both with its regional neighbors and the global community of nations. While this requires more modern finesse, it in no way signifies that Myanmar will become more democratic. The leader of the NLD, Aung San Suu Kyi, is no longer under house arrest but the NLD itself has broken up into squabbling factions. The junta has defeated and marginalized the panoply of insurrectionary movements that plagued the body politic ever since independence, in some 24 instances by entering into cease-fire agreements that merely turned them loose to fend for themselves. This is the most serious source of Myanmar's tensions with its neighbors today. Hundreds of thousands of people from Burma's border ("frontier") areas have been internally displaced or have fled into neighboring Thailand and Bangladesh as refugees. Those who remain often live off the production and trade of drugs, which have become more sophisticated and have doubled in the past decade. Thus, as Burma moves gradually from isolation to closer contacts with other Asian Pacific countries, it leaves behind a trail of problems that get exported to its neighbors.

With the end of the Cold War, the international environment seems much more benign for the Asian Pacific states. The diminution of external military threats, even to the still-divided states, holds out possibilities for cooperation in arms control and confidence-building measures aimed at constructing a common security system for the whole region. Relieved of the necessity to devote so much of available human and material resources to protecting national security by military means, countries may now be able to divert some of those resources to improving the quality of their citizens' lives and to reducing the substantial political influence of military officers. The disappearance of ideological correctness as the determinant of friend and foe opens up opportunities for forging relationships with new partners to their mutual gain. The changed context of international relations may stimulate the building of regional institutions, both private and intergovernmental, as stronger and more inclusive networks of economic, cultural, and environmental interdependence overcome the parochialism of national and subnational loyalties. The opportunities for all forms of creative cooperation are legion.

But it is also possible that the post–Cold War period will be marked by an upsurge in conflict, both between and within countries, as the restraints imposed by alliance loyalties and fear of being sucked into the maelstrom of superpower battles are lifted and governments have more latitude for risk taking in foreign policy. Old enmities may revive and new ones develop over issues of "turf" in the literal sense of land and territorial waters and extended economic zones, over place in the pecking order, over markets and resources and a whole host of other scarce "goods," material and intangible. Centrifugal forces that had been kept in check by appeals for national unity in the face of external threats may erupt in an orgy of destruction as they have in Eastern Europe. Already we see inauspicious signs in the shape of naval arms races, the threat of nuclear proliferation, antiforeign resentment, vituperative exchanges on human rights, charges of protectionism and unfair trading practices, suspicions of hegemonic designs, foot-dragging on regional institution building. In short, the post–Cold War period offers opportunities for more pervasive and more numerous conflicts in a whole range of relationships across and within national boundaries.

SUMMARY

The international political relations of Asian Pacific states since the end of World War II have been intimately connected to the global political environment. During the past half-century the world political system has undergone dramatic transformations that have both influenced and been influenced by the states in this region. The Cold War, the global contest between the communist and anticommunist superpowers, impinged on the ex-colonial states' struggle to consolidate their political independence and develop economically. For some, alliance with one or the other superpower brought substantial benefits, helping them to build their economies, although with some loss of autonomy in foreign policy choices. For others, the Cold War drew them into disastrous internal or external conflicts, or both, draining the lifeblood of winners and losers alike, dividing three of the Asian nations into two rival states. Even those who tried to remain aloof from the superpower contest were inevitably touched by it.

But the bipolarity that characterized world politics in the early phase of the Cold War began to erode, in part as the result of a new assertiveness by some ex-colonial states in Asia and elsewhere. China challenged Soviet leadership of the world communist movement, splitting it irrevocably, and the domination of world politics by the industrialized countries—both East and West—was challenged by a growing solidarity among "developing" states in Asia and other parts of what came to be known as the Third World. The Sino-Soviet rupture opened the way for accommodation across the ideological divide between China and the United States and set the two communist powers in competition for influence over other communist governments and movements. Recognition of common interests among them led to the creation of ASEAN by five noncommunist neighbors in Southeast Asia.

As the Cold War hostility between the United States and the Soviets diminished, opportunities opened up for Asian Pacific governments to move toward the resolution of long-standing regional conflicts of Cold War origin and to build political and economic bridges across the ideological divide. Koreans and Chinese began to talk about reunification, the American military involvement in Indochina finally ended, and Gorbachev took the initiative in proposing better relations with China, Japan, and other noncommunist states.

The breakup of the Soviet Union dealt the final blow to Cold War rationale for Asian Pacific foreign policy alignments and preoccupations and brought new opportunities and problems. The opportunities are for increased international cooperation within the region. The problems include the revival of old enmities temporarily held in check by Cold War obligations and the issue of what or who will fill the partial vacuum caused by declining American power in the region. China is a possible candidate, as is Japan, though that country is still committed to sheltering under the U.S. military umbrella, using economic levers as the major instrument of its foreign policy.

Whether the post–Cold War period in the Asian Pacific will bring increased cooperation or increased conflict or (more likely) some untidy mix of both, it seems reasonable to anticipate continuation of the trend toward greater importance of economic factors in shaping international relations in the Asian Pacific. Most of the countries are now so embedded in the world economy that issues of trade, aid, and investment are central to their foreign policy behavior. Analysis of regional economic relations is the subject of the next chapter.

QUESTIONS FOR DISCUSSION

1. Why were Asian Pacific countries drawn into the Cold War rivalry between the United States and the Soviet Union? Which countries benefited from that involvement? Which were adversely affected?
2. What instances do you see of the influence on the foreign policies of Asian Pacific governments of individual decision makers? Of internal factors? Of external factors?
3. China's relations with the USSR/Russia and the United States have undergone dramatic changes over the years since 1949. From the Chinese perspective, why did these changes occur? How have they served Chinese national interests?
4. The end of the Cold War transformed the global political system. What effects—positive or negative—has that had on international relations in the Asian Pacific?
5. In your view, does the Japan–United States political and security partnership still serve each partner's purposes in the 1990s as it did in the 1950s?

NOTES

1. William A. Williams et al., eds., *America in Vietnam: A Documentary History* (New York: Doubleday, 1985), pp. 156–57, citing Public Papers of the Presidents of the United States: Dwight D. Eisenhower, 1954 (Washington, D.C.: U.S. Government Printing Office, 1958), pp. 381–90.
2. Stanley Karnow, *Vietnam: A History* (New York: Penguin, 1984), p. 199.
3. Ibid., p. 534.
4. Williams, *America in Vietnam,* p. 309, citing *New York Times,* May 1, 1975, p. 16.
5. Marilyn B. Young, *The Vietnam War, 1945–1990* (New York: Harper Collins, 1991), p. 302.
6. Ibid., p. 280.
7. The text of the communique is in *Peking Review* 9 (March 31, 1972): 4–5.
8. *Peking Review* 51 (December 22, 1978): 8.
9. "U.S.–China Joint Communique, August 17, 1982," *Current Policy,* no. 413 (Washington, D.C.: U.S. Department of State, Bureau of Public Affairs, March 1982).
10. David J. Steinberg, ed., *In Search of Southeast Asia: A Modern History,* rev. ed. (Honolulu: University of Hawaii, 1987), p. 445.
11. Thanat Khoman, "ASEAN in a Regional and Global Context," in *ASEAN in Regional and Global Context,* ed. Karl D. Jackson et al. (Berkeley: University of California Press, 1986), p. 10.
12. Sudershan Chawla et al., eds., *Southeast Asia Under the New Balance of Power* (New York: Praeger, 1974), p. 119.
13. Evelyn Colbert, "ASEAN as a Regional Organization: Economics, Politics, and Security," in Jackson, *ASEAN in Regional and Global Context,* p. 200.
14. James C. Hsiung, "Asia Pacific in the Post–Cold War Order," in *Asia Pacific in the New World Politics,* ed. J. C. Hsiung (Boulder, CO: Lynne Rienner, 1993), pp. 3–4.
15. Ibid., p. 6.
16. Ibid., p. 9.
17. Tai Ming Cheung, "China's Buying Spree," *Far Eastern Economic Review* (July 8, 1993): 24.
18. Laura King, "Moscow-Tokyo Chill's Off," *Sacramento Bee,* October 14, 1993, p. A11.
19. Alex Pravda, ed., *Yearbook of Soviet Foreign Relations, 1991 Edition* (London: I. B. Tauris, 1991), p. 172, and "Secrets of the Korean War," *U.S. News & World Report,* August 9, 1993, pp. 45–47.
20. Shim Jae Hoon, "Russian Roulette," *Far Eastern Economic Review* (October 7, 1993): 30.
21. *Far Eastern Economic Review, Asia 1999 Yearbook* (Hong Kong: Review Publishing, 1999), p. 139.
22. Rhee Sang-Woo, "From National Unification to State Unification," in *North Korea in Transition,* ed. Chong-Sik Lee and Se-Hee Yoo (Berkeley: University of California Institute of East Asian Studies, 1991), p. 136.
23. *To Build a National Community through the Korean Commonwealth: A Blueprint for Korean Unification.* National Unification Board, Republic of Korea, September 1989.
24. An interview with Lee Hoi Chang, "Point of Departure: South Korea's Newly Empowered Opposition Leader Vows to Promote the Politics of Cooperation, Not Confrontation," in *Far Eastern Economic Review* (May 18, 2000): 22.
25. Maria Hsia Chang, "Relations Between Taiwan and Mainland China" (paper presented at the Western Political Science Association meeting, March 20, 1992), pp. 18–20.
26. Julian Baum, "Divided Nations," *Far Eastern Economic Review* (September 16, 1993): 10–11.
27. "Divided China in the United Nations: Time for Parallel Representation," paid advertisement in the *New York Times,* September 20, 1993, national edition, p. A13.
28. Ibid.
29. *Far Eastern Economic Review,* September 16, 1993, p. 11.
30. Hsiung, *Asia Pacific,* pp. 224–25.
31. William R. Nester, *Japan and the Third World* (New York: St. Martin's, 1992), p. 17.

32. Quoted in Charles P. Wallace, "Singapore Proves a Welcome Friend for the U.S. Military," *Los Angeles Times,* January 3, 1992, p. A4.
33. For recent events in the section that follows, we have relied on the *FEER Asia Yearbooks,* 1996–2000.

FOR FURTHER READING

Blackwill, Robert D. and Paul Dibb, eds. *America's Asian Alliances.* Cambridge and London: MIT Press, 2000.

Curtis, Gerald L., ed. *Japan's Foreign Policy After the Cold War.* Armonk, NY: M. E. Sharpe, 1993, parts 1, 3, 4, 5.

Fleming, D. F. *The Cold War and Its Origins.* vol. 2. Garden City, NY: Doubleday, 1961, chs. 20–23.

Hsiung, James C., ed. *Asia Pacific in the New World Politics.* Boulder, CO: Lynne Rienner, 1993.

Lee, Chong-Sik, ed. *In Search of a New Order in East Asia.* Berkeley: University of California Institute of East Asian Studies, 1991, parts 1, 3, 4.

McDougall, Derek. *The International Politics of the New Asia Pacific.* Singapore: Lynne Rienner and ISEAS, 1997.

Schwarz, Adam, *A Nation in Waiting: Indonesia's Search for Stability,* 2nd ed. Boulder, CO: Westview, 2000.

Wurfel, David, and Bruce Burton, eds. *The Political Economy of Foreign Policy in Southeast Asia.* London: Macmillan, 1990.

Yahuda, Michael. *The International Politics of the Asia-Pacific, 1945–1995.* London and New York: Routledge, 1996.

Young, Marilyn B. *The Vietnam War, 1945–1990.* New York: HarperCollins, 1991.

8

Political Economy of the Asian Pacific Region

By 1990 Asian Pacific countries had acquired a regional reputation for vigorous economic growth. This inspired claims of an impending "Pacific Century" in which the Asian Pacific would provide regional dynamism for the entire global economy. Popular in the mid-1990s, such expectations were buttressed by comparisons with other regions. Between 1980 and 1990, the average annual growth rate of real gross domestic product (GDP) among Asian Pacific countries was 8.4 percent, compared with 3 percent for the industrial countries of North America and Western Europe, 2.9 percent for the Middle East and North African regions, and 1.6 percent for Latin America. But by 1998 these "miracle economies" were being diagnosed as "crisis economies" suffering from a reputed regional affliction dubbed the "Asian flu." In its quest for an answer to what happened to the "miracle economies" of the Asian Pacific, the World Bank concluded, no doubt accurately, that there had never been any economic growth "miracles." Having grown accustomed to their economic accomplishments, Asian Pacific countries were suddenly faced with their first severe financial crisis and debilitating recession in the post-war era.

Although the scope and depth of recession came as a shock to the peoples of the Asian Pacific, depressions—or recessions as they are now called—are familiar occurrences in the global market. The irony of the economic downturn in the Asian Pacific was that it was a mark of successful regional integration into the world capitalist system. Those countries in the region with the most liberalized (open) market structures bore the brunt of the financial crisis while countries with more protected domestic economies remained relatively sheltered from disaster. But the impact of the economic crisis on the region as a whole has been to increase the level of awareness of regional vulnerability to the vagaries of the global capital market. The temptation today, therefore, is to see both the recession and the recovery as portending greater institutionalization of the Asian Pacific as a region: to fortify regional safeguards against the damage that can result from uncontrolled global capital flows, to defend its exports from protectionism on the part of other regions, to strengthen coordination of its internal resources, and to foster a more integrated domestic market for consumption of its own products.

The conditions for such regional coordination exist in the Asian Pacific. Intraregional trade, aid, and investment are extensive and increasing; the material and human resources to fuel production and furnish markets in the region are abundant; and regionally integrated manufacturing systems are already in operation and rapidly spreading. Now that the barriers separating communist from noncommunist nations have receded—the last one between North and South Korea vanquished at the historic summit of June 14, 2000—new markets are opening for trade and investments in China, Vietnam, Laos, Cambodia, Myanmar, and now even North Korea. Thus the incentives for Asian Pacific trading partners to increase their economic cooperation are likely to multiply as we move into the twenty-first century.

But it is premature to consider the countries of the Asian Pacific a region in any but the most general sense of geographical proximity. The political and economic obstacles in the way of regional coordination remain overwhelming: the geopolitical disparities among nations in the area; the immense cultural diversity that separates the subregions of East and Southeast Asia as well as the ethnic divisiveness that crosscuts national boundaries in much of Southeast Asia; the historical legacy of mistrust that exists among traditional enemies; the economic competition among nations competing for the same markets; and the political fractiousness of new nations maneuvering internal conflicts in an uncertain international order. And these impediments to cooperation pale by contrast to the mistrust all Asian nations share toward the one power that has already contributed substantially toward regionalization in the Asian Pacific; Japan.

In this chapter we focus on the political and economic linkages that currently exist among nations of the Asian Pacific. What patterns of economic interpenetration have emerged in relations among countries of the region? How do the economic bonds forged in the process of development intersect with the political interests that define their nations' objectives as sovereign entities? What are the politics of a complex system of economic interdependence that functions both regionally and globally, and how does it impact decision making at the national level? Exploring the answers to these questions involves a shift in our angle of vision: In place of comparing the domestic political economies of Asian Pacific countries from within, as we did in Chapter 5, we now view their political and economic interrelationships from outside and above, evaluating the bilateral and multilateral networks that both connect and divide countries of the region among themselves and within the larger global nexus.

We begin by analyzing the relevance of our theoretical models for understanding regionalism as an intermediate layer between the nationalism of the interstate system and the internationalism of the global economy. Then the economic linkages among countries in the Asian Pacific region are traced: the reemergence of regional ties and patterns of trade, investment, and aid both within the region and also between it and extraregional partners in the international market. In the last two sections we discuss the politics of economic interdependence, describing the various multilateral arrangements or regional associations that have been formed to further economic cooperation and speculate on the degree of regionalization likely to occur as a result of the patterns of economic growth in the Asian Pacific.

INTERNATIONAL POLITICS AND THE GLOBAL ECONOMY IN THEORETICAL PERSPECTIVE

International relations are composed of two disparate elements: (1) the configuration of nation-states' interrelationships—the interstate system—and (2) the economic interdependencies of a global production system—the global economy. The interaction between these two systems generates both conflict and cooperation and constitutes what has come to be known as the international political economy.

The International Political Economy

The global relationships among a variety of public and private "actors" is the focus of the international political economy (IPE), which addresses the fundamental reality of our times: that the economic and political decisions that affect our livelihoods as producers, consumers, and citizens transcend the boundaries of nation-states. Whether and how we are employed, the nature of our social and educational opportunities, the human "rights" available to us are no longer bounded by the jurisdiction of whatever nation-state defines our citizenship. Human choices and institutional policies are global in their reach, linking all of us economically and politically to one another's destiny.

It is bewildering to look at not only the scope of international political economy but also the large number of diverse actors involved on this global stage. They fall roughly into three categories. National governments (states) are still the principal actors; in the Asian Pacific setting they include not only the Asian states but also the G-7 (the United States, Germany, France, Britain, Italy, Canada, Japan), Russia, and Australia as makers of economic policies and as donors and recipients of aid. Intergovernmental organizations (IGOs) are a second, important set of actors; these include global financial institutions like the World Bank and the International Monetary Fund and regional organizations such as the Asian Development Bank (ADB), and the Association of Southeast Asian Nations (ASEAN). Finally there are transnational entities of a wide variety; these include multinational corporations (MNCs), nongovernmental organizations (NGOs), international (private) banks, overseas Chinese, and a variety of powerful illicit organizations like drug and arms traffickers or immigrant smugglers.

At the global level, the actors that most concern us in understanding the international political economy of the Asian Pacific are multinational corporations and nation-states because they cooperate and contend with each other. Multinational corporations, indifferent to national boundaries, expand operations and shift locations with extraordinary ease, wielding economic power no longer subject to the sovereignty of a single, even the most powerful, state. Using a technology that "renders industrial location and the direction of production less dependent on geographical distance," these multinational corporations become architects of a global economy that inevitably diminishes the capacities of nation-states to function in their traditional role as sovereign bodies.[1] As global entrepreneurs, multinational corporations rely on an organization of labor that decomposes complex production processes into tasks simple enough for an unskilled labor force to learn, giving them access to a worldwide reservoir of labor from which to choose. By contrast, nation-states are deprived of their economic base, left with communities abandoned by industries and citizens powerless to defend their livelihood.

Besieged by a combination of internal and external problems created by the blurring of national boundaries, and the uncertainty of "hegemonic stability" in a world without superpowers, nation-states have sought strength in numbers by increasing interactions with their nearby neighbors. These are the regional associations we know by their acronyms: the European Community (EC), renamed the European Union (EU) in 1994, the Association of Southeast Asian Nations (ASEAN), and the North American Free Trade Association (NAFTA). But regionalization today is an even more pervasive and often less institutionalized phenomenon than these regional organizations suggest. It grows out of the search for some form of mutual security on the part of states that experience increased demands from their citizens for a clean, safe, stable, and prosperous environment in an increasingly chaotic international situation.

The Thai peasant watching his Sony TV after driving home in a Toyota truck and the American suburbanite with a Japanese car, a Taiwanese computer, and a Malaysian-made VCR may be aware of the economic interdependence of prosperity in today's world. What is more obscure to them both is how this international production of prosperity comes into conflict with their national identity and the national community on which they depend for their livelihood. Because material prosperity is increasingly manufactured in component parts produced and assembled in disparate places around the globe, we are all dependent on international trade. But with the lifeline of national economies more than ever dependent on an international economy, there is no clear agreed upon understanding of how transnational economic actors, sovereign nation-states, and competing regional blocs or arrangements fit together as a world political order. Each of our three theories understands this relationship from a different vantage point; though in surveying the following summary, remember that our description of each of these approaches necessarily oversimplifies the variety of diverse interpretations that exist within each theoretical perspective.

Modernization Theory

Modernization theory ascribes the success of Asian Pacific economic growth to the adoption of rational market-oriented policies. The state's role is to enact domestic policies encouraging its entrepreneurs to produce for the market. For late-developing countries, this means orienting domestic economic production toward the international market. This ensures that each country will specialize in furnishing for export that which it produces best at the lowest possible price, which is called its *comparative advantage*. An international division of labor arises naturally from the principles of the market. When states engage in free trade on the basis of their comparative advantage, each expands its own national wealth through exchange in the international market. The success of newly industrializing economies (NIEs) in the Asian Pacific attests to the validity of these principles: By producing for export commodities of relatively high quality and low price, the NIEs discovered the secret of economic growth in the policy of subjecting their governments to the discipline of the international market, an idea captured in the phrase "getting the prices right."

If the market occupies the central position in an "open trade system," the state nonetheless has a definite if limited international role to play. States must agree to establish the rules and regulations—referred to as *international regimes*—that govern currency exchanges and other economic arrangements between sovereign national entities in order to ensure that no country or domestic group is hurt by "unfair" international competition. In the real world, of course, nation-states pursue a broad array of political and military as well as economic objectives in the international arena. How, then, are mechanisms of the international market safeguarded from the political interference of powerful states? Modernization theorists assume that each state maximizes its overall utility by calculating the cost-benefit ratios of a wide range of possible options, choosing the course that yields the highest reward or the least objectionable sacrifice. Trade-offs may be necessary and states can and do resort to forms of protectionism to defend or improve their domestic circumstances in certain situations. The essential element from the (neo)classical liberal perspective of modernization theory is that such instances of state intervention in the economic market remain exceptions or temporary departures.

But international trade in the modern age is complicated by the fact that not only goods and services but also capital and know-how move freely across national borders. From a modernization perspective the movement of capital and technology—*foreign direct investment* (FDI)—carries out an essential task: It transmits capital and ideas, spreading economic growth throughout the world. FDI enables economic actors in advanced nations to earn a return on their capital by promoting the economic growth and development of more "backward" areas of the world. Foreign capital brings modern technology, jobs, management skills, and marketing expertise to far corners of the globe, opening developing economies to the opportunities of the world market. As multinational corporations, to whom this missionary task falls, increasingly organize investment, production, and marketing on a global scale irrespective of the needs of isolated national economies, their indifference to national boundaries raises the question of what happens to the sovereignty of states. Because this issue frames the debates among advocates of the contending theories, it will be further discussed below.

World System Theory

To understand the international economy from the world system perspective is to view it as the cause rather than the consequence of nation-states trading with one another on the basis of comparative advantages. From this perspective, modern industrial capitalism, though organized politically in the form of sovereign nation-states, is economically an international division of labor that is continually expanding and changing its scope and pattern. Thus the world economy is "not . . . a simple addition of its national units, but . . . a powerful independent reality created by the international division of labor and by the world market which dominates all the national markets."[2] The individual nation-states, which are as much the creations as the architects of the international economy, do not interact as equals. Wealthy and powerful states at the core of the international economic system act like magnets, attracting the resources and reaping the profits from incorporating backward areas into the world economy, while peripheral states, instead of benefiting from the diffusion of capital and technology from the core, suffer an increasingly debilitating dependence on their benefactors.

But world system theorists view the international economy as historically evolving. The states comprising the core of the global system after the sixteenth century were Great Britain, joined in the mid-nineteenth century by France, with the United States, Germany, Italy, and Japan moving up from underdeveloped peripheral countries to the middle rank of semiperiphery. By World War II, Germany and Japan were contending with the United States and the Soviet Union for preeminence at the core of a vastly expanded world economy in which the states throughout the rest of Europe and Latin America as well as the colonies of Africa and Asia constituted the semiperiphery and periphery, respectively. This means that at any point in time, although core countries tend to get richer while those on the periphery get poorer, over the long haul major shifts do occur in which core countries descend from their pinnacle of power while countries at the semiperiphery ascend to replace them. In their historical depiction of this drama, world system theorists, though delineating the development of states as a consequence of an expanding international economy, rely on the empirical evolution of history for their analysis.

In general, however, world system theory, in contrast to modernization theory, views the terms of trade as fundamentally unequal, with wealth from the periphery flowing in the direction of the core as the world economic system expands. When capital, technology, and skills in the form of FDI by multinational corporations move from the core to the periphery, it is in search of cheap labor and easily accessible resources to produce goods for markets in the core. And without the capacity to reproduce or appropriate advanced technology for their own use, national economies in the periphery will generate neither an entrepreneurial class nor a self-sustaining economy to employ all their people. Multinational corporations, on the other hand, benefit from immense and movable assets, rapid changes in technology, worldwide communications and information sources, and ready access to resources, transportation, and competitive labor markets, enabling them to play countries off against one another.

Despite this rather bleak picture that world system theory paints of the marginalization of developing countries in the periphery, it recognizes the historical possibility that some states can move up the international hierarchy. The question this theoretical approach raises, then, is: What are the characteristics that enable some states to effect their own upward mobility in the world system? A similar question might be asked from the more sanguine outlook of modernization theory: Since international cooperation and trade at the international level enable countries to increase their wealth, why are these advantages so vastly underutilized? The developmental state approach, to which we now turn, offers an answer to these questions.

Developmental State Approach

In this view of the industrialization process, it is the systematic leadership of the state that explains how and why developing countries manage the difficult task of sustaining effective economic growth. The premise is deceptively simple: National policies that constructively promote industrialization do not follow automatically from either the international pressures of the advanced industrialized economies or the particular endowments of a particular country. In the absence of a self-confident entrepreneurial class, a state can be instrumental in generating production that is competitive on the international market. It does this by effectively intervening in domestic economic affairs, mobilizing and distributing resources from abroad as well as locally planning sectoral development in response to evolving international circumstances. To accomplish this end, a state must be capable of directing preferential investments; subsidizing unprofitable industrial ventures; providing infrastructure, technological leadership, tax and production privileges, and marketing assistance; promoting economies of scale in production; and withstanding the domestic political opposition to unpopular policies.[3]

If the developmental state plays the active, critical role in shaping the domestic political economy, it is also a principal player on the international scene. It must protect its national economic interests against the detrimental actions of outsiders while maximizing technological and economic integration into the international system. The underlying logic of this argument is similar to the Realist school of international political economy, which, as Frieden and Lake point out, makes three assumptions:

1. that nation-states are the highest authorities, dominant actors, and the sole judge of their own behavior *in the international economy;*
2. that each nation-state must always be prepared to defend itself by force, if necessary, because no other country or higher authority is obligated to come to its defense; and
3. that nation-states are rational actors in a zero-sum game, each choosing the course that yields the greatest value, in this case, the one that maximizes power.[4]

A developmental state demonstrates its strength in the international arena by controlling and managing foreign capital to enable its domestic economy's technological integration into the international market. Though proponents of the statist perspective share with modernization theorists the view that foreign capital inputs are essential to rapid industrial expansion, they nonetheless display the world system theorists' suspicion that foreign capital is apt to disproportionately benefit investors in the more advanced industrial economies unless the state is capable of breaking down the various components of the production bundle.[5] The "strength" of a developmental state, therefore, consists of having the resources, expertise, and authority to "decouple" foreign capital from its control and management by foreign investors. It must be able to selectively integrate those elements of production—capital and technology, for example—that fit the needs of domestic economic expansion in particular sectors by resisting demands that foreign investment directly control the entire production process from managerial operations and labor through marketing and the repatriation of profits. By restricting foreign direct investment to a particular sector, arranging for technology transfer through licensing or joint ventures, the developmental state protects future market shares and expansion for its domestic industries. But for it to implement such policies that employ foreign direct investment while reserving the domestic market for its own producers, the government must exercise extensive control over market forces within its territory.[6]

"Decoupling" by the developmental state is essential because it facilitates domestic capital accumulation, enabling one's own industries to move up the international product cycle whenever international circumstances present the opportunity. For developing countries to break out of their relative backwardness, according to the developmental state approach, sustained rapid growth is imperative. Only a strong state with centralized access to information, capital, and expertise can direct when and how to expand a nation's comparative advantage, helping to move its industries into new sectors and to acquire the latest technology. The government of a strong state can pursue commercial expansion abroad while providing protectionism at home. It is able to recruit foreign capital/technology with the promise of providing and regulating domestic inputs—a quiescent labor force, for example—while protecting and enhancing the competitive advantages of its domestic industries abroad. Thus the officials of a state can lead rather than follow, so long as they can exercise maximum control over both external and internal exigencies.

Applying the Theories to Regional Economic Growth

The actual strategies of Asian Pacific countries fall somewhere between these three theoretical models, mixing and matching on the basis of contingent factors, their own resources, and the degree and type of political integration obtained in each country. Despite their generally authoritarian adaptation to market systems, the differences among them are considerable, as detailed in Chapters 4 and 5. Most countries' policies acknowledge the market as instrumental for rapid economic growth, but no country is willing to entrust its economic fortunes entirely to unfettered market forces. In addition, each country empowers the state with significant control over economic affairs to discharge political objectives, albeit in ways different from one another. Yet in none of these countries, including Japan, does the state exercise the kind of independent political force claimed to be essential to the developmental state model.

The world system theory has an equally ambiguous applicability to Asian Pacific experiences. Its profound misgivings that an underdeveloped country can develop within the fold of international capitalism in any but the most crippled form of dependency is unsubstantiated in the outstanding economic performances of the principal players among Asian Pacific countries. Yet might it not be argued that Asian Pacific countries have succeeded precisely to the degree to which they heeded the theory's counsel against the debilitating effects of international capitalism? The impact of the global economy under colonial rule was, after all, the foundation of strong, centralized states throughout the Asian Pacific. Nationalistic sentiment, with the exception of Japan and Thailand, was nurtured on opposition to international capitalism, providing the vocabulary for newly independent nation-states as they pursued modernization in the postwar world. And where it has occurred, their rapid economic growth over the last 30 years is heavily indebted to the political economy of the Cold War and Japan's resurrection as a regional core of the expanding global economy.

For purposes of exploring the political economy of the Asian Pacific region, therefore, world system theory furnishes the most pertinent perspective for understanding because it underscores the mutual dependence of nations as part of the global economy.

U.S. HEGEMONY AND A REGIONAL GROWTH ECONOMY

Successful economic growth in the Asian Pacific has been distinguished by an export-oriented strategy pursued by strong nationalistic states and private firms operating in a capitalist market. Even the socialist countries—China, Vietnam, Laos, and even North Korea in its initial stages—have opened their economies to international trade and investment, adapting capitalist institutions into a hybrid form of socialist market. How do these countries, all of whom depend heavily on the United States to absorb their exports and on Japan to upgrade their technology and provide capital, relate to one another economically and politically within the larger global context? What underlying patterns have evolved out of their pursuit of prosperity within a postwar global context of expanding opportunities? These questions can only be answered against the backdrop of Japan's ascent to regional power status prior to World War II and the rise of the United States to hegemonic status in the postwar world.

Nationalism, regionalism, and the global economy appeared as a triumvirate on the Asian Pacific scene. Nationalism, as described in Chapter 2, was inspired by European political domination and economic exploitation of the region in the nineteenth century. And regionalism was the result of Japan's economic and political participation in the Western-sponsored dismemberment of China. In 1895 Japan acquired access to Korea and Taiwan. Subsequently, as Japan spread its control over northern China, these three territories were integrated into the East Asian Co-Prosperity Sphere, a highly centralized, regional economic empire. As protégé and beneficiary of Western imperialism, Japan enlarged its empire through regional conquest and military occupation so that prior to the end of World War II it encompassed the length and breadth of the Asian Pacific. Thus even before nationalist movements in the rest of the Asian Pacific succeeded in achieving independence from Western political domination, an endeavor in which they were often aided by the Japanese, the peoples of the Asian Pacific had imposed on them a substantial degree of regional integration with Japan at its core.

Japanese-centered regionalism was defeated at the end of World War II by the United States, the new economic center of world power. But with the Asian Pacific and Western Europe in ruins, the wealthy colossus and only creditor nation in the world had first to nurture not only its allies but also its vanquished enemies back to economic health to secure trading partners for itself. Toward this end, the United States organized and funded a new set of global institutions to establish a universal system of liberalized trade throughout the "free world." The International Monetary Fund (IMF), the World Bank (WB), and the General Agreement on Trade and Tariffs (GATT) were designed to promote strong capitalist economies with politically stable pro-American regimes, especially in the frontline states bordering the "communist world."

In conjunction with massive U.S. economic and military assistance, the global economy under the Bretton Woods system of fixed international exchange rates entered a period of robust growth and expansion. The results were immediately visible in the developed countries where annual economic growth (real GDP) grew at an average of 5 percent in the period between 1950 and 1970. This was "two and a half times the growth rate in the four preceding decades and twice as rapid as would occur later in the 1970s."[7] Thus the initial beneficiaries of this new international political regime were the developed countries.

Continuation of the prosperity of the developed world, however, depended upon political stability and the extension of economic development to the rest of the free world. Germany was rehabilitated as the core of an anticommunist Western Europe, and Japan was politically and economically reconstructed as the principal U.S. partner in the Asian Pacific. When the communists came to power in China, the United States dramatically expanded its economic and military assistance to South Korea and Taiwan as well as propping up the interests of the British outposts of Hong Kong and Singapore—together forming the "four tigers."

In Southeast Asia, the United States assumed responsibility for the political stability of countries along the entire perimeter of communist China, helping to negotiate the independence of colonies from European control, intervening in support of conservative pro-American elites when necessary to "contain communism," and waging war if those elites seemed in danger of collapse. But if the United States shouldered the political leadership and military protection of the noncommunist Asian Pacific, it delegated economic responsibility for its growth and development to Japan. Thus Japan emerged as a strategic economic partner of the United States in Pacific Asia, once again acting as the core of an East Asian regional configuration, this time only economically, with military security provided by the United States.

The U.S.-Japanese Partnership

The irony of postwar reconstruction of a global economy tied to the wealth and productivity of the United States was its ultimate enfeeblement of the giant on which the world depended. To protect its world order ("hegemonic stability") from the perceived threat of communism, the United States engaged in two costly wars in Korea and Vietnam, financed the military security of the entire "free world," and helped rebuild and construct the powerful economies that were to become its competitors.

Even the rules that the United States promoted to facilitate international trade in the postwar world, known as an *open trade regime*, proved to be a mixed blessing for the United States. Although designed to prevent national barriers from raising the costs of selling merchandise throughout the "free world," these rules, if they were to fulfill the multiple objectives of the United States, had to accommodate protectionist policies on the part of its allies while keeping the U.S. market wide open to their exports. Import substitution, after all, was essential for Japan, Taiwan, and South Korea to build the industrial strength necessary to be politically stable partners in the cold war. From the beginning, therefore, American policymakers used a double standard to measure "open trade," a policy referred to as *diffuse reciprocity*.[8] By relying on formal procedures rather than actual outcomes, the United States was able to overlook infractions of free trade rules when it suited the strategic purposes of maintaining "hegemonic stability."[9]

In the Asian Pacific, this meant a convergence of interests between postwar Japan and the United States: reviving the Japanese economy as a regional superpower dependent upon Southeast Asia for its source of raw materials. Toward this end, "Washington promoted a triangular economic division of trade between the United States, Japan and Southeast Asia in which America would provide high technology and capital goods, Japan intermediate and consumer goods and Southeast Asia raw materials and energy."[10] This policy was articulated by the Joint Chiefs of Staff in a July 1952 report and implemented in the American practice of linking American aid to the region to the purchase of Japanese goods and services.

The Japanese took advantage of the opportunity provided in the San Francisco Peace Treaty, which required them to pay war reparations to countries devastated in the 1930s and 1940s but left the amount and type to be determined by Tokyo. Between 1955 and 1965, Japan negotiated separate agreements with ten East and Southeast Asian countries, transferring about $1.5 billion in reparations and economic/technical assistance to Burma, Indonesia, the Philippines, South Vietnam, Cambodia, Laos, Malaysia, South Korea, Singapore, and Thailand. "By tying all this aid to purchases of Japanese goods and services, Tokyo opened up vast export markets as each country became dependent on Japanese corporations for spare parts, related products and technical assistance."[11]

From the world system perspective, this partnership between the United States and Japan, which provided the foundation of U.S. Cold War policy in the Asian Pacific, set into motion a subregional division of labor among the countries inhabiting this most recently incorporated part of the global economy. If the United States needed Japan to carry out its postwar mission in the Asian hemisphere, Japan needed Southeast Asia as a source of raw materials to replace its earlier colonial territories in China, Korea, and Taiwan. Accordingly, Japan's reindustrialization acted as a subregional core tied to the availability of raw materials and markets in a subregional periphery—namely, the countries of Indonesia, Malaysia, and Brunei. In between these two positions of "flying geese," an intermediate subregional semiperiphery emerged made up of the four tigers—South Korea, Taiwan, Singapore, and Hong Kong—also considered essential to the postwar hegemonic stability of the United States. Thus the regionalization of the Asian Pacific can be viewed, through the lens of world system perspective, as a consequence of the reconstruction of the global economy after World War II.

As long as the United States remained preoccupied with the war in Vietnam, the American economy was assumed to be so far ahead of the rest of the world that Japan's resurgence as an industrial giant attracted little attention. Fundamental cooperation between the victor and the vanquished of World War II was dictated by the defense of the "free world" in the Cold War against communism. In the global arena, Japan accepted its junior partnership with the United States while regionally exercising its own hegemonic power as senior partner to the Southeast and East Asian allies of the United States. But the United States found its economy perceptibly weakening under the twin burdens of a costly, not-so-cold war and an insatiable demand by U.S. consumers for goods manufactured in Japan. Alarmed by the relentless expansion of Japan's share of the American market, the United States began reversing its lax policy of tolerating the asymmetry in its trade relationship with Japan. During the 1970s, the United States won Japanese agreement to a series of compromises—trigger price mechanisms (TPMs) and voluntary export restraints (VERs)—curtailing the high volume of color televisions, steel, and automobiles it exported to the United States.

In retrospect the major disruptions in the world economy of the 1970s and the political reconfiguration of international relations they triggered set the stage for a new international political economy. Breakdown of the Bretton Woods system of fixed international exchange rates came in the early part of the decade, when the United States went off the gold standard. Two oil crises—in 1973 and 1979—sent shock waves of recession and inflation rippling through developed and underdeveloped countries alike. And in 1975 and 1979, respectively, the U.S. withdrawal from Vietnam and normalization of relations with the People's Republic of China resulted in similar political aftershocks for governments around the world. After Mao Zedong's death in 1976, China reversed its course, embarking on an economic reform program that by the mid-1980s brought it into the East Asian community of newly industrializing nations, whose primary market for manufactured goods was the United States. By the early 1970s Japan had surpassed the United States as the predominant trade power in East Asia and was accumulating a large trade surplus with the United States. And the U.S. trade deficit was beginning to threaten global financial stability. In this international context, the relationship of Japan and the United States entered a new, more confrontational phase.

By the 1980s, the United States was absorbing an estimated 71 percent of the manufactured exports of the Asian Pacific, with the contribution of the NICs having risen substantially alongside the exports from Japan. The new tensions raised by the Japanese trade surplus with the United States were addressed by the Plaza Agreement reached in February 1985, when the five key-currency countries then known as the Group of Five—made up of the United States, Britain, France, West Germany, and Japan—agreed to a policy of bringing the value of the dollar down in relation to the yen. This agreement to manage a depreciation in the American currency that would appreciate the Japanese currency was directed at reversing the enormous growth of Asian Pacific exports that had yielded Japan huge trade surpluses with the United States in the early 1980s. The expectation was that a stronger yen would make Japanese goods in the United States less attractive to consumers while increasing sales of American goods in Japan.

The results were mixed: The U.S. global deficit did decline as the Japanese yen appreciated from 230 to 120 to the dollar, but the Japanese trade surplus with the United States nonetheless remained high ($38 billion) while the NICs benefited by increasing their exports to the United States. Even though the costs of their imports from Japan rose, increasing the NICs' trade deficits with Japan, the NICs accumulated growing surpluses with the United States, edging in on the Japanese market share. Thus, the NICs, as part of a triangular trade relationship, have contributed to the increase in both the U.S. deficit and the Japanese surplus, simultaneously strengthening the regional hegemony of Japan and weakening the global hegemony of the United States. In seeking redress for its persistent overall trade deficits with the Asian Pacific, the United States has turned its attention to the value of other Asian currencies and the use of "specific outcomes" to open markets in Asian Pacific countries for American goods.

In the early 1990s, the United States and the European Community still found themselves with recessionary problems of high unemployment and underutilized productive capacity. Japan, with over 40 percent of its investments in the United States, was also in a recession, with substantial losses on its investments, the collapse of real estate and stock markets, and dramatic political turmoil attending the fall from power of Japan's long-standing ruling party. Although the United States was forced to grapple with large trade deficits, Japan had enormous trade surpluses. Despite these surpluses, however, Japan found itself in a sustained period of economic stagnation in the aftermath of the asset-price bubble while the United States recorded outstanding economic performance. From 1992 to 1997 annual real growth in Japanese GDP averaged 1.4 percent, which is poor not only compared to the United States but also to the slower-growth economies of the EU, which averaged 1.7 percent in the same period. In the boom period preceding this, from 1988 to 1991, Japan's GDP had averaged 4.9 percent. In any event, it is essential to clearly distinguish Japan's extended economic stagnation from the Asian financial crisis.

Japan's poor economic performance for six consecutive years prior to the 1997 financial collapse was critical because it precluded Japan from contributing in any positive manner to the region's ability to cope with financial collapse. If anything, Japan's powerful position as a regional economic hub made it more of a liability than an asset as its economy fell into official recession (negative growth rate) in 1998. Unable to move into positive growth territory until the rest of the region began its recovery in 1999/2000, Japan found itself ceding heroic regional leadership to China instead, which steadfastly resisted devaluation of its currency to prevent the region from falling deeper into the abyss. The question of what happened to Japan—why was it stagnating instead of prospering in the period leading up to regional financial collapse?—is important for our purposes because it addresses the issue of how prepared Japan is to exercise the regional and global leadership expected of the second most powerful economy in the world. In this context, one of the four explanations generally offered for Japan's economic misfortunes deserves mention before turning to a consideration of how Japan's trade, aid, and investment patterns contributed to its becoming the dominant economic power in the Asian Pacific region.

The most popular explanation for Japan's six-year stagnation and subsequent sharp contraction under the impetus of regional financial crisis is that the Japanese economic model (its structures and mode of operation) is to blame. Japan did not sufficiently "reform" its basic economic structure to meet the global standards for liberalization. A second explanation is that Japan's disappointing performance results from interest-group deadlock, which can only be overcome by a painful destruction of Japan's tightly woven and corrupt economic system. Yet a third explanation faults Japan's burdens of an aging society that acts as a constraint to short-run growth, prescribing macroeconomic austerity to provide for the long-run future of an aging society. A fourth explanation, offered by Adam Posen in a well-documented study, *Restoring Japan's Economic Growth,* is that Japanese policymakers mistakenly administered the wrong cure for what ailed the economy.[12] His analysis suggests that insufficient demand was the culprit for Japan's six years of low growth before the advent of the financial collapse. But by administering a laissez-faire financial strategy as part of a macroeconomic austerity program, Japanese policymakers were fighting the last war—the 1930s Great Depression—with the same weaponry that had lost the war last time. The distinctive feature of this explanation is that it focuses on policy rather than economic models as coherent national blueprints or determinants of short-run macroeconomic performance.

What we turn to now is an understanding of Japan's trade, aid, and investment policies and how they affected regional growth and development.

THE JAPAN-CENTERED STRUCTURE OF REGIONAL TRADE

Japan has become the major trading partner for all Asian Pacific economies. Japan not only exports more to each of those economies than does the United States, in 1997 it also exported more to the Asian Pacific region as a whole than it did to the United States. As recently as 1982, U.S. exports to South Korea and the Philippines were more than Japan's, and to Taiwan they were about the same level. By contrast, in 1997 Japan's exports to South Korea were more than three times those of the United States and one and three-quarters times more than U.S. exports to Taiwan. Even to the Philippines, which was for so long a traditional U.S. market, the United States now sells less than Japan, $2.27 billion versus $8.694 billion.[13] Although the United States continues to be the largest importer of goods from these countries, with the exception of Indonesia, Japan seems to be closing the gap in the case of Taiwan, South Korea, and Thailand. Only in Singapore has the United States continued to do very well, but even there Japan's 1989–1991 increase was 16 percent, compared to 11 percent for the United States. In the aftermath of Japan's adjustment to the yen appreciation by transferring production to "offshore" locations, the exports of Asian Pacific economies have increased and an increasing share of these exports is going to Japan.

This greater intraregional trade exhibited since 1985 seems to support the Japanese belief in the "flying-geese pattern" of economic growth in the Asian Pacific.[14] The striking aspect of this image applied to Asian Pacific countries is the diversity of "geese" that make up the flock. By their sheer size, capitalist Japan and more recently socialist China—more of a fellow traveler than a member of the flock—cast long shadows over both the more industrialized NICs and the more resource-rich Southeast Asian nations. In everything from size and population to politics and culture, the diversity of countries in the region militates against the kind of economic integration that has occurred in the EC (now the EU). Yet a regional economic pattern has emerged from the flow of merchandise, capital, and aid that links the developmental states of the Asian Pacific with one another and with the global economy. At the center of this regional economic formation is Japan, which acts as model, facilitator, and engine for growth in the region. Though its own growth rate today is lower than all the economies of East and Southeast Asia except Myanmar and Cambodia, Japan dominates the region by the staggering size of its productive output and per capita income. Its position as leader of "the flying geese" suggests two things: It sets the direction in which the flock moves and provides a structure for its economic interrelationships.

In the postwar world, Japan established its regional dominance by a capacity for rapid restructuring of its export-led production to keep one step ahead of technological advances on the global market and of protectionist devices against Japan exports. While producing toys, electrical appliances, and textiles in the 1950s and 1960s, Japan acquired the technology—through licensing, joint ventures, and "reverse engineering" rather than direct foreign investment—for producing ships, steel, heavy machinery, and automobiles to export in the 1960s and 1970s. When oil crises and protectionist pressures threatened the security of Japan's resources and markets in the 1970s, Japan was quick to alter the structure of its industrial production again, upgrading its technology to produce high-tech electronics like videocassettes and scientific equipment and adopting stringent conservation measures along with diversifying its sourcing for raw materials. Since 1980, Japan has upgraded its technology, shifting its comparative advantage once again, to knowledge-based or information and communication industries.

These shifts in comparative advantage by which Japan propelled itself into the forefront of industrialization are reflected in the composition of Japanese trade. According to data from the Keizai Koho Centre, exports of textiles, ships, and steel products dropped from 29 percent of Japan's total exports in 1977 to 10 percent in 1988, while automobiles increased throughout the 1980s, reaching 20 percent of Japan's total export value in 1986. The leap in Japan's technological sophistication as an industrial producer during this period is evidenced in the declining share of total imports, represented by foodstuffs, which remained constant in absolute terms as compared to manufactured goods, whose share of total imports increased from 19 percent in 1980 to 55 percent in 1996.[15]

As Japan restructured its own economy, it exported the capital, machinery, and know-how perfected in the previous phase to its developing neighbors, "the four tigers" or NICs, who could then promote a similar line of exports while avoiding the import restraints targeted at Japan. Most often, this involved Japanese companies moving their investments and production facilities "offshore" to locations in the NICs that offered lower wages and fewer deterrents to exports destined for the United States or the European Community. Offshore production in these so-called "sunset" industries, therefore, continued to profit the Japanese economy as well as boosting regional growth rates by increasing its neighbors' dependence on Japan for spare parts and components. In its move up the industrialization ladder, therefore, Japan not only elevated the economies of its neighbors but tied them more closely to its own. Though the Japanese contend that in this way other countries of the Asian Pacific will be able to "catch up" to Japan, the V-shape of the "flying geese" formation suggests no such closing of the ranks, a deduction many of Japan's Asian Pacific neighbors draw from experience. Equally clear, however, is the imprint the Japanese structure of economic growth and trade have had on the phenomenal development of the entire region.

Trade Patterns of the NICs

If domestic adaptation of the Japanese economy had the outcome of regionalizing economic growth during the 1960s and 1970s, the yen appreciation following the Plaza Accord in the mid-1980s had a similar if unintended effect. Designed to lower the Japanese trade surplus with the United States by making Japanese exports to the United States more expensive, its impact in the Asian Pacific was to accelerate the export-led industrialization of the NICs, linking their trade more closely to Japan. Because their currencies were either pegged to the dollar or appreciated only slightly, the NICs could increase their exports (especially consumer electronics) to the United States after 1985. This enabled them to achieve the highest growth rates in the region during the decade ending in 1990. Their combined exports to the United States almost doubled from 1984 to come within four-fifths of Japan's sizable exports to the United States in 1990. And in 1998 their combined exports to the United States have almost caught up with that of Japan, constituting 96% of Japan's exports to the United States.

But if the NICs gained the most from yen appreciation enlarging their trade surplus with the United States, they also increased their dependence on Japanese imports, forming a triangular relationship characteristic of growth in the region. To sustain a high level of exports to the United States, the NICs imported from Japan the intermediate components to produce their consumer and communications products for the American market. As a consequence, the NICs ran a trade deficit with Japan throughout the 1980s, despite an increasing level of exports to Japan.[16] NIC exports to Japan accelerated after the Plaza Accord, mounting from $11 billion in 1985 to $26 billion in 1990. A new element of this trade between the NICs and Japan was the growing proportion of manufactured goods, particularly consumer electronics, that began to make inroads into the Japanese home market. In place of the labor-intensive finished goods, there was a larger component of technology-intensive parts, even capital goods, that made up Japanese imports from the NICs, the proportion increasing from 58 percent in 1980 to 66 percent in 1987.[17]

Between 1984 and 1990 Hong Kong and South Korea substantially reduced their exports to the United States as a proportion of their total, while increasing their exports to Japan, the other NICs, and the European Community. As seen in Table 8.1, all four NICs are import-dependent upon Japan, which has consistently enjoyed large trade surpluses with them: in 1997, $11.491 billion with South Korea, $15.081 billion with Taiwan, $25.009 billion with Hong Kong, and $14.389 billion with Singapore. And though all are heavily export-dependent upon the United States, with the exception of Singapore, the huge investments of South Korea and Taiwan in heavy and high-technology industries and of Hong Kong in labor-intensive industries have made them even more dependent on imports of Japanese capital equipment.[18]

All four NICs have expanded their trade with China and the EC as well as with one another. With Taiwan and South Korea relaxing their political opposition to trading with China, Hong Kong became a major conduit for growing trade with China. By 1993, increasing investments from Taiwan and Hong Kong, which take advantage of cheap labor in the growing number of special economic zones set up by the Chinese government, have turned the major thoroughfares in and out of

TABLE 8.1   Japanese Trade with Asian Pacific and Global Partners, 1997 (in U.S.$ Millions)

Country/Group of Countries	Japan's Exports to	Japan's Imports from	Japan's Trade Balance
Hong Kong	27,257	2,248	+25,009
Singapore	20,264	5,875	+14,389
South Korea	26,097	14,606	+11,491
Taiwan	27,557	12,476	+15,081
NICs: Total	101,175	35,205	+65,970
Brunei	149	1,407	−1,258
Indonesia	10,190	14,605	−4,415
Malaysia	14,524	11,372	+3,152
Philippines	8,694	5,014	+3,680
Thailand	14,615	9,568	+5,047
ASEAN-5: Total	48,172	41,966	+6,206
China (mainland)	21,692	41,827	−20,135
EU	65,728	45,266	+20,462
United States	118,383	75,975	+42,408

Source: International Monetary Fund, *Direction of Trade Statistics, Yearbook,* 1998, pp. 271–273.

Hong Kong into parking lots. As increased trade between the NICs and China passed through Hong Kong, ASEAN's share of Hong Kong trade decreased somewhat during the 1980s. But in the 1990s the NICs' trade with ASEAN have increased slightly. Altogether, regional trade has become a more significant element in the NICs' overall trade picture, with slightly increased imports from other NICs (except for South Korea) and significantly expanded exports to China as illustrated in Table 8.2.

Just as Hong Kong's trade has been firmly linked to the continent of China, Singapore's retains its special relationship with Malaysia. Though its trade with Thailand and Taiwan grew between 1984 and 1990 from 3.4 percent to 4.5 percent and from 2.5 percent to 3.9 percent of total exports, respectively, Singapore's trade in the Asian Pacific region remains especially high with Malaysia: It was 15.6 percent of the total in 1984, and 15.1 percent in 1998. But significantly, Singapore's trade with the other NICs *collectively* increased during the period between 1984 and 1998 from 8 percent to 15.2 percent, surpassing its total trade with Malaysia of 15.1 percent in 1998 and with Japan of 12.1 percent. Compared to its trade with the NICs, however, Singapore's trade with the United States remains at roughly 18 percent (in 1998 it was 18.9 percent) while its trade with the EU initially increased from 10.3 percent in 1984 to 13.9 percent in 1997 and has remained at that level.[19] Overall, Singapore has moved in the direction of evenly distributing its trade not only throughout the Asian Pacific region but also globally.

TABLE 8.2   NICs Trade with Selected Partners, 1991 and 1997 (Percent of Total Exports and Imports)

Two-way Trade		Hong Kong	Singapore	South Korea	Taiwan
To Japan	1991	5.4	8.7	17.2	12.1
	1997	6.1	7.1	10.9	9.6 (8.4)*
From Japan	1991	16.4	21.3	25.9	30.0
	1997	13.7	16.9	19.3	25.4 (25.8)
To other NICs	1991	8.9	13.1	12.6	21.1
	1997	6.6	17.1	16.3	29.4 (26.6)
From other NICs	1991	18.1	10.0	4.1	8.2
	1997	17.2	10.3	3.9	8.9 (9.9)
To ASEAN-5	1991	3.5	23.2†	6.1	6.5***
	1997	3.6	25.5†	9.4	8.1 (6.4)
From ASEAN-5	1991	3.7	19.2†	6.3	5.5
	1997	5.4	21.9†	6.5	8.5 (9.1)
To ASEAN-7	1991	3.9	23.7†	6.4	—
	1997	4.0	27.4†	10.6	—
From ASEAN-7**	1991	3.9	19.3†	6.3	—
	1997	5.5	22.4†	—	—
To China	1991	27.1	1.5	1.4	—
	1997	34.9	3.2	10.0	—
From China	1991	37.7	3.4	4.2	—
	1997	37.7	4.3	6.9	—
To United States	1991	22.7	19.7	25.9	29.3
	1997	21.8	18.5	15.9	24.2 (26.6)
From USA	1991	7.6	15.9	23.2	22.4
	1997	7.8	16.9	20.7	20.3 (18.8)
To EU	1991	18.8	14.6	14.7	12.4‡
	1997	14.7	13.9	11.2	10.3 (11.9)
From EU	1991	9.7	13.0	13.1	9.7
	1997	11.0	13.9	13.0	11.9 (13.1)

*In parentheses are figures for 1998.
**ASEAN-7 includes Malaysia, Thailand, Philippines, Brunei, Indonesia, Myanmar, and Vietnam.
***This figure does not include Brunei (Indonesia, Malaysia, Thailand, and Philippines).
†These figures do not include Indonesia.
‡This figure only includes UK, Germany, France, and the Netherlands.
Sources: International Monetary Fund, *Direction of Trade Statistics Yearbook 1998*, pp. 161–163, 280–282, 397–399; *Taiwan Statistical Data Book, 1999*, pp. 217–220.

Trade Patterns of ASEAN

By the 1990s, the ASEAN-4 (Indonesia, Malaysia, Philippines, and Thailand) had joined the ranks of three newly industrializing nations (Malaysia, Indonesia, and Thailand) overtaking the NICs in their growth performance (see Table 8.3). From their early role as suppliers of raw materials and energy, principally to Japan, the resource-rich ASEAN nations have moved in the direction of diversifying their exports. When Japan and other industrialized countries reduced the proportion of raw materials and fuel per unit of production after the 1970s, ASEAN nations turned to Japanese and NIC foreign direct investments to upgrade their industrial base. Commodity exports, as a consequence, constitute a smaller share of total ASEAN exports. In 1991 more than half of the exports from Thailand, Malaysia, and the Philippines (as shown in Table 8.4) consisted of manufactures: 67 percent in Thailand, 61 percent in Malaysia, and 71 percent in the Philippines. Even with this shift in composition of trade on the part of the resource-rich ASEAN nations, their relationship with Japan has remained asymmetrical, with ASEAN depending on Japan to buy 35 percent of its commodity exports while Japan's commodity imports from ASEAN constitute only 15 percent of its total.[20]

One solution to the problem of asymmetrical trade relationships is to diversify trading partners. When Malaysia and the Philippines sought to alter their dependence upon their former colonial powers—Great Britain and the United States—however, they found themselves export-dependent on Japan instead. Japan's initial dominance in Southeast Asia both in the prewar and early postwar periods—as consumer of its natural resources and primary products—has been solidified rather than reduced by its becoming an investor rather than merely a consumer. The trade statistics in Table 8.5 attest to this, and individual country data bear it out. Of Malaysia's exports in 1984, 22.8 percent went to Japan with only 13.5 percent to the United States and 13 percent to Western Europe. In the same year, 26 percent of Malaysia's total imports were Japanese products, compared to 16.1 percent and 15.5 percent that were U.S. and Western European market shares, respectively.[21] Indonesia, until the late 1960s, was import-dependent on Japan but export-dependent on the United States. But by 1984, 47.3 percent of Indonesia's exports and 23.8 percent of its

TABLE 8.3   *Percent of Growth in Gross Domestic Product, NICs and ASEAN-4*

NICs	1990–96	1995–96	ASEAN-4	1990–96	1995–96
Hong Kong	5.5	2.2	Indonesia	7.7	5.8
Singapore	8.7	5.6	Malaysia	8.7	5.8
South Korea	7.3	5.6	Philippines	2.9	4.5
Taiwan*	6.5	8.2	Thailand	8.3	4.4
NIC average	7.0	5.4	ASEAN average	6.9	5.1

*Taiwan data for 1997.
Source: Far Eastern Economic Review: Asia 1999 Yearbook, pp. 12–13.

TABLE 8.4   ASEAN-4, NICs, China, Japan, and United States Exports by Sector, 1991 (Percent of Total Exports)

Country	Fuels, Minerals, Metals	Other Primary Commodities	Transport, Machinery	Textiles, Clothing	Other Manufactures
Indonesia	43	16	2	14	25
Malaysia	17	22	38	6	17
Philippines	9	20	14	9	48
Thailand	2	32	22	17	28
Hong Kong	2	3	24	40	32
Singapore	18	8	48	5	21
South Korea	3	4	38	21	34
Taiwan	2	6	38	16	39
China	9	15	19	28	29
Japan	1	1	66	2	29
United States	6	14	48	2	30

Source: World Bank, *Development Report,* 1993, Table 16.

TABLE 8.5   Destination of ASEAN-5 Exports, 1991 and 1997 (Percent of Total Exports)

Destination		Brunei	Malaysia	Philippines	Thailand	Indonesia
To Japan	1991	63.08	15.86	20.03	17.82	36.90
	1997	53.85	12.55	15.99	15.18	24.35
To NICs	1991	17.13	33.77	11.98	16.02	20.96
	1997	11.03	33.07	16.99	21.55	21.36
To ASEAN-4	1991	13.25	5.87	4.38	3.58	2.70
	1997	4.55	6.98	5.18	8.04	5.93
To China	1991	0.16	1.86	1.45	1.16	4.08
	1997	*	2.37	1.05	3.03	4.54
To United States	1991	1.06	16.88	35.65	21.06	12.03
	1997	2.23	18.57	34.43	19.39	14.41
To EU	1991	0.53	15.17	19.08	22.41	13.13
	1997	21.35	14.42	16.11	15.91	14.93

*Amount negligible.
Source: IMF 1998 Direction of Trade Statistics Yearbook.

imports were traded with Japan, while the United States took only 20.6 percent of Indonesian exports and provided 18.4 percent of its imports.[22] In the case of the Philippines, which has been export-dependent on the United States since independence, one-third of its trade deficit since the 1970s has been with Japan. Only Thailand, more recently, seems to have avoided being export-dependent on any single trading partner, though its import-dependence on Japan has grown. This "tilting" of ASEAN countries (with the exception of Singapore) "caught in a classical 'neocolonial' relationship with Japan in which they increase their dependency and Japan increases its surpluses."[23]

However, with the exception of the Philippines and Thailand, export figures for 1997 indicate a shift away from this dependence on Japan. During the 1980s, the most significant feature of ASEAN-5 trade was the growth in exports to the NICs compared to the relative decline in importance of exports to Japan. Now all of the ASEAN-5 countries—Indonesia, Malaysia, Thailand, the Philippines, and Brunei— are exporting proportionately less to Japan and more to the NICs than previously. All of them except for Thailand are trading more with one another. Proportionately, Indonesian exports to China have increased substantially, with only slight increases by Malaysia, the Philippines, and Thailand. Although Japan remains an important trading partner for members of ASEAN, its relative importance for ASEAN exports has remained the same or declined. For Thailand, Japan has increased dramatically as a trading partner, quadrupling its exports and increasing its imports by almost the same amount by 1990.[24] Apart from Japan, Thailand's trade in the Asian Pacific region is primarily with Singapore, though its trade with the NICs has increased, placing it just behind Singapore.[25]

In trade with extraregional partners, Indonesia, the Philippines, and Brunei exported a smaller proportion to the United States in 1997 than they did in 1984, while in the same period, all five of the ASEAN countries increased their exports to the EC. Combined exports from ASEAN-5 as a group to the United States and EC increased from 15 percent in 1984 to 18 percent in 1990 and to 17.2 percent in 1997. If we compare ASEAN-6 exports within the region (that is, with Japan, China, other ASEANs, and NICs), it is clear that only one-third of Philippine and Thai exports are intraregional, while two-thirds or more of the exports of Indonesia, Malaysia, and Brunei are intraregional. Singapore's exports are about evenly divided.

In summary, the pattern of trade that has emerged among Asian Pacific countries is clearly structured around the dominance of Japan's economy in the region but with strong extraregional dependencies on the part of most individual countries (including Japan) on core markets in the larger global economy, in the United States and Western Europe. Japan's economic behavior as regional hegemon has been marked by the inequality that world system theory predicts of core countries: It has preserved its own superiority as leading goose in the region, and by intensifying the trade dependency of the flock, has insured that the other geese will continue to fly in formation. The one exception is China, which will undoubtedly rival or surpass Japan as a regional economic hegemon. Hong Kong has already nominally returned to China's sovereignty though its political economy remains distinct as a Special Administrative Region (SAR) until 2047.

The questions we turn to now are what the pattern of investments is in the region and what it might indicate concerning the interrelationship of regionalization and globalization.

INVESTMENT PATTERNS IN THE REGION

Export-led strategy, which has become a trademark of Asian Pacific development, results not only in increased world trade and rapid economic growth for parts of the developing world but also in vastly expanded opportunities for capital investments from the developed world, the foreign direct investments (FDI) of transnational corporations. FDI in the postwar world has been the late-twentieth-century equivalent of the Portuguese and Spanish explorers of the late fifteenth century. It is capital in search of new economic horizons to chart, conveyed by computer rather than by ship. Among the factors influencing the transformation of today's world economy, FDI has assumed extraordinary importance because it is the medium of technology transfer, a form of DNA for human civilization in the twenty-first century. Not surprisingly, therefore, FDI has grown even faster than world trade and output. As developing countries intensify their efforts to attract FDI and transnational corporations adopt increasingly global strategies to survive and prosper, the gap between the growth rate of exports and that of foreign direct investment continues to widen. It has prompted one writer to observe that "as a means of international economic integration, foreign direct investment is in its take-off phase; perhaps in a position comparable to world trade at the end of the 1940s."[26]

The global pattern of FDI (inward and outward stock and flows) in the early 1980s can be depicted as bipolar, dominated by the United States and the EC, which by 1988 had achieved parity with the United States in terms of stock. In the 1990s the global pattern became tripolar, with Japan having emerged as an equally important FDI power, at least in terms of outward flows. Japan thereby constitutes the third member of a triad. The rapidly declining share of the United States in the triad's total outward stocks and flows has been taken up by the rising share of Japan, which, at least in terms of outward flows, surpassed the United States in 1993 by a substantial margin. In fact, the United States, by becoming a major host (recipient) country for FDI, has promoted the overall rise in world foreign direct investment located in the triad. By contrast, Japan, which has so far discouraged the inward flow of FDI, has contributed to the relatively low share (about one-half) of worldwide inward stock located in the triad as a whole.[27] As a host country for FDI, therefore, Japan is not yet considered an equal triad member, though through international mergers and acquisitions, that may be in the process of changing.

From a global perspective, then, the triad occupies a dominant position in the marketing strategies of Japanese transnational corporations: Of the total 10.5 trillion yen of manufactured goods sold by Japanese foreign affiliates in 1987, 54 percent were sales by affiliates located in the two other triad members (the United States and the EC), and 64 percent were sales to a triad country from affiliates in all countries. The second most important market for Japanese affiliates abroad is Asia, where regional core networks are strongly linked not only to Japan but also to the two other legs of the triad: Of the total exports of Asian manufacturing affiliates, 68 percent were to the triad, with 35 percent, 23 percent, and 10 percent exported to Japan, the United States, and the EC, respectively. A large percentage of these exports are semifinished goods exported from Asia for final manufacture or assembly by another affiliate in the triad or low-cost finished goods to be sold by an affiliated distributor in the triad.[28] This pattern integrates economic markets across regions so that low-cost suppliers based in Asia support the three-legged strategy in the triad. Japan plays an important role in supplying Asian affiliates, such as in some cases the electrical and electronic equipment industries, create low-cost supply networks to sell manufactured goods back to Japan, while in others, such as the automobile industry, supply low-cost components to sell to affiliates in the United States. A major question for the future is what would happen to this interregional economic integration should further regionalization of markets occur in North America and Europe.

The Regional Pattern of FDI

As Table 8.6 clearly indicates, the lion's share of foreign direct investment (FDI) in Asian Pacific countries, with the notable exception of China, comes from the developed countries of North America, Western Europe, and Japan. Shifts occurring between the early and late 1980s continue to distinguish subregional differences between ASEAN and NIC countries. For the NICs, excluding Hong Kong, FDI from developed countries has steadily increased as a share of the total, with a decreasing proportion of FDI coming from developing countries. Unlike the developing countries, for whom higher labor costs have eroded the advantages of the location, developed countries still find production costs lower than at home, with certain advantages such as access to a skilled labor force, available infrastructure, and an export orientation. However, they have shifted investments toward more technologically sophisticated industries, manufacturing high value-added products, and increasingly toward services.[29]

For ASEAN countries, with the exception of Malaysia, where the share from developing countries has remained constant, there has been a noticeable growth in FDI from developing countries, especially those within the region, and a corresponding decrease in the share from developed countries. China is the only country where the share of developing countries' FDI exceeds that of developed countries, reflecting the importance of investments coming from Hong Kong, Taiwan, and South Korea into the special economic zones in the coastal areas. The emergence of the NICs as a regionally significant source of FDI, specifically in China, has led some scholars to observe China's potential alongside the NICs to act as an economic counterpoint to Japan's predominance in the region.

Among developed countries, there has been a shift away from North America and Western Europe in favor of Japan as a source of FDI. Since 1989 Japan has become the largest single investor in the region as a whole. Its investments in Taiwan, South Korea, Hong Kong, and ASEAN in 1992 were over $60 million, an amount at least double the U.S. investment in the region.[30] More important than the sheer size of Japan's investments in the region's economies has been the dependence fostered by Japan in its relationships with other Asian Pacific countries. Investments flowing from Japan to each of its partners increase each of these countries reliance on Japan

TABLE 8.6   Distribution of FDI (Inward Stock) by Home Country, Region,
Various Years (Percentage)

		Share of Stock from Developed Area/Developing Area						
Countries	Years	All Developed Countries	North America	Western Europe	Japan	Other Developed Countries	All Developing Countries	Asia and the Pacific
Hong Kong	1989	83.1	38.6	20.0	36.0	5.4	16.9	88.2
	1984	92.0	58.8	16.2	22.9	2.2	8.0	76.5
South Korea	1988	92.8	29.9	13.8	56.1	0.2	5.8	66.5
	1980	89.9	21.9	10.7	67.3	0.1	8.2	26.1
Singapore	1989	94.6	35.1	32.4	32.5	...	5.4	...
	1980	88.5	33.4	47.7	18.9	...	11.5	...
Taiwan	1988	72.3	44.4	18.5	37.1	...	27.7	61.9
	1980	63.2	55.4	15.3	29.4	...	36.8	71.6
Indonesia	1988	72.8	12.2	34.4	38.4	15.0	27.9	82.8
	1980	77.1	6.3	14.0	48.6	31.1	22.9	70.6
Malaysia	1987	59.2	12.4	46.0	33.9	7.6	40.8	93.0
	1981	58.6	11.5	49.4	30.0	9.2	41.4	92.2
Philippines	1987	90.6	65.0	17.2	14.7	3.1	9.4	78.4
	1980	92.0	63.7	13.7	18.3	4.4	8.0	64.6
Thailand	1988	77.3	31.7	19.9	47.5	0.9	22.8	98.4
	1980	80.2	40.5	22.5	36.2	0.8	20.3	99.9
China (PRC)	1987	35.0	48.8	27.2	20.5	3.6	65.0	98.3
	1984	41.8	45.1	34.9	13.9	6.0	58.2	96.6
Vietnam	1989	80.5	0.6	72.7	17.9	8.8	16.1	99.3

Source: United Nations, *World Investment Directory 1992,* vol. 1, *Asia and the Pacific,* table 8, p. 19.

as a producer of capital-intensive, high-tech, manufactured goods and as a consumer of their largely labor-intensive intermediate products. The result is a regional network of economic ties comprising de facto economic integration in the region, one in which Japan is the dominant power.

Types of Japanese Investment

Postwar Japanese investments fall into four categories: (1) investment for resource development, (2) investments in import-substitution industries to maintain foreign market share, (3) investment in production for export to third countries, and (4) service sector investments.[31] Japan's earliest postwar foreign direct investment (FDI) was in resource-extraction development in Southeast Asia. Its purpose is to ensure supplies of minerals, oil, timber, and pulp for home consumption. Indonesia, the recipient of much of this investment, has remained Japan's second largest investment destination after the United States and, along with resource-rich Malaysia and Brunei, is one of the few countries in the region with which Japan consistently runs a trade deficit. A second type of Japanese FDI is in import-substitution industries. These are manufacturing firms that set up shop behind another country's import barriers to produce relatively standardized goods for local consumption: textile goods, toys, electrical appliances, consumer electronics, and metal products. Japan relocated much of its labor-intensive industries to South Korea and Taiwan in this way during the 1960s. An important characteristic of this type of Japanese FDI is the large number of small- and medium-sized firms that have invested abroad, often with the capital and technical assistance of Japan's large trading firms. Forty percent of Japan's foreign investments are still made by small- and medium-sized firms that inevitably follow abroad the large corporations with whom they have subcontracting arrangements.[32]

A third type of Japanese FDI is in production for export to third-country markets. The purpose of such investments is to take advantage of abundant cheap labor and the investment incentives—income tax exemptions, free plant sites, and duty-free importation of raw materials—provided by countries in export-processing zones. In the 1970s and 1980s, after the Japanese government eased its restrictions on overseas investment, investments of this kind were made in ASEAN countries and in the NICs as well as today in China. With the lifting of restrictions in 1969 and 1970, Japanese corporations launched large-scale overseas investments in minerals, oil, and raw materials. By 1979, of the Japanese foreign investments in Asia, 39.3 percent were in resources, 44.3 percent in manufacturing, and 16.4 percent in services.[33] And in 1987, according to Nomura Research Institute statistics, 59 percent of the production of Japanese manufacturing subsidiaries in Pacific Asia was for the local market, 17 percent for export back to Japan, and 24 percent for export to the rest of the world.[34]

The fourth type of Japanese FDI is in the service sector, which includes investments in finance, real estate, travel, and insurance. "In 1988, 32.4 percent of new Japanese foreign investments were in finance and insurance, followed by 17.9 percent in real estate, 17.1 percent in manufacturing, 8.7 percent in other services, 8.6 percent in natural resources, 8.3 percent in commerce, and 7 percent in other categories."[35] Fears that a lingering recession in the United States would preclude further expansion there prompted Japan's "Big Four" securities houses to undertake a major drive into Southeast Asia in the late 1980s, purchasing local securities firms and entering the region's small and volatile but growing stock markets. With Japanese banks, securities, and insurance companies expanding their operations, Singapore and Hong Kong have become major beneficiaries. Seventy-seven percent of Japanese investment into Singapore in 1988, according to government estimates, was in nonmanufacturing businesses.[36] Japanese department stores have opened branches throughout Southeast Asia, capturing increasing shares of the retail market as they force local department stores to sell rather than face bankruptcy. And Japanese tourists flock to these stores because their prices are lower than comparable items at home.

Three Waves of Japanese Investment.   Japanese investments have swept across the Asian Pacific in three successive waves. The first, starting in the early 1950s, occurred under restrictions imposed by the occupation authorities to keep capital from leaving Japan and to preserve Japan's balance of payments. Japanese investments abroad in this period were approved on a case-by-case basis and only if they promoted Japanese exports or resulted in overseas development of the natural resources Japan needed to develop its home industry. Other countries' investments in Japan during this time were prevented in favor of getting competitive foreign firms to sell their technology to infant Japanese industries. Altogether, however, Japanese FDI in both manufacturing and resource production in this first wave of investment abroad was small, amounting to $166 million in the ASEAN countries in 1966, which was only one-quarter of the American investment at the time.

A second wave of Japanese overseas investments, spurred by capital liberalization and yen appreciation in 1969 and 1970, saw Japanese investments throughout the Asian Pacific reach $4 billion, which was one-third larger than American investments in the area. By 1976, more than 75 percent of new foreign investment in the Asian Pacific region was Japanese, with eight major recipients—South Korea, Taiwan, Hong Kong, Singapore, Malaysia, Indonesia, Thailand, and the Philippines—having received cumulatively 27.2 percent of Japan's total FDI by 1980.[37] Three international events converged with domestic pressures in Japan in the late 1960s and early 1970s to bring about this shift in government FDI as part of Japan's comprehensive security policy. One was Nixon's devaluation of the dollar in 1971 and his subsequent decision to let the value of the dollar float. A second was the adoption of import-substitution policies by the NICs and ASEAN countries to foster foreign industrial investments in their countries. The third international event to push Japan into vastly expanded FDI was OPEC's temporary oil-export embargo and quadrupling of oil prices in 1973.

Domestic pressures for an easing of government restrictions on FDI in this second "wave" of investments overseas included a shortage of labor within Japan, the high cost of land, and a nationwide consensus to place restrictions on heavy polluting petrochemical and metal-refining industries in order to "houseclean Japan."[38] To circumvent Japanese vulnerability and spread around Japan's resource suppliers as strategically as possible, the government encouraged Japanese corporations to embark on large-scale oil, mineral, and raw material investments. When undertaken in joint ventures with host countries who depended upon Japan as a market for their abundant natural resources, the tactic provided leverage for the Japanese. This applied to Malaysia and the Philippines, from whom Japan imported 100 percent and 92.7 percent, respectively, of their bauxite exports. In a classic example of pursuing "comprehensive security," the Japanese government used a foreign aid program, its sponsorship of the Asahan industrial complex in Indonesia, to promote overseas investment in the construction of an immense dam and hydroelectric power station on the Asahan River, which fueled an aluminum refinery and other industries, to obtain low-cost resources.

To put in global perspective the flow of Japanese investment into the Asian Pacific region, however, it must be remembered that it was surpassed by the phenomenal growth of Japanese investments in the United States. Already the largest recipient of Japanese investment, the United States had absorbed $25.3 billion through 1986, a figure three times larger than the second-ranking country, Indonesia, with $8 billion.[39] Thus Japanese investment growth within the region, rapid as it has been, has declined relative to the extraordinary growth in Japan's extraregional investments. This expansion of intraregional economic ties accompanying an even greater interdependence tends to support Richard H. Solomon's observation of "a unique outward-looking regionalism" characteristic of the Asian Pacific, one that closely links the region to the global economy.[40]

A third "tidal wave" of investments was spearheaded by Japanese banks and securities corporations in the mid-1980s. These new Japanese investments, mostly in service industries, "totaled $1.43 billion, $2.32 billion, and $4.86 billion in 1985, 1986, and 1987, respectively, compared to new American investments in the area of $55 million, $405 million, and $2.2 billion in those same years. In 1988, the Ministry of Finance estimated that Japan's cumulative investments in East Asia were $30 billion or about 21 percent of Japan's total foreign investments."[41]

With the exception of resource-based industries, Japanese investments in the Asian Pacific go down the ranks of the "flying geese" as development among the countries in the region moves up the rungs of the international product cycle. Early waves of Japanese investment in non–resource-based industries were directed to the East Asian NICs, in particular South Korea and Taiwan. With rising wage costs and currency appreciation in the NICs after the mid-1980s, Japanese companies producing key technology-intensive products began moving their operations away from production in the NICs to ASEAN countries. Japanese FDI in South Korea in fiscal year 1988 decreased by about half, increasing more than threefold in Thailand. Mitsubishi Electric, for example, decided to reduce its audio equipment production at its Taiwan affiliate company, increasing its investment in its Thai joint venture, while Asics, the leading Japanese sports equipment manufacturer, shifted all its sports shoe production from South Korea to Indonesia.

As Japanese firms export higher value-added products out of the Asian Pacific region, their investments within the region are increasingly more sophisticated in their use of technology. Sony, for example, has upgraded its investments in Singapore by producing compact disc players that for the first time utilize a large-scale robotized production system for optical pickups, and Fujitsu's plans include building a $25 million semiconductor plant in Malaysia.[42] While the export of higher value-added products improves the trade balances of these host countries, the gain is offset by their increased dependence upon Japan for more, and more expensive, components. As much as Japan's Asian Pacific neighbors seek increased Japanese investments to help them develop, therefore, they are at risk of being compromised by Japan's "economic colonialism." Thus, to the extent that Japan's economic success has been accompanied by an accelerated economic hegemony in the region, it faces continuing political problems that arise from perceptions of its "arrogance and insensitive behaviour."[43] This configuration in the Asian Pacific, however, is likely to be significantly affected by two factors. One is the emergence of China as a regional economic rival; the second is Japan's capacity for political and institutional adaptation to the requirements of a rapidly changing global order.

The NICs' Investments

Until the 1980s, outward investment from the developing countries of the Asian Pacific was small. After the mid-1980s, however, in response to rising costs of labor and currency appreciation, Hong Kong, South Korea, and Taiwan became major foreign investors in the rest of the region, especially among the ASEAN-4 (Indonesia, Malaysia, Philippines, and Thailand) and the coastal provinces in China. Since 1985, Taiwan has invested more than $12 billion in Southeast Asia, becoming by 1991 the largest foreign investor in Indonesia and Malaysia, as well as one of the top investors in other ASEAN countries. Examples of Taiwan's investments include a $220 million petrochemical plant joint venture in the Philippines and a $1 billion "electronics park" in Malaysia. There is also a large capital flow in an ever expanding two-way indirect trade across the Taiwan Strait between Taiwan and the People's Republic of China. With little or no direct official contact, Taiwan's investments in the PRC in 1991 are said to have totaled $5.6 billion, with more than 3,000 Taiwanese firms in operation in China.[44] Hong Kong, reputedly the largest investor in the region, is reported by China as having invested (along with Macao) $15.5 billion between 1979 and 1987.[45] By the end of 1991, business firms from Hong Kong were employing over 3 million workers in adjacent Guangdong province. Although South Korea started to invest directly in China later than the other NICs, it had already contracted for 141 Korean firms to be established in China, an investment of $1.4 billion.

The NICs in the 1980s, replicating Japan's earlier transfer of its labor-intensive production technologies to the NICs in the 1960s and 1970s, were moving up the high-tech ladder, exporting their own labor-intensive enterprises to ASEAN countries and China as they attracted primarily technologically intensive FDI from Japan. Until the mid-1980s, NIC investments especially in ASEAN countries were primarily in labor-intensive manufacturing; in the case of Taiwan, for example, they were in textiles, chemical products, and electrical equipment. Since then, manufacturing as a proportion of NIC investments in ASEAN has begun to shift somewhat, with increasing diversification in the direction of construction and the service sector. For Taiwan, this has been particularly evident in the Philippines and in Thailand, where the construction industry has grown significantly. For Hong Kong and Singapore, FDI investment has been concentrated in services; for Hong Kong this has been apparent in Indonesia and in Thailand, and for Singapore in Malaysia.[46] In the 1990s, an increasing amount of NICs' FDI in labor-intensive manufacturing has gone to China, whose exports present a challenge to the ASEAN-4, since both China and the ASEAN-4 enjoy a comparative advantage in similar product lines. China's exports are predominantly labor-intensive light manufactures combined with resource-based products like crude oil and raw materials, which ASEAN-4 countries rely on for their foreign exchange.

In a study by Chow, applying the "export similarity index" to an evaluation of the overlapping of exports between China and ASEAN-4 in OECD markets, the conclusion was that among Asian Pacific countries Malaysia had the least export similarity with China, while the Philippines and Thailand displayed the greatest export similarity with China.[47] By 1990 more than 50 percent of China's exports overlapped with those from the Philippines and Thailand in the U.S. and EU markets, and greater than 40 percent with those from Indonesia in the same markets. This might suggest a potential competition between China and the ASEAN-4 countries over similar products sold in the United States and EU. By contrast, many business firms in the NICs—particularly Hong Kong, South Korea, and Taiwan—have instead exported various kinds of domestically produced industrial components to be processed at offshore assembly lines in the neighboring ASEAN-4 or China's coastal provinces for reexport to the world market. The resultant FDI from the NICs has generated an additional momentum in the direction of regional economic integration.

In summary, there has been a rapid growth of FDI in the Asian Pacific, principally as a consequence of the overall economic growth of countries in the region. Japanese TNCs have played the leading role, pursuing a regional core network strategy in their sourcing and supplying activities. Japanese affiliates have thereby contributed to the economic interdependence of Asian Pacific economies, acting as a force for integration in the region. NICs (except for Singapore) have also become major investors abroad, the outward investments of South Korea and Taiwan overtaking those of Hong Kong. The geographical distribution of FDI from the NICs exhibits a pattern similar to Japan's: a larger proportion going to developed countries, with a declining share of total FDI going to developing countries. In 1988, the percentage of total FDI to developed countries was 71.3 percent and 55.5 percent from Taiwan and South Korea, respectively, up from 56.5 percent and 31.8 percent in 1980. And for TNCs home based in South Korea and Taiwan, like those in Japan, the North American market, particularly the United States, is the most important location for outward FDI.[48]

The direction of overseas investments by Japan and the NICs differs according to the strategies and objectives of the home-based TNCs: Investments within the Asian Pacific region seek to maintain the competitiveness of exports while those to developed countries try to overcome existing or future tariff and nontariff barriers. Whether responding to internal and/or external factors, the increase in FDI of countries in the Asian Pacific grows out of the impetus to safeguard export markets, a motive that reflects as much as it affects trade. And if FDI is closely interrelated with trade, so is official development assistance (ODA), considered by some to be another form of investment.

FOREIGN AID

Bilateral foreign aid goes back to colonial rule, when the transfer of funds by governments to their colonial administrations was known as "infant colony subsidies." Once colonial territories became independent nation-states following World War II, the overseas economic aid provided by governments of rich countries to governments of poor countries became known as foreign aid or, more formally, official development assistance (ODA).[49] From a modernization theory perspective, such "foreign aid" is a way of providing new nations with the necessary financial and technical resources to ensure their economic viability and political stability. In the world system view, such financial assistance to new, weak players in the international market is a cost required to sustain and expand a world economy in which rich players, the core countries, are the major beneficiaries. Applying either schematic to the dynamics of foreign aid in the Asian Pacific subregion raises a central question about the purposes and efficacy of Japan's role as principal donor in the region: Does Japanese ODA contribute more to the independence (or dependence) of recipients or to the enrichment (or sacrifice) of Japan?

The Evolution of ODA

Japan views itself as having historical, geopolitical, economic, and strategic interests both in China and in the ASEAN states, each of which receives almost one-half or more of its bilateral ODA from Japan. They are not only an essential source of energy and raw materials but a significant market for both Japanese goods and Japanese capital. Often justified on these grounds, Japan's perception of its own vulnerability was magnified first by its devastating defeat in World War II and thereafter by the humbling experience of reentering the community of nations as a client-state of the United States. Besides its neighbors' fears of recurring militarism, its constituents' insistence on comprehensive security, and poor countries' expectations of financial help, there were continuous demands by the United States for Japan to be economically strong yet suitably accommodating to its patron's interests. This relationship between the United States and Japan has profoundly affected the ways in which Japan has grappled with the issue of foreign aid.

By 1961, when the Development Assistance Committee (DAC) of the OECD (Organization for Economic Cooperation and Development) began coordinating the donations of rich countries to assist developing nations, Japan was already a charter member. A minor aid donor at first, Japan rose rapidly to become, in absolute volume, the fourth largest donor in the DAC by the end of the 1970s and the first by 1989, with an annual ODA expenditure of $9 billion between 1988 and 1990.[50] In Asia, which Japan considers as vital to its own security as Latin America is to the United States, Japan surpassed the United States as principal aid donor by 1977. The heaviest concentration of Japanese ODA all along has been in the ASEAN states (and more recently, China) where Japan began outspending all other DAC donors by 1987 (see Table 8.7).

Compared to the 1960s and early 1970s, when as much as 90 to 100 percent of Japan's aid was concentrated in the Asian Pacific, Japanese aid to the ASEAN states as a proportion of its total aid has actually been reduced, reflecting Japan's

TABLE 8.7 Percent of Total Foreign Aid Received by ASEAN-5 (1987) and China (1979–1984) from Major Donors

	Donors		
Philippines	53.7 Japan	32.6 United States	13.7 others
Thailand	69.4 Japan	8.0 United States	6.9 West Germany
Malaysia	78.5 Japan	11.0 Australia	10.5 others
Indonesia	63.1 Japan	12.5 Netherlands	24.4 others
Singapore	50.6 Japan	20.2 West Germany	16.1 Australia
China	45.0 Japan	14.0 IMF	12.0 UN

Sources: Compiled from Japan's Ministry of Foreign Affairs, cited in Robert M. Orr, Jr., *The Emergence of Japan's Foreign Aid Power* (New York: Columbia University Press, 1990), table 4.3, p. 76. Information for China is from Zhao Quansheng, "Japan's Aid Diplomacy with China," in Bruce M. Koppel and Robert M. Orr, Jr., eds., *Japan's Foreign Aid: Power and Policy in a New Era* (Boulder, CO: Westview, 1993), p. 165.

increasing acknowledgment of its global responsibilities. After the international crises of the 1970s, Japanese ODA began to move out into the larger global arena, with larger donations going to the Middle East, Africa, and Latin America. As a result, its Asian share of ODA dropped to about 63 percent, with half of this, approximately 30 percent, going to ASEAN countries. This led to the 7:1:1:1 regional distribution formula widely believed to be employed by the Foreign Ministry, according to which roughly 70 percent of Japan's aid is set aside for Asia, with 10 percent each assigned to Latin America, the Middle East, and Africa.[51] Table 8.8 shows the actual figures for 1997.

The second major turning point for ODA policy, initiated by the United States, was the Plaza Accord, which decreased the value of the dollar by appreciating the yen. The net result was to precipitate an outflow of private sector FDI from Japan (and the NICs) as well as to change the focus of ODA in the ASEAN states from securing natural resources to assisting the development of export industries. Japan extended concessional loans for government projects to improve economic and social infrastructures in Indonesia, Malaysia, the Philippines, and Thailand. This raised the concerns of the United States because Japan, with its protected domestic markets, was unable to absorb additional manufactured goods, raising the likelihood that increased exports from ASEAN would end up in the United States with its already huge trade deficit. Among ASEAN members, complaints addressed both the indebtedness that high interest payments resulting from the rising value of the yen would exact on ASEAN nations and the "growing feeling that Japan has not adequately met ASEAN's request to dismantle its remaining trade barriers."[52] Clearly, the long-term pressure would be in the direction of Japan's replacing the United States as an import market for manufactured goods produced in Southeast Asia.

Another shift in direction of Japanese aid within the Asian Pacific occurred in the 1980s when the NICs, who had been early recipients of significant amounts of aid themselves, became donors. South Korea and Singapore, for example, were among the top ten recipients of Japanese aid in 1970 but no longer appear among

TABLE 8.8   Japan's Bilateral ODA by Region (1997)

Region	U.S.$ Millions	Percent of total Japanese ODA
Asia and Oceanic	6,724	62.8
South and Central Asia	1,907	17.8
ASEAN-4*	3,045	28.4
Sub-Saharan Africa	1,005	9.4
Middle East and North Africa	612	5.7
Latin America and Caribbean	1,041	9.7
Europe and unspecified	1,337	12.5

*ASEAN-4 includes Indonesia, Thailand, Philippines, and Malaysia.
Source: DAC 1998 Report: Development Co-operation (1999 edition), OECD 1999.

the top ten recipients in 1986. By contrast, aid to the Philippines and China has steadily, in some years even dramatically, increased. In fact, China became Japan's largest recipient of ODA from 1982 until 1987, when Indonesia resumed its number-one spot. In 1987 and 1988, the Philippines and China joined Indonesia as the top three recipients of bilateral Japanese ODA, receiving $534.72 million, $673.70 million, and $984.91 million, respectively, in 1988.[53]

Japan has grown into China's largest aid donor since 1979, when both countries set a precedent, Japan in providing and China in accepting for the first time a (yen) loan package from a DAC member. Having severed diplomatic ties with Taiwan, Japan was encouraged in this role by the United States, which had a strategic interest in promoting an open and moderate China but was prohibited from extending aid because the Foreign Assistance Act regarded China as a "member of the international communist movement."[54] Typical of Japan's overall ODA, only a very small proportion of Japanese ODA to China is in grants; the overwhelming proportion is in the form of concessional yen loans, which, to allay U.S. fears of Japanese domination of the fabled lucrative China market, is atypically untied to procurements.[55]

NICs' aid to the region, beginning in 1987, has exhibited the same clear-cut links with investments as Japan's. South Korea started an economic cooperation fund in 1987 to distribute 55 billion won of currency loans as part of a five-year 300 billion won foreign aid loan plan to developing countries, while Taiwan in 1988 established a soft-loan fund of $1.2 billion for disbursement over a five-year period to "friendly" developing countries in Southeast Asia and Africa. In Taiwan, it was hoped that foreign aid, including such projects as funding technical cooperation, would be beneficial in a number of overlapping ways: to offset the huge foreign-exchange reserves Taiwan had accumulated, to finance infrastructural projects that could assist Taiwanese investments abroad, to enhance trade, and to further diplomatic relations vis-à-vis China. Foreign assistance by the South Koreans was given to development projects and financing the purchase of capital goods from South Korea.

ODA: Attributes and Accusations

More important and controversial than the sheer size of Japanese aid have been the national objectives ODA serves as part of Japan's overall foreign policy. From the outset, Japan has openly acknowledged the close link between foreign assistance and its need to promote the Japanese economy. Japan's preoccupation with its vulnerabilities as a national entity has made its underlying objectives in providing ODA quite different from those of the United States. For Japan, trade, aid, and investment are essential for survival, a condition that by extension can be said to be true of its protégés, the NICs. This is expressed in the five policy objectives of Japanese foreign assistance programs:

1. to further Japanese economic interests by promoting exports, securing raw materials, and creating a favorable climate for commercial business activities in the recipient country;
2. to establish and strengthen diplomatic ties in order to counteract the lingering negative image of Japan that was the legacy of World War II;

3. to bolster the political stability of neighboring Asian countries;
4. to become a good partner of the other aid-giving, industrialized nations of the world; and
5. to establish Japan's status and influence in both regional and global international affairs.[56]

In its postwar reindustrialization, Japan once again confronted the necessity of cultivating markets both for resources and manufactured goods. Official foreign assistance was the form in which this was achieved. But an additional vulnerability had to be compensated by ODA: winning friends and acceptability among the nations of both the region and the world. This objective, embedded in Japan's postwar foreign policy, has coincided with the interests and needs of its principal partner. The United States, finding itself in retreat from the Asian Pacific theater after virtual defeat in Vietnam, needed a friendly and reliable power to fill the vacuum of its own diminished role. And if Japan's constitution (written and imposed by the United States) precluded military rearmament of the sort sought by the United States in the heyday of the Cold War, then Japan's presence as a source of foreign assistance in the region would have to suffice.

But winning friends with ODA has not been easy for Japan. Major criticisms have been voiced from all quarters on every aspect of Japanese foreign aid. First and foremost, Japan has been faulted for primarily considering her own national economic interests rather than the needs of recipient countries. At first criticism was directed at Japan's preference for commercially tied loans rather than concessional aid. Japan is notorious for offering the smallest number of grants as a proportion of total ODA. There is widespread suspicion that Japan uses foreign assistance simply to create markets for Japanese goods and services, and a number of attributes of the administration of Japanese ODA lend credence to this perception. Foreign aid is administered largely by bureaucrats in a bewildering number of competing ministries, each having its own agenda for evaluating the worth of foreign assistance projects. Those agencies with the greatest clout often have the least interest in overseas aid expenditures.

The party with the most interest in Japan's aid policy is business, and Japan's preference for infrastructural aid projects reflects the considerable influence of construction companies and engineering consulting firms in the determination of which projects to fund. Japan administers sizable amounts of aid money in recipient countries with extremely small staff contingents. The lack of trained development specialists means there are no field missions abroad. This results in the private sector's moving in to fill the void. "In 1986 engineering consulting firms alone did 43.7 billion yen worth of ODA-related business."[57] They often do the feasibility studies used to make project selections and then provide the contractors to do the work once they are approved.

The request basis of the aid process, which mandates that proposals for all aid projects come from the recipient government, enables Japan to justify maintaining such a small bureaucracy professionally trained to administer development assistance. In theory, the recipient governments are responsible for implementation of the projects. But since they too lack the requisite expertise, assistance on the part of the Japanese private sector fills a need. Thus the trading companies with their amply staffed overseas offices have played an active role in implementing Japan's aid program. It is hardly surprising, therefore, that this familiar cooperation between the public and private sectors in the determination and implementation of Japanese foreign aid has led some observers to view ODA as "a thinly disguised export promotion program."[58]

TRADE, AID, AND INVESTMENT AMONG THE NEWEST ENTRANTS TO THE REGION: MYANMAR, VIETNAM, LAOS, CAMBODIA, AND NORTH KOREA

The pattern of postwar trade, aid, and investment in the Asian Pacific was shaped, as we have seen, in the context of the Cold War. With Japan as Asian buffer between the United States and the Communist world, the political lines were drawn to isolate China, along with North Korea, North Vietnam, and Laos, from the rest of the Asian Pacific, which was to be a model of "free world" development. Cambodia remained in contention and wracked by war and political dissension as it was drawn into the strife between its neighbors—Thailand and Vietnam—and their powerful patrons, the United States and the USSR. Burma, like Cambodia, was not only wedged between even more gigantic powers—India and China—but also had similarly been the scene of massive destruction by both sides—Japan and the Allied forces—during World War II. But in contrast to Cambodia, which did not have the opportunity to remain above the fray, Burma chose self-isolation and neutrality. These five countries, then, for different reasons, had in common an antipathy toward the Western world. This placed them outside or with only tenuous ties to the flourishing international economy.

For all these countries, the end of the Cold War and the disintegration of the Soviet Union have meant fundamental changes in their international relations. The future of countries within the socialist orbit, whose trade, aid, and investment had been linked with the command economy of the Soviet Union, depended upon how determinedly they pursued a program of economic reform. China, having faced the most serious difficulties both domestically and in its relationship with the Soviet Union, was the first to implement economic reform, pursue an export-led strategy with an infusion of private investment capital, and receive large amounts of Japanese ODA. By the late 1980s, with a short hiatus in the aftermath of the Tiananmen affair, China was successfully incorporated in the Japanese regional orbit of trade, aid, and investment. Japan had assumed the role of mentor with the blessing of a more distanced United States. Vietnam and Laos also embarked on the path of economic reform in the 1980s, almost immediately inviting the economic attention of Japan and Thailand. In 2000 North Korea has come into the fold of the international market economy, as a result of the euphoric summit between Kim Il Jung and Kim Dae Jung in Pyongyang.

North Korea and Myanmar

At either end of the east-west arc of the Asian Pacific, North Korea and Myanmar are at the very periphery of postwar regional economic development. North Korea receives no ODA from Japan, though from a perspective of Japan's policy of comprehensive security it could well be argued that this is unwarranted. But it is likely to remain the case as long as three purely political conditions continue to exist: North Korea's militaristic rather than economic approach to international relationships, South Korea's opposition to Japan's establishing a diplomatic relationship with North Korea, and Japan's alignment with the U.S. Korean policy.

In light of the recent fragmentation of Japan's once-dominant Liberal Democratic Party, it may be significant that proponents of a closer relationship with North Korea have existed within Japan for some time. Not only the Japan Socialist Party and the Japan Communist Party but also the liberal faction in the Liberal Democratic Party, led by Masayoshi Ohira and Zenko Suzuki, have maintained for the last 20 years that the entire Korean peninsula was important to the security of Japan. This has occasioned diplomatic strain between South Korea and Japan, as when the then-minister of foreign affairs (a member of Ohira's faction) went so far as to state in 1974 that he believed North Korea had no aggressive intentions toward South Korea.[59] In late 1993 such expressions of optimism were overshadowed by concerns that North Korea may be arming itself with nuclear weapons. But in the aftermath of the 2000 summit agreement, the question of Japan's relationship to a reunified Korea, economically and politically as well as in terms of security, is probably back on the agenda not only of Japan but other Asian Pacific countries and the major global players as well.

Burma/Myanmar presents an equally paradoxical case study of Japanese foreign assistance because, despite its spurning of international assistance, it has been a recipient of large amounts of Japanese ODA since the November 5, 1954 signing of a peace treaty between Japan and the Union of Burma. Heedless of Aung San's written legacy warning against Burma's dependence upon foreign assistance, Burma received assistance from a number of different quarters: Initially there was minimal aid from the Colombo Plan nations, the United States, and even the Soviet Union, with quite substantial aid from Japan after 1954. Japan provided products and technicians for a total value of $200 million over a ten-year period, with $2 million of this amount for Japanese-Burmese joint ventures and an additional $5 million annual grant for technical assistance. In 1963 (after the military coup) Burma requested a renegotiation of the reparations agreement and received an additional $200 million over 12 years beginning in 1965; $140 million of the amount was in grant reparations and $60 million in concessional loans.[60] Since then, except for a brief hiatus during 1990, Japanese ODA has come to about $2.2 billion, one of the largest in the world measured on a per capita basis.

This Japanese aid was extended despite indications that, far from contributing to Burma's development, the aid was being siphoned into support of an increasingly militarized administration of a corrupt regime. Japan even admonished Burmese officials in "a dialogue" in 1988 on the need to engage in economic reform. After the Burmese military disallowed the 1990 elections, Japan did suspend its aid. But irrespective of SLORC, the inadequacies of economic reform, the failures of four major Japanese industrial projects, and the enormous debt burden that has led the Burmese government into destructive sales of forest resources and the drug trade, Japan has been Myanmar's sole source of assistance since independence in the full knowledge, apparently, of its inefficacy as a tool for that country's development. A new joint venture between the Burmese and Japanese was announced on April 11, 1990, a month before Myanmar's democratic elections were held and dismissed. According to that Myanmar-Japan Concord, the construction of seven major projects were to be undertaken, including new international airports in Rangoon and Mandalay, at a cost expected to be about $14 billion over a ten- to fifteen-year period and involving the participation of 240 Japanese firms.[61]

Japanese disbursements of these contractual obligations made in 1990 have waxed and waned with Myanmar's human rights violations. In 1995, when the National League for Democracy leader, Aung San Suu Kyi was released from six years under house arrest, it looked briefly as if Myanmar might be improving its dismal record of human rights violations in response to ASEAN's pursuit of a policy of "constructive engagement." But once Myanmar became a member of ASEAN in 1997, its military junta's human rights violations instead of disappearing turned into a gigantic headache for ASEAN because it undermined the organization's principled commitment to refrain from interfering in the internal affairs of its members. Just like ASEAN's political policies, Japan's economic assistance program to Myanmar was affected by the degree of offense Myanmar's leadership provoked in the international community. Whenever the Myanmar government blatantly offends international sensibilities, Japan suspends its financial assistance, resuming its loan disbursements only after the furor dies down. Thus in February 1999 when Japan announced it was providing a $20 million loan to Myanmar to finance work on Rangoon's international airport, it quickly pointed out that this was not a resumption of aid to Myanmar but merely a disbursement of old commitments.

A number of reasons are used to explain this symbiotic relationship between Myanmar and Japan, some that are singular to Myanmar, some that speak to the characteristics of Japanese ODA in general. There is first and foremost the intrinsic wealth of Myanmar, both as a source of rice and of energy. Second are the close personal ties of the Burmese nationalist leadership to Japan—General Ne Win was trained and supported by the Japanese prior to 1945—and the physical destruction at the hands of the Japanese that marred this relationship toward the end of the war. Third is the absence of any Japanese oversight for its aid or any third-party evaluation of its effectiveness, an intrinsic aspect of the recipient-request nature of the process as described earlier. But most importantly, it can be suggested, is that the Japanese have through their ODA made themselves indispensable to Myanmar. "Their relations are critical to Burma, their support vital to the Burmese economy, and their access exceptional. Should Burma prosper, both Burma and Japan will benefit."[62] And there are indications that other countries, South Korea prominent among them, are lining up to invest in Myanmar as soon as the political climate permits.

Vietnam, Cambodia, and Laos

Embroiled in war with the United States until 1975, these three countries have come within view of normalizing their international relations and being incorporated into the global economy. Principally this is due to the dramatic changes in the international circumstances surrounding the end of the Cold War. Even before U.S.

troops were withdrawn from Vietnam, Japan was prepared to normalize diplomatic relations with North Vietnam and provide economic aid to both North and South Vietnam as soon as the Paris Peace Accord was signed in January 1973. When laying out the nonideological principles on which economic aid to Vietnam would be based at the conclusion of the Paris Peace Accord between the United States and Vietnam in 1973, Foreign Minister Ohira disclosed that 500 million yen had already been given to Vietnam, as a whole, through the International Red Cross. Its first official aid package to North Vietnam was 8.5 billion yen in grants in 1975, with another 5 billion in 1976. When Vietnam invaded Cambodia in December 1978, however, Japan suspended its aid commitments, and the Cambodian imbroglio became the major stumbling block to Japan's resumption of aid to Vietnam.

Behind the conflicts raging in Cambodia and among the great powers over its destiny as a state was the economic and military presence of the Soviet Union as an ally of Vietnam. The Vietnamese economy was propped up by Soviet and East European aid and preferential trading arrangements after 1975. When these arrangements were terminated, therefore, Vietnam's difficulties provided the opportunities for resolving the Cambodia stalemate and bringing about an enduring stability in that troubled area of the Asian Pacific. Japan has contributed substantially to bringing this about by playing a more political role than ever before and using the prospect of economic aid to Vietnam as a lever to obtain Vietnam's cooperation. In turn, the ASEAN nations have reduced their mistrust of Vietnam in favor of changing Indochina "from a battlefield to a marketplace."[63] Thailand has become increasingly active in Indochina, former Prime Minister Chatichai Choonhavan personally requesting Japan in 1990 to resume aid to Vietnam. President Suharto of Indonesia visited Hanoi in the same year to sign an economic and scientific technology agreement and express interest in Vietnam's joining ASEAN. The following year, Singapore, France, and Italy all announced resumption of economic aid to Vietnam.

In 1993, as reported by the Vietnamese government, there was a total of 390 projects worth close to $3 billion invested in Vietnam by companies from Taiwan, Hong Kong, the Netherlands, Britain, Australia, Singapore, France, Japan, South Korea, Canada, Malaysia, Sweden, Thailand, and the Philippines. Of special interest is the development of Vietnam's offshore oil fields, an area in which joint enterprises have made their largest investments. Japan's private investments have been eighth among the largest investors, with only 24 projects valued at $160 million. But the Japanese government did provide $500 million a year in ODA through 1995 once two of its major conditions for resuming economic aid to Vietnam were met—a new coalition government in Cambodia and improved relations between the United States and Vietnam.

And despite the Vietnamese government's ambivalence about inviting in the capitalist world and losing control over disposition of its resources, relations between the United States and Vietnam have improved since normalization of diplomatic ties in 1995. American companies have signed business contracts and hope to have some advantages in construction, machinery, hotel development, and, given the large numbers of Vietnamese Americans, air travel. The United States also removed its objections to the IMF's granting loans to Vietnam, and in mid-2000 signed a lengthy trade agreement with Vietnam according to which the United States would substantially reduce its tariffs on Vietnamese imports in return for Vietnam making reforms that cover bank branches, customs fees, investment protections, publication of laws and regulations and tariffs on a list of goods and services. Vietnam, following the Chinese pattern of reform, insisted on a gradual timetable to enable its companies to adjust to foreign competition. For example, though American retailers are permitted to enter the market there for the first time, they will be limited to a single retail store indefinitely. American financial companies will be allowed to issue credit cards but only eight years after the agreement has taken effect. In enterprises like phone and Internet services, foreign companies will have to wait at least three years before embarking on joint-venture agreements with local partners and even then they will be permitted only minority equity stakes.

The trade agreement with the United States has taken a long time to reach fruition but shows signs that Vietnam too is learning how to pragmatically cope with its own political and social impediments to greater regional and global integtration, e.g., intra-Party conflicts over the scope and pace of economic reform, an abiding mistrust of banks among Vietnamese, and a bureaucracy plagued by corruption and inefficiency. In specific areas, Vietnam has compromised its cautiously deliberate approach: Vietnam has agreed to allow foreign banks to take deposits and make loans in local currency, the dong, relatively quickly. Before the trade agreement can be implemented, U.S. congressional approval is required, which would entail establishing so-called normal trade relations with the United States subject to annual review. U.S. congressional approval was granted in 2000 which will provide an incentive for Vietnam to proceed with the economic overhaul that would enable Vietnam to take a giant step further toward opening its economy to the outside world.[64]

As in the case of Vietnam, which liberalized its foreign investment policy in 1988, Laos has moved in a more market-oriented direction. It has been on the receiving end of trade agreements, substantial investment, and charitable aid projects from bilateral and multilateral aid-giving agencies. The Thais have extensive contracts to log Laotian tropical hardwood forests. Australia is helping to build a bridge across the Mekong, which widens the trade link with Thailand. American companies, until recently blocked from even making commitments to invest in Vietnam, have become the second largest foreign investors in Laos, concentrating on two oil-exploration contracts in southern and central parts of the country.

The Japanese government has provided Laos with economic aid in the form of grants and technical cooperation (economic consultants) amounting to a total of 2.6 billion yen since 1989. To address the Laotian need for educational opportunities Japan accepts foreign students from Laos. In August 1990, Foreign Minister Nakayama, in the first visit of a Japanese foreign minister to Laos in 31 years, announced a policy of wholehearted cooperation in helping Laos to develop a market economy.[65] The marked interest by Laotians in the benefits of a market economy has elicited a lively response on the part of some of its neighbors. While Vietnam's influence has waned, Thai and Chinese (PRC) influence has increased.

The political economy of Cambodia remains a glint in the eyes of its neighbors as a new constitutional regime takes shape. The new coalition government faces an economy in shambles, an empty government treasury, and the Khmer Rouge disbanded but still in residence in large areas of the country, profiting from the lucrative trade in timber and gemstones. Years of civil war destroyed much of the village-based economy, which the Draconian measures taken by the Pol Pot government failed to restore. The arrival of UNTAC brought a massive infusion of dollars into the Cambodian economy in the form of salaries and local purchases, overwhelming the Hun Sen government's precarious hold on the economy. In Phnom Penh this stimulated feverish private business activity in construction, hotels, and restaurants, partially financed by overseas Cambodian money. Runaway inflation prompted underpaid civil servants to take on sideline businesses in order to survive.

Many Cambodians remain in refugee camps along the Thai border; still to be paid for somehow are the costs of resettling those still resident now that UNTAC has departed. The new government faces great dependence on outside economic aid to create the conditions that will make direct foreign investment attractive. Like Laos, however, Cambodia suffers from the absence of a skilled labor force, and the virulent anti-Vietnamese sentiment among all political groups may deprive Cambodia of the skilled labor available from her more populous neighbor. These problems notwithstanding, with a political economy yet to be shaped in Cambodia, there is undoubtedly interest in expanding trade and investments among the French, who still have a presence in Cambodia, the Thais, the Japanese, and, unwelcome as they may be in Cambodia, the Vietnamese.

REGIONAL ASSOCIATIONS FOR ECONOMIC COOPERATION

Public Goods and the Leadership Role

Dictated by the sheer size of Japan's economy, there is no doubt it will continue to play the core leadership role in promoting economic growth of the Asian Pacific region. But exports, imports, and capital exports are the result of free trade in the private market that, in order to function smoothly, requires that certain international conditions, "international public goods," be provided. Among these are security, maintenance of a free trade system, and some mechanism for international redistribution of income. Overall security in the postwar world, as we have seen in Chapter 7, was largely provided in the context of the Cold War. Similarly, maintenance of the free trade system and an international redistribution of income was furnished by the international organizations set up under the aegis of the United States: GATT, the UN and its numerous agencies, the international financial organizations—the World Bank, the International Monetary Fund—and a variety of nongovernmental organizations.

With the United States no longer in the ascendance, Japan has taken over some of the financial burden of providing these public goods. We have seen this principally in the growth of bilateral official direct assistance for countries in the Asian Pacific. It is also argued that Japan's regional economic strategy of deepening asymmetrical trade and investment relationships is part and parcel of its policy of comprehensive security. In that case, Japan is providing quasi-hegemonic security not only for itself but for the region as a whole within the larger global hegemony of the United States. This is, of course, the central dilemma of the region: whether and in what manner Japan will be able to assume the political leadership role for the region while simultaneously accommodating its global political responsibilities as a major player on the international stage.

The demand for Japan to shoulder political responsibilities commensurate with its global role as an economic superpower is most vocal in the developed world, though domestic pressures in the same direction are increasingly visible. On the other hand, whether it is desirable or not for Japan to act as political leader for the region, and there is widespread ambivalence throughout the Asian Pacific over this question, Japan is likely to dominate the region with the sheer magnitude of its economic presence. Only China, when it catches up to Japan, will be in a position to counter or join Japan as a core economy in the Asian Pacific region.

Japan has, in fact, played an active role in furthering regional economic integration by initiating and encouraging the formation of regional organizations like the Asian Development Bank. But in promoting Asian Pacific cooperation, the Japanese have been keenly aware of the profound mistrust their weaker neighbors retain toward Japan's leadership in the region. This is apparent in both the rhetoric and caution with which all countries in the Asian Pacific have moved toward greater regional economic and political association. Japan's predilection to separate economics from politics in the "parallel development" of economic and political foreign relations is reflected in the process by which movement toward regional association has occurred in the postwar world.

The Stimulus Toward Cooperation

Economic growth in the Asian Pacific region has been both contagious and contingent on an expanding global economy. Though Japan, the NICs, and China all export the largest proportion of their products to North America and the EU, they have in the process of pursuing an export-led dynamic crisscrossed one another's territories with an increasingly integrated network of economic and political interaction. The rapidly multiplying private contacts, mostly economic and bilateral, among people of different nationality across the entire Asian Pacific have been accompanied almost from the start by a spirited awareness of the advantages of regional cooperation on a wide range of issues. This identification among academics, professionals, government officials, and business groups has resulted in the formation of a number of all-regional organizations to collect, assess, and disseminate information of mutual interest. These have been at the heart of a movement considered by some scholars as a potential foundation of Asian Pacific regionalization.

Despite its geographical location and obvious Asian identity, however, Japan's preeminent status as a highly developed state within the region sets its interests apart from, perhaps even in conflict with, its developing neighbors. As a global economic power, Japan plays a dual role as a "Western" extraregional partner of the United States and as a core of the dynamically growing Asian Pacific region, the leader in the "flying geese formation." It is necessarily Janus-headed, with one face in the direction of the global world economy, the other facing its home base, the Asian Pacific region. There is some tension, therefore, among those regional associations that were created at the initiative of one of the global powers, including

Japan, and/or that include powerful extraregional partners and those in which the Asian Pacific states, including Japan, as principal members have taken both the initiative for their formation and the command of their membership and internal organization.

Regional organizations in our usage are intergovernmental and nongovernmental organizations that are both geographically and substantively centered on the Asian Pacific. Both can be considered international; in some cases the term refers to the relations among states within the region, in other cases the term more broadly refers to all relations (official and unofficial) across national boundaries. The largest number of regional associations surveyed below fall into the category of nongovernmental organizations (NGOs); only ASEAN, APEC (Asian Pacific Economic Conference), and ADB (Asian Development Bank) are intergovernmental organizations (IGOs).

All-Regional Organizations

The forerunner of Asian Pacific nongovernmental organizations (NGOs) in the postwar period, the Institute of Pacific Relations (IPR) was a private regional forum in existence from 1925 until it fell victim to McCarthyism in 1961. IPR brought academics, journalists, and business and labor leaders together with politicians, bureaucrats, and state officials. Within a short period after the demise of IPR, two new NGOs appeared, one principally an academic forum, the other a business association.

PAFTAD.   The Pacific Free Trade and Development Conference (PAFTAD), originally convened in 1968 at the initiative of the Japanese to consider a proposal for a Pacific free trade area, invites academics to participate in research on economic policy issues of common interest to countries in the region. By bringing concrete research results to the attention of practitioners in government and the business world, PAFTAD hopes to be able to promote regional economic cooperation. Although dominated by liberal, market-oriented economists from the developed countries of Japan, Australia, New Zealand, Canada, and the United States, PAFTAD included academics with diverse views from countries in Southeast Asia, the Soviet Union, China, and Pacific Latin America. Early research focused on alternative trading arrangements; more recent research explores industrial policy, technology, and trade in services.

PAFTAD has played the role of trailblazer in the early stages of institutionalizing economic cooperation in the region. Given the age-old, colonial, and Cold War legacies of divisiveness and mutual antagonisms, PAFTAD as a nongovernmental structure bypasses the participation of states in any official capacity while still incorporating the policy viewpoints of political practitioners. The policy orientation of PAFTAD research has been strengthened by the government background of many of the delegates. They have brought to the organization an accumulation of expertise from a wide range of economies, an extensive network of societal and political contacts, and a commitment to regional cooperation. In the informal setting provided for by PAFTAD, these scholars were able to highlight significant areas of potential economic cooperation.[66]

PBEC.   A second commercially oriented NGO launched by business leaders from the same countries and at about the same time as PAFTAD is the Pacific Basin Economic Council (PBEC). Joined by firms and individuals from South Korea, Taiwan, Mexico, Chile, Hong Kong, Peru, Indonesia, Malaysia, the Philippines, Singapore, and Thailand, PBEC is nonetheless narrowly based among the business community. It also is torn by dissension among those members who see the organization as the voice of business in regional politics and those members who see it as a "rich man's club" for renewing contacts and professing their faith in free enterprise.

PECC.   PBEC and PAFTAD are full members of the third regional NGO that plays a role in influencing regional economic cooperation, the Pacific Economic Cooperation Conference (PECC). Growing out of a conference of scholars, business leaders, and state officials meeting in Australia in 1980, PECC is a logical next step in the institutionalization of regional cooperation. It is based on a principle of nonexclusiveness that promotes reaching out to representatives of any country or organization as long as it is dedicated to the cooperation theme. Currently it includes members from ASEAN (Brunei, Indonesia, Malaysia, Philippines, Thailand, and Singapore), the OECD (Japan, the United States, Canada, Australia, and New Zealand), South Korea, and the South Pacific islands as well as PAFTAD and PBEC. Its conferences and research programs are supervised by an international steering committee that includes many longtime leaders of PAFTAD and PBEC.

The tripartite membership structure of PECC brings together state officials acting as individuals in a nonofficial capacity (a polite fiction to circumvent protocol requirements) with scholars and business leaders. This ensures that state interests are expressed and defended alongside those of the private sector. The decision to form PECC as a new and more comprehensive type of cooperative forum was accompanied by a decision to make PECC an unofficial rather than an official organization. Based on a consensus that direct governmental interaction in the Asian Pacific area is premature, PECC solicits no formal consent by governments but uses task forces to "develop trusting relationships with government officials and researchers on an informal basis"[67] This unofficial mode of operating has enabled PECC to include both China and Taiwan as regular members, the Soviet Union now Russia with observer status, and the ASEAN states, a major step toward a more inclusive Asian Pacific forum for economic cooperation. Its informal nature promotes flexibility and depth of discussion, and a consensual style of decision making forces state participants to negotiate and compromise with their societal counterparts for the organization to move forward on any particular issue. PECC has begun the process of formal institutionalization with the formation of a Singapore-based permanent secretariat in 1990.

APEC.   Both the PECC and ASEAN are informally interlocked with two broader diplomatic forums that include the United States, Australia, Canada, and New Zealand along with the Asian Pacific nations. The 15-member Asia-Pacific Economic Cooperation forum (APEC), first convened in 1989, is composed of the six ASEAN nations along with South Korea, Taiwan, Hong Kong, China (PRC), and Japan and the United States, Canada, Australia, and New Zealand. Its principal focus on preserving an open trading system among its members was a response to a drift toward protectionism and the formation of regional trading blocs. Prime Minister Nakasone first floated the idea for a trans-Pacific alliance to protect the multilateral trading system, but it was Australian Prime Minister Bob Hawke who provided the impetus for the first ministerial-level conference in 1989. Despite the diversity of the group, agreement was reached on the following guiding principles, which were subsequently endorsed by ASEAN:

1. APEC was to be outward looking and not oriented toward the formation of a regional bloc.
2. The process of consultations was to be nonformal, based on building consensus on a gradually broader range of economic issues.
3. APEC would not develop into a formal intergovernmental negotiating process in which some sought to force their views on others.
4. APEC would complement existing regional organizations such as ASEAN and PECC.
5. Participation was to be open-ended, assessed on the basis of the strength of economic linkages with current participants rather than on ideological grounds.

A specific agenda of tasks was undertaken by APEC members in 1990. These included monitoring the regional and global economic outlook and improving data on regional trade in goods and services and on investment flows; technology transfer and trade promotion; and sectoral cooperation in telecommunications, energy, transport, fisheries, and marine resources conservation. The United States announced an initiative for regional human resource development, and Singapore was to set up a regionwide database on trading opportunities. An agreed-upon definition of trade liberalization was to be consistent with GATT principles and not to the detriment of other economies inside or outside the region. The agreement to avoid actions that would damage market access of those outside the region meant that APEC could not move in the direction of a trading bloc. At a special meeting of APEC trade ministers in 1990, agreement was reached on phasing out the trade-distorting multifiber arrangements and phasing in a comprehensive framework for subjecting trade in services to normal GATT disciplines.[68]

The APEC meeting in Seattle in November 1993, on the heels of successful passage of NAFTA in the United States, received much publicity. But despite the fanfare, the meeting did more to illuminate fundamental differences between the Asian and the Anglo-American contingents of the Pacific Rim than to move the organization toward agreement on trade procedures. Mexico, Papua New Guinea, and Chile gained entry, but Australia and Southeast Asian members raised objections to admitting other Latin American countries. A decision was reached to bar entry of new members for three years while the group better defined its mission. The most tangible outcome of this APEC meeting was to prod resolution of the subsequent Uruguay round of the GATT. The trepidation with which Asian Pacific "member economies" welcomed joint participation with the United States was captured by Pyong Hwoi Koo, chairman of the South Korean conglomerate, Lucky Star International, when he compared Asia's smaller nations to "shrimps" in danger of being devoured by the U.S. "whale."[69]

Leaders of APEC at November 1993 meeting in the United States. From the left are: Prime Minister Paul Keating, Australia; Prime Minister Goh Chok Tong, Singapore; President Suharto, Indonesia; President Fidel Ramos, Philippines; President Bill Clinton, United States; Chairman Vincent Siew, Chinese Taipei; Prime Minister Morihiro Hosokawa, Japan; Hong Kong Financial Secretary Hamish MacLeod; President Jiang Zemin, China; Prime Minister Chuan Leekpai, Thailand; President Kim Young Sam, South Korea; Prime Minister Jean Chretien, Canada; and Sultan Hassanal Bolkiah, Brunei.

Source: Photo from AP/Wide World Photos

This fear reflected a split within APEC between the developed and the developing countries over APEC's goal to establish a regional free trade area within 25 years. The developed countries pushed for a lowering of tariffs by 2010 for developed countries and by 2020 for developing countries. These deadlines were adopted at the 1994 Bogor Summit as voluntary targets rather than legal commitments. Among developing countries, however, there was a sensitivity to being pressured by the developed countries. This was expressed the following year at the Osaka APEC Summit (1995) when Malaysia and China insisted that each country should follow its own path rather than conforming to a grand timetable set by the developed countries. The members agreed that the individual action plans originally designed as transitions toward the free-trade goals of 2010 and 2020 become incremental two-year plans for each individual country, a process referred to as "concerted unilateralism." At each APEC summit meeting, countries announce the "down payments" they are making toward the eventual APEC free-trade area: In 1995, Japan announced the biggest liberalization of its markets in 16 years and in 1996, China promised to cut tariffs on 3,364 items. The split in outlooks, however, remains: the United States and other developed countries expect APEC to produce results while Asian developing countries look to APEC as a process of confidence-building.

was decided at this meeting to pursue new directions, in principle, in the forthcoming decade, despite serious disagreements on how these agreed-upon changes should be implemented. The membership called for an ADB-led multilateral dialogue to boost economic policies in developing member countries, encouragement for stepped-up environmental protection, and the creation of an Asian Finance and Investment Corporation (AFIC) to act as a bridge between ADB and commercial banks to expand participation in private enterprise.[71]

Retarded Regional Institutionalization.   What is apparent from the overview of regional associations is that formal institutionalization of regional economic cooperation in the Asian Pacific lags far behind de facto economic integration as measured by trade, aid, and investment patterns. As one might expect from the extreme diversity in size, population, resource endowments, cultural-historical circumstances, ideological bent, and stages of economic development of Asian Pacific countries, all-regional associations tend to be sprawling, amorphous bodies that are open-ended, outward looking, and largely consultative in nature. Regional organizations are for the most part NGOs that offer opportunities for academics with expertise, government officials, and businesspeople from throughout the Asian Pacific to interact, pool their resources, set up data banks, and seriously explore the issues, strategies, and obstacles involved in promoting greater regional economic cooperation.

Three factors perpetuate the reluctance on the part of Asian Pacific countries to move toward more formalized governmental institutions of a regional nature. One is the heavy economic dependence of these countries on markets outside the region, particularly in the United States and the EU, to buy their exports. A second is Japan's overwhelming economic dominance and its dual identity as a developed "Western" and an Asian regional power. The third factor is the difficulty of defining membership to accommodate two Chinas and three or more subregional and multinational entities in the process of formation.

Members of ASEAN, one of the region's most successful multinational organizations, are concerned that their newly found identity not be diluted by incorporation into a larger international organization. At the opposite end from this well-established regional organization are a number of new subregional growth triangles. The term, originally used to describe Singapore's plans to develop a subregional industrial park with Indonesia and Malaysia, has also been applied to the multinational development zone in northeastern Asia. The Tumen River Delta Project, where North Korea, China, and Russia converge, is a $20 billion development project initiated by China and sponsored by the United Nations Development Program. This multinational development zone has its roots in the same concept as the special economic zones (SEZs) established in the southeastern region of China. Hong Kong's return to China has occasioned speculation that the commercially developed southeastern region of China might join Hainan and Taiwan to force the regime in Beijing to acknowledge its special characteristics. The prospect of such subregional growth areas raises the novel question of how their participation in regional associations might be handled.

Given the enormous challenges to greater regional institutionalization in the Asian Pacific, what is remarkable is the widely expressed intuitive perception that regionalism is definitely on the Asian Pacific agenda. What are the origins of this perception, and does it have any validity? In the final section of this chapter we address these questions.

TO BE OR NOT TO BE: THE QUESTION OF ASIAN PACIFIC REGIONALISM

The core and cause célèbre of regionalization in the Asian Pacific is, of course, Japan. The dynamic postwar economy of Japan, which provided both the impetus and a model for development in the region, has made Japan the principal champion of greater regional association. Until the demise of the Soviet Union, the mere suggestion that Japan favored a particular regional formation was sufficient to heighten the suspicions of her neighbors. Since then, however, it is no longer commonplace to assume that Japanese domination of the region would always be opposed by the ever-watchful victims of earlier Japanese aggression. Japanese economic dominance of the region has appeared more benign, even advantageous, to other Asian Pacific countries than before, altering considerably their perceptions of a mutual common interest in regional development. By 1990, Japan's bilateral aid and foreign investments had stimulated a level of intraregional trade that surpassed that of any other region, creating a formidable economic network of regional interdependence.

But regionalization in the Asian Pacific must be understood as distinct from that in Western Europe since the 1960s. It does not occur as a result of attempting to coordinate fully developed national economies into a regionally more effective competitor in the global economy. Rather, regionalization in the Asian Pacific is itself the process by which national economies are enabled to grow and develop. As countries become incorporated into the dynamics of aid, trade, and investment not only in the region but also via the region into the global economy, they generate a virtuous circle of exports → capital goods imports → capital formation → productivity improvements → exports. The outcome of this export-led strategy has been the singular development of effectively organized national economies within the NICs, ASEAN states, and China.

However, it is not exports or trade alone that accounts for this development. A second aspect of this regionally based strategy of capital formation involves the dynamic process of an evolving international product cycle. Based on the ever expanding technological capacity of Japan to produce increasingly more sophisticated goods and services that lend themselves to production in different stages and in different places, adjacent national economies are able to import not only finished products but intermediate capital goods with which to embark on a vertical ascent from less capitalized, labor-intensive production to higher value-added, more capital-intensive production. The outcome of this international product cycle is an increasing horizontal trade within the region and between countries of the region and the global economy. Instead of operating on the basis of fixed comparative advantage(s) that countries use as a basis of exchange, this development of the capitalist market elevates mass production and assembly principles to a new international division of labor. As a result, the trade relationship between Japan and its regional neighbors has gradually been transformed from an interindustry vertical type, in which primary commodities, for example, are exported and manufactured products are imported, to an intra-industry horizontal type of division of labor, in which the intermediate goods to produce sophisticated products like automobiles are imported and finished automobiles are exported. Japan serves as the source of intermediate goods and the United States as the destination of exports.

With an increasing horizontal division of labor, the development of industrialization in one country induces the upturn of industrial production in another country. Horizontal trade in the Asian Pacific through this accelerating reciprocal interrelationship has benefited the development of national economies. The sizable trade in intermediate goods, for which the developing nations of the Asian Pacific depend on Japan, plays a pivotal role not only for reciprocally inducing increased production and high growth rates but also for ensuring a closer integration among trading countries throughout the region.

Thus the Asian Pacific may not have the conditions the European community had in its formative years—two nations (West Germany and France) of similar size and economic capacity—but it does offer an alternative model of regional formations that is closely tied to its innovative, state-centered, developmental strategy. With strong states capable of seizing the regional and global opportunities for development of their national economies, the countries of the Asian Pacific are presently contributing to a momentous global transformation. Frequently referred to as a new international division of labor, this unfolding transformation constitutes a new stage in the evolution of the world economic system.

Two general but necessarily speculative conclusions may be drawn with respect to the future of regionalization in the Asian Pacific and its challenge for the world system. One is that Asian Pacific regionalism may force us to think about regionalism in a different way. What may be emerging in the Asian Pacific is a new, dynamic regional economic structure encompassing a sizable number of nation-states, cutting across the territorial boundaries equated with national sovereignty throughout the nineteenth and twentieth centuries. It would be a mistake, however, to conceive of these regional formations as made up of equal members or as closed regional blocs. They are more likely to have the internal unevenness of present-day nation-states. With a highly integrated horizontal division of labor, these regional economies will have a capacity for autonomously generating continued sources of economic growth and technological innovation far greater than the nation-state.

Regions in this sense are not mere aggregations of nation-states for defensive purposes. Gilpin suggests they be called "trading regions" rather than "economic blocs."[72] But while they are "open," even interlocked with the global economy, in contrast to the colloquial connotation of "economic blocs," these regional centers can nonetheless be in competition with one another. This is the second conclusion to be drawn about the embryonic regionalism emerging in the Asian Pacific. If it develops along lines similar to the patterns described in this chapter, it is likely to engage with other regional centers of economic power in a struggle for control of the "world product." Such an economic struggle for control of the world product among regional centers may then be presented as a competition between various forms of capitalism organized on both a regional and global scale. As a replacement of the cold war clash of ideologies, therefore, this type of economic competition among regional centers of power, far from eliminating the existing power of military forces throughout the world, may be likely to use them in support of one or another system of political economy.

These speculative suggestions have avoided discussion of the fate of nation-states and the thorny question of their sovereignty. But they attempt to account for the widespread preoccupation with regionalization in the context of existing evidence. This includes the various ways in which protectionism is set into motion by what seems to be an inexorable process of globalization and transnational integration. Industrial planning, managed markets, and colossal mergers are the order of the day. As rapidly as tariff barriers come down, nontariff barriers are erected to take their place. What the United States calls "specific targets" in its demands for parity in trade with Japan are quantitative restrictions that are the functional equivalents of tariffs and operate on a regional as well as a national basis. Important sectors of the economy of Japan, the United States, and the EU are protected in this way. Gilpin estimates that "as much as 40 percent of world trade is 'managed trade' of some kind, rather than simply subject to market forces."[73]

SUMMARY

In this chapter, we have traced the patterns of trade, investment, and aid that have increasingly tied the countries of the Asian Pacific into a subregion of the world economy. With China and Vietnam embracing market reforms and participation in the global economy, the degree of de facto economic cooperation among businesses throughout the Asian Pacific has increased dramatically. By the early 1990s Japan's bilateral aid and foreign investments had stimulated a level of intraregional trade surpassing that of any other region and creating a formidable economic network of regional interdependence.

Among ASEAN states, those with a history of colonial subjugation to European powers—Malaysia, Singapore, and Indonesia—have diversified their trading partners within the region, hoping thereby to loosen the strings that bound them so implacably to a single Western power. By contrast, Thailand and the Philippines have two-thirds of their trade with extraregional powers. Yet all the countries in the region have found themselves increasingly dependent upon Japan as the regional economic superpower. Japan's economy, along with most of the countries in the region, is dependent upon the United States, whose hold on its hegemonic reins has weakened. The inevitable result has been a complex network of interdependence in which regional economic growth is contingent upon extraregional trade and investment. This interdependence of countries in the region upon one another and the developed countries is reflected in the growing significance of regional associations.

The question of whether or not the Asian Pacific moves in the direction of what is popularly referred to as a "yen bloc" is part of the larger question of regionalization throughout the global economic system. Though the manner in which globalization will proceed is a matter of pure conjecture, the process continues unabated, knocking the ground out from under many of our most comfortable suppositions. The challenge is to provide at least some heuristic ways of thinking about the implications of different paths that global events might take in the twenty-first century. These will be addressed in the final chapter.

QUESTIONS FOR DISCUSSION

1. How has the growth of trade, aid, and investment in the Asian Pacific promoted and/or impeded the institutionalization of regional associations?
2. What in your view are the opportunities and pitfalls of greater regionalization not only in the Asian Pacific but throughout the world?

NOTES

1. Michael Stohl and Harry R. Targ, *Global Political Economy in the 1980s* (Cambridge, MA: Schenkman, 1982), p. 15.
2. James Caporaso, "European Industrial Policy and the Evolving Global *Division of Labor,*" in *Global Political Economy in the 1980s,* ed. Michael Stohl and Harry R. Targ (Cambridge, MA: Schenkman, 1982), p. 81.
3. Russell Mardon and Won K. Paik, "The State, Foreign Investment, and Sustaining Industrial Growth in South Korea and Thailand," in *The Evolving Pacific Basin in the Global Political Economy: Domestic and International Linkages,* ed. Cal Clark and Steve Chan (Boulder, CO: Lynne Rienner, 1992), p. 150.
4. Jeffry A. Frieden and David A. Lake, *International Political Economy: Perspectives on Global Power and Wealth,* 2nd ed. (New York: St. Martin's, 1991), p. 10; emphasis added.
5. The term *production bundle* is used by Steve Chan to refer to the variety of inputs required for industrial production, in "Catching Up and Keeping Up: Explaining Capitalist East Asia's Industrial Competitiveness," *Journal of East Asian Affairs,* no. 5 (1991): 80.
6. Mardon and Paik "The State," p. 151.
7. Mark Borthwick, *Pacific Century: The Emergence of Modern Pacific Asia* (Boulder, CO: Westview, 1992), p. 508.
8. Stephen D. Krasner, "Trade Conflicts and the Common Defense: The United States and Japan," in *Pacific Dynamics: The International Politics of Industrial Change,* ed. Stephan Haggard and Chung-in Moon (Boulder, CO: CIS Inha University–Westview Press, 1989), p. 252.
9. Robert Keohane discusses the distinction between diffuse and specific reciprocity, indicating the implications of each approach, in his article "Reciprocity in International Relations," *International Organization* 40 (Winter 1986): 1–27.
10. William Nester, *Japan and the Third World: Patterns, Power and Prospects* (New York: St. Martin's, 1992), p. 121.
11. Ibid., p. 122.
12. Adam S. Posen, *Restoring Japan's Economic Growth* (Washington, D.C.: Institute for International Economics, 1998).
13. Bernard K. Gordon, "Japan: Searching Once Again," in *Asia Pacific in the New World Politics,* ed. James C. Hsiung (Boulder, CO: Lynne Rienner, 1993), p. 62.
14. K. Akamatsu is credited with having applied the term to the characteristic growth pattern of the region, in "A Historical Pattern of Economic Growth in Developing Countries," *The Developing Economies,* no. 1 (March-April 1962): 3–5.
15. World Development Report, *Knowledge for Development,* 1998/99, table 20, "Global Trade," p. 228.
16. Masahide Shibusawa, Zakaria Haji Ahmed, and Brian Bridges, *Pacific Asia in the 1990's* (London and New York: For the Royal Institute of International Affairs: Routledge, 1992), p. 12 and the IMFs *Direction of Trade Statistics Yearbook,* 1998, pp. 161–163, 280–282, 379–399.
17. Ibid., p. 13.
18. Nester, *Japan and the Third World,* p. 103.
19. Data are from the International Monetary Fund's *Direction of Trade Statistics Yearbook,* 1998 and *IMF Quarterly,* December 1999.

20. Nester, *Japan and the Third World*, p. 134.
21. Ibid., p. 135.
22. Ibid.
23. Ibid., p. 134.
24. See IMF, *Direction of Trade Statistics Yearbook*, 1991, p. 378.
25. Shibusawa, *Pacific Asia in the 1990s*, p. 16.
26. The quote, attributed to DeAnne Julius, *Global Companies and Public Policy: The Growing Challenge of Foreign Direct Investment* (London: Royal Institute of International Affairs/Pinter Publishers, 1990), is found in United Nations Centre on Transnational Corporations, *World Investment Report 1991: The Triad in Foreign Direct Investment*, p. 3.
27. United Nations, *World Investment Report 1991: The Triad in Foreign Direct Investment*, p. 33.
28. Ibid., pp. 46–47.
29. United Nations, *World Investment Directory 1992*, vol. 1, *Asia and the Pacific*, p. 18.
30. Gordon, "Japan," p. 62.
31. Shibusawa, *Pacific Asia in the 1990s*, p. 20.
32. Nester, *Japan and the Third World*, pp. 54–57.
33. Ibid., p. 65.
34. Quoted in Shibusawa, *Pacific Asia in the 1990s*, p. 20.
35. Nester, *Japan and the Third World*, pp. 65–66.
36. Quoted in Shibusawa, *Pacific Asia in the 1990s*, p. 20.
37. Nester, *Japan and the Third World*, p. 103, and Shibusawa, *Pacific Asia in the 1990s*, p. 20.
38. Nester, *Japan and the Third World*, pp. 60, 103.
39. Ibid., p. 65.
40. Richard H. Solomon, Director of the Policy Planning Staff, U.S. Department of State, "Pacific Development and the New Internationalism" (address before the Pacific Future Conference, Los Angeles, CA, March 1988), *Current Policy* No. 1060, Bureau of Public Affairs, U.S. Department of State.
41. Nester, *Japan and the Third World*, p. 103.
42. Shibusawa, *Pacific Asia in the 1990s*, p. 22.
43. Malaysian Prime Minister Mahathir, as quoted in Nester, *Japan and the Third World*, p. 116.
44. Gordon, "Japan: Searching Once Again," p. 199.
45. Shibusawa, *Pacific Asia in the 1990s*, p. 23.
46. Ibid., p. 24.
47. Gordon, "Japan," p. 200.
48. United Nations, World Investment Directory 1992: *Asia and the Pacific,* pp. 28–31.
49. Robert M. Orr Jr., *The Emergence of Japan's Foreign Aid Power* (New York: Columbia University Press, 1990), p. 2.
50. Orr, *The Emergence of Japan's Foreign Aid Power*, p. 3, and Yoshio Okawara, "Japan's Global Responsibilities," in *Japan's Emerging Global Role*, ed. Danny Unger and Paul Blackburn (Boulder, CO: Lynne Rienner, 1993), p. 61.
51. Orr, *The Emergence of Japan's Foreign Aid Power*, p. 55.
52. Quoted in Orr, *The Emergence of Japan's Foreign Aid Power*, p. 78.
53. The table listing the top ten recipients of largest amounts of Japanese bilateral ODA from 1970 to 1988 is found in Orr, *The Emergence of Japan's Foreign Aid Power*, pp. 70–71.
54. Ibid., p. 73.
55. Ibid., p. 74.
56. Bruce M. Koppel and Robert M. Orr, Jr. (eds.), *Japan's Foreign Aid: Power and Policy in a New Era* (Boulder, CO: Westview, 1993), p. 136.
57. Orr, *The Emergence of Japan's Foreign Aid Power*, p. 28.
58. This section has relied on Orr's analysis of the evolution of aid policy, pp. 52–68; the quote is on p. 59.
59. Hosup Kim, "Japanese ODA Policy to the Republic of Korea," in Koppel, *Japan's Foreign Aid*, p. 226, n. 38.

60. David I. Steinberg, "Japanese Economic Assistance to Burma," in Koppel, *Japan's Foreign Aid,* pp. 138, 142.
61. Ibid., p. 162, n. 44.
62. Ibid., p. 156.
63. Juichi Inada, "Stick or Carrot? Japanese Aid Policy and Vietnam," in Koppel, *Japan's Foreign Aid,* p. 124.
64. Joseph Kahn, "Vietnam and the U.S. Sign Historic Trade Agreement," *New York Times,* July 14, 2000, International Page.
65. Inada, "Stick or Carrot?" p. 129.
66. Lawrence T. Woods, "Non-Governmental Organizations and Pacific Cooperation: Back to the Future?" *Pacific Review* 4, no. 4 (1991): 313–14.
67. Norman D. Palmer, *The New Regionalism in Asia and the Pacific* (Lexington, MA: Lexington Books, 1991), p. 142.
68. Andrew Elek, "The Challenge of Asian-Pacific Economic Cooperation," *Pacific Review* 4, no. 4 (1991): 326–27.
69. Quoted in Karl Schoenberger and Leslie Helm, "Clinton Targets Pacific Rim for Trade Crusade," *Los Angeles Times,* November 19, 1993, p. A13.
70. Palmer, *The New Regionalism,* p. 72.
71. Ibid., pp. 148–51.
72. Robert Gilpin, "The Debate About the New World Economic Order," in *Japan's Emerging Global Role,* ed. Danny Unger and Paul Blackburn (Boulder, CO: Lynne Rienner, 1993), p. 26.
73. Ibid., p. 26.

FOR FURTHER READING

Brown, Richard Harvey, and William T. Liu, eds. *Modernization in East Asia: Political, Economic, and Social Perspectives.* Westport, CT: Praeger, 1992, ch. 2.
Dixon, Chris. *South East Asia in the World-Economy.* Cambridge, England: Cambridge University Press, 1991, chs. 5, 6.
Frieden, Jeffry A., and David A. Lake, eds. *International Political Economy: Perspectives on Global Power and Wealth,* 2nd ed. New York: St. Martin's, 1991.
Haggard, Stephan, and Chung-in Moon, eds. *Pacific Dynamics: The International Politics of Industrial Change.* Inchon, Korea and Boulder, CO: CIS–Inha University and Westview Press, 1989.
Higgott, Richard, Richard Leaver, and John Ravenhill, eds. *Pacific Economic Relations in the 1990s: Cooperation or Conflict?* Boulder, CO: Lynne Rienner, 1993.
Hsiung, James, ed. *Asia Pacific in the New World Politics.* Boulder, CO: Lynne Rienner, 1993.
Lee, Chong-Sik, ed. *In Search of a New Order in East Asia.* Berkeley: Institute of East Asian Studies, University of California, 1991, part 2.
Lele, Jayant, and Kwasi Ofori-Yeboah, eds. *Unravelling the Asian Miracle: Explorations in Development Strategies, Geopolitics and Regionalism.* Aldershot, Brookfield, USA, Singapore, Sydney: Dartmouth Publishing Co., Ltd., 1996.
Martin, Linda G., ed. *The ASEAN Success Story: Social, Economic, and Political Dimensions.* Honolulu: East-West Center, 1987.
Palmer, Norman D. *The New Regionalism in Asia and the Pacific.* Lexington, MA: Lexington Books, 1991.
Shibusawa, Masahide, Zakaria Haji Ahmad, and Brian Bridges. *Pacific Asia in the 1990s.* London and New York: For the Royal Institute of International Affairs, Routledge, 1992.
Unger, Danny, and Paul Blackburn, eds. *Japan's Emerging Global Role.* Boulder, CO: Lynne Rienner, 1993.

9

Summing Up and Looking Ahead

To appreciate the development of Asian Pacific nations, assess the "miracle" of their economic growth, and speculate on their increasingly interdependent destiny as a regional center of global economic activity, we have attempted in this book to weave the strands of our explorations into a single piece of fabric. Cut originally from the whole cloth of human history, this fabric is necessarily reconstituted out of the odds and ends, traces and fragments of human communities sometimes stitched together, sometimes torn asunder by events far beyond their control. With varied beginnings in precolonial villages, small kingdoms, and majestic empires, Asian Pacific people have passed from local and imperial traditions, through colonial rites of passage, into their place as modern actors on the global stage of history.

Comparing the politics of the Asian Pacific has been a vast and complex endeavor. The diversity of the thirteen countries and two territories included in our delineation of the region is extraordinary. In size, resource endowment, ethnic and religious configuration, and economic and political organization their differences defy categorization and resist attempts at generalization. Geographically, these countries range from the size of a city-state (Singapore) to the size of a continent (China), from one or more islands to a vast stretch of interior landmass. The cultural variation is equally daunting, from the intricate ethnic mosaic of Southeast Asia to the dense homogeneity of civilizations in China, Japan, and Korea. Yet despite the diversity, there are common threads that bind these disparate peoples together, distinguishing their development from that of the West. How those threads have interwoven with the patterns and designs coming from the West has fashioned the material of this book.

In Chapters 2 through 8, we followed the Asian Pacific peoples' experiences with colonialism, their nationalist struggles, their efforts to survive as modern states in a capitalist-dominated world economy, their adaptation to a global political system rent by cold war conflict, and then their adjustments to the fluidity and uncertainties of the post-Cold War era. This final chapter is devoted to summing up and looking ahead at the course of modernization and development in the Asian Pacific. How far have the people of these countries come since their encounter with the dynamic expansionism of a more technologically advanced West? How has their development been similar to and different from the Westerners from whom they learned the importance of becoming modern? How far do the theories of development explain what has happened in Asian Pacific countries? What problems will they confront in the twenty-first century? What is the future likely to hold in the evolving power relations between states in the region and between the region and the rest of the world?

In this chapter we offer partial and tentative answers to those questions for you to evaluate in the light of your own knowledge and insights. We hope that your reward for reading this far will be to discover that you have your own answers, drawing on your interpretation of what you now know about that fascinatingly complex and rapidly changing region of the world, the Asian Pacific.

THE RECORD OF POLITICAL AND ECONOMIC ACHIEVEMENTS

Survival as States

We begin with the obvious: All of the states that gained their independence still exist, with the sole exception of South Vietnam, now rejoined to the rest of Vietnam. None has reverted to colonial rule. The last two colonial possessions were returned to Chinese sovereignty and East Timor—forcefully incorporated into Indonesia—has gained its independence as a state. None of the states, despite deep cleavages among their people, has disintegrated into a number of quarreling successor states, as have Yugoslavia and the Soviet Union. Even in the case of Malaysia, its brief marriage with Singapore was annulled with a degree of civility that made subsequent cooperation between the two states possible. So the record of survival for Asian Pacific states is impressive.

Survival, like the process of liberation from colonialism, has not been without costs, many imposed by the international struggle between the superpowers and internal struggles between Communists and non- or anticommunists. The two Koreas fought a war with each other in which China joined, responding to what Beijing perceived as the beginning of an American campaign to "liberate" the mainland from the "Reds." The government on Taiwan has since 1949 felt its survival threatened by the possibility of attack from the mainland and so has built up its military strength, at first with generous American aid, now self-financed. The struggle for survival was particularly costly for the Indochinese states. All were embroiled politically and militarily in the contest between North Vietnam and Communist insurgents in South Vietnam, Cambodia, and Laos on one side and the United States and South Vietnam on the other, and all suffered heavy damage from ground and air warfare. Cambodia's independence was subsequently jeopardized by Vietnamese intervention and again by civil war, from which it began to emerge in 1993. In Malaysia and

Indonesia, communist movements once posed challenges before being forcibly suppressed. Communist and ethnic rebels have waged guerrilla war against the governments in Myanmar and the Philippines for decades, but negotiations seem to be bringing about an end to their armed opposition.

Sovereignty and Independence

But survival means more than just the *appearance* of independent statehood. A major objective of Asian Pacific governments in throwing off colonialism was to assert their national sovereignty in the international arena, to control their destiny through foreign policy decisions of their own making. Of the countries allied with the United States, the Philippines was least successful in escaping from the bonds of "neocolonialism," remaining under the American shadow at least until recently, when the country's strategic significance diminished and Japan's economic stake surpassed America's. Japan, while asserting its independence in economic matters, has chosen to follow U.S. leadership in most external political affairs. Its unprecedented self-abnegation on the use of military power as an instrument of foreign policy may be interpreted as evidence either that Japan is dependent on the United States for its security or that it is better able to achieve its foreign policy goals by purely economic means. The Japanese economic stake in many countries in the region carries with it the possibility of Japanese influence over their economic policymaking, but Japan's low profile in international politics seems thus far to have kept to a minimum any effort to extract obedience in foreign policy as the price for economic support.

South Korea's military dependence on the United States circumscribes its latitude for independence in external political affairs. American leverage over Taiwan since the termination of the alliance is difficult to judge; Taiwan's ability to *buy* expensive American military hardware and the American need to *sell* the excess output of the weapons industry may tip the balance of influence more to the island's favor. Although deprived of legal recognition as a sovereign state by the international community and thus of formal membership in most international intergovernmental organizations, the Republic of China government's de facto control of Taiwan is indisputable, however vulnerable it may be to takeover by the PRC. Thailand, another ally of the United States once quite dependent on American military aid and a staunch supporter of American policy in Indochina, has attempted to distance itself from Washington. It has diversified its weapons suppliers, moved toward accommodation with China and Myanmar, and reasserted its traditional influence in Laos and Cambodia.

The sovereignty and independence of Laos and Cambodia appear quite precarious. Laos's vulnerability stems from Vientiane's loose grip over the hinterland and the government's eager receptivity to almost any form of external help, whatever the source or terms, for the country's stagnant and backward economy. Cambodia's future depends on the ability of the two-headed coalition government formed in 1998 to wean itself from financial dependence on international aid, to gain control of areas that were under the Khmer Rouge (KR), and to put an end to Thai collaboration with the remnants of the KR in the timber and gem trade. Both states' prospects gain at least in the short run from Vietnam's abandonment of its aspirations to reassert the dominant role Vietnamese played in the rest of Indochina under French colonialism.

Hanoi's effort to establish its credentials as "good neighbor" to China and ASEAN, its military power, large population, and attractiveness to foreign investors all seem favorable to protecting Vietnam's sovereignty and independence.

Nonalignment and isolation bought Myanmar independence from outside control of its foreign policy, but limited the range of actions it could take. Brunei, Malaysia, and Singapore have managed to remain officially nonaligned while retaining a degree of security dependence on their former colonial overlord, Great Britain, supported by the United States, Australia, and New Zealand. In contrast, Indonesia's rupture with the Netherlands was quite abrupt, and Sukarno's promotion of nonalignment put him at loggerheads with the United States. Under Suharto's rule, however, Indonesia solidly allied itself with "the free world," benefiting from its close relationship with the United States. Strains on this relationship grew out of Indonesia's invasion and "occupation" of the Catholic-dominated former colony of Portugal, East Timor, in 1975. In the firm belief that Indonesia had the tacit support of both the United States and Australia for its intervention and annexation of East Timor, Suharto appeared to ignore mounting U.S. criticism of Indonesia's human rights violations in East Timor and elsewhere in Indonesia. Following Suharto's forced resignation, Habibie ordered the referendum on self-determination for East Timor after receiving notification that Australia had shifted its policy to join the international call for self-determination. On August 30, 1999 East Timoreans voted overwhelmingly for independence triggering a wave of violence against them by pro-Indonesian militia abetted by the Indonesian military. Within three weeks of the vote, the Indonesian government was forced to accept a heavily-armed, Australian-led U.N. peacekeeping force on its soil to restore order. Indonesia was approaching the nadir of its post–Cold War problems with this infringement of its sovereignty following on the heels of the country's economic subjugation to the IMF and its conditions for bailing Indonesia out of its economic disaster. A wave of violence among warring religious and ethnic communities and between separatist movements and the military in Aceh and Irian Jaya continues to threaten Indonesia's political stability.

Of all the countries, China—particularly after the break with the Soviet Union—seems to have most effectively pursued an independent course in its foreign relations. Even the opening to foreign business interests does not seem to have impaired significantly its determination to defy other governments' actions that appear to the Chinese as insults to their national sovereignty and prestige. North Korea, having kept a substantial margin of freedom from domination by either of its neighboring communist patrons by maneuvering between them, as of this writing has exhibited a determined if idiosyncratic self-assurance in its quest for international recognition. However intransigent and even irrational Pyongyang's behavior may appear to outsiders, the North's policies do demonstrate its independence of foreign domination.

National Unity

The degree of success attained by Asian Pacific states in "nation building," in creating or tightening the bonds of national unity, depends in large part on the extent of ethnic, regional, religious, and political diversity in each country when it achieved independence. Colonialism brought the gospel of nationalism everywhere in the region, catching on faster and winning more converts in some places than others. Sometimes the spread of modern nationalism reinforced bonds of solidarity already felt by the people, as in the case of countries with long histories of separate political identity (such as Japan, China, and Korea), national unity being equally fervently espoused by both Communists and anticommunists in China and Korea. In Indonesia and the Philippines, the potential for nation building was enhanced by colonial rule, which gave the people of those islands their first experience of union. However, the emergence of some form of pan-Malay nationalism uniting the people of Malay stock inhabiting what are now Malaysia, Indonesia, and the Philippines was foreclosed by their separate administration as colonies of three different Western powers.

Borders drawn around Laos and Burma by the colonial powers and the migration of foreign laborers into British Malaya meant that at independence the governments of Malaysia, Singapore, Burma, and Laos inherited ethnically diverse populations lacking a sense of common identity. In Malaysia, the Chinese and Indian minorities have accepted the government's policy of discrimination in favor of the Malay majority as the price they must pay for being left in relative peace to pursue economic activities. Singapore seems to have worked out an accommodation between the Chinese majority and the minority Malay and Indian citizens and claims to be aiming at greater psychological unity in the form of a Singaporean identity. Thus far, however, in both Singapore and Malaysia successful *state* building has not yet been matched by successful *nation* building. In Burma, divisions between the Burman majority and a daunting array of non-Burman groups, some in almost continuous rebellion against the central government, have made state building difficult and nation building impossible. By 1993 SLORC seemed to have negotiated an ad hoc form of shared sovereignty with all of the insurgents except the Karens, a compromise that falls far short of the goal of national unity. Similarly fractionated between Lao-speakers and non-Lao mountain people, Laos's identity as a nation after independence was further stalled by ideological divisions, and the abolition of the monarchy after the Communists consolidated power removed it as a possible symbol around which some semblance of national unity might be forged.

The monarchies in Thailand and Cambodia, on the other hand, have retained their potency as symbols of national unity and even preserved some of the political influence they once enjoyed in the era of unlimited royal power. The Thai king's contribution to national unity and stability was demonstrated in 1992, when he intervened after a bloody confrontation between rival political groups and insisted that peace be restored. Norodom Sihanouk, having survived four decades of assaults on the integrity and independence of Cambodia, returned to the throne in 1993, still the symbol (perhaps the *only*) of national unity for the Khmer people, the father of the Cambodia people. Ahead are the problems of overcoming political divisions within the Khmer majority and incorporating (or evicting) the Vietnamese minority. The 77-year old monarch's successor will be chosen from among his sons and half brothers, no doubt with an eye to avoiding anyone with his own political ambitions.

Some governments still face challenges from minority groups demanding autonomy or independence, such as China's Tibetan population, the Karens in Myanmar, Moslems in the Philippines and Thailand, and Acehnese, and Irianese in Indonesia. Brunei's sultanate has thus far escaped serious challenge from the large non-Malay minority, although it would be difficult to claim that all the residents of that ministate share a sense of Bruneian national identity or that the sultan's government wants them to.

Although the Chinese and Korean nations are still divided, the leaders of North and South Korea signed an accord in June 2000 establishing the groundwork for a process of reconciliation between them. With the possible exception of Indonesia, the general picture of Asian Pacific states is that they are reasonably in control of centrifugal forces and unlikely to disintegrate. Varying degrees of coercion underlie the extent of stability and cohesiveness their leaders have achieved since independence.

Political Leadership

Some form of authoritarianism has typically been chosen by postcolonial leaders as the means either to bring about political, social, and economic revolution or to make more modest economic and social progress or to defend the status quo against internal or external threat. In a few countries, such as South Korea, Taiwan, Thailand, and the Philippines, authoritarian rule seems to be in the process of self-transformation toward a more consensual, less coercive system. In others, such as China and Myanmar, the leadership has responded to challenges from critics and opponents by tightening, rather than loosening, political controls.

There has been a surprising continuity in leadership in the period since independence for most of the Asian Pacific governments. Communist parties have held the reins of power in China since 1949, in North Korea since 1948, in North Vietnam since 1945, and in all of Vietnam since 1975. Noncommunist one-party rule has prevailed in Singapore and Malaysia since independence, in Taiwan since 1945, in Japan until 1993, while in Brunei the sultan has reigned supreme since the end of the British protectorate. The military has been in power in Myanmar since 1962, in Indonesia since 1965, and in Thailand from 1932 to 1992. In Indonesia, a combination of military excesses, violent protests against the regime and international condemnation forced President Suharto to resign after 33 years in power. Amidst continuing turmoil, a new constitution and free elections brought President Abdurrahman Wahid into power but whether or not he will be able to survive this tumultuous transition to achieve a more unified basis for political stability among the 300 distinct ethnic groups that inhabit the 13,000 islands of Indonesia remains to be seen.

The four remaining states—Laos, the Philippines, South Korea, and Cambodia—have experienced more discontinuity in leadership than the others. Laos, after years of shifting coalitions among a trio of princes, has been led since 1975 by the Communist Party. The Philippines have gone from a competitive two-party civilian system to Marcos's dictatorship with major military participation to the post-Marcos multiparty civilian government with the military still politically significant. South Korea's political history since 1948 has seen civilian rule overthrown by the military, who dominated the government until the end of 1992. In 1997 South Koreans elected a former political dissident from the opposition party and he has taken the first step toward reaching a reconciliation of North and South Korea. Cambodia has had the most checkered history of all, going from limited monarchy to military dictatorship to Khmer Rouge Communists under Pol Pot to more moderate Communists to limited monarchy again under a coalition government of Communists and noncommunists.

Whether the continuity in leadership that characterizes most of the Asian Pacific countries will survive the passing of aging leaders, and whether the power holders will deal successfully with pressures for political change are problems that will be discussed below. But the continuity experienced thus far has brought the benefit of political stability (with some exceptions, like the upheavals of the Great Leap Forward and the Cultural Revolution and the periodic outbursts against military rule in Thailand and Myanmar). In the case of Japan, the NICs, the NECs, and now China, continuity of leadership and stability are thought to have contributed to their progress in economic development. Burma's economic stagnation, and North Korea's of late, suggest that the connection among continuity in leadership, political stability, and economic development is not a simple one.

Economic Progress

It is in economic development that Asian Pacific countries have excelled, redirecting world attention to the idea that manufacturing exports for a global economy provides an effective means for accomplishing sustained and rapid economic growth, even for countries with few natural resources starting out in a world dominated by rich and powerful developed nations. Although the region as a whole has astounded the world with its economic growth rates, the record of accomplishment is—as we have seen—mixed. Some countries have been gloriously successful, most have made considerable progress, substantially raising the standard of living of many (though not all) of their people, while a few are still no better off than they were at the time of independence.

While the market appears to have triumphed, even in the self-styled socialist countries, as the most effective mechanism for generating and distributing wealth, two questions present themselves. One concerns the costs or losses incurred by development. The physical quality of life in the Asian Pacific, improved in some respects, has also been adversely affected by runaway urbanization, unsafe working conditions, profligate consumption of forests and other natural resources, and environmental degradation on a scale equaling or surpassing that in the West. A 1993 report by the UN Economic and Social Commission for Asia and the Pacific pointed out that rapid economic growth has caused air and water pollution of crisis proportions and contributed to the large, ever increasing numbers of urban poor living in slums, even in high-income countries such as South Korea. In many countries the income gap between the newly affluent and the rest of the population has widened, and the focus on industrial development leaves the rural population behind. In recent years the economies in Japan and South Korea in particular have demonstrated that even those cases of "miracle" growth are subject to the boom-and-bust cycle well known in Western economic history.

The second question concerns the observation that dynamic development in the Asian Pacific, as in the West, is the result of adopting *market mechanisms*, even among former communist states. But in analyzing the success of markets in the Asian Pacific, one must ask whether the conception of "the market" is one and the same in the Asian Pacific and in the West? Or does the meaning of what a market is vary with the historical and cultural circumstances of the particular process of development in each case? Contending perspectives in addressing this question will be reviewed in the next section.

A Distinctive Pattern of Development

The costs notwithstanding, an impressive record of achievements followed the adoption of an export-led strategy lending support to the idea that a distinctive national-regional pattern of development has taken shape in the Asian Pacific. The roots of this strategy go back to Western colonial incorporation of the entire region into the imperialist world system. Under the impact of Western and Japanese imperialism, people in the Asian Pacific were introduced to the idea of the modern nation-state, to the global economy, and to the regional implications of economic integration as mutually compatible, perhaps even complementary, developments. When Asian nationalists pursued independence, therefore, they were keenly aware that the objective of national development facing them after liberation had to be undertaken within the larger context of the global economy.

In the aftermath of Japan's defeat, the United States became the economic center of power in a world ideologically divided into two armed camps. Although nationalism had not abated and strong states in the Asian Pacific retained their decisive role in guiding domestic economic development (with notable exceptions), they now pursued development on one or the other side of the political and military fence. Exempt from playing an independent political and military role in the world, Japan rapidly reemerged as a powerful engine of regional economic growth within an expanding global network of markets. While China, North Korea, and Vietnam, along with Laos and Cambodia, became embroiled in war against the United States, domestic political turmoil, and socialist economic planning (described in Chapters 4 through 7), the economies of Japan, South Korea, Taiwan, Hong Kong, and the ASEAN nations were beneficiaries of the boom in the capitalist world economy.

The political and economic relationships built up in the Asian Pacific during this era laid the foundation for the distinctive national-regional pattern of economic growth and expansion, described in Chapter 8 and variously alluded to as "the flying geese formation," the East Asian developmental model, or Confucian capitalist model of development. But the international context providing the incubator for this developmental pattern (described in Chapter 7) has now ceased to exist. Viewed against the backdrop of this shifting international context, how well do the four theoretical approaches covered throughout the book explain the nature of development in the Asian Pacific?

HOW WELL DO THE THEORIES EXPLAIN DEVELOPMENT?

One conclusion about the theories of development seems inescapable: The road to economic progress mapped out by the modernization theorists was not the one taken by Japan and the newly industrializing nations of the Asian Pacific, nor has incorporation in the global capitalist economy been the roadblock to development that dependency theorists predicted it would be. Contrary to modernization theory's assumption, Asian Pacific countries did not follow the incremental course presumed to have characterized Western nations. Rather then emulating the self-reliant, market-driven Western way of modernizing, Asian Pacific countries relied heavily on the world economy, their own interventionist states, and important elements of their traditional cultures to promote rapid sustained economic growth. On the other hand, despite dependency theorists' grim expectations that less developed nations would be prevented from improving their prospects, some developing countries, by adopting export-led strategies, have in fact been able to propel themselves into the middle rank of newly industrializing countries. What, then, of the other theories?

World System Theory

Existing evidence on the whole seems to corroborate the three-tiered hierarchy of core, semiperiphery, and periphery that world system theorists use to understand nation-states' development as parts of a single expanding world capitalist system.[1] Two additional elements of world system theory appear substantiated by the evidence. One is that countries do in fact move up and down the ladder of successful development, not as a simple consequence of their own domestic efforts, but as a complex response to a dynamically changing set of global opportunities. The second is that this upward and downward mobility is confined to a relatively small number of countries; worldwide, the larger number of peripheral countries remain at the bottom and the smaller number of core countries retain their advantageous positions at the top of the wealth and development hierarchy.

The central question, not only for theory but for the policymaking of state officials, therefore, is: What explains the successful upward mobility of Asian Pacific countries? The developmental state approach contributes significantly to answering this question.

The Developmental State Approach

This approach draws attention to the ways in which an effective, developmentally oriented state can facilitate a virtuous circle between the market decisions of domestic entrepreneurs and the global opportunities for economic expansion and upgrading. When a state has sufficient autonomy from partisan domestic interests to exercise national leadership closely attuned to the growth of a global economy, it can promote the country's rapid and sustained development and upward mobility in the international status hierarchy. The developmental state approach thus turns out to be a strategy for successful industrialization that places a premium on the political autonomy and economic leadership of the state. As a theoretical explanation of development, the statist or developmentalist approach rests on the opposite assumption from both modernization and world system theories: that economic power cannot exist outside the framework of politics provided by a state. What the theory proposes (and the Asian Pacific experience seems to support) is that the power of politics is autonomous and preeminent, the necessary precondition for harnessing and managing economic power organized on the basis of the market.

Critics of the developmental state theory, especially those who have studied Latin America, argue that which pattern of development a weak developing state chooses when it embarks on modernization may depend on the particular model provided by a neighboring core country. Fernando Fajnzylber suggests that a reason for the success of East Asian NICs may be that they took Japan as their model and followed its emphasis on strategic, long-term industrialization, high savings rates, international competitiveness, education as a national priority to compensate for the dearth of natural resources, the "conquest" of external markets, and social integration as a legitimating device for ruling elites.[2] Latin American countries, by contrast, followed the U.S. pattern of development based on a tactical, short-term orientation toward industrialization geared primarily toward the domestic rather than the international market, high levels of consumption rather than savings, reliance on natural resources in international trade, and a social order structured and legitimized largely by market forces, with the state playing a far less innovative and critical role in planning and financing development than in the Japanese model. "These models represent not only the ideological hegemony of the U.S. and Japan in propagating developmental paradigms but also the concrete historical impact of their colonial and neocolonial legacies in shaping the production, consumption. and distribution patterns in their respective follower nations."[3]

Cultural Theory

Criticism of the developmental state as the source of successful development comes from another direction: the adherents of a cultural theory of development. For cultural theorists, alternative types or models of development are shaped by the varying cultural environments of people. People's cultural beliefs and values set limits on and shape both their pattern of development and the kind of state that carries it out. Thus whether a strong or a weak state is employed as a framework for development is itself an outcome of a people's culture; different cultures produce different styles of modernization. Cultural theorists argue that cultural attributes like the relatively high social prestige of bureaucrats, the importance of education, frugality, deferred gratification, reciprocal social obligations, and an appreciation of the authority of the state promote development while others, like conspicuous consumption and unrestrained competition among self-interested individuals, do more to obstruct development. It is the Confucian-based culture of East Asian states that, for cultural theorists, accounts for their success in moving up the international ladder of economic achievement.

Although no one disputes the significance of culture as one of many variables explaining the success or failure of particular developmental states, advancing the nebulous concept of culture as the sole causal factor to explain differences in developmental patterns invariably results in contradictory arguments. Thus Confucianism has been used to explain both why China did not industrialize and why Taiwan and Hong Kong did. There is, in addition, the fact that a significant number of non-Confucian countries, Southeast Asian nations among them, have been able to adopt the pattern of development first exhibited by East Asian countries, which argues that culture may not be as essential a component for successful development as emulation of a regional patron-state and integration into the regional and global division of labor.

The cultural theory may nonetheless have explanatory value for the transnational economic role Chinese have played in fueling growth not only in Taiwan, Hong Kong, and Singapore but in the other countries of the Asian Pacific to which they have migrated for centuries. The contribution of "overseas Chinese" as a transnational economic force in the development of the region cannot be overestimated. They have energetically promoted business and trade in the development of nation-states throughout Southeast Asia and they continue to form an "invisible" regional network of economic activity linking development cross-nationally.

Having celebrated the impressive political and economic accomplishments of Asian Pacific countries and assessed the different theories' power to explain their development, we are ready finally to turn our attention to the future, to the problems these countries can expect to face in the twenty-first century. In the next section, the focus is on prospects for political change and in the concluding section on the region's place in the global economic and political system.

PROSPECTS FOR POLITICAL CHANGE: SUCCESSION, POLITICAL REFORM, AND HUMAN RIGHTS

Change is inevitable in human institutions as it is in the lives of individuals. Sometimes it occurs almost imperceptibly, at a glacial pace; at other times, like our own, the speed of change is dizzying. This is especially true for the people of the Asian Pacific, many of whom, in the span of a generation or two, have been swept from the familiar moorings of traditional society to the excitement, uncertainty, and opportunities generated by rapid modernization. In the midst of such rapid change, it is difficult to assess the ratio of opportunity to danger in the changes that confront us. This is true not merely for all of us living in and through this unparalleled period of human history, it is equally true for those of us claiming to observe and describe what we see transpiring. A good example is the first political change we will address: the problem of political succession. A scant six years ago, when the first edition of this book was being written, most political scientists observing the Asian Pacific ranked the problem of political succession as the major threat to political stability among a large number of Asian Pacific states. Today, in retrospect, the succession of political leaders like Kim Il Sung in North Korea (who died in 1996), Deng Xiaoping in China (who died in 1997), and Suharto in Indonesia (who was forced to resign in 1998) seems to have occurred without the collapse of political order.

This is *not* to say that political succession has had no ramifications of consequence. Clearly the aftermath of political succession brings with it innumerable challenges and conundrums. But political succession as such, even in authoritarian states with highly personalized rule by a "supreme leader" or where one group has monopolized power for a long time, does not *necessarily* threaten state sovereignty. In the Asian Pacific, as we have seen, authoritarian forms of rule are not the quixotic creations of despotic or dictatorial rulers; they are institutional arrangements that embody the sovereignty of the state (in Hobbes' terms) and under ordinary circumstances have their own political dynamic for enduring beyond the lifetime of any single leader. They may not have the transparent legal-rational rules of succession that we are accustomed to in western liberal democracies, but their institutions can exhibit "staying power" nonetheless. The political organization of states like that in China, North Korea or Indonesia may be said to have what Samuel Huntington referred to as *political institutionalization*—i.e., their political institutions "have acquired *value* in the eyes of the population and *stability* to withstand significant pressure" despite the fact that they are totally dissimilar, even inimical, to those of our own state.[4] This was touched on in Chapter 4 in the discussion of authoritarianism.

In the same way that individuals who provide the leadership required in the early stages of development face the reality of their own mortality, the political organizations through which they have exercised this leadership face growing pressures for change generated by the very economic and social transformations they themselves have brought about. After a brief description of political succession in the region, the two remaining problems we have chosen to address as the most likely prospects to challenge Asian Pacific leadership in the immediate future are political reform and human rights. Each poses a serious risk regardless of whether a state chooses to embrace or reject the challenge. We begin with the issue of political succession because it is often the catalyst for the other two.

The Issue of Political Succession

What actually happened in China when Deng "went to meet Marx," in Indonesia when Suharto was forced to retire, and in North Korea when Kim Il Sung departed? In all three situations, the succession went smoothly with no evidence of a bitter political struggle between contending forces. In China, Jiang Zemin was already ensconced in his official positions as General Secretary of the Communist Party and President of the PRC and Deng Xiaoping's death seemed anticlimactic rather than momentous, even though it truly signified the end of revolutionary leadership in China. Deng Xiaoping, like Mao Zedong before him, was a self-educated, peasant-revolutionary in sharp contrast to Jiang Zemin and Zhu Rongji who are engineers and technocrats, not revolutionaries.

The results were similar in the case of Kim Il Sung's death in North Korea. There were no outward signs of political struggle or opposition to Kim's son, Kim Jong Il, taking over, though the three-year period of mourning required of the younger Kim provided ample opportunity for speculation from afar. In Suharto's case, even though his forced retirement occurred in the midst of turbulent mass protests against his misrule, the transition went smoothly. Vice President Habibie assumed the presidency, but convinced he could not possibly win, withdrew from the election enabling a moderate Moslem and experienced politician, Abdurrahman Wahid, to be elected President by the Assembly, as constitutionally mandated. Megawati Sukarnoputri, who had received a plurality of the popular vote, as a woman and a political novice was unable to muster the votes to win in the Assembly election for president.

Political Reform: Democratization and Decentralization

The larger problem confronting Asian Pacific states, for which political succession is a convenient symbol, is that of political change, most often thought of as political reform. But why is political reform a problem one might ask? There is a widespread belief in the West that reforming politics, especially since it is assumed to apply to those political systems—other than our own—that require reforming, is a good idea. As the data suggest and even the World Bank—the foremost proponent of market-oriented liberalism—has acknowledged, the "high economic growth with equity" achieved by Asian Pacific countries was accomplished by strong developmental states pursuing industrial strategies.[5] If this is so, then political reform can only mean *reducing* the strength of these states by either making them more accountable to a wider set of constituents (democratization) or by abridging their involvement in managing the economy (decentralization of economic power).

To assess the prospects of political reform in Asian Pacific countries in the decades ahead we first review why and how democratization and decentralization pose critical problems for communist and noncommunist states in the region, and then look at the possible configurations political reform is likely to assume in these diverse countries in the Asian Pacific.

Both communist and noncommunist states in the region promoted economic growth within the context of authoritarian rule. In China, Vietnam, North Korea, Taiwan, Malaysia, and Singapore, it was the authoritarian leadership of a single party often headed by a dynamic, charismatic personality, that provided the initiative and coordination to promote national economic growth. In Thailand, Myanmar, the Philippines since Marcos, South Korea, Indonesia, and even pre-war Japan, it was the military that provided the ballast and unity of command for the ship of state to steer a course toward economic development. Among the exceptions in the Asian Pacific—Brunei, Hong Kong, Cambodia, Laos, and Japan—the truly extraordinary exception was Japan because it had already developed a modern economy only to be defeated in World War II. In rebuilding its modern economy as a vanquished world power, therefore, Japan was required to accomplish its task without a military to serve as rudder and with a democratic constitution imposed by the United States. The outcome was a developmental state, with its nondemocratic (bureaucratic) invulnerability to popular pressures that enabled a cross-sectoral elite to effectively instruct private market forces in a coherent, coordinated, and globally integrated development.

As we know, these developmental states in the region brought about a period of extremely high economic growth rates relatively unimpeded—though this differed from country to country—by any organized expression of political opposition. Indeed, this capacity to prevent open dissension of any kind from deflecting national energies is an important measure of the strength of developmental states. It was only after growth rates had succeeded in substantially raising the productivity and living standards of people in these countries that political reform was permitted any space in public discourse. This began in the 1970s and 1980s when manifestations of discontent with the political status quo bubbled to the surface—in 1973 in Thailand, 1976 in China, 1979 in South Korea, 1983 in the Philippines and so on. Almost certainly instances of "corruption" and "cronyism" existed before then, but they had reached some critical mass only with the rising tide of expectations brought about by successful economic growth. By the late 1980s, widespread perception of corruption—the misuse of public funds (resources) for private purposes (gain)—and "cronyism" (the term is western, the idea is expressed in varying ways depending on the language and culture of a country)—the mutually beneficial and self-serving relationships between public officials and their private clients—converged in organizations and movements to demand political reform.

Developmental states thus created the very opposition that sought to reform them. By enlarging the national economic pie, developmental states also generated new beneficiaries of this expanded wealth, raising peoples' expectations generally and multiplying the number and scope of demands made upon the state by a growing number of groups and individuals. Though the pressures for political reform vary in specifics from one developmental state to another, the long-run persistence of this movement for political reform exhibits certain commonalities: the demand for greater accountability to those enriched and empowered by rapid economic growth, the demand to include excluded groups and individuals in the processes of government so they too can increase their share of the national pie, the demand for fewer restrictions and greater latitude for individual opportunities, initiative, and actions. These demands for political reform fall into the category of "democratization."

Allied to but distinct from democratization are the ways in which government retreats from its broadly encompassing control of social, economic and political life. Because it usually requires the central government to shed some of its functions and activities—those thought to belong to the private domain of civil society—we refer to this aspect of political reform as "decentralization." It is not a demand for representation in the central government (e.g., calls for a direct vote for central government officials or calls for a competitive party system at the national level) but very often a de facto result of economic reform in communist countries, like China, and of "cronyism" in developmental states like Thailand and Indonesia.

Political Reform and the Asian Economic Crisis.   Although democratization and decentralization are distinct aspects of political reform, their consequences have much in common. Political reforms aimed at democratization dissipate the protective insulation of elite decision making thus fragmenting, diluting and otherwise diminishing the coherence of policy recommendations to accommodate divergent and often incompatible constituencies. Decentralization in the interests of loosening market forces from their state moorings threatens to bring about regional, sectional, or territorial fragmentation. Both of these facets of political reform pose serious problems for states in the Asian Pacific, principally because they threaten to erode the political unity and territorial integrity of nation-states that are relative newcomers to the global order. With the exception of North Korea, states in the Asian Pacific now appear to recognize the necessity of acceding to a wider and more heterogeneous array of constituents.

This acceptance by governing elites of their inescapable need to accommodate peoples' demands for political reform may be the most significant consequence of the Asian financial crisis of 1997–2000. To accord political reform the serious attention of government policymakers is to direct public energies to the internal exigencies that require "fixing" in a crisis rather than simply to divert public discontent onto external actors over whom one can have no control. In public reactions to the Asian crisis there was a clear divide between leaders in the Asian Pacific who pointed their fingers at foreign currency investors playing "casino capitalism" at the expense of Asian Pacific economies and Western political leaders and international economists who pointed their fingers at the "crony capitalism" and illiberal markets of Asian Pacific economies that prevented them from playing by the rules, thereby inviting such disasters on themselves. If the "Asian crisis" implicated international investors in "betting" or speculating on currency exchange differentials on a global scale, it was just as certainly the internal vulnerabilities of Asian Pacific political economies that provided the opportunities without being aware of the consequences. How, then, did the Asian economic crisis lead to the need for political reform?

The internal problems of governance in successful Asian Pacific states were insufficiently destabilizing on their own to be seriously addressed by governments content to bask in having stimulated high economic growth rates. But when they found their economies in danger of collapsing overnight as a consequence of the gambling habits of international capital investors, governing elites in these developmental states were forced to view their internal vulnerabilities in a new light. Political scandals, corporate bribery, banks that were "captives" of particular industries, financial institutions with mountains of unrecoverable debts and a general lack of oversight and transparency in the operation of the financial system could no longer go unheeded. The economic risks of integration in the global market were made palpable by the rapidity with which global currency transactions could detonate implosions that not only shattered domestic financial institutions but spread throughout the region. Largely unanticipated, the crisis and its domino effect on the region's political economies initially elicited inappropriate responses on the part of both Asian Pacific governments and the international institutions, like the IMF, that ran to the rescue, in some instances aggravating rather than alleviating the downward spiral into economic recession in the region.

In retrospect, the Asian economic crisis has had a greater impact on political reform than on economic restructuring. Though bankruptcy laws have been refined, new and more rigorous accounting procedures adopted, professionalism in the regulation of financial transactions increased, and mergers and acquisitions with foreign companies facilitated, there is little indication that the "fundamentals"—as economists call them—have altered dramatically. It is arguable how this is measured, of course, and in what time frame, but as of now in the immediate aftermath of the crisis, indications are that developmental states in the Asian Pacific are intact. What has happened in individual countries, however, is that an opening has been created for political reformers to get a hearing. What the prospects are for Asian Pacific states to accommodate political reform without risking serious political disruption will be the central challenge of all states in the region. How these diverse states are tackling this challenge of confronting demands for political reform in the aftermath of the economic crisis is the subject of the following section.

China.   Political reform in China has been a volatile issue with global linkages that make it extremely delicate for the Communist Party–state. Since the CPC's revolutionary embrace (under Deng Xiaoping's leadership) of commodity production for the international capitalist market (1978), China's path of development has been redirected away from revolutionary socialism to "market socialism." The similarities between "market socialism" and capitalism are studiously avoided in official rhetoric. But this radical departure of Chinese Communist Party policy since 1978 has left the party's legitimacy hanging by two threads: prosperity and national unity. Just as prosperity goes hand in hand with continued economic reform and governmental adaptation to its own shifting role in the economy, Chinese nationalism is intertwined with the issue of national political unity. Two policy consequences follow from this: there can be no alternative to reuniting Taiwan with the motherland and the line separating political reform from treasonous behavior is dangerously thin.

The extent to which political reform in any shape or form is couched in Western competitive electoral terms for national office makes it an anathema to the government of China. The *manner* in which the Chinese government suppresses such demands for political reform may be clumsy and costly—as in the case of the Tiananmen incident of 1989 when the international fallout was considerable—but the explanation for why the government is determined to suppress such opposition is transparent. Political dissidents are treated uniformly with harsh jail terms though they can also be used as bargaining chips in the game of international diplomacy. In similar fashion, the government suppresses opposition in which there is any suggestion of a link with Chinese or foreigners on the outside. This applies to large-scale religious demonstrations like that of Falun Gong adherents who surprised the leadership with the movement's scope and effective organization as well as its leader—an ex-Chinese army clerical employee currently living in exile in the United States.

There is, on the other hand, a vastly expanded latitude for personal freedom in China, which runs the gamut from individual protests against medical malpractice to demonstrations and strikes drawing attention to people's particular grievances and hardships. This is striking for Americans who live and work in China for extended periods of time, as this author has since 1976. Are these signs of an active civil society occasioned by political reforms? They may not appear so for people who identify politics and therefore political reform strictly in terms of competitive party politics and electoral behavior. But in China, the widespread perception that it is possible to actually engage in these individual and collective expressions of grievances or discontent is the result of a number of significant political reforms undertaken at the national level. One is in the area of strengthening the legal system. This means not only promoting the legal profession but passing legislation that clarifies and specifies what is and is not required of human beings in their economic and social conduct; promoting the courts as a way of resolving disputes and educating the population in the value of cultivating the rule of law. These reforms are all still in their infancy and, as with economic prosperity, social mobility, and educational opportunities, they are not evenly distributed among the 1.2 billion people in China.

Other areas in which political reforms have begun but are likely only gradually to develop are in reducing the size and scope of governmental involvement in economic and social life. In the activities of obtaining employment, schooling, housing, health care, the state has already retreated to a greatly narrowed arena of macro-managing the social system. This is where the adoption of a legal system becomes essential to create more transparency and uniformity in regulating the complex apparatus of a modern, legal-rational system of governance. But before a spirit of respect for the law can be institutionalized in China, there will be continuing, disquieting problems with the ongoing political decentralization of government functions. The major headaches accompanying this reform are posed by the capacity of more affluent regions with independent access to international markets "to go it alone" by ignoring the strictures of the central government. This opens up opportunities for corruption and malfeasance of all sorts—the single greatest source of public discontent and a potential weakening of the central government's control over its far-flung territory. Thus political reform as decentralization in China (which might be called liberalization in the west), as well as the inalienability of Taiwan hark back to fundamental anxieties about political disunity.

In the area of electoral reform, national legislation has been passed opening the most basic (village) level elections to more than one but still a limited number of candidates. One might expect future steps in such democratization to move up the political ladder from basic-level to county and provincial levels. But whether or to what extent political parties other than the Communist Party will be permitted to function is anyone's guess. Acceptable political reform has been and will undoubtedly continue to be defined largely in terms of decentralization and liberalization of state power rather than democratization in the sense of multiparty competitive electoral politics. Interesting in this regard is the dynamic between China and Taiwan on this issue of democratization. On the one hand, the current DPP leadership in Taiwan bolsters its justification for Taiwan's existence as "a separate state" on its claim of being a real democracy; on the other hand, China reinforces its claim for the viability of a negotiated reunification on the basis of "one country, two systems" by pointing to the fact that China on both sides of the straits is embarked on "democratization."

Within these limited boundaries political reform has occurred by default through the gradual elimination of all obstacles to the pursuit of private gain and freedom of personal expression. While the Communist Party remains the sole channel for becoming a professional politician and assuming high position in public office at the national level, democratic parties are allowed, even encouraged, to play an advisory role to the Communist Party. As political reform has moved slowly higher on the political agenda of the Communist Party leadership, these "democratic parties" have increased both their visibility and prestige as participants in the CPPCC (described in Chapter 4). Nonetheless, their role remains largely educational, not unlike that of third parties in the United States.

Other One-Party Communist States. While there is evidence of discontent and opposition from religious, ethnic, and political interests, the dominant position of the ruling parties in these countries seems unchallengeable for the present. Despite social changes occurring as a result of economic reforms in Vietnam, Laos as well as China, and differences of opinion within the parties in China and Vietnam about the pace of economic liberalization and even conflicts over the need for political reforms within the Communist Party, none of those parties seems headed for a breakup into contending parties. As long as they resist centrifugal forces, there is little or no chance for noncommunist opposition parties to organize in the face of government surveillance by police and military and government control of the media. In the absence of any alternative to it, the Communist Party, particularly in China, can play on the fear of descent into chaos and anarchy in appealing for public support for its continued leadership.

Taiwan.   Political reform in Taiwan is the result of a complex interplay of internal and external pressures. As long as Taiwan was under the single-party rule of the Guomindang whose mission was sustained by the myth of returning to the mainland, advocates of political reform were silenced. During the 1970s, however, as U.S. financial and ideological support for Taiwan declined, pulling down the myth of returning to the mainland with it, opposition to the regime grew, mostly among native Taiwanese resentful of mainlanders' domination, intellectuals, and some labor organizations. After the death of Chiang Kaishek and the accession of his son, Chiang Chingguo, a process of Taiwanization of the Guomindang (Nationalist Party) was undertaken (1978) to expand the base of the party to include Taiwan-born members. Although derecognition of Taiwan by the United States in 1979 fueled growing opposition to the Guomindang, public dissent was still forcefully suppressed, dissidents routinely jailed, and the opposition remained fragmented.

In 1983, elections were held, principally to appease domestic and international sentiment for liberalization. This prompted greater organization on the part of the opposition in the hopes of running candidates for local and state elections. When martial law was lifted in 1986, the opposition was able to field candidates and it formed a new party, the Democratic Progressive Party, committed to seeking democratic reform. On the basis of three major issues—a social policy, government support for small business and independence for Taiwan—the DPP had captured a number of seats in local government making itself visible by the time the younger Chiang died in 1988. He was succeeded by the vice president, Lee Teng Hui, who became Taiwan's first native-born president. That same year, constitutional rule was restored, followed by a series of democratic reforms: the official dissident blacklist was abolished; proceedings were undertaken to terminate the life-membership terms of the National Assembly, a select body with the sole power to elect and recall the president; amendments to the constitution were passed, guaranteeing a multiparty state and adoption of the French system of splitting the executive power between a prime minister and a president.

These reforms pushed through by the Taiwan-born president of the Guomindang ensured the party its future in a Taiwan increasingly dominated by Taiwan-born citizens for whom the mainland carried no personal history. Still in the lead over the DPP in the first full elections to Taiwan's legislative bodies in 1994, the KMT also captured the first directly elected presidential election of 1996, returning President Lee to office. The sea change brought about by political reform under the leadership of President Lee has been to demote the privileged political and social status of mainlanders so there is more of a level playing field between the native-born Taiwanese and the mainland Chinese. Although the differences between the two will die out with the passage of time, their dissimilarity culturally has been a complicating factor because it includes Japan as part of the problem. The 50-year development of Taiwan as a colony of Japan has left an indelible imprint on Taiwanese culture which continues to exacerbate the antagonisms between Taiwan and China. Native-born Taiwanese, like former President Lee Teng Hui, in many ways have a greater cultural affinity with Japan than they do with China. They speak Japanese fluently and grew up in an educational system indistinguishable from that of Japan at the time. Their distance from the lives of people growing up in revolutionary China is far greater than one would expect from the superficial observation that Taiwanese and mainlanders are both Chinese.

But political reform leaves Taiwanese on the horn of a dilemma by increasing the possibility of conflict with the PRC. The election in 1999 of a pro-independence DPP president immediately stiffened Beijing's resolve to reunite Taiwan by force, if necessary. Taiwan's President Chen Shui-bian responded with a conciliatory inaugural address, suggesting that like Nixon's unexpected rapprochement with China, he too might be able to cross the great divide to reach for a negotiated settlement with China. Though the prospects for a peaceful resolution clearly favor "the one country two systems" principle articulated by the PRC, the process is likely to be an extended, drawn-out affair marked as it was in the late 1990s by sharp swings between sabre-rattling confrontation and more peaceful accommodation. The decisive factor will be consideration of the *economic* interests of both sides.

North Korea. The prospects of political reform in North Korea need to be viewed through a zoom lens. Metaphorically this lens has materialized in the euphoric summit meeting June 12–14, 2000 between President Kim Il Jong of North Korea and President Kim Dae Jung of South Korea. Little is known about what, if any, factional disagreements exist between "conservatives" and "reformists" in the Korean Workers' Party but North Korea appears to be serious in its commitment to seeking peace on the Korean peninsula and joining the community of nations. Within two weeks of the summit meeting and signing the North-South accord in mid-June 2000, Red Cross officials from North and South Korea had set into motion the program for reuniting families and returning the 50 North Korean prisoners of war still held (since the Korean War) by South Korea home. North Korea has also established relations with a host of other countries, including Italy and Australia. The United States has loosened and is expected to drop its embargo against North Korea and joint business ventures between South and North Korea are likely to be in the offing. In a surprise visit to China just prior to the summit, Kim Jong Il had expressed admiration for the results of China's "successful experiment in socialism with Chinese characteristics."[6] But if North Korea were to follow the path already trodden by China—implementing economic reform gradually and leaving political reform until the last—it would have to be another experiment: in "socialism with Korean characteristics."

Compared to the six years it took since the elder Kim's death and the summit meeting of North and South Korea in 2000, the three days (and two weeks of preparation meetings) spent in reaching and signing the accord were astonishingly short.

It is foolhardy therefore to look ahead with any pretense of confidence. Instead we will point to several observations that might be helpful in following events as they unfold. One is that there are lessons to be learned from the experience of Germany's reunification which South and North Korea will undoubtedly apply to planning the process of Korean unification. Probably the most significant of those lessons pertain to what *not* to do. A second observation is that even if both South and North Korea engaged in the most meticulous planning humanly possible, it would be impossible to control the myriad domestic and international variables that are beyond human control in such a situation. And last but not least is the observation that there will be incalculable costs to both sides in this lengthy process. For South Korea, the sheer monetary costs are staggering while for North Korea, the impact of exposure to the jungle-like "freedom" of the global market is unimaginable.

South Korea.   Political reform in South Korea, as we have seen in some detail in Chapter 4, has gone through a number of stages of development. The most recent stage was ushered in by the election of President Kim Dae Jung who took office in 1998 supported by a coalition between his party, the National Congress for New Politics, and the conservative United Liberal Democrats; together they held a narrow victory. During most of his first term, instead of making headway on his twin objectives of economic restructuring and democratic reforms, President Kim Dae Jung expended his political energy in widening the margin of his coalition's support and battling the opposition, the Grand National Party, in the National Assembly. Not even his "sunshine policy" of reaching out towards North Korea met with any success when as part of its fiftieth anniversary celebration, the North Koreans fired a rocket that flew over Japan.

Under mounting criticism from all sides—charges of corruption, the backlash from a series of natural and manmade disasters, his populist image as antibusiness—President Kim Dae Jung launched a new broadly based political party in January 2000, the Millennium Democratic Party, to spearhead the parliamentary elections on April 13. On April 10, Seoul and Pyongyang announced that their two leaders would meet at a summit in Pyongyang in June. Though the promise of the summit was insufficient to give Kim Dae Jung's ruling coalition a working majority in the April elections, the results of the summit will more than likely strengthen his political party in the presidential elections of 2002. With the opposition Grand National Party capturing four seats short of a majority in the April elections, South Korea today is arguably closer to a credible two-party system than any other country in the region, and its opposition leader, Lee Hoi Chang, who was defeated by Kim Dae Jung in 1997, is poised to run for president in 2002.

Japan.   A few years ago a scholar of Japanese politics observed that Japan would go through a turbulent transition—much like a roller coaster—after the end of the Cold War. The question here is whether the roller coaster at the turn of the century is on an upswing or a downswing. In 1993 the Liberal Democratic Party, which had governed Japan (with a short break in 1955) since 1948, lost its majority, ushering in a period of great uncertainty. The country was in the midst of an economic slowdown for which there seemed to be no antidote. When the policies used by Japan's developmental state to "catch up" (described in Chapter 5) were no longer effective in sustaining high growth rates, both Japanese politics and the structure in which they were embedded came into question. What had been accepted as a strength during the Cold War years—the seamless web by which senior bureaucrats, leaders of the dominant LDP factions, heads of large companies and their constituents or clients made policy—was now perceived not merely as weakness but as crookedness (venality). This collaborative network that had provided a coherent and stable direction for developing Japan's national economy now appeared to be a self-perpetuating circle of corruption impervious to the public's wishes.

In 1996 and 2000, the LDP got back in and managed to retain its majority coalition, despite the electoral reforms that had been put in place. Though on the surface it looked as if nothing had changed, underneath a gradual transition was in motion. There is widespread disaffection with politics-as-usual, especially among urban voters, as expressed in the 2000 elections in which a third of the population didn't vote (high for Japan) and the LDP won only because of its traditional rural clientele. Liberalization of the financial sector has resulted in greater freedom from the constraints of the tradition-bound Finance Ministry. This has also spawned more innovative industries and start-ups. New accounting regulations require greater disclosure in financial transactions, making it harder for indebted or unprofitable companies to obtain loans from their group's main banks. One result has been a loosening of the cross-shareholding ties of the *keiretsu* (see Chapter 5). As weaker companies have been permitted to go under or get bought out, even by foreign investors, the *keiretsu* as a group of interrelated companies has been undermined. A related result is the increase in mergers and acquisitions with foreign companies, which in 1999 brought $23 billion of foreign investment *into* Japan.

These reforms in Japan's political economy are in line with both the urban Japanese peoples' and the IMF's concerns about the system we have been referring to as the developmental state. But to date, it is impossible to foretell whether and to what extent these changes will become extensive and have a marked impact on the system as a whole. Many of the scholars who have studied aspects of Japan's developmental state have strong doubts that Japan's fundamental structure will change anytime soon. As Mark C. Tilton observes from his study of regulatory reform in Japan, "there is no broad business mandate for usurping the role of bureaucrats, introducing rigorous market competition, or running uncompetitive strategic industries out of business in the name of efficiency."[7] This would suggest that at least in the area of regulatory reform, there will not be a dismantling of Japan's "system of dense, informal governance by bureaucracies and trade associations and open Japan's markets indiscriminately to imports." Does this mean that the LDP can return as a governing one-party dominant system with a renovated, more unified party, less corrupted by the scramble for individual campaign chests? Among Japanese today, there are more questions than answers. From the outside this may be seen as a belated "loss of innocence" but for some Japanese at least, it is likely to be seen as a loss of traditional Japanese virtues.

Indonesia.   Reluctantly and without anticipation of the necessity for political reform, President Suharto resigned on May 21, 1998, 32 years after taking power and just two months after being rubber-stamped for a seventh term. In the midst of economic collapse, financial ruin of the state, and riots calling for his blood or his (stolen) money, Suharto resisted stepping down until even his vice president and chosen successor, Habibie, publicly disavowed his rule. When Habibie took over as president, his attempts to plug the dike against the flood of pent-up discontents sufficed only to accomplish two things: (1) the passage and implementation of a new constitution that reduced the political role of the military and opened elective offices to the free competition among all political parties; and (2) the order for East Timorese to be given a referendum on independence or autonomy. The first political reform—a new constitution—gave Indonesia a plurality popular vote for Sukarnoputri (Sukarno's daughter) as president and a National Assembly election of the actual president, Abdurrahman Wahid with Sukarnoputri as vice president. The second political reform of Habibie's gave the people of East Timor both death and destruction followed by independence.

In the military state of General Suharto who became president in 1968 after the military coup and massacre of the Communists in 1965, economic growth and repression of all opposition went hand in hand in the name of democracy and anti-communism, all with the blessing of the United States. The ethnic and religious divisions with their roots in Dutch colonialism were kept down by the military, the flow of money was from the provinces, the outer islands, into Java and the Javanese promoted high economic growth, an emergent (and acquiescent) middle class and statehood-with-stability for Indonesia. In the late 1980s, however, as the Soviet Union began to unravel, Suharto's rule started to exhibit its fault lines under mounting external criticism of human rights violations both in industry and in East Timor. In 1994 and 1995 in response to protests the military would repeatedly go in, remove the troublemakers by the truckload and give them a course in "discipline." But when the financial crisis of 1997 hit Indonesia, central authority rapidly disintegrated. The military no longer went into trouble-spots promptly, permitting the conflicts to escalate before attempting to quash them. This was also the case in East Timor where the army simply allowed the paramilitary militia to kill off opponents of Indonesian rule—i.e., pro-independence supporters.

With the collapse of prosperity, support for Suharto evaporated. Mounting domestic pressures converged with external pressures—which now included the IMF, the U.S. government and human rights organizations—to throw the Suharto regime off balance. The resulting paralysis of will marked the end of Suharto's presidency and the beginning of an extended period of turmoil for Indonesia. Despite the orderly succession secured by the constitutionally mandated free elections that put President Wahid into office, the fabric of Indonesian nationhood continues to be torn asunder by economic hardship and ethnic conflict that feed into one another. The military has tried to maintain a low profile, having been discredited internationally and nationally for both their incapacity to maintain order and their gratuitous brutality when they attempted to impose it. But they are still sufficiently powerful (and are once again being trained and supplied by the United States) to attempt a military takeover if the United States were to deem it necessary for stability in the region. This in turn depends on the continually escalating violence of the conflicts between ethnic and religious groups. To understand the depth and complexity of these ethnic and religious conflicts requires an understanding of how *post-independence* policies and especially the rapid economic growth under President Suharto's rule exacerbated the tensions originally created by the Portuguese and the Dutch. We will focus on only one example, the Moluccan island of Ambon—the Moluccas or Malukus, which used to be called the Spice Islands.

Like many ethnic groups throughout the archipelago when Indonesia won independence from the Dutch in 1949, Christian separatists in Ambon sought to break away from the new (Muslim) republic, forming their own Republic of the South Moluccas. In doing so they burned down several Muslim villages leaving a legacy of bitterness in the same villages that in 2000 figured prominently in the conflicts on Ambon. In the intervening decades the relationship between Christian and Muslim communities has been further confounded by the successive influx of ethnic migrants from Sulawesi. When the devoutly religious Muslims—mostly ethnic Butonese, Bugis, and Makassarese from the island of Sulawesi (known collectively as BBM) who had wandered the vast archipelago for more than 400 years—began moving into Ambon, the central island of the Moluccas, at first in the 1950s, and then in greater numbers in the 1970s and 1980s, they thrived as they always had through a combination of business acumen and hard work. Migration was a symbol of pride for Sulawesan wanderers and if setting down roots meant taking "dirty jobs" that would have been considered beneath them in their own feudal culture, they were glad to do so in their adopted homes. As migrants, far from home they were free to accumulate capital for their own nuclear families without distributing their wealth among large extended families. Indeed, they developed no tradition of sending money back to Sulawesi. They preferred to intermarry with locals, and develop strong bonds with the communities that offered them new opportunities; there was no thought of ever returning to their homeland.

Buton migrants became vendors, trishaw drivers, and construction workers, and they tended to live separately in their own small enclaves (*kampangs*). The Bugis and Makassar migrants prospered as small merchants and shopkeepers and moved into Christian communities while the Chinese who were not recent migrants maintained their dominance in bulk imports and exports, living as they always did in their own communities. By the 1990s, the newcomers known as "BBM" had conquered the retail trade and all forms of transport. As long as the price of cloves remained high and the clove trade was booming, the landowning Christian Ambonese who produced the cloves were unperturbed by the growing riches of the BBM migrants. But in the early 1990s, when clove prices crashed, an Ambonese Muslim became governor of the island and a clove-purchasing monopoly led by Suharto's youngest son conspired to threaten the controlling position of Christian Ambonese, they aimed their animosities against the newly rich Sulawesi migrants. They resented the Bugis and Makassar in particular perhaps because they had violated decades of religious apartheid by building homes and mosques in the midst of Christian communities. The Buton still lived primarily in their own Muslim quarters (*kampungs*) where they had originally farmed the fertile soil. Despite the emergence of many interfaith friendships, therefore, the Christians and the Sulawesi migrants became enemies. Today whatever the traditional code of harmony (*pela gandong*) may have achieved under Suharto's rule by way of restraining mutual hostility has vanished and the polarization has led to outright civil war between the communities. Tens of thousands Bugis and Makassarese have flooded back to Sulawesi to avoid clashes between Ambonese Christian and Muslim mobs wielding spears and machetes.

With East Timor independent, Irian Jaya on record demanding independence, an Aceh separatist movement fighting for autonomy since before Indonesian independence and an additional half dozen or so other ethnic and sectional disputes to be sorted out, the threat of disintegration is likely to be an ongoing problem for the state of Indonesia. If the country is to secure and maintain its unity as a national economy in the long run, therefore, it may have to assume a more federal form. And if the thrust is toward greater regional autonomy, migration is likely to accelerate rather than abate as provincial governments with greater control over natural resources and development planning provide new opportunities. As new regional trade centers emerge outside Indonesia's main island, Java, new jobs and investment opportunities will serve as magnets for migrant families once again. Whether Indonesia will be able to retain its present governmental structure while adapting to changes that can increase its economic security and make it competitive in a rapidly changing global economy are questions that will take time to be answered in any shape or form.

Cambodia.   What will happen in Cambodia when Sihanouk dies will depend on whether the hybrid government first created in 1993 and recreated after Hun Sen's removal of his co–prime minister, Norodom Ranariddh—who also happens to be the King's son—survives. For the first time since King Sihanouk was ousted by the U.S.-backed Lon Nol in 1970, peace is a real possibility for Cambodians. The government under Prime Minister Hun Sen has effectively solidified its control over the whole country after the last remaining Khmer Rouge guerrillas surrendered in late 1998 and early 1999. If this government can also succeed in gaining legitimacy before Sihanouk dies, then who becomes king will be relatively unimportant; there might even be no need to continue the monarchy at all, especially since none of his children seems to have inherited Sihanouk's charismatic appeal to the Cambodian people.

Cambodia's history is one of more powerful countries encroaching on its dominion. Even Hun Sen's rule is tainted by association with the Vietnamese whose army installed him to replace the murderous regime of Pol Pot. And today when Cambodians want nothing but to put the horrific past behind them and move on to economic development, outsiders—human rights groups and the United Nations—continue to impose their own demands, in this case insisting that the Cambodian government hold war crimes trials for members of the Khmer Rouge. Hun Sen—himself a member of the Khmer Rouge at one time—has sought to negotiate a compromise to ensure that at least half of the judges in such trials are Cambodians. To truly exercise its sovereignty, Cambodia will require rebuilding the social fabric, organizing the government to promote economic development and social services, like education, for a poor, largely illiterate population. In his inaugural speech at the National Assembly, Hun Sen promised an ambitious agenda of reforms: of the civil service, the judiciary, the police, the military, and most importantly, of the economy. The rubber industry needs to be restored and there are al-

Norodom Sihanouk returned to the throne of Cambodia in 1993. It will be difficult to find a successor to the king who, for half a century, has been the symbol of national unity for his people.

Source: United Nations photo 178181/M. Grant Doc. 0058p.

ready 100,000 workers employed in 170 garment factories owned by South Koreans, Hong Kongers, Malaysians, Taiwanese and Singaporeans. To oversee a coherent economic development that will serve the Cambodian people, Hun Sen (or someone like him) is likely to remain the "strongman" of Cambodia for a considerable time while political reform in the sense of widespread participation in political decision-making will have a longer wait here than elsewhere in the Asian Pacific.

As we have already seen in the cases of Japan, Taiwan, and South Korea, where one group has monopolized political leadership for decades, pressures accumulate to depose that ruling party from its perch. Each case has its own particular features, but all share the risk that complacency, corruption, internal squabbling, loss of vision, and loss of touch with their constituents may undermine their capacity to rule effectively. Further, economic progress has had the effect of strengthening, diversifying, and multiplying a variety of interest groups that make demands on government to respond to their particular aims. Success in accommodating those interests within the ruling party is crucial to its continuing in power, for which the political assets of incumbency give it an advantage. We now turn to a consideration of the prospects of two other examples of such one-party dominant rule.

Malaysia and Singapore.   The dominant parties in both countries seem to be in solid positions. The minority populations lack the sheer numbers to oust them at the polls and opposition parties so far have not succeeded in breaking out of their separate ethnic bases and forming broad cross-ethnic coalitions to challenge either the National Front in Malaysia or PAP in Singapore. There are generational, regional, secular-Islamic fissures within UMNO, but there is no other party that has projected the credibility to attract large numbers of disaffected partisans who hope to have a share in exercising political power. The most recent attempt to mobilize a broad base of opposition to UMNO on the part of Keadilan, a party started in April 1999, illustrates the difficulty. Formed in response to Anwar Ibrahim's ouster as Deputy Prime Minister, Keadilan reflected Malay disenchantment with Mahathir's provocative manner of ridding himself of a rival. From a position as Prime Minister Mahathir's chosen successor, Anwar Ibrahim—after a trial, conviction and sentencing—found himself in jail on an eight-year sentence for treason. (The bizarre story of his two trials is a research project waiting to be undertaken.) The political party that took up his cause, headed by his wife Wan Azizah, attempted to broaden its focus but failed to make a dent in Mahathir's parliamentary majority in the fall 1999 elections. A similar situation prevails in Singapore, where people who object to the government's paternalism and curbs on freedom can emigrate. In both countries, government controls on the media and restrictions on political organizations inhibit the growth of opposition movements capable of mounting a serious challenge to the dominant party.

Although single party rule within a framework of electoral democracy is likely to remain unchallenged, at least in the near future, in both Malaysia and Singapore, there are nonetheless marked differences between these two single parties that will affect their long-term prospects. Singapore's PAP is a tightly knit organization built up on a foundation of one man's personality and competence but imbued with the principle of merit-based performance (see Chapter 4). Its identity as a party and therefore its ability to garner a majority of votes depend on its competence in governing, not the personal popularity of its leaders. Thus it is widely expected that as long as PAP provides the kind of leadership that secures the high standard of living to which Singaporeans have become accustomed, the PAP will more than likely choose Lee Kuan Yew's son (who has a military training) to be candidate in the next round for prime minister, which will probably do no harm to the party's chances for a solid majority.

Malaysia's UMNO, on the other hand, has become a ruling institution because it is less fragmented and more inclusive than the alternatives. Based on compromise and forging a national consensus to prevent a return to intercommunal violence, UMNO has acquired a reputation (among some observers) of being a "labyrinth of patronage." And in what is by many considered to be Mahathir's last term as prime minister, the issue of succession is problematical because of UMNO's loss of its Malay voting base in the last elections. The broad expectation of political reform within its own 2.4 million members has largely gone unaddressed under Mahathir's leadership and the spring 2000 election to the Supreme Council—the party's governing body—reflected their disaffection. Among its 25 elected seats most of which are filled by ministers, state chiefs and other luminaries, ten have been filled by younger representatives of a new generation that is openly critical of Mahathir.

Finally, the Military.   Even in governments now headed by civilians, such as Thailand and the Philippines, the military are not going to drop out of politics or let themselves be pushed aside in the drive for economic development. Post–cold war uncertainties have heightened interest in national security issues and increased military expenditures in a number of countries, and these developments enhance rather than diminish the political influence of the military. In Myanmar, for example, the junta seems to have professionalized its form of rule by removing military personnel from ministerial positions (the sole exception at present is Prime Minister Than Shwe who has indicated he may be stepping down from his political position). But the League for Democracy, the opposition party that won with a landslide in the only free election in recent years, seems to have been crushed by the generals. Although Aung San Suu Kyi upholds its significance, the League for Democracy as an organization capable of undertaking coherent political activity *inside the country* has been incapacitated through military intimidation and internal fragmentation while the generals continue to evoke preservation of national unity as their ultimate justification for staying in power.

In all of these countries the forces of change brought about by economic development are at work and are certain to have political effects. Tensions are inevitable not only among military leaders but between technocrats and ideologues, between bureaucrats and politicians, between central and local governments, between regions, between city and countryside, between industry and farmers, between business and environmentalists. Old leadership is being challenged to change from inside and outside, and human rights is one of the most controversial of those challenges.

Prospects for Expanding Human Rights

In approaching this subject, we need to acknowledge the human propensity to assume that our way of doing things is the right, the only, way to do things and that the persistence of others in doing things their way is perverse error from which they should be rescued by persuasion or even coercion. This propensity is particularly manifest where such emotionally charged issues as individual rights and democracy are concerned. Americans more than other Westerners seem to exhibit a special zeal for the mission of converting the rest of the world to their vision of those ideals.

Although governments everywhere endorse the principles of democracy and human rights, they do not agree on precisely what are the essential features of democracy, on which are the rights that ought to be protected, and even on whether any universally applicable standards are possible. Some argue that the Western emphasis on individual civil and political rights (such as freedom of expression, the right to vote, to equal protection of the laws) neglects economic and social rights (such as the right to a decent living standard, to a job, education, health care) and the rights of groups of people to keep their cultural identity, language, autonomy. Even when it is agreed that all of those rights are important, disagreement arises over which ones should be given priority, if they all cannot be promoted simultaneously.

In the Asian Pacific as elsewhere, that lack of consensus is a cause of controversy in both international and domestic politics, pitting governments, political parties, nongovernmental organizations, and individual citizens against each other in a struggle to have their own versions of democracy and rights prevail. Asian Pacific governments rarely criticize each others' practices, but that restraint is exercised selectively by Western governments. Their criticisms are most often directed against China, Indonesia, North Korea, Vietnam, and Myanmar, and the U.S. administration has only grudgingly and against strong congressional opposition relinquished its linkage of trade advantages for China to improvements in its human rights record. The most outspoken responses to Western critics have come from China, Singapore, Malaysia, Indonesia, and Myanmar. The differences center on three issues: cultural distinctiveness versus universality; economic development first versus full rights to political participation along with development; and respect for national sovereignty over internal affairs versus the right of governments to set conditions for amicable relations.

Universality Versus Cultural Distinctiveness.   To the Western argument in favor of the principle of universality, that human rights standards are or should be the same everywhere, Asians counter with the cultural distinctiveness argument, that Asian cultures and political traditions are different from the West's, so Asian concepts of rights and democracy are necessarily different too. As Kishore Mahbubani, deputy secretary in the Singapore foreign ministry, says:

> There is no unified Asian view on human rights and freedom of the press. These are Western concepts. Asians are obliged to react to them. Predictably, there is a whole range of reactions from total acceptance to total rejection. The truth is that in most Asian societies there is little awareness, let alone understanding, of these concepts. The vast and populous continent of Asia, preoccupied with more immediate challenges, has not had the time or energy to address these issues squarely.[8]

Even so, he continues:

> Both Asians and Westerners . . . can agree on minimal standards of civilised behavior that both would like to live under. For example, there should be no torture, no slavery, no arbitrary killings, no disappearances in the middle of the night, no shooting down of innocent demonstrators, no imprisonment without careful review. These rights should be upheld not only for moral reasons; there are sound functional reasons. Any society which is at odds with its people and shoots them down when they demonstrate peacefully, as Burmese did, is headed for trouble.[9]

Development Before Rights.   Some Asians reject the argument that the exercise of democratic rights to political participation and expression is a prerequisite for economic development, saying instead that development must take place first because exercise of individual rights is meaningless until people enjoy basic material well-being. Rapid economic progress requires stability and allowing dissenters to sabotage that effort is impermissible. For example, President Jiang Zemin, when asked about China since Tiananmen, responded:

China has enjoyed political stability, and economic development and living standards of the people have greatly improved. . . . China is constantly strengthening its democracy and legal system. It is not an easy job. Managing a country . . . to ensure food and clothing to China's 1.2 billion people is a contribution in itself [to world peace and stability].[10]

Implicit here is that when there is a choice between political freedom and material progress, most people will choose the latter; further, by meeting their expectations for improvement in their lives, government is in fact being responsive to the people it governs. An American journalist with years of experience in China comments:

From afar, it sometimes seems as if the fundamental dynamic in China is brutal repression of dissent. In reality, *political* dissent plays an inconsequential role in most people's lives, particularly in the countryside [where three-quarters of China's people live]. . . . Most Chinese say that if the Communist Party were suddenly to announce free elections, it could count on the votes of the peasants to win overwhelmingly.[11]

Criticism Infringes Sovereignty.   Finally, the principle of sovereignty is used against Western governments' criticisms of Asian governments' human rights records and in particular against efforts to make trade and aid conditional on changes laid down by the trade partner or aid donor. At the 1993 APEC meeting in Seattle, President Jiang reminded President Clinton that governments should show respect for each other and not meddle in each other's internal affairs. Prime Minister Mahathir of Malaysia has charged that the West uses human rights to reimpose dominance over other countries: "This is what the West wants—not democracy, not free trade and not human rights."[12] The writer of a letter to the editor of the *Far Eastern Economic Review* concurs in that assessment of Western motives: "It seems that free trade and human rights have replaced colonisation and Christianity as the new banners under which Western nations can continue to dominate the world."[13]

Singapore offered this parting shot against Western hypocrisy in criticizing others while ignoring conditions in their own countries:

In the face of growing evidence of social, economic and occasionally moral deterioration of the fabric of many Western societies, it would be increasingly difficult for a Westerner to convince Asians that the West has found universally valid prescriptions for social order and justice . . . the West should stop lecturing Asians.[14]

Conventional wisdom has it that greater affluence brings more widespread expectation of and pressure for participation in politics. In the cases of South Korea, Taiwan, and Thailand, this seems to have occurred and, if generalized to other countries, augurs well for the advancement of political and civil rights. But prosperity does not always follow an upward curve, and unless protection of rights becomes firmly entrenched in the political culture and effectively defended in political and legal institutions, their durability in times of economic adversity is uncertain. In a fundamental sense, citizenship requires constant vigilance to keep the governors responsive to the needs and wishes of the governed. In actuality, in the West as well as Asia, this responsibility falls most of the time on a few, those who are politically active in parties and other organizations. In some Asian Pacific countries, national NGOs have formed to monitor and advocate for human rights. If they can escape being seen as tools of foreigners trying to embarrass or subvert their governments, those NGOs have potential for promoting and protecting rights.

Outside pressures, on the other hand, particularly public government-to-government "shaming" exercises, are likely to be counterproductive. No government wants to appear to be caving in to foreign demands, and "face-saving" is important, in the West as well as in Asia. In our view, the prospects for improvements in economic and social rights for most of the people are good and for some, more opportunity to exercise political and civil rights is opening up—fitful and painful though progress may be.

THE NEW GLOBAL ORDER AND
PROSPECTS FOR THE REGION

The convergence of an economically vibrant Asian Pacific, the end of the cold war, the political dissolution of the Soviet Union and states in Eastern Europe, and a diminution in the economic base of U.S. power have set into motion a new international configuration of wealth and power. Although the United States remains the solitary hegemon of world order, it is principally on the basis of its political influence and military might. The dynamism for global economic growth no longer emanates from any one country or region, a situation that has led scholars to use "multipolarity" as a descriptive label for the emerging world order. Chapter 8 analyzed the distinctive regional growth pattern that evolved by using export earnings to import capital, intermediate goods, and technologies. The resulting intra-industry horizontal trade within the region has strengthened the international competitiveness of manufactured exports among an expanding number of countries in the region. By providing the capital goods and capital-intensive intermediate goods to its neighbors, Japan has induced industrialization among its trading partners and in the process has stimulated a transformation of trade relationships from the interindustry vertical type to an intra-industry horizontal type of division of labor.

The success of this regional development pattern has had a dramatic effect on international relations, changing not only the priorities from military to economic competition but potentially also the numbers and kinds of international actors as well as the nature of their interaction in pursuing cooperation and competition in the global economic arena. First we focus on some problems and dilemmas posed for international political economy by this global transformation from a Cold War international regime to one that will eventually reflect the emergent new international division of labor. Three interrelated problems will be addressed. One is the "Japanese problem," stemming from the perception that the Japanese have unfair trade advantages; the second is the dilemma of resorting to a strategy of aggressive unilateralism; and the third is the dilemma posed by globalization. In the final section, we discuss the impact of the new global landscape on the prospects for the Asian Pacific. Here we will concentrate on the political possibilities of alliances among Asian Pacific countries as they attempt to pursue two contradictory objectives: increasing market shares to sustain the international competitiveness of their national economies, and economic cooperation through regionalization to counter the potential challenges of the already institutionalized regions in Europe and the Western hemisphere.

The Dilemmas of a New Global Configuration

The cold war international regime established after World War II served as an incubator for the formation of an economically powerful Asian Pacific region with Japan at its core and a frontier for expansion in Myanmar, Vietnam, the newly constituted Cambodia, North Korea, and the northeastern region where China, Korea, and Russia converge. As the architect of this international regime, the United States used its special relationship as victor over a defeated Japan to construct a regional bulwark against communism in the Asian Pacific. In exchange for relinquishing autonomy over its own national security (Article 9 of the Japanese constitution), Japan would reap favorable conditions for economic growth along with military security from the United States. This "implicit bargain," built into the foundation of the postwar international system, set the parameters for what "free trade" was to mean in the postwar world.[15] The United States would tolerate Japan's restrictive and aggressive trade and investment policies while opening wide its own market to Japanese (and other Asian Pacific countries') exports because it served the best interests of both the United States and the "free world" to strengthen the economies of allies in the Asian Pacific region.

"The Japanese Problem."   From the start, therefore, what was heralded as a system of "free trade" was actually a complex historical compromise including a large number of "safeguards, exemptions, exceptions and restrictions—all designed to protect the balance of payments [of nation-states] and a variety of domestic social policies."[16] Though the objective of GATT was to lower tariff barriers and promote nondiscrimination in trade between nations, the right of national governments to protect their own domestic markets remained sacrosanct. The United States obtained a GATT waiver to exempt its own agricultural price supports from international negotiation; it also recognized Japan's protection of its postwar industries as national prerogatives implicitly protected by the framework of liberalization. But this system of "embedded liberalism" became problematic once Japan rather than the United States was the paramount exporter of industrial goods. At this point, the perception that imports were permitted by Japan only in areas where they did not compete with domestic production became "the Japanese problem."

Ironically, it was the very success of the international regime represented by GATT (now the WTO) that brought "the Japanese problem" into the limelight. As the vast majority of nations in the world, including Japan, successfully reduced and eliminated tariff barriers, the flood of exports into the United States, which it must be recalled was the biggest buyers' market in the world, submerged domestic industries' capabilities to compete. The result was a series of attempts on the part of the U.S. government to redress its own vulnerabilities in a world market with cost-effective competitors. Nontariff barriers (NTBs) were erected to slow down or limit the rate of increase in (Japanese) imports, Japanese currency was appreciated to increase American capital and goods exports to Japan, and the Japanese government's acquiescence to a series of quid pro quos within the framework of the Structural Impediments Initiative (SII) was obtained. When the United States still found itself stymied from lowering its deficits with Japan and significantly increasing its share of the Japanese domestic market, policymakers concluded that Japan's "unfair trade practices" stemmed from the unique nature of Japan's internal industrial structure.

Thus "the Japanese problem" refers to the fact that Japan's developmental political economy differs qualitatively from the political economy prevailing in other advanced capitalist countries. This difference between Japan's capitalist system and that of Western countries is perceived as a problem for the continued growth of both the U.S. and the world economy.[17] As we have seen throughout this book, there is no agreement on what explains the singular nature of the Japanese model of development. Some scholars argue that it is a distinctive cultural matrix, others argue that it is the industrial structure of a corporate economy informally wedded to the state bureaucracy. There is also no agreement on whether or not these structural differences are likely to diminish over time or remain as a more permanent feature of Japanese and some of the other Asian Pacific political economies. These uncertainties surrounding the intractability of U.S. deficits and Japanese current account surpluses have resulted in an endemic strain in the partnership between the two countries although it has been overshadowed in the last decade by the persistent stagnation and then brief recession that came over the Japanese economy in the 1990s. Interesting in this regard is the fact that the same argument made against Japan's success—namely, that it was a unfairly tied to the singularly insular nature of Japan's developmental state—was also used to criticize the extended economic downturn—namely, that Japan was unable to climb out of its economic weakness because of its distinctive developmental state.

But as John Ruggie surmises, a problem would exist with the GATT (now WTO) framework of international order regardless of Japan's situation. It was inevitable, once formal trade barriers were reduced to insignificant levels as intended by GATT, that the domestic policies and practices that shape the structure of foreign trade of different countries would assume center stage in international trade. At that point, whatever differences emerged in the domestic policies and practices among countries would be cause for an international problem. It is the consequence of an inherent conflict between the limited nature of the GATT/WTO mission "to maintain a balance of [external] concessions and obligations, not to restructure nations," and the increasingly interventionist objective of an international trade game in which powerful players in the global economy seek to harmonize the international effects of divergent domestic economic structures.[18] Because WTO relies upon multilateral agreements for reaching symmetrical quid pro quos, there is no way to use WTO to transform a fundamental asymmetry between Japan's domestic economic structure and that of the United States.

The Strategy of Aggressive Unilateralism.   This conflict between the asymmetry of Japan's domestic economy and that of the other capitalist countries led the United States unilaterally to undertake an aggressive form of "managed trade" by passing into law Section 301 of the Omnibus Trade and Competitiveness Act of 1988. In Super 301, as it is called, Congress mandates the executive branch of the United States to assess and take unilateral action against any policy it deems to be an "unfair trading practice." Thus, Super 301 targets Japanese (and others') trade policies unilaterally rather than through WTO-sponsored negotiations. And it targets Japan not because Japan is "cheating" on formal WTO rules but because "The structure of Japan's trade is simply, and importantly, different from the established norm around which the international trade regime revolves."[19] Japan's low level of manufactured imports, intra-industry trade, and preference for unprocessed or the least refined raw materials are used as evidence of a closed market. Super 301 is a form of retaliation for Japan's pursuing a policy to prevent U.S. corporations from establishing majority-owned subsidiaries within Japan.

The objective of such unilateral action on the part of the United States is to pry open the Japanese market, bringing Japan's trade structure into greater harmony with those of its trading partners. Though it may not in and of itself constitute protectionism, the policy evokes charges and countercharges of protectionism, portending continuing problems between Japan and the United States because some practices are clearly WTO-illegal and tend to erode the efficacy of the multilateral arrangements that are at the foundation of the existing international regime represented by the WTO. Although the danger is mitigated by Japan's continued acquiescence to U.S. demands in a manner that sidesteps Japanese refusal to formally negotiate under terms of Super 301, the underlying problem remains irresolvable within the confines of an international regime created to serve the Cold War configuration. International trade disputes that stem from fundamental differences in the way industries and trade are domestically organized and managed in different countries and regions are inherently beyond the scope of the WTO framework as it has functioned since the Cold War era. And forecasts that the end of the Cold War would usher in universal victory for liberal economics and democratic politics have been premature. It is far from clear what these terms mean in the global economy that has emerged while the world's attention was fixed on the possibility of nuclear annihilation.

Globalization.   Regional economic development in the Asian Pacific has coincided with an extraordinary period of technological innovation and foreign direct investments to fundamentally alter the structure of global relationships. Computer technology, the science and application of which have come to be known as cybernetics and cybernation, respectively, has generated new products and services, produced old ones with new processes, and brought about a new way of linking production systems internationally.[20] There are various terms to capture the newness of this global process we are witnessing: a new international division of labor, complex interdependency, a borderless economy. It is a transformation that breaks down production processes and fragments them so they are spread across a vast and shifting array of countries covering the entire surface of the globe. Production components are designed, manufactured, assembled, and marketed in different lo-cations. As a result, intra-industry trade grows more rapidly than inter-industry trade. And like traded services that have also expanded dramatically, intra-industry trade is not amenable to collecting uniform and universal statistics because it "does not exist in conventional economic theory."[21]

The effects of globalization on world markets have been drastic because of changes involving what, how, when, and where things are produced and distributed. Products have shortened lives, and choosing among a number of competing tech-nologies and production locales can have a rapid and profound effect on profits, losses, and the prospects that a firm will be taken over or disappear. The survival of firms increasingly dictates entering into cross-national alliances with competitors, which brings with it new problems and new demands on the abilities of executives. Diplomacy is no longer the specialized preserve of state officials but an attribute required of corporate managers when multinational corporations enter into negoti-ations with states to avail themselves of the best locations for different aspects of their production processes.

The global economy would not be possible if not for the changes in how firms organize their financial affairs. These have occurred with great rapidity in recent decades as nationally centered financial markets that engaged in some buying and selling of credit across the exchanges have grown into a closely integrated "global system, in which national markets, physically separate, function as if they were all in the same place."[22] New credit instruments have been devised by banks, transna-tional corporations, and states, all of which issue tradable commercial paper that acts as the equivalent of money to sustain investments and lubricate trade. The ex-traordinary mobility of capital and the creation of new forms of credit have been facilitated by the revolution in communications and information. This technology is capable of generating international financial flows in any week or month that are 50 times greater in value than the flow of goods.[23]

These structural changes in financial and production markets have only begun to have a noticeable impact on the policies of the United States. In contrast to the Asian Pacific, where inward foreign direct investment has been an integral part of postwar development, extensive foreign direct investment going into the United States has been of only small consequence until recently. The result has been dra-matic, though not necessarily widely understood among people. Generally de-scribed in the United States as a shift away from foreign to domestic policy, it is ac-tually a shift in priorities away from a foreign policy defined in military terms to a domestic policy defined in global economic terms. The melting of the cold war has exposed a new international rivalry among states that the Asian Pacific has helped to define: It is the development game.[24]

The development game is one in which states enhance their prestige by pursu-ing greater market shares of global economic development; economic rather than military weapons are critical to win in this game. Expressed somewhat differently, nation-states in the postwar world pursue higher standards of living for their popu-lations by actively involving themselves with multinational firms pursuing global strategies. In place of seeking control over more territory, the first priority of states now is to compete for the means to create wealth within their own territory. This leads states to interact with each other as well as with multinational corporations in pursuit of economic rather than military security. As they seek to arm themselves economically, they no longer employ the "blunt, unsophisticated and easily targetable weapon"—the tariff—substituting in its place the newer "stealth" weapons consisting of "that panoply of administrative arrangements and 'voluntary' agreements that exist under the collective title of the Non-Tariff Barriers (NTBs)."[25]

Since Japan has developed the equivalent of a "Star Wars" system to detect other countries' threats to its economic security, the new global configuration of political economy raises important questions of how Japan and the other countries of the Asian Pacific are likely to respond to the United States' having joined the development game. Which national populations will have the greatest advantages in attracting market shares of the global economy in the new "triangular diplomacy"—among states, among firms, and between states and firms? What alliances will be made or unmade in pursuit of winning? Will the EU and NAFTA develop as open trading regions or as protectionist regional blocs? Will the Asian Pacific move toward greater institutionalized economic and political cooperation? Or will the combination of old conflicts and new rivalries leave the Asian Pacific politically fragmented and economically contentious? These questions are, of course, unanswerable but tantalizing and we will in the final section indulge ourselves in that time-honored human need to gaze into the crystal ball or throw the I Ching.

Which Way the Asian Pacific?

How will the newly industrializing countries fare in the new global economy? With a regional pattern so dependent upon exports to the United States, what strategies can be developed to adjust to the increasing regionalization of the world's countries? Will the Japanese continue to have the advantages that have been attributed to their distinctive developmental system, or will they, as developed countries ahead of them, begin to suffer from the problems of old age and decay while the United States engages in its own restructuring to face the new tasks of the twenty-first century?

These questions draw attention to the possibility that what has passed for a superior model of economic growth and development among Asian Pacific countries may yet turn into the familiar capitalist system with all the flaws already afflicting developed capitalist countries. Japan's declining growth rates, its persistent decade-long economic stagnation, its increasing unemployment, and other dislocations of its current recessionary downturn are used as evidence for the argument. On the other hand, it is at least plausible that Asian Pacific development will continue to evolve in its own distinctive fashion while industrial restructuring in the United States will exhibit its own particular imprint. The purpose of this book has been to provide an understanding of the singular pattern of Asian Pacific development so readers can make their own comparisons. As all countries readjust to the new global economy, contrasts among different organizational models of production will become the basis for how countries attempt to restructure their advantages. Perhaps no single paradigm of perfection or universal agreement will emerge, but countries with sophisticated and well-maintained infrastructure, a highly skilled and well-disciplined labor force, a resilient educational system, and an effective and internationally savvy political leadership are likely to have a competitive edge in the contest for global market shares.

The Japan–United States Relationship.   At the heart of the question of the Asian Pacific future is the U.S–Japanese partnership that has provided the foundation for the region's development in the postwar period. Trade tensions between the two countries, as amply demonstrated, are bound to continue, especially if the gap between Japan's surpluses and the U.S. deficits continues to widen. Internal divisions among Japanese over the issue of opening Japan's domestic market to outsiders—which has already begun—are already complicated by the necessity of political reform. The dramatic ousting of the LDP from its political position of stable authority in the postwar world has had controversial consequences: The symbolically significant Japanese rice market has been opened for the first time, and electoral changes to undermine the dominance of the LDP have been introduced. But the internal structure of the Japanese political economy remains intact. It continues to enable Japan, as it has throughout the postwar period, to publicly acquiesce to pressures from the United States without actually implementing agreements so they achieve the desired outcomes. But it seems clear that if the openness of the Japanese market is measured by the United States in terms of outcomes rather than the formalities of bilateral agreements, the U. S.–Japan partnership will be in for some rocky times. Ironically, this result is equally likely should political reform in Japan succeed with the political system assuming a two-party form.

On the U.S. side, resistance to industrial restructuring to increase the country's international competitiveness is just as contentious. Judging from the divisiveness over NAFTA, advocates of protectionism are capable of mustering considerable national political support, as witnessed by the impressive demonstrations at recent WTO meetings. It is far easier, given historical prejudices and the transparency of the political system in the United States, to impose a "fairness" doctrine on Japan holding the Japanese responsible for U.S. deficits than it is to undergo fundamental domestic restructuring. But, as in Japan, though there is movement in the direction of industrial restructuring and some form of industrial planning as an instrument of national policy could shore up the partnership between Japan and the United States, the nationalistic sentiments that favor protectionism as a solution to trade problems with Japan are as powerful in the United States as they are in Japan. Thus the future of the U. S.–Japan partnership will depend ultimately on the capacities of both Japan and the United States to reform the historical and cultural biases underlying their relationship since World War II.

Regionalism Led by Japan and China?   The relationship between the United States and Japan is closely intertwined with the question of regionalism. Heightened tensions between Japan and the United States lead in the direction of more protectionist-oriented regional development on both sides of the Pacific Ocean. As we have seen, Japan has followed a course of trade, aid, and investment that has fostered economic regional integration. For Chalmers Johnson, "There is no doubt that Japan has the capacity to create a yen-based regional economic grouping in the Asian Pacific region."[26] How rapidly this occurs, what institutionalized shape such a regional grouping might assume, and what direction it moves in are contingent on all the interrelated domestic and international factors. If both the EU and NAFTA develop as open regions committed to multilateralism rather than as protectionist blocs seeking to exclude the exports of Asian newcomers, then more leeway will be available for Asian Pacific countries to develop a rather closely integrated economic cooperation while maintaining close dependent ties with the United States both militarily and economically. The successful conclusions of WTO negotiations in recent years interspersed by high-profile APEC meetings offer some promise for the openness of the regions being formed in Europe and the North American continent. But Asian Pacific countries will cautiously await the impact of these regional formations on their own export markets.

In the meantime, the Asian economic crisis of 1997–2000 with its disastrously "contagious" consequences for the region and the embarrassment of watching an armed, western-led U.N. peacekeeping force intervening in the internal affairs of one of ASEAN's major players has acted as a wake-up call for leaders of the region's states. Enhancing regional sensibilities can no longer be treated as a secondary concern to the domestic problems of individual nation states. The rapidity with which both these major crises escalated beyond the capacity of the region's countries to formulate—let alone act upon—a collective regional response, has raised awareness of the manner in which national vulnerabilities become regional liabilities. Protecting the national sovereignty of individual states in ASEAN and in the larger Asian Pacific region may require much greater regional responsibility for what transpires *within* the territorial borders of each sovereign member state than was ever previously conceivable. Alongside this inchoate notion there is an enhanced sense of urgency—almost palpable in the interactions of Asian Pacific countries today—for the need to expand and formalize regional mechanisms for collaboration.

China will play a principal role in affecting both the Asian Pacific's prospects for greater regionalization and the outcome of U.S.–Japan relations. By its size, resource endowments, historical importance in the region, global stature, and success at achieving economic reforms within a framework of political stability, China stands apart from and somewhat above the rest of the Asian Pacific, sharing this position with its former archenemy, Japan. This was clearly illustrated in the regionally responsible behavior of China in the depths of the economic crisis. Rather than devaluing its currency as many people feared, China stuck to its word by maintaining the value of its currency as an anchor with which the hardest-hit economies and the region as a whole could begin to recover. Alone among all the Asian Pacific countries, China has successfully pursued an independent foreign policy, first distancing itself from both the United States and the Soviet Union at the height of the cold war and then enlisting as a third party in disputes between the superpowers. The People's Republic is well qualified, therefore, to complement Japan's diffidence in its role as global leader while at the same time acting as a countervailing force to Japan's economic power in the region. As a third party in a triangular relationship with the United States and Japan, China's position on international issues can be pivotal in either increasing or decreasing tensions between the Asian Pacific and North American regions. By asserting its independence or throwing its weight behind one or the other economic superpower, China is likely for the foreseeable future to act in a stabilizing manner to further its ambitious economic development plans. Essential to these plans are the successful integration of Hong Kong and the de facto merging of Taiwan with the economy of the mainland.

Pressures toward increased regionalization seem certain to continue in the coming years. Of major importance in deciding the pace of change toward greater institutionalization of regional cooperation will be the degree of openness or protectionism of the U.S. market. The persistently successful economic growth experienced by the United States at the turn of the century while it has not substantially diminished the intensity of protectionist sentiments has redirected its energies in the direction of the WTO. And in the long run rising protectionism on the part of the United States can act as a unifying force among the disparate Asian Pacific countries. There is already some overt sentiment, as indicated earlier in this chapter, for excluding the United States from any Asian Pacific organization. This could be strengthened by heightened tensions between the United States and Japan. A possibility that their exports would no longer find an outlet in the United States might prompt the governments of Asian Pacific countries to open their domestic markets to one another. Increased formal agreements regarding the creation of such a "common market" may be little more than a glimmer on the horizon, along with Korean unification but all the countries of Southeast Asian have by now joined ASEAN, and discussions have already yielded an agreement on Japan's proposal for a regional currency fund to act as a lender of last resort for countries, like Thailand, that find themselves under siege by unregulated capital flows in and out of domestic markets.

Clearly, the obstacles to an Asian Pacific region taking shape in the manner of the EU are formidable. How Japan carries out its leadership role in the region will be critical. But judging the effectiveness of Japanese leadership can be culturally biased. It may be, as Alan Rix points out, that Japan's style of "leadership from behind" will make Japanese economic and political power in the region more acceptable than any overt dominant behavior would allow.[27] A style of leadership that stresses negotiation and skill in brokering the interests of many actors may be more appropriate to the task of forming the equivalent of an "international regime" at the regional level.

Conjecture about the short-term outlook of the U.S.–Japan partnership runs the gamut: Some argue it will result in bigemony or "Amerippon," others suggest either a Pax America II or a Pax Nipponica. In the long run, regionalism as a way of increasing the market size of nation-states will mean a great many more regions in the world. Multipolarity might take the form of a sizable number of regional nodes of power, not in isolation from each other but in competition and collusion over the resources of the global economy.

But getting from here to there is a daunting enterprise, the possibilities or impossibilities of which are beyond the scope of this book. Trying to understand development in and among Asian Pacific countries will be a continuing quest. What we have attempted in this book is to provide a historical and cultural context for understanding the issues and problems that face each of these countries. We have not shied from covering the breadth of the terrain, an endeavor we hope has not prevented our doing justice to our neighbors across the Pacific.

QUESTIONS FOR DISCUSSION

1. Looking back over their record of political and economic achievements during the last four decades, what grade would you assign to each of the 15 Asian Pacific countries and Hong Kong? Why?
2. Imagine that you, an expert on theories and models about development, have been hired by the government of one of the less affluent Asian Pacific countries (such as Vietnam or Myanmar) to brief top officials on what lessons are to be learned from other countries' experience in development and modernization. What important points about each of the various theories or models of development would you point out to them as relevant guidelines to consider in policy making?
3. What (if anything) should the U.S. government, private organizations, and individuals do about human rights in Asian Pacific countries?
4. Do you agree with some who forecast that the twenty-first century will be the "Pacific Century"? What role will the United States have in the region? Japan? China?

NOTES

1. Steve Chan and Cal Clark, "The Rise of the East Asian NICs: Confucian Capitalism, Status Mobility, and Developmental Legacy," in *The Evolving Pacific Basin in the Global Political Economy: Domestic and International Linkages*, ed. Cal Clark and Steve Chan (Boulder, CO: Lynne Rienner, 1992), p. 39.
2. Fernando Fajnzylber, "The United States and Japan as Models of Industrialization" in *Manufacturing Miracles: Paths of Industrialization in Latin America and East Asia*, ed. Gary Gereffi and Donald Wyman (Princeton, NJ: Princeton University Press, 1992), pp. 323–52.
3. Chan and Clark, "The Rise of East Asian NICs," p. 43.
4. James N. Danziger, *Understanding the Political World: A Comparative Introduction to Political Science* (New York: Addison Wesley Longman, 1998), p. 276.
5. See the World Bank Report, *The East Asian Miracle (EAM)* (N.Y.: Oxford Univ. Press for the World Bank, 1993).
6. Shim Jae Hoon and Adrian Edwards, "Korea Summit: No Turning Back," *Far Eastern Economic Review* (June 22, 2000): 17.
7. Lonny E. Carlile and Mark C. Tilton, eds., *Is Japan Really Changing Its Ways? Regulatory Reform and the Japanese Economy* (Washington, DC: Brookings Institution Press, 1998), pp. 188, 190.
8. Kishore Mahbubani, "Live and Let Live," *Far Eastern Economic Review* (June 17, 1993): 26.
9. Ibid.
10. Stephen Magagnini, "Chinese Leader Scores PR Coup at Conference," *The Sacramento Bee*, November 21, 1993, p. A32.
11. Nicholas D. Kristof, "Riddle of China: Repressions As Standard of Living Soars," *New York Times*, September 7, 1993, p. A6, national edition.
12. Michael Vatikiotis and Robert Delfs, "Cultural Divide," *Far Eastern Economic Review* (June 17, 1993): 20.
13. T. P. Huang, Letter to the Editor, *Far Eastern Economic Review* (August 26, 1993): 4.
14. Mahbubani, "Live and Let Live," p. 26.
15. A point made with respect to Europe by B. J. Cohen in 1974, quoted in *Pacific Economic Relations in the 1990s: Cooperation or Conflict?* ed. R. Higgott, R. Leaver, and J. Ravenhill (Boulder, CO: Lynne Rienner, 1993), p. 3.
16. John Gerard Ruggie "Unravelling Trade: Global Institutional Change and the Pacific Economy," in Higgott, *Pacific Economic Relations*, p. 16.

17. An article that details evidence for the existence of the "Japan problem" is "'Japan Problem' in Pacific Trade" by John Ravenhill in Higgott, *Pacific Economic Relations*, pp. 106–32.
18. Ruggie, "Unravelling Trade," p. 29.
19. Ibid., pp. 25–26.
20. The best work on the subject, to which this entire section is heavily indebted, is *Rival States, Rival Firms: Competition for World Market Shares* by John M. Stopford, Susan Strange, with John S. Henley (Cambridge, England: Cambridge University Press, 1991).
21. Ruggie, "Unravelling Trade," p. 33.
22. Stopford, *Rival States, Rival Firms*, p. 41.
23. Ibid., p. 44.
24. Shumpei Kumon and Akihiko Tanaka use the concept of "the development game" in their alternative framework to the hegemonic power explanation of changes in the current world system; see "From Prestige to Wealth to Knowledge," in *The Political Economy of Japan*, vol. 2, *The Changing International Context*, ed. Takashi Inoguchi and Daniel I. Okimoto (Stanford, CA: Stanford University Press, 1988), pp. 66–82.
25. Richard A. Higgott, *Some Alternative Security Questions for Australia, Canberra Papers on Strategy and Defence*, No. 51 (Canberra: Australian National University, 1989), p. 21.
26. Chalmers Johnson, "History Restarted: Japanese-American Relations at the End of the Century," in Higgott, *Pacific Economic Relations*, p. 53.
27. Alan Rix, "Japan and the Region: Leading from Behind" in Higgott, *Pacific Economic Relations*, pp. 62–82.

FOR FURTHER READING

Akaha, Tsuneo, and Frank Langdon, eds. *Japan in the Posthegemonic World*. Boulder, CO: Lynne Rienner, 1993.
Caporaso, James A., ed. *A Changing International Division of Labor*. Boulder, CO: Lynne Rienner, 1987.
Drysdale, Peter. *Europe, East Asia and APEC: A Shared Global Agenda?* Cambridge, England: Cambridge University Press, 1998.
Dutta, M. *Economic Regionalization in the Asia-Pacific: Challenges to Economic Cooperation*. Northhampton, MA: Elgar, 1999.
Hersh, Jacques. *The USA and the Rise of East Asia Since 1945: Dilemmas of the Postwar International Political Economy*. New York: St. Martin's, 1993, chs. 3 and 4.
Morley, James W., ed. *Driven by Growth: Political Change in the Asian-Pacific Region*. Armonk, NY: M. E. Sharpe, 1993.
Nanda, Ved P., et al. *Global Human Rights: Public Policies, Comparative Measures, and NGO Strategies* (Boulder, CO: Westview, 1981).
Stopford, John M., Susan Strange, with John S. Henley. *Rival States, Rival Firms: Competition for World Market Shares*. Cambridge, England: Cambridge University Press, 1991.
Stubbs, Richard and Geoffrey Underkill, eds. *Political Economy and the Changing Global Order*. New York: St. Martin's Press, 1994.

Acronyms

ADB	Asian Development Bank
AFIC	Asian Finance and Investment Corporation
AFPFL	Anti-Fascist People's Freedom League, Burma
ANZUS	Australia-New Zealand-United States security treaty
APEC	Asian Pacific Economic Cooperation forum
ARATS	Association for Relations Across the Taiwan Straits, China
ARVN	Army of the Republic of (South) Vietnam
ASEAN	Association of Southeast Asian Nations
BIA	Burma Independence Army
BSPP	Burma Socialist Programme Party
CPC	Communist Party of China
CPF	Central Provident Fund, Singapore
CPPCC	Chinese People's Political Consultative Conference
CPSU	Communist Party of the Soviet Union
DAC	Development Assistance Committee, OECD
DAP	Democratic Action Party, Malaysia
DLP	Democratic Liberal Party, South Korea
DPP	Democratic Progressive Party, Taiwan
DPR	People's Representative Council, Indonesia
DPRK	Democratic People's Republic of Korea
DRV	Democratic Republic of (North) Vietnam
DSP	Democratic Socialist Party, Japan
EAEG	East Asia Economic Group
EC	European Community, now European Union (EU)
EOI	export-oriented industrialization policy

FDI	foreign direct investment
FUNCINPEC	United Front for an Independent, Neutral, and Free Cambodia
GATT	General Agreement on Trade and Tariffs
G-7	Group of seven major industrialized countries
GCBA	General Council of Buddhist (Burmese) Associations
GCP	gross domestic product
GNP	gross national product
IAEA	International Atomic Energy Agency
ICP	Indochinese Communist Party
IGO	intergovernmental organization
IMF	International Monetary Fund
IPE	international political economy
ISDA	Indies Social Democratic Association
FY	fiscal year
JCP	Japan Communist Party
KMT	Guomindang
KPRP	Khmer People's Revolutionary Party
KR	Khmer Rouge
KWP	Korean Workers' Party
LDP	Liberal Democratic Party, Japan and Philippines
LPRP	Lao People's Revolutionary Party
MCA	Malay Chinese Association
MCP	Malayan Communist Party
MIA/POW	missing in action/prisoners of war
MIC	Malaysian Indian Congress
MILF	Moro Islamic Liberation Front
MITI	Ministry of International Trade and Industry, Japan
MNC	multinational corporation
MPAJA	Malayan People's Anti-Japanese Army
MPR	People's Consultative Assembly, Indonesia
MRLA	Malayan Races Liberation Army
NAFTA	North American Free Trade Association
NAM	Non-Aligned Movement
NATO	North Atlantic Treaty Organization
NEC	newly-exporting country, referring to Indonesia, Malaysia, and Thailand
NEP	New Economic Policy, Malaysia

NGO	nongovernmental organization
NIC	newly industrializing country, referring to Hong Kong, Singapore, South Korea, and Taiwan
NIE	newly industrializing economies, both NIC and NEC
NLD	National League for Democracy
NLF	National Liberation Front, South Vietnam
NPC	National People's Congress or National (Communist) Party Congress, China
NTB	nontariff barrier
ODA	official development assistance
OECD	Organization for Economic Cooperation and Development
OPEC	Organization of Petroleum Exporting Countries
OSS	Office of Strategic Services, Myanmar
PAFTAD	Pacific Free Trade and Development Conference
PAP	People's Action Party, Singapore
PAS	Pan Malaysian Islamic Party
PAVN	People's Army of Vietnam
PBEC	Pacific Basin Economic Council
PCI	per capita income
PDI	Indonesian Democratic Party
PECC	Pacific Economic Cooperation Conference
PKI	Indies (later Indonesian) Communist Party
PLA	People's Liberation Army, China
PLAF	People's Liberation Army Force, Vietnam
PNI	Indonesian Nationalist Party
PPP	Islamic United Development Party, Indonesia
PRC	People's Republic of China
PRG	Provisional Revolutionary Government, South Vietnam
RAM	Reform the Armed Forces Movement, Philippines
ROC	Republic of China
ROK	Republic of Korea
SALT	Strategic Arms Limitation Talks
SEATO	Southeast Asia Treaty Organization
SDPJ	Social Democratic Party of Japan
SEC	State Economic Commission, China
SEF	Straits Exchange Foundation, Taiwan
SEZ	special economic zone

SI	Sarekat Islam, Indonesia
SII	Structural Impediments Initiative
SLORC	State Law and Order Restoration Council, Myanmar
SOC	State of Cambodia
SOEs	State-Owned Enterprises
SPC	State Planning Commission, China
SPDC	State Peace and Development Council, Myanmar
TMD	Theater-Missile Defense Shield
TNC	transnational corporation
TPM	trigger price mechanism
TVEs	Township and Village Enterprises
UMNO	United Malays' National Organization
UNCOK	UN Commission on Korea
UNCURK	UN Commission for Unification and Rehabilitation of Korea
UNTAC	United Nations Transitional Authority in Cambodia
UNTCOK	UN Temporary Commission on Korea
USDP	United Social Democratic Party, Japan
VER	voluntary export restraint
WB	World Bank
YMBA	Young Men's Buddhist Association, Burma
ZOPFAN	zone of peace, freedom, and neutrality

Index